solutions@syngress.com

With more than 1,500,000 copies of our MCSE, MCSD, CompTIA, and Cisco study guides in print, we continue to look for ways we can better serve the information needs of our readers. One way we do that is by listening.

Readers like yourself have been telling us they want an Internet-based service that would extend and enhance the value of our books. Based on reader feedback and our own strategic plan, we have created a Web site that we hope will exceed your expectations.

Solutions@syngress.com is an interactive treasure trove of useful information focusing on our book topics and related technologies. The site offers the following features:

- One-year warranty against content obsolescence due to vendor product upgrades. You can access online updates for any affected chapters.
- "Ask the Author" customer query forms that enable you to post questions to our authors and editors.
- Exclusive monthly mailings in which our experts provide answers to reader queries and clear explanations of complex material.
- Regularly updated links to sites specially selected by our editors for readers desiring additional reliable information on key topics.

Best of all, the book you're now holding is your key to this amazing site. Just go to **www.syngress.com/solutions**, and keep this book handy when you register to verify your purchase.

Thank you for giving us the opportunity to serve your needs. And be sure to let us know if there's anything else we can do to help you get the maximum value from your investment. We're listening.

www.syngress.com/solutions

SYNGRESS®

Check Point™ NG VPN-1/FireWall-1

Advanced Configuration and Troubleshooting

Jim Noble CCSI, CISSP, Technical Editor

Doug Maxwell CCSI, NSA

Kyle X. Hourihan NSA

Robert Stephens CCSI, CISSP

Barry J. Stiefel CCSI, CISSP

Cherie Amon CCSI

Chris Tobkin CCSI

KEY	SERIAL NUMBER
001	YV4PK9H7G3
002	TKXD37T6CVF
003	8J9HF5TBAA
004	Z2BMQUH89Y
005	U8MPT3L33T
006	HAXXR54ES6
007	G8D4EPQLUK
008	EJ69BKMRD7
009	579KP7V6FH
010	TRCA7UM39Z

PUBLISHED BY
Syngress Publishing, Inc.
800 Hingham Street
Rockland, MA 02370

Check Point NG VPN-1/FireWall-1 Advanced Configuration and Troubleshooting

Printed in the United States of America

1 2 3 4 5 6 7 8 9 0

ISBN: 1-931836-97-3

Technical Editors: Jim Noble, Doug Maxwell, Victor Chang
Technical Reviewer: Kyle X. Hourihan
Acquisitions Editor: Jonathan Babcock
Cover Designer: Michael Kavish
Page Layout and Art by: Shannon Tozier and Patricia Lupien
Copy Editors: Darlene Bordwell, Darren Meiss
Indexer: Rich Carlson

Distributed by Publishers Group West in the United States and Jaguar Book Group in Canada.

Acknowledgments

We would like to acknowledge the following people for their kindness and support in making this book possible.

Karen Cross, Lance Tilford, Meaghan Cunningham, Kim Wylie, Harry Kirchner, Kevin Votel, Kent Anderson, Frida Yara, Jon Mayes, John Mesjak, Peg O'Donnell, Sandra Patterson, Betty Redmond, Roy Remer, Ron Shapiro, Patricia Kelly, Kristin Keith, Jennifer Pascal, Doug Reil, David Dahl, Janis Carpenter, and Susan Fryer of Publishers Group West for sharing their incredible marketing experience and expertise.

The incredibly hard working team at Elsevier Science, including Jonathan Bunkell, AnnHelen Lindeholm, Duncan Enright, David Burton, Rosanna Ramacciotti, Robert Fairbrother, Miguel Sanchez, Klaus Beran, and Rosie Moss for making certain that our vision remains worldwide in scope.

David Buckland, Wendi Wong, Daniel Loh, Marie Chieng, Lucy Chong, Leslie Lim, Audrey Gan, and Joseph Chan of STP Distributors for the enthusiasm with which they receive our books.

Kwon Sung June at Acorn Publishing for his support.

Jackie Gross, Gayle Voycey, Alexia Penny, Anik Robitaille, Craig Siddall, Darlene Morrow, Iolanda Miller, Jane Mackay, and Marie Skelly at Jackie Gross & Associates for all their help and enthusiasm representing our product in Canada.

Lois Fraser, Connie McMenemy, Shannon Russell, and the rest of the great folks at Jaguar Book Group for their help with distribution of Syngress books in Canada.

David Scott, Tricia Wilden, Marilla Burgess, Annette Scott, Geoff Ebbs, Hedley Partis, Bec Lowe, and Mark Langley of Woodslane for distributing our books throughout Australia, New Zealand, Papua New Guinea, Fiji Tonga, Solomon Islands, and the Cook Islands.

Winston Lim of Global Publishing for his help and support with distribution of Syngress books in the Philippines.

Acknowledgments

Contributors

Cherie Amon (CCSI, CCSA, CCSE, NSA) is technical editor of and contributor to the best selling *Check Point Next Generation Security Administration* (Syngress Publishing, ISBN: 1-928994-74-1), as well as the *Nokia Network Security Solutions Handbook* (Syngress, ISBN: 1-931836-70-1). Cherie is a Senior Professional Security Engineer at Integralis, a systems integrator specializing in IT and e-commerce security solutions. She is both a Check Point and Nokia Certified Security Instructor and has been installing, configuring, and supporting Check Point products since 1997. Cherie currently provides third-tier technical support to Integralis clients and acts as Technical Lead for many managed firewall accounts. Cherie is a member of USENIX and SAGE.

Chris Tobkin (CCSI, CCSE+, CCSE, CCSA, MCP) has over eight years of security-related experience in a wide range of products and technologies. Chris is currently employed as a Security Engineer for Check Point Software Technologies, Ltd. His career began in programming C, C++, and Perl. While studying for his MIS degree, his job at the University of Minnesota included systems and network administration, and later, database administration and project management. His interest in security was recognized and applied to each of these areas. Chris later moved on to a security services company where he was able to hone his skills in social engineering, penetration testing, firewalling, policy development, intrusion detection, and teaching courses in security, including Check Point.

Simon Coffey (CCSI, CCSA, CCSE) is a support consultant based in the Integralis European Support Centre in Reading, United Kingdom. Integralis is one of Europe's leading specialists in the IT security market. Simon has many years experience providing support, training, and installation services for security products, specializing in Check Point solutions and Nokia firewall appliances. He is also a member of the Theale

Volunteer Networking Group, a local forum for discussing current real-world issues.

Robert Stephens (CISSP, CCSI, NSI, NSA-IAM) is a Senior Security Consultant with VigilantMinds, where he provides enterprise security assessments and penetration services, along with engineering services, for managed Check Point VPN-1/FireWall-1 solutions for VigilantMinds clients. Prior to this he was the Technical Lead for Check Point and Nokia training and courseware development with VeriSign. Robert holds a bachelor's degree in Criminology from the University of Pittsburgh and a master's degree in Management Information Systems from Duquesne University.

Barry J. Stiefel (CISSP, CCSI, MCSE, CCSA, CCSE, CCNA, A+), co-author of the best selling *Next Generation Check Point Certified Security Administrator*, is the founder of Information Engine, Inc., a San Francisco security training and consulting firm (www.Information-Engine.com). Previously, he was the Founding Manager of Information Systems at Galileo Technology, an instructor at the University of California, and President of the Windows NT Engineering Association. Barry has developed and teaches the only independent Check Point FireWall-1 training course and is developing CPUG.org, the Check Point User Group. Barry has earned a bachelor's of Science, as well as a master's in Business Administration. In his lab, he has more firewalls and routers than he needs, but not as many as he wants.

Yinal Ozkan (CISSP, CCSE) is a Senior Security Engineer at Integralis. He currently provides low level troubleshooting support for enterprise level customers. Yinal is a strategic contributor for large scale deployment projects and security awareness implementation initiatives. His specialties include smart cards, financial systems security, and network security systems. He enjoys focusing on financial sector clients. Yinal holds a bachelor's degree from Istanbul Technical University, and is a member of the ISSA and ISACA. Yinal lives in Manchester, CT.

Thorsten Behrens (CCSE, CCNA, CNE-5, CNE-4) is a Senior Security Engineer with Integralis. Thorsten provides technical expertise to all of Integralis' Managed Security Services and Support clients. He is responsible for complete client satisfaction on a technical and support level for clients, and is a leading member of the Integralis QA team. Thorsten's specialties include Check Point FireWall-1, Cisco PIX and routers, network design and troubleshooting, and communications infrastructure (including Frame Relay, ISDN, and ATM). Thorsten is a German national who currently resides in Springfield, MA with his family, Christopher, Amberlea, and Caitlin.

Kurt Falde (MCSE, MCSA, MCP, CCSE, CCSA, A+) is the Senior Systems Engineer for INFO1 Holding Company, Inc., located in Atlanta, GA. Kurt is responsible for maintaining the corporate Active Directory network and the Check Point Firewall structures throughout the company's multiple sites. He provides direction, implementation and troubleshooting for the numerous VPN's that the company maintains for business-to-business connectivity. He is currently engaged in managing the merging of several new sites into the corporate Active Directory network as well as security infrastructure. Kurt has spent the last nine years working in the IT industry. His enthusiasm with using computers, however, goes back about fifteen years. Kurt holds a bachelor's degree in Mechanical Engineering from Pensacola Christian College. Kurt currently lives in Sugarhill, GA with his wife, Tara, and their cat, Mr. Kitty.

Daniel Kligerman (CCSA, CCSE, Extreme Networks GSE, LE) is a Consulting Analyst with TELUS Enterprise Solutions Inc., where he specializes in routing, switching, load balancing, and network security in an Internet hosting environment. Daniel is a contributing author for *Check Point Next Generation Security Administration* (Syngress Publishing, ISBN: 1-928994-74-1). A University of Toronto graduate, Daniel holds an honors bachelor's of Science degree in Computer Science, Statistics, and English. Daniel currently resides in Toronto, Canada. He would like to thank Robert, Anne, Lorne, and Merita for their support.

Martin Summers (CCSA, CCSE) is a consultant with Integralis, where he provides technical support for Integralis customers and the Articon Integralis group. His specialties include UNIX and troubleshooting network systems. Martin has previously worked as Project Manager and Senior Engineer at BBC Monitoring, part of the BBC World Service. Martin currently resides in Reading, United Kingdom with his wife, Julie.

Jamie Caesar (CCSE, CCNP) is the Senior Network Engineer for INFO1 Holding Company, Inc., where he is responsible for enterprise network design, deployment, and security for voice and data networks, as well as developing secure, highly available solutions for client connectivity. Jamie is also a co-author of *Managing Cisco Network Security, Second Edition* (Syngress Publishing, ISBN: 1-931836-56-6). Jamie holds a bachelor's degree in Electrical Engineering from Georgia Tech and he resides outside Atlanta, GA with his wife, Julie.

Technical Reviewer

Kyle X. Hourihan (NSA) is the Course Development Manager and a Senior Technical Trainer for Nokia Internet Communications in Mountain View, CA. He designs, writes, and teaches Nokia Internet Division's internal and external training material. He conducts Train-the-Trainer sessions for Nokia Authorized Training Partners as well as high-end training for Nokia's internal R&D and TACs (Telephone Assistance Centers). Kyle has been working in Network Security since 1999, and previously worked for 3Com as a Senior Instructor and Developer for their Carrier Systems Division (Commworks). He began his career working as a programmer writing code for Cisco IOS, implementing minor routing protocols, and performing software QA on their routers. Kyle earned a bachelor's of Science in Computer Science from the University of Maryland, College Park. He is a co-author of the highly acclaimed *Nokia Network Security Solutions Handbook* (Syngress Publishing, ISBN: 1-931836-70-1), and he is also a co-author of Freesoft.org (www.freesoft.org), a comprehensive source of Internet engineering information. Kyle resides in Palo Alto, CA.

Technical Editors

Jim Noble (CISSP, CCSA, CCSE, CCSI, CCSE+, CNX) is the Network and Security Director for INFO1 Holding Company, Inc. He and his team are responsible for the design of the company's networking infrastructure, security architecture, telecommunications strategy, and data center design. He comes from an Army Intelligence background, and has 11 years of Information Systems experience. Jim has five years experience with Check Point FireWall-1 and is very interested in securing information. INFO1 Holding Company, Inc., an information technology company, is one of the four largest credit information providers to the mortgage industry. The company provides credit information and other related services including flood certifications, fraud detection, tax return verifications, and business reports to mortgage and banking clients throughout the country. The company is known for its industry leading technology, and through its nationwide processing centers, has earned a reputation for excellent customer service. INFO1 uses advanced electronic data exchange in XML, X12 and other standard and proprietary formats over secure Internet and Private Wide Area Network connections.

Victor Chang (CCSA, CCSE, CCNA) is the Product Line Support Team Lead for IPSO and Hardware with Nokia. He currently provides Product Line Escalation Support for the Nokia IP Series Appliances and assists Product Management in new product development. Victor currently resides in Fremont, CA. He would like to thank his parents, Tsun San and Suh Jiuan Chang, Ricardo and Eva Estevez, as well as the rest of his family and friends. Without their love and support none of this would have been possible.

Doug Maxwell (CCSI, NSA) is a Senior Professional Services Engineer with Integralis in East Hartford, CT. He primarily designs and implements the integration of Nokia and other Check Point firewalls, as well as IDS solutions into enterprise networks, and teaches Nokia Security

Administration and Check Point NG to clients. He is also the Lead Engineer for the Integralis-US S3 team, which provides network security auditing, penetration testing, and computer forensic services. His specialties include UNIX network security and firewall/IDS network integration. Doug holds a bachelor's of Science degree in Computer Science from the University of Massachusetts at Amherst, and is a member of the Association for Computing Machinery (ACM), USENIX, and the System Administrator's Guild (SAGE). Doug is a contributing author for *Check Point Next Generation Security Administration*, (Syngress Publishing, ISBN: 1-928994-74-1). He happily resides in Ellington, CT with his wife and two-year-old son.

Contents

Foreword

Security of corporate networks has become big business. Many companies are willing to provide hardware, software, consulting, design, and implementation services. The product space is vast, offering many different levels of products that claim to provide all manner of solutions. The problem with the current state of the security space is that it can be a difficult sea to navigate. The vast range of companies and products as well as the ever-growing number of consulting companies can make choosing a network security product a grueling process. However, for the past six years Check Point has stood out as a leader in security solutions. Check Point software, certified consulting, support, certification, and authorized training provide a solid solution for securing any network environment. Check Point OPSEC partners (www.opsec.com) provide additional solutions to augment Check Point's security solutions.

In addition to providing corporations and large enterprise solutions, Check Point's FireWall-1 NG has products that range from five-user small office solutions to multifirewall, load-balanced systems with bandwidth management for unlimited user enterprises. This vast coverage of the market also allows organizations to start small with FireWall-1 products and grow their security system investments as their organizations grow.

Since the NG product is a completely new architecture, Check Point can very easily provide new features for the product. FireWall-1 feature packs are the new method to receive new features and minor hotfix rollups. This book uncovers the advanced features of Check Point FireWall-1 NG, specifically focusing on the Feature Pack 3 (FP3) release. Check Point has led the firewall and virtual private network (VPN) market for the past four years, and this latest release provides more leading-edge features that should keep FireWall-1 in the market lead for some time to come. This book provides you with a firm picture of the new features of NG FP3 and how to best utilize these features in securing your environment.

We designed this book to provide you with resources to further your expertise with NG, which introduced changes to existing methods of functionality; we review these changes in Chapter 1. New client-side NAT and automatic ARP features are detailed, so you can make the right decisions for deploying these tools in your environments.

Other changes in the software, including the new names for the old GUI clients, are covered in Chapter 2. The SMART Clients provide new names and new features for the management of the FireWall-1 NG product. Understanding these new interfaces is critical to the ongoing management of the NG product. Some of the new features include the use of certificate-based authentication of firewall administrators.

Certificate-based authentication can also be used for other purposes and is easily integrated into NG. NG can even be your certificate authority. Chapter 3 covers these new additions for authentication and reviews how RADIUS, TACACS+, and other types of authentication can be used in your environments.

Since 4.*x* of FireWall-1, CheckPoint has provided many VPN deployment options. Designing large-scale VPN environments has mainly been the work of consultants. We reveal these VPN concepts in Chapter 4 to ensure that you choose the right ones to use in your environment. A discussion of advanced VPN client installations follows in Chapter 5, to assist you in deploying SecuRemote and SecureClient.

NG adds new strengths to the firewall market by providing easy solutions for high-availability and load-sharing configurations. The ability to scale out your firewall infrastructure provides a new range of options for hardware, deployment scenarios, and scalability. Chapter 6 covers these options and provides clear information on how to deploy these new features.

FireWall-1 NG can operate on many platforms, such as Nokia IPSO, Solaris, Windows, Linux, and now a Check Point-specific operating system, SecurePlatform. Chapter 7 covers the SecurePlatform product. SecurePlatform is a hardened version of Linux, specifically designed to run Check Point software. Although many organizations are wary of deploying Linux solutions due to supportability issues, Check Point provides support for SecurePlatform running FireWall-1. In addition to this support, SecurePlatform provides incredible throughput at excellent prices, achieving new levels of protection and value.

In addition to these new features, the management server has not been forgotten. FireWall-1 4.*x* contained tools that many administrators created with scripts, batch jobs, and other tools to make the process of maintaining a management server easier. Check Point took notice of all those activities. Chapter 8 covers the new features of the management server, including automatic log rotation and advanced management server high availability, to name a few.

Other options available with NG include Check Point Vectoring Protocol and URL Filtering Protocol options that allow OPSEC partner integration for advanced security controls. Chapter 9 provides details on how to use these features in your environment.

To enhance your experience with NG, Chapter 10 delves into the methods of deploying VPN clients using the new SecureClient Packaging tool. With this tool, you can provide prepackaged installations for your remote VPN deployments. We provide new insight into the options for deployment with SecureClient and SecuRemote.

NG includes new elements that allow you to create a more defensive posture with your networks. Chapter 11 reviews how the Smart Defense features provide you a stronger posture by protecting your network from new attacks as they are identified. Now you can stop Code Red and other Web server attacks by configuring the Smart Defense features.

New features that allow updating of firewall and management servers provide the capability to upgrade and control hotfix deployment, software updates, and feature pack installations. Smart Update, covered in Chapter 12, shows how this tool is used to manage software updates. The Smart Update tool also centrally manages licensing for one or multiple firewalls and other Check Point software. This tool is the foundation for the new licensing model introduced in FireWall-1 NG.

The final three chapters of this book cover Performance Pack, User Authority, and advanced troubleshooting methods and provides insight into how these additional features are used in a real-world network. Performance Pack provides advanced throughput for your firewall needs; installing it on the Solaris platform is covered in Chapter 13. The User Authority allows you to combine Check Point user authentication into Web applications in your environment. Chapter 14 covers this new feature. Lastly, in Chapter 15 we review how to troubleshoot your firewall when all else fails, discussing the features that are available to you for troubleshooting your installations.

It is our hope that this book provides you with a guide to these new Check Point FireWall-1 features so that you can make the best decisions for your situation.

—Jim Noble, CCSI, CISSP, CCSA, CCSE, CCSE+, CNX
March, 2003

Chapter 1

FW-1 NG Operational Changes

Solutions in this chapter:

- Static NAT Changes from 4.x to NG
- Automatic ARP
- Upgrading 4.x to NG

☑ Summary

☑ Solutions Fast Track

☑ Frequently Asked Questions

Introduction

In the latest release of FireWall-1 NG, Feature Pack 3 (NG-FP3), Check Point Software has introduced many new features. This chapter discusses some fundamental changes in software's methods of operation from 4.*x* to NG. Chapter 2 discusses the new SMART Clients introduced in FP3. Some of the key changes in NG include a much faster kernel, a revamp of static Network Address Translation (NAT), and the introduction of automatic Address Resolution Protocol (ARP), to name just a few. We will highlight the new features of the NG product and how these changes affect your FireWall-1 environment. For readers who are new to FireWall-1, this section outlines the ways that some of these key features function and what they can provide for your deployment.

NG is not an upgrade from 4.*x*. Check Point has spent a number of years redesigning the FireWall-1 product; NG represents that redesign. Some of the functions that were available in the 4.*x* version have been removed, replaced, or simply restructured from the ground up. NG contains new features that existing administrators will need to review before implementing.

The first area in which the NG product has significantly improved is in its throughput. NG increases the throughput on all platforms. (Visit www.checkpoint.com/products/choice/platforms/platforms_matrix.html for the specifics on platform and performance numbers.) For example, the Windows platform with Dual Xeon processors, 1GB RAM, and two 64-bit PCI Gigabit Ethernet cards will provide approximately 625Mbps throughput, with a platform price of around $5,000. This is a substantial improvement over the 4.*x* platform. Check Point also has added SecurePlatform, which provides a secure operating system to use with the Check Point software. If the hardware is used with SecurePlatform, NG can provide greater than 3+Gbps for the same $5,000 hardware cost!

Static NAT has also changed. With the ability to perform NAT on the client side of the connection, Automatic ARP functions, NG can make your Static NAT creations on hosts very quick and simple operations. In some areas, the NAT changes could change the way your network needs to be configured, so be sure to review this section well if you plan to utilize client-side NAT.

Lastly, in some environments, upgrading your product might not be the best solution. Rebuilding your firewall might be a better solution. We dig into these scenarios and provide insight into how best to get your 4.*x* firewall up to NG. Now let's review these changes.

Static NAT Changes from 4.x to NG

You have installed your firewall and are now configuring the Rule Base, objects, and systemwide parameters. Although the process of configuring the rules is relatively straightforward, the NAT configuration always seems to increase the frustration level for firewall administrators. The security policy is a top-to-bottom list of matching criteria for packets that reach the firewall. With a rule in place to accept the desired traffic, the "What happens next?" question complicates matters when you're implementing NAT. We have two basic methods of applying address translation: Static and Hide. In Hide mode, you are using one IP address to serve as the source IP for multiple clients—a many-to-one substitution. The common application of Hide mode is to provide clients with a legal IP address to be able to access resources on the Internet. Check Point's Hide mode NAT is synonymous with Port Address Translation (PAT). Static NAT replaces the physical IP address of a single device with a different IP address, a one-to-one substitution. Typically, this method is used for making resources available from the Internet.

NAT does not require us to use valid Internet addresses as the translated address. Although this is the most common application, there are no restrictions on using non-routable IP addresses for the translation. For the examples that follow, the translated addresses are routable.

Both Hide and Static NAT can take place on either interface of your firewall with NG-FP3. This does not imply that you only have two interfaces on your firewall; typically, there are three or more. For an individual packet traversing a firewall, there are only two interfaces. The first interface is where the packet arrives at the firewall and makes a comparison to either the Rule Base or the firewall state table in the inbound direction. The second interface is where the firewall forwards the packet after being accepted in the outbound direction. The origin of the packet is the determinant for referring to an interface to as either inbound or outbound. Version 4.*x* did not provide the flexibility to modify where the translation occurred; it was always on the outbound interface. Pre-NG-FP3 manual NAT rules applied only to the outbound direction. NG-FP3 has an option for translating manual rules on the inbound interface.

Tools & Traps…

Address Translation Rules: Automatic vs. Manual

There are two options for creating address translation rules: automatic and manual. *Automatic rules* are created from an object by selecting the check box for **Add Automatic Address Translation Rules** in the NAT configuration options of that particular object. These rules may not be modified or deleted from the SmartDashboard Address Translation rules screen. The comment will say Automatic Rule (see the network object data). Automatic rules will always

Continued

be contiguous, and Static NAT rules will appear above Hide NAT rules. As long as an object has automatic NAT enabled, these rules will exist in any security policy created.

Manual rules are created by inserting rules in the SmartDashboard Address Translation rules screen. Manual rules can only be inserted before or after the automatic rules. You must create an object for the node or network and an object that represents the NAT address. This increases the number of objects that need to be created and managed. Pre-NG-FP3 manual Static NAT rules did the destination address translation only on the server side. NG-FP3 has an option for enabling destination translation on the client side. Both types may be used in the same security policy; however, manual NAT rules will not carry over when you create a new policy.

Reasons for creating manual NAT rules are influenced by your production requirements. One common scenario is using a manual NAT rule to not do address translation between networks. This situation could occur where a virtual private network (VPN) is configured and the encryption domain is defined using the internal addresses or where there is a wide area network (WAN) connection. Add a manual rule, configure the source and destination section for the original packet, and leave the settings as original in the translated packet. This rule must come before the automatic rules.

Another scenario for using manual NAT rules is one in which you want to translate the destination address based on the service type. You have a limited number of legal IP addresses and need to have different server types using the same IP. It is important to remember the change in FP3 allowing for destination translation on the client side when you upgrade from earlier NG versions.

You must account for certain considerations within your infrastructure when you're selecting either mode. The changes are not intended to make your life more difficult as a firewall administrator or to provide job security. These features are intended to allow the flexibility necessary for the complexity of our network topologies. Static NAT in 4.*x* is very rigid, with specific configuration steps. NG is designed to provide dynamic and automatic configuration parameters to support simple and complex network designs.

Server-Side NAT

Server-side NAT is the default when you're using static NAT in version 4.*x*. Say that we have a server that we want to make available using a different IP address from the one physically assigned. The reasons for doing this are either to provide a legal address where there is currently an illegal address or to mask the physical address. The translation of the destination address takes place on the interface on the server side of the firewall, the outbound interface.

Let's look at the flow of a packet through this process and the configuration steps necessary to make this work. We have a Web server www.newyork.com with a physical address of 10.1.1.3 that we want to make available to the Internet with a 38.1.1.3 address. Once the valid IP address is selected and added to the Domain Name Server (DNS) record, we need to configure the firewall so that the communication functions properly.

The first step in either version is to create the workstation object using the physical, nonroutable IP address, as shown in Figure 1.1. The second step is to define the NAT configuration settings for this object using a legal IP address with Static NAT, as illustrated in Figure 1.2. Checking the box for **Add Automatic Address Translation Rules** will generate the inbound and outbound rules. The third step is to configure a rule that accepts traffic destined for this server—in our case, http or https, as shown in Figure 1.3.

Figure 1.1 Web Server Object

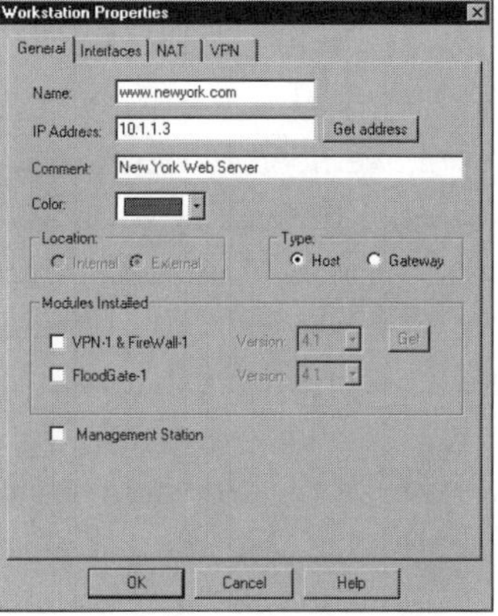

Figure 1.2 Web Server NAT

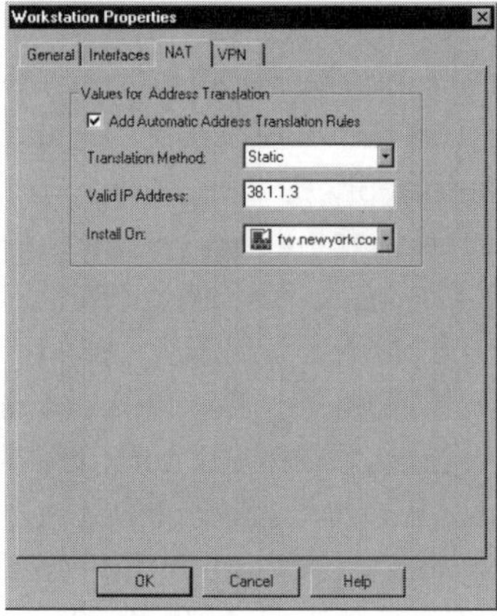

Figure 1.3 Firewall Rule

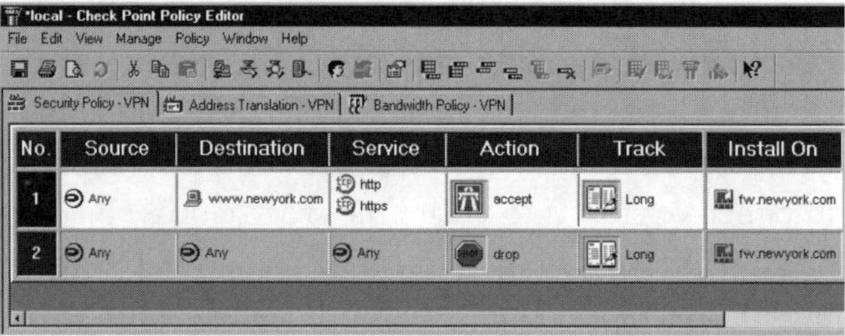

If you are using NG with default settings with a functional Automatic ARP environment, you are done with the process. The 4.*x* environment has a few additional steps. For seasoned veterans, the next couple of sections are merely a review.

Version 4.*x* Destination Static NAT

This section follows the configuration steps relative to the packet flow. No Automatic ARP is available when 4.*x* is used; we need to define a means to let the border router know where to send the packet—the firewall's external network interface card (NIC). Accomplishing this goal requires creation of an ARP entry with the legal NAT IP address and the MAC address of the external NIC on the firewall. Another method is to add a static host route on the border router that routes the legal NAT IP to the firewall's external interface.

Now that the packet has arrived at the firewall, we need to make sure that the firewall knows where to forward the packet. No translation has taken place, so the network layer on the firewall will want to send the packet back out the external interface. The destination address is still the legal IP that is part of the network between the border router and the firewall. Create a static host route on the firewall routing the legal IP address to the internal host address. This forwards the packet out the internal interface.

Finally, at the internal interface on the server side of the firewall, the destination address is changed from the legal to the nonroutable IP address. The server then receives the packet. The server then sends a reply packet, the source address being the nonroutable IP, to the default gateway. The firewall then changes the source IP back to the legal address at the internal interface. The packet is dropped here based on Rule 0 unless the antispoofing is modified to accept packets with a source IP from the network address range and the legal IP. Properly configuring the antispoofing requires you need to complete the following steps. First you must create a network object to represent the IP network physically connected to the internal interface of the firewall (see Figure 1.4). Next you must create a workstation object representing the NAT (legal) IP address being used for the Web server, as shown in Figure 1.5. Add both of these objects to a group, and use this group for the antispoofing settings on the internal interface (see Figure 1.6). Finally, you need to select the **Specific** option on the Security tab for the internal interface, then use this object you just created, as shown in Figure 1.7. *It is very important to set the **Spoof Tracking** settings to **Log**. The default setting is no tracking; choosing the default would make troubleshooting this problem a little difficult.* The reply packet is then routed back to the client.

Figure 1.4 Network Object

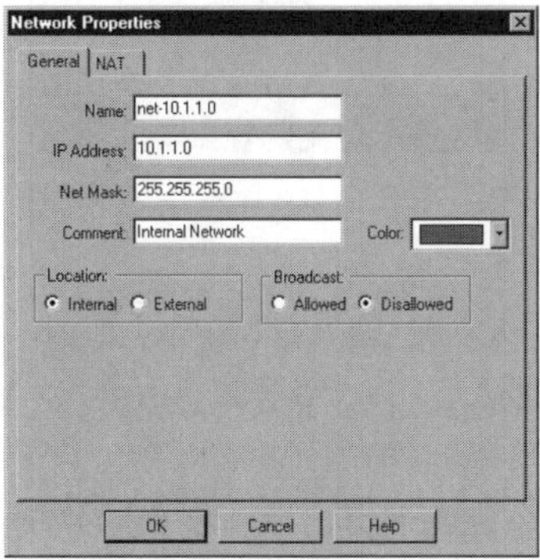

Figure 1.5 Workstation Object for NAT(Legal) IP

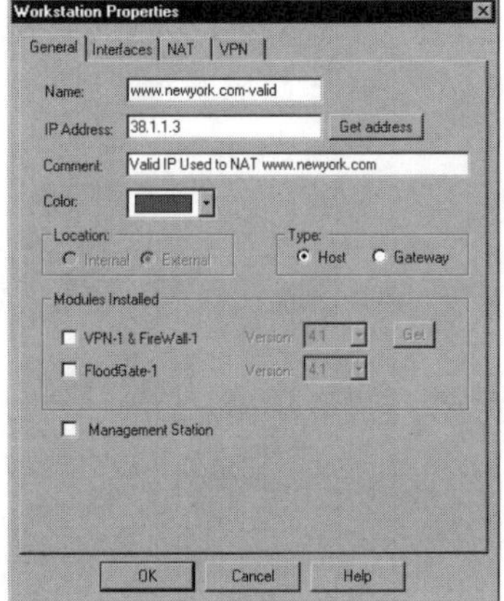

Figure 1.6 Group Object

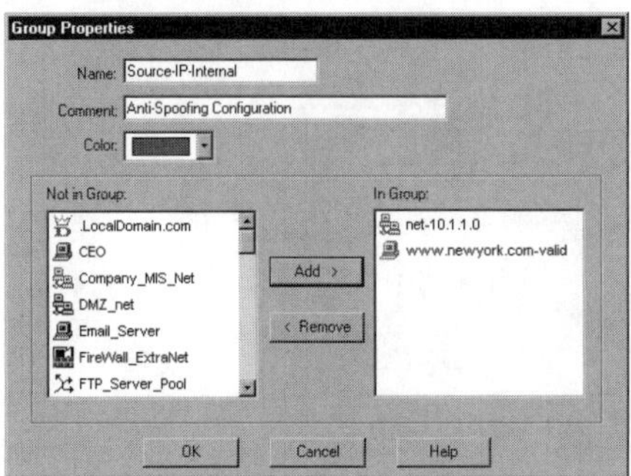

Figure 1.7 Antispoofing

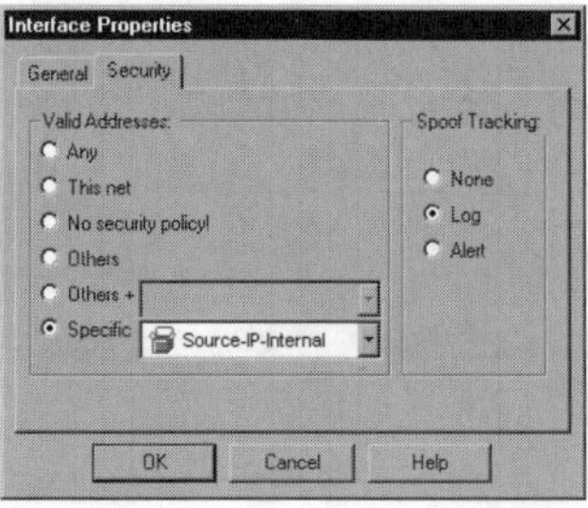

How It Really Works

In the scenario diagrammed in Figure 1.8, a client wants to connect to the www.newyork.com server. Provided the DNS is configured properly, a packet is created with a source IP (SIP) of 4.3.2.1 (Client IP) going to a destination IP (DIP) of 38.1.1.3.

Figure 1.8 Server-Side Static NAT

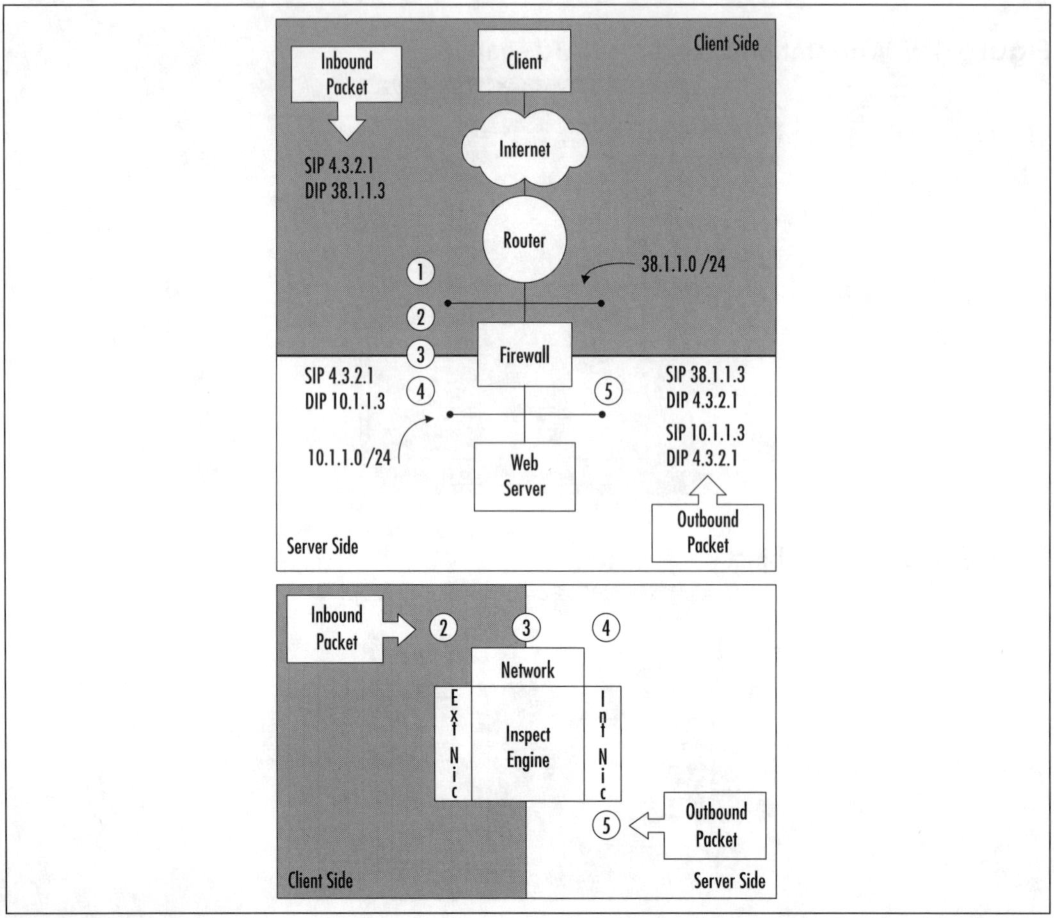

Through the magic of the Internet, the packet is routed along to the external router as follows:

1. The router has a packet with a DIP of 38.1.1.3, a network to which it is directly connected. If there is no specific route in place, the router will ARP asking for the MAC address of this IP. The firewall must be configured to reply to this ARP request with the MAC address of the external interface. The packet is then forwarded to the firewall.
2. The firewall now has a packet to match against the Rule Base, provided a rule is configured to accept the communication. (Yes, this implies that 4.3.2.1 is a valid SIP on the external interface.)
3. The packet is then passed up the stack to the network layer to determine routing. Internally the firewall will have a route for the 38.1.1.0 network back through the external interface. Because the DIP has not yet been modified, a host route is needed on the firewall. In this case, we want to route 38.1.1.3 via 10.1.1.3 so the packet is then directed out the internal interface.
4. At the internal (server side) interface, the DIP is now changed to 10.1.1.3 and the packet is forwarded to www.newyork.com.
5. Being a friendly Web server, a reply packet is then sent with SIP-10.1.1.3 to DIP-4.3.2.1. In this configuration, the default gateway is the firewall. The packet is modified before inspection by changing the SIP from 10.1.1.3 to 38.1.1.3. Now think back to Check Point 101 class. Before matching a packet to the state table or Rule Base, the SIP is checked against antispoofing settings. Without NAT, this interface should be configured as this net, meaning that an inbound packet to the firewall on this interface must have a SIP of 10.1.1.*x*. The packet has already had the SIP changed to the 38.1.1.3 address; unless we create a group containing the 10.1.1.0 network and 38.1.1.3, the antispoofing configuration will drop the packet.

Client-Side NAT

Client-side NAT occurs when the destination address is translated on the client-side interface of the firewall, the inbound interface. This removes the need for the static route required when you use the server side, the host route on the firewall, and the modification of the antispoofing feature. This option is new in NG and prior to FP3 was only available when you used automatic rules. FP3 adds the ability to do client-side translation for Manual NAT rules as well. The previous NG releases only use server-side NAT when manual rules are used. Enabling client-side translation is done in the

Global Properties | Network Address Translation screen by selecting **Translate destination on client side**, as shown in Figure 1.9.

Figure 1.9 The Global Properties Network Address Translation Settings

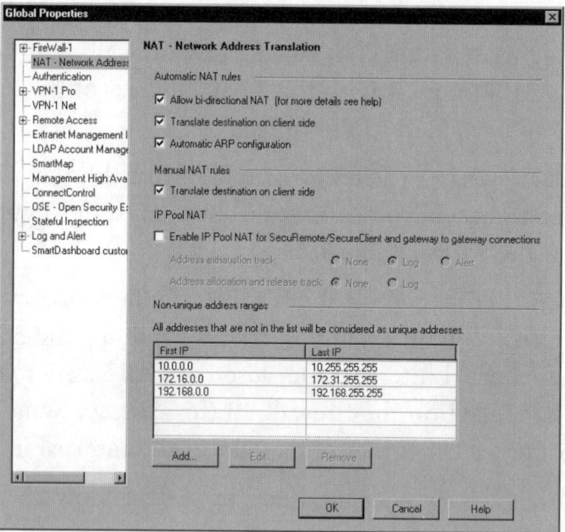

How It Really Works

The packet flow is not different, only the interface where the actual translation occurs (see Figure 1.10). The DIP on an incoming packet and the SIP of the reply packet are both modified at the external or client-side interface. A reminder for readers who are using a pre-FP3 version of NG: This function is only available for automatic NAT:

1. The router has a packet with a DIP of 38.1.1.3, a network to which it is directly connected. If there is no specific route in place, the router will ARP asking for the MAC address of this IP. The firewall must be configured to reply to this ARP request with the MAC address of the external interface. The packet is then forwarded to the firewall.
2. The firewall now has a packet to match against the Rule Base, provided a rule is configured to accept the communication. Now on the client-side interface, the DIP is changed from 38.1.1.3 to the illegal internal address of 10.1.1.3.
3. The packet is then passed up the stack to the network layer to determine routing. Because the DIP has already been modified, the packet is then forwarded out the internal interface; no host route is necessary.
4. A reply packet is then sent with SIP-10.1.1.3 to DIP-4.3.2.1. In this configuration, the default gateway is the firewall. The internal interface receives the

packet; a valid response to a connection request, and routes it to the default route. Before the packet is sent out the external interface to the destination, the SIP is changed back to 38.1.1.3.

Figure 1.10 Client-Side Static NAT

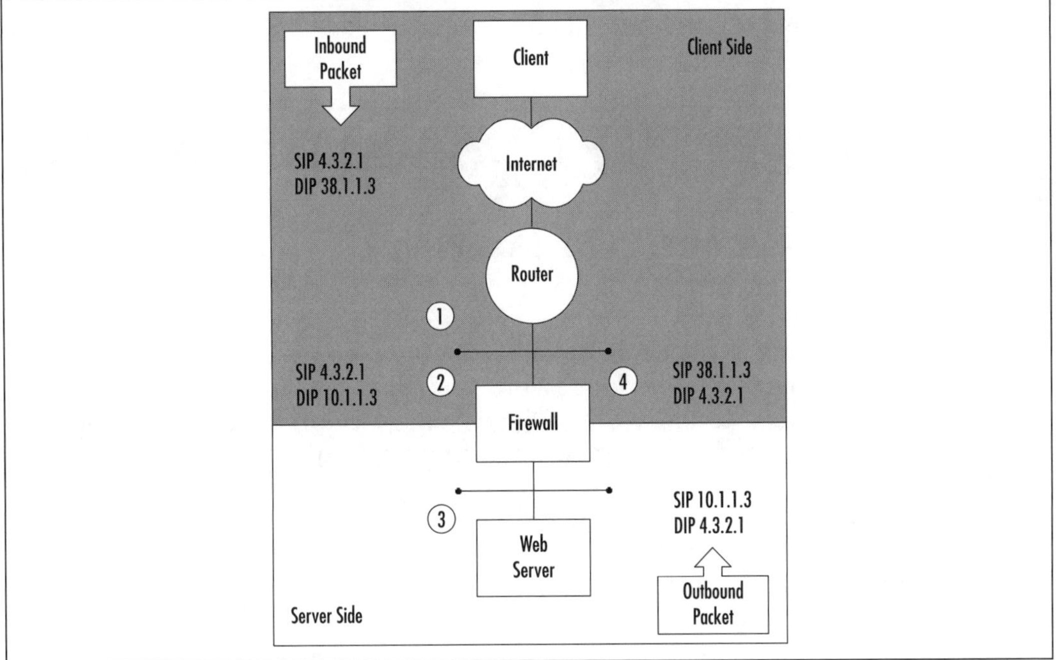

Bidirectional NAT

The one option in Figure 1.9 to enable bidirectional NAT is another new option. This option allows two NAT rules to apply to a connection. It is useful when you need to translate both the source and destinations. One scenario for using this option is when a remote location is using identical address space. For example, both the corporate office and remote office have used the 10.1.1.0/24 IP address space and communicate through an internal WAN connection. Both networks need static translation to different address ranges in order to talk with each other. This is only one particular scenario that might be applicable for your environment, and you should know the available options.

Automatic ARP

Next Generation adds the Automatic ARP configuration setting for Static NAT. This setting eliminates the need to create the ARP entry in the firewall operating system. This option is intended to overcome different nuances in the various operating systems on which NG is supported. The function of the ARP entry is to ensure that the router knows the firewall Media Access Control (MAC) address for the next hop in routing a packet. The Automatic ARP feature only works when automatic NAT rules are used. The main reason for maintaining this functionality is when an entity does not have configuration rights on a router connected to a network segment connected with the firewall. This includes an Internet service provider (ISP) or a partner or remote office with connectivity through a dedicated link.

Tools & Traps...

When Does Automatic ARP Not Work?

There are a few scenarios in which Automatic ARP does not work. One such configuration is when Manual NAT rules are used. If you use Manual NAT, you must define the ARP entry within the firewall operating system. Another solution in which Automatic ARP doesn't work is when a static route on the router is configured to point to the IP of the firewall interface on the connected network. The other scenarios involve issues with operating system compatibility or functionality.

Automatic ARP is not currently supported when a Nokia appliance is used. You must create a manual proxy-only ARP entry. The MAC address to use in creating this entry depends on the configuration. If you are using a single Nokia, use the interface's MAC address. If you're using Virtual Router Redundancy Protocol (VRRP), make sure you use the VRRP MAC address.

Windows 2000 presents a few issues. By default, you have an adapter labeled *NDISWANIP,* with no address assigned. This adapter must not exist on the firewall object for Automatic ARP to work. There cannot be an interface without an IP address assigned. You should disable this adapter from the operating system before installing Check Point software. To do so, in Device Manager select **View | Show hidden devices**. Under Network Adapters you will see an interface, **WAN Miniport(IP)**. Right-click this device and select **Disable**. In addition to disabling this port, you must make sure **Routing and Remote Access** is disabled.

In addition to the aforementioned configuration issues, you should be aware of other restrictions:

- Automatic ARP is not supported in performing Manual NAT.
- Automatic ARP is not supported on Linux implementations or when SecurePlatform is used (Check Point Knowledge Base Solution sk8022).
- Automatic ARP is not supported when IP Pool NAT is used (Check Point Knowledge Base Solution sk5751).

When ARP Is Automatic

Provided the operating system is both properly configured and supports Automatic ARP, this feature is available for use. Automatic ARP works only with automatically generated NAT rules, either Static or Hide. The benefit of Automatic ARP is that it eliminates a step in the NAT configuration. This feature works only in Solaris and Windows environments, so it might not necessarily be applicable to the entire audience. (This functionality of this feature on the many currently available appliances is unknown at the time of this writing.)

The command *fw ctl arp* is used to verify whether the Automatic ARP is working in Windows NT or 2000. The results list the resolved name, IP, MAC, and the interface IP that is advertising this information.

In a Windows 2000 environment, Check Point uses an application programming interface (API) provided by Microsoft for the Automatic ARP to function properly. The FireWall-1 software tells the operating system the IP addresses for which it is responsible in controlling ARP requests. A confusing symptom of this functionality is that when you type **arp –a**, you will not see the IP(s) listed with a **fw ctl arp** command. This situation is explained in Check Point Knowledge Base Solution sk13212.

When ARP Is Manual

There are a few different areas in which the ARP entries need to be defined manually. When using Manual ARP in your configuration, it is important that you uncheck **Automatic ARP configuration** in the Global Properties | NAT page. Making the decision to use Manual ARP or not really depends on your architecture. If the operating system of your FireWall-1 enforcement point does not support this feature, the decision has been made for you. The next contributing factor lies in the administrative control of the router(s) involved. If you do not control the router, you have no choice but to create an ARP entry on the firewall. The commands for creating an ARP entry in the more common operating systems are as follows:

- **Solaris** `arp -s <ip_address> <ethernet address> pub`
- **Windows** Create a local.arp file in the $FWDIR\state directory:

  `<ip_address> <ethernet address>`

- **IPSO** Create a Proxy Only ARP entry

An important consideration to keep in mind is that NAT is not always done solely on the Internet-facing side of the firewall. In some situations, you are using NAT across internally connected networks. In this situation, make sure you use the correct or MAC address from the interface facing the respective router. In some situations, you will not use the physical MAC address but a virtual one.

For example, in a High Availability (HA) configuration, the MAC address to use depends on the solution used for HA. The first consideration is whether you are implementing an active/standby or load-sharing configuration. With ClusterXL, there may be a virtual or physical MAC address serving an interface. In FP3, there are two modes available for HA: New mode, as it is called, or Legacy mode. In Legacy mode, a Unicast MAC address serves a physical IP address; New mode uses a multicast MAC serving a virtual address, the same way that the load-sharing mode works. Earlier NG versions only used the Legacy mode for HA. If you're using a Nokia configuration, you can use VRRP for active/standby or the new Clustering mode for load sharing. Determine the actual or virtual MAC address needed. In the second consideration; network infrastructure aside, you need to make sure that the router will accept ARP replies in the form used. By default, a Nokia will neither accept multicast ARP replies nor allow a multicast ARP entry to be configured locally.

This chapter spent a great deal of time covering ARP and the different methods available in NG FP3. You can make NAT work just fine without configuring any kind of ARP entries. All you need to do is configure a static host route on the router that will be sending out the ARP request. Configure these routes for the NAT IP addresses sending the packet directly to the firewall; after all, that is what the ARP entries are designed to accomplish in your environment.

Upgrading 4.x to NG

Firewall administrators commonly have questions about upgrading to NG, such as: What versions can I upgrade from? What version should I upgrade to? Should I upgrade or rebuild? When will I have to upgrade? There are no absolute answers for every configuration. A great deal of confusion over whether or not to try and upgrade Check Point 2000 (4.*x*) to NG originated with NG FP0, the initial release. The initial release did not consistently upgrade to the new version cleanly, leaving a bad initial reaction to NG on the part of users.

Check Point has implemented quite a few new features in FP3, as you will see throughout this text. There are many improvements in documentation, features, flexibility, and performance. The fear over newsgroup postings or other information sources available on the Internet discussing issues with NG and the upgrade process is unfounded. Shortly, we'll discuss the steps in the upgrade process, but there is one dominant reason Check Point administrators must consider upgrading their infrastructures: The end of life for version 4.*x* is scheduled to occur on June 30, 2003.

There are three paths to take for the upgrade process: upgrade your existing management server, build another server to be used for the upgrade process, or use this opportunity to rebuild from scratch. The amount of work involved increases with each of these choices. The significant advantage for the parallel server choice is the ability to roll back if you do encounter a problem. The third choice could involve a significant investment of time and will test your meticulous nature. The new rebuild option is discussed at the end of this chapter. Ultimately, the choice is yours to make. Considering that your management server is the most important component of your firewall architecture, you might want to avoid a potential career-limiting move and choose the second or third options.

The quickest and easiest method to upgrade is to use a Check Point CD and select the Upgrade option directly on your live management server. This is by far the riskiest method of upgrading, because there is no quick and easy method to back out of the process. Tools are available to mitigate some of the risk in using this option. There is a Pre-Upgrade Verifier tool and a Post-Upgrade Verifier tool to assist in providing a clean upgrade. The Pre-Upgrade tool uses read-only access to analyze the database for potential issues that could interfere with a clean upgrade. It gives you an opportunity to address any necessary changes. If errors are encountered during the upgrade, the Post-Upgrade tool is designed to fix these problems or to verify the upgrade process. It is important to note that Check Point recommends that you make a backup copy of your $FWDIR\conf directory before running the Post-Upgrade tool. The reason for this is that this tool accesses the database with the ability to make changes. You can access the Pre-Upgrade an d Post-Upgrade Verifier tools by following this URL: www.checkpoint.com/techsupport/downloadsng/utilities.html (available with public access).

The most appealing option is to build a parallel system and take advantage of the upgrade utilities in a manual or automatic process. The automatic process involves making a copy of the existing management server's contents and performing the upgrade directly from the CD. To assist in this process, you'll find some Check Point Solutions invaluable for guidance. The first is the Check Point Knowledge Base Solution ID, sk11635*: How to Upgrade from VPN-1/FireWall-1 4.1 to VPN-1/FireWall-1 NG FP1 and Above.* This solution provides a step-by-step process for replicating an existing management server. Within this solution are two hyperlinks; click to get the Upgrade Verifier Utility that links to www.checkpoint.com/techsupport/ng/fp3_updates.html and the Upgrade Guide that links to https://support.checkpoint.com/public/idsearch.jsp?id=sk16625 (both available with public access). The first link is a one-stop page for FP3 documents, tools, and applications. The Upgrade Guide link to Solution ID sk16625 is discussed in the next section.

The 4.*x* Upgrade Process

Let's say that you have an existing 4.*x* installation and the time has come to upgrade to NG FP3. There is a specific order you must follow to upgrade: management server (SmartCenter Server), then graphical user interface (GUI) clients (SMART Clients), and then firewalls (enforcement points). The upgrade of the 4.1 management server to the FP3 SmartCenter Server is the most critical step, as mentioned earlier; SmartCenter Server is the new name for the management server. (The functionality and a complete list of name changes appears in Chapter 8.) Once this component is upgraded, you need to upgrade the GUI clients. Upgrading the enforcement points can be done manually or scheduled automatically using the SmartUpdate tool, as described in Chapter 8. An NG management server can manage version 4.1 firewalls provided that you select backward compatibility during the installation.

Let's now look at sk16625, *The Ultimate Upgrade Guide: How to Upgrade a Management Server from 4.1 to NG.* A hyperlink in this resolution, *How to Upgrade the Management Server,* links to http://support.checkpoint.com/kb/docs/public/firewall1/ng/pdf/upgrade_mgmt_srvr.pdf, a file that is indeed the ultimate upgrade guide for taking a 4.1 through NG FP2 management server to FP3. This date for this PDF file is February 2003. At the time this chapter was written, this file had recently replaced a version from December 2002. This document contains detailed systematic processes to replicate your existing management server and then use automatic or manual methods to upgrade.

The main premise of this document is based on upgrading without changing the operating system, name, or IP address of the existing management station. If you are using the upgrade opportunity to migrate to a different platform, change the name or change the IP of the current management server. There are appendices in the document highlighting the differences in the process.

When to Rebuild

You might be thinking that you would rather have a tooth pulled without Novocain than completely rebuild your management server. If your environment includes thousands of objects and dozens of rule bases, you could find an upgrade option more appealing. The main benefit of this option is to enjoy the luxury of starting with a clean slate. You can define common standards for naming and color designation. Eliminate the unused or unnecessary objects, services, and rules by not creating them. This option requires an additional server for rebuilding, so the option involves less risk. One last point to keep in mind is that naming conventions are not quite as important in NG as they are in 4.*x*. Using some type of naming convention such as *h-hostname, net-x.x.x.x,* or *fw-fwname* helped with using the network objects manager. This tool sorts the objects alphabetically, regardless of type, and using a naming convention means that similar types of objects are listed together. In SmartView Dashboard, the new name for the Policy Editor in FP3, the order that objects are displayed in the Objects list can be sorted by type, name, and even color. However, using a standard naming convention is still beneficial for providing a level of clarity and consistency.

The next reason that makes a rebuild the option of choice deals with Rule Base optimization. Two different Rule Base scenarios make this option more viable. The first is when you are dealing with a legacy of policy generation without maintenance. Firewall administrators often forgo deletion of old rule sets. Every single rule of every policy ever saved exists in the rulebases.fws file. When a large number of legacy Rule Bases are present, you can use the rebuild option to avoid carrying antiquated polices along for the upgrade. The other appropriate situation is when you are looking to improve performance with a more streamlined rule set; the fewer the number of rules that exist, the better the performance. You might want to recreate new policies using a more streamlined Rule Base.

The aforementioned reasons for rebuilding versus upgrading are noncritical. Eliminating unused objects and old Rule Bases helps shorten compilation and installation time.

There is a stateful relationship between the objects.C and rulebases.fws files. Performing a manual backup by copying off these configuration files requires synchronization of these files. For example, if a Rule Base contained objects that were created today and you copied a version of the objects.C from a week ago, the Rule Base would no longer be able to load. Another type of corruption occurs when a group object no longer matches traffic correctly against the objects it contains. This and other types of corruption may be related to drive or memory errors. This problem is not specific to 4.*x* but also occurs in NG. If you have corruption issues, it can be impossible to locate the source of the problem. In this scenario, a clean rebuild is a necessity.

Summary

This chapter was designed to introduce you to Check Point Next Generation Feature Pack 3. In particular, we discussed the changes in Network Address Translation followed by the possible upgrade paths. Many enhancements are included for each FP release of the NG code. It is important to realize that the design modifications are engineered to improve the security of your VPN-1/FireWall-1 architecture. In doing so, the means by which the inspect engine makes decisions regarding packet flow have changed. Whether upgrading from the Check Point 2000 (4.1) version or within NG feature packs; a firewall administrator needs to understand the potential impact to his or her environment.

The configuration of NAT will always be one of your most important tasks. The changes in where this translation occurs on your gateway now depend on the default properties or your customization. These modifications are intended to remove complexity while providing additional flexibility. Your job is to implement these options successfully into your environment. Understanding how and why will give you the necessary tools to be successful.

An important element for packet flow with NAT is the ARP entry on the firewall. This entry is necessary for the router to forward packets to the firewall for translated addresses. Although there is an automatic option for the firewall in some configurations, it is important to know when this feature will not function. Equally important is to understand which MAC address is necessary for creating Manual ARP entries for special configurations. Ironically, you can avoid all the ARP issues by simply using static routes on the router to forward the packets to the firewall.

Upgrading the management server in your environment can be an intimidating process. The early issues of the initial NG release and the horror stories of failed upgrade attempts have made this task even more overwhelming. The functions of an NG management server are more numerous than a 4.1 management station. The underlying database structure is entirely different as well. Check Point provides utilities and documentation to guide you through the upgrade process. The recommended practice is to replicate the management server before performing the upgrade so that you have a rollback option. Additionally, you may chose the upgrade as an opportunity to rebuild the configuration from scratch. Knowing your options and selecting the best choice will depend on your specific goals and requirements.

Throughout the remainder of this text, we highlight additional changes and configuration options that will impact your Check Point solution. Although these changes are subtle in comparison with the major version changes from 4.*x* to NG, consider FP3 a substantial version upgrade. The chapters that follow walk you through various options and changes. This guide is intended to inform you of how the environment changed and to make you comfortable with making the decisions that lie ahead of you.

Solutions Fast Track

Static NAT Changes from 4.*x* to NG

☑ The new default Global Properties are configured to perform address translation on the client-side interface of the firewall for automatic NAT rules defined on the object.

☑ When Manual NAT rules are employed, the default setting in FP3 is to perform the translation on the client side of the connection; this can be modified to work like the earlier NG releases, which only changed the address on the server-side interface.

☑ It is possible in NG to have more than one NAT rule apply to a packet. This function is enabled by default and can be toggled off in the Network Address Translation section of the Global Properties.

Automatic ARP

☑ Instead of having to create an ARP entry in the firewall OS when you're using NAT in NG, the firewall software can do this for you automatically. This is the default setting.

☑ This feature is *not* supported on the Nokia, Linux, and SecurePlatform installations; on those, you must manually configure ARP settings.

☑ Windows 2000 installations require no interfaces to be active without an IP address in order for Automatic ARP to function properly.

☑ The command *fw ctl arp* will display the Automatic ARP entries functional on Windows NT and 2000 installations.

Upgrading 4.*x* to NG

☑ The firewall database can be checked for configuration settings that could interfere with the upgrade process using the Pre-Upgrade Verifier tool available from Check Point.

☑ The Post-Upgrade Verifier tool can be used to fix database conversion errors that occurred during the upgrade process.

☑ The upgrade can be done automatically or manually, at your discretion.

- ☑ It is recommended that you perform the upgrade on a parallel system rather than on the live management server.
- ☑ Detailed steps are available with public access from the Check Point SecureKnowledge Web page, Solution ID sk16625.

Frequently Asked Questions

The following Frequently Asked Questions, answered by the authors of this book, are designed to both measure your understanding of the concepts presented in this chapter and to assist you with real-life implementation of these concepts. To have your questions about this chapter answered by the author, browse to **www.syngress.com/solutions** and click on the **"Ask the Author"** form.

Q: What does the option for **Allow bidirectional NAT** on the NAT Settings page of Global Properties do?

A: This setting allows for two different NAT rules to apply to a packet in cases in which both the source and destination IP addresses need to be changed.

Q: What are the default settings for NAT when I'm installing or upgrading to FP3?

A: On the NAT Settings page of Global Properties, all features are enabled for a new install, and an upgrade will leave the client side disabled for compatibility.

Q: If I am upgrading a system to FP3 and I have already configured ARP entries in the operating system, do I need to use the Automatic ARP feature?

A: No, but in some cases, manually configured ARP settings will not work unless you disable the Automatic ARP feature.

Q: Do I have to upgrade to an earlier Feature Pack of NG before upgrading to FP3?

A: No, you can go directly from 4.1 to FP3.

Q: Can I just build a new FP3 management server and copy my 4.1 database files?

A: No, the whole architecture has been modified in NG. There have been modifications between the NG Feature Packs as well.

Q: If modifications are made to the $FWDIR/lib/base.def file prior to an upgrade, will this hold across a Feature Pack upgrade of NG?

A: No, you will need to make these changes to the new base.def file after upgrading.

Q: At the end of building a new NG management station from the FP3 CD, a window opens reminding me to remove the CD before rebooting. I remove the CD and click OK. Why do I get an error message looking for a file from the CD?

A: There is a bug with the CD. The installation script still needs access to files from the CD after the popup window tells you to remove the CD. You can either reinsert the CD or not remove it until the machine begins rebooting.

Chapter 2

Smart Clients

Solutions in this chapter:

- SmartDashboard
- SmartView Status
- SmartView Tracker
- SmartView Monitor
- User Monitor

☑ Summary

☑ Solutions Fast Track

☑ Frequently Asked Questions

Introduction

With the introduction of the FireWall-1 NG product, Check Point has separated the new feature releases from the product fixes. With Feature Packs, Check Point is not simply providing "bug fixes" or "service packs," as the company did with its older software. Feature Packs (FPs) bring new features such as the new log management interface in FP3. The NG FP is now the method by which Check Point will provide cumulative updates and new features to the product.

In NG FP3, Check Point has launched "smart" clients. We focus on the new features of this Security Management Architecture's smart clients and correlate the new client names to the Check Point clients that you have used in the past. Be sure to review this section well because there are some major differences between these new clients and the old. In the past, these user interfaces were called *GUI clients*. The three main clients were Policy Editor, Log Viewer, and System Status. For those sites that deployed SecuRemote and/or SecureClient, the SecureClient Packaging Utility was also a GUI client.

As shown in Table 2.1, now there is the SmartDashboard, SmartView Status, SmartView Tracker, SmartView Monitor, and User Monitor. The SmartDashboard is used to modify security policy, just as did the Policy Editor of previous versions. SmartView Tracker is the new Log Viewer, and SmartView Status is the new System Status.

There are some new tools as well, including the User Monitor. This client allows you to view the current users connected through your firewall using SecuRemote and/or SecureClient. This chapter does not cover the SecureClient Packaging tool; Chapter 11 is solely dedicated to that topic.

Table 2.1 New FireWall-1 NG FP3 Client Names

New Client Name	Prior Corresponding Client Names
SmartDashboard	Policy Editor, Policy Manager
SmartViewTracker	Log Viewer, Log Manager
SmartView Status System	Status, Status Manager
SmartMap	Visual Policy Editor (VPE)
SmartView Monitor	Real-time Monitor, Traffic Monitor

SmartDashboard

The most apparent enhancement in the NG series is the management interface. The new Smart-prefixed clients' center console is named SmartDashboard. SmartDashboard answers the needs of a busy security administrator with plenty of new features. The new pane-based dashboard features new functions such as extended search, collapsible rule base and object trees, and dynamic toolbars. These enrichments address an enterprise-level complex firewall installation's administrative necessities.

We address the new features of the SmartDashboard in two categories:

- What's new in the NG dashboard?
- A GUI overview of new FP3 features

What's New in NG SmartDashboard?

The changes in the management GUI are not limited to the new menu items in NG. The change covers a major upgrade in the interface. The new interface offers multiple shortcuts to firewall functions while trying to keep the security desktop organized. The new GUI SmartDashboard's enhancements are summarized in the following sections.

New Panes

The Object Tree, Object List, and SmartMap are the new panes in NG. These panes accelerate access to security policy and the objects. All screens are modifiable. Although it is possible change the visibility properties of the panes through the View menu, we recommend using the Panes toolbar, which offers shortcuts to managing panes.

The Object Tree

The Object Tree (see Figure 2.1) is the new object explorer of the GUI. This expandable/collapsible left pane is a very handy alternative to the previous "manage-object" menus. When you're editing an object, the Manage menu requires a minimum of six clicks, but you may execute the same operation with four clicks on the Objects Tree. The Object Tree is also helpful in organizing the objects. When the Sort by Type option is chosen, all the objects are displayed in a collapsed view. So, instead of facing hundreds of objects in the initial manage network objects menu, you may directly go to Check Point nodes in the Object Tree. You still have the option to list the objects in an ungrouped order when the Sort by Name option is checked. The new NG features, such as Where Used, Query Objects, or SmartMap Connection are also accessible through right-click menus of the Object Tree.

The Object Tree has a tabular view. Each tab has its own group of objects, which are expandable under their parent object types.

The Object List

The Object List is the center pane window for accessing the objects. As shown in Figure 2.2, the Object List displays the brief properties of the objects in its own view.

The contents of the Objects pane change dynamically with the chosen groups in the Object Tree pane. This list is helpful for reviewing the existing objects at a glance. The Object List view cannot be grouped under object types, so all the objects are displayed in the same window (unlike the Object Tree). It is also possible to sort all the objects in descending or ascending order via a single click on the column name.

Figure 2.1 The Object Tree

Figure 2.2 The Object List

Name	IP	Comment	Behind NAT	Version	Net Mask
Alaska.DMZ.CVP	172.31.254.35	Hide Nat for online AV updates	Yes	N/A	
Alaska.DNS.virtualIP	10.100.254.119	For DNS LB	No	N/A	
Alaska.Fin.Deasel	10.112.254.70		No	N/A	
Alaska.Fin.Devek	10.112.254.7		No	N/A	
Alaska.IT.alfa	10.100.137.200	Terminal Server	No	N/A	
Alaska.IT.Bentli	10.100.137.201	Terminal Server	No	N/A	
Alaska.IT.smf	10.100.137.117		No	N/A	
Alaska.LAN.Chincilla	10.100.254.111	File and Mail Server 3	No	N/A	
Alaska.LAN.Gozilla	10.100.254.100	File and Mail Server 1	No	N/A	
Alaska.LAN.Mozilla	10.100.254.101	File and Mail Server 2	No	N/A	

If your screen resolution does not support higher resolutions, we recommend keeping this Object List pane closed in order to have a crisper view of the policy pane.

SmartMap

When firewall administrators were discussing the pros and the cons of graphical user interface (GUI) versus command line interface (CLI), Check Point moved to the next level: the visual interface. SmartMap (see Figure 2.3) allows administrators to implement security policies, managing objects in a visual environment. The SmartMap interface, which comes with a separate license from Check Point, brings plenty of new built-in functions. The visual topology is calculated automatically with the *topology creation algorithm*. The SmartMap interface is tightly integrated with the other components of the dashboard, such as bidirectional drag-and-drop actions, right-click object editing from SmartMap, or visual topology views from the Object Tree and Rule Base.

Figure 2.3 The SmartMap Pane

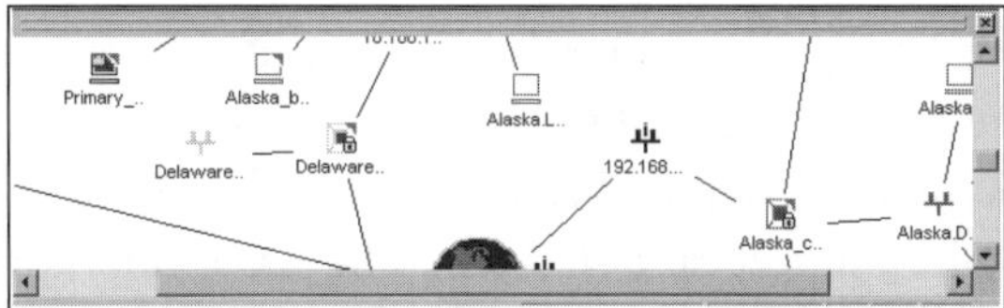

It is recommended that you view SmartMap in undocked mode in order to optimize usability of the dashboard desktop in limited screen resolutions.

We do not cover SmartMap in depth since this feature is an optional add-on and a different approach to managing the FireWall-1 NG. This interface is new, and it is expected to have greater functionality in upcoming versions.

Tools & Traps...

What Do I Get If I License SmartMap?

Licensing SmartMap adds the following features to NG SmartDashboard:

- Dynamic visual policy creation
- Management of security policy through the visual interface (limited)
- Expandable and collapsible map views of your Check Point network
- Bidirectional interaction with the other components of GUI Object Management
- Recognition of implied and ambiguous networks; actualization of implied networks
- Exportable topology map; support for various image types and Visio
- Undockable window; ability to work in a separate window
- SmartMap helper for solving duplicated networks and unsolved object interfaces
- Other fancy features such as navigator window, zoom, customization

New Policy Tabs

The Rule Base and the Network Address Translation (NAT) are not the unique policy tabs anymore. With the new functionality, the policy tabs (see Figure 2.4) are extended with Desktop Security, VPN Manager, Web Access, and QoS tabs. The functionality of these policy tabs is detailed in relevant chapters. The basic functionality of the tabs is listed here:

- **Desktop Security** The policy server rule base for SecureClients.
- **QoS** The bandwidth management rule base for the FloodGate-1 product.
- **Web Access** Granular access policies for Web applications with the User Authority product.
- **VPN Manager** SmartMap-style visual community editing.

Figure 2.4 Policy Tabs

Each policy tab serves a different product and purpose, but all the interfaces share common, unique components to easily manage the policies. All policy tabs carry the simple, column-based colored Check Point Rule Base properties.

The new GUI functionality of the policy tabs for FireWall-1 product is listed in Table 2.2.

Table 2.2 GUI Options

Policy Tab	Security Rule Base	Address Translation	Desktop Security
Query Rules	Yes	No	No
Query Objects	Yes	No	No
Drag&Drop rules and objects	Yes	Yes	Yes
Multiple Cut&Paste	Yes	Yes	Yes
Rule Summarization	Yes	No	No
String Search	Yes	Yes	Yes

New Menu Items and Toolbars

The menus and toolbars in FP3 are completely restructured. In the 4.x interface, there was a single toolbar and status bar; in the NG FP3 dashboard, we have 12 toolbars and the status bar. The dashboard exploits all Windows GUI features to manage these toolbars.

You may align the toolbars on the left, right, or bottom of the interface via drag-and-drop actions, you may have floating toolbars, and you may arrange the order of the toolbars.

The main menu items have also expanded from seven to nine, excluding the SmartMap. Some of the old functionality has been shifted to the new menu items. For example, the rule-editing submenus under the Edit menu in 4.x are organized under the Rules root menu. The changes are summarized in the following sections.

File

NG introduced revision control for security policies. The new functionality is accessible through the File menu. The printing functions now cover SmartMap:

- **New Menu Items** Revision Control, Print Controls, and Delete
- **Removed Menu Items** None
- **Transferred Menu Items** None

Edit

Menu items for rule editing are transferred to the Rules menu. FP3 supports copying multiple objects:

- **New Menu Items** Paste Object
- **Removed Menu Items** None
- **Transferred Menu Items** Add Rule, Delete Rule, Hide Rule, and Disable Rule

View

There is a massive change in the View menu. Toolbar changes are listed in a separate item. Queries are transferred into the Searches menu item:

- **New Menu Items** Products, Toolbars, Object Tree, Object List, Rule Base, SmartMap, VPN communities, Topology VPN view, List VPN view, Reset Column Width, Sort Tree, Community Rules, Object Status in SmartMap
- **Removed Menu Items** None
- **Transferred Menu Items** Mask (hiding rules), Queries

Manage

UFP and CVP servers are created in OPSEC applications:

- **New Menu Items** OPSEC Applications, Permission Profiles, Users and Administrators, VPN Communities, QoS, Remote Access, SmartView Monitor, User Authority
- **Removed Menu Items** Users, Real-Time Monitor, Credential Manager, and Web Access
- **Transferred Menu Items** None

Rules

The Rules menu is a new root-level menu; all items are new. In previous 4.x versions, the Rule Management menu items were in the Edit menu. The items in the Rules menu are Add Rule, Disable Rule, Add Section Title, Add Sub Rule, Add QoS Class, Hide, Delete, and Select All.

Policy

Policy Installation Targets, SmartDefense, and Management HA are managed through the Policy menu:

- **New Menu Items** Policy Installation Targets, Convert to, View Policy of, Management HA, SmartDefense
- **Removed Menu Items** None
- **Transferred Menu Items** None

Search

This is a new root-level menu in FP3. Query rules directly displays the Query Clause screen. The old Query Rules screen is accessible through the Manage Query Rules item.

Toolbars

As shown in Figure 2.5, there are 12 new toolbars in NG. These organizable, floating toolbars create shortcuts for most of the menu items. The Setup VPN, Setup Extranet, and Certificates icons of prior NG versions are no longer valid. The floatable menus are:

- **New Toolbar Items** Global Properties, Help, Objects, Panes, Policy, Rules, Search, Standard, Visual Tools, VPN Manager, Smart View
- **Removed Toolbar Items** Certificates, VPN View, and VPN Communities

There are no major changes in the Window and Help menus. When SmartMap is licensed, a full-featured SmartMap menu is also displayed.

Figure 2.5 SmartDashboard Toolbars

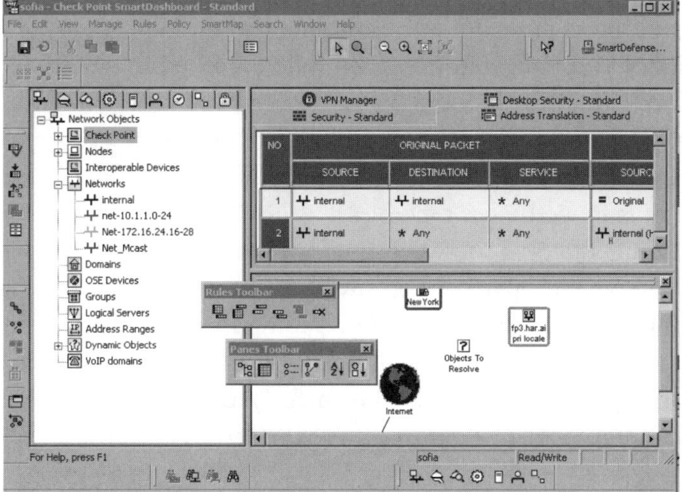

New Object Types

Object types help firewall administrators have organized control over the various objects. Obsolete object types are retired, but the new NG object types truly reflect Check Point's approach to granular firewall administration. This massive change required a change in the underlying file types such as objects. C file. There are three new object type categories: OPSEC Applications, Virtual Links, and VPN Communities. The 4.x Object Type categories User on Account Unit and Keys are not valid in NG. All the changes in each object type category are summarized in the following sections.

Network Objects

"I can't define my third-party firewall" is a typical discussion group post for the experienced 4.x firewall administrator. The missing workstation object is the next question.

In the new NG network object type hierarchy, all Check Point installed products are under Check Point object types. This includes single interface boxes, clusters, embedded devices (also known as integrated firewalls), routers, and switches. The remaining network components can be defined under "Node," which replaces the old workstation and gateway products.

If VPN is required between a third-party node and the FireWall-1/VPN-1 protected network, the external node must be defined as an interoperable device, such as Cisco PIX. The access control list (ACL)-based routers and switches are defined as

Open Security Extension (OSE) devices. The new object type categories are dynamic objects and the voice over IP (VOIP) domains.

Services

There isn't a significant change under this category at the object type level. When you browse this category, you will notice a group called Compound TCP Services. This type is a predefined group for FloodGate-1. DCE-RPC services have been recoded in NG and they are much more functional. Although they need to be defined explicitly in the Rule Base, they have a finer control on the traffic. DCE-RPC is now a separate object type. The port range object type of 4.x is not valid in NG. In NG, port ranges are defined by adding a hyphen between the lowest and the highest port numbers in the TCP or UDP service properties window's port field. When you're defining port ranges, it is possible that two services could be using the same port number. If the service field of a rule is Any, all services will match this rule, including the ones with port ranges. To avoid this problem, uncheck **Match for Any** for the services, which use the same port. This property is defined in the TCP Properties window.

NOTE

If **Keep connections open after policy has been installed** is checked, all control and data connections will remain open until the connections have ended, even if they are not allowed under the new policy. This overrides the settings in the gateway's Connection Persistence page.

If you change this property, the change will not affect open connections, only future connections.

Resources

Besides URI, SMTP, and FTP resources, NG offers three new resource object types:

- **URI for QoS** A resource for FloodGate-1 Rule Base.
- **TCP resource** Any generic TPC service traffic may be piped to CVP or UFP traffic with this resource.
- **CIFS resource** A resource for stateful inspection of the new disk share access over Common Internet File Sharing (CIFS) protocol.

OPSEC Applications

The process of defining a CVP or UFP server has been changed. The new CVP, UFP, or AMON servers should be defined under OPSEC Applications. Another supported feature is the support for multiple OPSEC servers. You may scale your OPSEC-based servers via chaining or load sharing. Chaining requires splitting the inspection tasks on multiple servers, but load sharing distributes the requests on identical servers with a round-robin algorithm. The server groups are also formed under the OPSEC Applications menu.

Servers

Though the basic server types remain unchanged, the submenus are more stable. It is easier to define directory servers under LDAP Account Unit. The UFP and CVP server definitions have transferred to OPSEC Applications, and Defender and Policy Server types are no longer valid. SecuRemote DNS Server may be defined through the Servers menu as well.

Users and Administrators

Managing administrator users through SmartClients was an eagerly awaited functionality. It is now possible to define administrator users and user groups through SmartDashboard (see Figure 2.6).

Figure 2.6 Users and Administrators

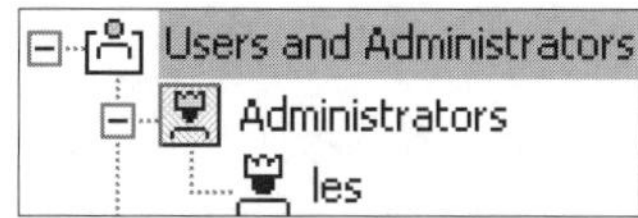

Another important change in FP3 is the Generic* user. If you try to create this user, your request will be denied since it is predefined. To manage Generic* users, you should use the External User Profile object type.

When you define directory services through servers, you will be able to modify the user settings through the Users and Administrators category under the Object Tree.

Time

Time objects and groups are accessible through the Time menu. The new Time object type is Scheduled Event. Scheduled Event objects are used to trigger processes, for example, in the Management High Availability page of the Global Properties window and in the Logging Policy page of the Workstation Properties window.

Virtual Links

The new virtual links are created in SmartDashboard. With virtual links, it is possible to monitor traffic and service-level agreements (SLAs) between two network entities. Monitoring virtual links is detailed in the "SmartView Monitor" section later in this chapter.

VPN Communities

The new VPN Communities, which allow VPN Communities as a matching factor in Security Rules may be defined through this object type category. Site-to-Site, Extranet, and Remote Access are the available object types.

The Extended Object Properties Screen

The Global Properties window in Check Point GUI client 4.1 release had 13 tabs layered in three lines. Check Point's GUI developers have addressed this problem by introducing "Windows-style" expandable left pane navigation trees. The tabular GUI view in the overpopulated menus of Global Properties, Check Points, Nodes, Interoperable Devices, Time, and VPN Communities windows have been replaced by a expandable tree pane on the left side of the window. You may manage all properties from this expandable GUI (see Figure 2.7).

Figure 2.7 The New Menu Style in Global Properties

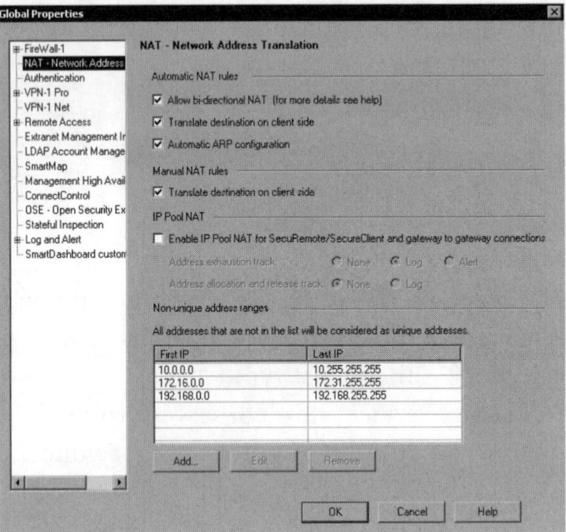

Extended Administrator Access

Now it is possible to use your certificates to authenticate your GUI access. In the SmartDashboard login screen, you may choose to use your certificates or change your certificate password (see Figure 2.8).

Another important improvement is the Demo Mode. Every SmartClient installation comes with a predefined demo network. When the Demo Mode check box is selected, the other options are grayed out and you make a local logon to the demo security rule base. This semifunctional rule base is very helpful for learning the features when lab facilities are limited.

Figure 2.8 The GUI Client Login Window

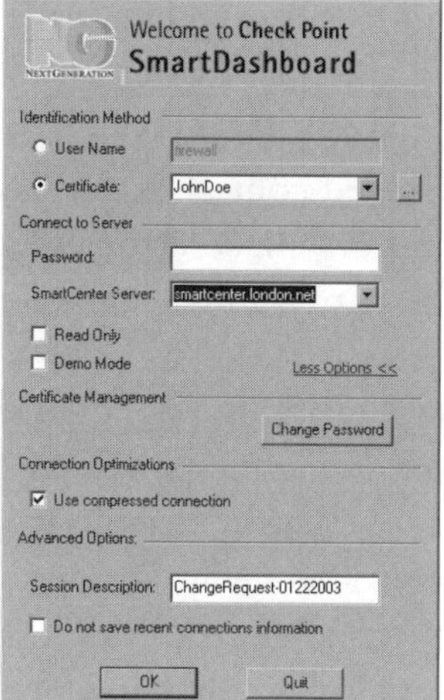

Tools & Traps...

Editing the Demo Database

The SmartClients installation folder contains the demo database in the following folder:

```
%Installation Path%\SMART Clients\NG FP3\PROGRAM\cpml_dir\conf
```

This folder contains authentic objects_5_0.C and other files so you can modify and change the actual demo files. For troubleshooting purposes, you may view other policies simply by changing the contents of this folder.

The last new function on the logon screen is the Session Description. This free text area is very useful when combined with the security policy. This text is directly logged under audit log type when logout is executed. In other words, it is possible to comment the SmartDashboard sessions in the log database. This text is visible when **Session ID** is checked in SmartTracker.

A GUI Overview of New FP3 Features

Besides basic object and rule management properties of SmartDashboard, new tools and windows accelerate the daily life of an administrator. The new policy installation interface aims to remove the burden of policies on multiple firewalls by classifying the installation targets. The Sections feature simplifes the view of complex rule bases by organizing the rules under certain section headers. Furthermore, the database revision tool is Check Point's first attempt to control change management on the rule bases.

The New Policy Installation Interface

The new user interface offers detailed control of the installation process. The installation targets, live process indication, and organized error indication lists are the new extended features in policy installation. The new features make SmartDashboard installations cleaner.

You'll see four main windows during the policy installation. In the Install Policy window (see Figure 2.9), you can define the policy types to be installed. NAT policy and Security policy are installed together by default. It is possible to install Desktop Security and VPN-1 Net policies individually. Depending on your deployment's complexity, you have an option to choose Select All or Clear All. In the Installation Mode properties, you may choose to install the policy independently or dependently. This option enables you to specify what to do if the Security Policy installation is unsuccessful for one or more of the selected modules. When dependent installation is chosen, the policy will not be installed if any of the installations fail. These rules do not apply to pre-NG gateways.

Figure 2.9 The Install Policy Window

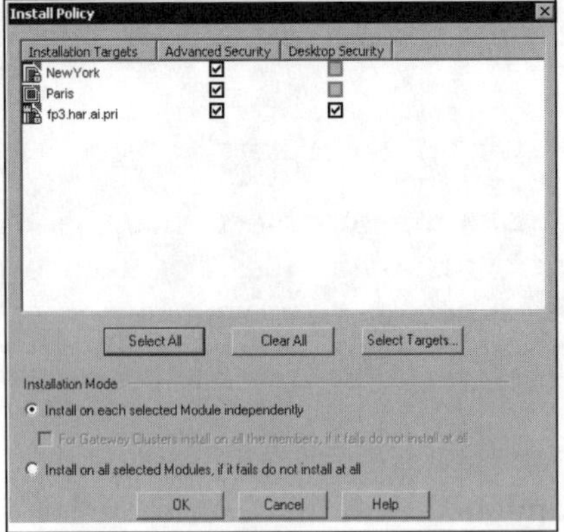

Select **Installation Target Window**. This window (see Figure 2.10) is very useful if you install policy on specific servers. Once you set the installation targets, you don't have to deselect each host in your objects database. You may define the installation targets per policy. This feature is very helpful if you are managing multiple firewall networks from a single management server.

During the installation, you can view the stages and percentage of the operation in the Installation Process window (see Figure 2.11).

Figure 2.10 The Installation Target Window

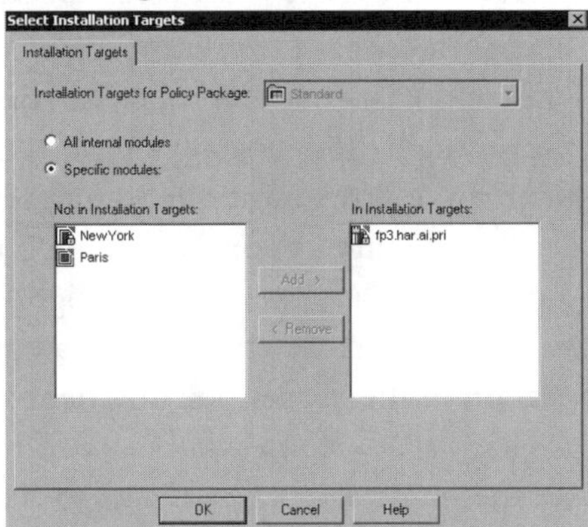

Figure 2.11 The Installation Process Window

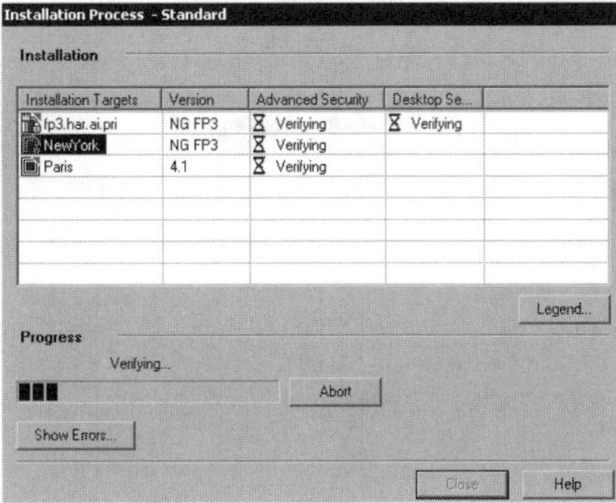

When you click the **Show Errors** button, you can see the processes in real time from the Verification and Installation Errors screen (see Figure 2.12). If the installation completed successfully, this button disappears.

Figure 2.12 The Verification and Installation Errors Window

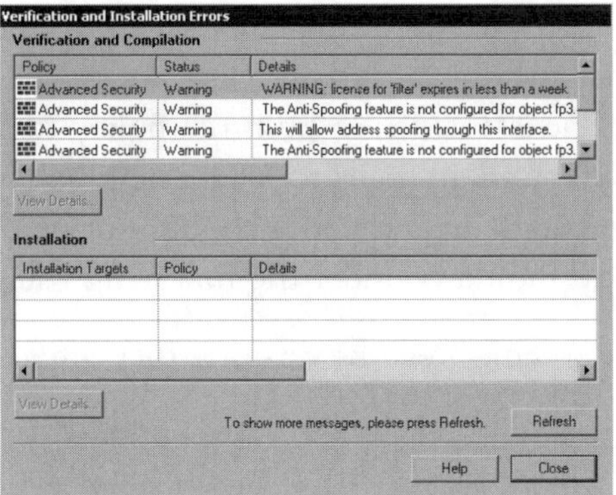

Using Sections in the Security Rule Base

Although search functions release the pain of navigating a Security Rule Base, navigating a complex Security Rule Base with more than 30 rules is a continuing problem. With FP3, Check Point addresses this issue by simply applying the same expand/collapse logic to its Security Rule Base. Now you can organize rules under sections.

Applying a section is simple. Highlight the rule where you want to add a section. From either the Rules—Add Section Title menu or the right-mouse-click Add Section Title menu, you can choose to add a section above or below the highlighted rule.

Enter the name of the section in the header pop-up menu, and that is all you need. Remember that all the rules below that section will be added to the new section. You do not have an option to choose the number of rules to add, so starting from the bottom is a good idea. Since rule base order must remain intact, you may not deploy logical sections and reorganize the rules in different sequences; you may only summarize the existing rules in existing order. Collapsed rules organized under sections are shown in Figure 2.13.

Figure 2.13 Sections of Rules on SmartDashboard

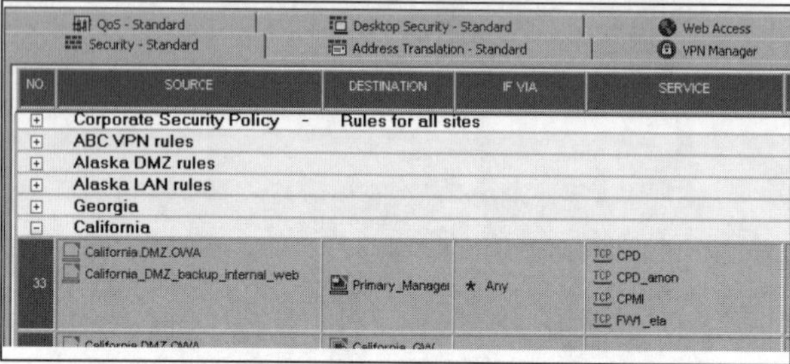

Version Control with Database Revision Control

With FP3, Check Point improved the revisioning system. You may save an existing database on SmartCenter Server. Once it is saved, you can go back to the previous states of the database.

With revision control you can create, view, restore, and delete the previous database versions. If you want to deactivate this feature, you need to uncheck **Revision Control** from the Global Properties window. You then need to save the policy and unload the policy from the module. The last step is to push the policy to the module again. If you do not unload the policy first, all attempts to load a new policy will fail.

This tool requires a separate license, and it should not be considered a complete version control system. You should consider the following issues before deployment:

- It is not possible to edit previous versions; they are accessible only in read-only mode.
- Only FP2 backward compatibility is supported. Restoring FP2 databases on the remote module is possible only through the command line.

- You may not compare the changes with the Database Revision Tool.
- Key management is not versioned.

SmartView Status

Integration of the new application-monitoring standard AMON brought a solid base to the Check Point system status manager. The new modular architecture of the Check Point base and all certified products can now be monitored to a greater extent. It is easy to notice the effects in the new SmartView Status: pane-based tabular screen organization, adjustable window sizes for panes, search functions, collapsible menus, and all-new interface gizmos are used in the new GUI. A new Disconnect Client feature has also been added to the interface.

What's New in SmartView Status?

More status data is available in NG. You can access real status details such as virtual private network (VPN) statistics from the SmartView Status interface. The good news is that all information is accessible through CLI, so system administrators can integrate in-house monitoring systems with Check Point status data. System alerts are more useful with NG since SVN foundation monitors the critical resources of the systems beneath the VPN-1/FireWall-1 firewall.

The Panes

There are two main tabular screens in SmartView Tracker: System Status and System Alert. System Status, with its three panes, is very useful for gathering real-time availability data in a hierarchical view. On the other hand, Systems Alert helps administrators set predefined alert thresholds for various cases. Let's look at each screen in more detail.

System Status

System Status has three synchronized panes (see Figure 2.14). The heart of the status-monitoring system is the top-left Modules pane. This pane has the hierarchical brief information of all the products installed. On a tree-based view, it is possible to monitor time-stamped status and IP addresses of all Check Point products. Each product is listed under its parent product. The hierarchy is as follows: Network Objects | Members | Products installed on the members. When any of the products or subcomponents is highlighted, the left Details pane displays all known status details. All problematic modules are relisted in the bottom Critical Notifications pane so that you can isolate the problems. All views are synchronized, so if you choose one product in the Critical Notifications pane, the contents of the other two panes change dynamically, or vice versa.

Figure 2.14 SmartView System Status

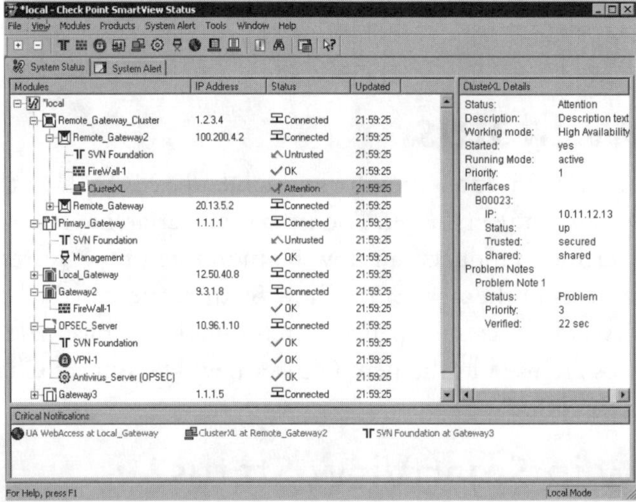

Tools & Traps…

Status Information from the Command Line

Check Point NG applications are monitored through the AMON protocol (TCP 18192). This makes it easy to troubleshoot data-gathering problems in SmartView Status. The *cpstat* command returns the same information that you see on the Details pane. The syntax of the *cpstat* command is as follows:

```
#cpstat [-h host] [-p port] [-f flavour] [-d] entity.
```

The entity and available flavors for FP3 are listed in Table 2.3.

Table 2.3 *cpstat* Command Options

Entity	Available Flavors
fw	default, all,policy,performance,hmem, kmem, inspect, cookies, chains, fragments, totals, ufp_caching, http_stat, ftp_stat, telnet_stat, rlogin_stat, ufp_stat, smtp_stat
vpn	product, general, IKE, ipsec, fwz, accelerator, all
ha	default, all
mg	default
os	default, routing
fg	all

System Alert

The second screen of SmartView Status (see Figure 2.15) allows administrators to define threshold values and possible counteractions. As of NF FP3, only FireWall-1, FloodGate-1, SmartCenter Server, and SVN Foundation support system alerts. The screen is divided into two panes: Modules and Alert Definition. There are three system alert definition options for each component. These options can be checked under the General tab of the Alert Definition pane:

- **Global** Description pane is grayed out. The Global entries of the System Alert menu are valid.
- **Custom** The description can be defined through the Alert Definition pane.
- **None** No alerts are applied for the given network object.

Figure 2.15 The System Alert Tab

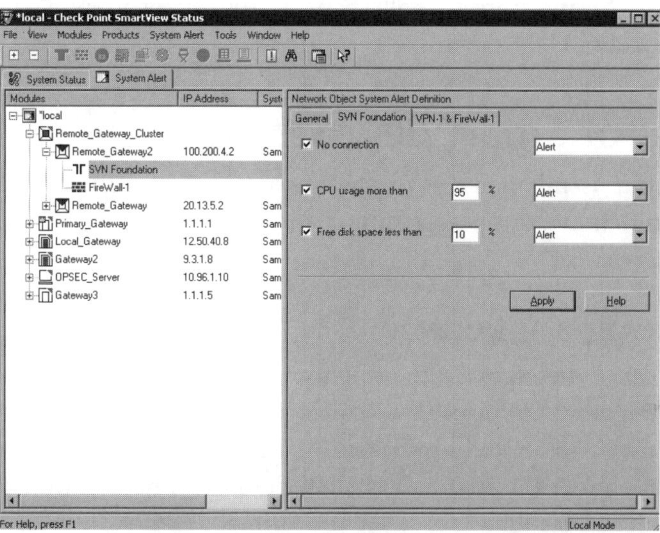

The predefined alert triggers per product are listed in Table 2.4. Alert actions are the same as those for SmartDashboard.

Table 2.4 Alert Triggers

Product Name	Alert Triggers
SVN Foundation	No Connection, Max. CPU Usage, Min Free Disk Space
FireWall-1	No Policy Installed, Policy Name Change, Policy Installed
FloodGate-1	No Policy Installed, Policy Name Change, Policy Installed
SmartCenter	Not Synchronized (for ClusterXL)

Changes in the Menu and the Toolbar

The four-item menu of 4.x is gone. The overpopulated View menu of the 4.x Status Manager is enhanced in FP3 by four new root-level menus: Modules, Products, System Alert, and Tools. The new locations of the previous View menu functions are:

- **Removed menu items** Show/Hide Objects, Icons View, Compression Details.
- **Transferred to toolbar** Automatic Update as Active Update, Alerts (pop-up).
- **Transferred to Products menu** VPN Details, FloodGate Details, HA Module Details.
- **Transferred to Modules** Update Status as Update Selected.
- **Transferred to System Alert** Options and Global.
- **Existing Menu Items** Toolbar and Status Bar of View Menu, File Menu, Window, and Help menus.

Highlights of SmartView Status

There are small but useful additions to the SmartView Status interface besides basic status and alert functionality. These additions include displaying and disconnecting clients or auto reconnect.

Disconnecting a Client

No more "read only" messages for the mighty firewall administrators. The Disconnect Client tool (see Figure 2.16) displays all current GUI connections with the host as well as client name and database status information. In addition, if you have the proper permissions, you can choose the session and click the Disconnect button to guarantee your next read/write access session.

Figure 2.16 Disconnect Clients

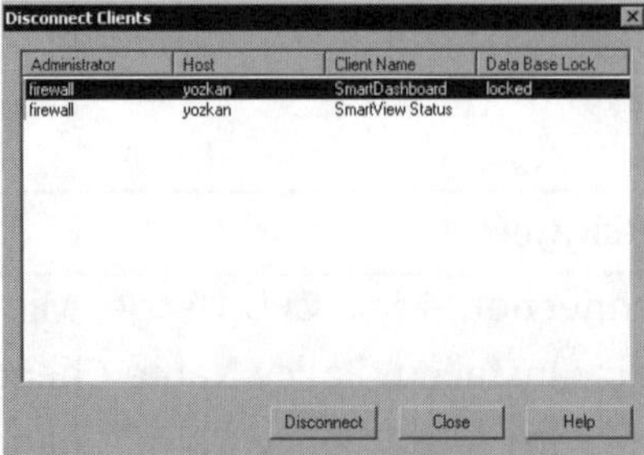

Other Fancy Features

The following features are also integrated the SmartView Status interface:

- **Auto Reconnect** If the connection is lost, SmartView Status tries reconnect in 15-second intervals.
- **System Alert Monitoring Mechanism** With Start and Stop buttons, you can emulate alert actions.
- **Find** Text-based search in the SmartView Status GUI.
- **Active Update** Updates the status dynamically.

SmartView Tracker

With the release of FP3, the firewall administrators are released from the legacy restraint of the old log viewer. All the GUI interface changes, which serve for a faster and better-organized desktop in SmartDashboard and SmartView Tracker, have been implemented in the new SmartView Tracker Client. This interface supports the three modes of log types in different tabular screens. Each screen is fortified with two additional panes and a more useful status bar. Extended free text search and remote file management are also newly enhanced features. Previous functions such as blocking connections in active mode or resolving addresses and services are also accessible through the toolbar and the menus.

What's New in SmartView Tracker?

Actually, everything is new in FP3. The outlook and the organization features are original. Let's take a closer look.

The Panes

Figure 2.17 SmartView Tracker Windows

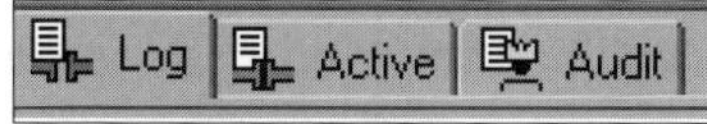

The panes are available for all three log types: Log, Active, and Audit (see Figure 2.17).

The Query Tree Pane

If you are using plenty of custom predefined queries or switching between VPN and regular views, activating the Query Tree pane will be very helpful. As shown in Figure 2.18, this left pane has predefined product queries, too. The product queries are not simple filter-by-product queries. Remember that each product query has different fields. It is recommended to keep this pane closed if your screen resolution is limited. You may toggle between views from the toolbar toggle buttons.

Figure 2.18 The Query Tree Pane

NOTE

The predefined default query "All records" does not drawn on all entries in the log database. You still need to check the necessary field types from the Query Properties pane to display the hidden fields.

The Query Properties Pane

This filter screen (see Figure 2.19) is very useful. You may visually define your queries, design your screen layout, and enter your subqueries. The only drawback is the order of the query variables. You cannot sort the variables by clicking on the columns, so you need to know the order of the query properties. You may drag and drop the fields on the Query Properties pane. Of course, scrolling down the whole list is always a valid option. The default firewall queries do not contain the NAT-related fields, so you need to add them manually. This pane is accessible through the Menu and Toolbar option. It is recommended that you use toolbar Show and Hide options for a crisper log view.

The Records Pane

The old log viewer window is now the Records pane. The logs are more versatile in this GUI. You have the following options in the new Records pane:

- Link to related Security Policy Rules.
- Copy cell or whole record options.

- When records are double-clicked, record details are displayed in a pop-up window.
- There's free text search on all columns.

Figure 2.19 The Query Properties Pane

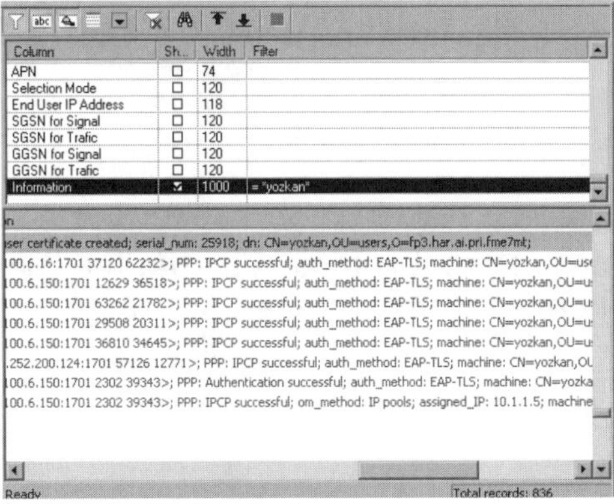

Menu Changes

Firewall administrators who are familiar with the 4.x interface will not find the Edit, Select, and Mode items in the new menu bar. The Edit menu is no longer required, since Find is integrated with the right-click. The old expanding Select menu has been divided into two menus. The Query Properties pane has all the filter options. On the other hand, the Query menu has the necessary menu items for basic query management, which includes the functions such as save as, copy, delete, and rename. The Mode menu has been transferred to the main interface as the tabular screen switches.

Highlights From the SmartView Tracker

Besides managing regular log files, some additional features make firewall administrators' lives easier. Fetching log files from remote enforcement modules or viewing a historical rule in SmartDashboard are very helpful features, as we see in this section.

Remote File Management

SmartView Tracker allows administrators to fetch log files from remote enforcement points. The interface has organized subscreens for remote log file management. This is done in three steps:

1. **Choose the enforcement point.** This screen allows you to choose the modules from which you will fetch the log files. It is also possible to execute a log switch on the remote module via the Log Switch button.

2. **Get a file list.** All log files on the remote station are listed in a scroll-down menu. You may choose multiple log files, except the active log file. To get the active file, you must first perform the Log Switch operation.
3. **Monitor file fetch progress.** This screen is simply a download screen. You have real-time access to the status of the log file fetches from the remote modules. The remote log filenames are prefixed with the module name to prevent mix-ups.

NOTE

Using remote log management commands from the command line or using Remote Files Management from the SmartView Tracker is always a better alternative to simple file transfer, since the log files are automatically compressed with the LZ77 (gzip) standard.

View in SmartDashboard

If you're wondering who allowed this connection and you don't want to track the rule number that existed six weeks ago, the new SmartView Tracker offers a convenient function. As shown in Figure 2.20, it is possible to display the related rule base and the rule via the View in SmartDashboard option. Of course, you must have the revisioned databases to use this function. The process is as follows:

1. Open an historical log file.
2. Highlight a record in the Records pane.
3. Click the **View in SmartDashboard** item on the right-click menu. A new SmartDashboard will be opened in read-only mode, displaying the rule that created the related record. This view displays a previous database version if the log record does not belong to the current security policy.

Figure 2.20 View in SmartDashboard

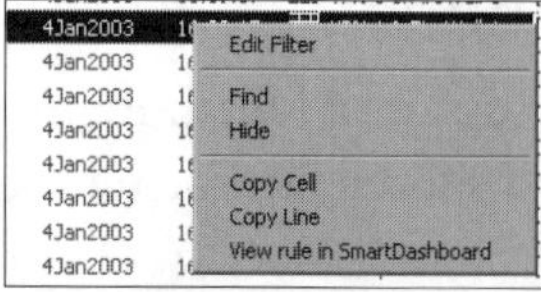

Command-Line Options

In an enterprise environment, most security policies require a centralized logging system. Although OPSEC-based products help firewall administrators manage the files through the LEA protocol, sometimes it is necessary to use simple scripts to automate tasks or troubleshoot some basic problems. NG offers the following flexible command-line logging utilities, which complete the SmartView Tracker:

- **fwm log** Displays logs with the given switches. For example:

  ```
  #fwm log -c reject -h London -n
  ```

- **fwm logexport** Exports log contents to ASCII format. Useful for third-party integration. For example:

  ```
  #fwm logexport -d : -n
  ```

- **fwm logswitch** The command-line logswitch, useful for batch scripts. For example:

  ```
  #fwm logswitch -h London old.log
  ```

- **fwm repairlog** Very useful when you only have the log file but not the PTR file. For example:

  ```
  #fwm repairlog backup.log
  ```

- **fwm mergefiles** Merges multiple log files into single files and unifies the records. For example:

  ```
  #fwm mergefiles -s 101.log 102.log final.log
  ```

- **fwm lslogs** This is the command line *Get File List*. For example:

  ```
  #fwm lslogs London
  ```

- **fwm fetchlogs** This is the command line *File Fetch*. For example:

  ```
  #fwm fetchlogs 101.log  London
  ```

- **fw lea_notify** Notifies all LEA clients for log collection. For example:

  ```
  fw lea_notify
  ```

- **log_export** Exports logs to an Oracle database. Requires configuration file and an Oracle client. For example:

  ```
  log_export
  ```

SmartView Monitor

Seeing is believing. Check Point has an easy-to-use network-monitoring tool. SmartView Monitor, which is the FP3 marketing brand name of the previous Real-Time Monitor, answers most enterprise monitoring needs of a mission-critical distributed Check Point deployment. Besides real-time monitoring, SmartView Monitor offers recording of sessions and historical views. With the utilization of system counters generated by SVN Foundation and the application of virtual links, SmartView Monitor delivers simple, readable visual results on its own interface.

SmartView Monitor basically has two main sources of information: system counters and the flow of the traffic analyzed by the Check Point products. This data source is used to generate specific views for availability and SLA monitoring.

Installation

Since SmartView Monitor is not a built-in product, it must be checked during the installation. Remember that if you are deploying SmartView Monitor on a different server than the SmartCenter, you should also choose SmartView Monitor in the SmartCenter installation.

The Interface

SmartView Monitor has a very user-friendly interface. The application flow is as follows:

1. Define a new session.
2. Choose a real-time or historical session type.
3. Configure your session.
4. Adjust the graphical interface.
5. Record, play, fast forward, or pause the display.
6. Open, save, or delete the previous sessions.

SmartView Monitor has five toolbars (see Figure 2.21). The standard toolbar has the session management functions. You can view, edit, open, or delete a session; suspend a QoS policy; or pause the real-time monitoring. It is possible to change the graph type from the standard toolbar, but more options area available on the View menu.

On the Recording menu, you can actually record the session with the data and replay, fast forward, or pause as needed.

If you want to change the view scale of the graph or optimize it automatically, you can use the Scaling option.

Locking services is very useful when you're monitoring real-time traffic. When all the services change dynamically in real-time monitoring, you can lock the services by clicking the Lock the Services button and continue monitoring in a more stable environment. Another useful feature is sorting on a data column.

Figure 2.21 SmartView Monitor

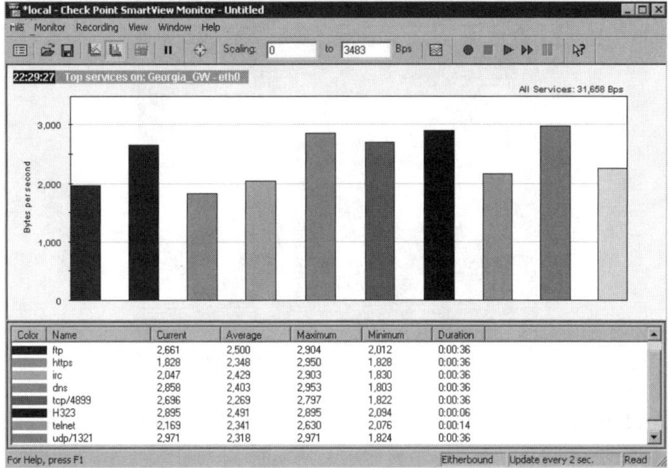

Traffic Monitoring

Real-time traffic is monitored on a session basis. There are three main session types:

- Check Point System Counters, which rely on counter variables
- Traffic Sessions, which accumulate the traffic information on interfaces
- Virtual Links, which measure traffic between two modules

Monitor Using Check Point System Counters

When creating a new session, you may chose to monitor the systems with system counter values, which are collected from the Check Point products. If you are familiar with the Microsoft platform's PERFMON performance monitor product, you won't face any difficulties in understanding the logic of Check Point's system counters. Basically, Check Point collects the SNMP variables and displays them in an organized visual display along with related statistical data.

There are two main configuration screens for system counters:

- **The Counters tab** In the Counters screen (see Figure 2.22), you can choose your categories and view the available counters by category. If you want to add a counter to the session, all you need is to select it and click the Add button. It is also possible to view a short description of the counters on the bottom part of the screen.

Figure 2.22 Counter Categories

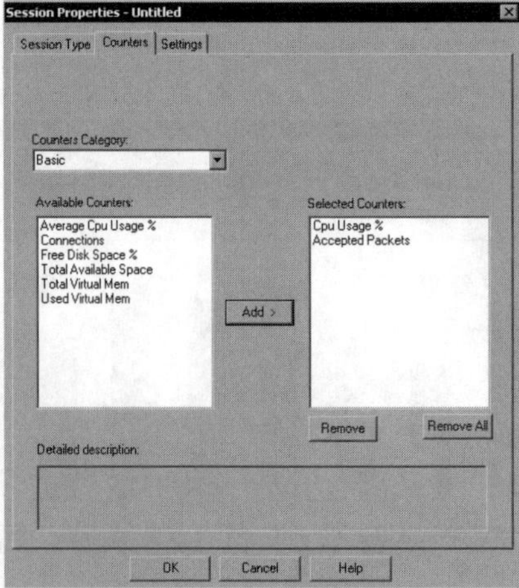

- **The Settings tab** You can define the update interval and chart type (bar/line) from this tab.

Monitor by Service

When your traffic should be monitored on a service basis, you can choose a Check Point FireWall or FloodGate product or just a single interface to generate the real-time monitoring output. There are two configuration screens:

- **Monitor by Service** In this configuration tab, you have to decide to monitor either top services (see Figure 2.23) or the specified services that are available for monitoring. It is also possible to define the data direction.

Figure 2.23 Monitoring Top Services

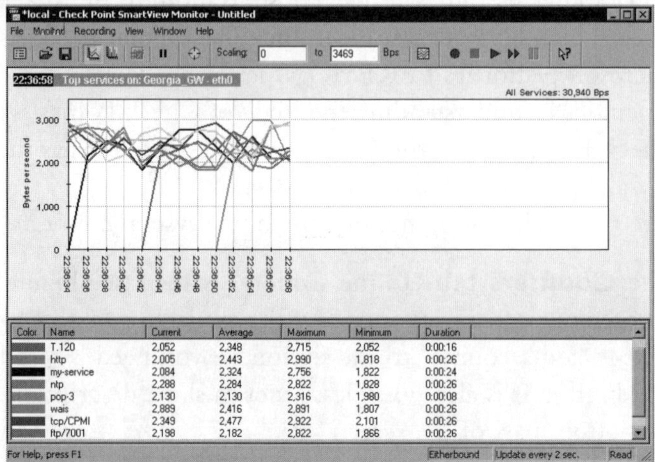

- **The Settings tab** You can define the update interval and chart type (bar/line), measurement unit, and scale options from this tab.

Monitor Using Network Objects

When your traffic should be monitored on a network object basis, you can chose a Check Point FireWall or FloodGate product or just a single interface to generate the real-time monitoring output. There are two configuration screens:

- **Monitor by Network Objects** Traffic can be monitored for top objects or the specified objects in the session. It is possible to define data direction and the origin of the traffic as well.
- **The Settings tab** This tab is the same as the Monitor by Service Settings tab. You may define the update interval and chart type (bar/line), measurement unit, and scale options from this tab.

Monitor by QoS

If FloodGate-1 is installed, you can watch the quality-of-service (QoS) variables from SmartView Monitor. Unlike the other session types, this one limits the number of monitored interfaces per product. There are two configuration screens:

- **Monitor by QoS Rules** All QoS rules are populated in this screen. You can refresh the list to update the rule set. By choosing the appropriate rule to monitor from the expandable tree view and specifying the data direction, you can monitor the QoS data.
- **The Settings tab** This menu is the same as the other Settings tabs.

Remember that it is possible to suspend a FloodGate-1 policy from the SmartView Monitor interface to understand the effects of the QoS rules. To suspend or resume QoS Policy, select **Suspend QoS Policy** from the Monitor menu.

Monitor Using Top Firewall Rules

If you want to detect your active rules and monitor them, you should define a session based on firewall rules and the traffic allowed by the selected rules. There are two configuration screens. The Monitor by Top Firewall Rules setting screen does not allow you to chose specific rules; as stated in its name, you can configure only the quantity of the top rules to be monitored. It is also possible to define the data direction. There is no difference in the Settings screen. When you complete the settings, you may monitor the activity based on your rules, as shown in Figure 2.24.

Figure 2.24 Monitoring Rules

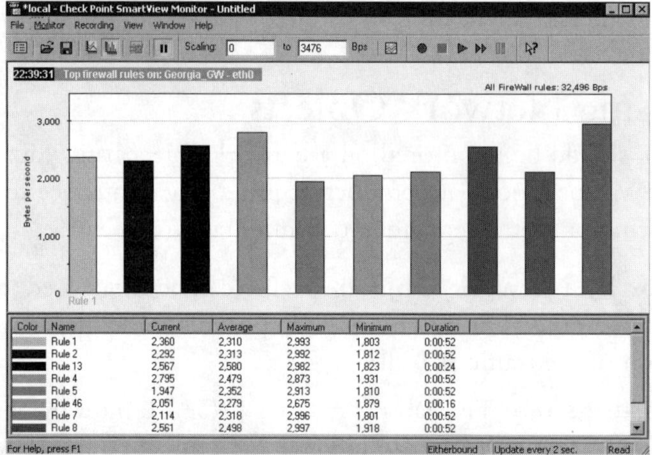

Monitor Using Virtual Links

The trail between two Check Point VPN firewalls or FloodFate Modules is defined by a virtual link. To define SLA parameters, virtual link objects are created in the SmartDashboard application. Virtual links are monitored through SmartView Monitor.

When you create a virtual link between two modules, you should define the SLA parameters as well. The thresholds cover availability, round-trip time, bidirectional committed information rate (CIR), and bidirectional bandwidth loss. The alert and logging action can be defined from the Global Properties menu of the SmartDashboard.

NOTE

Virtual Link Monitoring is implemented using the E2ECP service, a Check Point protocol. Make sure there is a rule on each of the Virtual Link gateways that allows the E2ECP service between them. For example:

- **Source** Local_Gateway
- **Destination** Remote_Gateway
- **Service** E2ECP
- **Action** Accept
- **Track** Log
- **Install On** Gateways

To monitor virtual links from the SmartView Monitor, the Activate Virtual Link check box must be checked in the Virtual Object properties. In SmartView Monitor, the monitoring setting can be defined from the following screens:

- **Virtual Link Monitoring** You must decide which data type to display. It is even possible to define the direction of the monitored traffic for bandwidth and bandwidth loss. The other option is round-trip time. Another decision is the source of the traffic. *Application data* is the data as the application sees it, uncompressed and unencrypted, but if you are interested in the data on the wire after compression or encryption for SLA purposes, choose **Wire Data**.
- **The Settings tab** You may define the chart type, measurement units, and scale from this tab.

Generating Reports

Although the product was once called Real-Time Monitor, SmartView Monitor can be used to generate historical activity reports. When creating a new session, you may choose History Report to see previous activity. There are two main report types: Check Point Systems Counter Reports and Traffic Reports.

Check Point Systems Counter Reports

It is possible to receive counter-information from all Check Point monitored systems. On the initial report page, after you choose the monitored module, select the related categories and the available counters to be included in the report. It is not possible to generate a consolidated report for all the modules on SmartView Monitor. When the selection process is over, the report will be generated for the predefined time range, which is also selected in the Counters setting tab.

Traffic Reports

To generate reports on Check Point VPN/FireWall or FloodFate Modules traffic, simply chose the module and open the Traffic History configuration tab. You should choose a time frame and the traffic type from the Select Throughput Report box.

User Monitor

If you need real-time monitoring for your remote access users, User Monitor is the tool for you. On a new interface, you will be able to view all your SecureRemote users currently logged on to specific policy servers, and you will be able to define queries and export your query results for reporting. This tool centralizes the monitoring for enterprises that have multiple policy servers.

User Monitor allows you to define queries, refine results, and view the active policy servers in a single interface.

Tools & Traps...

Fixing User Monitor in FP3

A common problem you could face is that the User Monitor does not work in VPN-1/FireWall-1 NG FP3. The User Monitor GUI sometimes fails to synchronize with the policy server, and therefore it is not possible to perform any queries. You'll see the "EnableUserMonitor is still set to false" error message in the $FWDIR/log/dtpsd.elg file. User Monitor shows 0 users. Policy Server is displayed in random status, when no SecureRemote users are connected to this policy server. When connecting with the User Monitor client to the management, FWM crashes on UNIX. If this is the case, follow these steps to resolve the problem:

1. Install FireWall-1 NG FP3 HotFix 1. Then, on the SmartCenter (Management) Server, do the following:
2. Stop FireWall-1's processes by issuing *cpstop*.
3. Rename the $FWDIR/conf/objects_5_0.C.bak file.
4. Open the objects_5_0.C file with DBedit editor and, to the *:properties* section, add the following line:

```
:EnableUserMonitoring (true)
```

5. Save the objects_5_0.C file.
6. Edit the $FWDIR/conf/tables.C file with a text editor, and change the *read_only* attribute of the "end_point_status" table to *false*.
7. Save the tables.C file.
8. Start VPN-1/FireWall-1's processes by issuing the *cpstart9* command. Reinstall Security Policy on the Policy Server modules.

The Interface

As shown in Figure 2.25, the User Monitor interface consists of four panes. View options can be changed with the toggle toolbar button or the View menu:

- **The Query Selector pane** You can create, view, or delete queries from this pane. When a query is selected, it is possible to edit, save, save under a different name, rename, export, or delete from the right-click pop-up menu.
- **The Query Results pane** When the query is run, the matching items are listed in columns on the right results screen. You can limit the number of records displayed with the Records Limitation function.

- **Query Editor** This is very similar to the Query Properties pane of SmartView Tracker. On a visual interface, you may define the filter criteria for the query.
- **The Policy Editors pane** This pane displays the list of active policy servers. When detailed view is chosen, it is possible to see the synchronization status of the policy server. Synchronization represents the alignment between SmartCenter and the policy server.

Figure 2.25 User Monitor

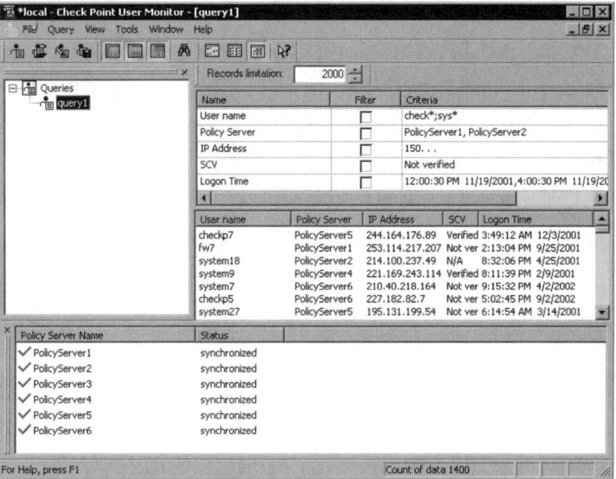

Managing Queries

Once you define and save your queries, User Monitor has the following options to manage your saved queries:

- **Defining a Query** You may create a new query either from the toolbar, the menu bar, or the Query Selector pane. The following filters are available: User Name, Policy Server, IP Address, SCV, and Logon Time. Using wildcards is not possible on most of the filters.
- **Editing a Query** When a query is selected, these options are available: edit, save, save under a different name, rename, export, or delete. The export function allows the exporting of the current result set into an MS Excel compatible (*.xfw) file format.
- **Running a Query** You may run a new query from the toolbar, the menu bar, or the Query Selector pane.

Summary

The NG GUIs cannot simply be called a face-lift and a bunch of fancy tools. Check Point listened to systems administrators' details of chronic problems and tried to address most of the problems with the new interface set. With the introduction of SmartTracker, the new log management console in NG FP3, Check Point introduced new terminology. The "Smart" clients are fortified with the new monitoring tools such as SmartView Monitor and User Monitor. Integration of strong authentication and certificate support in Smart Clients management is a major milestone.

SmartDashboard, the old policy editor, has become a central management console with the integration of LDAP GUI, administrator user management, and revision control. The new panes and configurable toolbars are notable. The only problem using SmartDashboard is the amount of space it requires. Larger screen resolutions make it easier to access the functions. Although Motif GUI is still supported, you could feel that the strong influence of Windows GUI functionality in the SmartClients all-drag-and-drop functions, expandable trees, and tabular view change the GUI experience. Using sections in NG FP3 for Security Rule Base is a very practical solution for busy rule bases.

SmartView leverages the architectural changes. The application-monitoring functionality shaped around SVN Foundation delivers fine status information about the Check Point network. More data is available to the administrators if connected/disconnected status views of 4.x versions are taken as a base. Status information is also available from the command line. Alerts are more mature with NG; you can collect alerts based on connectivity disk usage and CPU utilization. Global configuration options are available for system alerts.

NG FP3's major client impact is the SmartView Tracker. The new log interface has a lot of fresh features. Besides the organizational changes of the screen, using the new query filter alters your filtering habits. Within access to all log fields, Query Editor offers a long list of choices. The problem of choosing the required fields on a long list of options is solved by visual filters of Query Editor. There are also new features like viewing multiple log files concurrently and integration of previous policies in the revision database. It might be obvious, but the cut-and-paste functionality of the logs is a very useful feature.

If you are familiar with the Windows platform Performance Monitor, it won't take too much time for you to figure out the logic of SmartView Monitor. Finally, Check Point offers a native system-monitoring tool. SmartView Monitor delivers real-time and historical monitoring functionality. Though not complete, this information is a good start. Most of the monitoring options are also available from the command line. User Monitor, another tool to monitor remote access in real time, also tries to fill the enterprise-monitoring gap while client VPNs' importance and vitality grow every day.

The SmartClients are better than before, though not perfect. The biggest questions in administrators' minds are related to Check Point's support for other platforms. With the increased usage of Linux-based firewalls and appliances, it is time to reconsider a Linux desktop for Check Point.

Solutions Fast Track

SmartDashboard

☑ Object Tree makes it easier to access all objects.

☑ Authentication is more sophisticated with SmartDashboard. You can choose certificates or strong authentication.

☑ Administrator users can be defined from the SmartDashboard. There is no need for *cpconfig*.

☑ There are new GUI add-ons such as policy revision control and enhanced policy install windows.

SmartView Status

☑ SVN-supported detailed status information is available.

☑ Alerts can be defined as global. CPU, disk, and connectivity thresholds can generate alerts.

☑ Command-line status monitoring is also possible with the AMON protocol.

SmartView Tracker

☑ The new GUI is faster. You can monitor the speed from the status bar as you read the logs processed.

☑ A new pop-up window enables you to view the log details.

☑ All log fields are available for filtering when the GUI-based query filter is selected.

☑ There are three log formats: Log, Audit, and Active.

SmartView Monitor

- ☑ Besides real-time monitoring, historical reports are also available.
- ☑ All Check Point system counters can be monitored graphically.
- ☑ Virtual links enable SLA monitoring.
- ☑ QoS monitoring is also integrated.

User Monitor

- ☑ User Monitor enables real-time client VPN activity monitoring.
- ☑ The wildcard option in queries allows detailed query filtering.
- ☑ The User Monitor provides multiple options for sorting query results.

Frequently Asked Questions

The following Frequently Asked Questions, answered by the authors of this book, are designed to both measure your understanding of the concepts presented in this chapter and to assist you with real-life implementation of these concepts. To have your questions about this chapter answered by the author, browse to **www.syngress.com/solutions** and click on the **"Ask the Author"** form.

Q: What is audit mode?

A: Audit mode displays administrator-level activity in SmartView Tracker, such as policy changes and object modifications.

Q: How can I run SmartMap?

A: You need a separate license to activate SmartMap.

Q: Where do I define SmartClient Administrators?

A: You can define SmartClient Administrators from the Object tree or the Manage | Users menu. However, in order to define an administrator, you should first create a Permission Profile from the Manage menu.

Q: What is a virtual link?

A: Virtual links are defined in order to monitor traffic between two VPN-1/FireWall-1 gateways, monitor SLA violations, and log traffic data.

Q: How can I define a non-Check Point firewall in SmartDashboard?

A: Select **Manage | Network Objects | New | Interoperable Device** to create a third-party firewall.

Q: Why I can't see client VPN connections on User Monitor on my FP3 box?

A: You need to apply a specific hotfix to correct the synchronization problem.

Q: Why are my logs are off by one hour on NG FP3 SmartView Tracker?

A: This problem occurs on NT SP6a. You need a specific fix.

Q: I can't run Remote Files Management on the cluster. I get a "Check if the module is up" notification, even if the module is up.

A: Run the following command from the command line:

```
fw fetchlogs -f *.log <firewall object name>
```

Chapter 3

Advanced Authentication

Solutions in this chapter:

- Active Directory
- Standard LDAP
- RADIUS
- TACACS+
- General User Management

☑ Summary

☑ Solutions Fast Track

☑ Frequently Asked Questions

Introduction

"Who is coming through my firewall?" is one of the most frequently asked questions in our security space today. Managing access through FireWall-1 has not always been glamorous or even exciting. With NG, most of the issues relating to authentication and user management are diminished. Now managing users can be accomplished in a centralized Lightweight Directory Access Protocol (LDAP) database with all of the security rules and access in the store and can be used to authenticate users through FireWall-1. With this support comes the ability to utilize Microsoft Active Directory (AD) integration for shops that use the AD exclusively.

This chapter walks you-through the use of LDAP, MS-AD, RADIUS, and TACAS+ integration for user authentication. The primary focus is how to integrate the components, not how to manage the users. User management is accomplished in the source directory, LDAP, not in FireWall-1. For readers who used the old account management client, it is now integrated into the SmartDashboard.

This chapter also points out some pitfalls and other ideas that you might want to use to make your administration of users against a centralized directory less of a headache. Today most organizations can create Web sites that enable end users to modify or change their passwords; we discuss the integration of this feature to make your deployment of user authentication and centralized user management a reality. Overall, the use of these features will assist any organization that seeks to enable a more centralized security and authentication model.

Active Directory

Proprietary systems are not welcome in heterogeneous computing environments. Microsoft was criticized for its limited directory service capabilities in the NT operating system, just as Check Point has been hit by the lack of full support for a directory service. But lessons have been learned, and with NG, Check Point VPN-1/FireWall-1 has native authentication services support for Microsoft's Active Directory Server, the standards-compliant directory server.

A *directory service* is a database that contains information about every object in the network. When AD is used for authentication in Check Point deployments, the Check Point administrators eliminate the need for multiple directory management and authentication services are centralized. Another benefit is the real-time integration with corporate identity management systems, which allows real-time user provisioning. AD brings the following technical benefits for the authentication services:

- **Active Directory is fault-tolerant.** Domain controllers use multimaster replication to replicate Active Directory data. Check Point has fault-tolerant setup for LDAP-based account units.

- **Active Directory is extensible.** All objects in AD are defined in the Active Directory Database. When extension is required, as with the Check Point integration case, the schema can be modified dynamically and the new attributes will be immediately available. Check Point delivers a ready-to-use Active Directory extension.
- **Active directory is scalable.** Windows NT's 40,000-object limit is not valid for AD. The unlimited objects allow corporations to utilize Check Point's authentication at the security perimeter.

On the Check Point side, the following technical benefits are apparent:

- AD has inherent redundancy.
- High performance is gained by geographically distributing the authentication load.
- Standards-based SSL protected LDAP queries.
- Integrated AD user management is available in SmartDashboard.
- Granular password policy management is available.

The effort required to integrate AD services with NG decreases when the deployment is divided into two main sections: configuring Active Directory Server and configuring Check Point FireWall. Although these two processes are tightly integrated, it is recommended that you complete AD configuration before Check Point configuration.

Setting Up Active Directory for FireWall-1 Authentication

To use AD directory services on Check Point, you should allow schema modifications. SSL communication should also be activated over LDAP. This functionality requires Microsoft Certificate Server. For encryption compatibility, you need the Microsoft High Encryption pack. Of course, you should have a properly configured Active Directory and DNS.

The following steps describe Active Directory configuration on a Windows 2000 server. The instructions cover basic Active Directory installation procedures:

1. Create and configure AD services if they do not exist.
2. High Encryption Pack must be pre-installed.
3. Verify DNS services.
4. Enable SSL over LDAP. Install and configure Microsoft Certificate Server.
5. Install the Microsoft High Encryption pack.

6. Allow modifications on schema.
7. Modify AD schema for additional Check Point fields (optional).

Active Directory Installation and Basic Configuration

When Active Directory is chosen for a VPN-1/FireWall-1 user database, it is assumed that the target network has a working AD base. But due to corporate security policy restrictions or lab installations, you might need to configure Active Directory from scratch. The following steps describe a brief procedure for AD installation with the DCPROMO utility:

1. Start DCPROMO (see Figure 3.1) from the **Start | Run** prompt by entering the command **dcpromo**. This command initializes the Active Directory Installation wizard. You can also initialize the wizard through **Start | Programs | Administrative Tools | Configure Your Server and Active Directory**. An NTFS formatted disk partition is required for Active Directory installation.

Figure 3.1 The Active Directory Installation Wizard

2. You can install the domain controller for either a new or existing AD domain. Assuming that you do not have an existing domain, choose **Domain controller for a new domain**, as shown in Figure 3.2, and click the **Next** button.
3. Since this is a new domain root, choose **Create a new domain tree**, as shown in Figure 3.3, and click the **Next** button.
4. Create a forest by choosing **Create a new forest of domain trees**, as shown in Figure 3.4, and click the **Next** button.

Figure 3.2 Choosing to Install a New Domain Controller

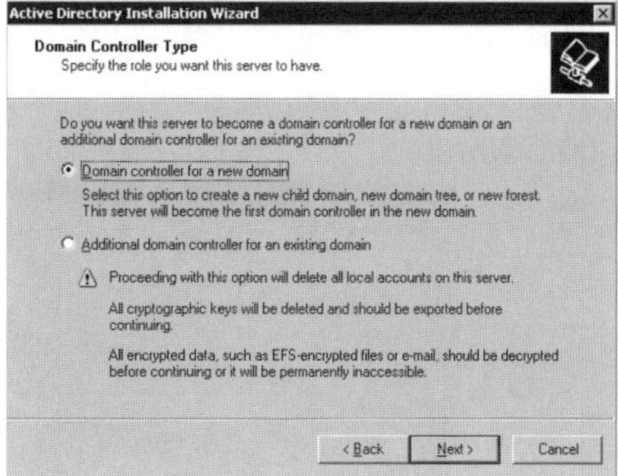

Figure 3.3 Domain Tree Options

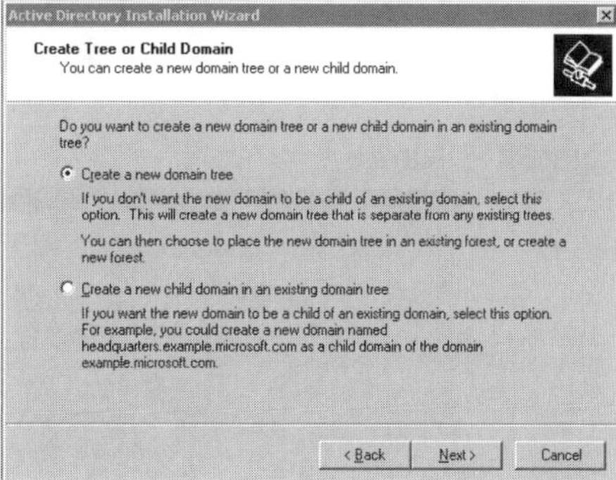

Figure 3.4 Forest Options

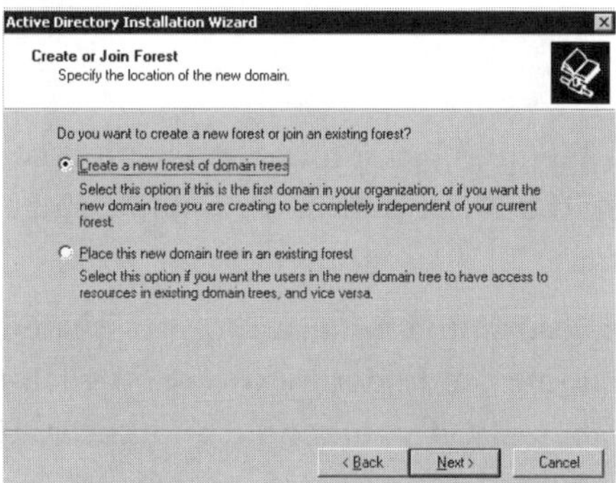

5. As displayed in Figure 3.5, we will use a domain called *hq.net* for this chapter. Enter the desired domain name for the AD root and click the **Next** button.
6. Type your domain's NetBIOS name in the box (see Figure 3.6). The initial NETBIOS name will be extracted from the domain name, but you may change it. All NT and Windows 9x clients will recognize this domain controller with

the NETBIOS name. This is not critical for VPN-1/FireWall-1. We use the default name *HQ* for the NETBIOS domain name. Click the **Next** button to continue.

Figure 3.5 DNS Name

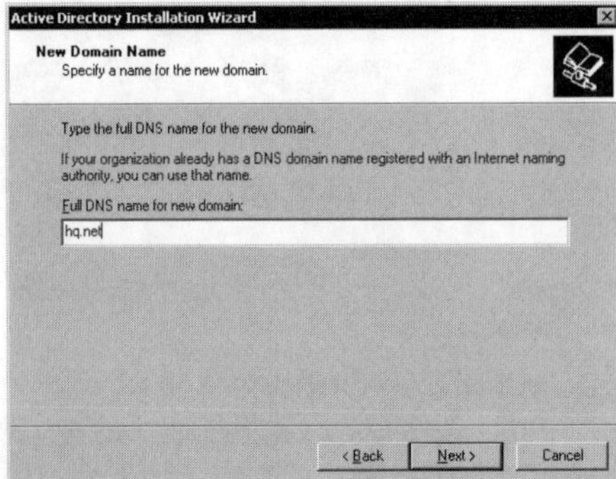

Figure 3.6 NetBIOS Name

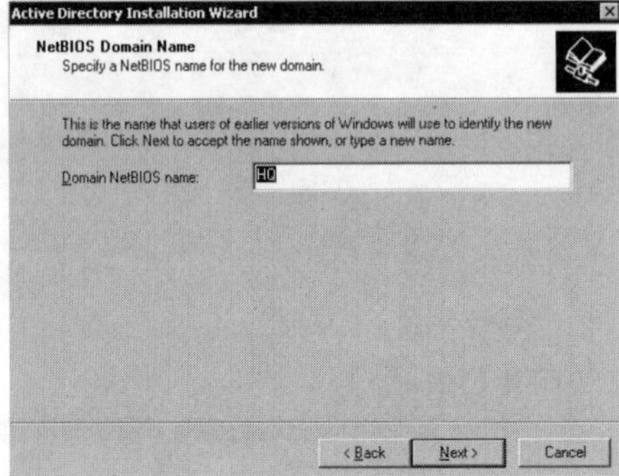

7. As shown in Figure 3.7, approve the location of the critical Active Directory files and click the **Next** button. You may change default location using the **Browse** button.
8. If you have a distributed installation, your shared system volume should be replicated. Choose the folder location and click the **Next** button (see Figure 3.8). Remember that if you choose another volume, the target folders should be NTFS formatted, too.
9. At this point, the Active Directory Installation will search for the DNS information. Active Directory is tightly integrated with DNS. Windows 2000 Server has a built-in DNS service, which is interoperable with other DNS systems. If you want to use a non-Windows 2000 DNS server, you must ensure that your third-party DNS server supports the following properties:
   - Support for SRV records—BIND 4.9.6 or later

- Incremental zone updates—BIND 8.2.1 or later
- Dynamic Update—BIND 8.1.2 or later

Figure 3.7 Paths for the Active Directory

Active Directory Installation Wizard
Database and Log Locations
Specify the locations of the Active Directory database and log.
For best performance and recoverability, store the database and the log on separate hard disks.
Where do you want to store the Active Directory database?
Database location:
C:\WINNT\NTDS
Browse...
Where do you want to store the Active Directory log?
Log location:
C:\WINNT\NTDS
Browse...
< Back
Next >
Cancel

Figure 3.8 Shared System Volume

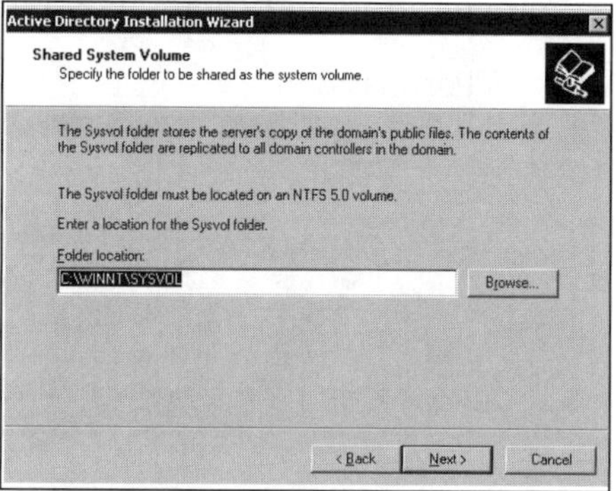

If you do not already have a DNS server for Active Directory, there are two methods of installation. The first method is using the Add/Remove Programs applet from the Control Panel. You should choose **Windows Components | Network Services** and then click the **Details** button.

Luckily, DCPROMO has a built-in DNS installation and configuration wizard, which will start DNS configuration automatically (see Figure 3.9). If you do not have a DNS server in place, DCPROMO will display the warning message shown in Figure 3.9.

Figure 3.9 DNS Prompt

10. As displayed in Figure 3.10, we choose the first option, to utilize the built-in wizard configuration. Click the **Next** button to continue.

Figure 3.10 The DNS Installation Wizard

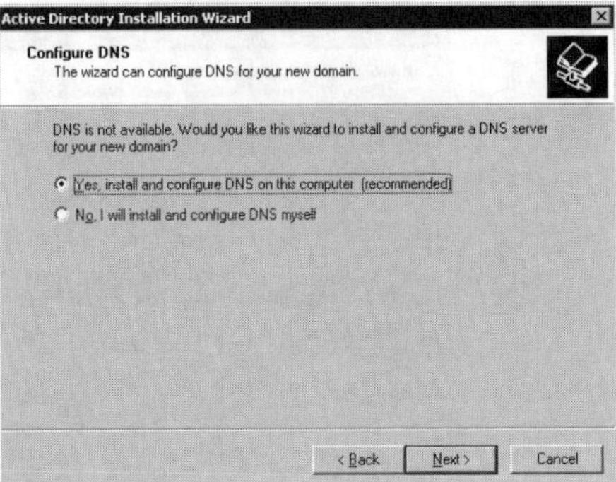

11. Select backward compatibility (see Figure 3.11), which will allow unauthenticated DNS communication, and click the **Next** button.

Figure 3.11 DNS Permissions

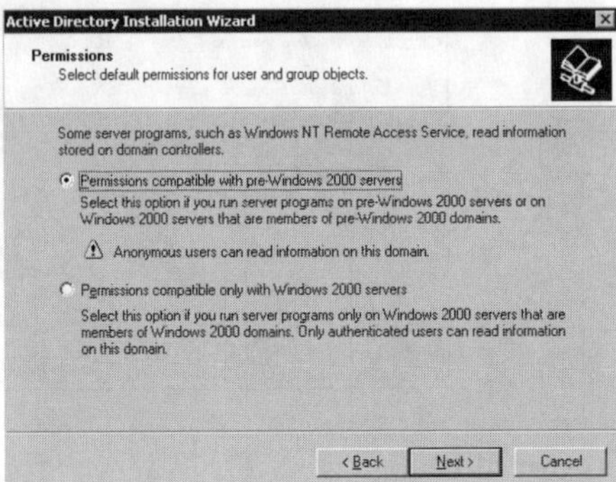

12. Active Directory contains a Restore mode option for disaster recovery. As shown in Figure 3.12, type and confirm the Administrator password for Restore mode and click the **Next** button.
13. The Active Directory Installation wizard will display the summary of your decisions. If you find anything irregular, you may roll back to the relevant configuration screen with the Back button (see Figure 3.13).
14. Click the **Finish** button to complete Active Directory installation (see Figure 3.14).

Figure 3.12 Restore Mode Password

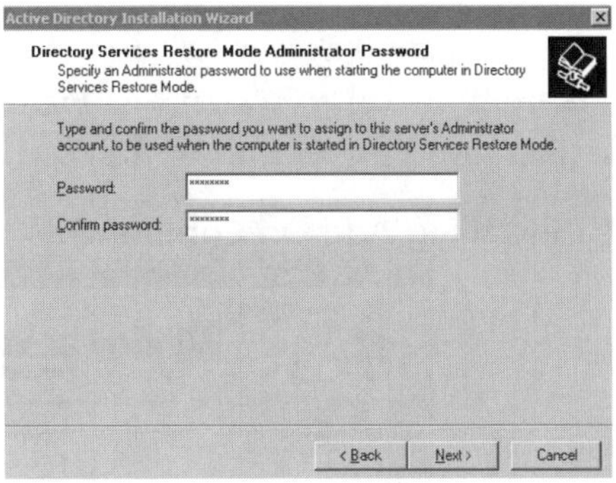

Figure 3.13 Installation Wizard Review

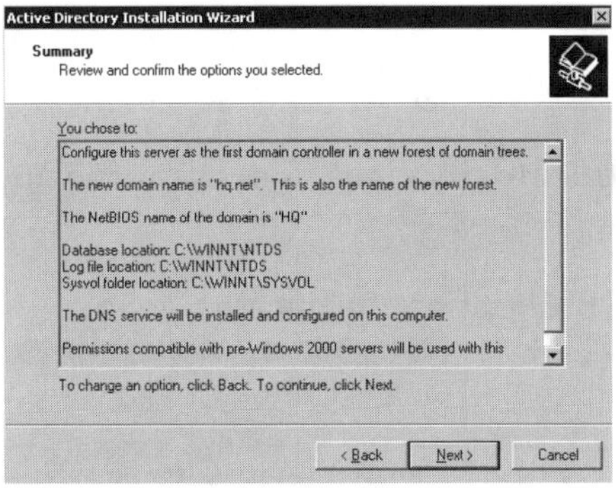

Figure 3.14 End of Installation Wizard

Enabling LDAP Over SSL

When you leverage the security standards of AD, having all encrypted traffic is the first step. The traffic between Check Point SmartCenter and Active Directory should be authenticated and encrypted.

To enable Secure Sockets Layer (SSL), follow these steps:

1. Insert your Windows 2000 Server CD and choose **Install Add-On Components** from the splash screen (see Figure 3.15). Or you may go through Add/Remove Programs from the Control Panel.

Figure 3.15 Installing Add-On Components

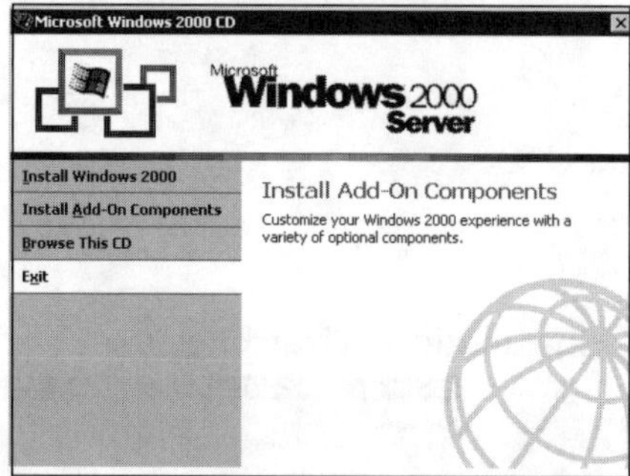

2. Select **Certificate Services** from the menu and click the **Next** button (see Figure 3.16).

Figure 3.16 Choosing Certificate Services

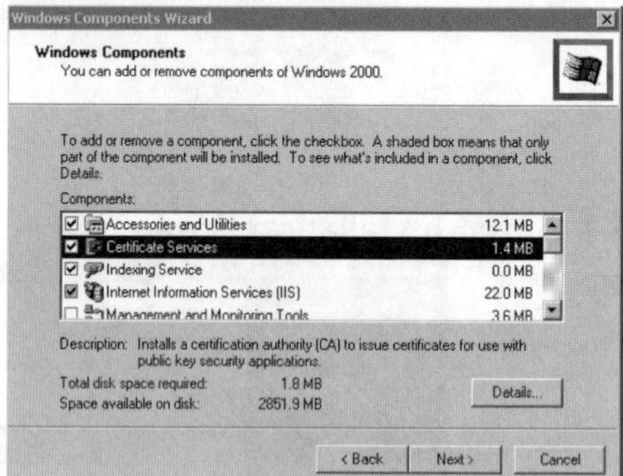

3. Choose **Enterprise root CA** from the CA types menu (see Figure 3.17). Click the **Next** button.
4. Define CA information and click the **Next** button (see Figure 3.18).
5. Approve storage locations (see Figure 3.19) for the CA database and click the **Next** button.
6. As displayed in Figure 3.20, the files will be copied to your server. This process will take some time. Click the **Finish** button when copying is completed. A notification window will acknowledge the installation, as shown in Figure 3.21.

Figure 3.17 Choosing CA Type

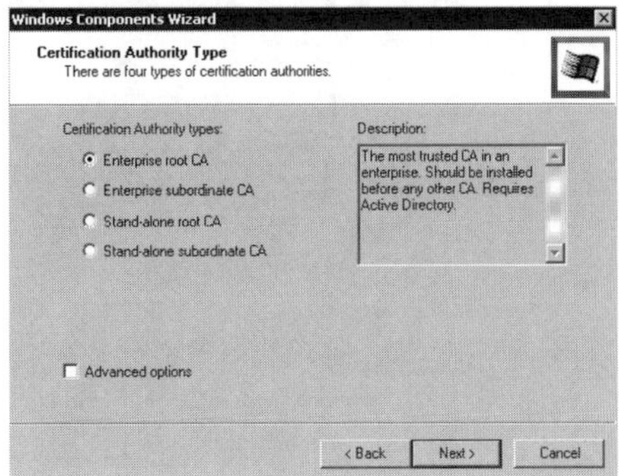

Figure 3.18 CA Identifying Information

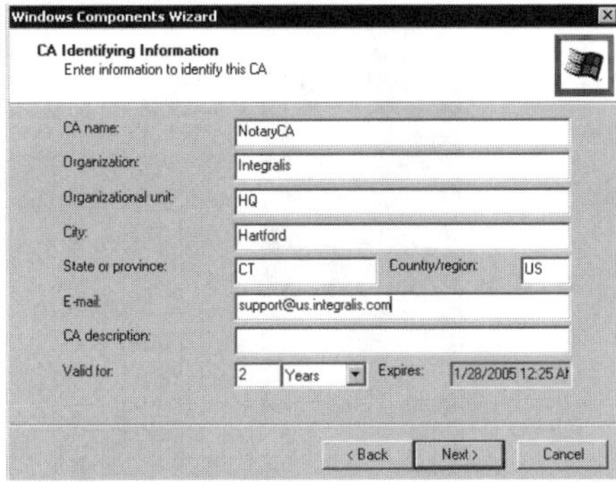

Figure 3.19 Database Storage Locations

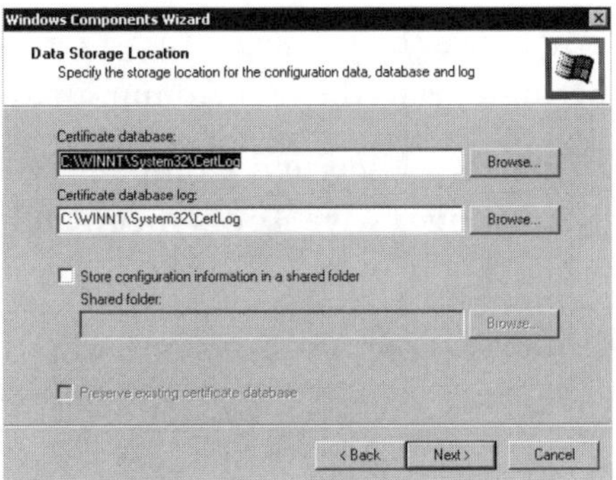

Figure 3.20 Configuring Components

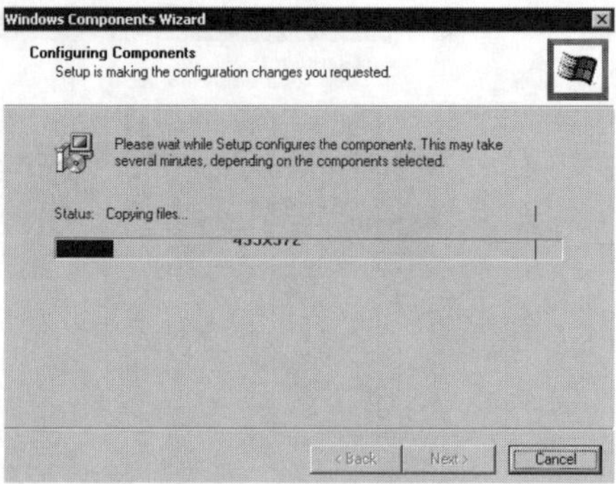

Figure 3.21 Completing the Certificate Services Installation

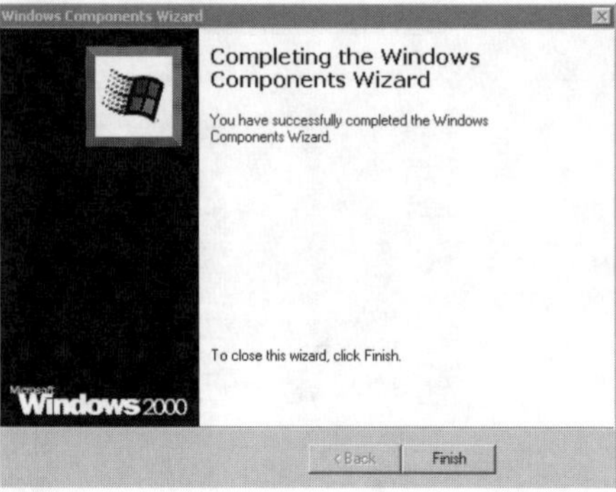

Delegation of Control

Administrator users do not have the privileges that are required to manage Active Directory. To change permissions to the user Administrator, use the following procedure:

1. Open Active Directory Users and Computers from the Windows 2000 **Programs | Administrative Tools** menu and choose **Delegate Control** (see Figure 3.22).

Figure 3.22 Active Directory Users and Computers

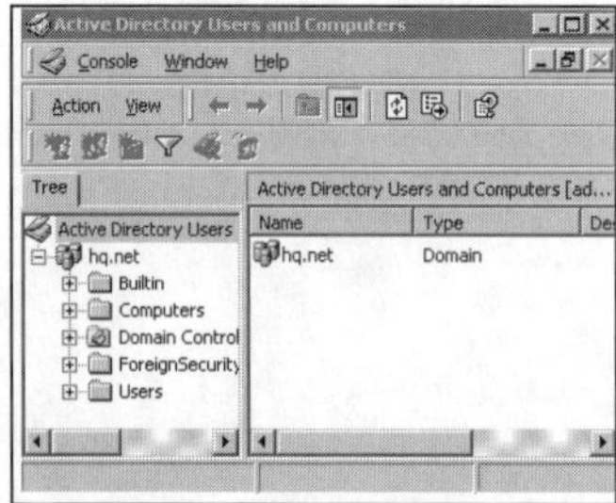

2. A wizard pops up (see Figure 3.23) with the "Delegation of Control Wizard" title. Click the **Next** button to continue.

Figure 3.23 The Delegation of Control Wizard

3. Select the groups to which you want to give privileges. Depending on your security policy, choose the user groups to assign privileges (see Figure 3.24). Click the **Next** button to continue.

Figure 3.24 Selecting Users or Groups

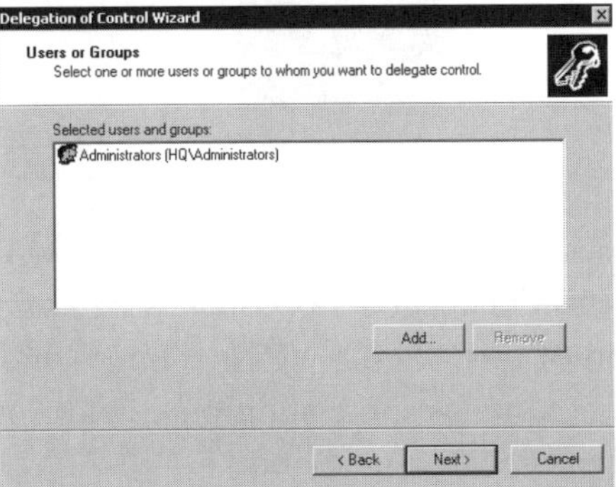

4. As displayed in Figure 3.25, choose both boxes to assign common tasks to the chosen group. You do not need to delegate additional tasks for Active Directory integration. Click the **Next** button to continue.
5. Click the **Finish** button to complete the delegation process (see Figure 3.26).

Active Directory Schema Management

Active Directory schema is a metadata repository of all objects, attributes, and the classes to which objects belong. The schema determines the location and the property of Active Directory database contents. In other words, the schema can be defined as the rules that determine what can be stored in Active Directory.

Figure 3.25 Delegating Tasks

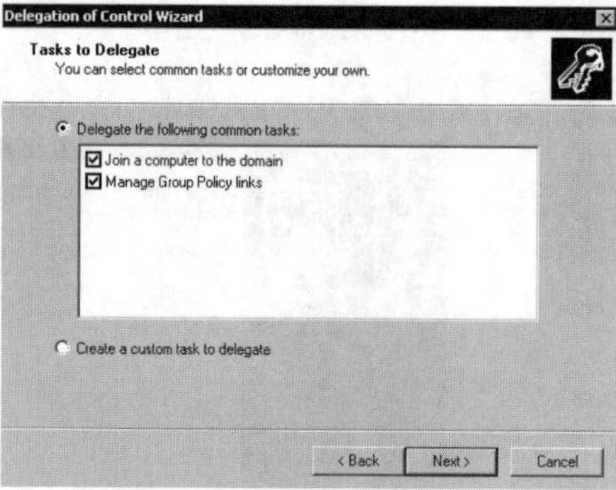

Figure 3.26 Completing the Wizard

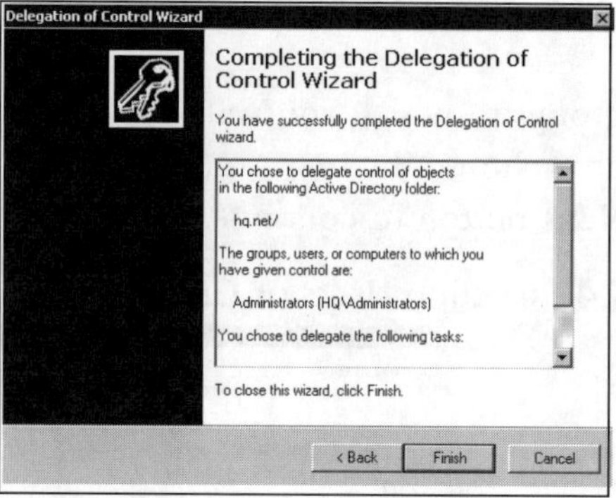

Windows 2000 is shipped with a default schema, which is installed with Active Directory. Although this default schema contains basic fields, third-party applications may require extension of this schema. VPN-1/FireWall-1 is a good example for this case: The user database contains some additional fields that might be useful (optional) for extended control of user management.

Active Directory supports multimaster replication of the directory data store between all domain controllers in the domain. As a result, all Active Directory database and transaction logs are replicated on all servers, but not the schema. Some changes are impractical to perform in multimaster fashion; however, only one domain controller, called the *operations master*, accepts requests for such changes. Because the operations master roles can be moved to other domain controllers within the domain or forest, these roles are sometimes referred to as *flexible single master operations (FSMOs)*.

To manage the schema, you can use Microsoft Management Console (MMC). To access schema properties through the MMC, you need to first register the schmmgmt.dll:

1. From the **Start | Run** menu, type **Regsvr32 schmmgmt.dll** and click **Run**. You will then see the pop-up screen shown in Figure 3.27. After you

complete the registration, you may view the schema properties (see Figure 3.28) from the MMC.

Figure 3.27 DLL Registration

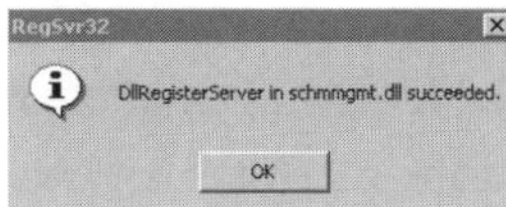

Figure 3.28 Schema Snap-In

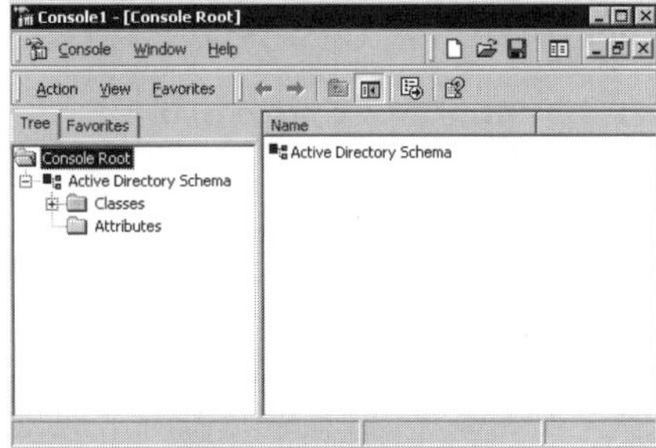

2. To add the MMC snap-in to your MMC console, open the MMC from **Start | Run**. Type **mmc** in the Run box.
3. On the MMC console, select **Add/Remove Snap-in** from the **File** menu.
4. Click the **Add** button.
5. On the pop-up screen, select **Active Directory Schema** and click **Add**, then click **Close**.
6. Click **OK** on the Snap-in page. You will get the schema management controls as a snap-in module on your Microsoft Management Console.

Troubleshooting with Schema Masters

There is only one domain controller for Active Directory schema. As explained, the schema master cannot be used in multimaster mode, and it may be referred to as an FSMO. To identify the schema master:

1. Open **Active Directory Schema**.
2. In the console tree, right-click **Active Directory Schema** and then click **Operations Master**.

The name of the current domain-naming master appears in Current Operations Master. Every forest has only one schema master. To identify the schema master in a different forest, target the appropriate forest before clicking Operations Master.

Schema Master Failure

Temporary loss of the schema operations master is not visible to network users. It will not be visible to network administrators either unless they are trying to modify the schema or install an application that modifies the schema during installation. If the schema master will be unavailable for an unacceptable length of time, you can failover the role to the standby operations master. However, transitioning this role is a drastic step that you should take only when the failure of the schema master is permanent.

To failover the schema master role, follow these steps:

1. Click **Start**, click **Run**, and then type **cmd**.
2. At the command prompt, type **ntdsutil**.
3. At the ntdsutil prompt, type **roles**.
4. At the FSMO maintenance prompt, type **connections**.
5. At the server connections prompt, type **connect to server**, followed by the fully qualified domain name.
6. At the server connections prompt, type **quit**.
7. At the FSMO maintenance prompt, type **seize schema master**.
8. At the FSMO maintenance prompt, type **quit**.
9. At the ntdsutil prompt, type **quit**.

Extending Your Schema

Check Point VPN-1/FireWall-1 does not require modification of an Active Directory schema. Check Point account management can leverage existing Active Directory objects. If you do not want to have granular control of users, you may choose to employ user templates instead. User templates assign generic properties to all users created from those templates—at least those which do not have similar properties defined in the Active Directory schema. (Use of templates is summarized in the "Defining the Active Directory Account Unit" section of this chapter.) Whether or not your schema needs to be extended depends on your requirements. For example, not all VPN-1/FireWall-1 user properties are defined in the Active Directory schema because these variables are VPN-1/FireWall-1 specific attributes. If your security policy requires defining Authentication schemas per user, you need to store the authentication schema attribute on Active Directory, and this extra feature requires extension of your Active Directory schema.

Modifying AD schema is a one-way function. There is no schema Delete function. It is irreversible and must be avoided if it's not necessary. If you decide to extend your schema, you should first try this process in an isolated lab environment. Once modified in production, all your enterprise servers will receive the replicated metadata, and you will receive inconsistency errors if the modification is not successful. This error will bring down all your directory implementation, and you will need to reinstall everything.

WARNING

This section contains information about modifying the Active Directory schema. If problems occur, a system backup or reinstallation of your system might be the only way to recover data. You should use extreme caution when you make any changes to the Active Directory schema, because the changes will occur forestwide, and you cannot remove objects and attributes that are added to the schema.

So think twice and carefully justify whether you really need the additional properties in Active Directory (shown in Figure 3.30 for FW-1) for VPN-1/FireWall-1. It is relatively safe to use predefined modification script from Check Point, which we examine in a moment. Depending on your current schema implementation, a bad modification has the potential to devastate your entire network. Proceed with caution!

The extension or modification of the Active Directory schema requires write access to the schema. Schema updates may be enabled by means of the Schema Management Console (Schema Manager) or directly in the Registry. Schema updates can only be enabled on the domain controller that holds the schema master role.

Open the Schema Manager, which you configured as a snap-in MMC in the previous section. Right-click **Active Directory Schema** and select **Operations Master**. You will see the "Change Schema Master" screen, as displayed in Figure 3.29.

Figure 3.29 Change Schema Master

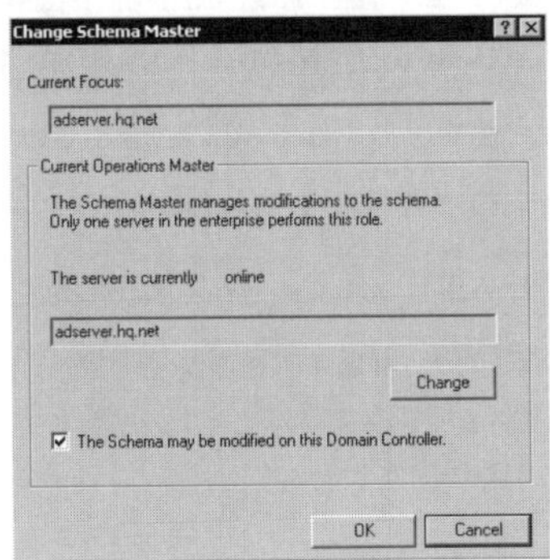

Check the box labeled **The Schema may be modified on this Domain Controller**.

It is not recommended that you enable schema updates by directly editing the Schema Update Allowed Registry key. Schema updates should be enabled through the console method whenever possible. If for some reason the console method cannot be used, the following Registry key may be edited directly:

```
HKEY_LOCAL_MACHINE\SYSTEM\CurrentControlSet\Services\NTDS\Parameters
```

To add Check Point attributes to your Active Directory schema, you can use a pre-defined configuration file from Check Point. You should test the ramifications of using this extension in your lab before applying the change in your production environment. The modification file is located in the $FWDIR/lib/ldap directory of your SmartCenter. This file (schema_microsoft_ad.dif) is generic and does not contain your domain name. The variable *DOMAINNAME* is used instead of your own domain name. Open your favorite text editor and replace all instances of *DOMAINNAME* with your fully qualified domain name. In our example, we used *HQ.NET*.

In the following example, the schema extension is executed for the HQ.NET domain. Here are some sample schema extensions:

- **Active Directory Server** ADSERVER.HQ.NET
- **SmartCenter** SMARTCENTER.HQ.NET
- **Administrator FQDN** cn=administrator,cn=users,dc=HQ,dc=NET
- **Administrator User** administrator
- **Administrator Password** abc123
- **Modified LDIF with Full Path** C:\winnt\fw1\ng\lib\ldap\schema_microsoft_ad.ldif

AD should be on a remote server, and hostnames must be resolvable. Run the following command from the SmartCenter in one line from the command prompt:

```
Ldapmodify -c -h ADSERVER.HQ.NET -D "cn=administrator,cn=users,dc=HQ,dc=
    NET" -w abc123 -f  C:\winnt\fw1\ng\lib\ldap\schema_microsoft_ad.ldif
```

You will see the output of modifications on your screen. To check the changes, go back to your Active Directory server, open the Schema Manager from the MMC, and examine the new FW-1 attributes. Figure 3.30 displays a modified Schema Manager screenshot with FW-1 modifications.

Figure 3.30 Modified Fields in AD Schema

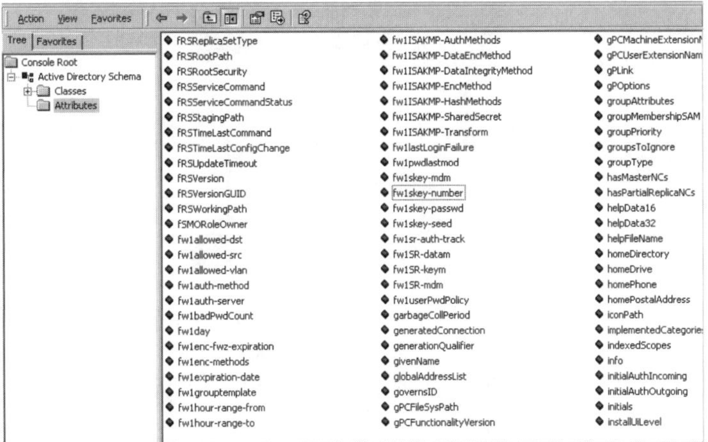

Enabling SSL Communication Between VPN-1/FireWall-1 and Active Directory

SSL is used to encrypt the traffic between VPN-1/Firewall-1 and Active Directory. The steps that follow summarize the SSL configuration procedure:

1. Open **Domain Security Policy** from the **Start | Programs | Administrative Tools** menu (see Figure 3.31).

   Figure 3.31 Domain Security Policy

   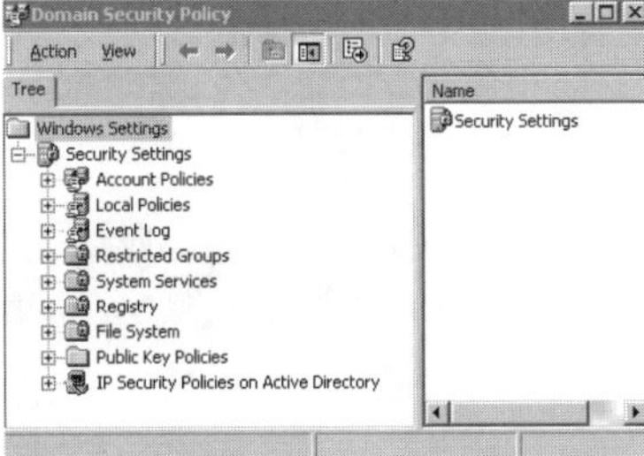

2. As shown in Figure 3.32, select **Security Settings | Public Key Policies | Automatic Certificate Request Settings**. Right-click **New Automatic Certificate Request**.
3. The Automatic Certificate Request Setup wizard will pop up automatically (see Figure 3.33).

Figure 3.32 Automatic Certificate Request Settings

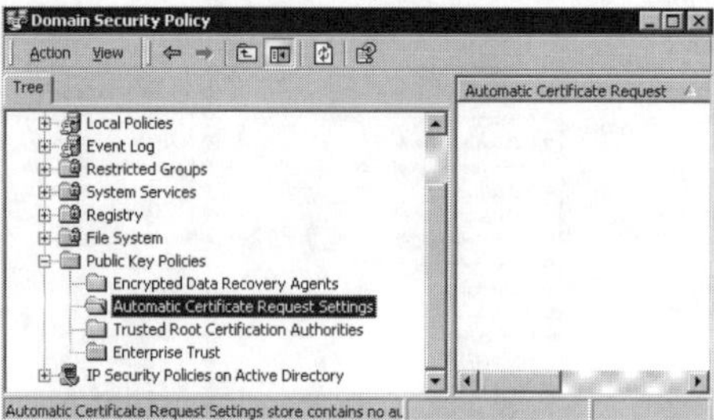

Figure 3.33 The Automatic Certificate Request Setup Wizard

4. As displayed in Figure 3.34, select **Domain Controller** for client/server authentication.

Figure 3.34 Certificate Templates

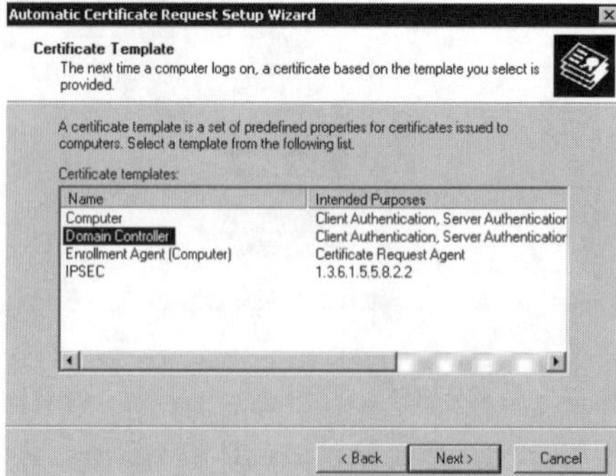

5. Choose the CA server (see Figure 3.35) that you created in the previous steps.
6. Click the **Finish** button (see Figure 3.36) to complete the process.

Figure 3.35 Certification Authority

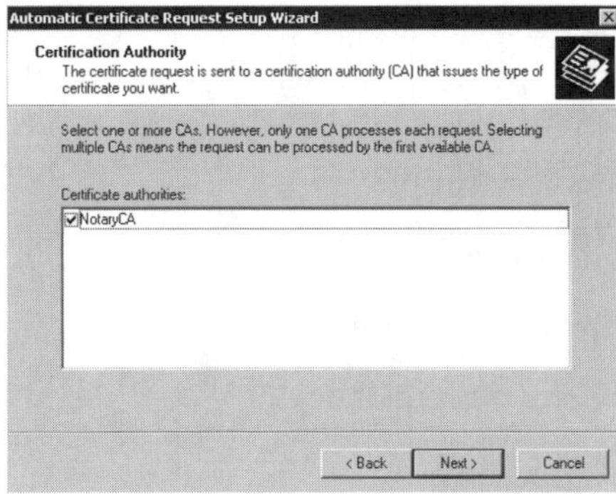

Figure 3.36 Completing the Automatic Certificate Request Setup

When the process is completed, in the Domain Security Policy window you should see an entry named *Domain Controller* on the right pane when Automatic Certificate Request is highlighted (see Figure 3.37).

Figure 3.37 Displaying Automatic Certificate Request Settings

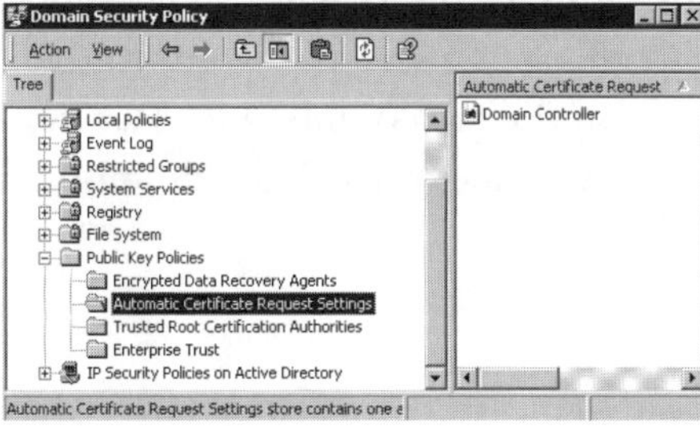

Setting Up the Firewall for AD Authentication

Setting up your firewall for Active Directory is easier than 4.1 configurations. With the help of the integrated LDAP account management GUI, you need nothing but the

SmartDashboard. The extended properties of the Account Unit object in VPN-1/FireWall-1 allow load sharing and high availability. On the other hand, it is possible to delegate account units per gateway, which will ease the geographically distributed configurations.

The setup steps are very simple:

1. Configure Global Properties.
2. Configure the account unit.
3. Configure LDAP administrators.
4. Configure user groups.
5. Configure the Rule Base.

Configuring Global Properties for Active Directory

When you have the proper license from Check Point, you can activate LDAP Account Management from the SmartDashboard. The SmartDashboard imports a limited number of users from the LDAP source at a time; you may define the size and the timeout variables for the imported list. After a timeout, you need to fetch the user table again. If authentication is set through the Active Directory unit properties, this action will require entering the password each time.

The Password Expires variable is FW-1 specific. This variable is introduced to Active Directory with schema modification so the third-party user management tools or original Microsoft user administration utilities are not aware of the *fw1pwdLastMod* variable. During the implementation, you may choose not to use this property. Users can log on with either their usernames or logon names.

When password strength is configured from Global Properties (see Figure 3.38) on FireWall-1, the configuration does not affect Active Directory security policies. During password-related operations, all LDAP users will be checked against these Global Properties. When you try to change a user's password, you will get the *ldap error -10* message (see Figure 3.39) if you do not comply with Password Strength settings rules. You have an option to force these rules on LDAP administrators, too.

Figure 3.38 LDAP Account Management Global Settings

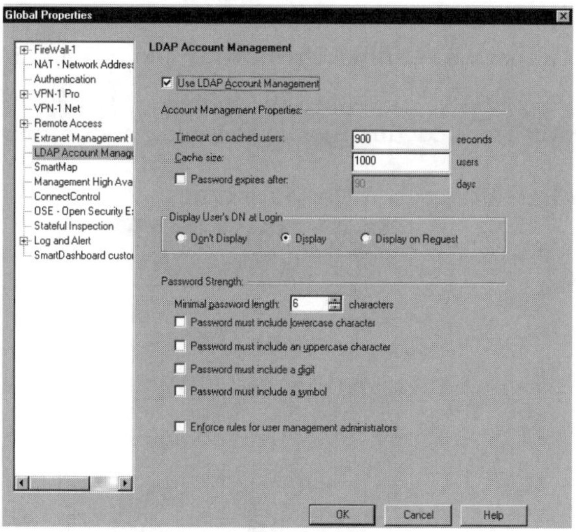

Figure 3.39 The Password Strength Error Message

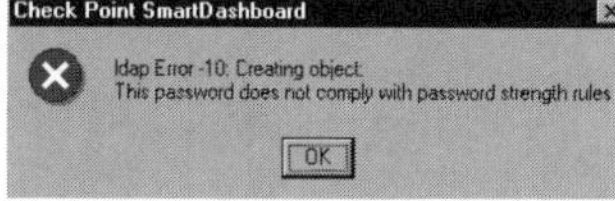

Defining the Active Directory Account Unit

Here are the basic steps in defining the Active Directory account unit on Check Point FireWall-1:

1. From the **Objects** tree (shown in Figure 3.40) or the **Manage | Servers** menu, create an Active Directory unit. For high availability and load sharing, LDAP account units allow grouping of multiple LDAP servers in a single server object.

   Figure 3.40 The Object Tree Servers Tab

   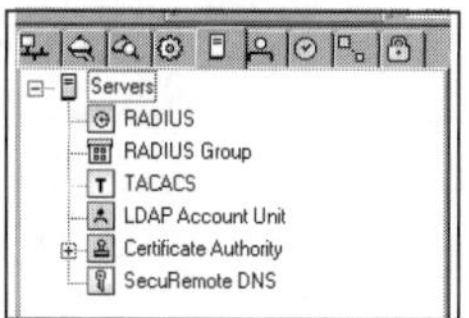

2. On the initial definition screen (see Figure 3.41), define the unit properties, usage type, and matching profile for the unit. OPSEC PKI based CA servers are able to store and retrieve CRL's from LDAP trees. This function is enabled only if the CRL Retrieval property is checked. In our case, we will use the

account unit for user management. If this property is not modifiable, that indicates Global Properties setup for LDAP account management has not been completed. Go back to **Global Properties** and enable LDAP account management to activate these fields. In the objects.C file, the attributes for each directory server are predefined, so you should choose the matching profile.

Figure 3.41 LDAP Account Unit Properties

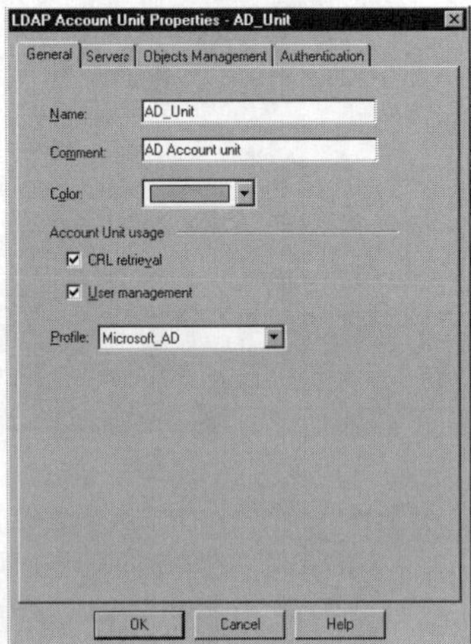

3. Prior to NG FP3, LDAP account units had identical priorities; gateways would query all servers, and once the first answer was received, the rest of the queries were dropped. In NG FP3, it is possible to add multiple replicated directory servers. If load sharing is desired, all LDAP servers should be defined with identical priorities, but for failover purposes, lower priorities are always an option.

   It is also possible to use external user (LDAP) groups in place of regular user groups, which will ease security management. Since the administrators can restrict the account units to be queried, it is possible to direct authentication requests to predefined servers and optimize your network traffic to build an optimized network.

   All gateway objects can be configured to use specific account units with specific priorities. In geographically distributed installations or under heavy load, you can configure your LDAP account units. Apply your localized units from your gateway's properties under **LDAP Account Management**.

   From the **Servers** tab, click the **Add** button to define your LDAP servers. If you have a previous version of NG FP3 gateways in your network, they won't be able to recognize multiple servers and the priorities, so you should assign a specific server for your "aged" gateway. Choose this gateway from the **Early Versions Compatibility Server** drop-down list, available from the Servers tab. (See Figure 3.42.)

Figure 3.42 LDAP Account Unit Properties Servers Tab

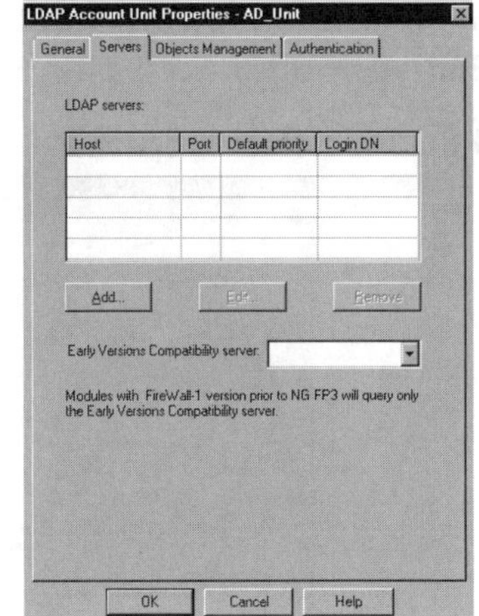

4. Click the **Add** button to add LDAP servers to the account unit. In the LDAP server definition screen (see Figure 3.43), you should describe the LDAP host and the access privileges to connect to the directory services. The Login DN will be used to connect to the directory services. This Login DN serves another purpose, too. If LDAP user management is handled by a different organizational group, the Login DN may add additional security. Accessing directory information is bound to Login DN and the password. Since this value is also kept in the management server, you can restrict querying LDAP servers based on Login DNs.

Figure 3.43 LDAP Server Definition

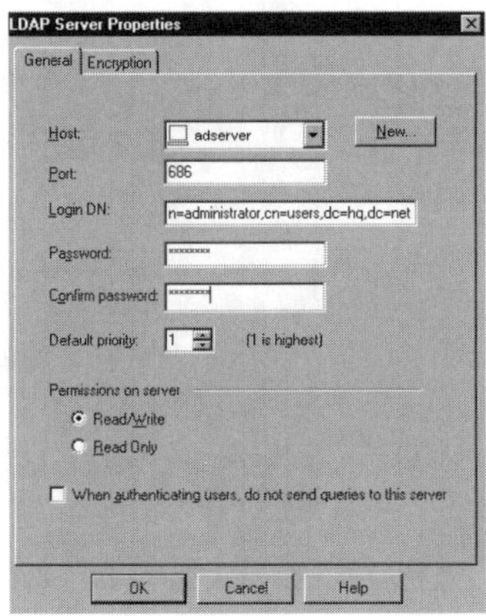

5. SmartDashboard and account unit communication can be encrypted with LDAP SSL. The default SSL port is 686. You can verify the LDAP server's

fingerprint with the **Fetch** button. For Active Directory, you must choose **Strong** for **Min/Maximum Encryption Strength** from the **LDAP Server Properties | Encryption** tab (see Figure 3.44).

Figure 3.44 The LDAP Server Properties Encryption Tab

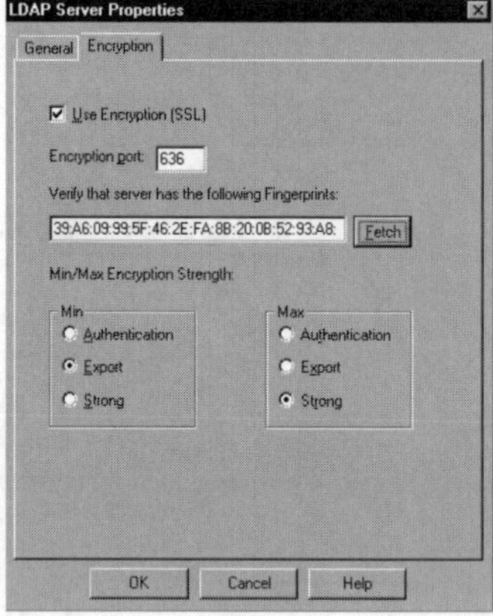

6. As shown in Figure 3.45, when displaying users on the on GUI, you can define the branches to be fetched. Clicking the **Fetch** button gets the default list. You may also limit the number of users to be returned. As discussed, you can enforce authentication on the account unit by checking the **Prompt for password when opening this Account Unit** option.

Figure 3.45 The LDAP Account Unit Management Objects Management Tab

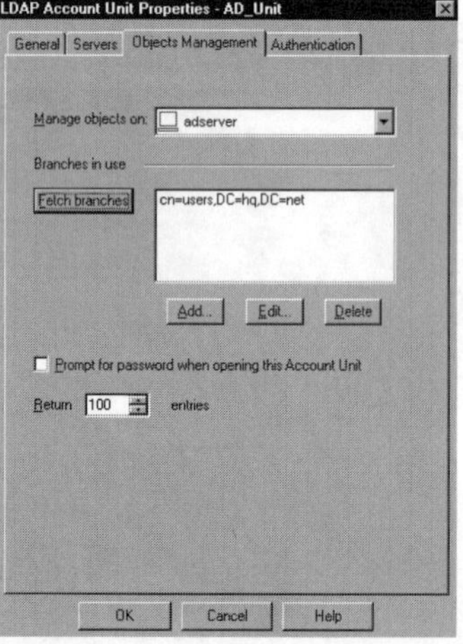

7. It is possible to filter the authentication methods on the account unit. This tab is critical for Active Directory integrations. When AD does not have the

VPN-1/FireWall-1 specific attributes in its schema, VPN-1/FireWall-1 will use the default templates. The user template chosen in the Authentication tab will apply to all users authenticated from the account unit. User templates have many options, and you may utilize these features without modifying your schema. The most important setting is authentication. If you need to integrate certificate or pre-shared, secret-based authentication, you can choose this global property. Another option is to choose Default Authentication Schema. This option is feasible when basic Active Directory authentication is required. The following authentication methods can be used with AD integration. If you choose a RADIUS or TACACS server, you need to define the server as well. The authentication options are:

- SecureID
- RADIUS
- TACACS
- OS Password

Tools & Traps…

Verifying the Fingerprint of the Certification Authority

Authenticity of the certificate authority is verified by the fingerprint. To verify the CA fingerprint, follow these steps:

1. On the Active Directory server (or your CA), run the **Certification Authority** console.
2. In the **Issued Certificates** list, double-click the certificate issued to the domain controller serving as the LDAP account unit.
3. In the **Details** tab, click **Copy to File....**
4. Make sure the **DER encoded binary X.509(.CER)** option is selected and click **Next**.
5. Specify a name for the file that the certificate will be written to. (The extension .CER will be added automatically.)
6. Click **Finish** and then click **OK** to close the Certificate Export wizard.
7. Use any MD5 utility to calculate the exported file's MD5 fingerprint. The fingerprint fetched in the Encryption tab of LDAP Account Unit should be compared to the output string.

To use IKE preshared secrets or public key certificates, you should use user templates. When SecureID is used, usernames are checked against the user's AD personal identification number (PIN) and the tokens are checked against the ACE server. There are other user control options, such as limiting login failures in the Authentication tab. Secure Authentication API (SAA) supported applications can also be integrated with Active Directory.

S/Key is not an option in Default Authentication Schema, since it cannot be used globally. It is not recommended that you use S/KEY in security policy authentication rules, since S/Key authentication will be phased out by the upcoming FP4 release.

When an IKE secret key is used for SecuRemote users, the user's password must be stored encrypted in the Active Directory database. To do this, first define the secret key in the account unit by selecting the **Properties | Authentication | Encryption | IKE pre-shared secret authentication key** field (see Figure 3.46). Then you can generate the encrypted passwords with the *fwm ikecrypt* command. The resulting string is then stored in Active Directory. The syntax for *fwm ikecrypt* is as follows:

```
#fwm ikecrypt SharedSecret userpassword
```

Figure 3.46 The LDAP Account Unit Management Authentication Tab

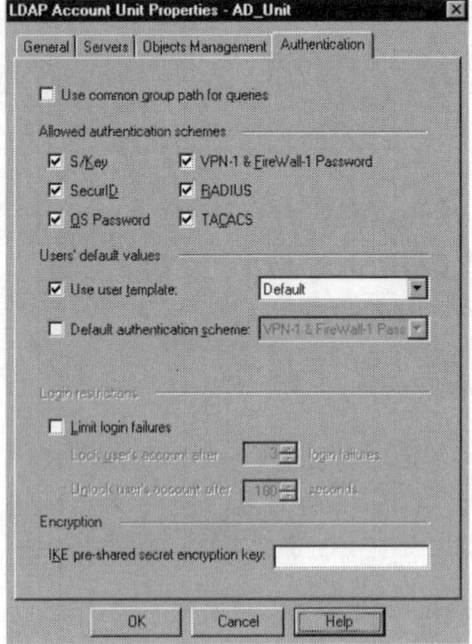

After you finish configuring your account unit, you will notice that your LDAP tree appears on the Users and Administrators tab of the Objects tree (see Figure 3.47). When you open the tree by double-clicking it, you will see your Active Directory users and groups in your SmartDashboard.

Figure 3.47 Displaying Active Directory in SmartDashboard

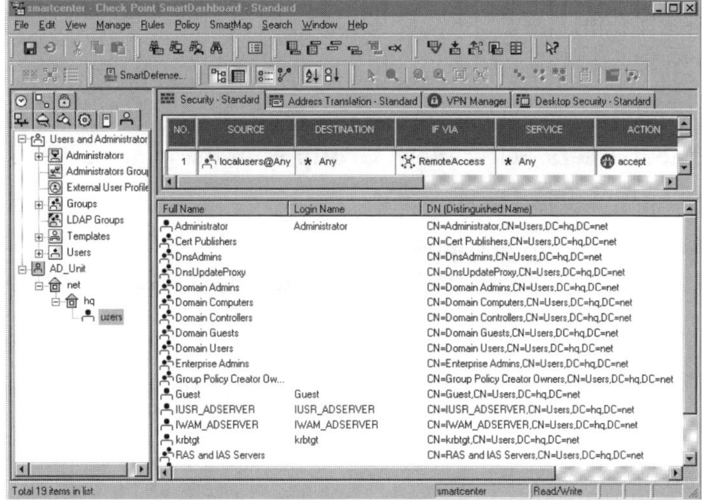

Configuring LDAP Administrators

Once you define your Active Directory unit and establish the connection to it, SmartDashboard becomes your user manager, or the Active Directory User Management console becomes your VPN-1/FireWall-1 user management console. Your changes on both consoles will take effect on the Active Directory database that is defined as your account unit. VPN-1/FireWall-1 assumes that all servers in the account unit are replicated, and it does not control the accuracy of the data in the AD servers. Access order to the account units is based on the priorities. When there are identical priorities, round-robin load distribution is used.

Generally, firewall administrators do not handle user management. Assigning access privileges in SmartDashboard can be a problem, especially when you have multiple administrators with different access rights. To handle this problem, you should define specific LDAP administrators in the SmartDashboard user management interface and delegate only LDAP user database **Read/Write** or **Read Only** access to these users. With these options, LDAP administrators will not be able to make changes to the security policy. You may define a specific permission profile from the **Manage | Permission Profiles** menu. Then you can define multiple account units with different DNs. In the **Object Management** tab of account unit descriptions, check **Prompt for password when opening this Account Unit** to enable password protection on user databases.

User Management on Active Directory

You may use SmartDashboard to manage your users in Active Directory. To do so, follow these steps:

1. From your SmartDashboard, open the **Object tree** and go to **Users | Your AD Tree | Users**. Select **New Group** from the context menu to create a new user group (see Figure 3.48).

Figure 3.48 Group Properties

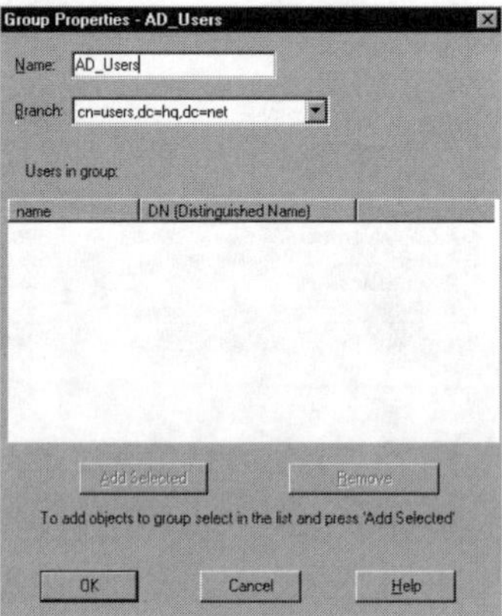

2. You will see that the group AD_Users has been created in the SmartDashboard central pane, as shown in Figure 3.49. If you open the AD user management GUI, you will see that the group information is accessible from there as well.

Figure 3.49 Displaying Users from SmartDashboard

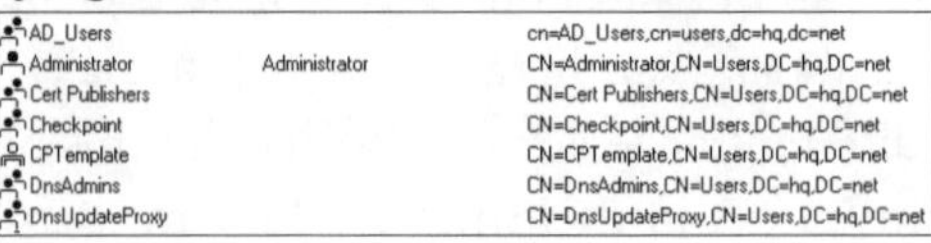

3. You are now able to use the group you have created. To define the group members, choose an existing user from the SmartDashboard, as displayed in Figure 3.50, and add the user to the groups that you have created.
4. Open your **Active Directory Users and Computers** console on your AD server and verify the changes on the Active Directory database (see Figures 3.51 and 3.52).

Figure 3.50 Modifying User Groups from SmartDashboard

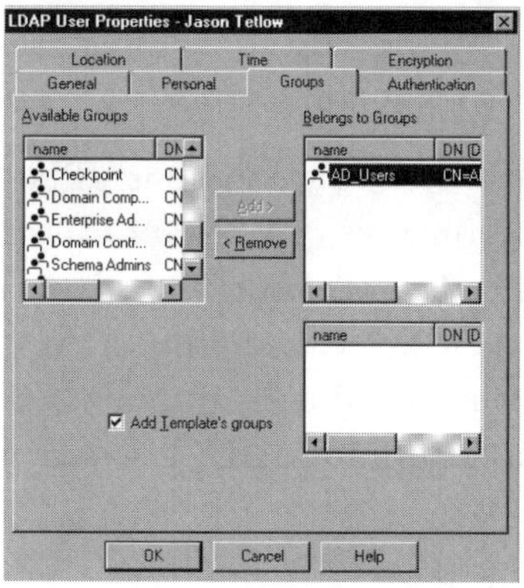

Figure 3.51 Displaying Changes in Active Directory

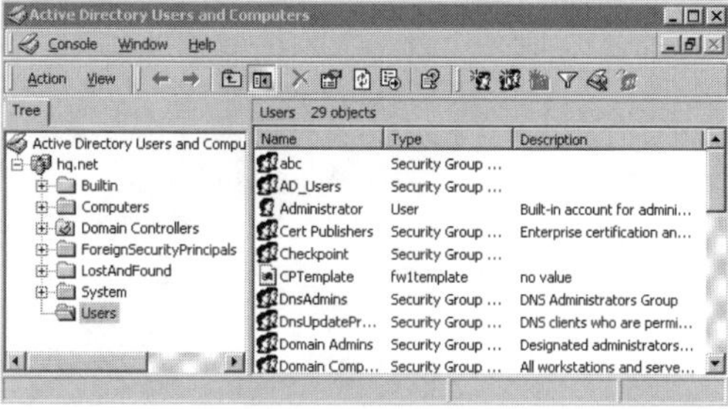

Figure 3.52 Group Details in Active Directory

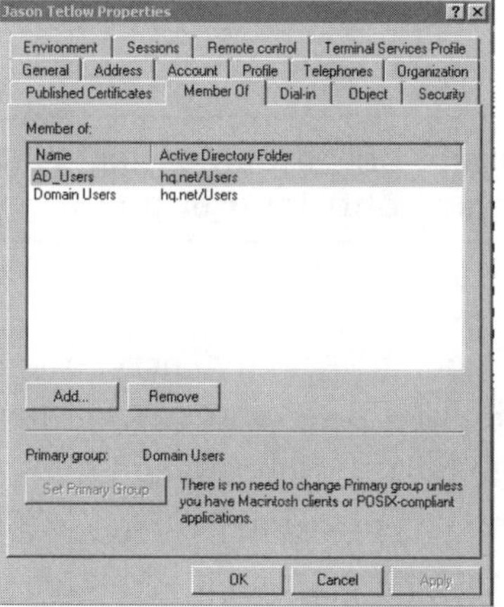

You may conduct further tests on bidirectional interaction. Since SmartDashboard and Active Directory Native interface interact with the same data source, all changes will be transparent to users on both sides.

Configuring the Rule Base

When you complete your Active Directory Integration, you may use the Active Directory user groups in your Rule Base for authentication.

1. To use your users and groups in your VPN-1/FireWall-1 Rule Base, define an LDAP group (see Figure 3.53) from **Object Tree | Users | LDAP Group** or the **Manage | Users** menu. The advantage of creating these groups is the ability to limit their scope. Defining LDAP groups allows you to apply granular filters on your LDAP users through a defining scope. In the following example, only users from the AD_Users group are allowed to be members of the LDAP group.

Figure 3.53 LDAP Group Properties

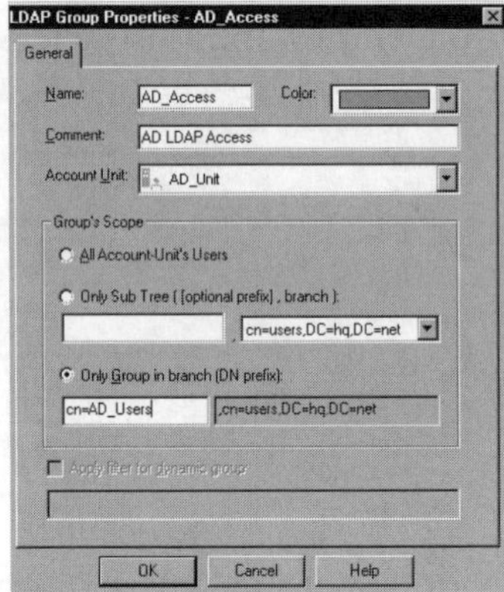

NOTE

Define external groups only if they are actually used in your Rule Base. LDAP enforces membership rights for user groups.

2. As shown in Figure 3.54, verify encryption properties from user properties. Use of user templates is recommended when a large number of users will be defined through SmartDashboard.
3. Check your VPN-1/FireWall-1 gateway's configuration before pushing policy. As displayed in Figure 3.55, your gateway must support the encryption and authentication schemes used by your users. If you are using a policy server for SecureClient authentication, the AD user group must be listed under the **Policy Server | Users** drop-down menu of your gateway object's properties.

Figure 3.54 LDAP User Properties

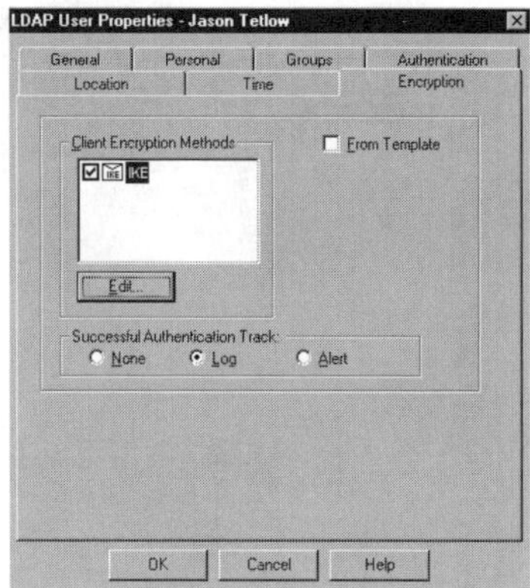

Figure 3.55 The Gateway Properties Authentication Tab

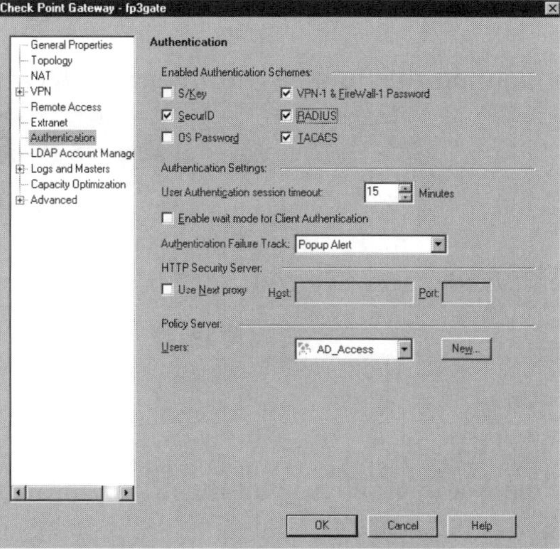

4. If you use remote access communities for SecuRemote or SecureClient, users using simplified security policies will ease the configuration (see Figure 3.56). To allow remote access, simply add the participating user groups to the Remote Access Community page.
5. Configure your Rule Base and add the authentication (see Figure 3.57). Allow your LDAP user group to access services via the Remote Access community.

On the client side, your users will be authenticated against Active Directory, and as shown in Figure 3.58, you will get successful authentication entries in SmartView Tracker. For Remote Access, SmartView Tracker generates detailed troubleshooting information on the Info tab.

Figure 3.56 Remote Access Community Properties

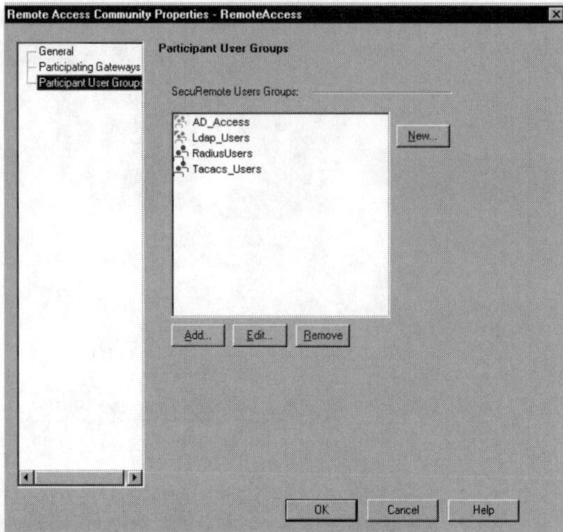

Figure 3.57 Configuring the Rule Base for Remote Access

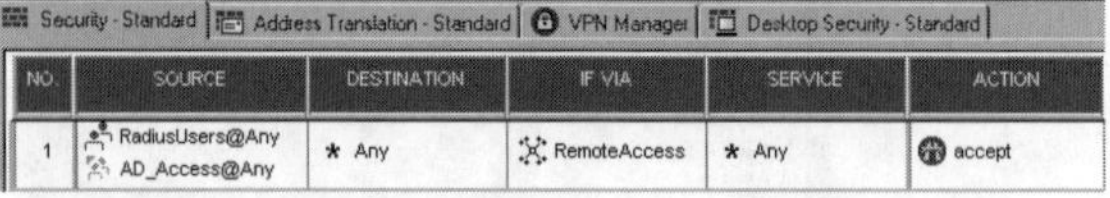

Figure 3.58 SmartView Tracker Output for Successful Authentication

Troubleshooting

This section describes some problems you might run into and some of the possible solutions for them.

Schannel.dll Error

If you are receiving an schannel.dll error (with a source of *Schannel*) in the Windows 2000 Event Viewer logs (see Figure 3.59), there are two possibilities for what is happening:

- You do not have the Windows 2000 High Encryption Pack.
- You did not set the minimum or maximum encryption strength to **High** in the **LDAP Server Properties | Encryption** tab.

Figure 3.59 The Schannel Error Message

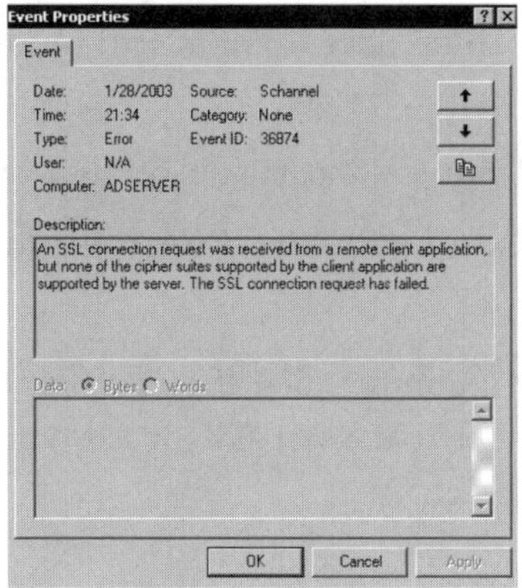

Unable to Find the Correct User Group in Active Directory

If you have difficulty finding your users in Active Directory, you have more than one option on VPN-1/FireWall-1. You may use either the GUI, as displayed in Figure 3.60, or the command line. The *Ldapsearch* command uses RFC-1558 compliant LDAP search filters. Or you can go to the **Search | Query LDAP objects** menu and enter your search query. The results will be listed in SmartDashboard.

Figure 3.60 LDAP Query Search

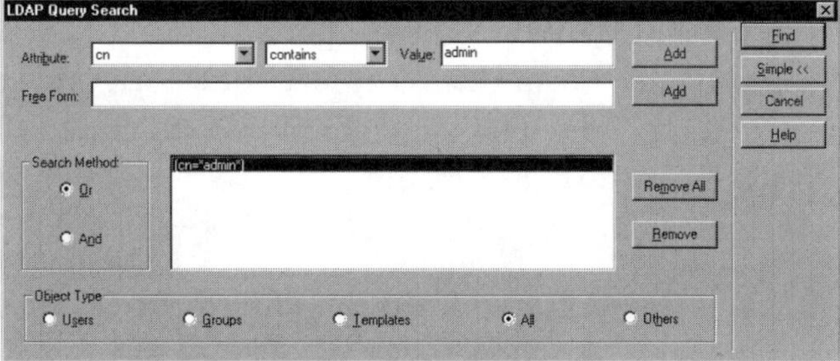

Suggested Uses of MS-AD Authentication

Active Directory and VPN-1/FireWall-1 integration could be useful in the following scenarios:

- You have an enterprise MS AD implementation and you do not want to duplicate your efforts for user management on the firewall.
- High availability and geographical load balancing are your prerequisites.
- You do not want to deal with user database administration issues such as replication or backup.

- You need to access your user database from various interfaces.
- Your requirements include development and modifications of the user management system.
- Your security policy requires separation of duties for user management.
- You want to utilize existing tools and solutions that are already available for Active Directory.

MS Active directory is *not* recommended if you are not familiar with the Microsoft platform. In any event, remember that SmartClient Administrator access cannot be authenticated against Active Directory.

Standard LDAP

Directory access became critical after the rapid expansion of information services. The requirements for managing large sets of users on multiple platforms increased the demand for standardized user management.

In order to answer the need for white pages for information systems, an open international standard named *X.500* was developed. Due to complex requirements of this standard's heavy client Directory Access Protocol (DAP), a new lighter protocol had to be developed. LDAP, or Lightweight Directory Access Protocol, is a subset of the original DAP. LDAP enables you to locate resources and resource types on public or corporate networks. You can use an LDAP directory to perform searches or store user-specific data. Using LDAP, companies can map their corporate directories to actual business processes rather than arbitrary codes. The hierarchical tree structure of LDAP is a good base for storing enterprise directory information.

Using LDAP brings the following advantages to VPN-1/FireWall-1 administrators:

- Integrate VPN-1/FireWall-1 with existing directories—unified authentication.
- Eliminate the burden of multiple directory management.
- Enhance performance and scalability.
- Achieve industry-based standards compliance.
- Use third-party user management tools.
- Separate duties to increase the security level.

LDAP is based on entries for objects, with each entry having corresponding *attributes*. Attributes can be types or values. All entries and the relations among them are regulated with a Rule Base called *schema*.

As stated earlier, a schema is a metadata repository of all objects, attributes, and the classes to which objects belong. The schema determines the location and the property of LDAP database contents. Each entry in LDAP database is associated with a distinguished name, which is concatenated from distinguished names.

With the standard LDAP tools, you can search, add, modify, and delete information from an LDAP database. Check Point currently utilizes an LDAP database to store user and authentication information. In the future we expect to fetch object information from the LDAP sources.

Setting Up the LDAP for FireWall-1 Authentication

Setting up an Enterprise Directory Service is a complex process. Each detail must be planned carefully. We do not cover the details of installing and managing an LDAP server here. Integration of your existing LDAP server with VPN-1/FireWall-1 for storing your user information and authenticating users requires the following steps:

1. Verify that you are using an OPSEC certified LDAP server. You can obtain the full list of certified OPSEC directory servers from the following URL: www.opsec.com/solutions/sec_authentication.html. Using an OPSEC-compliant directory server is recommended, since Check Point delivers predefined profiles for these directory servers. Although LDAP is standard, each vendor's implementation varies with organization of object types, relations, and attributes. In addition, the query types do not match. To ease this difficulty, Check Point has predefined profiles in the Objects_5_0.C file. We will use the Netscape Directory Server default installation and modify the default Netscape DS schema to work with VPN-1/FireWall-1. More information about the server architecture, deployment, and administration is available at the following URL address: http://enterprise.netscape.com/docs/directory/index.html.
2. Back up your directory server. If your organization relies on LDAP, you should be cautious before making any changes. Most of the LDAP servers are based on open LDAP projects, and they have similar configuration files. Netscape Directory Server's schema can be backed up by saving all slapd.* configuration files.

You should also back up your database from the Netscape DS GUI or command-line utilities such as *db2bak* and *db2ldif*. To back up your entire configuration, follow this procedure:

1. On the Directory Server Console, select the **Tasks** tab.
2. Click **Back Up Directory Server**. The Backup Directory dialog box is displayed.

3. Enter the full path of the directory where you want to store the backup file in the **Directory** text box, or click **Use default**, and the server provides a name for the backup directory. If you are running the console on the same machine as the directory, you can also click **Browse** to locate a local directory.
4. If you choose to use the default, the backup files will be placed in the following location: /usr/netscape/servers/slapd-serverID/bak/backup_directory, where *serverID* is the name of your directory server. The *backup_directory* variable names a directory using the name of the backup file. By default, the backup directory name contains the time and date the backup was created (*YYYY_MM_DD_hhmmss*).
5. Click **OK** to create the backup.

Now extend the LDAP schema. To add Check Point attributes to your Netscape Directory schema, you can use a predefined configuration LDIF file from Check Point. *You should test the ramifications of using this extension in your lab* before applying this change to your production environment. The modification file (schema.ldif) for Netscape Directory Server is located in the $FWDIR/lib/ldap directory of your SmartCenter. The variable *DOMAINNAME* is used instead of your own domain name in the schema.ldif file. Open your favorite text editor and replace all instances of *DOMAINNAME* with your fully qualified domain name. In our example, we used *HQ.NET*.

In the following example, the schema extension is executed for HQ.NET domain for Netscape Directory Server. Here are some sample schema extensions:

- **LDAP Directory Server** LDAP.HQ.NET
- **SmartCenter** SMARTCENTER.HQ.NET
- **Administrator FQDN** uid=admin,ou=people,dc=HQ,dc=NET
- **Administrator User** admin
- **Administrator Password** abc123
- **Modified LDIF with Full Path** C:\winnt\fw1\ng\lib\ldap\schema.ldif

AD should be on a remote server, and hostnames must be resolvable. As shown in Figure 3.61, run the following command from the SmartCenter in one line from the command prompt:

```
Ldapmodify -c -h LDAP.HQ.NET -D "uid=admin,ou=people,dc=HQ,dc=NET" -w
    abc123 -f  C:\winnt\fw1\ng\lib\ldap\schema.ldif
```

Figure 3.61 Schema Modification for LDAP Server

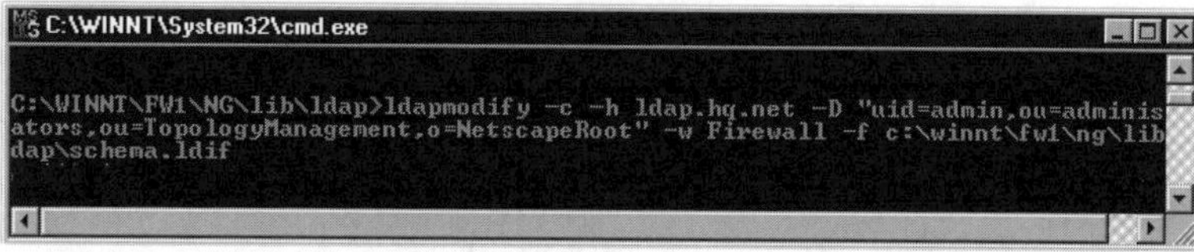

C:\WINNT\System32\cmd.exe
C:\WINNT\FW1\NG\lib\ldap>ldapmodify -c -h ldap.hq.net -D "uid=admin,ou=adminis
ators,ou=TopologyManagement,o=NetscapeRoot" -w Firewall -f c:\winnt\fw1\ng\lib
dap\schema.ldif

You will see the output of modifications on your screen. To check the changes, go back to your Netscape Directory Server, open the GUI console, and examine the new FW-1 attributes.

NOTE

The LDAP Data Interchange Format (LDIF) standard is used to describe a directory and directory entries in text format. LDIF is commonly used to build the initial directory database or to add large numbers of entries to the directory all at once. In addition, LDIF is used to describe changes to directory schema. For this reason, most of Directory Server's command-line utilities rely on LDIF for either input or output. LDIF consists of one or more directory entries separated by a blank line. Each LDIF entry consists of an optional entry ID, a required distinguished name, one or more object classes, and multiple attribute definitions. The LDIF format is defined in RFC-2849, *The LDAP Data Interchange Format.*

Setting Up the Firewall for LDAP Authentication

The process of defining an LDAP server in FireWall-1 is very similar to defining the Active Directory components. We will use an OPSEC compliant directory server, Netscape Directory Server, in our examples. The directory server LDAP schema should be updated before it is defined in VPN-1/FireWall-1.

Here are the basic steps in configuring VPN-1/Firewall-1 for LDAP authentication:

1. Enable Global Properties to support user authentication from **Policy_Global Properties | LDAP Account Management**.
2. Define an LDAP account unit (see Figure 3.62) from the SmartDashboard **Object tree** using **Servers | LDAP Account Unit** or from the **Manage | Servers** menu. Choose your predefined directory server profile from the **Profile** drop-down menu.
3. Click the **Add** button to define your LDAP server in the next screen. You will see the LDAP server properties. Select your LDAP server host in the **General**

tab of the LDAP server properties. In the **General** tab (refer back to Figure 3.48), describe the LDAP host and the access settings that will be used to connect to the directory services. Login DN will be used to connect to directory services. This Login DN serves to another purpose, too. If your LDAP user management is handled by a different organizational group, the login rights are set with this Login DN and password. This value is also kept on your management server, so you can avoid having to query your LDAP server for administrator logins. As shown in Figure 3.63, on the **Encryption** tab, if you uncheck **SSL**, the default access port for LDAP will be 389. On Netscape Directory Server, the default DN for the administrator user is uid=admin, ou=administrators, ou=TopologyManagement, o=NetscapeRoot.

Figure 3.62 The LDAP Account Unit Properties General Tab

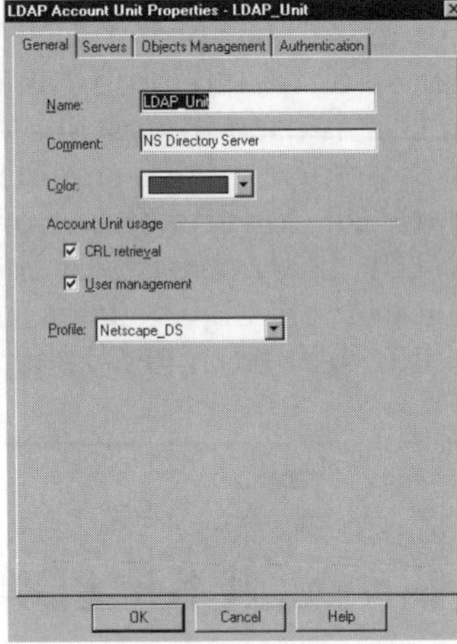

Figure 3.63 LDAP Server Properties

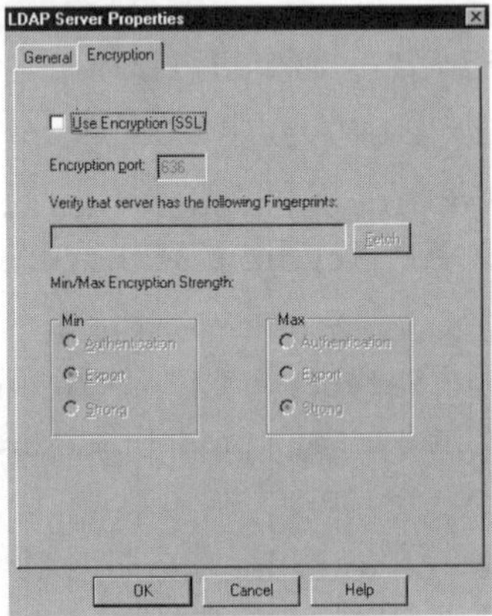

4. When you complete your LDAP server configuration, you will be back at the LDAP Account Unit definition screen, displayed in Figure 3.64. On the **Servers** tab, you should see the LDAP server that you have defined. You must choose **Early Versions Compatibility server** to support pre-NG FP3 gateways, which do not support multiple servers. Configure your high-availability settings by giving priorities to the LDAP servers you have defined.

Figure 3.64 The LDAP Account Unit Properties Servers Tab

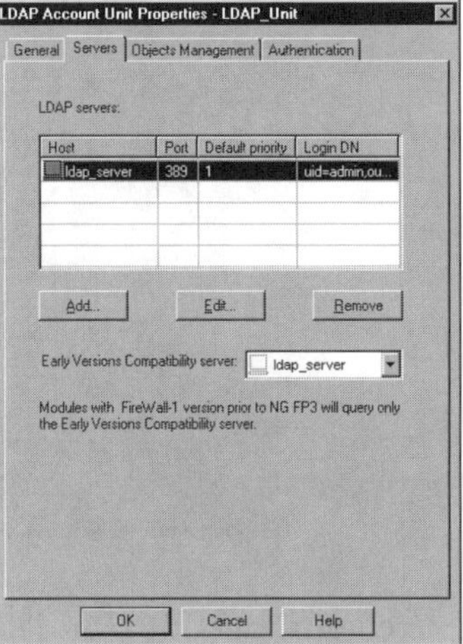

5. After the schema modification, you should be able to fetch the domain information as the branches in the **Objects Management** tab (see Figure 3.65).

Figure 3.65 The LDAP Account Unit Properties Object Management Tab

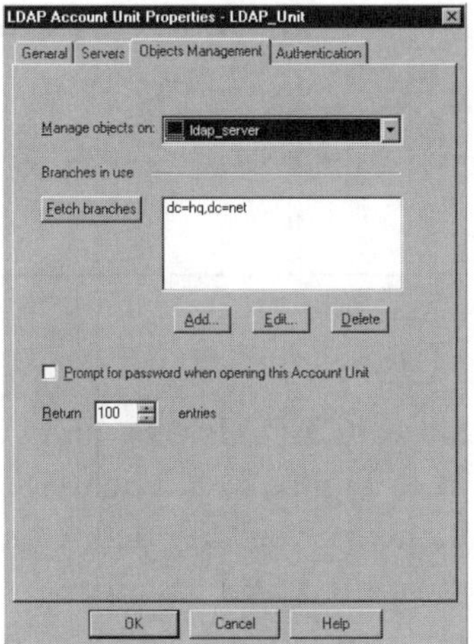

6. The default LDAP user authentication schema is **VPN-1 & VPN-1/ FireWall-1 Password** (see Figure 3.66). When this option is chosen, users will be authenticated against the LDAP user database. It is possible to use hybrid authentication methods as described in Active Directory services.

Figure 3.66 The LDAP Account Unit Properties Authentication Tab

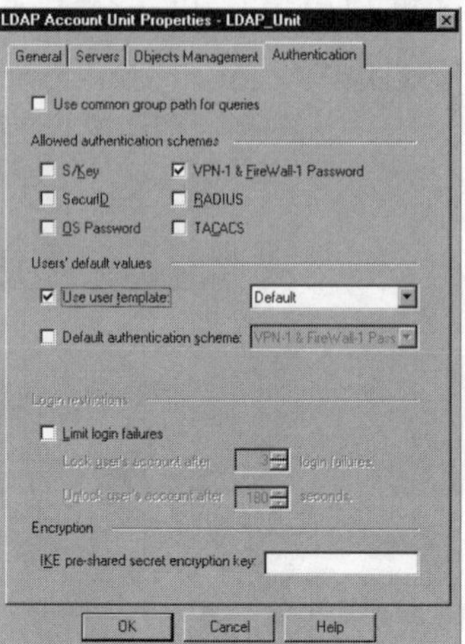

7. When you complete your account unit definition, you should be able to see your LDAP tree on **Objects Tree | Users**, as displayed in Figure 3.67. You may view, modify, or delete objects from the SmartDashboard integrated LDAP GUI client.

Figure 3.67 Displaying LDAP Users in SmartDashboard

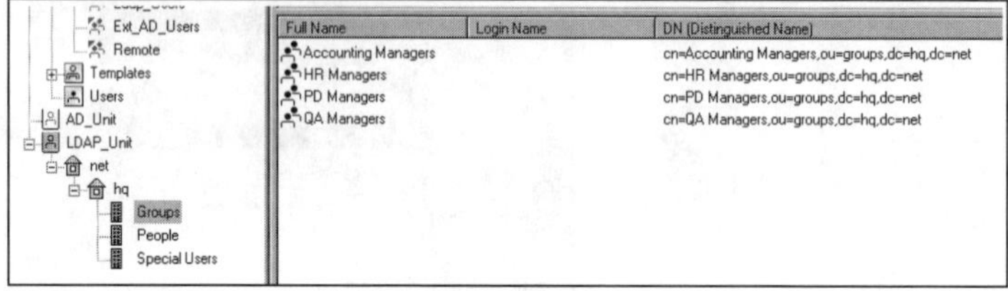

Defining a New User

In SmartDashboard, expand your **LDAP tree**, and go to the **LDAP_Unit | net | hq | People** object, as shown in Figure 3.68. Right-click to create a new user. Since you have extended the LDAP schema, you may define and store the FireWall-1 related properties of the new user on the LDAP database.

When you click the **Groups** tab, you will notice that your user groups in the LDAP account unit have already been populated in the Available Groups list (see Figure 3.69). Add your user to the related groups. Since we want to use this user in remote access with SecureClient integration, we should define the IKE settings in the Encryption tab. You should use user templates to ease the administrative burden of multiple users having similar settings.

Figure 3.68 LDAP User Properties

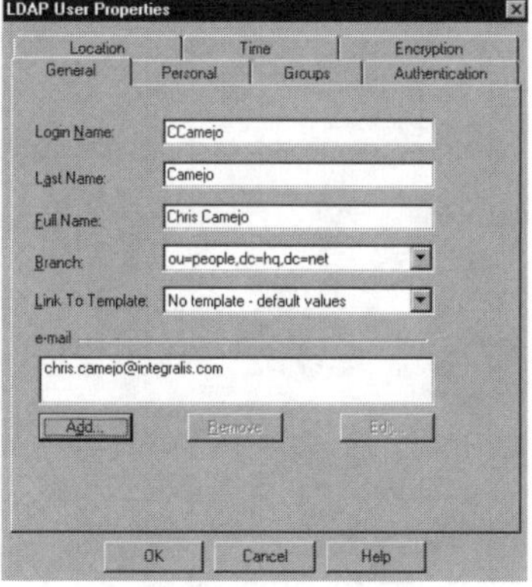

Figure 3.69 The Groups Property for LDAP User

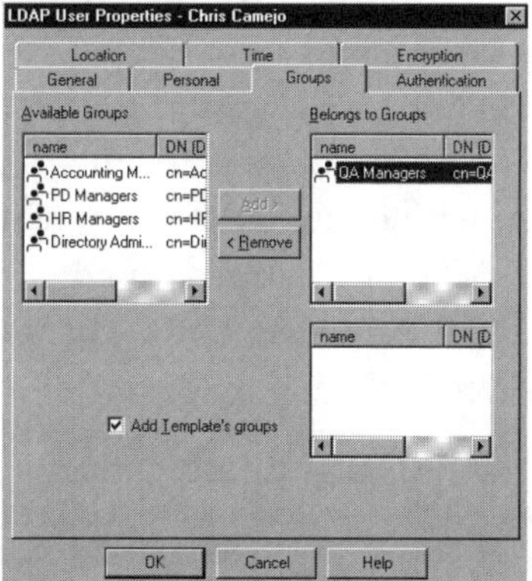

After you have defined your user, you may view (see Figure 3.70), edit, or delete the user from either the LDAP GUI or SmartDashboard.

Figure 3.70 Displaying LDAP Users from SmartDashboard

Full Name	Login Name	DN (Distinguished Name)
Chris Camejo	CCamejo	cn=Chris Camejo,ou=people,dc=hq,dc=net
Jason Tetlow	JTETLOW	cn=Jason Tetlow,ou=people,dc=hq,dc=net

To use your LDAP users in your security policy, define an LDAP group and add your LDAP users to this group (see Figure 3.71). Instead of using all users in the LDAP database, you may use a subbranch to define the LDAP user group and allow granular access. It is possible to define the members of the user group using existing LDAP name prefixes in the Group's Scope. It is even possible to define a filter for the matching. For example, you may choose a regional subtree such as *ou=NewEngland* and apply a filter such as *extranet_access=true*.

Figure 3.71 LDAP Group Properties

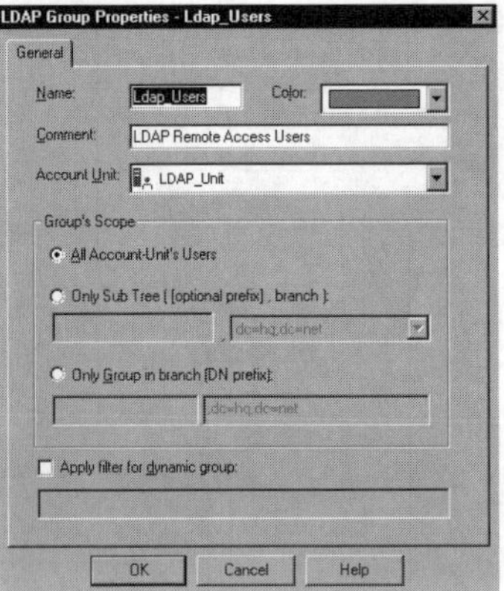

When you finish defining your LDAP user group, it is a simple process to use your group in a security policy. For example, in a simplified Rule Base, modify your remote access community and add your LDAP groups to the Participating User Groups. If your gateways are also participating gateways (i.e., members of the remote access community), you need nothing else. The settings are identical to regular SecureClient/SecuRemote definitions. The default LDAP user database is used when **VPN-1 VPN-1/FireWall-1 Password** is chosen in **LDAP Account Unit Authentication** properties. A sample remote access rule is displayed in Figure 3.72.

Figure 3.72 Rules for LDAP User Authentication

If your gateway's VPN domain is set as exportable, your user's encryption settings comply with the client's IKE requirements, and the authentication method matches what is available on your gateway, you will be authenticated promptly. In the SmartTracker, you will see the LDAP account unit with your user's DN and standard authentication information. Using an LDAP account unit for authentication is transparent to end users.

Suggested Uses of LDAP Authentication

LDAP is the de facto directory access standard, and its open architecture allows for easy third-party integration. VPN-1/FireWall-1's extensive support for LDAP, showcased by a native GUI, load-balancing options, templates, and ready-to-use schema extensions, makes LDAP a better alternative than legacy authentication servers such as RADIUS and TACACS+.

Consider LDAP authentication if:

- You prefer nonproprietary solutions and you do not want to duplicate your efforts for user management.
- High availability and geographical load balancing are your prerequisites.
- You do not want to deal with advanced user database administration issues such as replication, backup, or upgrade.
- You need to access your user database from various interfaces.
- Your requirements include development and modifications of the user management system.
- Your security policy requires separation of duties for user management.
- You want to utilize a rich set of existing tools and solutions from the industry.

On the other hand, LDAP implementations may be more complex than planned and could create additional management overhead if you do not have the required experience. Although LDAP is an open standard, remember that it is not easy to change server platforms.

RADIUS

Remote Authentication Dial-In User Service, or *RADIUS*, is one of the most common authentication and accounting services used on the Internet. The main driver behind RADIUS development was serving dialup users, as implied in the service's name. Over time, RADIUS has evolved into an enterprise authentication, authorization, and accounting (AAA) product.

Nowadays it is possible to integrate most of the commonly used authentication schemes with RADIUS servers. Since the RADIUS standards are open (IETF RFC-2058), most manufacturers of new products (including Check Point) chose to integrate with RADIUS..

RADIUS work principles are very simple. The RADIUS protocol defines a client and server. VPN-1/FireWall-1 acts as a network access server (NAS)—the client part of the setup. Client and server communicate on UDP port 1645. Communication is partly hashed by MD5, to provide some level of message integrity. When VPN-1/FireWall-1 receives a request that matches a RADIUS authentication rule, the firewall sends an access-request packet to the RADIUS server. The access-request packet contains the username, encrypted password, NAS IP address, and port. The RADIUS server returns "access-reject" or "access-accept" messages, depending on the validation of the request. Check Point does not utilize other challenge/response authentication protocols (such as PAP/CHAP) over the RADIUS protocol. Authorization and accounting features are also not functional for VPN-1/FireWall-1. FireWall-1 logs successful or failed RADIUS authentication attempts with its native logging facilities.

Setting Up the Firewall for RADIUS Authentication

The RADIUS protocol is included in VPN-1 and VPN-1/FireWall-1 Control Connections, but remember that in NG, Accept VPN-1 and VPN-1/FireWall-1 Control Connections only applies to VPN-1/FireWall-1 installed devices.

The basic steps to define RADIUS authentication for FireWall-1 are as follows:

1. Define a RADIUS server. From the **Objects** tree. select **Servers | RADIUS**. Enter the host description service and the shared secret, as displayed in Figure 3.73. The shared secret will be used to authenticate with the RADIUS server. In NG you may define multiple RADIUS servers in a single group. To define a RADIUS group, select **Servers | RADIUS Group** and add your servers one at a time. A RADIUS group is for simple high availability only; for sophisticated chaining options, use a third-party RADIUS proxy.

Figure 3.73 Radius Server Properties

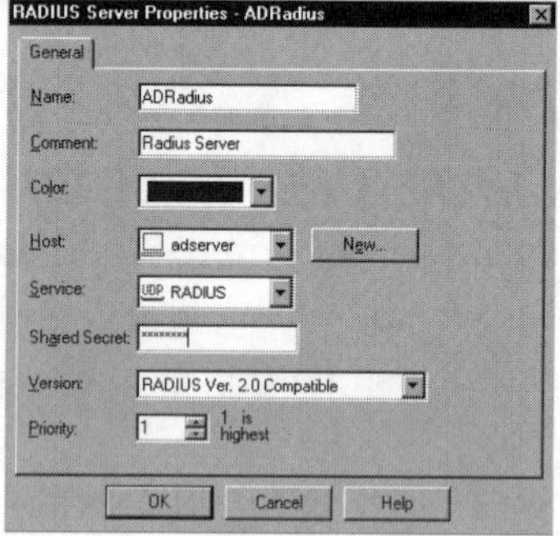

2. You have two options for defining users. You may either define your users in the firewall's user database and control authentication from the firewall, or you can use external user profiles. With external profiles, authentication requests are checked not on a per-user basis, but on a per-profile basis. When **Match All** is chosen, all unknown users will be matched against the Generic* profile, which eliminates the need for redefining each user on FireWall-1 (see Figure 3.74).

Figure 3.74 External User Profile Properties

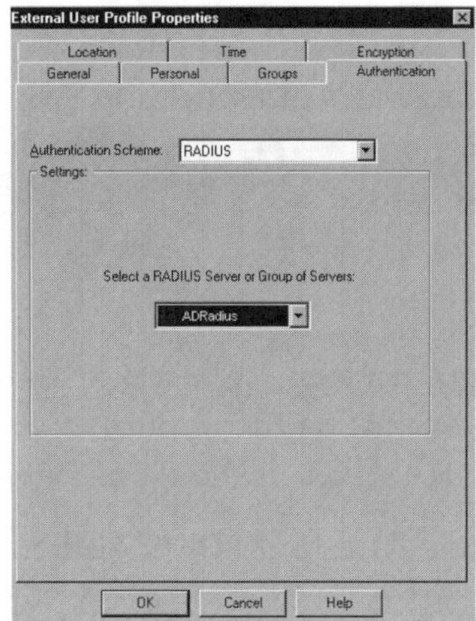

Tools & Traps...

The Order of Authentication Schemas on VPN-1/FireWall-1

If the same username is defined in multiple user databases, VPN-1/FireWall-1 searches the databases in the following order: FireWall-1 user database, LDAP, then Generic*. With NG FP3, when external user groups are defined, this limitation becomes obsolete with domain matching.

3. Create a regular user group (see Figure 3.75) for your RADIUS users, and then add the RADIUS users to this group. If external user profiles are used, profiles should be added to user groups. The **Encryption** tab should be configured if SecureClients will be used with IKE. Choose the related RADIUS server or group from the **Authentication** tab.

Figure 3.75 The Object Tree Users Tab

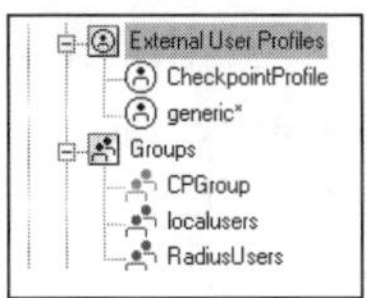

4. As displayed in Figure 3.76, allow RADIUS authentication on the gateway's **Authentication** tab. If a policy server is used, RADIUS user groups should

also be added to the Policy Server group on the Authentication tab of the gateway.

Figure 3.76 Gateway Authentication Properties

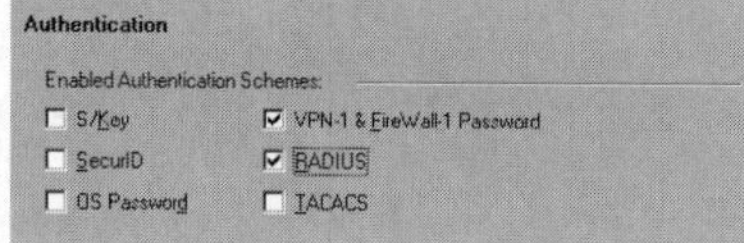

5. For SecureClient/SecuRemote access in a simplified policy, add a RADIUS user group to participating user groups in your Remote Access Community and define your Rule Base as shown in Figure 3.77.

Figure 3.77 Rule Base for RADIUS Authentication

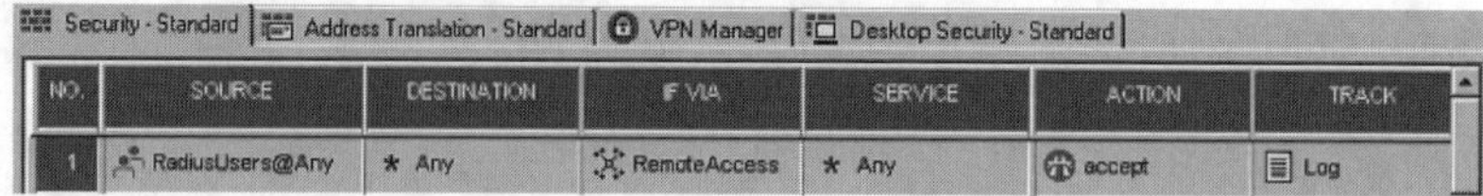

6. On your VPN client, you will get an "Authenticated by RADIUS" message if you successfully complete the settings. In SmartTracker, you should see the log entries shown in Figure 3.78.

Figure 3.78 SmartView Tracker Entries for RADIUS Authentication

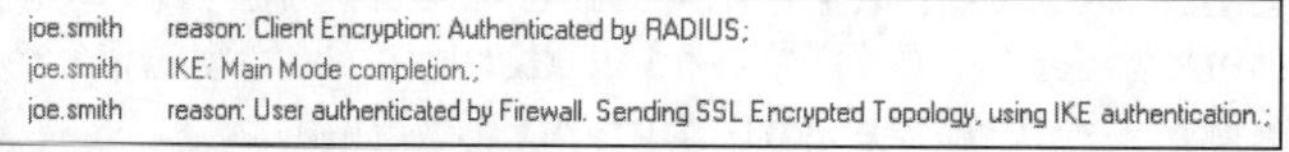

Setting Up RADIUS for FireWall-1 Authentication

Since RADIUS is an industry standard, there are plenty of RADIUS server vendors on the market. Using an OPSEC certified RADIUS solution is recommended. We used OPSEC certified Steel-Belted RADIUS software when running tests for this chapter. Besides serving standard RADIUS requests, most of the AAA servers can pipe authentication requests to proprietary systems. For example, if you want to use NT 4.0 user groups in your authentication, the AAA server can act as a proxy. A free software RADIUS implementation can also be downloaded as source code from the GNU project's pages (see www.gnu.org/software/radius/).

Configuring Steel-Belted RADIUS for standard RADIUS authentication is very simple. Simply define your VPN-1/FireWall-1 as a RAS client and select **Check Point FireWall-1/VPN-1** in the Make/Model drop-down list (see Figure 3.79). When you enter your shared secret for RADIUS in the appropriate box, you are all set. This shared secret should only be used for RADIUS authentication on the FireWall-1 side.

Figure 3.79 Configuring Steel-Belted RADIUS for Standard RADIUS Authentication

Once the firewall is defined as a RAS client, all RADIUS access-requests from VPN-1/FireWall-1 will be authenticated in the RADIUS user database (see Figure 3.80). You may either define your usernames in the native RADIUS DB or use existing user repositories. To back up all your configuration, simply export your configuration to a RADIUS information file (*.rif) from the RADIUS GUI. Database files are specific to implementation.

Figure 3.80 RADIUS User Database

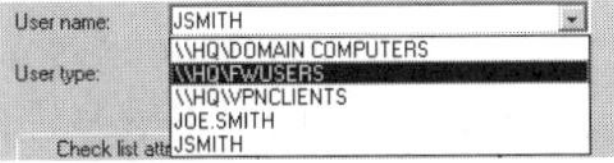

Suggested Uses of RADIUS Authentication

A RADIUS server could be a good choice for the following reasons:

- It accommodates existing user database integration.
- Most third-party strong authentication systems are integrated with RADIUS servers.
- It provides a unified AAA server.
- SmartClient Administrator logins are supported.

A RADIUS server has the following disadvantages when used with VPN-1/FireWall-1:

- Granular control policies cannot be applied, since the IP address of the gateway is unique and only a single policy can be applied for all users of VPN-1/FireWall-1.

- RADIUS has many attributes that are defined for authorization and accounting of dialup connections. These attributes are not used by VPN-1/FireWall-1.
- Database access is not standard and requires specific interfaces.
- RADIUS does not support IKE natively (although this was extended by RFC-3162). VPN-1/FireWall-1 handles authentication with Hybrid mode support. Client/server communication between the firewall and the RADIUS server is encrypted by MD5.

TACACS+

The *Terminal Access Controller Access Control System*, or *TACACS,* is one of the Internet's oldest AAA protocols. The initial TACACS protocol has evolved into XTACACS and TACACS+, which we use today. TACACS+ was developed and backed by Cisco Systems and was initially designed to provide dialup Point-to-Point Protocol (PPP) and terminal server access. Although efforts have been waged for public versions of TACACS+, it is still Cisco's proprietary AAA protocol.

VPN-1/FireWall-1 interfaces only with the authentication piece of TACACS+. Authorization and accounting features are not used. The authentication process is very straightforward. The VPN-1/FireWall-1 gateway acts as a NAS client. When the user sends his or her username and password, VPN-1/FireWall-1 relays the information in a hashed packet over TCP port 49 to the TACACS server. This packet is called a *start packet*. The TACACS+ server responds with reply or continue packets. Since VPN-1/FireWall-1 does not use extended features of TACACS+, the response packet usually contains "authentication-status-pass" or "authentication-status-fail" messages.

TACACS+ and RADIUS are very similar protocols. The story of both protocols resembles the Beta/VHS market penetration wars in the realm of home videos. RADIUS has wider support from industry, but Cisco Systems claims that TACACS is a better protocol. Lately Cisco Systems AAA servers support both TACACS and RADIUS protocols. Differences can be summarized as follows:

- TACACS supports Transmission Control Protocol (TCP). RADIUS runs over User Datagram Protocol (UDP). TACACS protocol is reliable.
- RADIUS encrypts only the password in the access-request packet; TACACS+ encrypts the entire message body.
- RADIUS has extensions for Internet Protocol Security (IPSec); TACACS+ doesn't.
- RADIUS has industry standards; TACACS is still in the draft stage.

Setting Up the Firewall for TACACS+ Authentication

The TACACS+ protocol is included in VPN-1 and VPN-1/FireWall-1 Control Connections, but remember that in NG, Accept VPN-1 and VPN-1/FireWall-1 Control Connections only applies to VPN-1/FireWall-1 installed devices.

Here are the basic steps to define TACACS authentication:

1. Define a TACACS server, as shown in Figure 3.81. From your **Objects** tree, select **Servers | TACACS**. Enter the host description service and the shared secret. Choose your protocol. TACACS+ is strongly recommended. The shared secret will be used for authentication on the TACACS+ server. In TACACS, you do not have an option to group servers for high-availability purposes.

   Figure 3.81 TACACS Server Properties

   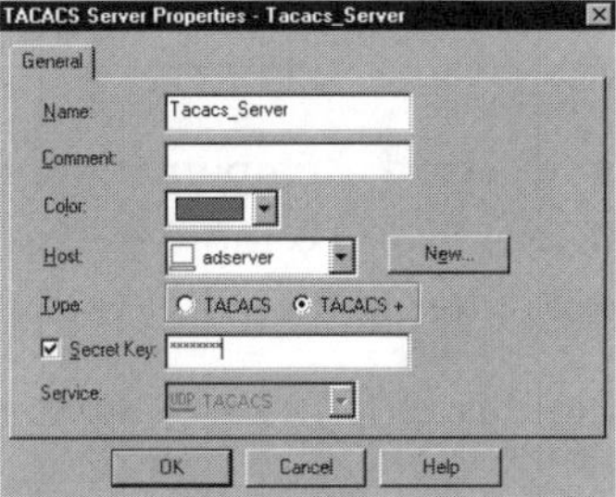

2. You have two options for defining users. You may either define your users in the firewall's user database and control authentication from the firewall, or you can use external user profiles. With external profiles, authentication requests are checked not on a per-user basis, but on a per-profile basis. When **Match All** is chosen, all unknown users will be matched against the Generic* profile, which eliminates the need for redefining each user on FireWall-1 (see Figure 3.82).

   Figure 3.82 The Authentication Tab

   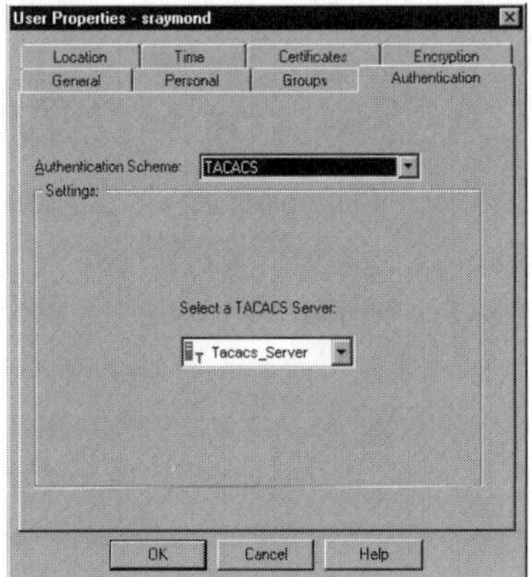

3. Create a regular user group (see Figure 3.83) for your TACACS users, and then add the TACACS users to this group. If external user profiles are used, profiles should be added to user groups. The **Encryption** tab should be configured if SecureClients will be used with IKE. Choose the related TACACS from the **Authentication** tab.. Allow TACACS authentication on the gateway's **Authentication** tab. If a policy server is used, TACACS user groups should also be added to the policy server group in the **Authentication** tab of the gateway. TACACS cannot be used for SmartClient Administrator users' authentication purposes.

Figure 3.83 Object Tree View for Users

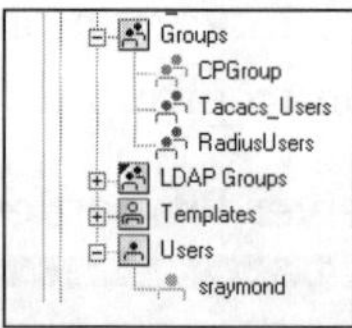

4. For SecureClient access in a simplified policy, add the TACACS user group to participating user groups in Remote Access Community and define your Rule Base, as shown in Figure 3.84.

Figure 3.84 Rule Base for TACACS Authentication

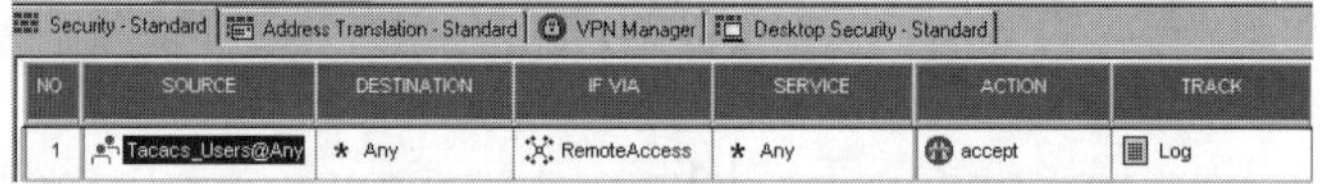

5. On your VPN client, you will get an "Authenticated by TACACS" message if you successfully complete the settings. On SmartView Tracker, you should see the log entries shown in Figure 3.85.

Figure 3.85 SmartView Tracker Entries for TACACS Authentication

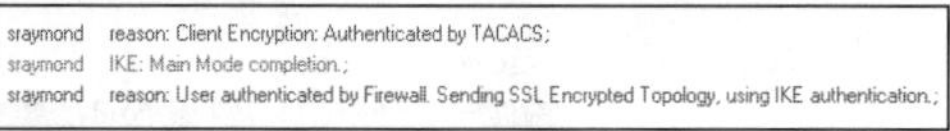

Setting Up TACACS+ for FireWall-1 Authentication

Most TACACS+ server solutions support multiple authentication protocols, including Cisco's. To download the source code for TACACS+ and examine the latest draft from 1998, point your browser to the following FTP URL: ftp://ftp-eng.cisco.com/pub/tacacs.

We used the best-known TACACS+ server, which is the Cisco Access Control Server (ACS). Installation is straightforward. During the installation, you should create your NAS as the firewall gateway and enter the TACACS secret key, as shown in Figure 3.86. It is possible to modify these values after the configuration. ACS has a simple Web interface. You can create users from the administration interface.

Figure 3.86 CiscoSecure ACS Configuration

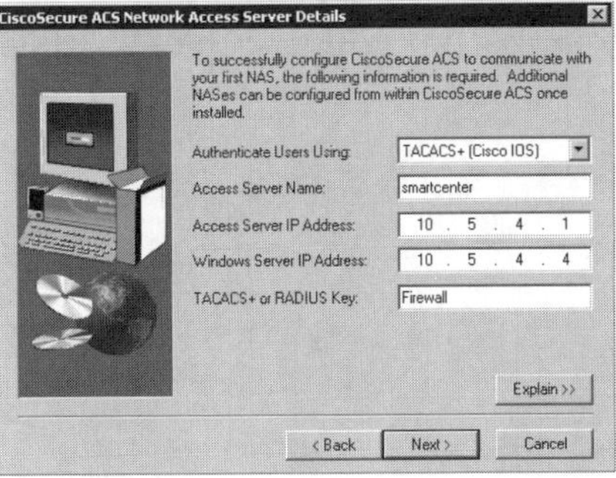

Tools & Traps...

How to Back Up the ACS User Database

Backing up the Cisco ACS is very simple. To facilitate backup and restoration of the CiscoSecure ACS configuration data and database, the CSUtil.exe utility is provided in the CiscoSecure ACS UTILS directory:

- **C:\csutil –b** Creates a complete backup of all CiscoSecure ACS data.
- **C:\csutil –r** Restores a CiscoSecure ACS from the backup file.

To perform a backup of the CiscoSecure ACS user and group data, execute the following instructions from the Windows NT command prompt (a DOS window):

- **C:\Net stop csauth** Stop the CSAuth authentication service to allow backup to take place.
- **C:\Csutil -d users_and_groups.txt** Back up the users and groups data to a text file called users_and_groups.txt. To back up only the group data, use the command with a *-g* instead of a *-d* command switch.
- **C:\Net start csauth** Restart the CSAuth authentication service.

Continued

The users_and_groups.txt file can then be backed up to tape and stored somewhere safe. To use *CSUtil -b* to create a backup file, enter the following command:

```
C:\csutil -b directory name
```

This command creates the following files in Utils\SysBackups\directory_name:

- REGISTRY.DAT
- USER.DAT
- USER.IDX
- VARSDB.MDB

The result is a compressed backup file named with the current date and time in the format *yyyymmddhhmm.zip*. This file is written to the CiscoSecure ACS\utils\dbcheckpoint directory. Each backup creates a new file that does not overwrite existing files. The data is stored in compressed format and therefore takes up very little space. The system administrator must still perform the necessary file management to maintain adequate disk space.

Suggested Uses of TACACS+ Authentication

There are proven attacks against TACACS+' existing encryption deployment, so it should not be used where security is an issue. TACACS+ is a viable alternative when there is an existing TACACS+ deployment. TACACS+ could be very useful when other systems authentication clients (such as access servers) require TACACS+ attributes. If it is possible, TACACS+ server and firewall communication should be tunneled.

General User Management

Using third-party authentication solutions makes VPN-1/FireWall-1 administrators' lives easier. Imagine an enterprise with 30 locations on all over the world, with more than 1000 remote access clients. Managing the profiles of 1000 users is a real problem. User creation and termination, automatic user provisioning, password management, database replication, load balancing, and hundreds of other enterprise networking problems will pop up with the deployment. Integrating your perimeter systems' identity management systems with mature enterprise directory services will solve most of your problems. Using an enterprise directory service with VPN-1/FireWall-1 will bring the following advantages:

- Automatic user provisioning
- Advanced database replication
- Ready-to-use third-party management tools
- Self-service password management
- Granular control with group-specific policies
- Load balancing the authentication overhead
- Enforcing of local password security policies

Here we examine a sample Active Directory deployment, keeping in mind the preceding points. Figure 3.87 is an illustration of the VPN user deployment for Acme Corporation.

Figure 3.87 VPN User Deployment for ACME Corporation

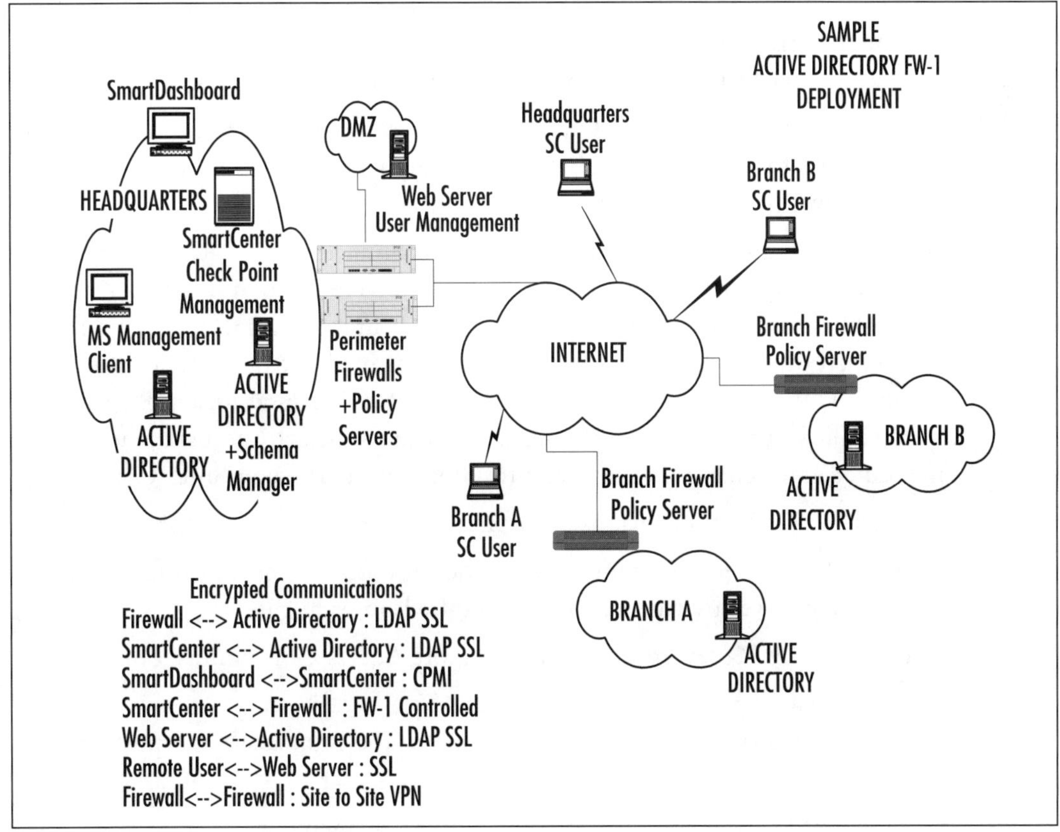

To avoid the management burden of 1000 users, systems administrators decide to utilize Active Directory services. The geographically distributed branches of Acme Corporation require remote users to log into their regional policy servers. The company's audit department requires all communication to be encrypted with the high-availability prerequisite. Furthermore, all the managers are asking for speed and ease of use without compromising security.

To solve the problems and meet the requirements, Acme administrators deployed the following infrastructure:

1. Established site-to-site VPNs to allow secure corporate communication.
2. Deployed Windows 2000-based Active Directory services on all locations and integrated all corporate identities and object profiles with the Active Directory. Then they optimized and verified the directory services' administration issues such as replication, backup, and security policies.
3. The project team tested the compatibility of the Check Point Active Directory Schema Extension. After the verification, Active Directory schema was extended on the Schema Manager and replicated throughout the enterprise.
4. Certificate services in Active Directory were configured for automatic certificate requests for the domains, and the MS High Encryption Pack was installed on all Active Directory servers.
5. After the load and traffic analysis, separate account units for each branch were defined. Headquarters Active Directory servers were defined in lower priority in branches for failover purposes. Each account unit has a specific scope for the branch or the organizational units. This was made possible by fetching the required DNs from the Active Directory database. Necessary user templates were applied during the creation of account units. To activate user management, necessary changes were made to Global Properties on SmartCenter.
6. Created the LDAP user groups according to the remote access policy.
7. Defined the allowed encryption and authentication properties on the gateways. Policy server user groups were modified on each gateway.
8. Added the LDAP user groups in the Remote Access Community object. Defined the participating gateways.
9. Added the generic remote access VPN rule in the Rule Base and pushed the policy.
10. Created an SSL Web site for self-service user management.

Self-Service User Management with ADSI

User management is a resource-intensive process. With a scarcity of resources, automating the user management functions and sharing the load with users are excellent ideas. However, since security is a prerequisite, allowing direct user access on VPN-1/FireWall-1 managed GUI clients is not a good approach. When authentication services are offloaded from the firewall with Active Directory services integration, a new, easy-to-use opportunity arises. The *Active Directory Service Interface*, or *ADSI*, is a common set of objects that enable administrators to write scripts that can manage the information stored on the directory services. This is an opportunity to automate all user management-related tasks.

Since Active Directory infrastructure supports platform-independent access, it is not very difficult to develop a Web interface with ADSI. ADSI accepts all scripting and programming languages, as long as the requests are sent in the correct syntax. Integrating VPN users' profile management should not be the weakest link in the security chain, but all encrypted and authenticated communication on an SSL Web site protected by a VPN-1/FireWall-1 presents a relatively secure approach. ADSI allows administrators and developers to utilize most of the details of Active Directory security policies.

Here is an active server page (ASP) test code for IIS 5.0—page 1 of a Post.asp, which collects the data via a simple HTML form,—to demonstrate the simplicity of ADSI. The code demonstrates simple Web-based password management. The form asks for the username/password/new information for an HQ.NET user and changes the password when submitted. Remember that this is a test code and no string manipulation or error checking is used:

Post.asp code

```
<html>
<head>
<title>Test Password </title>
</head>
<body bgcolor="#ffffff">
<center>
<font face="times new roman">
<i><h1>Change Password</h1></i>
</font>
<table width=300>
   <tr>
     <td>
```

```
        <font face="arial" size=2>
        <b>Username:</b>
        </font>
       </td>
       <td>
        <form action="answer.asp" method="post">
        <input type="text" name="username">
       </td>
   </tr>
     <tr>
     <td>
       <font face="arial" size=2>
       <b> Old Password</b>
       </font>
     </td>

     <td><input type="password" name="password"></td>
  </tr>
  <tr>
     <td>
       <font face="arial" size=2>
       <b> New Password</b>
       </font>
     </td>

     <td><input type="password" name="password2"></td>
  </tr>
     <td><br>

       <input type="submit" value="Submit">
       <input type="button" value="Clear"></form>
     </td>
  </tr>
 </table>
 </body></html>
```

The HTML output of Post.asp is displayed in Figure 3.88. User *jsmith* enters the current and new password.

Figure 3.88 Output of Post.asp

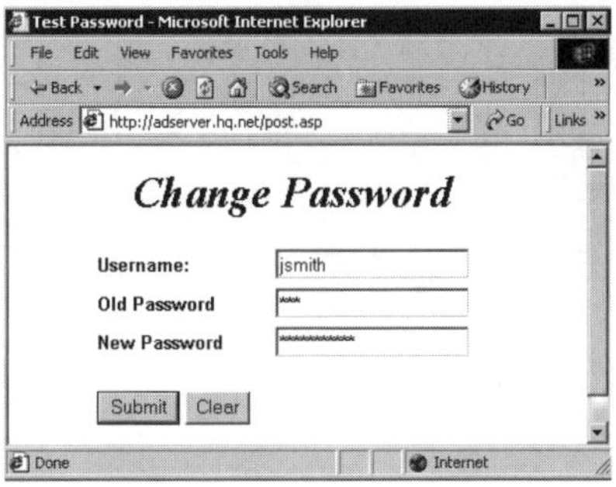

When Post.asp is submitted, Answer.asp is executed. Answer.asp creates an LDAP object that connects to Active Directory via LDAP. Using ADSI features password is changed within the script:

Answer.asp code

```
<HTML lang=en><HEAD><TITLE>Change Password</TITLE></HEAD>
<BODY>



<%
'Declarations
Dim sCN
Dim sOldPass
Dim sNewPass
Dim domain
Dim path



'Get passwords and other values from previous page
sCN = Request.Form("username")
sOldPass = Request.Form("password")
sNewPass = Request.Form("password2")



'form query
```

```
'hq.net is the domain name
domain = "hq\" & sCN
path = "LDAP://hq.net/cn=" & sCN & ",cn=Users,DC=HQ,DC=NET"

'execute
Set objAds = GetObject("LDAP:")
Set objUsr = objAds.OpenDSObject (path, domain, soldpass, 1)
objUsr.ChangePassword soldpass, sNewPass

'fin
Set objAds = Nothing
%>
<br><br><hr><br><br>
<%
Response.write ("User " & sCN & ": Your password has been changed!!" )
%>
<br><br><hr>
</body>
```

As shown in Figure 3.89, Answer.asp displays the results in simple HTML form.

Figure 3.89 Output of Answer.asp

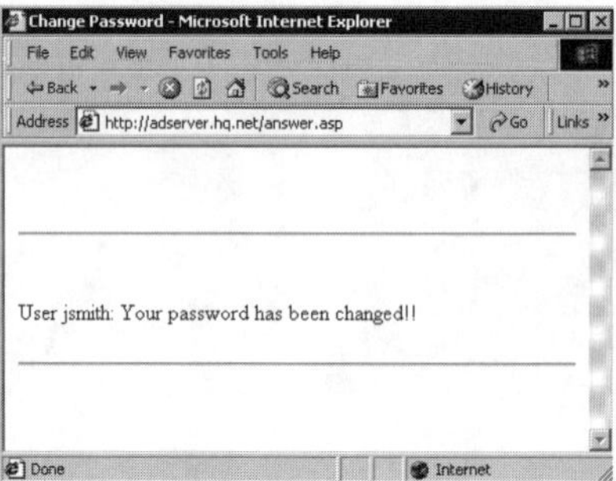

Summary

Keep it simple and secure, or KISS, is a well-known motto for security administrators. With the growing number of secure remote access demands, perimeter security devices are becoming critical authentication points. With increasing flexibility, reliability, and scalability requirements, using a built-for-purpose third-party authentication service provider is a good idea.

Administrators of VPN-1/FireWall-1 can integrate their authentication services with existing directory services or legacy AAA servers. This opportunity presents endless combinations, from tokens to LDAP directories.

Active Directory integration is more mature than ever with the integrated GUI and easy setup. Check Point introduced its own load-balancing and configuration options to Active Directory. Administrators are able to use AD without modifying the Active Directory schema. Even if you choose to support all features of Active Directory, Check Point delivers a predefined modification template. Installation is uncomplicated and all GUI based. One of the major user management problems, password management, is not a real issue with Active Directory, since it allows simple interfaces for developing a user management interface. Furthermore, if you have already deployed your directory services on Active Directory, your next step is obvious: Integrate the authentication services!

Native LDAP authentication support is as simple as can be. The same high-availability options, granular user policy designs, and ready-to-use schema extensions are built into the Check Point firewall. Using SmartDashboard as an LDAP client and being able to define LDAP administrators with different access rights are nice features. If you have implemented LDAP authentication prior to installing NG, you can still upgrade your setups with update_schema.ldif. Hybrid Authentication and Secure Authentication API (SAA) is supported on LDAP user groups.

Authentication, authorization, and accounting (AAA) servers are still on the market and evolving. There might be less need for dialup authentication, but the wide deployment base and the industrial support for the RADIUS protocol make RADIUS servers an integration point. Today you can access multiple authentication protocols over RADIUS. RADIUS has a very simple configuration and supports basic load balancing. TACACS+ is still the de facto choice for Cisco shops, and VPN-1/FireWall-1 offers full support for TACACS authentication.

With Check Point's familiarity with directory services, we can expect to see directory servers as object repositories in a future release, but for the time being, even user management is an important enhancement, especially when user management efforts are integrated with a self-service portal. Microsoft and Check Point integration will be more rewarding in the future with the introduction of .NET Active Directory. Full PKI and Smart Card integration, use of e-mail addresses as DNs, and schema delete functionality are all expected with the next releases of the products.

Solutions Fast Track

Active Directory

- ☑ Configure your Active Directory first. Enable CA, install the High Encryption pack, and organize your console.
- ☑ *Proceed with caution!* There is no schema delete in Active Directory. Be sure about the results before trying this in the production environment.
- ☑ Configure your account units, high-availability options, and user groups. Life is easier with simplified VPN rules.
- ☑ Consider building a user management portal with ADSI support.

Standard LDAP

- ☑ Define your account units, high-availability options, and LDAP user groups.
- ☑ Configure your remote access community, add your LDAP user groups in the simplified rules—and that is all you need to do.
- ☑ Consider defining LDAP administrators with different access levels. Define multiple account units and enable password authentication for connection.
- ☑ Optimize LDAP searches by eliminating unused user groups.

RADIUS

- ☑ RADIUS groups are supported. Configure your high availability.
- ☑ You can use RADIUS as SmartClient administrator authentication.
- ☑ RADIUS servers may bridge VPN-1/FireWall-1 server authentication with third-party AAA servers.
- ☑ FP3 supports external user profiles. You can have profiles to use the same usernames with different authentication methods.

TACACS+

- ☑ Simply define your TACACS server and enter your shared secret on both sides.

- ☑ TACACS and RADIUS protocols are enabled by default if you allow **Accept VPN-1/FireWall-1 connections**.
- ☑ Generic* user is predefined in **External User Profiles | Match all users**.
- ☑ Do not forget to allow TACACS+ in your gateway's accepted authentication schemas.

General User Management

- ☑ Using third-party authentication solutions can simplify the task of VPN-1/FireWall-1 administration.
- ☑ The Active Directory Service Interface (ADSI) is a common set of objects that enable administrators to write scripts that can manage the information stored on the directory services.

Frequently Asked Questions

The following Frequently Asked Questions, answered by the authors of this book, are designed to both measure your understanding of the concepts presented in this chapter and to assist you with real-life implementation of these concepts. To have your questions about this chapter answered by the author, browse to **www.syngress.com/solutions** and click on the **"Ask the Author"** form.

Q: Can I use Active Directory for SmartClient Administrator authentication?

A: No. Administrator users cannot be authenticated against LDAP resources.

Q: What is the order of authentication schemas?

A: FireWall-1 user database, LDAP, then Generic*.

Q: What is Hybrid Mode Authentication?

A: Check Point Hybrid Mode Authentication for IPSec enables the use of widely deployed authentication techniques such as token cards, RADIUS, and TACACS+ within IPSec VPNs.

Q: Does VPN-1/FireWall-1 support CHAP?

A: No.

Q: I have L2TP clients but I cannot authenticate when using LDAP user database. What should I do?

A: This is a known NG FP3 error. Contact your reseller for a remedy to the "illegal DN given as user name *xxx*" error message.

Q: How can I use LDAP command-line utilities to connect SSL ports of directories?

A: This is not supported. Try using third-party tunneling software.

Q: How can I create a Generic* user?

A: Go to **External User Profiles** and choose **Match all users**. You cannot create a Generic* user.

Chapter 4

Advanced VPN Concepts

Solutions in this chapter:

- What Are SEP and MEP?
- SEP Configuration Examples
- MEP Configuration Examples
- Combinations of MEP and SEP
- VPN Modes
- Routing Between VPN Connections
- Dynamic IP Address VPN Connections

☑ Summary

☑ Solutions Fast Track

☑ Frequently Asked Questions

Introduction

OK, here we go… another chapter of VPN technology with more three-letter acronyms (TLAs). Some of the TLAs that we cover are MEP and SEP, but where does it end? We focus on the VPN functionality that Check Point has added to its FP3 product. We hope to show you how to utilize Check Point FireWall-1 NG to enable easy VPN deployment with high throughput while presenting solid return on investment.

From an encryption standpoint, we focus only on IPSec VPNs. The industry has come together around IPSec as a standard for layer 3 VPNs in the past five years. Check Point has been on the forefront of that standard, designing, implementing, and enhancing the roles that VPNs can provide for securing network communications. It is also clear that Check Point has one of the most flexible VPN platforms on the market today.

With FireWall-1 NG, Check Point has created some new VPN features, including the ability to modify specific configuration settings on a per VPN tunnel basis, the ability to route traffic within meshed VPNs, and enhanced client VPN/Firewall solutions. Check Point Multi–Entry Point VPN (MEP) and Single Entry Point VPN (SEP) are deployment options that you need to be familiar with if you are going to design highly available Check Point VPN solutions.

What Are SEP and MEP?

Many companies have installed a single firewall to a single Internet connection and have been very satisfied with their configurations. As the company begins to use the Internet firewall and bask in the serenity of its newfound Internet security, it will add some new feature or process that will rely on this new Internet connection. Then the inevitable occurs. The firewall fails, or the local electric company digs up the local loop to your Internet connection. Or something else causes the failure of the Internet connection leading to the critical business process being unavailable. Now the fur begins to fly…. Well, there is a way out of this morass of problems, by deploying a high availability (HA) solution for your firewall and Internet connections. Check Point has two types or models of high availability options for the NG product: SEP and MEP.

The SEP (Single Entry Point) model is designed so that there is a "single" egress point between the "protected" and "unprotected" networks. This single egress is comprised of at least a two-system firewall cluster, since SEP is a high availability method of connectivity. SEP configurations normally have the following features:

- Cluster members share information regarding connections and availability to all cluster members.
- SEP is normally localized to one physical facility (or at most, single-mode fiber distances apart).

- Connections are not lost during a host failure, they are simply reassigned to the remaining host(s) that participate in the SEP cluster.

MEP (Multi–Entry Point) is a method where there are many points of entry between the "protected" and "unprotected" networks. MEP designs increase complexity of routing, because the internal network has many ways to get to the same external resources.

To relate this to medieval security structures, a SEP model is where there is a single castle with high walls, a moat, portcullis, and a drawbridge. The design of this is shown in Figure 4.1. The moat and high walls keep people out, and the portcullis and drawbridge are the main entry point of the castle structure. This allows all things entering and leaving the castle to be inspected prior to entrance or exit, and the surrounding structure and guards provide the high security necessary. The portcullis is specifically where there is an "airlock" type of entryway where inspections can take place.

Figure 4.1 Castle with Portcullis Security

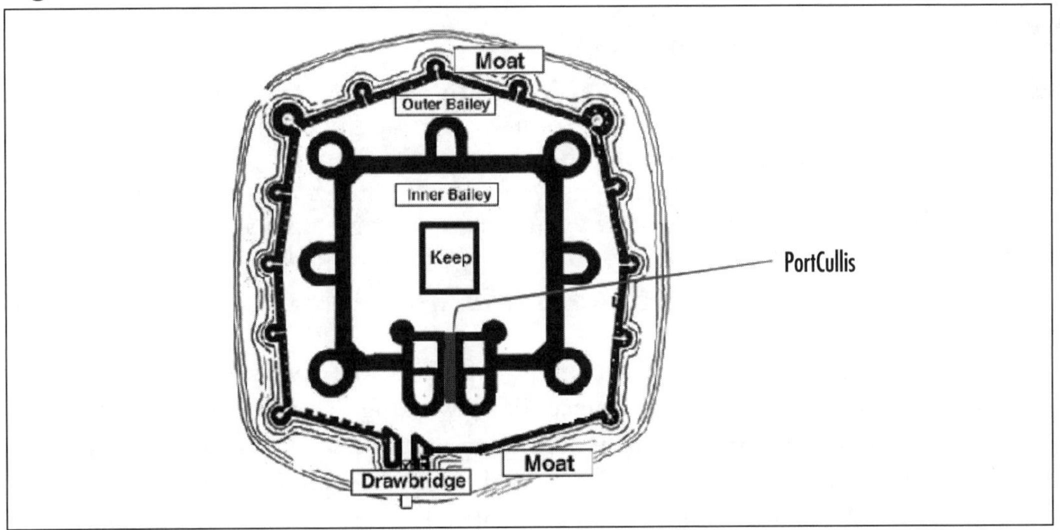

A MEP configuration would be more like a walled city, as shown in Figure 4.2. The walled city shares many features of the castle—the high walls, perhaps surrounding water on one or two sides—yet there is more space, and many different ways to get into the city, making it more convenient to the outside traveler. Also, anyone can leave the city out any exit. This also means that one could enter one gate and exit the other. From a packet standpoint, this could be a problem, because this would be asymmetric routing.

Figure 4.2 Walled City—Charleston S.C. from 1690 to 1720.

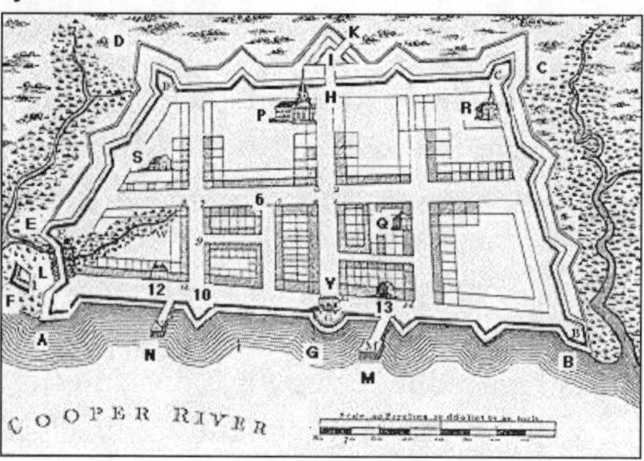

Notes from the Underground…

HA Isn't Just for Internet!

Although this chapter focuses on using HA for Internet connected or Internet "facing" solutions, all of these HA solutions can be utilized in many different architectures. HA can be configured in any direction where you need to secure, monitor, throttle, and provide continuous communications. For example, if your Firewall protected your environment from a value added network, you could perform SEP on your firewall for a HA solution.

Make sure that you understand these types of HA before you begin your design efforts, because there are many other pieces of networking that must be considered. Simple connectivity will turn complex depending on the type of HA that you deploy. Routing will also be directly affected by your choices of design. Lastly, maintaining this configuration will also carry a higher administrative burden. These considerations should not taint your desire or focus to deploy a HA solution, they are merely pointed out for your review. In order for the next sections to make sense, we first set up a sample scenario.

Sample Scenario

Company X has two offices and is growing quickly. There is a need to build a better security infrastructure, and the existing routers and access control lists are going to be upgraded. A Check Point firewall has been deployed to New York. The team has been asked to consider the following information:

- Offices located in New York and London
- WAN connection between offices
- Business connectivity:
  - Hosting of business presence Web site
  - Hosting a business FTP site
  - Business-to-business connectivity via FW-FW VPN
  - Home users with SecureClient VPN connectivity

Exploring SEP

With SEP, it is important to understand the methods that you would like to use. Within a SEP environment, you can use the Check Point product suite method, which is to deploy ClusterXL. ClusterXL provides HA by allowing you to configure two or more Check Point firewall enforcement points to provide secure connectivity from a "trusted" to "untrusted" network. An example of this is diagrammed in Figure 4.3. Also note, although it is not depicted in any diagrams in this section, SEP requires that the management station be separate from the enforcement points.

Figure 4.3 SEP Example

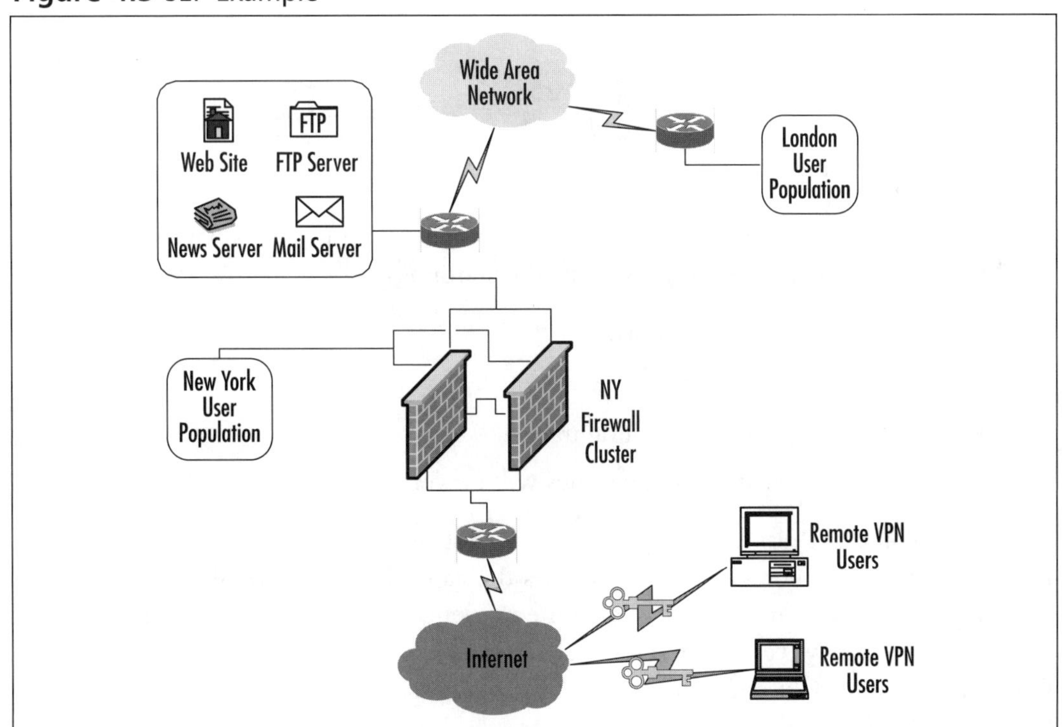

Many hardware product vendors on the market today will also tell you that you can utilize their hardware and obtain the same type of SEP HA, without having to purchase Check Point licenses, or even to have one Check Point and another vendor firewall. Their sales diagram would look similar to Figure 4.4.

Figure 4.4 Hardware SEP Solution

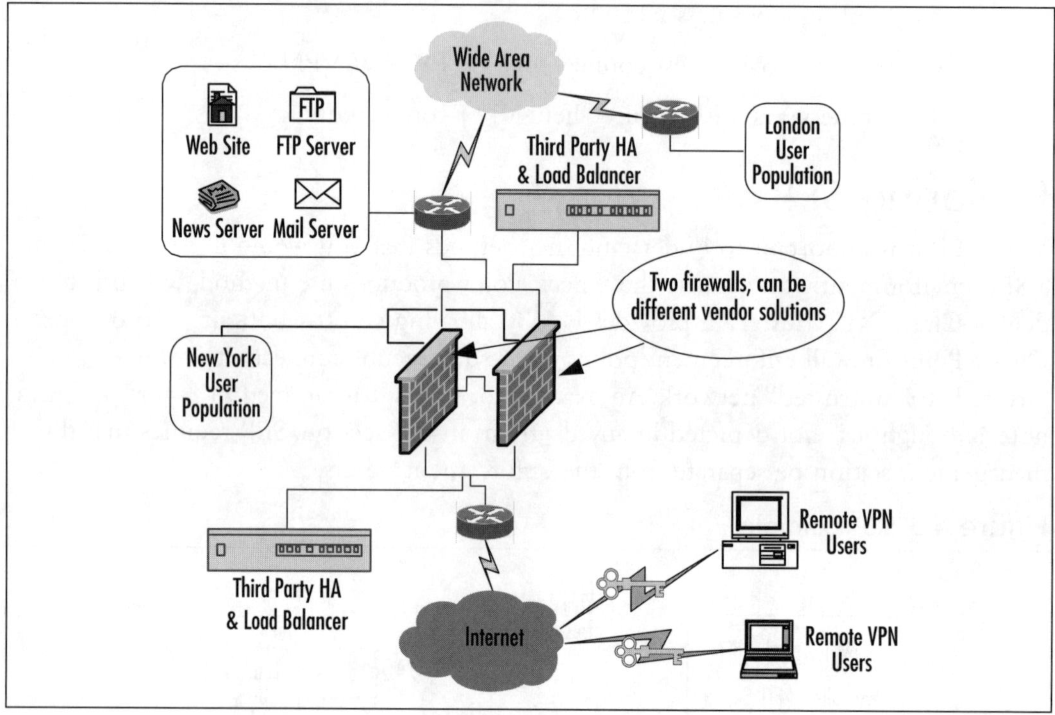

Be very cautious when considering this approach, because it does have some major disadvantages, and may suffer some serious shortcomings:

- Lack of IPSec VPN support.
- Connections will *not* fail over.
- Requires major DNS reconfiguration.
- Maintaining separate vendor rules will be very difficult.

Check Point SEP using ClusterXL provides a strong solution that will not suffer from these disadvantages. ClusterXL provides the capability to create SEP configurations with new ease. For those of you with experience with Check Point clustering, you will find the new version much easier to set up, deploy, manage, and support. Chapter 6 explores ClusterXL in detail.

Exploring MEP

MEP allows you to have a number of entry points into your network, to provide alternate access in the event that one fails. By using MEP, you can have VPN connections automatically rerouted *through* an alternate path within your network. Primarily, MEP is discussed as a VPN high availability solution, but with the right networking design and hardware, it can also be for your entire network.

SEP Configuration Examples

In this section, we review a few short examples of network designs that would benefit from SEP configurations. We start with the simplest and move towards the advanced. Note that these are simply examples, and your configurations will need to be reviewed closely, with a thorough understanding of the environment, prior to deploying SEP.

Scenario One

You are in charge of a small company that only needs to have outbound Internet access and a single VPN connection to one of your trading partners. The trading partner connection is considered to be of high business value, as is the Internet connection. You have only one location, a handful of remote VPN users (the IT staff), and choose to deploy SEP. Your environment might look like Figure 4.5.

Figure 4.5 Two-Firewall ClusterXL SEP configuration

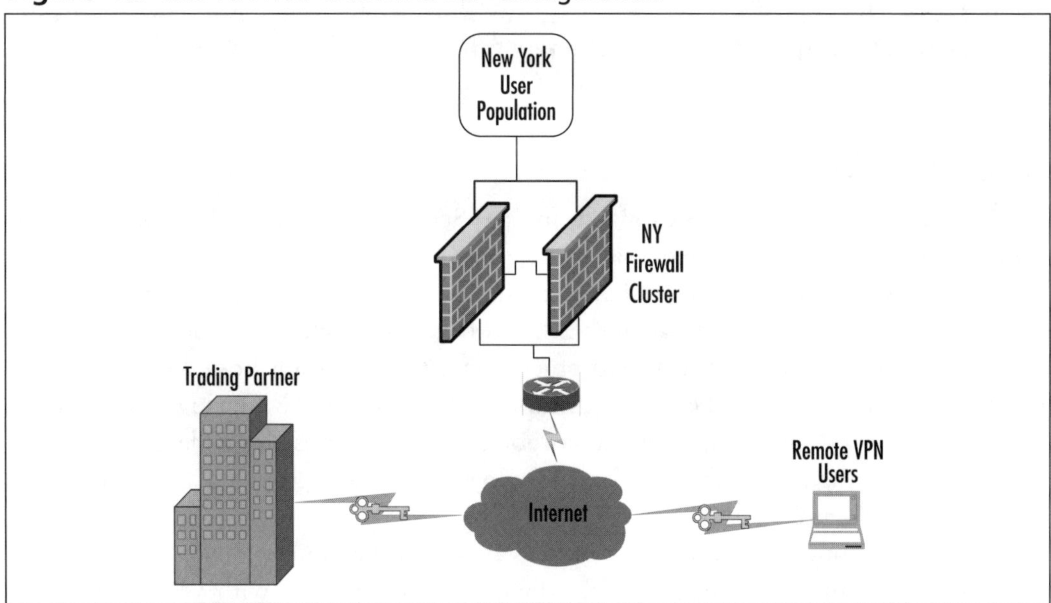

SEP here is a simple ClusterXL with OfficeMode enabled for the SecuRemote users. This environment can be expanded, as the business expands, and provides for many capabilities along with HA:

- Ability to perform maintenance on one system without severely impacting connectivity
- Load sharing to ensure that the trading partner receives the best response for communications
- Transparent solution to the trading partner and internal users

Notes from the Underground…

Load Sharing and FloodGate-1

Load sharing in SEP configurations is not fully supported in Check Point FireWall-1 NG. You may not be able to limit the bandwidth of connections or enforce Floodgate-1 SLAs while performing load sharing in FireWall-1 clusters. It seems that when you begin to load share connections, Floodgate-1 cannot keep up with the distribution of load between the firewalls *and* perform the traffic shaping/throttling functions of Floodgate-1. However, as Check Point has been making great strides in its software, this should be a temporary shortcoming; expect to see this change in future Feature Packs (FPs).

Scenario Two

The Company you work for is growing, and has Scenario One from the preceding section deployed. You have acquired a sales office in San Diego and need to provide Internet access to that office, as well as increase your remote user presence to support the roving sales force. With this acquisition, you have also gained four more customer VPN connections. Also, the San Diego office Web site, which was hosted by a third-party hosting company, will be brought into the New York office. During this transition, the decision to deploy an internal corporate mail system is also added. The existing SEP configuration that you have employed may be augmented as shown in Figure 4.6 and Figure 4.7.

SEP configurations can also grow in size when load becomes an issue. As a last example, assume that the configuration in Figure 4.7 is deployed, with a Web farm, and the traffic load into the Web farm is being slowed down by the Internet connection and the two firewalls. We have reviewed all of the traffic statistics and determine that the best way to resolve this problem is to increase the number of nodes in our ClusterXL cluster and bring in two more T-1 Internet connections. We can multiplex (MUX) the Internet connections for a maximum throughput of 4.6 Mbps (1.544 Mbps × 3) and utilize BGP routing on the Internet routers for failover. Figure 4.8 shows how this example might look.

Figure 4.6 Scenario Two—Remote Office via WAN Connectivity

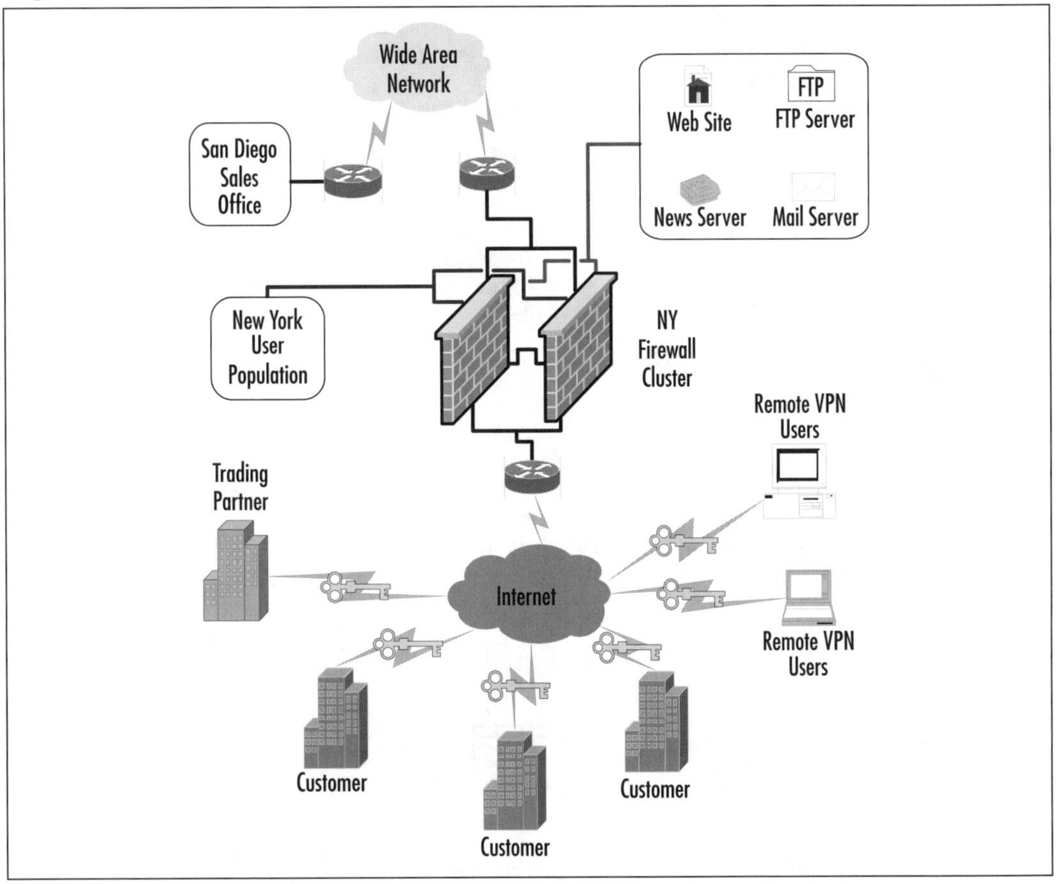

As this environment grows, we would have to look at alternate methods of providing fault tolerance and high availability. Of course, there are many other issues when determining which systems need to be redundant, and by which methods. In Figure 4.7 it is assumed that the infrastructure for power, Web, news, mail, and FTP are also configured to be HA, as well as the local loop for the multiple T-1s, through different carriers. If we then need to enhance this configuration, we can integrate MEP with this SEP architecture, making this environment even more robust.

Figure 4.7 Scenario Two—Remote Office via Firewall VPN

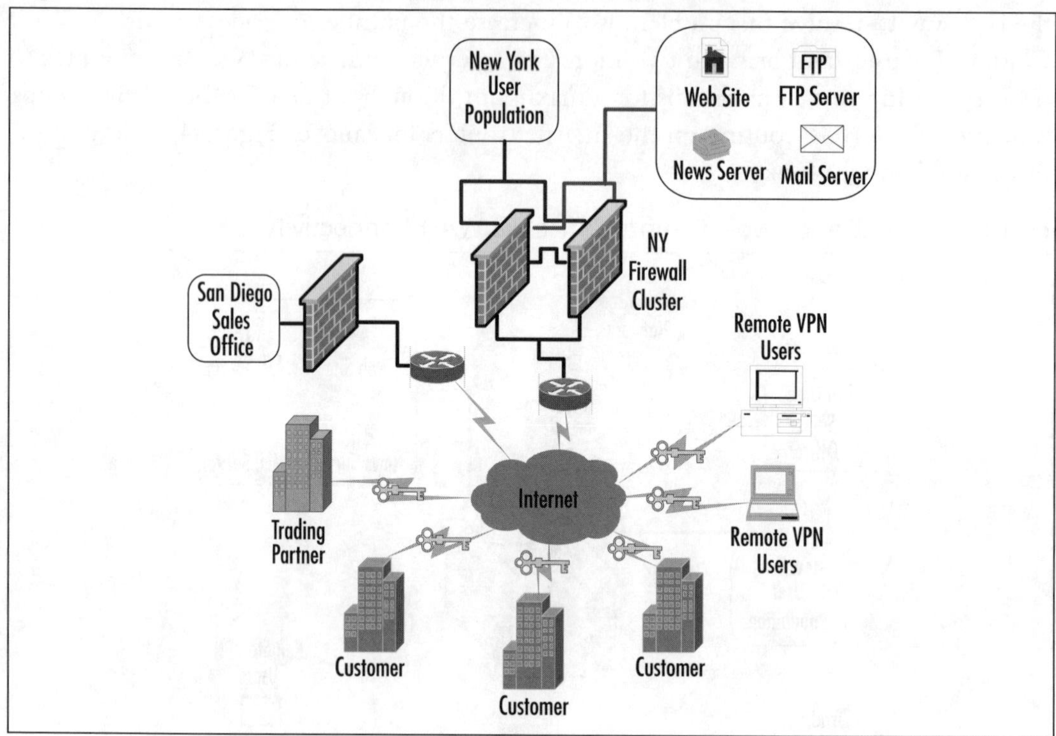

Figure 4.8 Large ClusterXL SEP Configuration

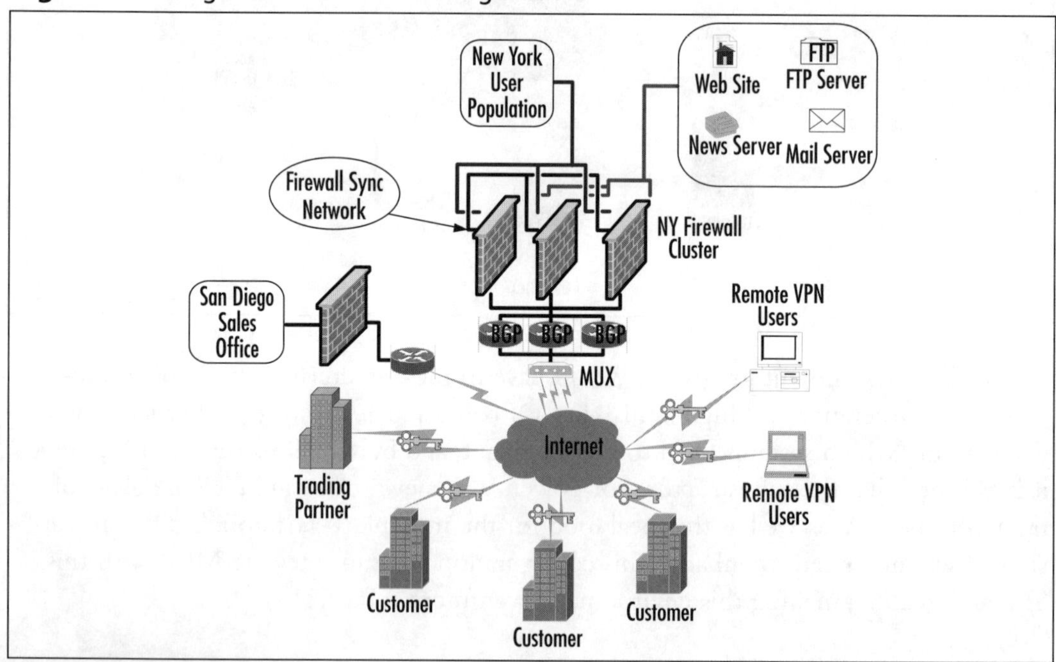

MEP Configuration Examples

Multi–Entry Point VPN configurations are designed to assist an organization that has many locations with Internet access to leverage these connections to provide HA for VPN and other remote connectivity. MEP can be complicated, depending on the routing infrastructure in place in the environment. For the sake of the examples, we assume the following:

- Internal control of all routers, switches, and firewalls.
- All internal IP addresses are private as defined in RFC-1918, including Web-accessible systems.
- All external IP address ranges contain 254 usable addresses (/24 or Class C mask).
- We will *not* multihome *any* internal hosts or servers.

Scenario One

You are in charge of a small company that is growing and has the following needs:

- Outbound Internet access
- VPN connection to one of your trading partners
- Remote sales office in San Diego with Internet access
- Remote VPN users (the IT staff and sales users)
- Internal hosting of business-centric Web site
- Internal corporate mail system, FTP, and news services

You have been directed to make this environment as robust as possible, and the company desires to keep the existing WAN connectivity to San Diego for emergency purposes. You may decide to deploy a MEP configuration as shown in Figure 4.9. There are a few important things to note here. The IP addresses inside the network must be NATed to the correct locations within the network, an external intelligent DNS load balancing device (F5, Cisco Distributed Director, Foundry ServerIron, or similar) must be used to direct all Internet DNS to the available servers. Table 4.1 contains the interface details for the gateways and routers depicted in Figure 4.9.

Figure 4.9 Basic MEP Configuration with IP NAT Pools

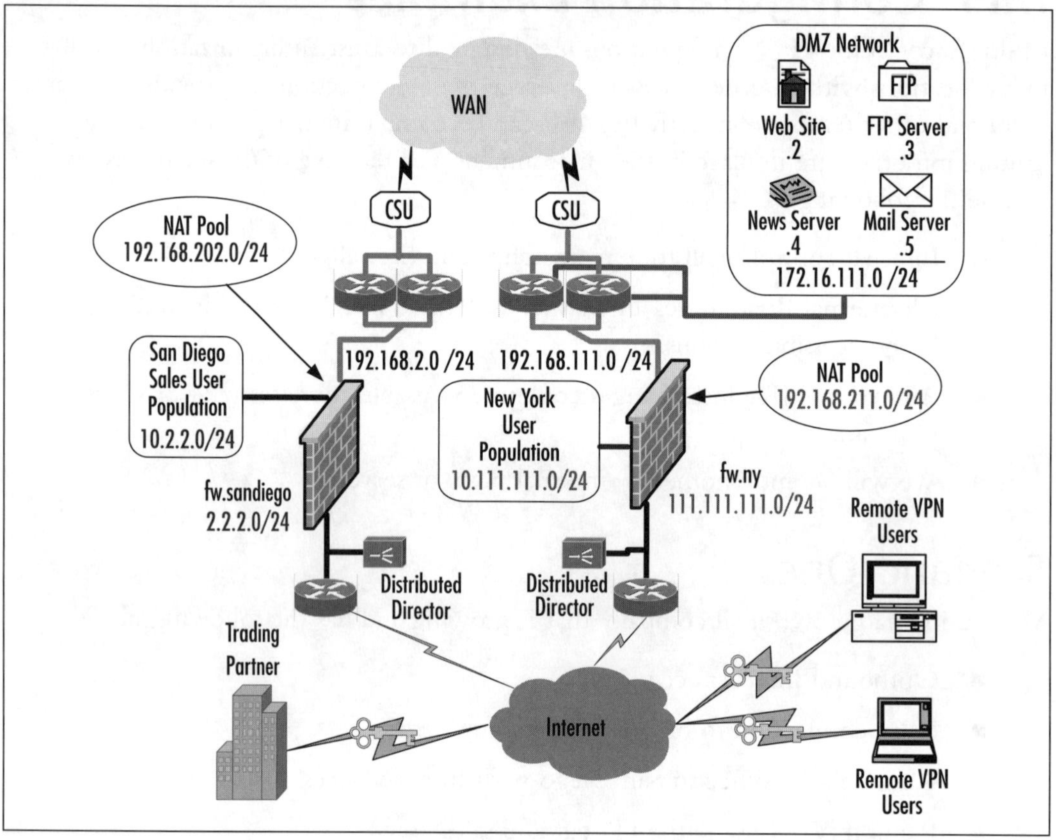

Table 4.1 IP Address Ranges and Their Purposes

IP Address/Mask	Name	Description
111.111.111.0 /24	New York Internet Address Range	The range of IP addresses from the ISP in New York.
192.168.211.0 /24	New York NAT Pool Address Network Address Range	Used for inbound VPN connections; allows NAT to be accomplished regardless of the source IP address.
172.16.111.0 /24	New York DMZ Network Address Range	DMZ host IP address range. All Traffic from the Internet will be NAT'ed to these addresses
10.111.111.0 /24	New York User Network Address Range	All end users would receive these addresses for use on the New York local network.

Continued

Table 4.1 IP Address Ranges and Their Purposes

IP Address/Mask	Name	Description
192.168.111.0 /24	New York WAN Router IP Address Range	IP address for firewall to WAN network interface.
2.2.2.0 /24	San Diego Internet Address Range	The range of IP addresses from the ISP in San Diego.
192.168.202.0/24	San Diego NAT Pool Address Network Address Range	Used for inbound VPN connections; allows NAT to be accomplished regardless of the source IP address.
10.2.2.0 /24	San Diego User Network Address Range	All end users would receive these addresses for use on the San Diego local network.
192.168.2.0 /24	San Diego WAN Router IP Address ange	IP address for firewall to WAN network interface.
192.168.254.0 /30	WAN IP Range	Used for the connection between New York and San Diego over the WAN connection.

Now we can begin to see the complexity of MEP. This is not to imply that MEP is difficult, but it can be cumbersome if you are not well versed in IP routing. We go into the detail of the routing tables on all of the devices in a moment. Please note that although we have decided to deploy two routers on the WAN to provide fault tolerance, we do *not* discuss the HA configuration of those devices here. As well, we have chosen to utilize a network interface off of the router pair in New York to host the DMZ for the Web so that this would be available in the event of a firewall failure in New York.

In order to have this configuration work properly, the following routes must be in place properly. The firewall and WAN routers, as well as the distributed directors, must be configured to forward traffic around outages. The interface tables are listed in Table 4.2, and the route table for the routers and firewalls is depicted in Table 4.3.

Table 4.2 Interface Table

Device	Interface	IP Address	Net Mask	Gateway
fw.ny	Internet	111.111.111.2	255.255.255.0	111.111.111.1
	WAN	192.168.111.1	255.255.255.0	
	Local Users	10.111.111.1	255.255.255.0	
fw.sandiego	Internet	2.2.2.2	255.255.255.0	2.2.2.1
	WAN	192.168.2.1	255.255.255.0	

Continued

Table 4.2 Interface Table

Device	Interface	IP Address	Net Mask	Gateway
	Local Users	10.2.2.1	255.255.255.0	
New York WAN routers	Ethernet 0	192.168.111.2	255.255.255.0	192.168.111.1
	Ethernet 1	172.16.111.1	255.255.255.0	
	Serial 0	192.168.254.1	255.255.255.252	
San Diego WAN routers	Ethernet 0	192.168.2.2	255.255.255.0	
	Serial 0	192.168.254.2	255.255.255.252	

Table 4.3 IP Routes (Assuming Static Routes on Firewalls)

Device	Network	Mask	Gateway	Metric
fw.ny	0.0.0.0 (default)	0.0.0.0	111.111.111.1	1
	2.2.2.0	255.255.255.0	192.168.111.2	1
	10.111.111.0	255.255.255.0	10.111.111.1	1
	10.2.2.0	255.255.255.0	192.168.111.2	1
	111.111.111.0	255.255.255.0	111.111.111.2	1
	172.16.111.0	255.255.255.0	192.168.111.2	1
	192.168.111.0	255.255.255.0	192.168.111.1	1
	192.168.2.0	255.255.255.0	192.168.111.2	1
	192.168.202.0	255.255.255.0	192.168.111.2	1
fw.sandiego	0.0.0.0 (default)	0.0.0.0	2.2.2.1	1
	2.2.2.0	255.255.255.0	2.2.2.1	1
	10.111.111.0	255.255.255.0	192.168.2.2	1
	10.2.2.0	255.255.255.0	10.2.2.1	1
	111.111.111.0	255.255.255.128	192.168.2.2	1
	111.111.111.128	255.255.255.128	192.168.2.2	1
	172.16.111.0	255.255.255.0	192.168.2.2	1
	192.168.111.0	255.255.255.0	192.168.2.2	1
	192.168.2.0	255.255.255.0	192.168.2.1	1
	192.168.211.0	255.255.255.0	192.168.2.2	1
New York WAN routers	0.0.0.0 (default)	0.0.0.0	192.168.111.1	1
	0.0.0.0	0.0.0.0	192.168.254.2	5

Continued

Table 4.3 IP Routes (Assuming Static Routes on Firewalls)

Device	Network	Mask	Gateway	Metric
	2.2.2.0	255.255.255.0	192.168.254.2	1
	10.111.111.0	255.255.255.0	192.168.111.1	1
	10.2.2.0	255.255.255.0	192.168.254.2	1
	111.111.111.0	255.255.255.0	192.168.111.1	1
	172.16.111.0	255.255.255.0	172.16.111.1	1
	192.168.111.0	255.255.255.0	192.168.111.2	1
	192.168.2.0	255.255.255.0	192.168.254.2	1
	192.168.202.0	255.255.255.0	192.168.254.2	1
	192.168.211.0	255.255.255.0	192.168.111.1	1
San Diego WAN routers	0.0.0.0 (default)	0.0.0.0	192.168.2.1	1
	0.0.0.0	0.0.0.0	192.168.254.1	5
	2.2.2.0	255.255.255.0	192.168.2.1	1
	10.111.111.0	255.255.255.0	192.168.254.1	1
	10.2.2.0	255.255.255.0	192.168.2.1	1
	111.111.111.0	255.255.255.0	192.168.254.1	1
	172.16.111.0	255.255.255.0	192.168.254.1	1
	192.168.111.0	255.255.255.0	192.168.254.1	1
	192.168.2.0	255.255.255.0	192.168.2.1	1
	192.168.202.0	255.255.255.0	192.168.2.1	1
	192.168.211.0	255.255.255.0	192.168.254.1	1

As shown in these tables, the routing can be a bit cumbersome. Note the dual default gateways defined in the WAN routers. This will provide failover routing in the event of a primary default gateway not being available. Also note where the NAT Pool IP addresses are defined in the route tables. To enable Internet failover, configure the distributed directors to maintain communications with each other, and periodically check the existence of several hosts in your network, via alternate paths through the New York and San Diego firewalls. In the event that one path is not available, they will stop serving the external DNS response that is associated with the failed path, then directing the traffic down the still functional path. Configuring your firewalls will be the next step.

Setup of New York Firewall

First, you must configure the firewall object itself. Ensure that the configuration of the topology is correct for the enforcement points. We start with the firewall in New York. Figure 4.10 shows the basic information on the General Properties tab of firewall definition.

Figure 4.10 New York Firewall General Properties Tab

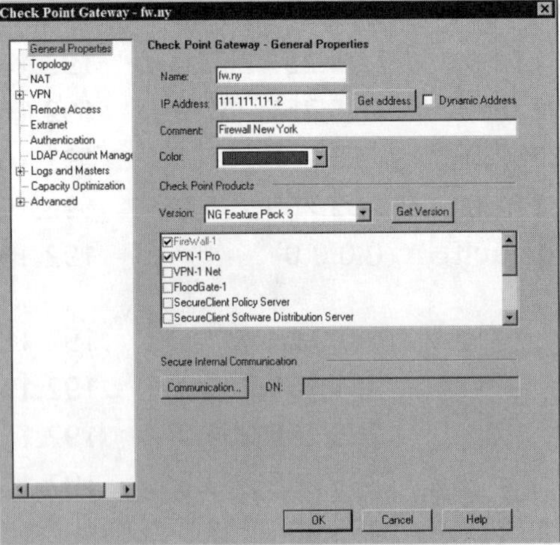

Figure 4.11 displays the Topology tab for the New York firewall. Take special note, we cannot use the automatic topology, because we plan to create this as a MEP configuration. We must create a manual encryption domain. Note that we have set up the New York DMZ as our encryption domain, meaning that we will encrypt traffic for those hosts only for incoming VPN connections.

Figure 4.11 New York Firewall Topology Tab

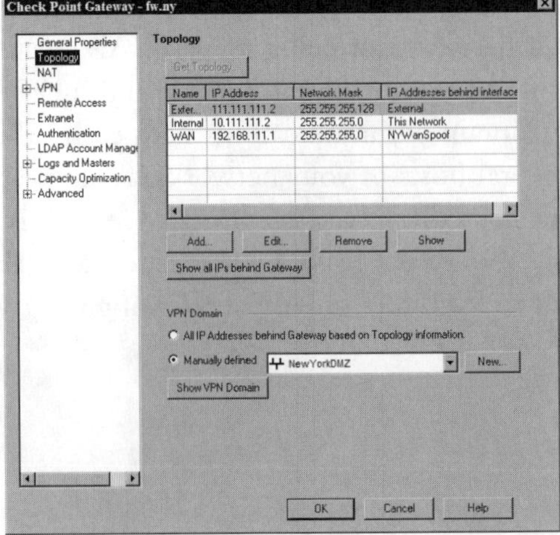

The important things here are the configuration of IP pool usage, as seen on the NAT tab of the firewall properties. By configuring this firewall to provide IP pool NAT to remote users, and to gateway-to-gateway connections, all inbound Firewall VPN traffic will be NATed to the IP pool that is created on the New York firewall. Figure 4.12 shows these settings.

Figure 4.12 New York Firewall NAT Tab

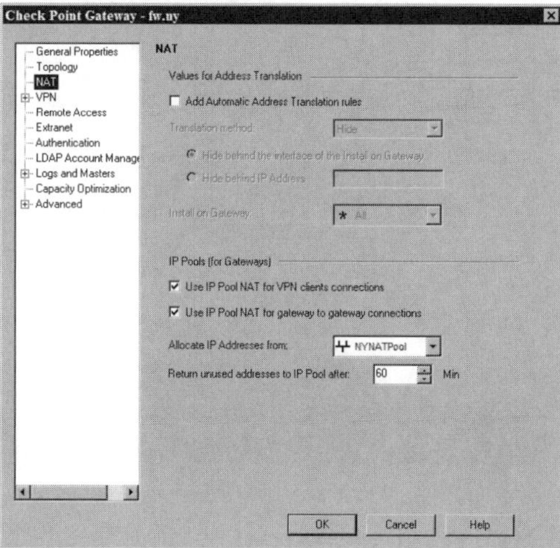

As well, this firewall is added to a firewall community with San Diego. By adding a VPN community, this firewall can route its traffic over the WAN or over the VPN to communicate with the San Diego site. This is shown in Figure 4.13.

Figure 4.13 New York Firewall VPN Tab

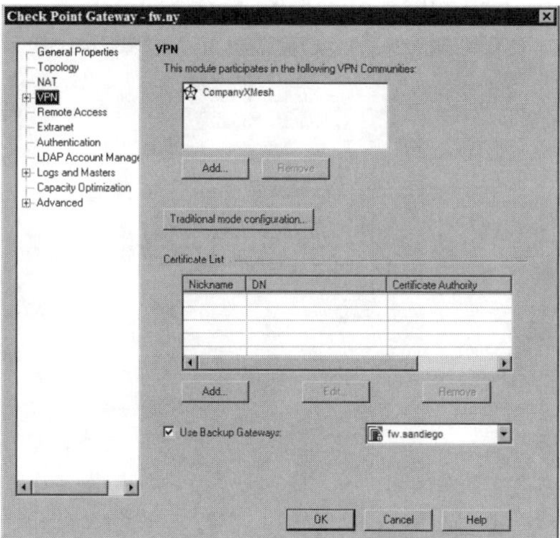

Lastly, office mode options are shown on the Remote Access tab. In Figure 4.14, you can see that we have selected that all remote users be given IP addresses from the NAT pool, which enables us to better control the traffic that we allow into our network.

Figure 4.14 New York Firewall Remote Access Tab

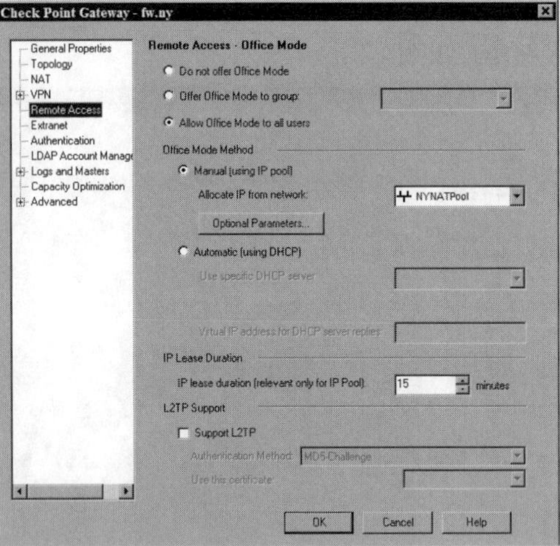

Setup of San Diego Firewall

Now we have to review the San Diego configuration. It is very similar to the New York configuration, with the obvious changes to topology; however, the encryption domain *must* be the *exact same* as the one for New York for the design to work. This is shown in Figures 4.15 through 4.19.

Figure 4.15 San Diego Firewall General Properties Tab

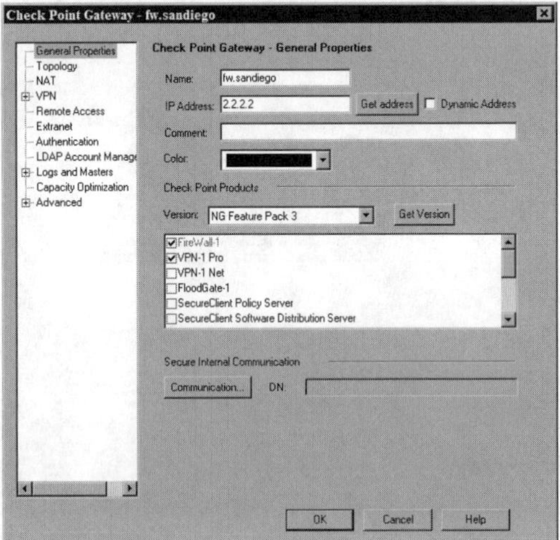

Figure 4.16 San Diego Firewall Topology Tab

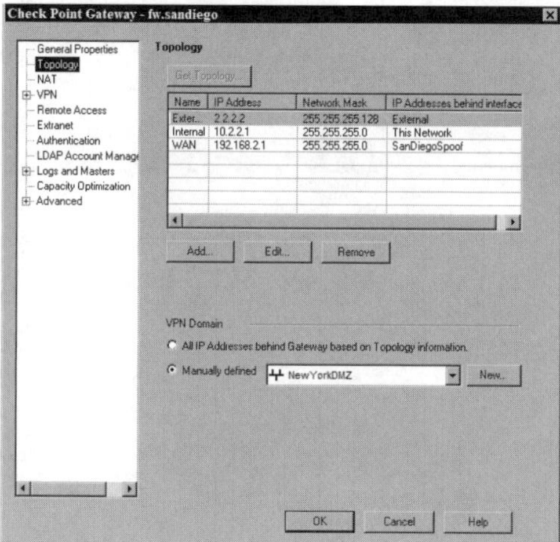

Figure 4.17 San Diego Firewall NAT Tab

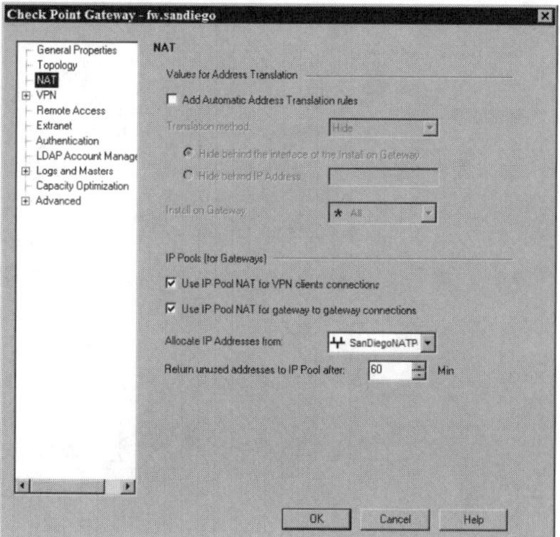

Figure 4.18 San Diego Firewall VPN Tab

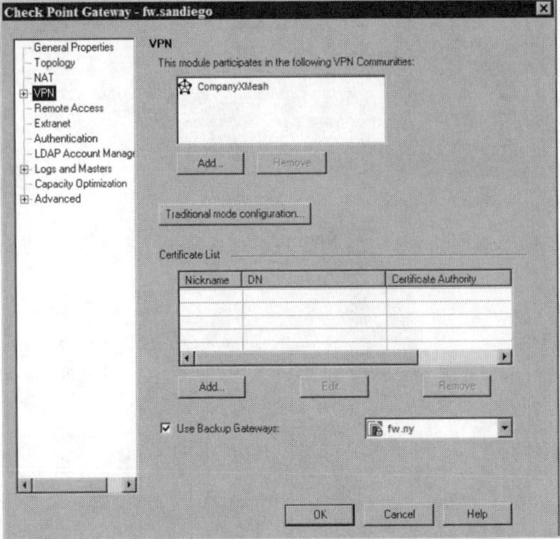

Figure 4.19 San Diego Firewall Remote Access Tab

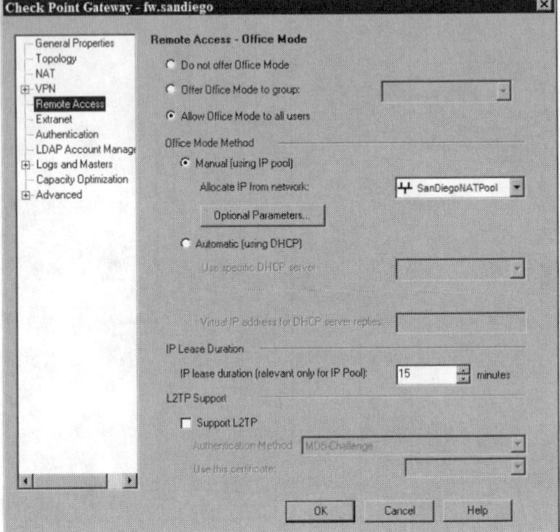

Lastly, you would have to create the rules in the rule base to allow all of the necessary traffic into the networks. You will have to pay close attention to your rules and ensure that you allow inbound traffic on both firewalls to the DMZ network in New York. A sample rule base is depicted in Figure 4.20.

This rule base could be installed on both firewall enforcement points, because it is clear enough for general traffic. However, it does not specifically contain or show the rules for remote access.

Figure 4.20 Sample MEP Rule Base

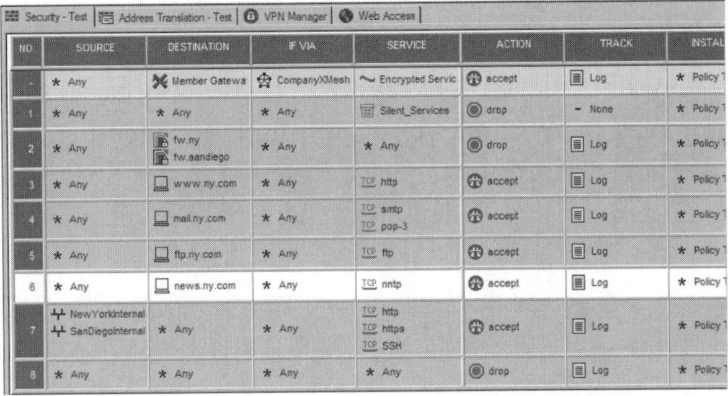

Security - Test | Address Translation - Test | VPN Manager | Web Access

NO	SOURCE	DESTINATION	IF VIA	SERVICE	ACTION	TRACK	INSTAL
-	* Any	Member Gatewa	CompanyXMesh	Encrypted Servic	accept	Log	* Policy T
1	* Any	* Any	* Any	Silent_Services	drop	- None	* Policy T
2	* Any	fw.ny fw.sandiego	* Any	* Any	drop	Log	* Policy T
3	* Any	www.ny.com	* Any	TCP http	accept	Log	* Policy T
4	* Any	mail.ny.com	* Any	TCP smtp TCP pop-3	accept	Log	* Policy T
5	* Any	ftp.ny.com	* Any	TCP ftp	accept	Log	* Policy T
6	* Any	news.ny.com	* Any	TCP nntp	accept	Log	* Policy T
7	NewYorkInternal SanDiegoInternal	* Any	* Any	TCP http TCP https TCP SSH	accept	Log	* Policy T
8	* Any	* Any	* Any	* Any	drop	Log	* Policy T

Tools & Traps…

Encryption Domains

Getting your encryption domains correct in MEP configurations is essential. There are four types of encryption domains:

- **Fully overlapping** When all firewalls that participate in a MEP configuration deliver the exact same encryption domain to all remote clients.
- **Proper subset** When one encryption domain contains *all* of the hosts of the second. This is normally used when there are two gateways, one behind the other, in a layered fashion, and both gateways perform VPN tunnel termination. The encryption domain of the first gateway contains all of the objects contained within the second gateway's encryption domain. Check Point FireWall-1 NG does support proper subset encryption domains. (Note: Proper subset is not used specifically for MEP configurations.)
- **Partially overlapping** When the MEP firewalls deliver different encryption domains. This would mean that depending on which firewall you connect to, you would have a different encryption domain, although some hosts may be contained within *both* encryption domains. Check Point FireWall-1 NG does *not* support partially overlapping encryption domains.
- **Non-overlapping** When each MEP firewall delivers a different encryption domain to its connecting clients, and they connect based on the encryption domain received. Check Point FireWall-1 *does* support non-overlapping encryption domains, sometimes referred to "dis-jointed encryption domains."

Combinations of MEP and SEP

When we were discussing SEP, we created an environment where we had a remote sales office with a firewall deployed (see Figure 4.7). We also had a somewhat complicated MEP configuration. Now, think about putting them together. All we would have to do is add a cluster at each location, and we have MEP and SEP. Again, we add complications to the environment, but if deployed correctly, we will then have a very robust environment.

Tools & Traps...

Documentation

It may sound like overkill, but you must heavily document an environment that contains MEP and SEP. Troubleshooting an environment that contains MEP and SEP without adequate documentation will lead to catastrophe. You will forget where and what is configured and lose track of where your traffic is going. The moment that you allow that to happen, you will also lose your security. If you cannot show where your traffic is coming from or going to, you should simply go home and start getting your resume ready.

Recommendations for documentation include the following:

- Design documents—start from the beginning.
- Textual descriptions of all interfaces, objects, and rules. Keep it short, use bullets.
- Diagrams.
- Diagrams.
- More diagrams!

VPN Modes

SecuRemote/SecureClient (SR/SC) software has also gained new functionality in FireWall-1 NG. There is a new way for the client to connect with the firewall. Traditionally, when SR/SC are installed on a system, it automatically starts every time the system starts. This method of operation now has a name, Transparent mode. As well, there is a new mode of operation, Connect mode.

Transparent Mode

In Transparent mode, SR/SC works just like the older versions. It starts when Windows starts, and will provide communications into the encryption domain once authenticated. You can view this configuration setting by opening SR/SC and choosing **Tools | Configure Client Mode**, as shown in Figure 4.21.

Figure 4.21 SR/SC Configure Client Mode

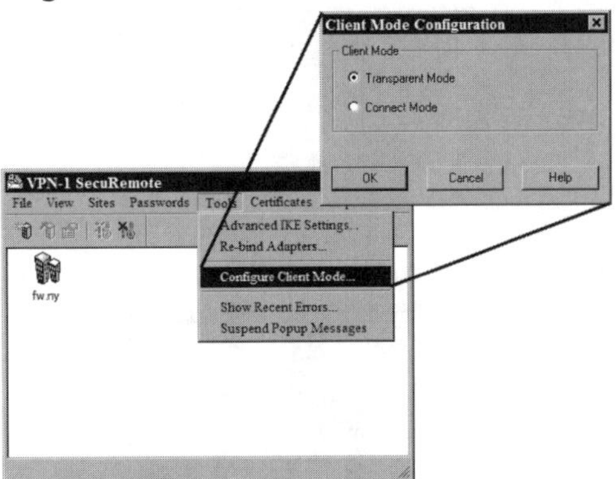

As you can see, there are two simple selections. When you have **Transparent Mode** selected, SR/SC simply works with the encryption domain, and will "transparently" determine if your traffic needs to be encrypted, based on the downloaded topology.

Connect Mode

When you select **Connect Mode**, you then have two states of SR/SC connectivity. These are Connected and Disconnected. In order to change to Connect mode, open SR/SC, choose **Tools | Configure Client Mode** (as shown in Figure 4.21), then select **Connect Mode**. When you select this option, you will receive a message that informs you that you must restart SR/SC in order for this to take effect, as shown in Figure 4.22.

Figure 4.22 Restart SecuRemote / SecureClient

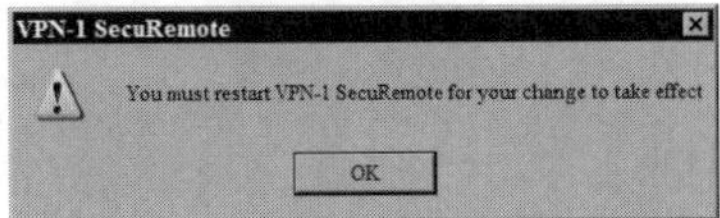

Simply choose **File | Stop VPN-1 SecuRemote**, as shown in Figure 4.23.

Locate the SR/SC shortcut and restart SR/SC. Once the icon is on your taskbar (see Figure 4.24), select it and you will be presented with the VPN-1 SecuRemote Connection window shown in Figure 4.25.

Figure 4.23 Stop VPN-1 SecuRemote

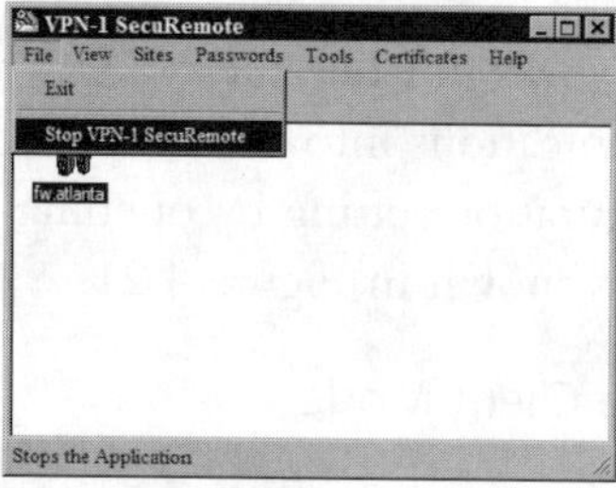

Figure 4.24 SecuRemote Taskbar Icon

Figure 4.25 VPN-1 SecuRemote Connection Window

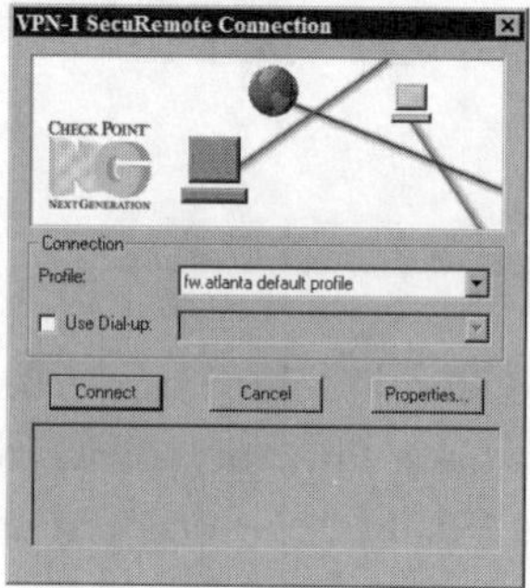

You are not connected to the VPN encryption domain until you force the software to connect to the firewall. Once you press the **Connect** button, you will receive the authentication window, shown in Figure 4.26, as you would in Transparent mode when the application starts.

Figure 4.26 VPN-1 SecuRemote Authentication

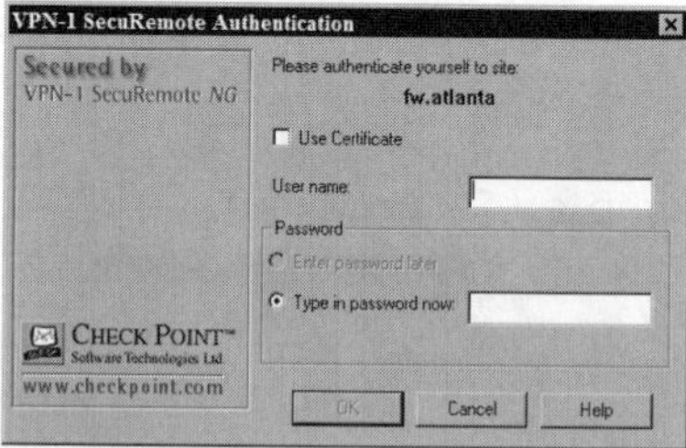

Once you have provided your certificate or username/password combination, you will be authenticated, and see the VPN-1 SecuRemote Connection window again, with a status of connectivity displayed in the lower portion of the window, as highlighted in Figure 4.27.

Figure 4.27 VPN-1 SecuRemote Connection Window

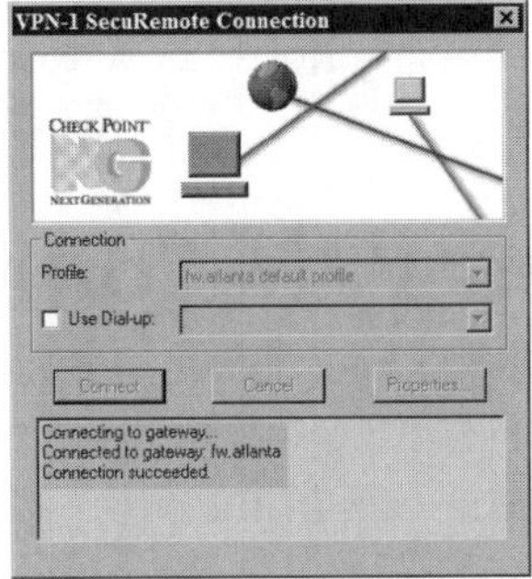

Once connected, you can select the SecuRemote icon on the taskbar to see the status of the connection. Figure 4.28 shows the initial connection page, and Figure 4.29 shows the Details tab of the connection page.

Figure 4.28 Connection Status General Tab

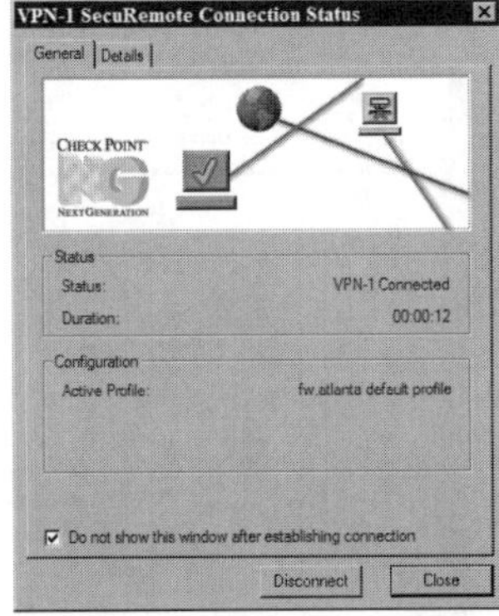

Figure 4.29 Connection Status Details Tab

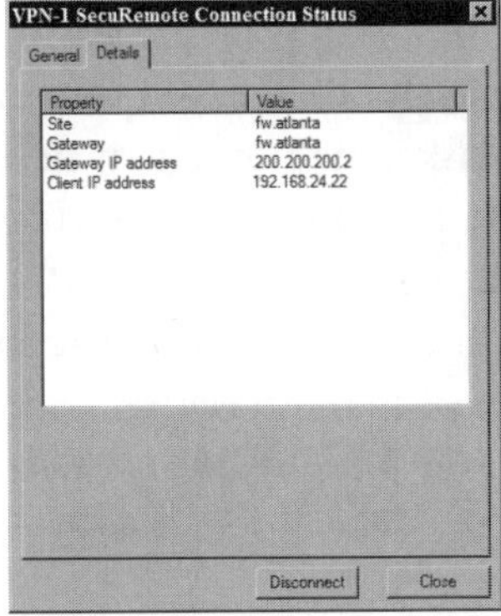

With Connect mode, you can disconnect your VPN at any time, and thereby directly control your access into your VPN connections. When a manual disconnect is selected, the username and password or certificate credentials are flushed from memory, and you must then log on again to authenticate again. With the new Connect mode or the existing Transparent mode, you can choose how to manage your connections into your network.

Routing Between VPN Connections

Check Point has introduced a new feature in NG FP3, the ability to route within VPN "domains." This will allow a managed firewall to route traffic from one firewall to another, bypassing an unavailable firewall in the process. This meshing of VPN connections allows a higher degree of fault tolerance than was available in earlier versions.

NG has a new mode of VPN configuration to go along with these new features. In the SmartDashboard there is a new tab to create these VPN configurations—VPN Manager (see Figure 4.30).

Figure 4.30 VPN Manager Tab

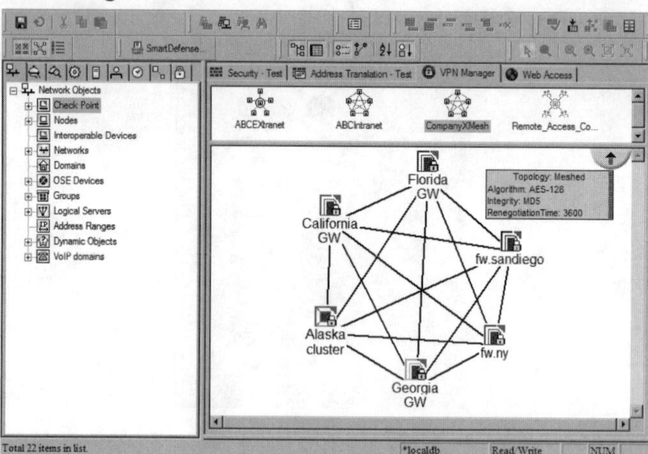

As you can see in Figure 4.30, six firewalls are participating in a VPN mesh. These firewalls can communicate with each other, and if one of the firewall connections fail, perhaps between Georgia and Alaska, the traffic that needs to flow between those sites will find the next fastest alternate path in the mesh to communicate. This feature of the VPNs in FireWall-1 NG is a very large advance in VPN deployment.

This allows organizations to utilize VPN-connected offices with multiple tunnels to remote sites, much like a traditional frame relay network with multiple PVCs (thus making the Internet the largest available WAN provider!). The California gateway could be connected via DSL, whereas the New York firewall could be connected with a T-3.

The VPN will still function properly and route traffic as necessary. This ability to use the firewall as an endpoint and starting point for your network connectivity is truly groundbreaking.

Tools & Traps...

VPN Modes

NG provides two modes of operation for configuring VPNs. There is a Traditional mode, which is very similar to the method of VPN configuration in the FireWall-1 4.*x* product, and the new Simplified VPN mode. Simplified VPN mode allows you to create meshed, star, and remote access VPNs, simply by adding objects to the VPN Manager tab. More than likely, traditional mode will be phased out some time in the future.

Dynamic IP Address VPN Connections

Dynamic VPN addresses? Can it be true? Yes. Check Point has provided a fantastic feature for its firewalls: you can now have a Check Point FireWall-1 box obtain a dynamic IP address and still participate in a VPN. It can even participate in a VPN meshed community! Figure 4.31 has six FireWall-1 gateways participating in a VPN meshed community, and two of them have dynamic IP addresses. The Toronto_GW and Florida_GW are both dynamic IP gateways, as shown in Figure 4.32 and 4.33.

Figure 4.31 Meshed VPN Community

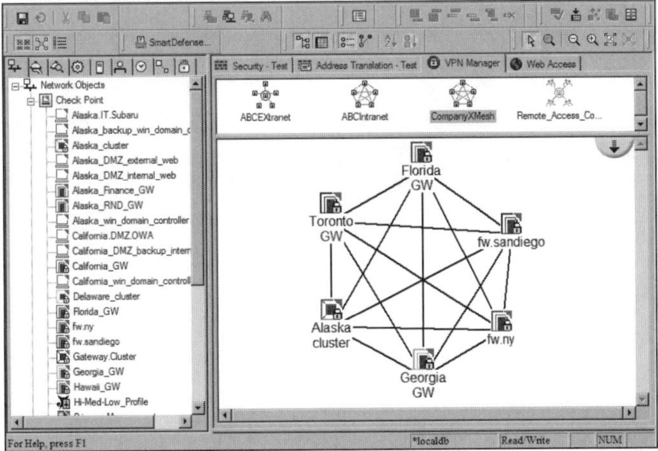

Figure 4.32 Toronto_GW General Tab

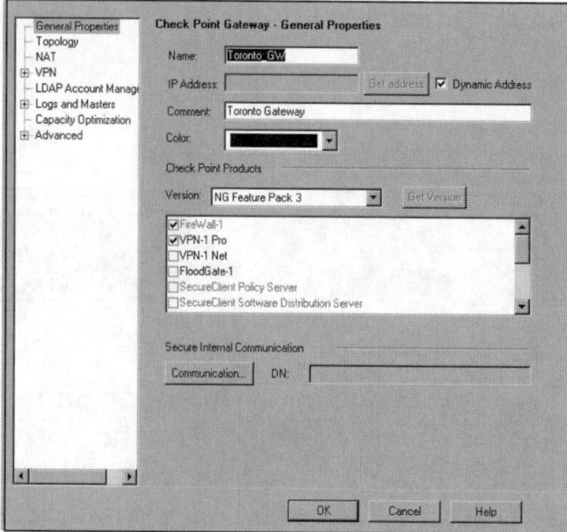

Figure 4.33 Florida_GW General Tab

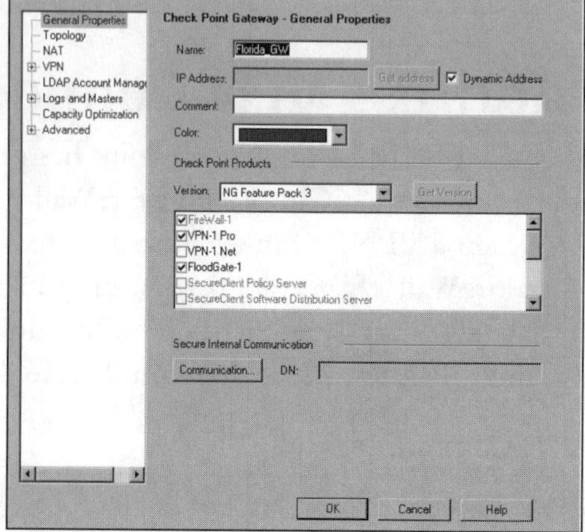

Summary

Check Point has provided many new advanced VPN functions for use in the NG product. In order to fully understand these, it is important to review the fundamental VPN modes of operation. NG now has new capabilities, which can expand the deployment options for organizations. With SEP and MEP, high availability is now a reality for most organizations and is not too expensive to deploy. SEP, using ClusterXL, is fully supported on all platforms, and it will provide a very cost-effective HA environment for a majority of organizations. Other benefits of SEP, such as the ability to perform maintenance during daylight hours, make it a very desirable solution for many organizations.

There are Check Point FireWall-1 upgrade bundles that will include copies of ClusterXL; speak to a sales representative to see what options your organization may have to upgrade and obtain this feature. Combinations of MEP and SEP can be utilized to provide an extreme HA system. The new VPN modes, Traditional and Simplified, provide a legacy method of operation while providing new features to create advanced VPN designs. With the ability to create meshed, star, and remote VPN communities, Check Point has provided a very powerful VPN platform. With the dynamic IP address features of Check Point firewalls and new VPN client connectivity modes, NG provides just about anyone, anywhere the capability to utilize a Check Point product for their secure connectivity needs.

Solutions Fast Track

What Are SEP and MEP?

☑ SEP and MEP are high availability solutions.

☑ They are non–Check Point specific.

☑ SEP is two gateways working in "tandem."

☑ MEP is physically dispersed and is primarily for remote user HA.

SEP Configuration Examples

☑ ClusterXL is the Check Point solution.

☑ It provides stateful failover of all connections and also provides high availability or Load Sharing modes.

☑ It must have a stand-alone management server.

☑ Load sharing and Floodgate-1 are currently mutually exclusive.

MEP Configuration Examples

- ☑ Provides HA across physically disparate NG firewalls.
- ☑ Offers VPN failover for client VPN connections.
- ☑ Can be used with third-party external load balancers for a very robust solution.

Combinations of MEP and SEP

- ☑ A combination of MEP and SEP provides the greatest level of availability but adds a great deal of complexity when used together.
- ☑ These combinations are recommended for environments when the firewall simply "cannot be down."

VPN Modes

- ☑ Transparent mode is identical to legacy SecuRemote/SecureClient functionality.
- ☑ Connect mode allows the end user to control when to have the VPN connected or disconnected.
- ☑ VPN modes provide alternate methods for VPN Client Deployment.

Routing Between VPN Connections

- ☑ NG FP3 has a new feature, the ability to route within VPN "domains." This will allow a managed firewall to route traffic from one firewall to another, bypassing an unavailable firewall in the process.
- ☑ This allows organizations to utilize VPN-connected offices with multiple tunnels to remote sites, much like a traditional frame relay network with multiple PVCs. This in effect makes the Internet the largest available WAN provider.

Dynamic IP Address VPN Connections

- ☑ DHCP and PPPoE dynamic gateways are now supported.
- ☑ Dynamic objects must be Check Point FireWall-1 gateways *only*.
- ☑ Dynamic IP address VPN connections are supported under SecurePlatform.

Frequently Asked Questions

The following Frequently Asked Questions, answered by the authors of this book, are designed to both measure your understanding of the concepts presented in this chapter and to assist you with real-life implementation of these concepts. To have your questions about this chapter answered by the author, browse to **www.syngress.com/solutions** and click on the **"Ask the Author"** form.

Q: Which type of high availability configuration should I use?

A: What type of network you have deployed today will determine what type of HA you should pursue. The following questions may help you:

- Do you have a single location (SEP) or multiple locations (MEP)?
- Do you wish to provide HA for all connections (SEP) or only VPN (MEP)?

Q: I have a MEP configuration, and I cannot seem to get it to work. Where do I start troubleshooting?

A: There are many things that should be reviewed, starting with the encryption domains. Ensure that they are a supported type, not partially overlapping. Check and double-check all of the routes, and if using a dynamic routing protocol, ensure that this traffic is allowed to the firewall for updates. Routing is the most critical piece of MEP configurations. It is recommended to log all traffic, including all implied rules (**Policy | -Global Properties | Log Implied Rules**). Also ensure that the NAT pool configurations are correctly configured, and review the SMARTView Tracker for the NAT traffic. If you feel that everything is configured correctly, it is time to pull out the larger tools, such as a network sniffer, on each side of the firewall, or utilize the *fw monitor* command. Also, enable router decodes to confirm that the traffic is flowing as expected within the network.

Q: I want to use a partially overlapping encryption domain, so that some of my systems are always available to all of my users. Is this something that I can configure manually?

A: No. Check Point does not support partially overlapping encryption domains. Instead, create a fully overlapping encryption domain and write separate rule bases on each firewall to provide the limitations that you desire in your environments.

Q: My VPN client users are complaining that they want to control the way they connect via VPN. What options do I have with FireWall-1 NG?

A: By enabling the client mode connection type, the end user can control when she is and is not connected to the VPN tunnel.

Q: I have a remote user who works on Web site development. The Web server is NATed to the Internet, and this user cannot gain access to the Web server when his SecuRemote is enabled. How can I correct this?

A: There are a number of methods to correct this issue. First, you may wish to modify the VPN client hosts file (%WINDIR%/system32/drivers/ect/hosts) and add the unregistered IP address of the Web server, and have DNS name resolution resolve that host locally. You also may wish to configure DNS for SecuRemote/SecureClient so that the DNS server inside your firewall responds to all DNS requests, thereby providing the internal IP address to the VPN client. Connect mode may also assist in this configuration, as when the SecuRemote is disconnected, all traffic goes out the default gateway of the VPN client system, even if it is inside the encryption domain.

Q: Does the policy on SecureClient remain in effect if the VPN user is configured for Client mode connections and is disconnected from the policy server?

A: Client mode has no effect on how a policy server and policy are handled on the SecureClient desktop. If your user has connected, and you have placed a policy on that client, when the client disconnects from the site when Connect mode is selected, the last known policy will be in effect. The only way to "disable" the policy is to Stop VPN-1 SecureClient.

Chapter 5

Advanced VPN Client Installations

Solutions in this chapter:

- The Difference Between SecuRemote and SecureClient
- Using DNSInfo Files
- Encrypting Internal Traffic
- Using SR/SC from Behind a CP-FW-1 System
- Using SecureClient
- Creating Rules for Internal Connections to Remote Clients
- Examples of Common Deployments
- L2TP Tunnels Terminating on a Check Point FP3 Box
- Office Mode SecureClient
- FP3 Clientless VPNs

☑ Summary

☑ Solutions Fast Track

☑ Frequently Asked Questions

Introduction

Check Point SecuRemote and SecureClient are excellent tools provided by Check Point for remote VPN connectivity. We reintroduce the differences between SecuRemote and SecureClient, and once we cover the differences, we discuss some of the advanced deployment options for both clients.

There are myriad options for the configuration and deployment of the NG client VPN. Some of these include using split DNS, encrypting internal traffic, and a number of other options. SecuRemote and SecureClient can also utilize AES-128 and AES-256 encryption. SmartDashboard adds new functionality with bidirectional rules to the SecureClient system, allowing applications to open connections to client VPN hosts through the existing encrypted tunnels.

Other options that NG provides also bear review, as Check Point has included the capability to terminate L2TP tunnels on the Check Point box. In addition, NG provides the capability to perform a clientless VPN. Overall, the new features in SecuRemote and SecureClient bring even tighter control, security, and flexibility to client VPN deployment.

The Difference Between SecuRemote and SecureClient

The first difference with SecuRemote and SecureClient that comes to mind is money. SecuRemote is the poor man's VPN solution, although FW1 does not come by default with a license for SecuRemote the license is free for using it. To obtain a SecuRemote license all one needs to do is log into your Check Point User Center and download a license for it. On the other hand, SecureClient will cost you to deploy. As of this writing, the prices for SecureClient range from $25 to $92 per seat of SecureClient that you deploy depending on how many licenses you buy. Leaving the money issues aside, though, one of the main differences between the two products is the inclusion/lack of a personal firewall in one versus the other. The SecureClient product has a fully functional firewall built into the product. You can actually write rules and push them to your clients to allow/disallow them from performing various IP-related activities. Some of you might say "okay, that's fine if my client is directly connected to the Internet, but my client is sitting behind an already fully functional firewall or NAT device. Why would I want to deploy another firewall directly on the client?" This question can be answered by another feature offered in SecureClient that is not an option in SecuRemote: Office Mode, which allows you to virtually establish a new network connection on the client machine and specify all the IP settings that are assigned to this adapter. This allows you to have multiple clients using the same private IP ranges within their respective networks. Imagine telling your CFO that you cannot expedite a business opportunity because new customer B has the same IP address range as existing customer A. Needless to say, investing the money in SecureClient here begins to become a non-issue.

Using DNSInfo Files

The use of DNSInfo files is necessary if you plan on allowing your remote users to do DNS lookups based on your internal DNS servers. DNSInfo files can also be used to push NetBIOS names into the local lmhosts file to help with internal name resolution. Please note however that use of DNSInfo files can be avoided by using SecureClient in Office Mode. To implement dnsinfo.C files, you will first need to create the dnsinfo.C file with the info that you want in it. Make sure that you use Wordpad if you are using built-in Windows editors and not Notepad, which will add extra formatting to the document that will cause it to not function properly. Format the dnsinfo.C file as shown in Figure 5.1.

Figure 5.1 dnsinfo.C File

dnsinfo.txt - Notepad

File Edit Format Help

```
(
	:dns_servers (
		: (Primary_DNS_Server
			:obj (
				: (192.168.1.2)
			)
			:topology (
				: (
					:ipaddr (192.168.1.0)
					:ipmask (255.255.255.0)
				)
			)
			:domain (
				: (
					:dns_label_count (5)
					:domain (.corp.com)
				)
			)
		)
)
:encrypt_dns (true)
:LMdata (
		: (
			:ipaddr (192.168.1.3)
			:name (ADDC)
			:domain (CORP)
		)
		: (
			:ipaddr (192.168.1.4)
			:name (ADDC2)
			:domain (CORP)
		)
	)
)
```

The first section of the file will allow you to specify what domains that the SecuRemote client will consider to be internal to the client and resolve via the internal DNS server. The first entry is the IP address of your internal DNS server. The second entry specifies the network and subnet mask that is considered internal to your network. The third entry "domain" specifies the URLs that the client should consider to be internal to it; for example, www.mycompany.com would be resolved internally via the client instead of via the normal DNS server by specifying that "mycompany.com" is an internally resolvable domain name. The *dns_label_count* parameter specifies how deep you want it to resolve for mydomain.com; for example, do you want to be able to just resolve www.mydomain.com, which would be three levels deep as opposed to resolving server21.Atlanta.mydomain.com, which would be a four levels deep. If using child Windows 2000 domains, keep in mind that each child domain adds another DNS label count. The *encrypt_dns (true)* parameter tells the SecuRemote client to encrypt DNS traffic to your internal DNS servers when the client is doing lookups based on the previously set up parameters.

The second section of the file is the LMdata section of the file. LMdata allows you to specify NetBIOS names and their IP address mappings. A good example would be to include the mappings for your PDC and BDC in a Windows NT network or the PDC emulator role on a Windows 2000 domain controller. Another valuable use of LMdata is to put in a mapping for your MS Exchange server. This allows you to easily configure Outlook clients on remote laptops, for example, without having to send or install an actual lmhosts file on the individual computers. One word of warning about LMdata, though, is that this is manually configured; do not forget settings that you have assigned to this file when you change a NetBIOS name or IP address mapping to a server. If you have a WINS server or Dynamic DNS, it is all to easy to change names and know that it will not affect your internal networks severely as clients are using normal name resolution services, but changing names and not keeping up with them in your LMdata files may cause you hours of grief trying to troubleshoot.

Encrypting Internal Traffic

In certain scenarios, there may be reason to encrypt traffic that crosses your internal networks. For example, your accounting department may be on the same network segment as your normal floor users, but they are accessing sensitive data on a database on a different segment and you/your company feels the need to keep this data from being sniffed on the wire while being accessed.

In order to implement this scenario, the clients will all need to have SecuRemote or SecureClient installed on them. The target servers will also need to exist on a network that has to be accessed through the firewall by the client; if you are really short on firewall interfaces, this could be performed using vlan tagging on the interface you have, or it could be done by multihoming the interface and doing one-armed routing on that interface. For an example of this configuration, see Figure 5.2.

The destination hosts should be set up as the internal encryption domain, and the users should be set up as normal SecuRemote/SecureClient users. Transparent connection mode should probably be used because this will make it more transparent for the users that are using this setup. Traffic rules should probably allow all protocols, but depending on the use that is needed, you may want to limit this down to NetBIOS traffic types and SQL or any other traffic that is required by the clients. Using a setup like this can also be made more transparent by the use of certificates that tie in with the Active Directory if you are using a Windows network. If using a setup like this extensively, be sure to look into using either accelerator cards for cryptography or possibly the use of Performance pack if you are not running on a Windows platform; for example, the SecurePlatform deployment has Performance pack included and gives even more performance gains for cryptography than using accelerator cards on Windows.

Figure 5.2 Encrypting Internal Traffic

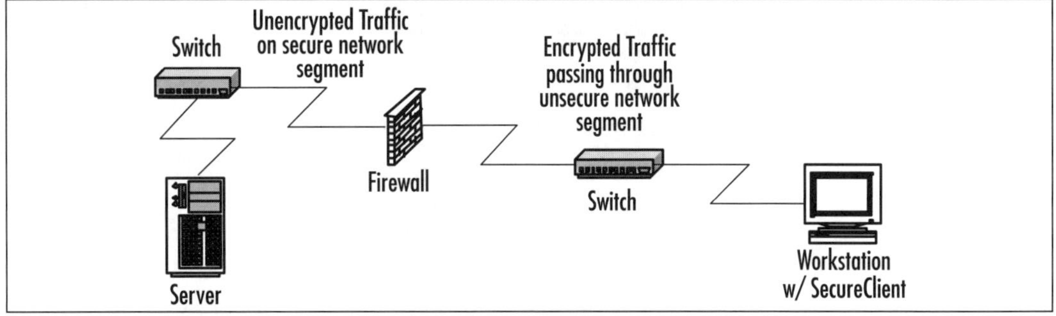

Using SR/SC from Behind a CP-FW-1 System

There are many different ways to configure SR/SC for the type of protocols that it will use for connectivity. The older more established methods include using Authentication Header (AH) or Encapsulating Security Payload (ESP). The AH method can be dismissed summarily; AH does not permit any tampering with the packets, so if your client is behind any type of hide NAT firewall, the client VPN will not work. The ESP method on the other hand is a little more forgiving and will allow your client VPN to work through a firewall. The newer and currently more widely used method is UDP encapsulation. UDP encapsulation allows the client to encapsulate the payload inside a UDP packet on a port that you specify and uses that port to send all the normal IPSec payload.

Allowing ESP mode client VPNs to work through your firewall is going to require three protocols outbound. The first protocol will be TCP port 264. This is also known as FW1-topo, and you can find this service description by clicking **Manage | Services** and looking for **FW1-topo**. See Figure 5.3 for an illustration of the protocol.

FW1-topo is used to allow the client to download site topology to create a new site as well as to update the site if any changes are made to the encryption domain on the server side. The second port that will need to be opened is for IKE, which you can see by clicking **Manage | Services** and clicking **Edit** for the IKE protocol (see Figure 5.4).

Figure 5.3 The FW1-Topo Protocol

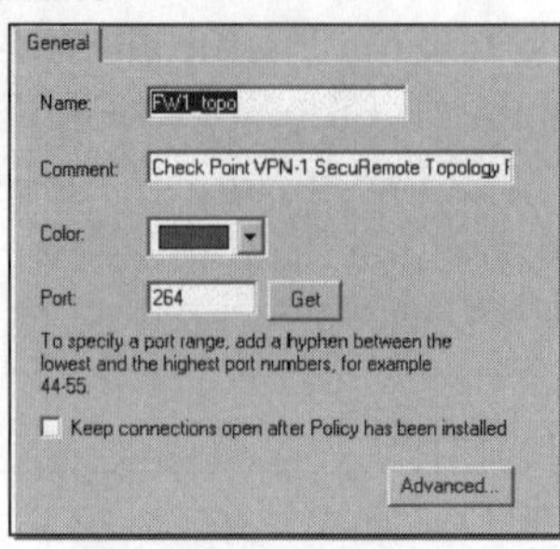

Figure 5.4 The IKE Protocol

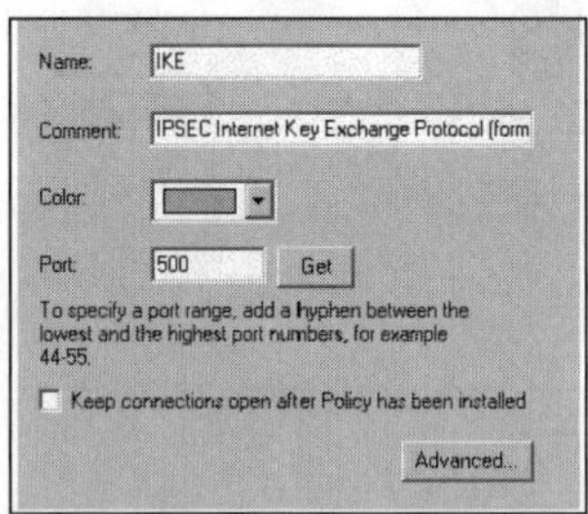

IKE is the first phase of a VPN setup; traditionally IKE has been over UDP 500, but since SP5 of FW1 4.1 there has been the option to do IKE over TCP 500. Verify which port you are using for IKE and allow that port outward bound on your firewall. If you need to lock it down to a certain destination firewall, do that as well. The third protocol used is IP protocol 50, also known as ESP (see Figure 5.5).

Figure 5.5 The ESP Protocol

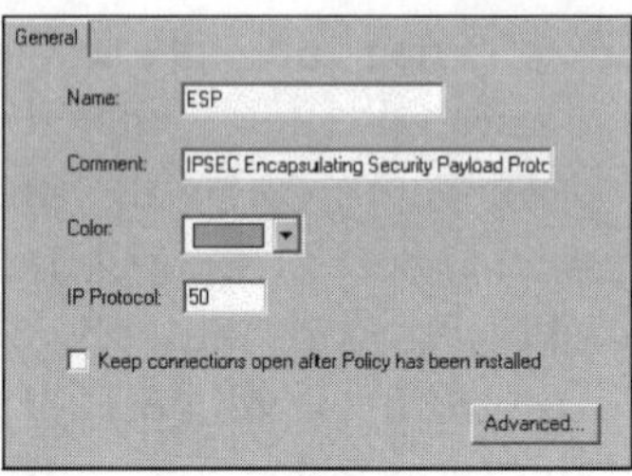

Do not mistake ESP for TCP or UDP 50. ESP is an IP protocol in a manner similar to the way that IMCP, TCP or UDP are IP protocols. That is to say that it resides below the Transport layer of the OSI model (See RFC-2401). The ESP protocol is the actual core of the connection—this is the tunnel down which your application data is flowing. Make a rule as well for outbound access for ESP. Typically, you could probably make a group of services and call it SR-SC-ESP. You can see an example rule allowing an outbound connection for a client using the ESP method without encapsulation in Figure 5.6.

Figure 5.6 Rule for Allowing Client VPN Using ESP without Encapsulation

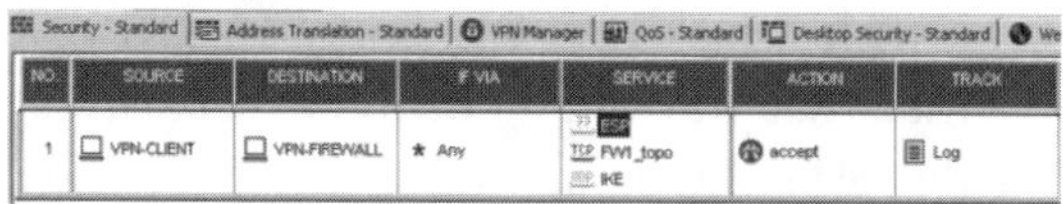

NO.	SOURCE	DESTINATION	IF VIA	SERVICE	ACTION	TRACK
1	VPN-CLIENT	VPN-FIREWALL	Any	ESP FW1_topo IKE	accept	Log

Allowing UDP encapsulated client VPNs is essentially similar to allowing ESP VPNs. You will still need to allow FW1-topo traffic out of your network to allow topology updates and installs. You will also need to allow TCP or UDP port 500 for IKE depending on the configuration of the host firewall for the VPN. The main difference, however, is that the ESP IPSec traffic that previously was in the clear is now encapsulated in a UDP packet that "normally" is on port 2746 (2746 is the default port used for UDP encapsulation on FW1; check with your host firewall manager to make sure that this is correct, though, because this is configurable). If you would like more information as to how UDP encapsulation works, refer to Daemon Welch's FAQ at http://www.phoneboy.com/fom/fom.pl?file=510.

Notes from the Underground...

New Traffic Method Coming Soon!

At the time of this writing, there is a new feature in beta testing by Check Point called *TCP tunneling*. TCP tunneling will allow the client VPNs to be totally encapsulated in a standard TCP port (443) so that it will be easier to deploy client VPNs to locations that have locked down policies on Internet access without having to have rule changes or intervention on the side of the firewall management team where the client VPN is installed. TCP tunneling should be available with the release of FP4 for Check Point NG.

Using SecureClient

In this section, we will present some various SecureClient usage scenarios. Many people seem to understand the basics of what a client VPN is utilized for, but many implementations fail to utilize the full functionality that Check Point has placed in the product.

One of the current trends in many offices today is to implement a wireless access point for being able to connect machines without having to go through the hassles of running cables all over the place. On the surface, this plan seems admirable. For example, the benefits of picking up your laptop to go to a conference room and staying connected the whole time without wires is extremely attractive. Wireless networks, however, are still in their infancy, and from a corporate security perspective are a complete nightmare. The WEP protocol for encrypting wireless networks has long been proved flawed, and even with it enabled, the traffic can be decrypted within a short amount of time if there is consistent network traffic going across the link. Normally the push for wireless comes from upper management as well. Think about it for a second—who accesses the most private documents on your network? You guessed it—upper level management; not the sort of stuff you want the script kiddie in your parking lot pulling up on his laptop by sniffing your wireless network. Until some of the newer wireless security initiatives take a better foothold and start being implemented on wireless devices, SecureClient can play a major part in securing the laptops throughout your company. One way of doing this is by segregating an interface of the firewall to be specifically for wireless traffic; call it a DMZ if you want to, but it really is just another segment. Enable some obscure IP range used on the wireless access point and laptops just make sure it is not one currently in use throughout your networks. Install SecureClient in Office Mode on all the laptops and allow them to pull DHCP from an internal DHCP server that is specifically set up for this segment. This ensures that they have IP addresses that will be recognizable throughout the rest of the corporate domain. Make sure to enable back connections to the clients. You can do this by setting the tunnel refresh rate for the clients to a low interval, and your wireless connections are secured, or at least as secured as they will get by today's standards. As of yet, there are no known cracks for AES encryption, but 10 years from now we may want to re-evaluate this. For an example of a network configuration done this way, see Figure 5.7.

Figure 5.7 Encrypting Wireless Networks

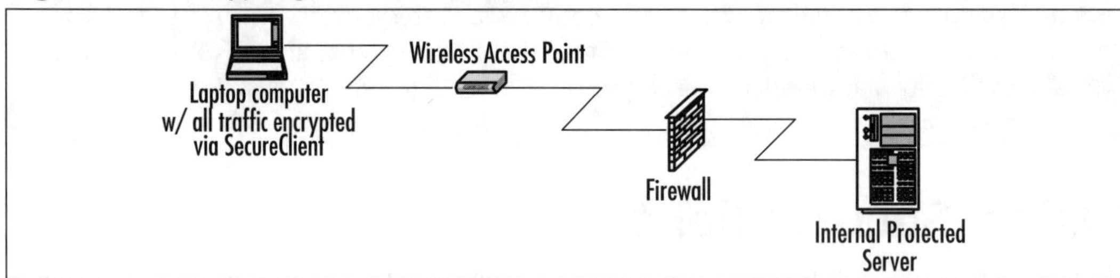

Another good scenario for using SecureClient is for setting up B2B network communications. Normally this would be used when the client wants to set up a quick temporary connection, and you are dealing with someone who is not the network engineer on the opposite side, and for whatever reason dealing with the correct individuals will take more time than is available to get the connection up and running. If the firewall on the opposing side has an any outbound rule with hide NAT for their internal clients, it is relatively simple to set up a VPN client on a machine and allow a prospective business customer to test applications with your company for a temporary period of time using a client VPN. This can make life much easier at times because many companies may have firewalls installed by outside contractors, and getting changes made, especially one as technical as setting up a FW-FW VPN, can be very time consuming.

Creating Rules for Internal Connections to Remote Clients

When using Office Mode client VPNs, you may find the want/need to initiate connections to the VPN clients with the connection originating from an internal network. Creating this sort of connection is fairly straightforward in NG. In Smart-Dashboard, you will notice a tab called Desktop Security in the rule base window. This tab allows you to specify rules for your various SecuRemote/SecureClient connections (see the example in Figure 5.8).

Figure 5.8 Picture of Desktop Security Tab / Rule Base

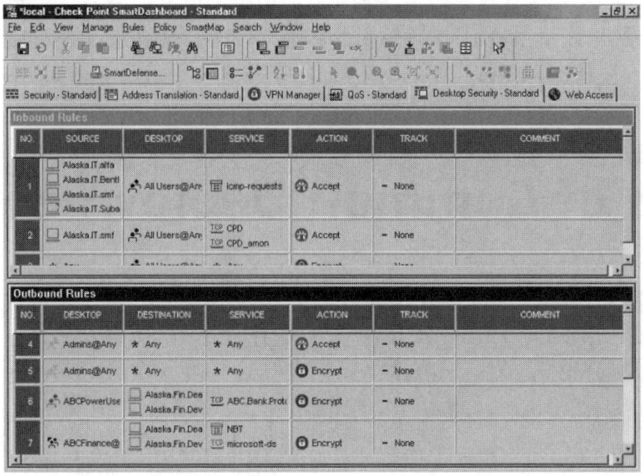

One common use of an internally initiated connection would be to facilitate connections from Exchange Instant Messaging servers to the clients because this service requires server initiated connections from time to time. Another setting that should also be enabled when trying to facilitate connections to clients is the **Enable tunnel refresh** setting. You can find it by going to **Policy | Global Properties** and highlighting the **Remote Access** setting (see Figure 5.9).

Figure 5.9 Remote Access on Global Policy Properties

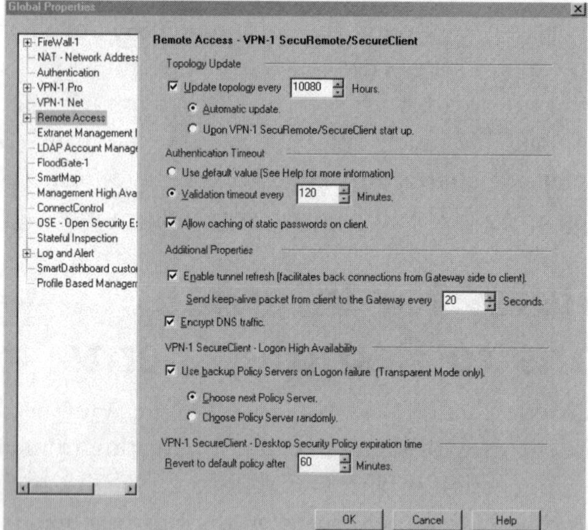

The default setting of 20 seconds should be fine for most cases, although you may want to lower it if you are having issues with not being able to connect to clients. Enabling this setting causes the VPN client to ping the gateway every *x* number of seconds, (in this case 20). Pinging the gateway every 20 seconds causes the session key information between the gateway and the VPN client to be kept current, which will allow connections back to the client at any time.

Examples of Common Deployments

When deploying SecuRemote or SecureClient to your remote workers it is normal to try to establish a base install that you use with all your users. The base install of the client from Check Point is sufficient for simple IP connectivity with a network administrator who knows what he/she needs to do. However, for the normal end user it will usually require some time on phone with your local help desk, which is a cost that can be easily defrayed by taking some time and preconfiguring the client install before deploying it to your end users. Since the release of NG, Check Point has included the SecureClient Packaging Tool (see Figure 5.10), which makes it much easier to configure the base install of the client. The following is a quick walk-through tutorial of what the settings are in the SecureClient Packaging Tool. This utility is described in detail in Chapter 10.

Figure 5.10 SecureClient Packaging Tool

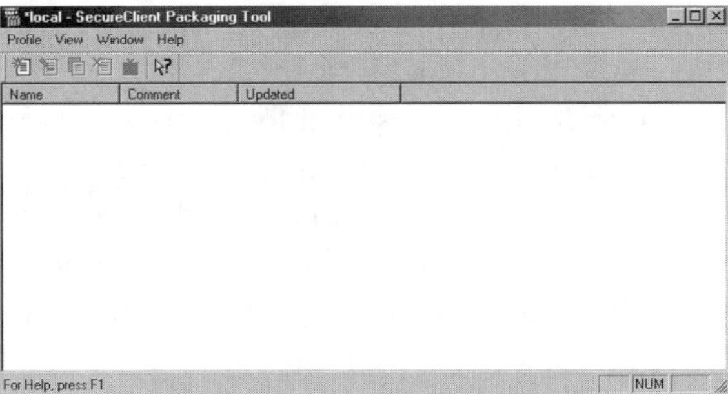

Start off by selecting **Profile | New**. Enter a **Profile name** and a description, as shown in Figure 5.11, and click **Next**.

Figure 5.11 Selecting a Profile Name and Description

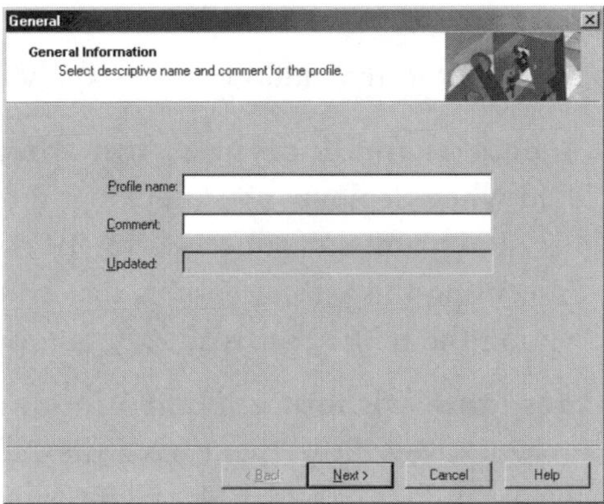

The next screen (Figure 5.12) deals with which type of connection mode that the client runs in.

Figure 5.12 Choosing a Connection Mode

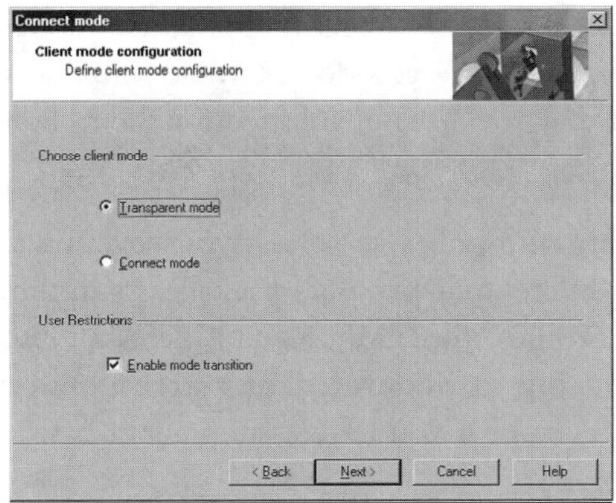

If you are used to previous versions of SecureClient/SecuRemote, the one that you are most familiar with is the Transparent mode. In Transparent mode, the client is constantly running, and the encryption tunnel is normally open once a first connection has been made. The client recognizes traffic destined for internal networks and automatically encrypts and delivers the traffic to the tunnel. The other option new in NG is the option for Connect mode. Connect mode still has the client running in the system tray, but the client is not always connected, nor will it send any traffic to an encryption tunnel until the user actually decides to tell the client to connect the tunnel manually. Although this may seem like extra difficulty, it does have its uses. For example, if you want to firewall your users' PCs while they are connecting to internal networks, the Connect mode ensures that someone is not remotely controlling a user's PC while she is connected to you. But at the same time, you can allow your user the flexibility to do what she wants/needs to do when she is not connecting to internal networks. The second option on this screen allows you to control whether or not the end user can control which connect mode he uses.

The next screen (Figure 5.13) mostly addresses issues applying to SecureClient:

- **Allow clear connections for Encrypt action when inside the encryption domain** Used when deploying SecureClient internally on your LANs/WANs. This allows authenticating uses for IP connectivity purposes, but at the same time, using this setting ensures that you don't add the extra overhead of encrypting the traffic that is already on your local networks.
- **Accept DHCP response without explicit inbound rule** Allows clients to still be DHCP clients even if the client has a firewall rule sets applied to it. Without this enabled, the PC on which the client is installed would not be able to be a DHCP client. This can be conversely done by implementing a desktop security rule which allows DHCP traffic to be accepted by the clients.
- **Restrict SecureClient user intervention** Removes the ability for your end users to disable the policy that is applied to the SecureClient. Normally from a security perspective you do not want your users disabling the firewalling rule set that you have established for their clients so this is a good setting to check.

The next section deals with policy servers. If you have multiple policy servers installed, you can create different client install packages with different policy servers defined as the default, or you can install the default here but also check the **Enable Policy Server Load sharing at SecureClient startup** option, which will reduce the load on the default policy server if you have a large client base.

Figure 5.13 Defining Policy Options

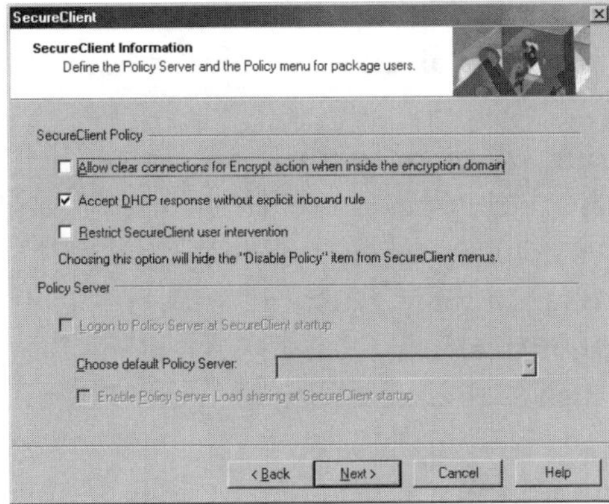

The next screen (Figure 5.14) provides additional options that apply to both SecuRemote and SecureClient.

Figure 5.14 Additional Options

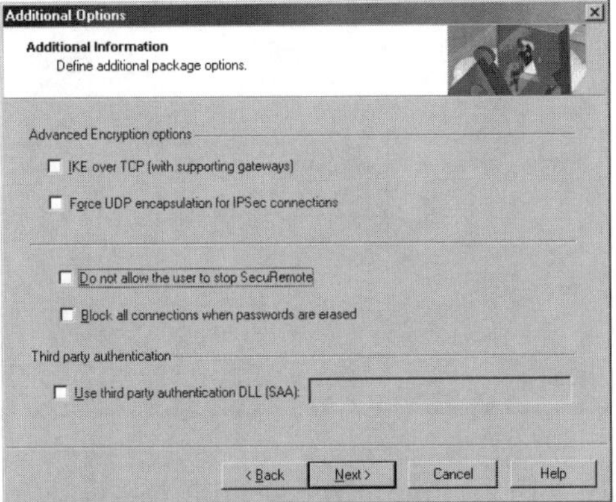

The first option is **IKE over TCP**. Normally IKE traffic travels over UDP port 500. However, not all NAT gateways and routers handle IKE over UDP well, and sometimes it can be fragmented and packets drop. Using IKE over TCP basically ensures that you will have more compatibility over a wider range of devices and is a good option to select and use.

Then next option is for forcing the use of UDP encapsulation on your client VPN tunnels. By default, you will want to check this. If you do not use UDP encapsulation, your clients will have all sorts of issues running from behind firewalls and other NAT devices. UDP encapsulation takes the usual IP protocol 50 IPSec traffic and encapsulates it in UDP packets on UDP port 2748. This will normally work through any SOHO NAT device or firewall that allows outbound UDP. If your connection does not work, see the "Using SR/SC from Behind a CP-FW-1 System" section.

The option **Do not allow the user to stop SecuRemote** basically means what it says. This is normally used on company-issued laptops to ensure complete control. Setting this on an install that is on an end user–owned home PC, however, is not such a good idea.

Block all connections when passwords are erased will immediately stop current connections from transmitting any more data when the end user clears passwords. This prevents another user from physically walking up to a PC and using an existing connection that they have not authenticated to.

Use third party authentication DLL (SAA) allows the use of third-party authentication methods, such as the use of smart cards, USB tokens, or some type of biometric reader.

The next screen (Figure 5.15) will bring up options dealing with topology and the SecuRemote/SecureClient client.

Figure 5.15 Topology Options

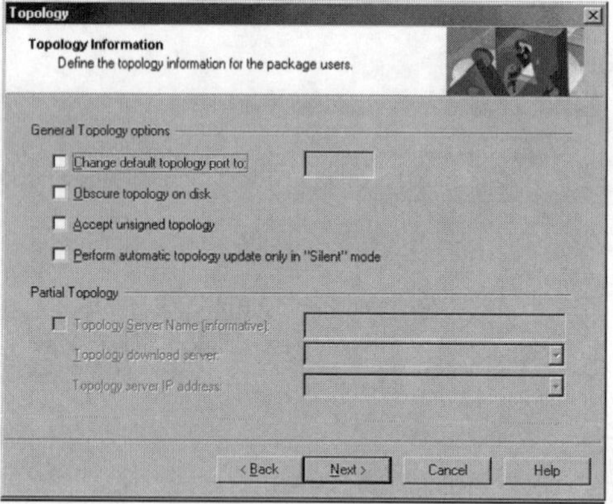

The first option deals with changing the default topology port. By default this is TCP 264. For security reasons, you may wish to change this on your firewall because known default ports always leave the possibility that some vulnerability will be discovered to easily utilize that port/service. Even though changing the port may not make the service less vulnerable, it will cut down the amount of scans that will automatically determine that you have a Firewall-1 firewall at this address because of the simple fact that it is responding on that port.

Obscure topology on disk will ensure that the topology file is not left in clear text format on the hard drive of the client. Previously, this file has always been clear text, which provides an easy method for an attacker to begin to determine internal targets if they gain access to this file. Obscuring the file encrypts it to a format that is readable only by the SecuRemote/SecureClient client.

The next setting is to allow the client to accept unsigned topologies. Normally you will not want to use this setting because it opens up a means that an unsecure topology could be installed on a client and force an end user into connecting to an unknown location for data requests. Topology should be either be installed with the initial install provided by the company or should be downloaded directly from the enforcement points with authentication provided by the company.

Perform automatic topology update only in "Silent" mode will allow you to push a topology update each time the user exchanges keys with the firewall. The process happens in the background and will not affect the user. This is normally a good option to select, especially if your internal networks are changing on a regular basis. For example, you have just added a new branch office with a new network range and although you have done your due diligence in adding the network object to the firewall and the encryption domain on the firewall, you neglected to inform the VPN client users that they needed to update their topology. With this setting in place, it will automatically update for them, which cuts down held desk support calls and the time involved with troubleshooting why they cannot connect to said network.

The next section on this page deals with partial topology. First, a little background information. There are three methods for deploying topology to the clients. The first would be a full topology deployment, but this poses a security risk if you are placing the client fully configured on an external http or FTP server for your clients to download. The second method would be not to deploy the client with any topology in it. However, this creates more deployment work because you'll have to provide good documentation to users and hope that they will understand how to establish and download the topology, or technical support personnel will have to spend a lot of time with the end users walking them through downloading topology. The third method is what this option details, the partial topology deployment.

Partial Topology allows defining the topology server to the client and its IP address and nothing else. This creates a minimum site setup within the client so that the site is set up, but the user will have to update it once to download the full topology. Although this does place the IP address of the topology server in the configuration of the client, it is less of a risk then placing your full internal topology on the client if you are placing the deployment files on an external Web or FTP server. Conversely a full topology could be deployed as well by using an obscured topology, but if the files are being deployed via Web or FTP services, it still places the full internal topology in an easily accessible file, which an attacker then could crack at their convenience.

The next page (Figure 5.16) deals with the use of certificates.

If you're using certificates for your users, go through and define these options. Input the **CA IP address** and **Port** as well as inputting the **LDAP server IP address** and **Port** that it uses. The third option enables the use of the Entrust Entelligence toolkit if it is installed (some deployments remove the entrust portion because doing so reduces the size of the install package).

Figure 5.16 Certificate Options

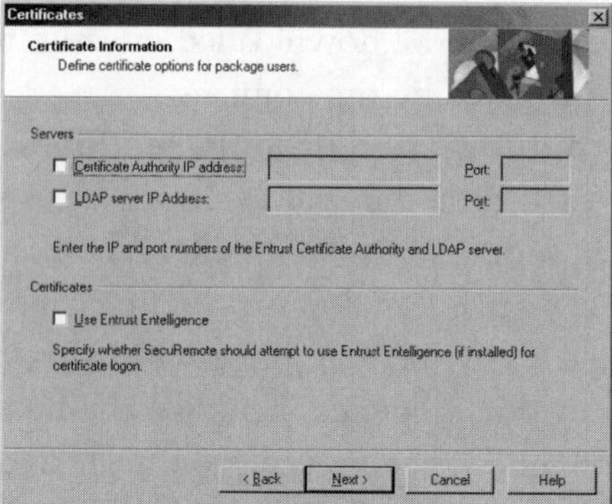

The next screen (Figure 5.17) deals with the options for the actual installation of the client itself. There are two options from which to select: **Don't prompt users during installation** or **Choose prompts that will be shown to users**. Normally when deploying to a large base, the best option is to use the **Choose prompts** method and only show the user the option to reboot at the end of the install. Allowing the user to see the rest of the prompts usually creates support calls for issues that the administrator should already have set in the install options.

Figure 5.17 Silent Installation Options

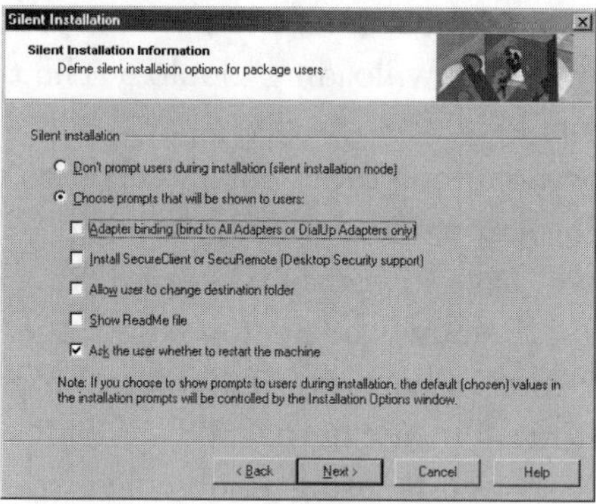

The next screen (Figure 5.18) deals with what the options will be as defaults when the client is installing.

The first section of the screen allows for specifying the use of either the default or a different folder for the actual install location of the files for the client.

The **Adapters installation** option allows selecting whether to install on all adapters or on dial-up adapters only. Typically this will be to install on all adapters so that end user will be able to use the connection over any type of fast access connection or dial-up while they are remote from the office.

Figure 5.18 Installation Options

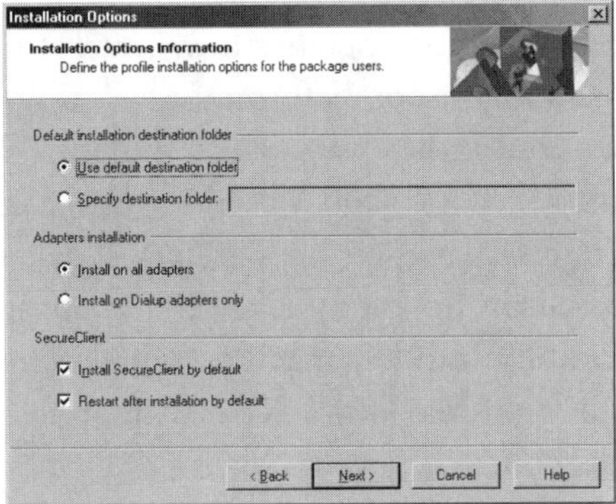

The next section specifies whether the client is going to be SecureClient or SecuRemote. Make sure this is specified. This should also be placed in the comment for this package build. I have seen many hours of troubleshooting that were finally resolved quickly once it was determined that the user was not using the proper client.

Restart after installation by default specifies that the machine should reboot once finished installing. If you have this selected and do not present the user the reboot prompt, they might be quite surprised and upset when suddenly their machine reboots with all their work still open after installing the client, which could lead to some upset calls coming to the local firewall administrator.

The next page of options (Figure 5.19) deals with operating system logon settings. This feature allows the client to log on to the internal NT network via the SecuRemote or SecureClient connection.

Figure 5.19 Operating System Logon Options

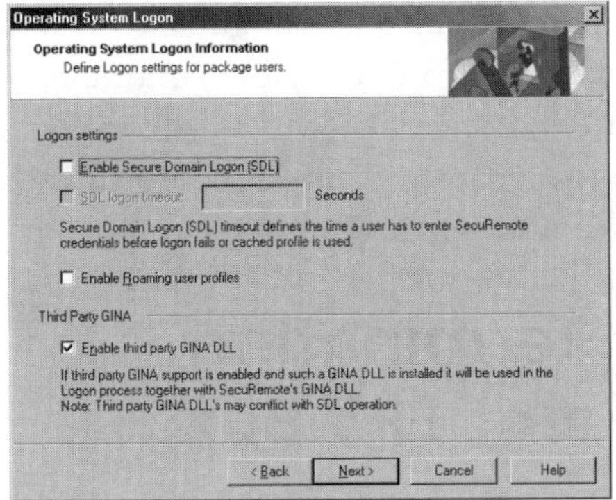

Enable Secure Domain Logon (SDL) allows a Windows client to log on securely to the internal network. Enabling this setting changes the client to start before the logon process so that the machine logon traffic can be encrypted to the domain controllers to allow proper logon to the NT domain.

The **SDL logon timeout** feature specifies how much time the user has to input his password on the Windows logon box before the session will expire and not allow him to log on to the domain but rather use cached credentials for locally logging on. For example, if this is set to 60 seconds and a user boots her laptop and walks away and returns to the laptop five minutes later, chances are good that she is not going to be logging into the domain based on how long it takes her laptop to boot but rather that she is going to be logging locally into her machine with cached credentials.

Enable Roaming user profiles allows SecureClient/SecuRemote to keep a connection open to the domain controller even after it has been closed down to allow the operating system to write any final changes to the profile while it is logging off of the network. Without this setting enabled, do not consider using roaming profiles because they will constantly have issues as the operating system will hang trying to write the profile on system shutdown.

The second section on this page deals with third-party GINAs. Typically you will not use this, but there are certain scenarios where it is useful. The gina.dll file on a Windows machine is responsible for the initial authentication to either the local machine or the network. Normally you will always use the Microsoft GINA, but there are times you might not. For example, I know of a company where they want to have a branded login prompt with company logo, graphics, and so on. Making this happen requires the use of a third-party GINA, which you can modify to do such things. Unless you specifically know you are using third-party GINAs, I would not recommend setting this setting.

The last screen (Figure 5.20) of the package creation presents the option to only create the profile or to actually build an install package. If you select to build the package, you will need to have obtained a configurable SecuRemote/SecureClient package from Check Point's download site before continuing.

Specify where the source package is as well as where you want the compiled package, and the program will generate a single file install package preset with all of the install options that you have just specified.

L2TP Tunnels Terminating on a Check Point FP3 Box

Although Check Point allows terminating client VPNs using L2TP as the encryption protocol, I personally would not recommend this approach to the user. The install is fairly complex, and there are still issues with the connectivity, the main one being that it will not work behind NAT devices. For example, all your home users behind their home firewalls will not be able to utilize this nor will any client connecting from behind a corporate firewall unless they specifically have a static one-to-one NAT established. With that being said, here is how you configure a L2TP client VPN terminating on a Check Point box.

Figure 5.20 Operating System Logon Options

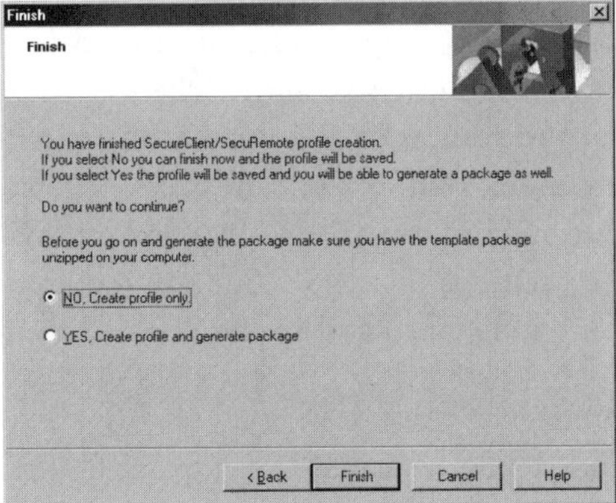

Begin by opening the **Remote Access** section on the properties of your enforcement point (see Figure 5.21).

Figure 5.21 Remote Access Section of an Enforcement Point

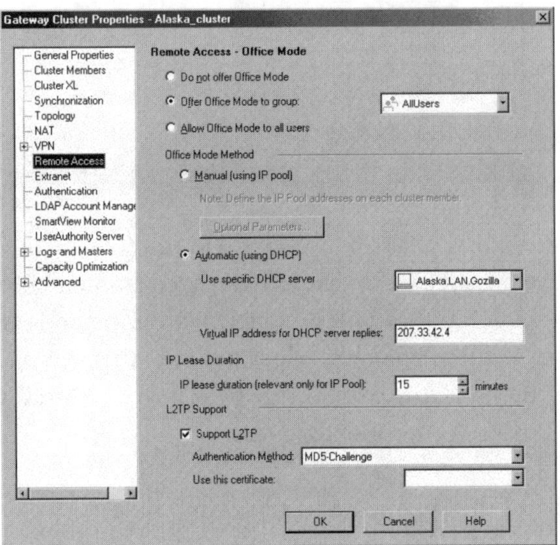

If you already have client VPNs configured for using Office Mode (OM), leave the OM section as it is, otherwise make sure to offer OM to a group of users that you will be using for L2TP connections. Make sure to define how you will be assigning IP addresses to the clients, whether it will be manual or through the use of an internal DHCP server. The next setting will be for you to enable the LT2P support, make sure to check the **Support L2TP** checkbox and select **MD5-Challenge** for the authentication method. Certificates can be used for authentication as well, but since you will already have to use certificates for the workstations assigning certificates for logons as well is kind of overkill, as well as adding significant time to your deployment. The next step requires that you deploy certificates to all the clients that you will be using; note that the certificates are for the computer account not the user account in Windows when you get to installing them. Before you can issue certificates from your Check Point CA, you will need to modify the $FWDIR\conf\internalca.c file in order to allow the CA to issue extra settings that MS Windows requires in certificates that it utilizes. The settings that you will need to add to the internalca.c file are the following:

- :ike_cert_extended_key_usage (1)
- :user_cert_extended_key_usage (2)

See an example of the file with the lines added in Figure 5.22.

Figure 5.22 InternalCA.C File

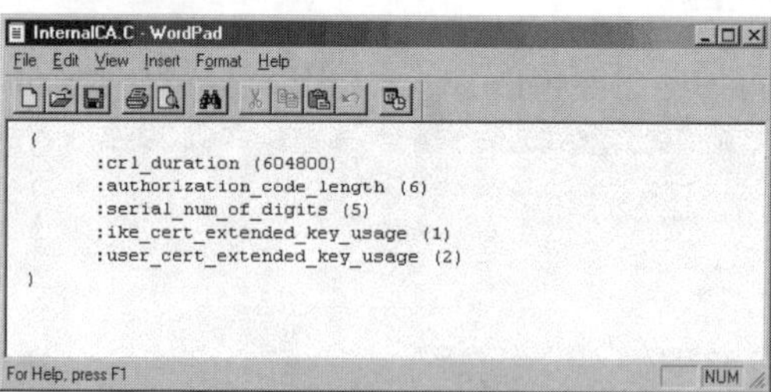

Make sure to have your CA stopped when you implement the changes and to restart it once you have finished. After these have been implemented, you can issue certificates to the client machines that will be participating in the L2TP VPNs.

Once you have made these changes, select the user that you wish to set up and assign a certificate to the user. You can do this by going to **Manage | Users and Administrators** and going to the **Certificates** tab on the user you are configuring (see Figure 5.23).

Once you have saved the certificate to file, you will need to install this certificate on the client VPN host. For Windows 2000/XP/2003 server machines, open the **Certificates MMC** snap-in. Do this by clicking **Start | Run** and enter **MMC** and click **OK**. Once you have the MMC console open, Click **Console | Add/Remove Snap-in** (see Figure 5.24).

Figure 5.23 Certificate Generation for Client VPN User

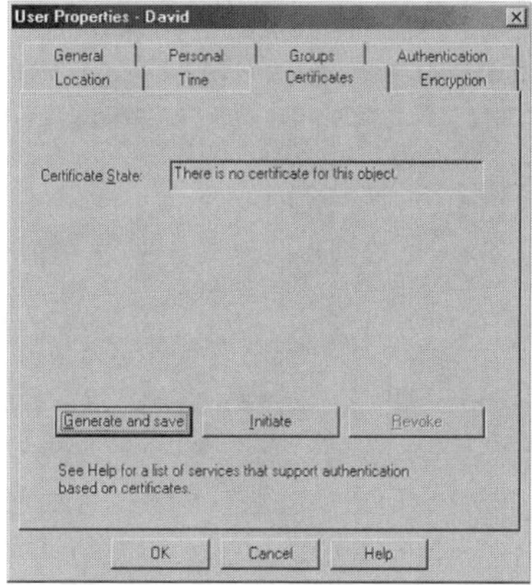

Figure 5.24 Adding MMC Certificate Manager Snap-In

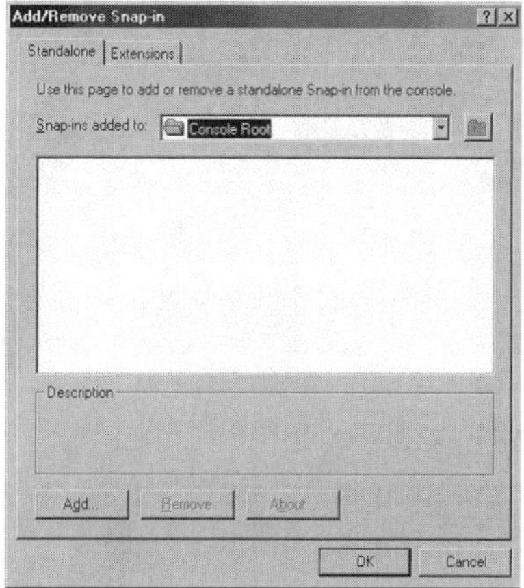

Click **Add...** once again and you will receive another window that will allow you to select which snap-in you would like to utilize. Select the **Certificates** snap-in and click **Add....** Select **Computer account** on the next screen (see Figure 5.25) and click **Next**.

On the next screen, select the **Local Computer** radio button and click **Finish** (see Figure 5.26). Click **Close** and **OK** to close the remaining two windows to get to the Certificate manager snap-in.

You should technically be able to do this by clicking **Start | Run** and entering **certmgr.msc**, but there is a bug in Windows 2000 that prevents this from running correctly (see MS Q228819 for more information). Once you have the Certificates Snap-in opened for managing your local computer, expand the tree in the left pane and right-click on the **Personal** folder and select **All Tasks** and click **Import**. Follow the walk-through and select the certificate file that you have generated from the firewall. Input the **Password** for the certificate and select the box to **Mark the private key as exportable** (see Figure 5.27).

Figure 5.25 Selecting Computer Account

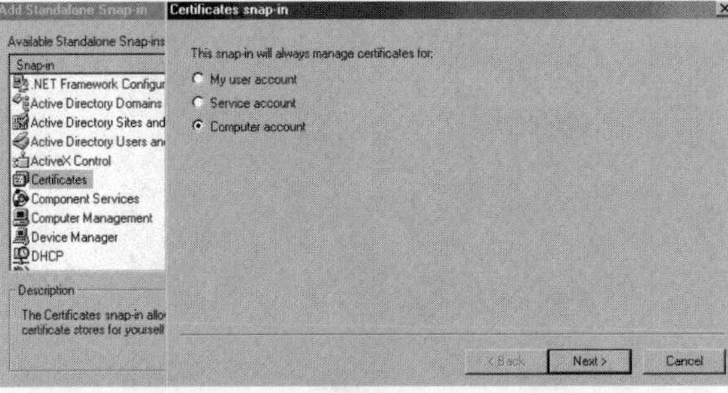

Figure 5.26 Configuring Certificate Manager Snap-In for Local Computer

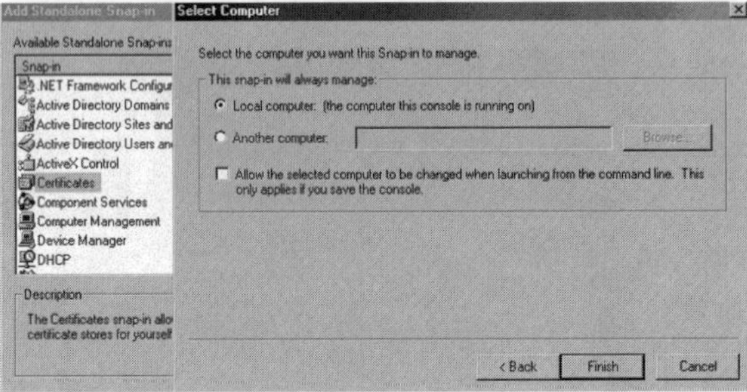

Figure 5.27 Importing Certificate

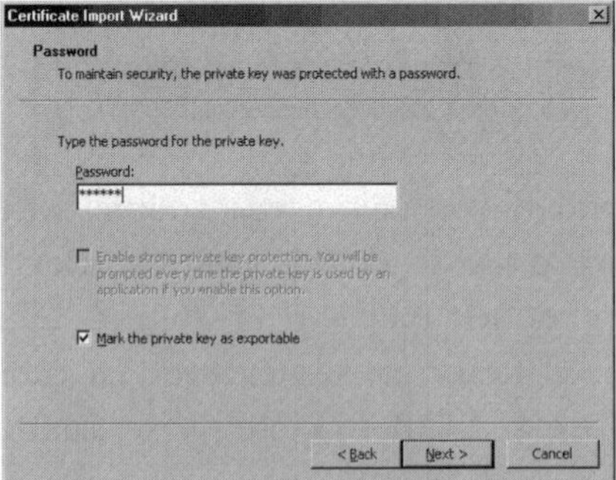

On the next screen, when prompted for which certificate store that the certificate should be placed in, select **Automatically select the certificate store based on the type of certificate** and click **Next** (see Figure 5.28).

Figure 5.28 Importing Certificate

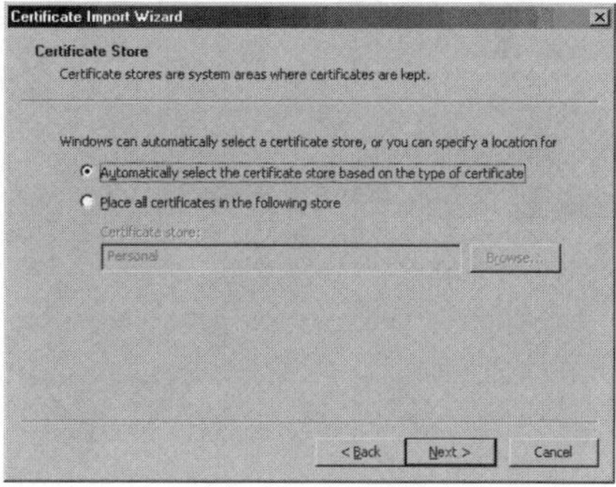

The next step in the process is creating the connection properties on the VPN client. Click **Start | Settings | Network and Dialup Connections**. Click on **Make New Connection** (see Figure 5.29).

Figure 5.29 Creating Client VPN

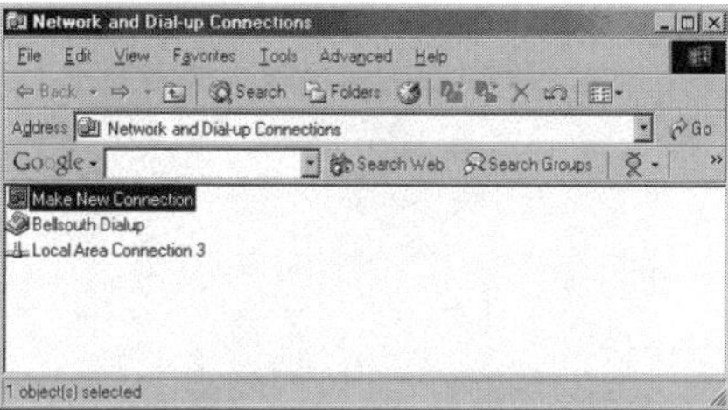

Click **Next** on the first screen then choose **Connect to a private network through the Internet** and click **Next** (see Figure 5.30).

Figure 5.30 Creating Client VPN

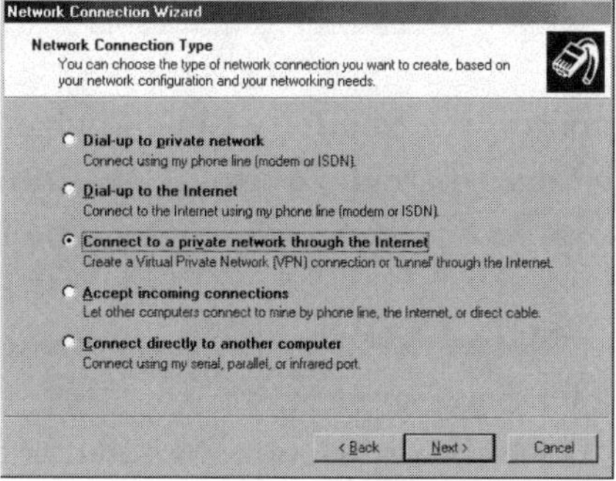

Input the IP address for the enforcement point that the user will be connecting to and click **Next** (see Figure 5.31). On the next screen, select whether or not the connection will be available to all users and then assign a name to the VPN connection.

Figure 5.31 Input Enforcement Point Address

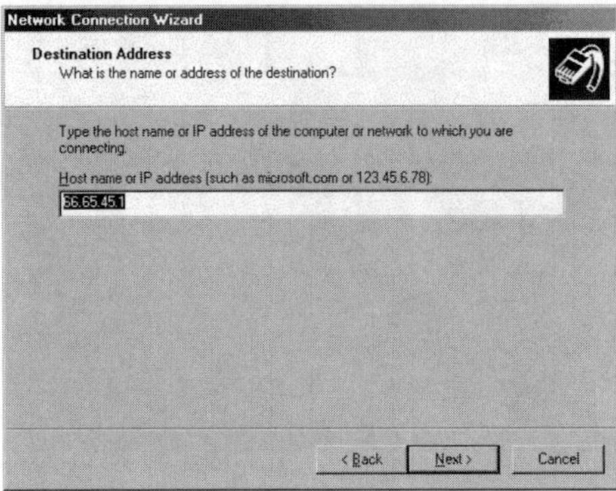

After you have created the connection, go back to the **Network and Dial-up Connections** window and right-click on the connection that you have just created and click **Properties**. Go to the **Security** tab and select **Advanced** (see Figure 5.32).

Figure 5.32 Creating Client VPN

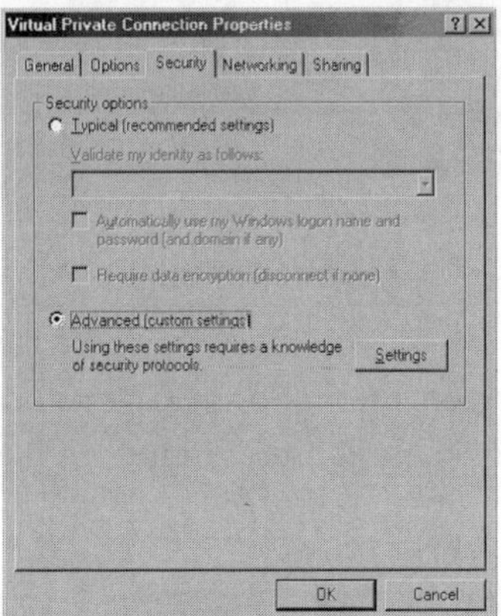

Click the **Settings** button on the **Security** tab and change the drop-down to **No encryption allowed**. Then select the radio button **Use Extensible Authentication Protocol (EAP)**. In the drop-down, change the logon type to **MD5-Challenge** (see Figure 5.33).

Click **OK** and select the **Networking** tab. Change the drop-down to be **Layer-2 Tunneling Protocol (L2TP)**. See Figure 5.34.

Click **OK** and attempt to use the connection. As stated at the beginning of this section, it is handy that this compatibility feature is included, but this is not meant for very widespread deployment because the manual intervention required at the client host is too intensive to make it worthwhile in an enterprise client VPN deployment scenario.

Figure 5.33 Client Advanced Security Settings

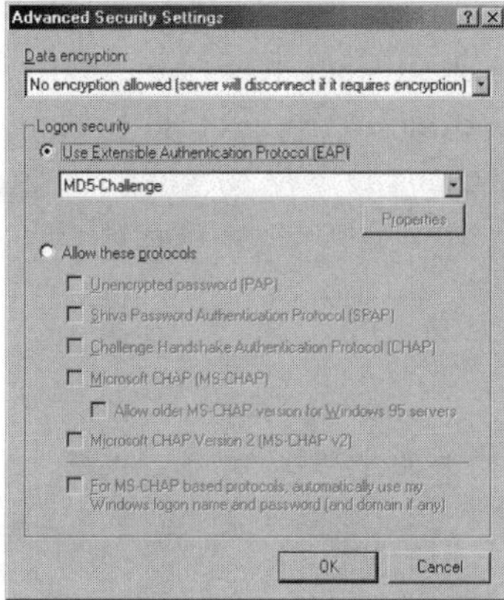

Figure 5.34 Networking Settings

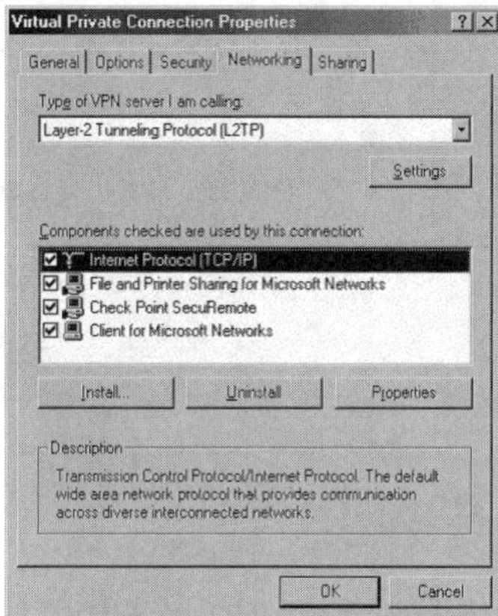

Office Mode SecureClient

Office Mode (OM) is solely a function of Secure Client (once again another reason to use SC over SR). The purpose of OM is to allow your client to have a virtual adaptor that you can provide IP settings to. Previously the only methods to allow your VPN clients to do internal name resolution was to use dnsinfo.c files, push lmhosts entries, or possibly to manually set the WINS server settings on the client. The dnsinfo.c method is not bad for internal DNS resolution, but pushing lmhosts entries or manually defining WINS entries can be a nightmare. OM lets you overcome some of these previous limitations by allowing you to pretty much treat your VPN clients just like a DHCP client. With OM you can specify all the settings that the virtual adapter will receive including DNS entries WINS entries and DNS suffix name.

One other issue that OM mitigates is the possibility that two of your VPN clients have the same IP address. With the multitude of home cable/DSL routers that generally tend to use 192.168.1.0/24 for their default subnet, many home users tend to have the same IP address of 192.168.1.2 or something close to that. By using OM, you can assure that each virtual adapter that the FW sees will be a totally different IP address range. This can also be very useful for business connections where multiple clients may use the same range.

Notes from the Underground…

Lockdown IPs Used by Clients Even While Using DHCP

A white paper on Check Point's support site details how in FP4 you will be able to lock down SR/SC clients to a certain assigned IP address. This is done by generating a pseudo-MAC address by using a command-line tool within the management station, which you can then use on your DHCP server to create reservations for that MAC address allowing you to specify a host for the user's workstation. This will allow IP allocation to be a little easier if using client VPNs for customer connectivity in that you will be able to quickly determine what customer is accessing various systems based on the IP address connecting to them.

FP3 Clientless VPNs

As of FP3, Check Point is promoting what they term as *clientless VPNs* as part of FW1. The idea behind clientless VPNs is that you are able to access some resource via a secure connection that is already built into the client machine. The secure connection in this scenario builds on the fact that most clients can take advantage of SSL sessions for HTTP and in the future for other TCP protocols such as POP3 and SMTP. In essence, Check Point is enabling FW1 to be a termination point for SSL tunnels. In conjunction with being the SSL termination point, it is also providing features that normal SSL accelerators do not, such as the ability to use the built-in authentication integration features of Check Point. One of the more common uses for clientless VPNs is setting them up to make intranet Web pages available externally via an SSL interface with combined authentication against your integrated authentication methods.

In order to configure a clientless VPN resource, you will need to perform the following steps. First you will need to open the properties of the enforcement point that will be doing the SSL termination and check the **VPN | VPN Advanced** properties (see Figure 5.35).

Figure 5.35 VPN Advanced Properties

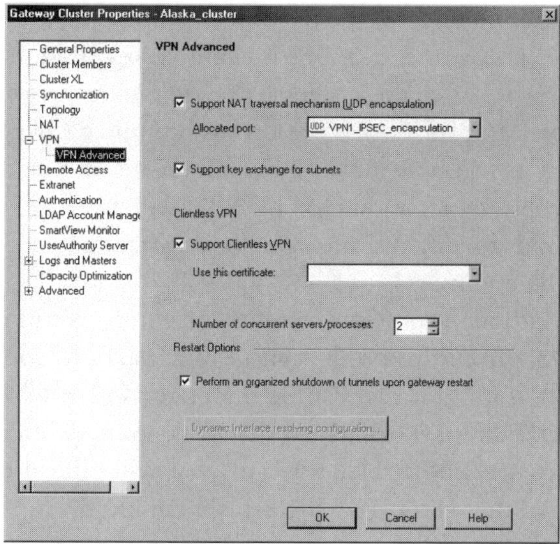

Check the **Support Clientless VPN** option and then use the drop-down to select the certificate that will be associated with the site for which the clientless VPN is being set up. The certificate can be one assigned from either the internal CA or any standard PKCS#12 certificate (such as a Web site certificate). Preferably the name should match up with the site; for example, www.yourcompany.com should be on the certificate if that is the site to which it is connecting so that no errors will appear on the client machines. Also on this screen is an option to select the amount of concurrent servers/processes to use for the clientless VPN. If you have an SMP server, you should take advantage of this by changing this to **2** or more depending on how many clients will be connecting to the resource (each process can support 500 simultaneous connections, and the processes will run on separate CPUs when using a SMP server). After changing these settings, click **Manage | Services** and edit the HTTP service. Click **Advanced** and make sure that the **Protocol Type** is set to **HTTP** (see Figure 5.36).

Figure 5.36 Advanced HTTP Protocol Properties

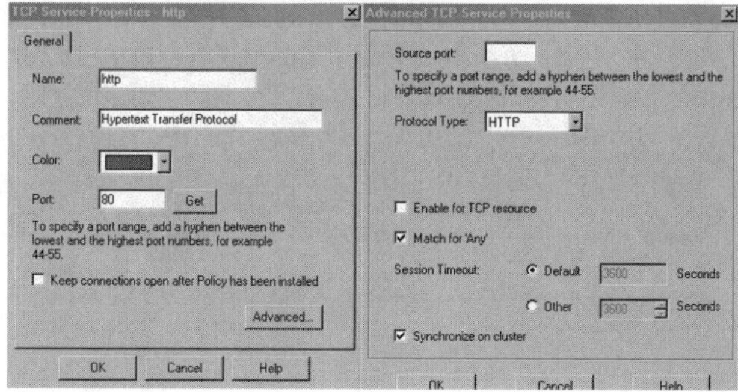

Once these changes have been implemented, the final step is to create a rule for an http destination. The rule should consist of source, destination, a service type of **HTTP**, and an action of either user authentication or client authentication with the sign-on method set to **Automatic**. After these steps have been taken, test connecting to the Web site with a browser and verify that the user is prompted for a username and password. The authentication will be handled by whatever means you have set up in your environment; for example, tacacs, radius, or LDAP integration are some of the more commonly used methods to authenticate against corporate networks to provide a single sign-on method for the end users.

Clientless VPN—although somewhat useful currently—is still in its fledgling stages. Expect to see a lot more from this product in Feature Packs to come. Currently there is no hardware acceleration for SSL that can be integrated into a Check Point enforcement point, but Check Point is working on that with some different vendors to provide something similar to their VPN accelerator cards that will offload the SSL acceleration from the main CPUs of the server on which this is running.

Notes from the Underground…

Thoughts on the Current State of Check Point's Client VPN Solutions

I personally have an affinity for the SecuRemote/SecureClient product line having used it for a long time. I can also say that I have used many other VPN clients. Though some may appear more simple to the end user, the amount of flexibility and overall control in the SecureClient product cannot be matched by any of the others out there currently. It has come a long way since its beginning where it was technically unusable due to constraints with no NAT traversal and issues with conflicting IP ranges. Check Point has done an excellent job in working diligently on any issues that have blocked the easy use of VPNs. If you ever encounter something that you feel could be modified, and you have a good idea of how you would like it to be in the Check Point product, don't neglect to submit an RFE (Request for Enhancements), you can find the form at www.checkpoint.com/cgi-bin/rfe.cgi. In this current dot-bomb era that we find ourselves in, Check Point listens very well and is doing everything they can to facilitate anything the customer needs.

Summary

Hopefully this chapter has provided some useful thoughts about the implementation of client VPNs with the Check Point NG product. The differences between the SecureClient and SecuRemote features can basically be boiled down to the capability to be able to firewall your clients if using SecureClient or not have that feature if relying on SecuRemote. If you are going the route of using SecuRemote throughout your networks, dnsinfo.c files can make the ability to have your clients use internal resources much easier. However, if you are going with SecureClient it would be better to use Office Mode because it will provide the features of SecureClient and much, much more. We have also covered a couple of thoughts on how to use SecureClient/ SecuRemote to encrypt internal connections on LAN networks when you need to be extremely secure with some clients' communications across not-so-trusted networks. One of the all-time hassles of client VPNs has been using them through firewalls; this has been covered with what you need to do to make the current implementations of SecuRemote/SecureClient work through firewalls. Be on the lookout for FP4, which will make client VPNs through firewalls much easier. One of the features with client VPNs configured correctly is the ability of internal machines to initiate connections back to client VPN hosts, with Office Mode this becomes much easier through the use of internal DHCP and DDNS. L2TP tunnels provide a method for configuring tunnels with the built-in VPN client of Windows 2000 and above, but the implementation for large numbers of clients is cumbersome. Look at using SecuRemote if faced with more then a few L2TP implementations. One of the best features of NG client VPNs is the capability to use the Office Mode feature. Office Mode provides a means of assigning internal IP ranges to clients, which will allow the clients to more easily integrate into the internal IP structure as well as name services structures. If you have the ability to use SecureClient and Office Mode, you will be doing yourself a disservice if you do not.

Clientless VPNs are currently a convenient method of allowing HTTPS tunnels to internal HTTP resources while securing them with the use of all the integrated security that Check Point provides. Be on the lookout for new protocols other than HTTP that clientless VPNs should cover in the future.

Solutions Fast Track

The Difference Between SecuRemote and SecureClient

- ☑ SecureClient has a built-in host firewall; SecuRemote does not.
- ☑ SecuRemote licenses are free; SecureClient is not.
- ☑ SecureClient has the capability to do Office Mode; SecuRemote does not.

- ☑ SecuRemote requires use of dnsinfo.c files for DNS resolution, whereas SecureClient can use Office Mode for DNS resolution.

Using DNSInfo Files

- ☑ Keep your files up to date; they are easy to overlook if you are using dynamic name registration services.
- ☑ DNSInfo files are useful if you're not using Office Mode; they can help with items normally handled by WINS resolution.
- ☑ If using Office Mode and SecureClient, dnsinfo.c files are not needed because a virtual interface is defined with all the appropriate settings anyway.

Encrypting Internal Traffic

- ☑ Encrypting internal traffic is useful for sensitive data crossing internal "sniffable" networks.
- ☑ You must have SecuRemote/SecureClient installed on the client machine.
- ☑ Make sure to use Transparent connect mode to make it more seamless/invisible to the end user.
- ☑ Servers must be on different segment than the clients, and the server segment must be trusted because the data will no longer be encrypted on it.

Using SR/SC from Behind a CP-FW-1 System

- ☑ You must allow IKE and FW1-Topo for both methods.
- ☑ Allow ESP for non-encapsulated ESP tunnels.
- ☑ Allow VPN1_IPSEC_encapsulation when using UDP-encapsulated ESP tunnels.
- ☑ Use UDP encapsulation, if possible, because it is easier to allow through firewalls.

Using SecureClient

- ☑ SecureClient is useful for securing wireless networks.

- ☑ SecureClient is useful for temporary B2B network connections or quickly getting connectivity running.

Creating Rules for Internal Connections to Remote Clients

- ☑ Make sure to enable Tunnel Refresh.
- ☑ Create rules allowing internal traffic needed to go down the tunnel.
- ☑ Useful for allowing traffic that needs to be initiated server side, such as Exchange Instant Messenger traffic.

Examples of Common Deployments

- ☑ Use the SecureClient Packaging tool to make packages.
- ☑ Deploy partial topology for security reasons.
- ☑ Obscure topology on disk to keep topology info secure.
- ☑ Automate the install as much as possible to keep it simple for your users.

L2TP Tunnels Terminating on a Check Point FP3 Box

- ☑ This requires installing certificates on client machines.
- ☑ It allows using the built-in Windows VPN client for connections.
- ☑ Client VPN installation at the client PC is time-consuming.
- ☑ This does not work well through NAT devices in the current implementation.

Office Mode SecureClient

- ☑ This assigns a virtual adapter to each client machine.
- ☑ Virtual adapter can be assigned all settings from either the firewall or a DHCP server.
- ☑ Virtual adapter allows you to have clients using the same IP address on their normal IP interface.
- ☑ Currently, you cannot specify which user gets which IP address when using DHCP for the IP address allocation.

FP3 Clientless VPNs

- ☑ FP3 clientless VPNs are currently available only for HTTP sessions.
- ☑ FW1 acts as an SSL termination point for SSL tunnels.
- ☑ Allows SSL tunnels to be authenticated for any HTTP site using the built-in methods of authentication that FW1 supports.
- ☑ Support for SMTP and POP are being implemented soon supposedly.
- ☑ This requires modifying the objects.C database in certain cases.

Frequently Asked Questions

The following Frequently Asked Questions, answered by the authors of this book, are designed to both measure your understanding of the concepts presented in this chapter and to assist you with real-life implementation of these concepts. To have your questions about this chapter answered by the author, browse to **www.syngress.com/solutions** and click on the **"Ask the Author"** form.

Q: My client VPN tunnel is up and certain applications are working but some aren't (usually on PPPoE connections). What should I do?

A: This is the *most* frequently seen question and also why it is at the top of the list. The normal MTU for most machines by default is set at 1500 bytes. PPPoE uses 8 bytes for authentication purposed out of that 1500. This technically should leave you with 1492 bytes for your IP payload, but depending on which PPPoE client you are using there possibly can be even more bytes used; for example, Microsoft's built-in PPPoE client on Windows XP uses 20 bytes, which would leave you with 1480 bytes for the IP payload. When your adapter is still trying to send out a payload of 1500, but the full 1500 is not available, the IP stack begins fragmenting the packets. Many NAT devices, however, do not handle fragmented IP packets and begin to drop some, which results in certain applications not working correctly. The way to fix the issue is to modify the MTU on the client adapter. From personal experience, 1400 is a good starting point, but you may have to experiment to get a working setting for your environment. Check Point also includes a new utility in the SR/SC package called *mtuadjust*, which will adjust this for you without you having to go into the Registry. However, the application currently works only on Win2k/XP.

Q: How can I troubleshoot whether or not UDP encapsulated client VPN traffic is getting to my firewall?

A: The most effective means I have seen of doing this is using a freeware utility called netcat. It can be found at www.atstake.com in the network utilities section. Since Windows does not have any built-in method to test a UDP connection, you have to use a third-party product to test them (simple *telnet* works fine for TCP). You will have get the netcat utility on the client machine and then have it open a connection on UDP port 2746 to a host that is protected by your firewall. (Note: Do not open a connection directly to the firewall because this is not always interpreted correctly in the logs.) If you can see the connection being logged for UDP 2746, you can be fairly sure that the phase 2 traffic is getting to your firewall.

Q: It seems like the UDP traffic is getting to me when doing a simple netcat test, but when I try to use the client I'm still not getting the actual UDP phase 2 traffic. Why?

A: A few times I have seen situations like this where it turns out that there was an IDS between the client and the terminating firewall. Some IDSs interpret the UDP traffic as a UDP bomb attack; in particular, I have seen a PIX firewall that had the limited IDS portion turned on it, which was blocking the UDP traffic. In a scenario like this, verify with the network administrators on the client side that there are no IDSs between the client and the firewall, and if there are, make special provisions on the IDS allowing the traffic.

Q: I'm running Norton Personal Firewall with SecureClient/Remote and am not able to connect. Why?

A: First of all you shouldn't need it while you are using SecureClient if you have a rule base configured for SecureClient. If you are using it while using SecuRemote make sure to go into Norton Personal Firewall and enable fragmented IP packets to pass through. If this is disabled, it will drop the UDP encapsulated traffic for SecuRemote and the connection will not work.

Q: What are some of the built-in utilities for troubleshooting SecureClient connections?

A: As of FP3 there two good utilities for testing your VPN client connections that are included with the install of SecuRemote/SecureClient. Make sure to check the \bin directory in the client installation directory, and you will find a program called *srfw*. The actual command for utilizing this is *srfw monitor*, which basically opens a sniffer to monitor the traffic from the client to the firewall. Also in this same directory is the *mtuadjust* utility, which can adjust the MTU settings for your interface. The SecureClient/SecuRemote client itself also has some built-in diagnostics that you can use from the GUI itself.

Q: I have two clients behind a personal firewall that are not able to connect simultaneously, but if only one of them connects the connection works fine. Why?

A: This is usually a limitation found in cheap home firewalls where the device does not do port translation on the source port so both clients are showing the same source port on the SOHO firewall for their connection attempts. This can be remedied by adding the setting *ChangeUDPsport* with a setting of TRUE to the userc.c file. This will automatically change the source ports for IKE and UDP encapsulation at the client machine itself negating the effect of the SOHO firewall not changing the source ports for you.

Chapter 6

High Availability and Clustering

Solutions in this chapter:

- Designing Your Cluster
- Installing FireWall-1 NG FP3
- Check Point ClusterXL
- Nokia IPSO Clustering
- Nokia IPSO VRRP Clusters
- Clustering and HA Performance Tuning

☑ Summary

☑ Solutions Fast Track

☑ Frequently Asked Questions

Introduction

In Chapter 4, we reviewed Single Entry Point (SEP) VPNs. The key to a SEP VPN is to utilize high-availability (HA) and clustering solutions. Of course, if you choose not to utilize the VPN features of FireWall-1, you can still use the HA and clustering features described in this chapter. Check Point, Nokia, and other third-party companies offer many methods for deploying HA solutions. Here we focus on the Check Point ClusterXL product, review the new Nokia IP clustering and VRRP solutions, and discuss the performance of these solutions. We also spend some time describing how each solution actually works and what the "life of a connection" is like through each clustering solution.

When you set up a cluster, one of the first things you want to do is test that it is working as expected. In this chapter, we cover a quick list of tests that you can do on each cluster to make sure you get the right responses. We also cover some of the command-line tools you can use to check the status of each node in the cluster.

Designing Your Cluster

There are a number of issues to be considered and decisions to be made when you're designing a cluster solution. It's worth keeping in mind that a resilient solution is worthless if poor design makes the clustering mechanism result in more downtime than would be expected with a single system.

Why Do You Need a Cluster?

It might be safe to say that the majority of this chapter's readers have already made the decision to install a clustered firewall, and so those readers know why this is a good idea. For readers who are not yet decided or aren't sure why they are installing a cluster, let's look at the reasons a cluster might be a good option.

The concept of any cluster solution is that the cluster itself appears on the outside as a single system. In the case of a firewall cluster, this system is a secure gateway, possibly providing a VPN end point and other services. There are two key benefits of a cluster that consists of multiple physical hosts: resilience and increased capacity.

Resilience

A cluster of multiple hosts should have the advantage of being able to provide continuous service, irrespective of whether members of the cluster are available or not. Even the best cluster will struggle if every member is unavailable, but as long as one member is running, service should continue if other members have failed or are down for maintenance.

Increased Capacity

According to some pretty simple logic, if we have three active hosts in a cluster, we can push three times as much traffic through it. Things are not quite that simple, however; there can be significant overhead in operation of the cluster technology itself, which tends to increase in proportion to the number of members and could become a bottleneck. Other bottlenecks could be the network bandwidth available on either side of the cluster and the performance of servers protected by the cluster. This concept might appear obvious, but it could be overlooked during the calculations of the incredible throughput theoretically possible if a further five members are added to a cluster!

High Availability or Load Sharing?

There are two distinct models for clustering solutions: HA and load sharing. Let's take a brief look at each.

Load Sharing

In a load-sharing cluster, all available members are active and passing traffic. This setup provides both resilience and increased capacity due to the distribution of traffic between the members. Some load-sharing solutions can be described as load balancing because there is a degree of intelligence in the distribution of traffic between members. This intelligence might be in the form of a performance rating for each cluster member or even a dynamic rating based on current load.

High Availability

In an HA cluster, only one member is active and processing network traffic at any one time. This solution provides resilience but no increased capacity. The choosing of HA is often due to the simpler solutions being easier to manage and troubleshoot and sometimes more reliable than a load-sharing solution due to the latter's additional complexity. The simplicity of these solution often means that they are a cheaper option financially.

Clustering and Check Point

Let's now look at design issues that arise in planning Check Point firewall clusters.

Operating System Platform

Depending on the operating system platform, different options are available for clustering solutions, including Check Point solutions and those from Check Point OPSEC partners. Here we look at Check Point's ClusterXL solution, which is available on the usual NG platforms—Windows, Solaris, Linux, and SecurePlatform—with the exception of Nokia IPSO. The IPSO platform offers the IPSO clustering load-balancing solution and VRRP HA, both of which we also cover in this chapter. We do not cover OPSEC partner solutions other than references given toward the end of this chapter.

Clustering and Stateful Inspection

Key to the operation of FireWall-1 is the stateful inspection technology that tracks the state of connections. If a cluster solution is to provide true resilience, a connection should be preserved irrespective of which cluster member its packets are routed through. In order for stateful inspection to deal with connections "moving" between members, a method of sharing state information must be provided. This method is known as *state synchronization* and is an integral part of FireWall-1 clustering. A dedicated network, known as the *sync network* or *secured network,* is used for the state synchronization traffic. Note that it is possible to configure a cluster without state synchronization if no connection resilience is needed.

Desire for Stickiness

Although in theory state synchronization allows each packet of a given connection to pass through any one of the cluster members, it is far more desirable to ensure that each connection "sticks" to a specific cluster member where possible. This is due to timing issues; there is inevitably some delay between one cluster member seeing a packet and that member passing its updated state information to other members. This delay can cause a subsequent packet to be dropped because it appears to be invalid—out of state—to the other members. The problem is particularly likely to be an issue during connection establishment, where a quick exchange of packets must adhere to strict conditions—in the case of TCP connections, the three-way handshake. Fortunately, once a connection is established, it is more resilient to packet loss, and the state is not so strictly enforced. This allows connection failover, where connections stuck to failed members can be moved to other cluster members with minimal disruption.

In an HA solution, stickiness is no problem; all connections naturally stick to the one active member. In a load-sharing environment, stickiness requires some intelligence from the clustering solution. It must ensure that there is stickiness, but the members should each have roughly equal numbers of connections stuck to them.

Location of Management Station

If you want a clustering solution, you must install an NG distributed management architecture, or in other words, your Check Point management station (also known as the *SmartCenter Server*) must be installed on a dedicated host, *not* on a cluster member.

Beware of upgrading FireWall 4.1 HA configurations that perform state synchronization but were not part of a cluster object. It was possible in version 4.1 to make one of the state synchronized firewalls a management station as well, but you cannot do this in FireWall-1 NG.

You must make a decision regarding which network the management station resides on. It is clearly desirable that each cluster member is reachable from the management station, irrespective of whether that member, and other members, are currently active in the cluster. Conversely, irrespective of which cluster members are active, the management station requires normal network connectivity to allow remote management, access to DNS servers, and so on. This decision will depend largely on the type of clustering solution implemented. Let's now look at two options for location, with examples of a simplified network topology.

A Management Station on a Cluster-Secured Network

The traditional configuration for many HA solutions has been to place the management station on a dedicated, "secured" network (sometimes shared with cluster control and state synchronization traffic). The network topology is shown in Figure 6.1. Each cluster member is reachable over the secured network, whether the members are in active or Standby mode. This configuration will be a requirement if members running in Standby mode are only contactable on this secured network interface; other interfaces are down while the member is in standby.

NOTE

This is the required configuration in which Check Point ClusterXL HA Legacy mode is implemented.

A limitation of this configuration is that the management station does not have reliable connectivity with any other networks, because its default gateway must be configured to one of the member's secured network IP addresses. Therefore, the management station relies on that member being active in order to "see" the outside world. To work around this problem, the management station can have a second interface that connects to an internal network. The management station default gateway can then be configured as the gateway on the internal network—possibly the internal IP address of the cluster itself. Alternatively, the second interface could be external facing, with a valid Internet address. This solution might be desirable if the management station manages remote firewall gateways. If the second interface is external facing, it *must* be firewalled in some way. A possible solution is to install a FireWall-1 enforcement module on the management station (at the time of install) and license it with a SecureServer (non-routing module) license.

If you run a backup management station, it also needs to be on the secured network.

Figure 6.1 A Management Station on a Secured Network

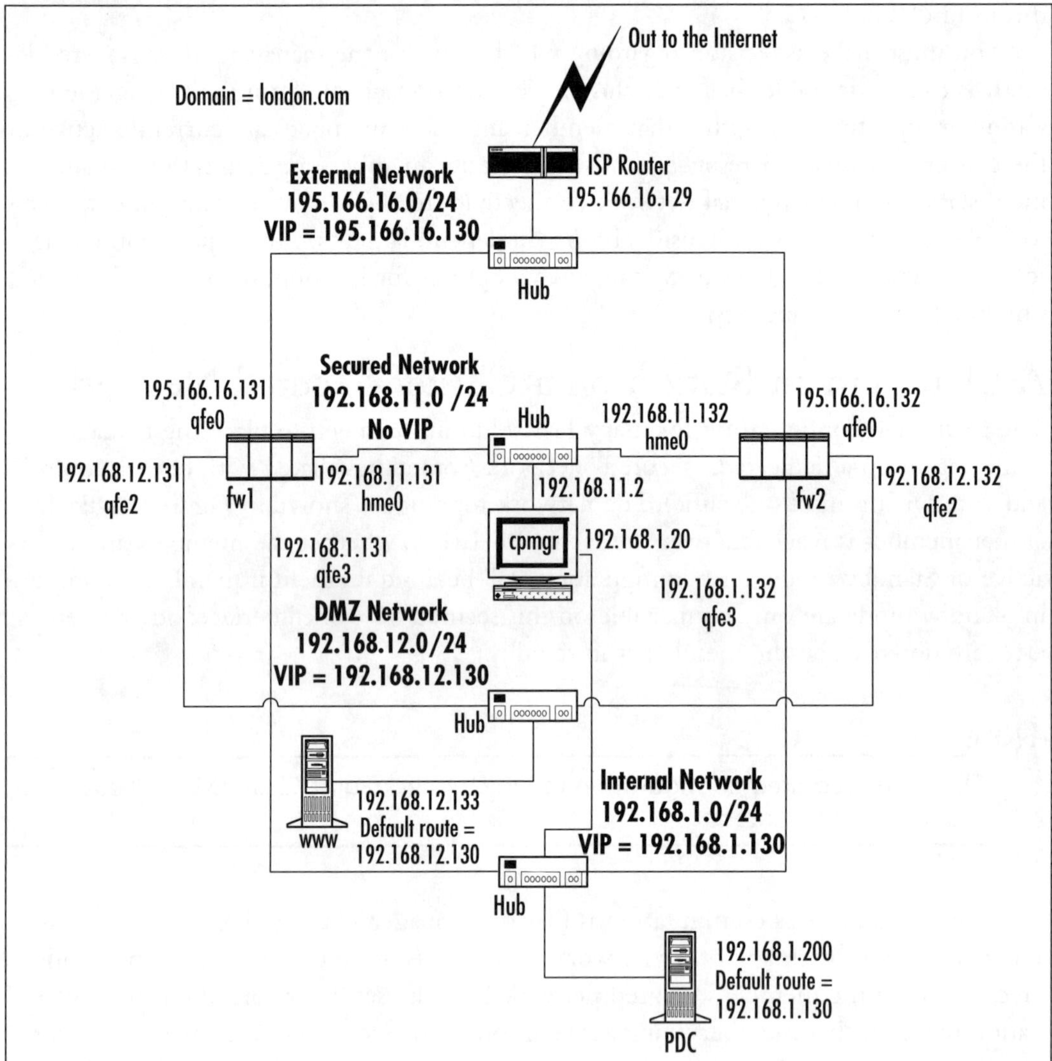

Management Station on Internal Network

The complications of placing the management station on a dedicated network can be avoided if the cluster solution allows members to be reachable on all interfaces, whether the member is active or not. This is achieved where members each have a unique IP address in addition to an IP address shared over the cluster.

Happily, all the other solutions we discuss—ClusterXL HA New mode, load sharing, IPSO clusters, and IPSO VRRP—behave in this way. These solutions can support a management station located behind any interface. Figure 6.2 shows a typical network topology, with the management station located internally. If the management station also manages a cluster at a remote site, it can do so by connecting via the Internet to the external interfaces of that remote cluster's members.

Figure 6.2 A Management Station on an Internal ("Nonsecure") Network

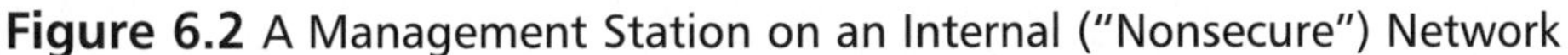

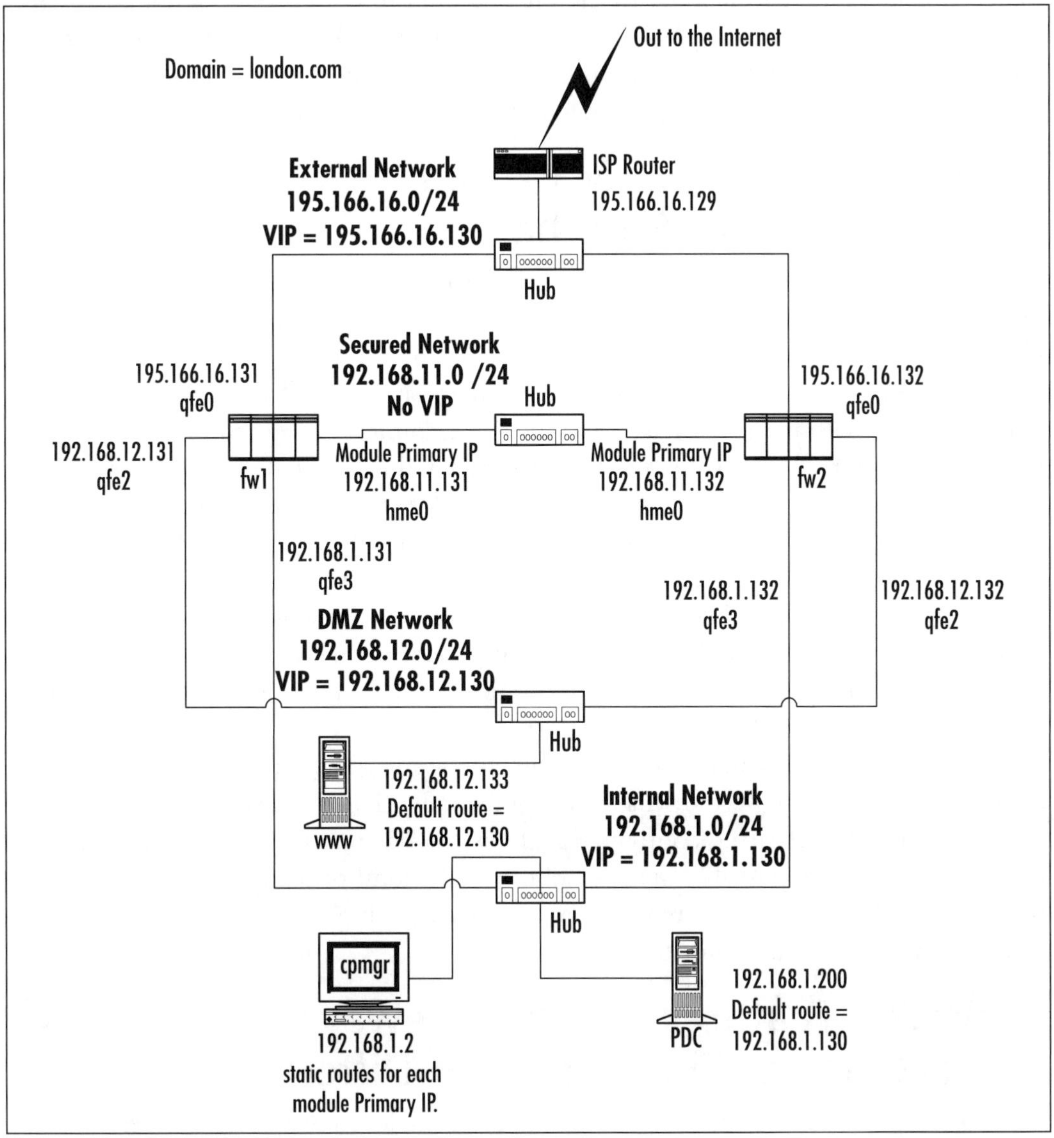

There are some routing factors to consider in using this topology. Some hosts on the internal network will often need to make connections to individual cluster members, including Check Point policy installs and administrative connections such as FTP

or SSH. Where these connections are made to the "nearest" IP address, this is no problem. However, if an IP address other than the "nearest" is specified—for example, the external IP address of the member—the packet will probably be routed via the default route (the cluster virtual IP address). There is a good chance that the packet will route through a different member to the one we want to connect to, resulting in asynchronous routing at best and possibly no connection at all. To avoid this situation, static host routes are required on adjacent hosts/routers that ensure that packets destined for each member's unique addresses are routed via that member's nearest unique IP address.

Connecting the Cluster to Your Network: Hubs or Switches?

The nature of clustering—several devices trying to act as one—tends to throw up some unusual network traffic, which invariably upsets some other network devices in one way or another. The most vulnerable devices involved will be any network switches that are connected to cluster interfaces, because by their nature the switch wants to track which devices (with particular MAC addresses) are connected to each of their ports. If we have a number of cluster members, each connected to a different switch port, but each pretending to be the same device, it is no wonder that an unsuspecting switch might struggle. In addition, cluster solutions often use multicast IP and MAC addresses—requiring switch reconfiguration in order to work.

In summary, most switches can be persuaded to cope with cluster configurations, but some can't. More important, the cluster solution provider is likely to have a list of supported switch hardware—and if your switch is not on that list, you might find yourself in trouble. Always check to find out the supported switches for your chosen configuration.

Hubs, on the other hand, really don't care about any strange protocols that the cluster might be talking, so they make life a lot simpler. The downside is throughput; particularly in a load-sharing configuration, hubs can become a bottleneck. Even so, although switches are probably the best solution, a handful of spare hubs nearby are useful for troubleshooting. Do remember to disable full-duplex settings on network cards before dropping in a hub, though.

FireWall-1 Features, Single Gateways versus Clusters: The Same, But Different

The concept behind the cluster is that it replaces a single gateway but provides resilience and possibly increased capacity. In reality, some FireWall-1 features will behave differently or require different configuration in a clustered environment.

Network Address Translation

When you're configuring NAT, you always need to ensure that packets on a NATed connection are correctly routed to the firewall from adjacent routers. A typical single gateway configuration, with Static NAT performed on an internal server, has the firewall performing proxy ARP for the legal (virtual) IP address, advertising the gateway's own external MAC address. In a cluster environment, it is vital that these packets are routed to the cluster MAC address, not the MAC address of a cluster member. Similarly, if a static host route for the legal IP address is added on adjacent routers (e.g., the ISP router), the destination gateway for the route must be the cluster IP address, not a cluster member IP address.

Security Servers

FireWall-1 uses security servers for user authentication and content scanning (i.e., where resources are used in rules). These servers run at the application level and are effectively transparent proxy servers (or mail relays, in the case of SMTP). These applications are not based on stateful inspection, and their state is not part of the synchronizing Stateful Inspection process. Security servers can still be used in a clustered solution, but the clustering solution must maintain connection stickiness, and connections will not survive member failure. Whether this limitation is a problem will depend on the applications involved:

- **Relay-to-relay SMTP** Deals with connection failure cleanly, with the sending relay retrying the connection later.
- **Client-to-server SMTP** Shows the user an error if their mail client was in the process of sending a message at the time of failure—but the chances of this are fairly slim.
- **General HTTP Web browsing** Users are accustomed to the odd connection failure on the Internet from time to time, and one more when a cluster member fails should not be an issue.
- **Authenticated HTTP** Users (using user authentication and proxying *to the cluster*) throw up an additional complication. While each individual HTTP connection will stick to its cluster member, the browsing session consists of multiple HTTP connections, and each may stick to a different member. As the authentication takes place at the application level, users will need to authenticate against each member they connect to. Fortunately, Web browsers cache the proxy password that the user supplies, so this occurs transparently—unless a one-time password authentication method is in use (e.g., RSA SecurID). The nature of one-time passwords means that a different password is required for

each cluster member, and in the case of SecurID, this requires a delay of a minute between each attempt! In a load-sharing solution, this is unworkable.

- **File downloads over FTP (or HTTP)** Failures here are more likely to cause upset, particularly failure of long downloads that were 95 percent complete. A possible solution for FTP downloads is using client authentication (and not configuring a proxy for FTP).

NOTE

If the security server is used as a traditional proxy server or mail relay (in other words, connections are made directly to the gateway), the cluster IP address should be used as the target proxy address or mail relay address.

Remote Authentication Servers

Where the gateways must connect to a remote server to perform authentication—for example, RADIUS servers or RSA ACE server—the remote server will often verify the request based on the source IP address of the connection. In some cluster environments, implicit address translation will occur so that this connection will appear to have come from the virtual cluster address. It might be that the remote server will be happy to treat the cluster as a single entity, but this will often cause problems—for example, authentication credentials might include one-time passwords that are maintained locally by the cluster members. In this scenario, we need each cluster member to communicate with the remote server as a separate client. In ClusterXL solutions, this can usually be achieved by creating explicit address translation rules that specify that the connections to remote authentication servers are translated to the real member addresses, as defined in the cluster member object. An example of NAT translation rules to avoid this problem is shown in Figure 6.3.

Figure 6.3 NAT Rules That Ensure No NAT for Authenticating Servers

ORIGINAL PACKET			TRANSLATED PACKET			INSTALL ON
SOURCE	DESTINATION	SERVICE	SOURCE	DESTINATION	SERVICE	
fw1	pdc.london.com	UDP RADIUS	fw1	Original	Original	fwcluster
fw2	pdc.london.com	UDP RADIUS	fw2	Original	Original	fwcluster

External VPN Partner Configuration

When participating in VPNs, the cluster appears as a single virtual gateway. External gateways should be configured appropriately, with references to the cluster address only, not member addresses.

Installing FireWall-1 NG FP3

We start the practical side of our clustering discussion by running through installation of the Check Point enforcement modules that will form our cluster. This process is not exceptionally different from installing on an ordinary module, but we highlight the areas of the installation that are relevant to clustering. It's also a good refresher to make sure that you have not forgotten to do something important! We are assuming that we have a healthy management station already running.

Checking the Installation Prerequisites

Follow these steps to check the installation prerequisites:

1. Ensure that your OS meets the requirements documented in the Check Point release notes. On the Windows 2000 platform, make sure that SP2 or SP3 is installed. On Solaris, make sure that the latest cluster patch its installed (e.g., solaris8_Recommended.zip—about 80MB). Make sure that the SUNWter package is installed on Solaris. You need this package before you can run UnixInstallScript from the NG FP3 CD or wrapper.
2. On the Nokia platform, download the latest version of IPSO that is compatible with NG FP3.
3. It strongly recommended that you have all your interfaces configured and working on the firewall modules and your management server before you install FireWall-1 NG FP3. Make sure that you have tested that each interface is up and running.
4. Make sure that the member clocks are synchronized; see the sidebar "The Importance of Time."
5. Carefully read the Check Point NG FP3 release notes before proceeding. This is important!

Tools & Traps...

The Importance of Time

It is important to ensure that the correct time, date, and time zone are set on each of the cluster members and on the management module. The time on the cluster members needs to be synchronized as accurately as possible for the purposes of state synchronization and cluster control protocols. The time

Continued

needs to be in step with the management module as the trust relationships between modules (SIC) is certificate based and time sensitive. The logs seen in SmartView Tracker are time-stamped with the local module's time, so these logs can be misleading if time settings are incorrect.

You should also take into account daylight saving time. If your platform does not automatically adjust for daylight saving (IPSO included), make sure that you set the time for the "unadjusted" time zone. This does mean that your local module time appears "wrong" by an hour during the summer months. SmartView Tracker will adjust the displayed time correctly, based on the time zone of the management station.

Given the importance of time synchronization, it should be automated using standard NTP. Obtain details of how to configure NTP on the platform chosen for your modules from your OS provider. (In the case of IPSO, this is configurable via Voyager.) When you're configuring NTP, it is recommended that only one of the cluster members synchronizes its time with an external source, whereas other members synchronize with that selected "master" member. This is because the priority is to ensure that all members are time synchronized with each other, rather than synchronized with an external source. Finally, don't forget to allow NTP as required in your FireWall-1 security policy.

Installation Options

Before installation, you need to be aware of some of the questions that you will be asked during the install. You need to have made a decision about the following points before starting the installation so that you answer correctly:

1. Each module needs to have VPN-1 SecureClient Policy Server installed if you want to use VPN-1 SecureClient later.
2. FloodGate-1 can be installed on the management and modules if required.

During installation of the enforcement module, you are asked if you would like to install a Check Point clustering product (CPHA, CPLS, or state synchronization). Answer **yes** to this option, even if you're installing a third-party clustering solution, because it is required for state synchronization.

Installation Procedure

The installation procedure is slightly different depending on which operating system you are running. With Windows, the installation procedure is a more visual experience, whereas with UNIX, it is a text-based installation. The UNIX installations are reasonably similar in the types of questions you will be asked and at what point you will be asked them.

To begin the installation:

- **Windows** Insert the FP3 CD. The installation wrapper should automatically launch. Alternatively, download the FP3 wrapper package and run **setup.exe**.
- **Solaris/Linux** Use the appropriate commands to mount the CD. Change directory to the mount point, and at the root of the CD, you should find a script called UnixInstallScript. Run this script: **./UnixInstallScript**.
- **IPSO** Use the *newpkg* command to install FP3 from an ftp server, CD, or the local file system.
- **SecurePlatform** Insert the FP3 CD and reboot.

In our example, we assume you are installing FireWall-1 NG FP3 on a Solaris host, but the questions are similar to what you would expect while installing on all platforms. On Windows the same procedure applies but via an installation GUI.

NOTE

On IPSO, the installation process can be automated by Nokia's Horizon Manager, which is a mid-level manager that allows for the installation of software, updates, and cpconfig information without having to use the CLI or Voyager.

The first screen you will see when running the UNIX wrapper is shown in Figure 6.4.

Figure 6.4 Introduction Screen When Running UnixInstallScript

```
Check Point Software Technologies Ltd.
Welcome to Check Point Next Generation Feature Pack 3 Enterprise Suite!
 We recommend that you close all other applications while running
 this installation program.
 This product is protected by copyright law and all unauthorized
 reproduction is forbidden.
V-Evaluation Product U-Purchased Product N-Next H-Help E-Exit
```

Press **U** for purchased product. All this means is that you will be asked for the license during install, but you can install the license later on NG FP3. (It will work for 15 days with a fully featured evaluation license.)

Pressing **U** will display the next stage of installation, which is shown in Figure 6.5.

Figure 6.5 The Purchased Product Screen

```
Check Point Software Technologies Ltd.
Purchased Products.

 Before you continue, please ensure you have obtained a license.

 You can obtain license from your reseller or from
 www.Check Point.com/usercenter

                         N-next B-go back C-contact information H-help E-exit
```

Press **N** to go to the next screen, shown in Figure 6.6, which will install the Secure Virtual Network (SVN) foundation. Note that just before the SVN foundation install, the installation scripts checks to make sure that the prerequisite patches are installed.

Figure 6.6 SVN Foundation Installation

```
Check Point Software Technologies Ltd.
Please wait while checking Check Point products installed...

 Installing Check Point SVN Foundation NG FP3...
                                    Please wait!
```

Once the SVN installation is complete, the next screen will display (see Figure 6.7).

Figure 6.7 Selecting Products to Install

```
Check Point Software Technologies Ltd.
The following products are included on this CD.
Select product(s)
 1.[*] VPN-1 & FireWall-1.
 2.[*] FloodGate-1.
 3.[ ] SMART Clients.
 4.[*] VPN-1 SecureClient Policy Server.
 5.[*] UserAuthority.
```

Continued

Figure 6.7 Selecting Products to Install

```
 6.[ ] SmartView Monitor.
 7.[ ] Performance Pack.


     N-Next C-Contact information R-Review of products H-Help E-Exit
```

After the SVN has installed, select the packages that you would like to install (using the numeric keys) as shown in Figure 6.7. Option 1 is mandatory for a firewall module, but all the others are optional. Press **N** for the next screen.

The next screen asks if the installation will be a firewall module, a management station only, a management and module, and so on (see Figure 6.8).

Figure 6.8 Module or Management Installation Screen

```
Check Point Software Technologies Ltd.
Installation type


 1.(*) Enforcement Module.
 2.( ) Enterprise Management.
 3.( ) Enterprise Management and Enforcement Module.
 4.( ) Enterprise Log Server.
 5.( ) Enforcement Module and Enterprise Log Server.


                         N-next B-go Back H-help E-exit
```

Select **Enforcement module** only. The installation script will then display a validation screen to confirm the options you have selected before proceeding with the install. This process is shown in Figure 6.9.

Figure 6.9 Verifying Your Selections So Far

```
Check Point Software Technologies Ltd.
Validation

 You have selected the following products for installation:
 * VPN-1 & FireWall-1 Enforcement Module
```

Continued

Figure 6.9 Verifying Your Selections So Far

```
 * FloodGate-1 Enforcement Module
 * VPN-1 SecureClient Policy Server
 * UserAuthority


                               N-next B-go Back H-help E-exit
```

Press **N** for the next screen. This will move you onto the screen shown in Figure 6.10. The installation script will then start installing the products you selected.

Figure 6.10 Products Installing...

```
Check Point Software Technologies Ltd.
Check Point Installation Program


 Installing VPN-1 & FireWall-1 NG FP3...

                                     Please wait!
```

Wait while the installation completes (see Figure 6.11).

Figure 6.11 Initial Configuration

```
Welcome to Check Point Configuration Program
=================================================


**************** VPN-1 & FireWall-1 kernel module installation **********


Installing VPN-1 & FireWall-1 kernel module...
Done.



**************** Interface Configuration ****************


Scanning for unknown interfaces...
Would you like to install a Check Point clustering product (CPHA, CPLS or
    State Synchronisation)? (y/n) [n] ? y
```

When installation has completed, you will be prompted to choose whether you would like to install the Check Point Clustering product, as shown in Figure 6.11. Answer **y**. Following this screen, you'll see a number of configuration questions that you should be familiar with from a standard FireWall-1 installation.

You will be prompted to supply a secret key password that will be used to communicate with the firewall management station. This password will be used when you define the cluster object in SmartDashboard. Make a note of your chosen password! The installation will then complete, and you will be asked if you want to reboot. Answer **y**.

Now repeat the installation procedure for the other members of the cluster.

Check Point ClusterXL

We now take a look at the Check Point ClusterXL clustering solution. ClusterXL FP3 can actually be configured to work in three different modes. Each mode provides different functionality and has differences in the underlying clustering mechanisms:

- **HA New mode** New mode gateways maintain online, unique IP addresses in addition to Virtual IP (VIP) addresses that are shared over the cluster. Traffic for the VIP is handled by the master gateway only.
- **HA Legacy mode (as available in previous versions of ClusterXL)** Provides HA by providing standby gateways configured with the same addresses as the master gateway. The standby gateway interfaces remain disabled unless the master fails, and the gateway is promoted to master.
- **Load Sharing mode** As with HA New mode, all gateways have unique IPs and shared VIPs. However, all gateways are "live" and share the traffic load.

NOTE

Nokia does not support Cluster XL. Load sharing/balancing has to be done via VRRP or Nokia's IP Clustering (ISPO 3.6 and later).

We begin by looking at HA New mode.

Configuring ClusterXL in HA New Mode

In this section, we describe how to configure Check Point FireWall-1 ClusterXL in HA New mode. In this example, we set up a two-member HA cluster using ClusterXL. Before we proceed with configuring the cluster, we need to make sure that we are starting from a point at which all the other essential tasks have already been completed.

Prerequisites for Installing ClusterXL in HA New Mode

Before configuring the cluster for HA New mode, you need to complete the following tasks:

- Design your cluster and know all the IP addresses and VIP addresses that your cluster will have. (You need one VIP per connected network other than the sync net. For details, see the "How Does ClusterXL HA New Mode Work?" section of this chapter).
- Plug all your multihomed hosts together using hubs (or switches) and checked IP connectivity between them.
- Make sure that your routers and adjacent hosts either side of your cluster have default routes set to the adjacent VIP of the cluster (even though the IP address does not exist yet!).
- Make sure that you have added hostnames that resolve to IP addresses in the hosts files on all the hosts that will be part of the cluster—including the host that will be the management station.
- Your firewall modules should be installed and ready to communicate with your firewall management station (SmartCenter Server).
- Make sure that your management station is operating correctly. You can connect with the SmartDashboard GUI and see the object for your management station.
- If you're working on the Solaris platform, it is strongly recommended that you configure the network interfaces to use unique MAC addresses (they are the same by default). This can be done using the command:

  ```
  eeprom local-mac-address?=true
  ```

- You would then need to reboot the Solaris host for the change to take effect. Type **ifconfig –a**. You should see that each interface now has a unique MAC address. This step will simplify testing and prevent problems that might occur if you are using switches.

Once this process is completed, you should have something looking similar to Figure 6.12. In our example, hubs have been used, so obviously no special switch configuration is required.

Figure 6.12 A Simple Topology for ClusterXL in HA New Mode

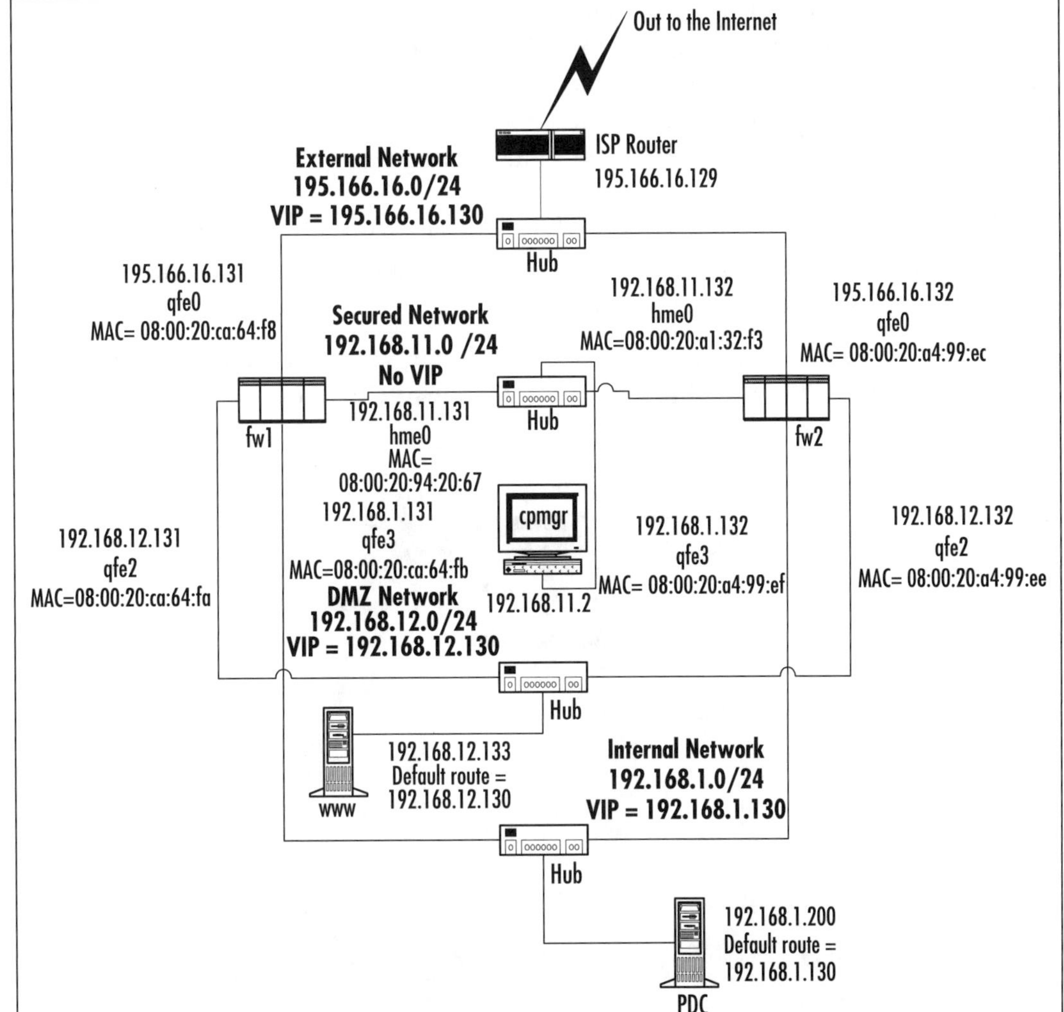

Configuration of ClusterXL HA New Mode

There are a number of ways in which you can create the cluster configuration and end up with the same results. When creating a new cluster in NG FP3, you can decide to create your firewall modules first and then add them to a cluster object, or you can create the cluster object first and define the firewall modules directly in the cluster object. Usually, if you are setting everything from scratch, it is probably quicker to create all your modules and trusts directly in the cluster object.

In this example, we create a cluster object first and define our first module (referred to as fw1 in this example) and make sure we can push a policy just to this new cluster object. We then configure the second module (referred to as fw2) as a standalone module, set up the trust, and push a policy to that. The final stage is to add the fw2 module to the cluster and then install the policy.

The following steps will enable us to achieve this goal.

Step 1: Creating a Gateway Cluster Object and Setting Up the Trust

Our first configuration steps aim to build a cluster consisting of just one enforcement module and test it by installing a policy:

1. In SmartDashboard, create a Gateway Cluster object (**Manage | Network Objects | New | Check Point | Gateway Cluster**.) You will see the Gateway Cluster Properties window pop up, as shown in Figure 6.13.

Figure 6.13 Gateway Cluster Properties Screen

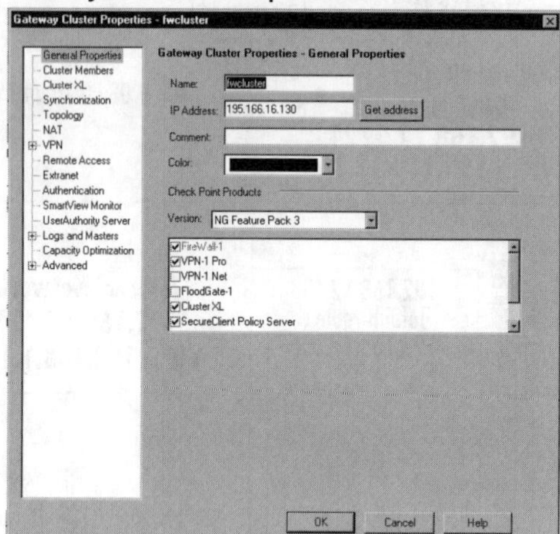

2. Fill in the name of the cluster. In our example, we called it *fwcluster*. We gave the object primary IP as the external VIP address—195.166.16.130. We then checked the boxes for **FireWall-1** (which is mandatory), **VPN-1 Pro** (because we plan to set up VPNs), **ClusterXL** (because we want to use the Check Point cluster solution), and SecureClient Policy Server (because we want to use SecureClients).
3. Click Cluster Members on the left side of the screen. This is where we add the enforcement modules into our new cluster. See Figure 6.14.
4. Clicking the **New** button will allow you to define a new firewall enforcement module that will be part of the cluster. In the **Name** field, enter the hostname

of this module. The IP address is the one chosen as the primary IP for that module, and the hostname should resolve to this address consistently across all modules. Usually, the primary IP is that of the Internet-facing interface. In our example, the name is fw1 and the address is 195.166.16.131, as shown in Figure 6.15. Note that it would not be possible to use the external IP as the primary address if you were using HA Legacy mode, because the module's only unique address is that of the secured interface.

Figure 6.14 The Cluster Members Screen Before Any Members Have Been Added

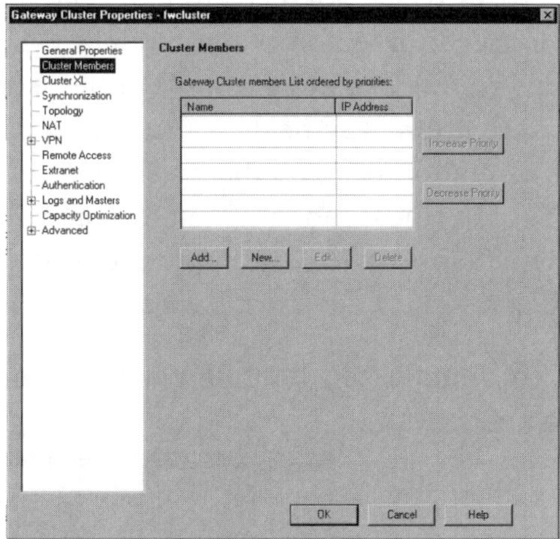

Figure 6.15 Defining the Cluster Member

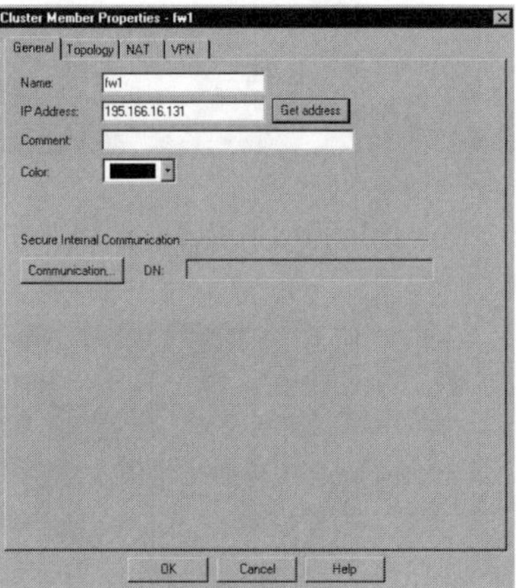

WARNING

Always use the member hostname as the object name and then use the **Get address** button to test that the management station resolves the member hostname correctly. If it does not, investigate this problem before proceeding further.

5. You now need to establish communication with the module. Click the **Communication** button. Clicking this button will pop up a window shown in Figure 6.16, in which you need to enter the secret password that you used when you installed this enforcement module. (Make sure that the module is started at this point.) Use this password in the **Activation Key** field and the **Confirm Activation Key** field. At first the trust state is *Uninitialized*. Click the **Initialize** button to set up the trust between the management station and the firewall enforcement module. Wait a short while, and then you should then see the window change to update the trust state to *Trust established*, as shown in Figure 6.17. Once trust has been established, click the **Close** button.

Figure 6.16 Uninitialized Trust Between the Management Module and a Cluster Member

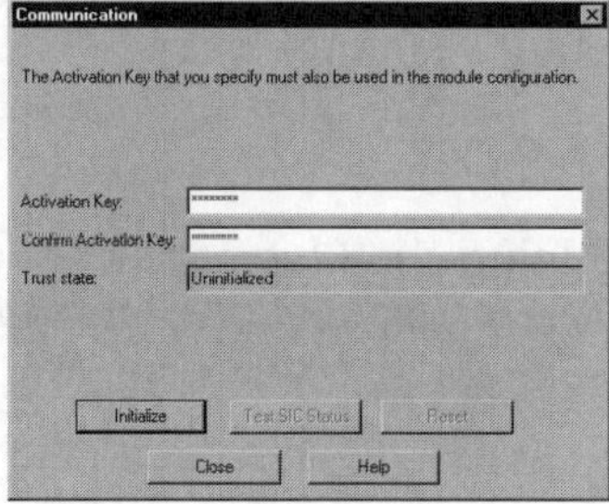

Figure 6.17 Trust Established Between the Management Module and a Cluster Member

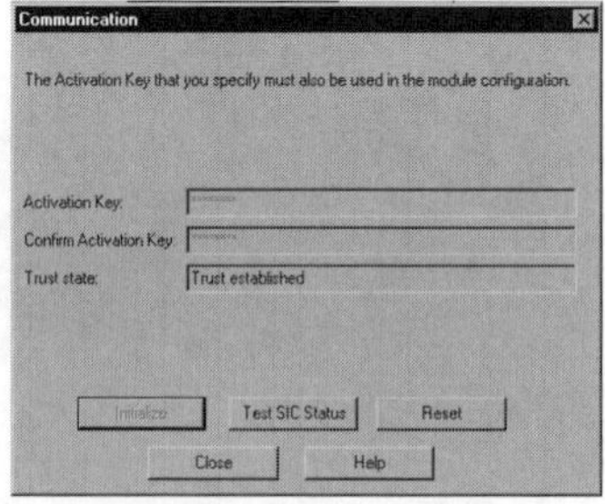

NOTE

It's a good idea to click the **Test SIC Status** button to ensure that the trust is working. When you click this button, you should get a popup window that reads, "SIC Status for fw1: Communicating." If you do not, you have a problem with the management station communicating with the firewall enforcement module and this situation will need to be rectified. Check routing and any intermediate firewall policies. If you manage intermediate firewalls from this management station, you should save the new cluster object without configuring communication, and then push a policy to those firewalls.

6. Click the **Topology** tab of the cluster, and click **Get topology**. This step should get the topology of your module, including IP addresses, netmasks, and IP addresses behind interfaces, where appropriate; an example is shown in Figure 6.18. Click the **Accept** button once you are happy with the topology obtained. Now select the interface that you are going to use as your *sync interface*—referred to as the Secured Network in the Check Point manuals. In our example, our sync network is on 192.168.11.131, on interface hme0. Double-click this interface. You will be presented with a new popup window, as shown in Figure 6.19.

Figure 6.18 Module Topology

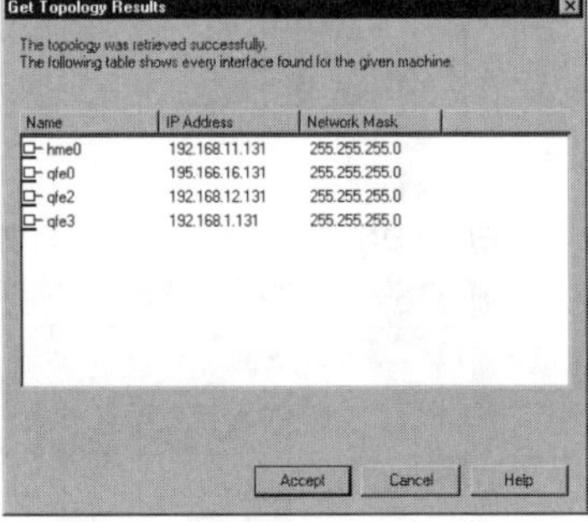

Figure 6.19 Defining the Secured Interface on One Member of the Cluster

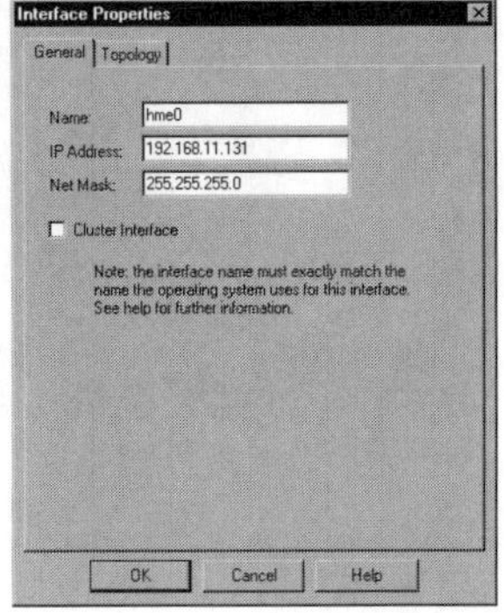

In the popup window, make sure that you uncheck the **Cluster Interface** check box so that the firewall module knows that this network will not have a VIP address. If you don't uncheck this box, you will receive a warning later in the configuration.

Click the **Topology** tab of this window. This allows you to define anti-spoofing for this interface. Select **Network Defined by the interface and netmask** for this example (see Figure 6.20).

Figure 6.20 Antispoofing Properties of the Secure Interface of a Module

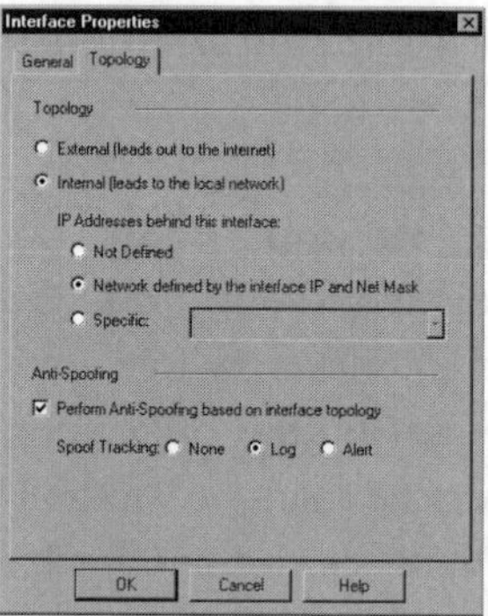

Click **OK** when finished. You should now be on the Topology tab of the Cluster Members Properties window. Don't worry about the VPN and NAT details for now. Click **OK** again, and you should be looking at the Cluster Members screen (see Figure 6.21). You should see that the first cluster member has been defined.

Figure 6.21 Cluster Members Screen After First Member Has Been Defined

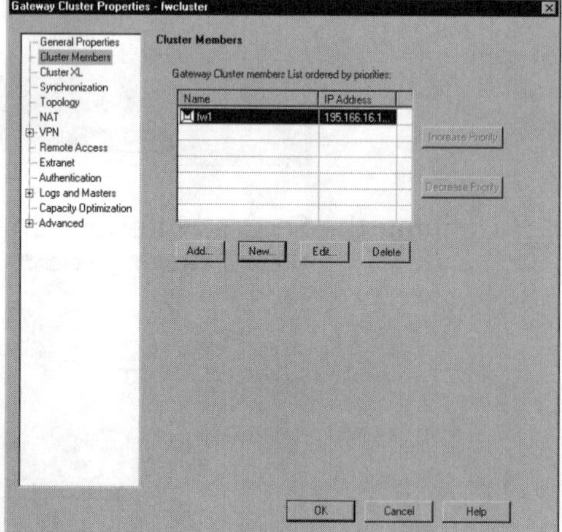

At this stage, you could add further cluster members using the **New** button, but we will use the **Add** button later to add an existing firewall enforcement module to the cluster.

7. Click **ClusterXL** on the left side of the screen. This screen shows you the mode that ClusterXL will work in (see Figure 6.22). In this example, the defaults are High Availability in New mode, which we have selected. We have also left the "Upon Gateway recovery" setting at **Maintain current active gateway**. This means that when a member in the cluster fails and then the member returns, all the traffic will still go through the second firewall member. The effect of this choice is that failback is a manual process.

Figure 6.22 Configuring the ClusterXL Mode of Operation

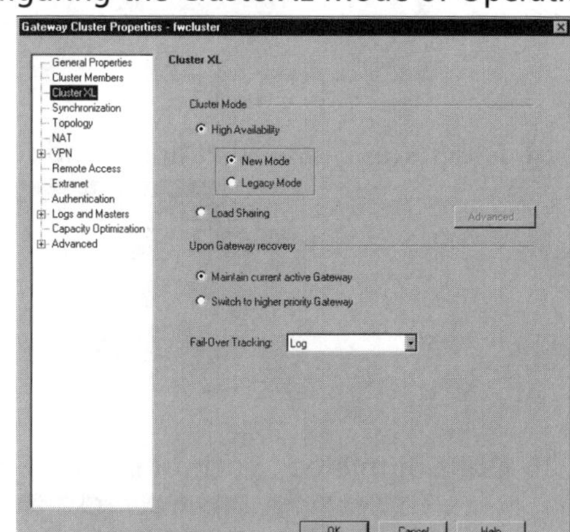

8. Now click the **Synchronization** tree item. This screen, as shown in Figure 6.23, allows you to define the sync network. The cluster members should have interfaces on this network that are not cluster interfaces (defined in the cluster member interfaces details). It is possible to define multiple sync networks here in order to provide resilience. In our example, we define a sync network 192.168.11.0, subnet mask 255.255.255.0. To do so, click the **Add** button. A popup window will appear (see Figure 6.24). Enter the network name (of your choice), network address, and subnet mask. Click **OK** when you're done. Once this process is completed, you should see something similar to Figure 6.25.

WARNING

State synchronization must be used if connection resilience is required (i.e. connections are maintained during a cluster failover).

Figure 6.23 Defining the State Synchronization Network

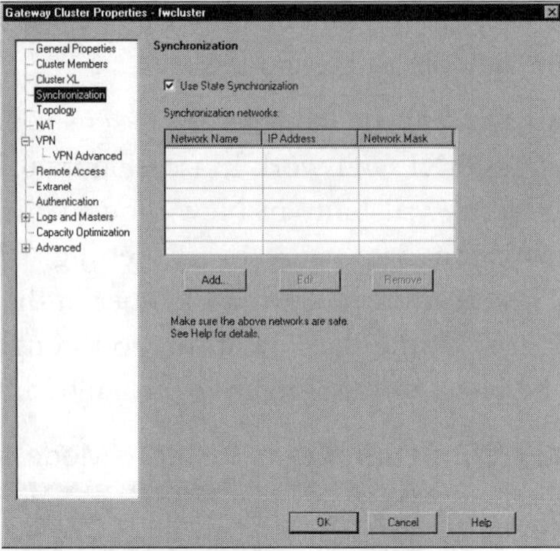

Figure 6.24 The State Synchronization Window

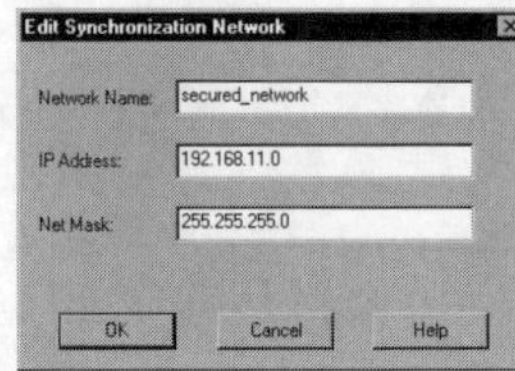

Figure 6.25 Our Completed Synchronization Network Definition

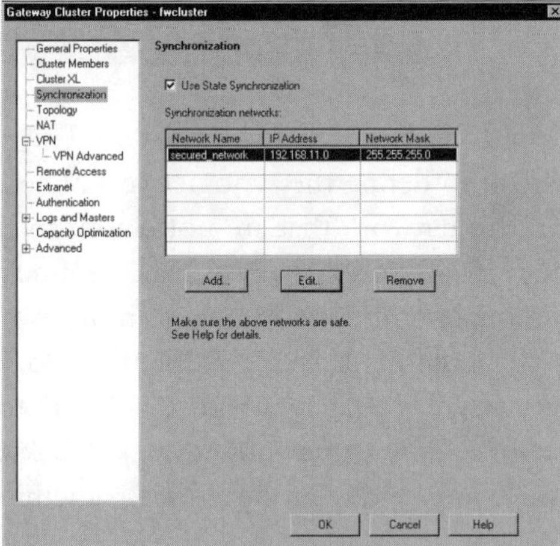

9. We now need to define the cluster's network topology. This is where you define the cluster's VIP addresses. Click the **Topology** item on the left side of the screen (see Figure 6.26). Click the **Add** button. A popup window (see

Figure 6.27) will appear to allow you to create a VIP address and provide it with a netmask.

Figure 6.26 The Topology Screen of Cluster Before Topology Has Been Defined

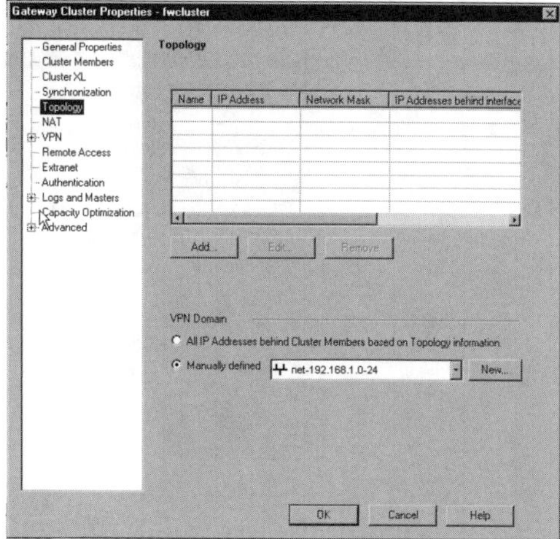

Figure 6.27 Cluster Topology Definition: Defining the External Virtual IP Address

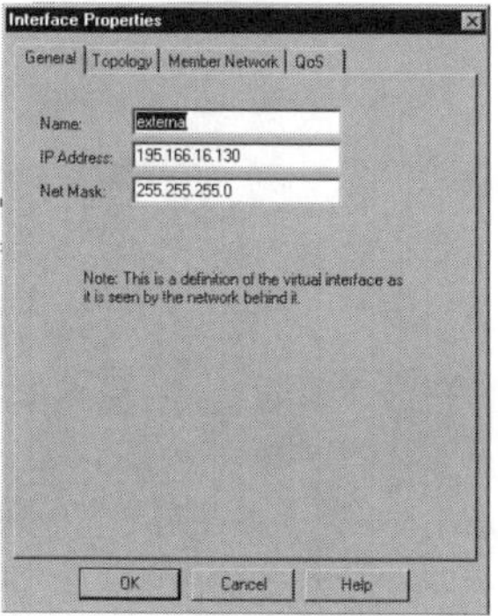

10. Next, click the **Topology** tab of the **Interface Properties** window (see Figure 6.28). Select this as the external interface because this is the Internet-facing VIP address on our cluster and we need to make sure that antispoofing is enabled.

11. Select the **Member Network** tab of the **Interface Properties** window (see Figure 6.29). This tab determines which interfaces the VIP address will function on. By default, it picks up the network and subnet mask of any interfaces you have already defined in the same subnet. However, the VIP address and

the physical interfaces that the VIP address will "listen" on do not have to be the same subnet. In our example, the VIP address is in the same subnet as our external interfaces.

Figure 6.28 Topology of Cluster: External Interface Definition of the Cluster

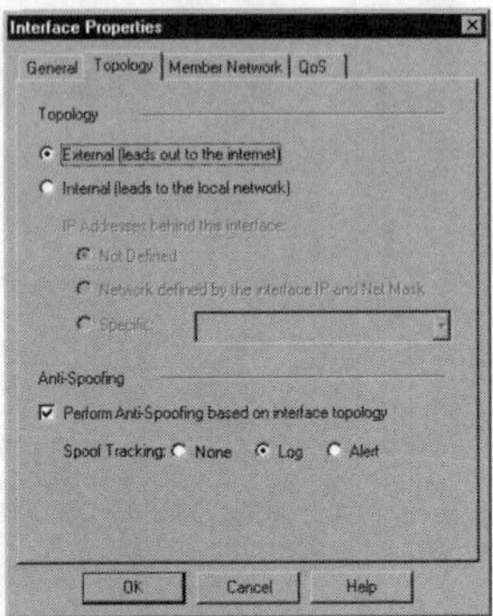

Figure 6.29 The Member Network Tab of the Cluster's Interface Properties

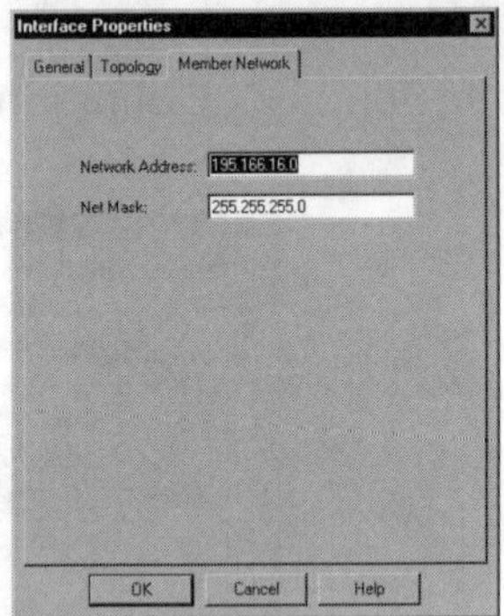

12. Click **OK** when you have defined the network. Doing so brings you back to the screen in Figure 6.26, but this time, you will have the external VIP address of the cluster defined. You need to repeat Steps 9–11 for all the interfaces of the cluster. In our example:

    - DMZ, Virtual IP = 192.168.12.130, internal, network defined by this IP address and subnet, member network = 192.168.12.0, subnet = 255.255.255.0.
    - Internal, Virtual IP = 192.168.1.130 , internal, network defined by this IP address and subnet, member network = 192.168.1.0, subnet = 255.255.255.0.

When this process is completed, the cluster topology screen should look like Figure 6.30.

Figure 6.30 The Completed ClusterXL Topology Definition

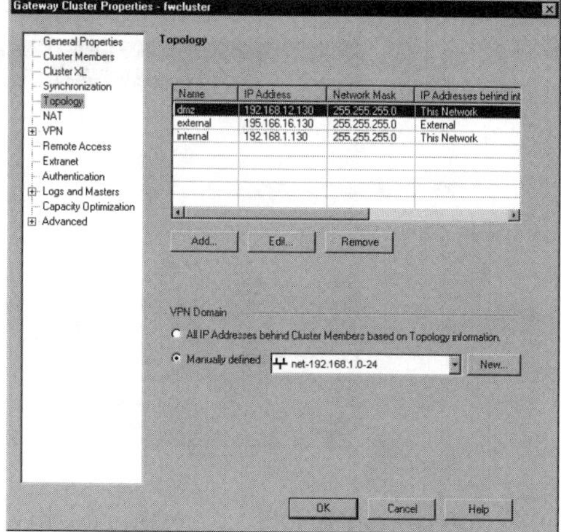

13. This completes the definition of the cluster module for just one cluster member. Click **OK** to complete the creation of the Cluster Gateway object. When you click OK, you will see the message shown in Figure 6.31. An IKE certificate is being created for the cluster object itself. Note that this would replace any IKE certificates that existed for any enforcement modules if we had added them to the cluster.

Figure 6.31 The IKE Certificate Message Displayed When You Click OK

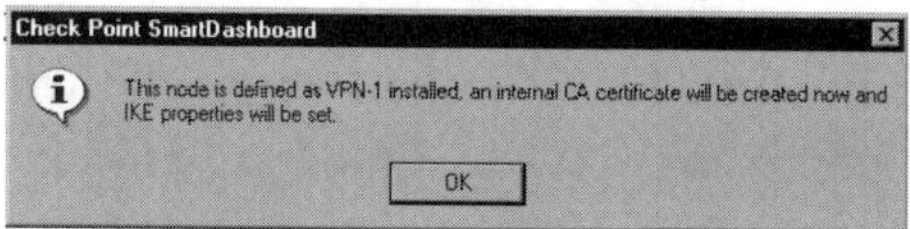

Step 2: Installing a Simple Security Policy to the New Cluster

Create a simple policy—perhaps even "Any source, any destination, any service, accept, log." At this point, we won't try any NAT or VPNs or otherwise run before walking. As we installed Policy Server on the module, we will also create a simple "open" desktop security policy. These policies are clearly insecure; don't connect the cluster to untrusted networks yet, but do keep all its interfaces "up." The idea here is to create a very simple Rule Base for testing the cluster:

1. Once the policies are ready, click the **Policy | Install** menu, as shown in Figure 6.32. The new cluster object should appear in the possible targets.

Select the cluster object (only) and click **OK**. The FireWall-1 SmartCenter Server will then proceed to compile and install the policy to each cluster member (of which there is only one defined at present!).

Figure 6.32 Policy Install to the Cluster: Single Member Only

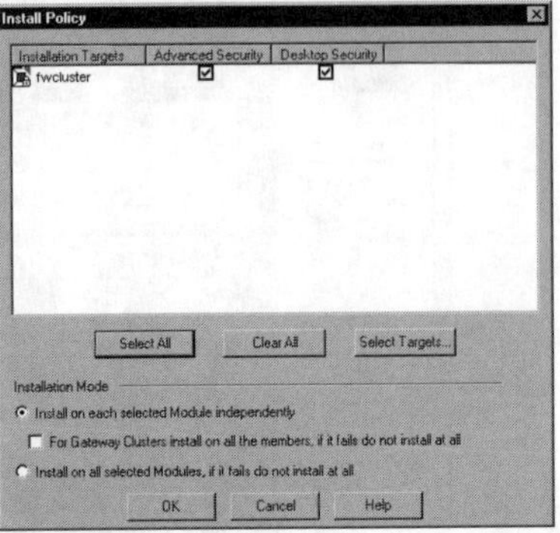

2. Hopefully the policy will install successfully. If it does not, possible causes could be a configuration error in the cluster object (although this is usually indicated at the time of configuration) or connectivity to the cluster. Assuming all went well, you now have configured a one-member ClusterXL HA New mode cluster. At this point, it is a good idea to check the cluster's health. You can start the SmartView Status client, and you should be able to see the status, as shown in Figure 6.33. Check that the cluster member is active and that all the components in the cluster object show a green tick, which indicates that they are functioning correctly. You might see a warning against ClusterXL; possible causes are that an interface is down or HA is not enabled on the cluster member. In addition, take note of the working mode stated in the ClusterXL Details window. It should say *High availability*.

Figure 6.33 SmartView Status Showing Cluster with Single Member

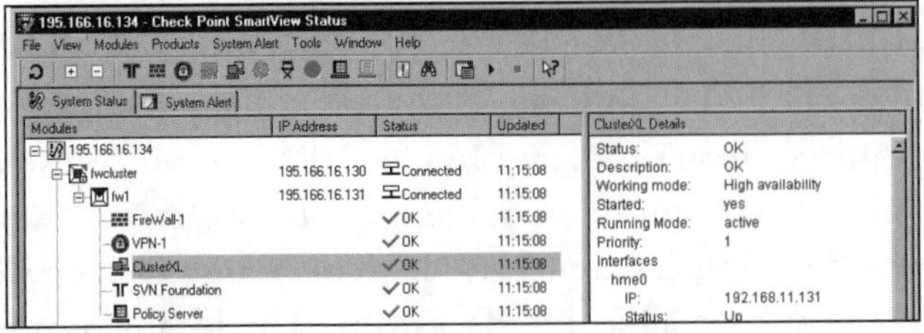

Step 3: Adding a Second Enforcement Module to the Cluster

We are now in a position where a Gateway Cluster object has been defined and has one member, and all appears to be working fine.

In our example, let's add an existing enforcement module to the cluster. If there were no existing module, we would add a new enforcement module to the cluster, following the same steps we used to add the first member. We will then push a policy to our newly expanded cluster.

Our existing enforcement module object is shown in Figure 6.34. Before proceeding, it is important to be happy that this module is working fine as a standalone gateway. Ensure that the Check Point products installed on this gateway (in reality and on the object!) match those of the new cluster object.

Figure 6.34 Existing FireWall-1 Gateway Object

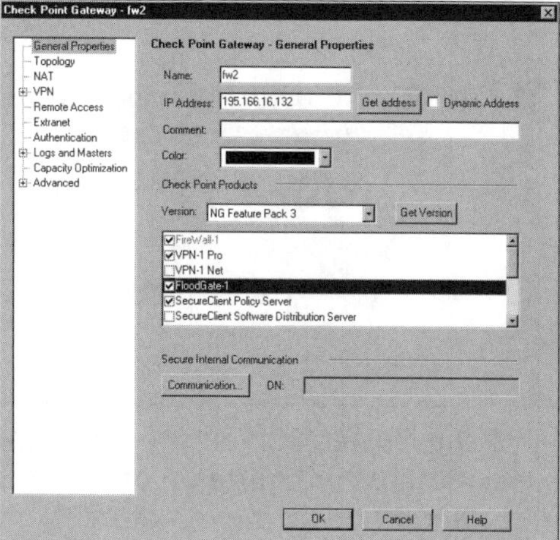

1. To start the process of adding the existing gateway into our cluster, edit the **Gateway Cluster** object. Click **Cluster Members** in the left side menu. Click the **Add** button to add an existing firewall module to the cluster. Select our existing **fw2** gateway module and click **OK** (see Figure 6.35).

Figure 6.35 Adding a Firewall Gateway to a Cluster Object

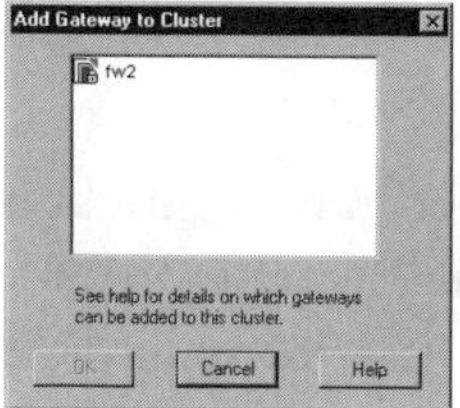

WARNING

You might not see an existing gateway object when you attempt to add a gateway into the cluster. This could be due to the gateway being a member of a VPN community. The procedure of adding the gateway to a cluster removes the gateway VPN configuration, so this is not allowed while the gateway is a community member. You must remove the gateway from the community using VPN Manager before adding the gateway to the cluster.

2. When you select OK, you will receive the warning shown in Figure 6.36. Click **Yes** to proceed.

Figure 6.36 fw2 Adding to Cluster Warning Message

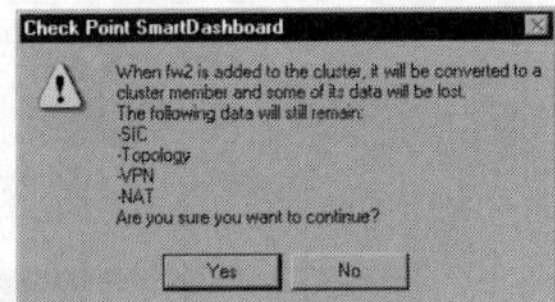

WARNING

Adding the gateway to the cluster will remove the gateway VPN configuration. Restoring the VPNs will require configuration of the cluster VPN settings, but it could also require reconfiguration at the remote VPN end points. They will need to refer to your VPN gateway using the new VIP address of the cluster, and if the VPN is certificate based, the new IKE certificate must be distributed.

3. We need to identify which of this member's interfaces is on the secured network. Edit the member and click the **Topology** tab. Double-click the interface that is going to be on your secured network (in this example, hme0, which is on 192.168.11.132). Make sure you uncheck the **Cluster Interface** check box (see Figure 6.37).
4. Your Cluster Members screen should now have two modules as members (fw1 and fw2), as shown in Figure 6.38. Note that if you click one, you can then promote or demote its priority in the cluster. This determines which one will be online initially.
5. Click **OK**. You can now install the test policy to the cluster gateway module, which now has two members.

Figure 6.37 Selecting the Interface That Will Be the Secured Network

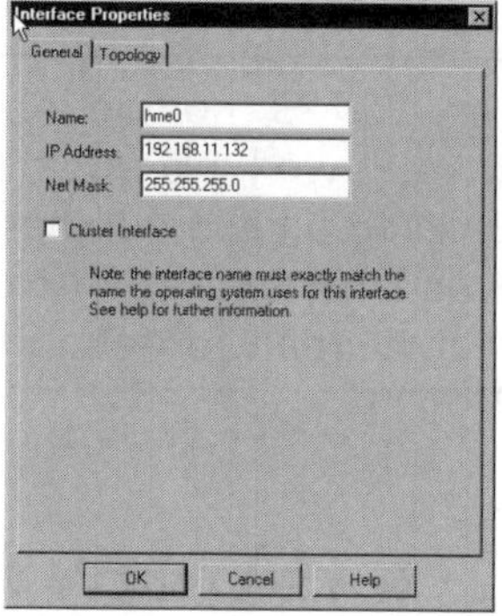

Figure 6.38 A Cluster Gateway Showing Two Cluster Members

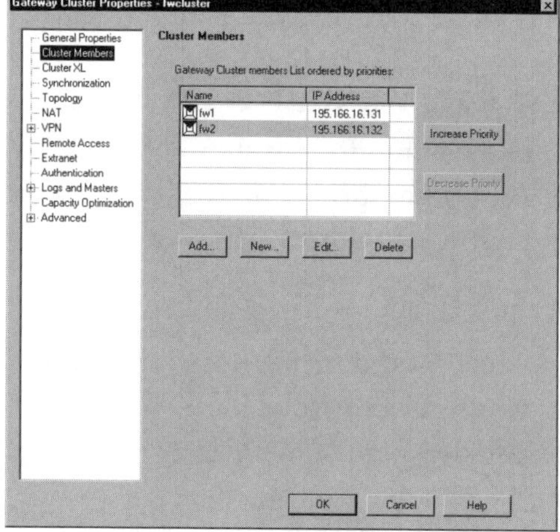

WARNING

It is recommended that you reboot the module that you have just added. After pushing a policy to a standalone module that requires that it becomes a cluster member, the ClusterXL module might not fully configure itself immediately. You could find that the active online member complains about the status of this new inactive member of the cluster (use the *cphaprob state* command on the online member or the SmartView Status GUI). Rebooting the offline member should remedy this situation.

NOTE

A new installation of an NG FP3 module inherits a full license for a 15-day trial period. It could well be that we have got this far in installation and configuration without actually adding a valid purchased license. Now is a good time to use the SmartUpdate management client to attach your purchased licenses to the cluster members, rather than forget and get a nasty surprise in 15 days.

Testing ClusterXL in HA New Mode

Once you have ClusterXL in HA New mode up and running, you will want to test it to ensure that it is functioning properly. There are many ways in which you can do this; we now look at three simple tests that you can perform.

Test 1: Pinging the Virtual IP Address of Each Interface

With ClusterXL in HA New mode, you should be able to ping the VIP address of each network from an adjacent host—providing that your security policy allows such an action. This is a useful test for a number of reasons:

- It tests that the VIP address is up and running.
- It identifies which of the members is replying to your ping. Look at the MAC address that you receive in your local workstation ARP cache. To view the ARP cache, use the command *arp –a*.

In our example (based on Figure 6.12), we log on to the host on IP 192.168.1.200 (PDC) and ping the VIP of 192.168.1.130. If host fw1 is active (therefore fw2 is on standby), we would expect to see the MAC address of 08:00:20:ca:64:fb in the ARP cache of 192.168.1.200. The reason that we know that fw1 is active is that the MAC address 08:00:20:ca:64:fb is the internal interface (qfe3) MAC address for fw1. If there was a failover to fw2, we would see the MAC address of the internal interface of member fw2 (08:00:20:a4:99:ef).

Test 2: Using SmartView Status to Examine the Status of the Cluster Members

When using ClusterXL, we use the SmartView Status GUI to monitor what each member in our cluster is doing. We are also able to stop and start the ClusterXL module on a member from this GUI. This tool can be used to manually fail over from the active member, perhaps before performing some maintenance. For example, in

Figure 6.39, we can see that member fw2 is active. If we right-click fw2 and select **Stop Member**, we will force fw1 to switch to active. This assumes that fw1—or another cluster member—is available. Be sure to check this status before stopping the current active member!

Figure 6.39 SmartView Status GUI Showing ClusterXL HA New Mode with Member fw2 Active

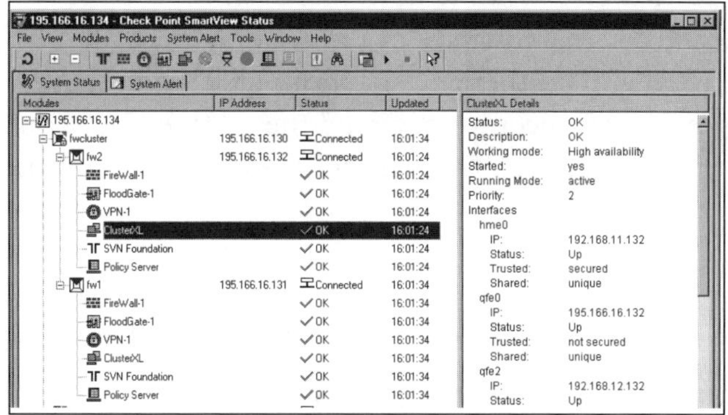

Take note of the Running Mode field, which states whether the member is active or not.

NOTE

Note that if a member has been disabled using "Stop member," the ClusterXL Details pane might still show the member as active. This is because we have lost contact with the ClusterXL module on that member, and the GUI is still displaying the last known status. It is worth checking the last updated time for the ClusterXL status and forcing an update (right-click **ClusterXL** and select **Update**).

A stopped member can be revived by right-clicking the member name and selecting **Start Member**. Note that it will stay in Standby mode irrespective of its priority if **Maintain Current Active gateway** is set in the cluster object.

Test 3: FTP Session Through the Cluster When an Interface Fails

As with all cluster solutions, the best tests are those simulating real-world failure. Physically damaging cluster members is probably the most challenging test but probably not a popular option, either. A more acceptable test is disconnecting a network cable from the current master member during a file download through the cluster.

In our example, we initiate a command-line FTP session from the internal host on 192.l68.1.200 to 192.168.12.133 (refer to Figure 6.12). The default gateway of host 192.168.1.200 will be the cluster VIP address for that subnet (192.168.1.130). The default gateway for 192.168.12.133 will be VIP 192.168.12.130.

We will use the *ftp hash* command in order to display the blocks downloaded so we can see the download's progress. A large file should be chosen that will take at least a minute to download; that gives us time to test failover.

If you pull out the external interface of the active member (for example, if member fw1 were active, removing the Ethernet cable from qfe0 would cause a fail condition), you should see member fw2 become active and the FTP session should continue, probably after a pause of a few seconds. This particular test is useful because it tests the following things:

- The hosts communicating have the correct default gateway.
- The hubs and switches are working correctly in an HA environment.
- The firewall members are failing over correctly.
- The hosts on the local subnet respond to the failover gratuitous arp.
- The firewall members' state tables are fully synchronized.

Command-Line Diagnostics on ClusterXL

Let's take a look at some useful command-line tools that can be used to monitor ClusterXL.

fw hastat

The *fw hastat* command can be used to check the basic status of each cluster member locally or remotely. The *fw hastat* command has the following syntax:

```
fw hastat <hostname / or IP address>
```

A typical response if this command is run on a local firewall cluster member module is:

```
    HOST           NUMBER       HIGH AVAILABILITY STATE          MACHINE STATUS
localhost1           1                   active                            OK
```

cphaprob

The *cphaprob* command is probably the most versatile command that can be used to monitor and manipulate ClusterXL. Here we cover just a few of the common syntaxes of this command, but it can do a lot more than merely show information about the cluster. This command can be used in order to integrated tailored status checking—maybe checking hardware health of a member.

The command can be used on either of the cluster members (not on the firewall management module). Running *cphaprob stat* on either of the firewall cluster members should tell you the status of each of the cluster members from the point of view of the cluster member you are running the command on. Here is an example output:

```
Working mode: Active up (unique IPs)

Number          Unique Address          State

1                192.168.11.132          active
2 (local)             none*              standby
```

NOTE

If you see *none* in the unique address for one of the cluster members, you need to reboot the module, then run the *cphaprob state* command again. It can also mean that the member is not correctly configured in the SmartDashboard GUI and that no secured interface exists on the member.

You can also use this command with different arguments to provide details of interfaces. The syntax for examining the interfaces on the local member is *cphaprob -a if*. The command will tell you the status of each interface and the virtual cluster IP addresses.

In this example, the local cluster member is in Standby mode:

```
Required interfaces: 3
Required secured interfaces: 1

hme0        UP                              (secured, unique)
qfe0        DOWN (2505.8 secs)            (non secured, unique)
qfe2        UP                              (non secured, unique)
qfe3        UP                              (non secured, unique)

Virtual cluster interfaces: 3

qfe0            195.166.16.130
qfe2            192.168.12.130
qfe3            192.168.1.130
```

In this example, we can see that the interface qfe0 is down—probably a cable or interface problem. Looking at the information further down, we see that qfe0 is associated with the VIP address of 195.166.16.130, the external interface, so that is where we should start looking for network problems. Until this problem is resolved, we expect this member to stay in Standby mode; hopefully another member in the cluster will be active.

cpstat ha

The *cpstat ha* command gives detailed status details from the local member—similar information to that displayed by the SmartView Status GUI. Run without arguments, the output to this command is something like:

```
Product name: High Availability
Version:       NG Feature Pack 3
Status:        OK
HA installed: 1
Working mode: High availability
HA started:   yes
```

More usefully, you can use the syntax *cpstat –f all ha* to get this:

```
Product name:           High Availability
Major version:          5
Minor version:          0
Service pack:           3
Version string:         NG Feature Pack 3
Status code:            0
Status short:           OK
Status long:            OK
HA installed:           1
Working mode:           High availability
HA protocol version: 2
HA started:             yes
HA state:               active
HA identifier:         1


Interface table
```

```
---------------------------------------------------
|Name|IP              |Status|Verified|Trusted|Shared|
---------------------------------------------------
|hme0|192.168.11.131|Up    |       0|      1|     0|
|qfe0|195.166.16.131|Up    |     500|      0|     0|
|qfe2|192.168.12.131|Up    |       0|      0|     0|
|qfe3| 192.168.1.131|Up    |       0|      0|     0|
---------------------------------------------------



Problem Notification table
-----------------------------------------------
|Name           |Status|Priority|Verified|Descr|
-----------------------------------------------
|Synchronization|OK    |       0|     198|     |
|Filter         |OK    |       0|     188|     |
|cphad          |OK    |       0|       0|     |
|fwd            |OK    |       0|       0|     |
```

How Does ClusterXL HA New Mode Work?

In HA New mode, on each member of the cluster, each interface that will share a VIP address will keep its existing MAC address. No additional shared MAC addresses are used. When a client that is on the nonsecured network ARPs for the virtual IP (which will be the client's default gateway IP address), the cluster member that is active will reply with its MAC address and so will receive the through routed traffic.

Note that a client should still be able to connect to any of the valid IP addresses of the cluster on the same local subnet, regardless of which member is active (assuming that the interface is not down, the OS hasn't crashed, or the local firewall policy does not prevent it).

Because all members are "live" but only one handles traffic, HA New mode could be seen as load sharing but with 100 percent of the traffic going through one member only and all other members on standby having 0 percent of the traffic. This is opposed to traditional HA solutions in which the standby members are "offline" and unreachable.

If we consider the diagram in Figure 6.40, we can see that member fw1 is active and fw2 is in Standby mode.

Figure 6.40 Active Traffic Routing Through the Active Cluster Member

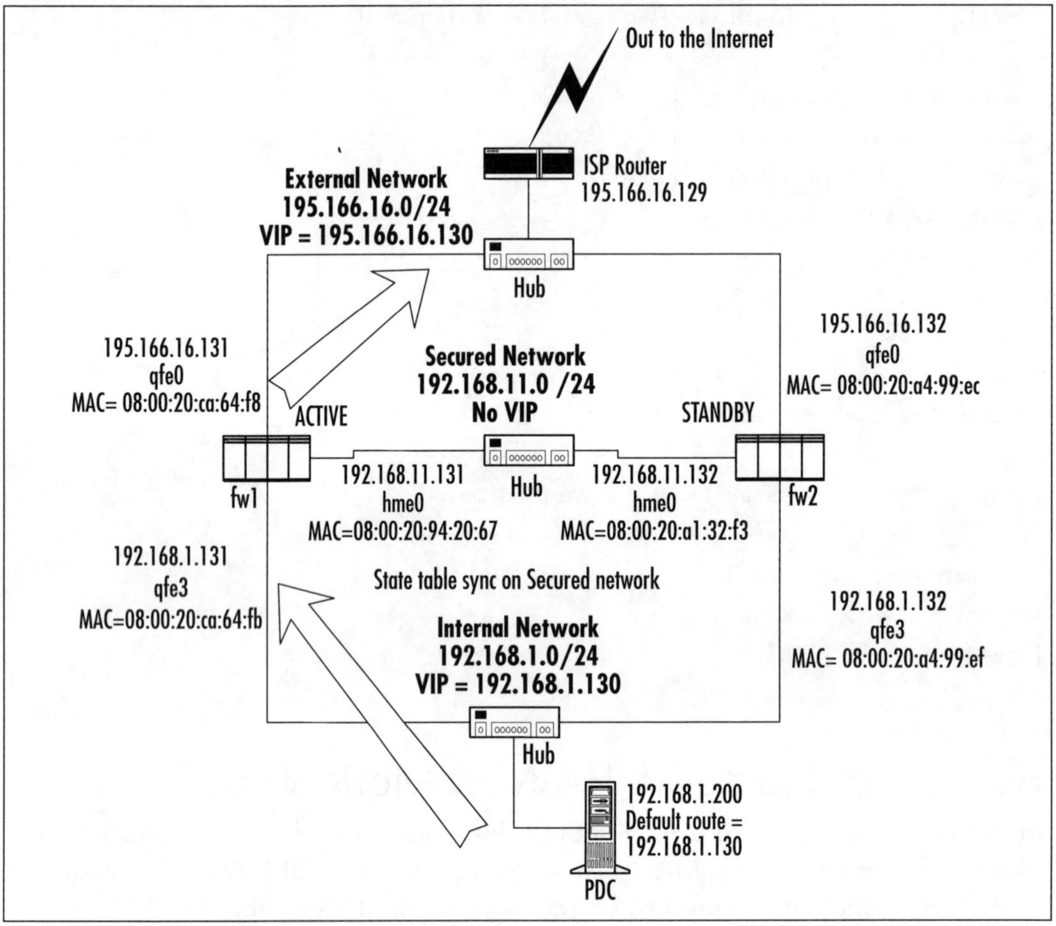

All network traffic should be routed through firewall member fw1—but only if its default gateway is set to the VIP address of 192.168.1.130.

If we take an example in which host 192.168.1.200 initiates a connection to a host out on the Internet and we are using Hide NAT behind the external cluster IP of 195.166.16.130, it will first ARP for the default gateway IP address. Host fw1 should respond because it is the active member in the cluster, with its internal interface MAC address of 08:00:20:ca:64:fb. This will be put in the ARP cache table of host 192.168.1.200, and a TCP connection—source IP 192.168.1.200, destination IP = 216.238.8.44, destination MAC 08:00:20:ca:64:fb—will originate from the host.

It is normal to use Hide NAT when internal hosts access the Internet, and this also makes it easy for replies to get back to your site. When the packet from host 192.168.1.200 leaves host fw1, the source IP will be address translated to 195.166.16.130

(and the source port will also change). The packet will then be routed out toward the ISP router (based on the default gateway of member fw1).

The reply packet will come back through the ISP router, which will ARP for a MAC address for 195.166.16.130. The fw-1 member is active and will respond with its external interface MAC of 08:00:20:ca:64:f8. The ISP router adds this into its ARP cache and sends the reply packet for the session back to 195.166.16.130, MAC address 08:00:20:ca:64:f8.

Member fw-1 then uses its stateful inspection to address translate the existing Hide NAT session so that the destination IP is changed from 195.166.16.130 to 192.168.1.200. The reply is then sent from interface qfe3 on fw1, source MAC address 08:00:20:ca:64:fb, to the host on 192.168.1.200.

ClusterXL HA New Mode Failover

On failover from the active cluster member to the standby member, adjacent routers and hosts still maintain the MAC address for the failed member in their ARP caches. Packets sent at this point arrive at the failed host and probably go no further. The cluster member that has just come active resolves this problem by issuing a "gratuitous ARP." The ARP is broadcast on the local subnet of all interfaces that have a VIP and will have the MAC address for the local interface of the new active member in the cluster. This should mean that adjacent routers will learn the new MAC addresses for the VIP addresses.

NOTE

Under some circumstances in NG FP3, there is a problem where the cluster member that comes online does not always issue a gratuitous ARP. This should be resolved in hotfix releases. It is a good idea to obtain and apply the latest released hotfix.

Let's now look in detail at what happens if the active member fails. If we consider the diagram in Figure 6.40, we can see that traffic is routing through the active member, and Hide NAT is being done to hide the internal host of 192.168.1.200 behind the cluster IP address of 195.166.16.130. Should an interface fail (as shown in Figure 6.41, for example), all traffic from 192.168.1.200 will not be able to get through to the qfe3 interface on member fw1, and traffic that is coming back will not get back to 192.168.1.200 because the interface is down.

At this point, fw2 will notice that fw1 is not responding on the qfe3 interface and will take note of this situation. If the interface stays down for a period of time, fw2 will start running its pre-online tests. These pre-online tests allow fw2 to determine if it is healthy enough to take over from host fw1. (We discuss these tests in more detail in the "Nokia Failover Conditions" section of this chapter.) Once fw2 has determined that it is able to take over from fw1, it will issue a gratuitous ARP on all its interfaces that have a VIP address (see Figure 6.42).

Figure 6.41 Interface Failure on Active Member

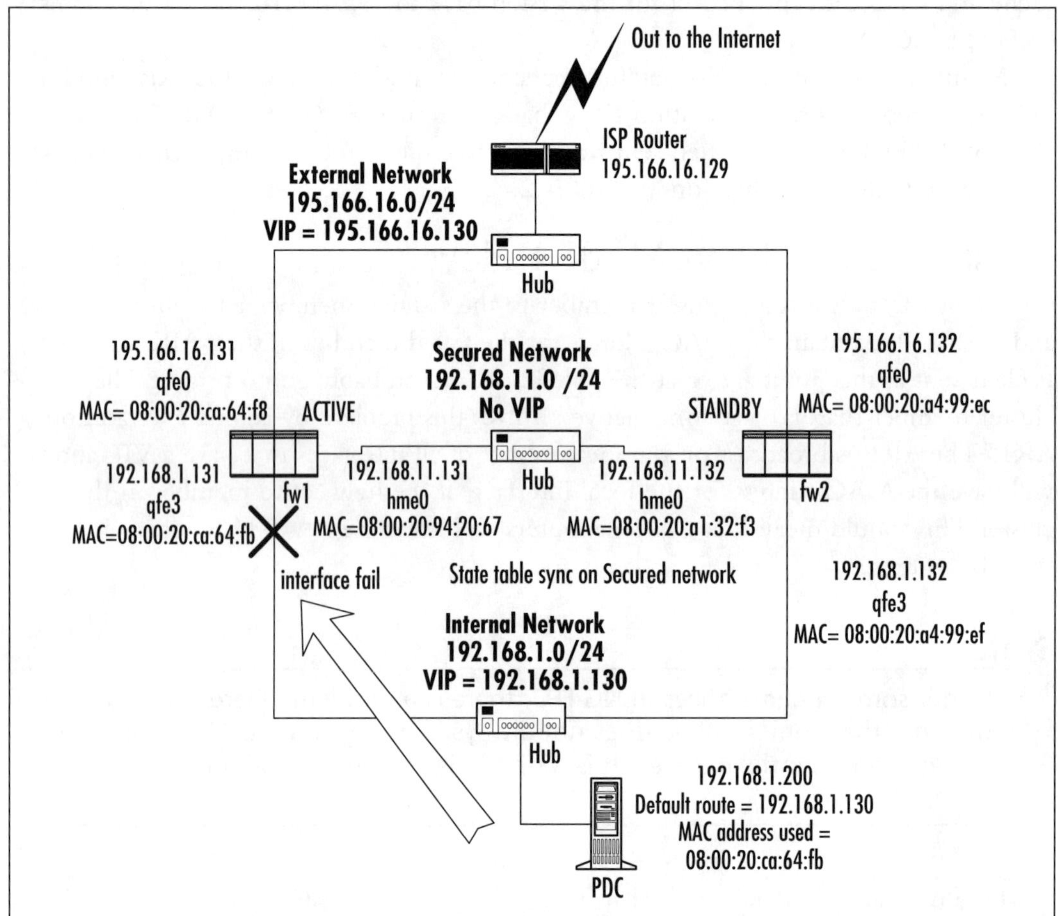

This will be cached by all devices on the local subnet of the interfaces of the firewall cluster, and they will update their ARP tables appropriately. This means that host 192.168.1.200 will now have a MAC address of 08:00:20:a4:99:ef in its ARP cache for IP address 192.168.1.130, so current through connections—perhaps an FTP session—should be able to continue.

On the external interface of the cluster, the ISP router would also have received a gratuitous ARP, updating its ARP table for 195.166.16.130 with MAC address 08:00:20:a4:99:ec—the external MAC address of qfe0 of fw2. At this point, fw1 will have considered itself offline in the SmartView Status GUI, stating that interface qfe3 is down.

Figure 6.42 Gratuitous ARP by fw2 to Take Over from fw1 on Failure

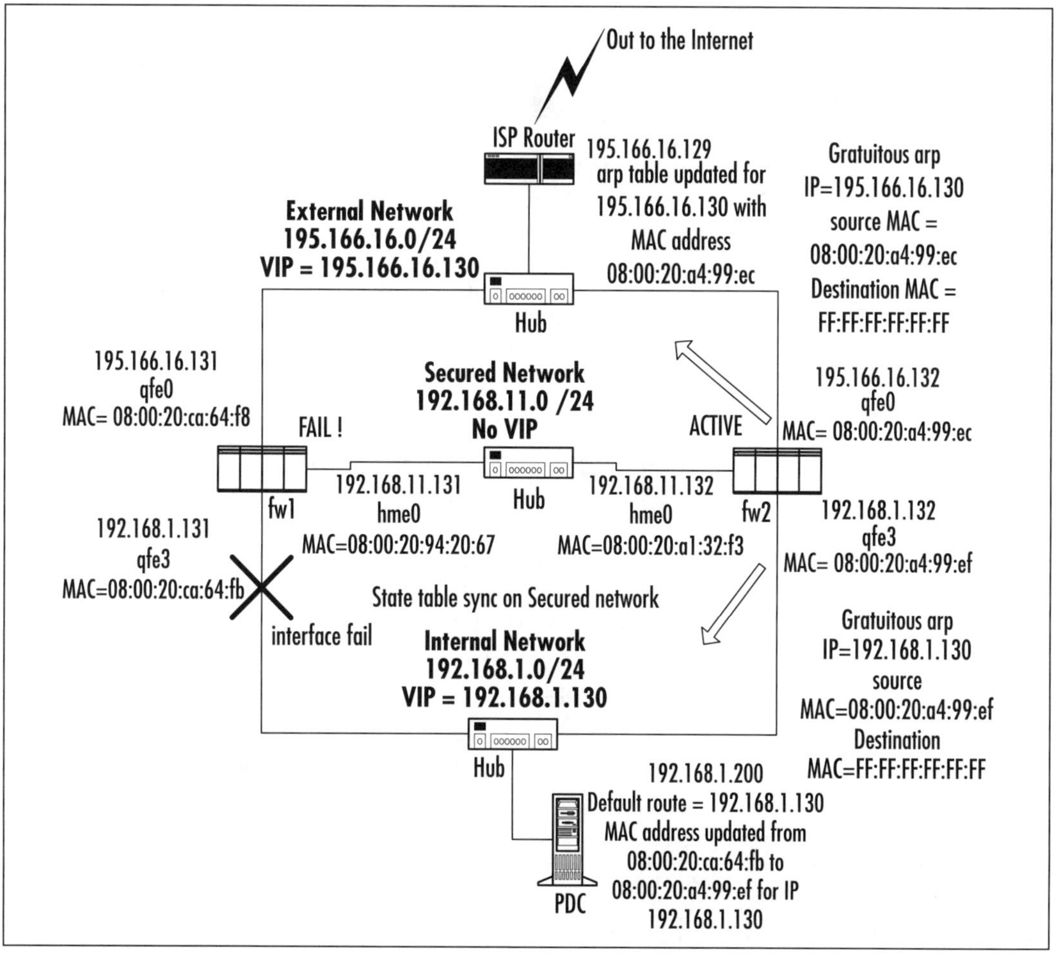

Once the FTP session recovers (which will only be the case if the gratuitous ARP is issued by fw2 and if state table sync is enabled between member fw1 and fw2), all traffic will continue to go through member fw2, as shown in Figure 6.43.
Should member fw1 recover, the cluster can be configured to either fail back to fw1 (which will have the highest priority) or continue working through fw2, which could have a lower priority. This can be configured in the **Cluster Gateway Object | Cluster XL Screen** (see Figure 6.22).

Figure 6.43 ClusterXL in HA New Mode, with Maintain Current Active Gateway Set After Failover

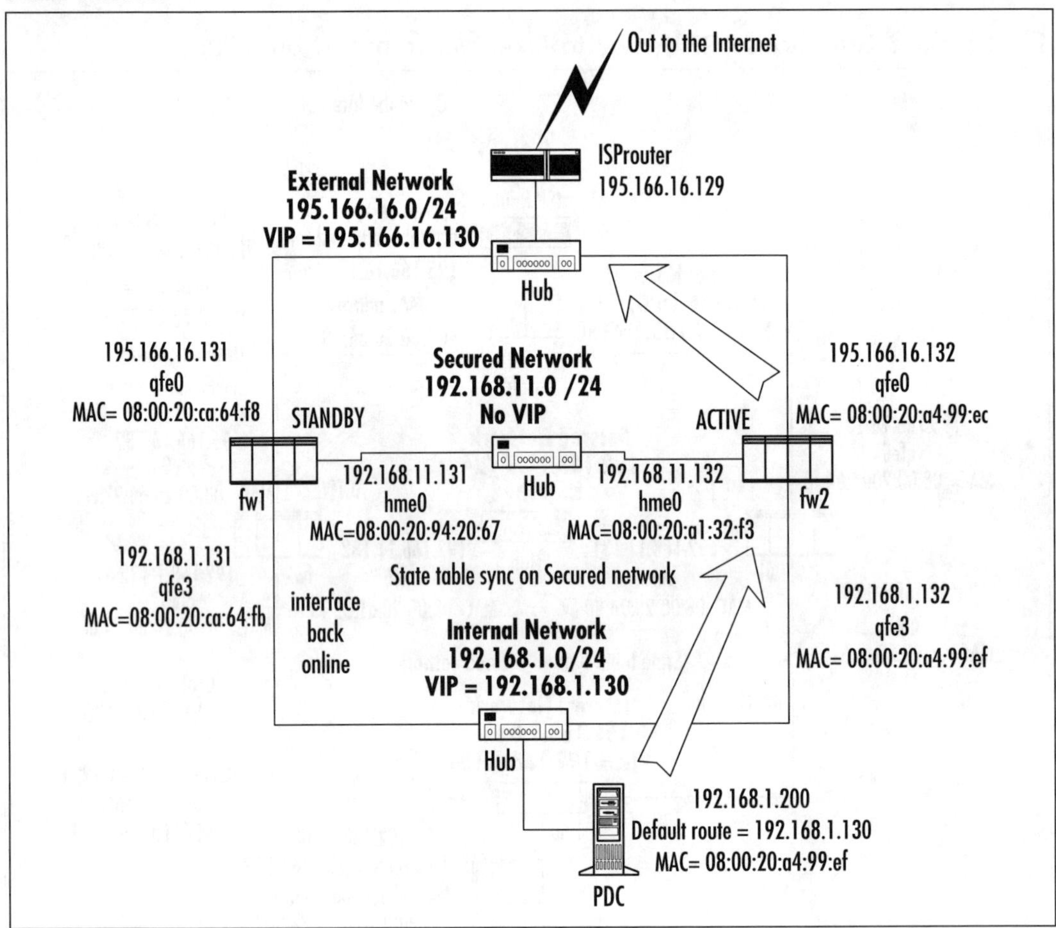

ClusterXL Failover Conditions

There are a number of conditions in which failover from one member to another will occur. These are:

- An interface or cable fails.
- Security policy is uninstalled.
- The machine crashes.
- Any process or device that specified with the *cphaprob* command (such as the *fwd* process) fails.

These conditions can be listed using the command *cphaprob list*.

But how does fw2 know to take over from fw1 when one of these conditions is met? How does a member in the cluster know that it can take over? These questions are answered when you analyze the CPHA protocol packets that each member sends to other members on each interface that has a VIP address.

TIP

Ethereal, a free network protocol analyzer, can decode the CPHA protocol from v0.9.8 upward. This can be very useful when investigating low-level ClusterXL issues. Ethereal is available at www.ethereal.com.

When a member of a cluster comes online, it issues an IGMP packet in order to advertise its membership of a multicast group. Connected switches with IGMP snooping ability can use this feature when deciding how to forward multicast traffic.

Status updates are sent from each member at regular intervals. Analysis shows the following properties of the update traffic for NG FP3, HA New Mode:

- At the data link layer (Layer 2 of the OSI model), the originating MAC address is always *00:00:00:00:fe:<member number>*, where member 1 in the cluster would be 00 and member 2 in the cluster would be 01—i.e., *member number - 1* is the last digit in the source MAC address.
- The destination MAC address is the multicast MAC for that VIP. For example, 01:00:5e:26:10:82 is the destination MAC seen on the external interface of our example network. The last two digits represent the VIP address's last two octets (16.130 where the entire VIP is 195.166.16.130).
- At Layer 3, we see the source IP is always 0.0.0.0 and the destination IP is the network address (195.166.16.0 in our example).
- Layer 4 shows that the transport is UDP with the source and destination port of 8116. The payload of the UDP packet is CPHA, which contains the following information:
  - Source machine ID is the same as last octet in the source MAC address of the packet.
  - Protocol version is 530 for NG FP3.

The rest of the UDP payload determines whether the member is sending out its status as a member on the cluster (there are other types). This includes each member's status as perceived by the member originating the packet and the last time it heard from the other members. This mechanism allows all members of the cluster to share their system status information.

WARNING

The multicast groups selected for intercluster communications are based on the last three octets of the VIP address. With this in mind, avoid using VIPs that end in the same three octets as other VIPs in the same broadcast domain.

Once an interface stops sending out status updates to the other members of the cluster, actions will start to be taken so that the highest-priority member that is active can then take over. When a member stops seeing status updates from the other member (or all the other members), it starts running a series of tests to determine the problem.

NOTE

CPHA protocol in NG FP2 (HA Legacy mode) is different from NG FP3 HA New mode in a number of ways. For one, the destination MAC address is a broadcast, not a multicast.

It will see if it can reach any other hosts that are valid on its subnet by ARPing for a selected range of IP addresses. A response suggests its own networking is good; no response could mean that it is disconnected from the network itself. It will attempt to ping the cluster IP address to see if it can receive any response from an active member; it will also attempt to ping the physical real IP of the other cluster member members. (For example, member 195.166.16.132 would ping 195.166.16.131 to see if it gets a response.) The member will also ping its default gateway.

Once these tests have completed, the member will make a decision as to whether it might be eligible for being a master and announces that it is active—and that the other member is dead—via the CPHA protocol.

The final step is that the member then issues a gratuitous ARP to the local subnets for the VIP (195.166.16.130 on qfe0 and 192.168.1.130 on qfe3 in our example)—and hopefully traffic resumes normally through this new active member.

NOTE

Now that you know that the firewall member that is in standby will issue ICMP echo requests to the default gateway—and other hosts on the local subnet as well as to the cluster IP and the other members in the cluster—it is a good idea to make sure that there are no access control lists on neighboring equipment on the same subnet that would block ICMP. The FireWall-1 policy on the cluster members themselves will not be a problem, because this CPHA module traffic bypasses the firewall filtering.

In Figure 6.44, we can see that the CPHA packet originated from the primary member. We can deduce this because the last octet in the MAC address source is 00. This is also confirmed in the CPHA protocol at a higher level, where the packet identifies the Source Machine ID as 0.

Figure 6.44 Breakdown of a CPHA Packet from Our Example

```
⊞ Frame 3 (78 bytes on wire, 78 bytes captured)
⊟ Ethernet II, Src: 00:00:00:00:fe:00, Dst: 01:00:5e:26:10:82
    Destination: 01:00:5e:26:10:82 (01:00:5e:26:10:82)
    Source: 00:00:00:00:fe:00 (00:00:00:00:fe:00)
    Type: IP (0x0800)
⊞ Internet Protocol, Src Addr: 0.0.0.0 (0.0.0.0), Dst Addr: 195.166.16.0 (195.166.16.0)
⊞ User Datagram Protocol, Src Port: 8116 (8116), Dst Port: 8116 (8116)
⊟ Check Point High Availability Protocol
    Magic Number: 0x1a90 (correct)
    Protocol Version: 530 (NG Feature Pack 3)
    Cluster Number: 2525
    HA OpCode: 1 (FWHA_MY_STATE - Report source machine's state)
    Source Interface: 2
    Random ID: 16251
    Source Machine ID: 0
    Destination Machine ID: 65534
    Policy ID: 65535
    Filler: 256
  ⊟ FWHA_MY_STATE
      Number of IDs reported: 2
      Report Code: Interface information included
      HA mode: 4 (FWHA_ONE_UP_MODE)
      HA Time unit: 0 miliseconds
    ⊟ Machine states
        State of node 0: 2 (Standby)
        State of node 1: 4 (Active/Active-Attention)
    ⊟ Interface states
        Interfaces up in the Inbound: 4
        Interfaces assumed up in the Inbound: 0
        Interfaces up in the Outbound: 4
        Interfaces assumed up in the Outbound: 0
      Cluster 0: last packet seen 0 time units ago
      Cluster 1: last packet seen 1 time units ago
```

Other areas to take note of are the source and destination MAC addresses, the IP addresses, and the port numbers used by the CPHA protocol.

The "Machine states" field shows what member 0 in the cluster thinks the status of the other members in the cluster are. Of course, member 0 could be incorrect.

Special Considerations for ClusterXL in HA New Mode

As with all clustering solutions, ClusterXL requires that you must always take into account some special considerations. These are usually based on the way that the clustering solution functions and can cause limitations when attempting to use certain functions of the firewall.

Network Address Translation

When using NAT on a cluster, you have to consider carefully how you are address translating and how it will be affected by the way the cluster works—especially when failover to another member occurs.

In ClusterXL in HA New mode, the original MAC addresses of the physical interfaces are used. When using static destination NAT, this will cause a problem if you have *manual* proxy ARP entries for the NAT addresses. This causes a problem because each member in the HA cluster would be advertising its own physical MAC address, and all may respond when an adjacent router ARPs for the NAT address. There is no control over which of the members will receive traffic for the NAT address.

Warning

Manual proxy ARP entries in the ARP table of a cluster member's operating system will not work with HA New mode.

In Figure 6.45, we can see the types of problems that manually added static ARP entries for Manual NAT might cause. In Figure 6.45, each member in the cluster is proxy ARPing its own local MAC address for the qfe0 interface for the NAT IP address of 195.166.16.133, which the firewall modules will have a NAT rule to translate to the real IP address of 192.168.12.133.

Figure 6.45 Possible Scenario If Manual ARP Entries Are Used for NAT

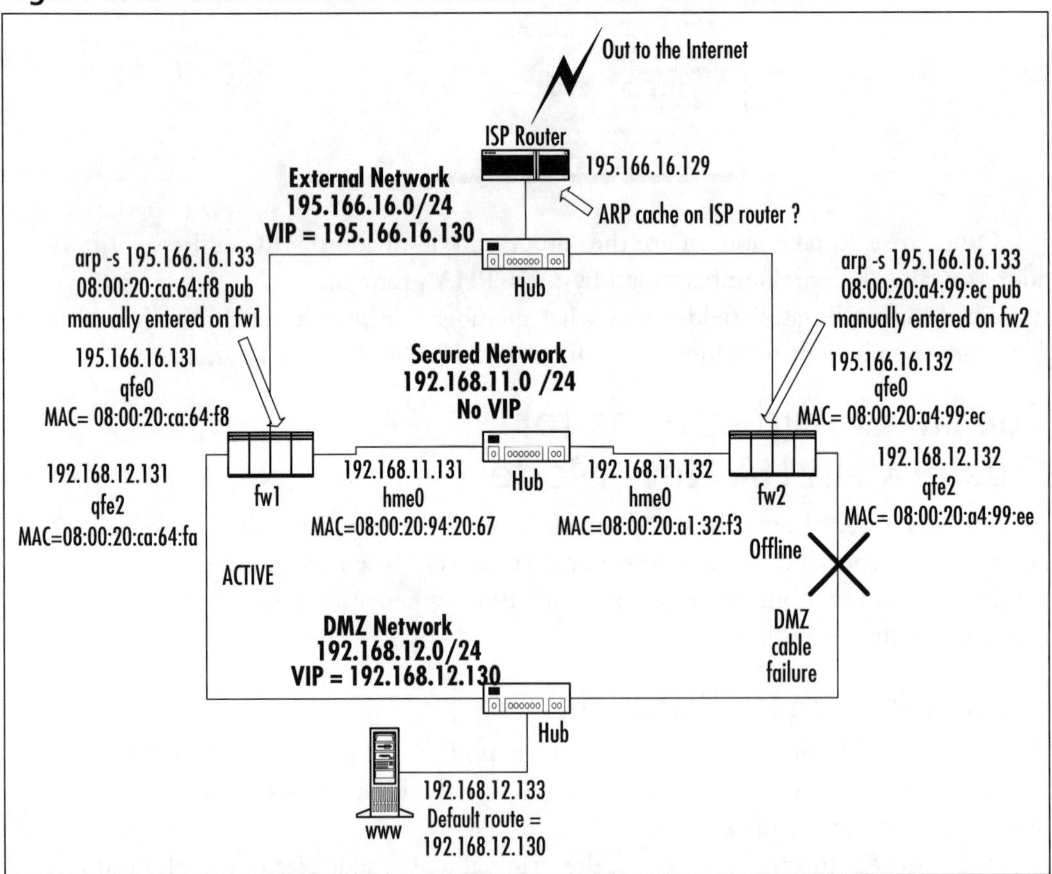

This will cause undesirable effects in an HA environment. You have no easy way of determining which MAC address the ISP router will have cached for the IP address 195.166.16.133. If you are unlucky, it could be the member that is in Standby mode.

In this scenario, and if the member in standby is "fit" and there are no faults, the packet will travel through the member as normal (even though it is on standby) and reach the internal host 192.168.12.133. However, because the default gateway of host 192.168.12.133 is the DMZ VIP of 192.168.12.130, the www host will have the MAC address of qfe2 of member fw1 in its ARP cache, so the reply packet would travel via member fw1. This means that you have asymmetric routing occurring.

If we take this scenario one step further, where qfe2 fails (as shown in Figure 6.45), the NATed packet would not get through at all. What are the alternatives to manual ARP entries?

With Manual NAT Rules

If you want to keep using Manual NAT rules, you only have one option, which is to enter routes on the adjacent router(s). This would be a static host route entry forcing the NAT IP address to forward to the cluster VIP. For example, on our ClusterXL example, if you had a manual static destination NAT rule to NAT 195.166.16.133 to 192.168.12.133, you would add a route on the ISP router that looks something like:

```
195.166.16.133 , netmask 255.255.255.255 gateway 195.166.16.130
```

This states that to get to IP address 195.166.16.133 as a host route, the next hop is the VIP address of the cluster (see Figure 6.46).

With Automatic NAT Rules

If you are using Automatic NAT, you have some options. You can still use static routes on the ISP router to get the packets onto the active member of the cluster, as described in the Manual NAT section, but you also have another useful alternative.

If you are using Automatic NAT and you have the Automatic ARP Configuration set in the SmartDashboard menu **Policy | Global Properties | NAT – Network Address Translation | Automatic Rules** section (see Figure 6.47), a firewall member switching to Active mode will issue a gratuitous ARP for all the Automatic NAT objects as well as the cluster VIP.

Configuring ClusterXL in HA Legacy Mode

HA Legacy mode is the technology that has existed in earlier versions of Check Point NG (and, in fact, late versions of FireWall-1 4.1). From FP3, we have the option to use HA New mode, which provides the same functionality but improved underlying technology. For this reason, Check Point suggest that New mode is used in FP3 installations.

Figure 6.46 Using Static Routes on the ISP Router for NATed IP Addresses

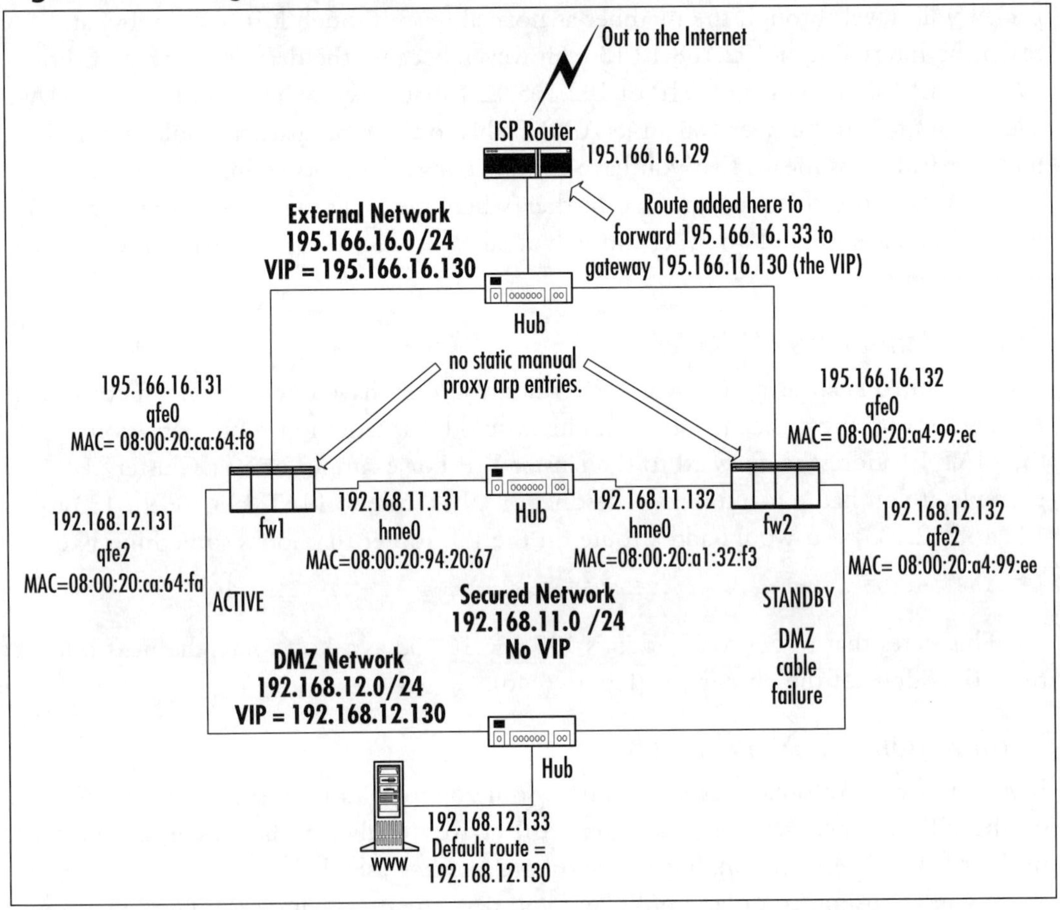

Out to the Internet
ISP Router
195.166.16.129
Route added here to
forward 195.166.16.133 to
gateway 195.166.16.130 (the VIP)
External Network
195.166.16.0/24
VIP = 195.166.16.130
Hub
no static manual
proxy arp entries.
195.166.16.131
qfe0
MAC= 08:00:20:ca:64:f8
195.166.16.132
qfe0
MAC= 08:00:20:a4:99:ec
192.168.11.131
hme0
MAC=08:00:20:94:20:67
Hub
192.168.11.132
hme0
MAC=08:00:20:a1:32:f3
192.168.12.131
qfe2
MAC=08:00:20:ca:64:fa
fw1
fw2
192.168.12.132
qfe2
MAC= 08:00:20:a4:99:ee
ACTIVE
Secured Network
192.168.11.0 /24
No VIP
STANDBY
DMZ
cable
failure
DMZ Network
192.168.12.0/24
VIP = 192.168.12.130
Hub
192.168.12.133
Default route =
192.168.12.130
WWW

Figure 6.47 Automatic NAT Settings for Cluster Member to Issue a Gratuitous ARP on Failover

Global Properties
FireWall-1
NAT - Network Address
Authentication
VPN-1 Pro
VPN-1 Net
Remote Access
Extranet Management I
LDAP Account Manage
FloodGate-1
SmartMap
Management High Ava
ConnectControl
OSE - Open Security E
Stateful Inspection
Log and Alert
SmartDashboard custo
NAT - Network Address Translation
Automatic NAT rules
Allow bi-directional NAT (for more details see help)
Translate destination on client side
Automatic ARP configuration
Manual NAT rules
Translate destination on client side
IP Pool NAT
Enable IP Pool NAT for SecuRemote/SecureClient and gateway to gateway connections
Address exhaustion track: None Log Alert
Address allocation and release track: None Log
Non-unique address ranges
All addresses that are not in the list will be considered as unique addresses.
First IP
Last IP
10.0.0.0
10.255.255.255
172.16.0.0
172.31.255.255
192.168.0.0
192.168.255.255
Add...
Edit...
Remove
OK
Cancel
Help

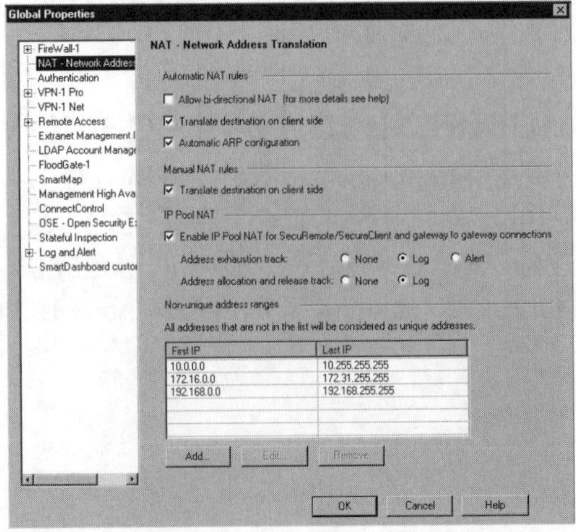

We do not discuss Legacy mode in detail; instead, we look at a summary of how Legacy mode differs, in terms of configuration procedure and operation:

- Cluster members should be prepared with identical IP addresses, with the exception of the secured network.
- When adding a cluster member, connect it to the secured network only until a policy has been installed to it, to avoid IP address conflicts.
- To select Legacy mode operation, select that mode in the gateway cluster object ClusterXL tab.
- Cluster object topology is configured implicitly by the duplicated IP addresses over the members.
- Standby members are reachable via the secured network only, so the management station must be connected to that network.
- The ClusterXL module configures all cluster members to use the same MAC address on their connected interfaces, so a single MAC address is presented to adjacent network devices.
- The CPHA protocol uses a broadcast destination MAC address.

Configuring ClusterXL in Load-Sharing Mode

In this section, we configure and test ClusterXL in Load-Sharing mode. As you will see, ClusterXL in Load-Sharing mode has a lot in common with ClusterXL HA New mode—especially its configuration. For this reason, it is a good idea to digest the contents of the HA New mode section of this chapter first! This mode also has a great deal in common with Nokia clustering in terms of how the cluster operates and appears to adjacent network equipment. These similarities will become apparent as we proceed.

Prerequisites for Configuring ClusterXL in Load-Sharing Mode

The configuration of ClusterXL in Load-Sharing mode is so similar to ClusterXL in HA New mode that all the HA prerequisites apply. Our example network topology is also identical (refer back to Figure 6.12).

You must make sure that your ISP router (and any adjacent routing equipment that is physically connected to the load-sharing interfaces) will accept an ARP reply with a multicast MAC—even if the IP address is not a multicast IP address. There are various ways of doing this, depending on the specific networking equipment. The reason for doing so is that ClusterXL in Load-Sharing mode allocates a multicast MAC address to the VIP address. This means that for a specific VIP address, the MAC address will stay the same. This means that all members in the cluster receive the network traffic, but only one will route the traffic based on a load-sharing algorithm that takes into account which members are available and properties of the traffic.

Configuration of ClusterXL in Load-Sharing Mode

In order to configure load sharing, follow the steps as you would for HA New mode, but when you come to configuring the Gateway Cluster object ClusterXL mode, select the **Load Sharing** radio button (see Figure 6.22).

Installing the policy will then make the cluster behave as a load-sharing cluster as opposed to an HA cluster. If the cluster was previously operating in HA mode, it is wise to reboot each member after the new policy install, to ensure that the ClusterXL modules are configured correctly.

Testing ClusterXL in Load-Sharing Mode

Once you have configured your ClusterXL in Load-Sharing mode, you will want to perform some tests to determine that your load sharing is working properly and to make sure that it functions as you expect under failure conditions. We can use the same tests we used for HA New mode, but we should see some differences in results:

Test 1: Pinging the Virtual IP Address for Each Interface

You should be able to ping the VIP address for each network. The main difference between this test and the HA test is that the MAC address of the VIP address is a multicast MAC address. When you ping from a host that is on the same local subnet as a VIP of the cluster, you should receive an ARP reply from one of the members of the cluster (not necessarily the member that will take the traffic; this is based on the load-sharing algorithm). The MAC address that you receive in the ARP cache will be a multicast MAC address.

If you were to run a packet trace while pinging the VIP address of the cluster, in the ping echo response packet from the cluster you will see the *real* MAC address of the member that responds as the source MAC address.

Test 2: Using SmartView Status to Examine the Status of the Cluster Members

As with HA modes, the SmartView Status GUI allows detailed monitoring and manual stop and start of the cluster members.

Looking at Figure 6.48, you can see that ClusterXL on member fw1 has a problem. If you examine the ClusterXL Details on the right side of the screen, you can see that interface qfe3 (the internal interface) is down. In this particular case, because it is a test, this was the interface we unplugged, so this was the expected result.

Figure 6.48 SmartView Status Demonstrating a Problem with an Interface

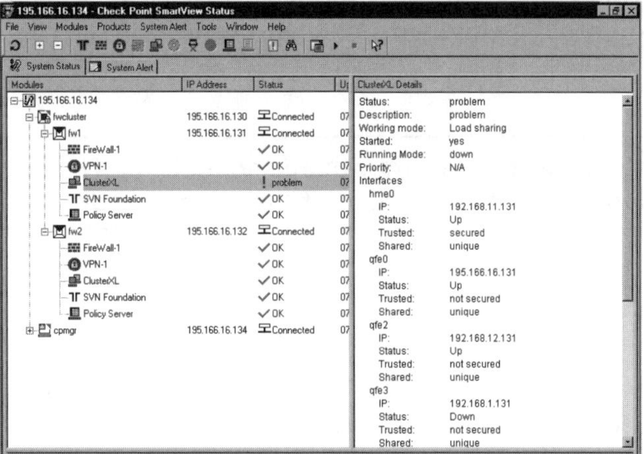

If you click **ClusterXL** for member fw2, you will see all the details of this member as well. You can see the details regarding the status of fwd and policy loaded if you scroll down a little further in the ClusterXL Details. The details show that the Working mode is Load Sharing and that the Running mode is *down* for member fw1. As with ClusterXL in HA New mode, you can right-click the **ClusterXL** icon and take that particular member down or start it up again. Be wary that if you do this, the SmartView Status will no longer receive updated information from the ClusterXL member, so it might still state that the member is up and running.

Test 3: FTPing Through ClusterXL Load Sharing During Failover

This test applies to load sharing as it did for HA mode; we still want connection resilience, so if a member fails, the load-sharing algorithm reallocates those connections to other members, and they are preserved. One snag with performing this type of test on a load-sharing cluster is this: How do we know which member the FTP traffic is going through? If you have the Real Time Monitor package installed on the modules, you could use that, as demonstrated later in the "How Nokia Clustering Works" section of this chapter. Another alternative is to watch the SmartView Tracker firewall logs and note which member logs the Accept of the FTP connection. However, in NG FP3, logging from cluster members is identified by the cluster name only, not the member name, so this is no help. Your other—rather unpleasant—option is to run a packet trace while the FTP download is taking place, identify a packet on the FTP connection that has come from the cluster, and check the source MAC address. This process will tell you which member the traffic is going through. You can then pull an interface cable out of the correct member in the cluster to observe failover. Take care not to stop the FTP session after taking the packet trace, and then start the FTP session again, because the new connection could go through a different member in the cluster!

NOTE

Happily, by the time you read this, there should be an FP3 hotfix release that will result in logging with the origin of the member, not the cluster name.

Command-Line Diagnostics for ClusterXL

The command-line diagnostic tools for ClusterXL in Load-Sharing mode are the same as ClusterXL in HA New mode, but the responses are different. Here, we take a quick look at how they differ.

fw hastat

When you run the *fw hastat* command on the cluster members, they should all respond with a status of active. In our little example, you would see something like:

```
fw2 #fw hastat


HOST        NUMBER      HIGH AVAILABILITY STATE          MACHINE STATUS
localhost 2             active                             OK
fw2 #


fw1 # fw hastat


HOST        NUMBER      HIGH AVAILABILITY STATE          MACHINE STATUS
localhost 1             active                             OK
fw1 #
```

If there was a problem on a member, for example, and interface was down on member fw2, *fw hastat* would produce an output that looks something like:

```
HOST        NUMBER      HIGH AVAILABILITY STATE          MACHINE STATUS
localhost 2             not active                        problem
fw2 #
```

cphaprob

We explored two variations of this command when we looked at ClusterXL in HA New mode. The first was the *cphaprob state* command. On a load-sharing cluster, you would see an output such as:

```
fw1 # cphaprob state

Working mode:   Load Sharing

Number       Unique Address   State

1 (local)   192.168.11.131   active
2            192.168.11.132   active

fw1 #
```

Note that both members have a state of active as opposed to active/standby in a ClusterXL HA New mode cluster. Should there be a failure on one of the members, you would see something like:

```
fw1 # cphaprob stat

Working mode:   Load Sharing

Number       Unique Address   State

1 (local)   192.168.11.131   active
2            192.168.11.132   down

fw1 #
```

In this example, member fw2 was taken down (an interface connection was removed), but the command was run on member fw1. All members in the cluster should report the same state for a member in a correctly working cluster.

cpstat ha

The information returned using the *cpstat ha* command is similar to the ClusterXL in HA New mode, but it reports on the load-sharing aspect of the cluster. The command *cpstat ha* will give you an output such as:

```
fw1 # cpstat ha

Product name: High Availability
Version:      NG Feature Pack 3
Status:       OK
HA installed: 1
Working mode: Load Sharing
HA started:   yes

fw1 #
```

The only differences here worthy of note are the working mode and the status. Predictably, if there is a problem, you will see the status change to:

```
Product name: High Availability
Version:      NG Feature Pack 3
Status:       problem
HA installed: 1
Working mode: Load Sharing
HA started:   yes
```

The other syntax of this command is *cpstat –f all ha*. An example of the output is as follows:

```
fw1 # cpstat -f all ha

Product name:        High Availability
Major version:       5
Minor version:       0
Service pack:        3
Version string:      NG Feature Pack 3
Status code:         2
Status short:        problem
Status long:         problem
HA installed:        1
Working mode:        Load Sharing
HA protocol version: 2
HA started:          yes
HA state:            down
HA identifier:     1
```

```
Interface table
---------------------------------------------------------
|Name|IP              |Status|Verified |Trusted|Shared|
---------------------------------------------------------
|hme0|192.168.11.131|Up      |        0|        1|     0|
|qfe0|195.166.16.131|Up      |        0|        0|     0|
|qfe2|192.168.12.131|Up      |        0|        0|     0|
|qfe3| 192.168.1.131|Down    |    32000|        0|     0|
---------------------------------------------------------



Problem Notification table
----------------------------------------------------
|Name           |Status|Priority|Verified|Descr|
----------------------------------------------------
|Synchronization|OK     |        0|    1618|      |
|Filter          |OK     |        0|    1618|      |
|cphad           |OK     |        0|       0|      |
|fwd             |OK     |        0|       0|      |
----------------------------------------------------


fw1 #
```

From this output, we can see that there is a problem with the local member (fw1 in this example) and that the status of interface qfe3 is down.

How ClusterXL Works in Load-Sharing Mode

ClusterXL in Load-Sharing mode works in a very similar way to ClusterXL in HA New mode but with the following unique distinctions:

- The MAC address used for the VIP address is shared among cluster members for that subnet. This means that there is no MAC address change on failure of a member as far as the network equipment on the local subnet of the cluster is concerned.

- The MAC address of the VIP address is a multicast MAC address. (i.e., its first octet is an odd number).
- In a healthy load-sharing cluster, all members of the cluster should be active and routing a portion of the active traffic.

Connections through the cluster are managed on a per-connection basis. For example, if a host on 192.168.1.200 initiates a connection through the cluster to 195.166.16.129 and member fw1 takes the connection, the connection will just go through member fw1 unless a failure of member fw1 occurs. The connection will continue through member fw1 until the session has completed. No asymmetric routing should occur on this particular connection.

The member in the cluster a new connection will go through is based on a hash of specific parameters defined in the Advanced section for ClusterXL Load Sharing (see Figure 6.49).

Figure 6.49 A Load-Sharing Algorithm Hash Can Be Based on These Parameters

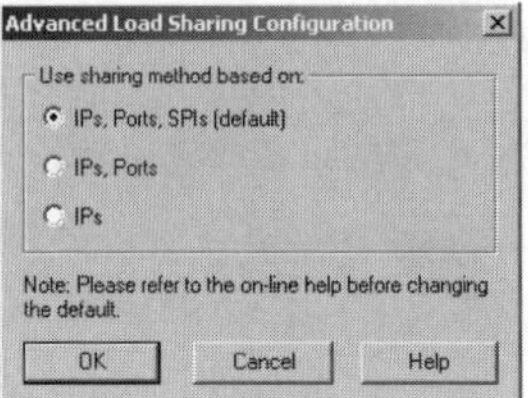

Assuming a "normal" connection passing through the cluster, all the packets involved will have the same hash value. For an Internet firewall, this means that, for a particular connection, a packet arriving from the internal network and a packet arriving from the Internet will have the same hash value. However, if the cluster is performing NAT or if VPNs are involved, we have a potential problem. The IP addresses and ports will be different on the "inside" and "outside" of the firewall. FireWall-1's stateful inspection helps us out here; because it understands what changes have been applied to connections, it can adjust the hashing accordingly.

As with ClusterXL in HA New mode, the members of the cluster still have their real IP addresses bound to their interfaces. This is particularly useful when the SmartCenter Server is communicating with the cluster members, because it need not be located on the secured network. This makes it easier for the SmartCenter Server to manage other firewall modules as well as the cluster.

Although all members are live and handling traffic, who should respond to ARP requests for the VIP address? The members in the ClusterXL cluster will agree on which member in the cluster will respond to the ARP request; however, that choice is not based on the member priority in the cluster, and even if a member is designated as having a problem but the interfaces on the member are active, the problem member may still respond to the ARP request. Within the ARP reply packets is the multicast MAC address for the VIP.

NOTE

You need to make sure that adjacent hosts and routers will accept a multicast MAC reply for a nonmulticast IP address. For example, host 192.168.1.200 would ARP for 192.168.1.130—the VIP address of the cluster—in order to route packets through the cluster. The ARP response would contain a multicast MAC address. Different systems respond in different ways: Windows is generally fine, but Cisco routers on the same subnet will not accept the ARP reply and will not cache the multicast MAC address, so steps need to be taken to circumvent this problem for Cisco routers. These steps usually involve entering a static entry into the ARP table of the router for the multicast MAC address.

ClusterXL Load-Sharing Mode Failover

As with ClusterXL in HA New mode, the key to how failover works is in the CPHA protocol that the members send to all the other members in the cluster, using multicasts.

There are a lot of similarities between ClusterXL HA New mode and ClusterXL Load-Sharing mode CPHA protocol packets. In fact, they are identical in the way they work, apart from some details in the UDP data payload. The similarities include these:

- The source MAC address of the CPHA update packet is always 00:00:00:00:fe:<*member number*>, where member 1 would be 00, member 2 would be 01, and so on.
- The destination MAC is always a multicast MAC address, ending with the VIP address in the last two octets of the MAC address.
- The source IP of the CPHA update packet is always 0.0.0.0.
- The destination IP address of the CPHA update packet is always the network IP address.
- Layer 4 (the transport layer of the OSI model) is always UDP, source port 8116, destination port 8116.
- The first part of the CPHA payload within the UDP header packet is the same as ClusterXL in HA New mode, and the format of an FW_HA_MYSTATE payload is the same parameters but *different data* for these parameters.

If we focus on the last point, we can see from Figure 6.50 how the data for the same parameters differ.

Figure 6.50 Packet Structure of a CPHA Packet When a Cluster Is in Load-Sharing Mode

```
⊞ Frame 4 (78 bytes on wire, 78 bytes captured)
⊟ Ethernet II, Src: 00:00:00:00:fe:01, Dst: 01:00:5e:26:10:82
    Destination: 01:00:5e:26:10:82 (01:00:5e:26:10:82)
    Source: 00:00:00:00:fe:01 (00:00:00:00:fe:01)
    Type: IP (0x0800)
⊞ Internet Protocol, Src Addr: 0.0.0.0 (0.0.0.0), Dst Addr: 195.166.16.0 (195.166.16.0)
⊞ User Datagram Protocol, Src Port: 8116 (8116), Dst Port: 8116 (8116)
⊟ Check Point High Availability Protocol
    Magic Number: 0x1a90 (correct)
    Protocol Version: 530 (NG Feature Pack 3)
    Cluster Number: 2527
    HA OpCode: 1 (FWHA_MY_STATE - Report source machine's state)
    Source Interface: 2
    Random ID: 18098
    Source Machine ID: 1
    Destination Machine ID: 65534
    Policy ID: 65535
    Filler: 256
  ⊟ FWHA_MY_STATE
      Number of IDs reported: 2
      Report Code: Interface information included
      HA mode: 2 (FWHA_BALANCE_MODE - More than one machine active)
      HA Time unit: 0 miliseconds
    ⊟ Machine states
        State of node 0: 4 (Active/Active-Attention)
        State of node 1: 4 (Active/Active-Attention)
    ⊟ Interface states
        Interfaces up in the Inbound: 4
        Interfaces assumed up in the Inbound: 0
        Interfaces up in the Outbound: 4
        Interfaces assumed up in the Outbound: 0
      Cluster 0: last packet seen 1 time units ago
      Cluster 1: last packet seen 0 time units ago
```

The main areas of note here are the HA mode, which states that the mode is mode 4 FWHA_Balance_mode—more than one member active. ClusterXL in HA New mode is referred to as mode 2 in this field.

The other field of note is "Machine states." This field communicates what the member originating the CPHA packet thinks the status of all the other members is. As we can see in Figure 6.50, the sending member is aware that member 0 is active. This packet was originated from member 1, or fw2 from our example.

Under normal operation, these CPHA packets are multicast to all the other members in the cluster. Each member multicasts its perception of the state of the rest of the members in the cluster. This process occurs on each interface of a cluster member and is sent at regular intervals, several a second.

Examining the CPHA protocol between cluster members, we see that if there is a problem on the member, the other members will show a "Machine states" value for that the member as *down/dead*. The member that is taking over a particular connection will then ARP for the MAC address of the local host it needs to push a packet to, and on response, it will continue the session. Note that the hosts on the local subnet do not notice any change in MAC address or IP address on failover. You could notice a small glitch in the data transfer while the failure occurs and failover to another member takes place, but the period of disruption should always be less than 3 seconds and is usually just over 1 second.

Note that when a member in a load-sharing cluster takes over from another member, there is no gratuitous ARP broadcast, unlike HA mode. This is because it is unnecessary since there has been no MAC address change.

Special Considerations for ClusterXL in Load-Sharing Mode

We have covered the principles of how ClusterXL in Load-Sharing mode works. We now contrast and compare how the special considerations for ClusterXL in Load-Sharing mode differ relative to other cluster modes.

Network Address Translation

ClusterXL in Load-Sharing mode is actually quite forgiving with regard to NAT and how proxy ARP is performed, unlike HA mode. It will handle manual proxy ARP entries fine for NATed IP addresses, as long as you proxy ARP for the cluster multicast MAC address. You enter these static published ARP entries on all members in the cluster. Automatic ARP configuration can be selected in the **Policy | Global Properties | Network Address Translation** area of the SmartDashboard GUI. This works fine because the multicast MAC address is used for all the automatic ARPs that are required. Manual routes on the ISP router can also be used instead of using proxy ARPs.

To summarize, as long as the multicast MAC address is used in any manual proxy ARPs, there should be no issues with Load-Sharing mode and NAT.

User Authentication and One-Time Passcodes

Like all HA and Load-Sharing clustering solutions, if you are using the Check Point security servers (for SMTP, HTTP, or FTP services) and a failover occurs, you will lose the connection and have to start again through the new member that the traffic is now going through. The security server and remote authentication issues discussed earlier in this chapter (comparing single gateway and clustering functionality) apply particularly to Load-Sharing mode, because sessions—with multiple connections—are always likely to be shared between all cluster members, unlike HA, when problems only occur on failover.

Nokia IPSO Clustering

ClusterXL is not available for the Nokia platform. This is because Nokia provides its own HA and load-sharing solutions. In this section, we look at the load-sharing cluster solution that Nokia provides on IPSO 3.6-FCS4, how to configure it, and how to configure FireWall-1 NG FP3 so that you have a complete Nokia load-sharing solution. We then talk about how you can test the cluster and go over any special considerations for this solution.

Nokia Configuration

To configure a Nokia load-sharing cluster, you need to take the following steps:

1. Configure the interfaces of a Nokia.
2. Configure FireWall-1.
3. Configure clustering in Voyager.

We assume that you have installed the latest version of IPSO 3.6 on your Nokia and that you have the Check Point FireWall-1 NG FP3 package installed and configured. As with setting up all clusters, it is recommended that you complete and test the physical connectivity first so that any problems that you encounter later aren't due to a misconfigured switch or interface, because these could be difficult to spot later.

In our example shown in Figure 6.51, you can see a sample Nokia cluster topology.

Figure 6.51 Our Example Nokia Clustering Topology Setup

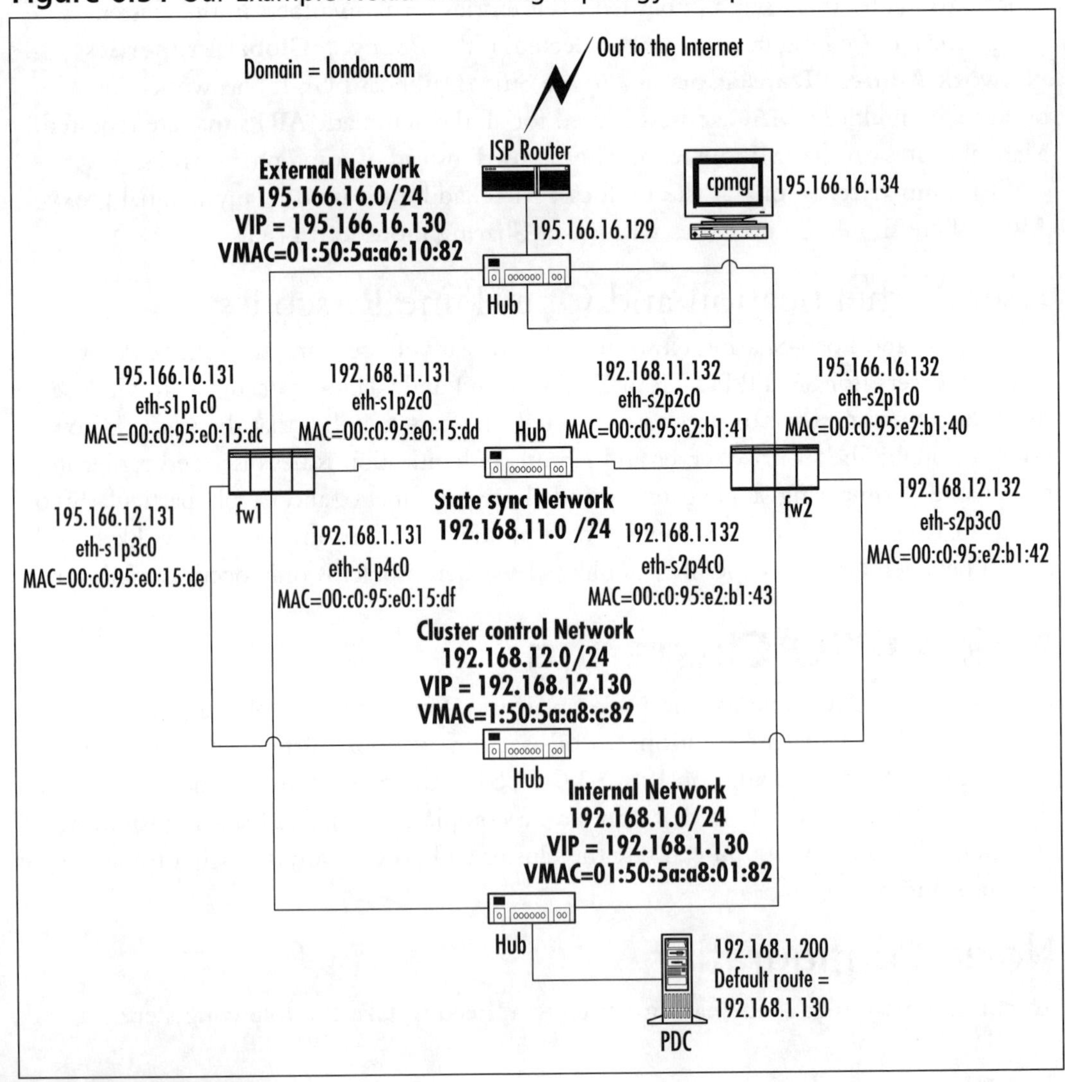

The main difference in network topology between Nokia clustering and using Check Point ClusterXL is that you require a dedicated network for Nokia cluster control communications. This is in addition to the Check Point state sync network.

As you can see from Figure 6.51, each network that has a VIP also has a virtual MAC address—a multicast MAC which is used for the VIP. From a network perspective of neighboring equipment on the same network as the cluster interfaces, it looks very similar to Check Point ClusterXL in Load-Sharing mode.

You should ensure that you have configured all the following using Voyager on each of the cluster members:

- Make sure that interface speeds are consistent across host and switches on the subnet. Only use full-duplex where connected directly to full-duplex-enabled switches!
- Make sure you have entries in each hosts file for the FireWall-1 management station and the other modules in the cluster.
- Make sure you have the correct time and date and the correct default local for each member in the cluster and on the Check Point management station.
- Make sure that the FireWall-1 NG FP3 package is installed.
- Read the Nokia IPSO and Check Point NG FP3 release notes!

A Few Points About Installing an Initial Configuration of NG FP3 on Nokia IPSO

Installing software packages on the Nokia platform is very different compared to installing on other platforms. Packages are added to Nokia and "enabled" using the Voyager interface. However, that is not the end of the process of installing FireWall-1 NG FP3. You need to log out after the package install and run the *cpconfig* command on the Nokia console. The output you will see is fairly similar to the output you would see in the UNIX installation of a cluster, and the choices you would make are identical.

One section during the install is specific to clustering:

```
Would you like to install a Check Point clustering product (CPHA, CPLS or
    State Synchronization)? (y/n) [n] ? y
```

Even though you will be using the Nokia clustering solution, make sure you answer **y**. This will make sure that you have the state synchronization available when you set up your cluster. That is essential for ensuring that connections continue through another member when failover occurs.

Check Point FireWall-1 Configuration for a Nokia Cluster

We will run through the most direct method of configuring FireWall-1 objects and rules for a Nokia cluster. This means that we will create the cluster member objects via the gateway cluster object directly and set up the SIC trusts between the management station and the cluster members within the cluster gateway object. Once the cluster gateway object is configured, we will install a basic policy to the cluster. If you have not already done so, it's a good idea to look through the "Configuring FireWall-1 for ClusterXL in HA New Mode" configuration procedure described earlier in this chapter, because there are many similarities.

Configuring the Gateway Cluster Object

Within the NG FP3 SmartDashboard GUI, click **Manage | Network Objects** and click the **New** button. Select **Check Point | Gateway Cluster**. You will be presented with a popup window (see Figure 6.52).

Figure 6.52 Defining General Properties of the Nokia Cluster

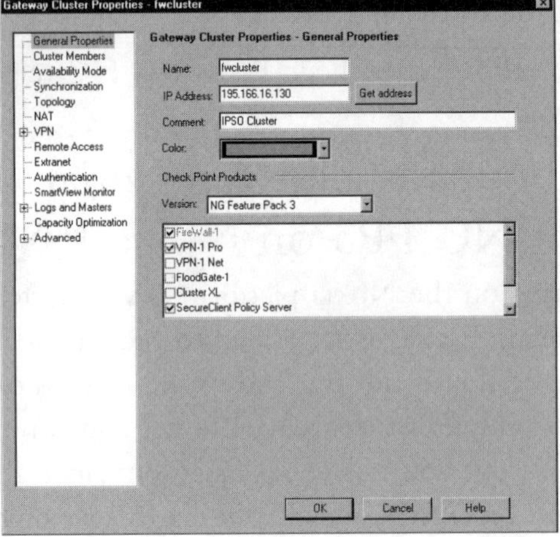

Particular areas of note here are that the IP address stated in the General tab is the external interface. The other important points to note are that the ClusterXL check box is *unchecked*.

Now click the **Cluster Members** menu option on the left side of this screen. Run through the steps for creating a new member, as we did when configuring Cluster XL HA New mode.

After the trust has been set up between the management module and enforcement module, click the **Topology** tab and click **Get Topology**. For each interface that is received, click it and set the topology for it. For example, the eth-s1p1c0 interface has IP address 195.166.16.131 assigned to it, and this is marked as our **External** interface in the topology. All the others are defined as **This Network** (see Figure 6.53).

Figure 6.53 Topology of a Cluster Member

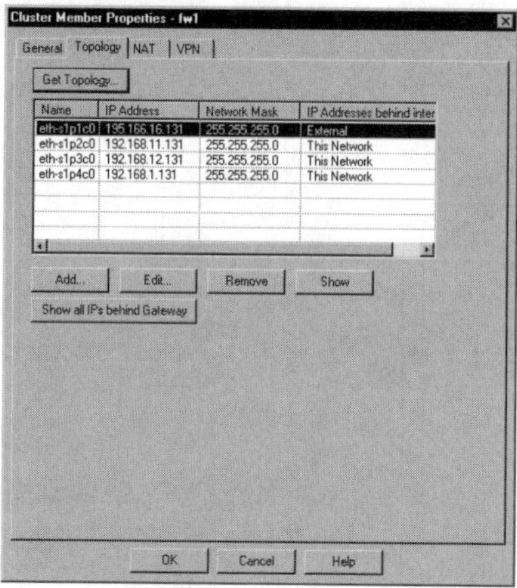

Click **OK**. You should now have the first member of the cluster defined and trusted. Repeat the procedure again in the **Cluster Members** menu to add the second cluster (and third, fourth, and so on). Use the **New** button each time. Once complete, you should have a list of cluster members defined.

Click **Availability Mode** on the left side of the screen to select which mode the Nokia cluster will operate in. Make sure you select **Load Sharing** (see Figure 6.54). Note that in Nokia clustering, this setting has no functional effect, but it is useful to select the correct one so that when you look at it again, you know what mode you are operating your Nokia cluster in! It is also useful to avoid any confusion if you need to seek technical support.

Click the **Synchronization** menu option on the left side of the screen. You need to add the network you are going to use for synchronizing the FireWall-1 state tables. Note that this network should not be the same as your Nokia cluster control network.

Click the **Add** button to add a synchronization network. In our example, the IP address is 192.168.11.0 , and the netmask is 255.255.255.0. (See Step 8 and Figure 6.23 of "Configuring ClusterXL in HA New Mode" for an example.) Click **OK**.

It is possible to add backup synchronization networks here; it would be acceptable to include the Nokia control network as a backup sync network, but if you do, the cluster should be monitored carefully so that a failover to this network is quickly identified and addressed.

Configuring topology in the cluster object when using Nokia clustering is not mandatory—in fact, *it is not recommended*. Doing so will change the behavior of the cluster with regard to packets originating from a member in the cluster. The effect of configuring a topology is covered in "Special Considerations for Nokia Clusters" later in this chapter.

Figure 6.54 Availability Mode Configuration for a Nokia Cluster

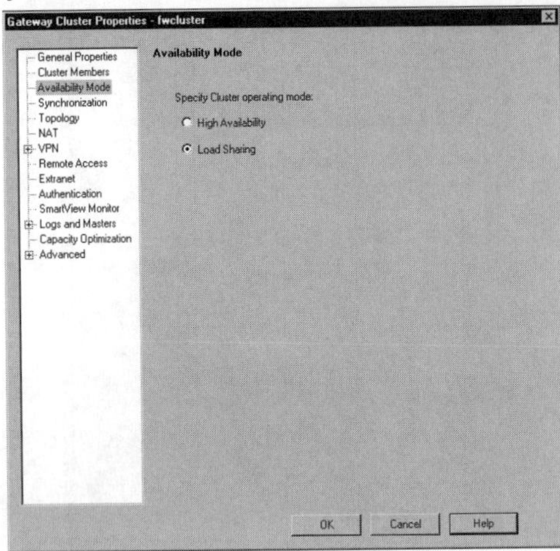

Once this process is complete, you are ready to click **OK** and start defining your security policy.

Configuring the Nokia Cluster Rule Base

You have some choices as to the Rule Base you want to install. You can either see if the configuration of your cluster object is going to work and install an open policy, or you can create a strict policy now. Remember, there is still one more step to do, which is to configure the clustering on Nokia using Voyager. This being the case, you might want to install an open policy now and then tighten it later once you are happy that your clustering is working correctly.

You need to allow IPSO cluster control protocols between each IP address of the Nokia cluster. This means you will have a rule, close to the top of your Rule Base, that will look something like Figure 6.55.

Figure 6.55 Rule Showing Communication Between Cluster Members

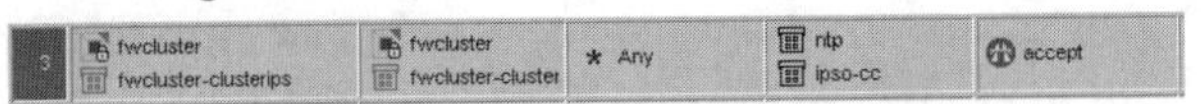

The group *fwcluster-clusterips* is made up of node host objects, one for each VIP address (195.166.16.130, 192.168.12.130, and 192.168.1.130 in our example).

The *ipso-cc* group is made up of two services that we will call IPSO Cluster Control Protocol 1 and IPSO Cluster Control Protocol 2. You define these by clicking

Manage | Services | New | TCP. The definition of these services is shown in Figures 6.56 and 6.57, respectively.

Figure 6.56 Defining Service for IPSO Cluster Control Protocol 1

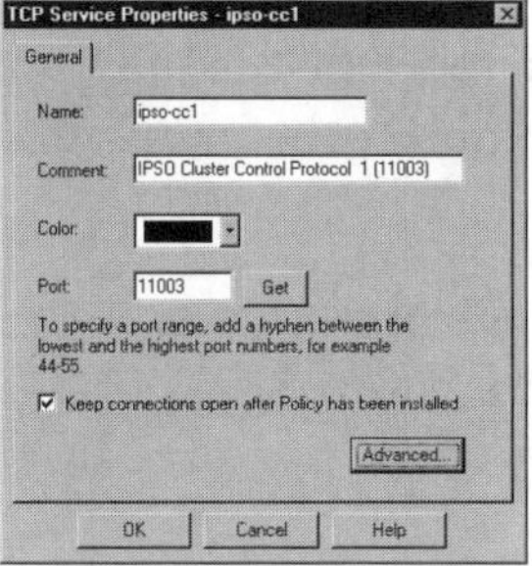

Figure 6.57 Defining Service for IPSO Cluster Control Protocol 2

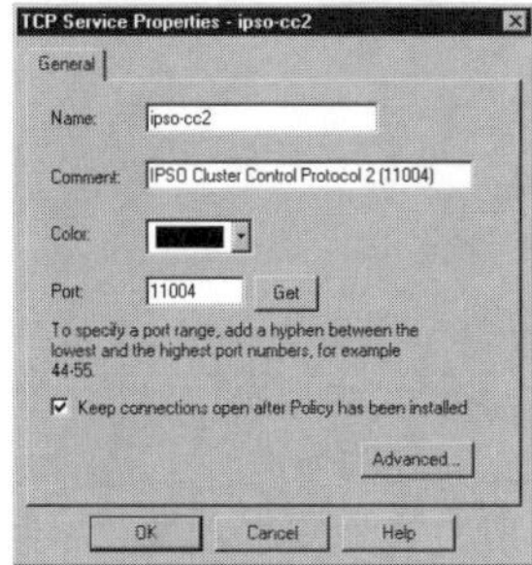

WARNING

It is vital to add the *fwcluster-clusterips* group to security policy rules wherever you use the cluster object as a destination. This is because the cluster object does not include the VIP addresses, since we have not defined the cluster topology information. However, it is possible to connect to the VIP addresses. This is most important when defining the "stealth" rule (see Figure 6.57).

Once defined, these services can be added to a service group (defined as *ipso-cc* in our example).

In addition to the *ipso-cc* services, we have also accepted the Network Time Protocol (NTP). Running NTP is a good idea to make sure that the time between the Nokia cluster members does not drift.

When you define the "stealth" rule in order to explicitly protect the cluster members, add the cluster object *and* the group of VIPs, *fwcluster-clusterips,* as shown in Figure 6.58.

Once you have configured your policy, install it to the cluster object. Note that in Figure 6.59, we can see that the policy will fail to install if it does not install to all members of the cluster. One thing to be acutely aware of here is that if a member in the cluster is down or switched off and later comes online and becomes functional, it will first look at other members of the cluster to compare the policy that it has against the policy that the other cluster members have. If the other cluster members have a more recent policy, the cluster member that has just come up will download the policy from one of the other cluster members—before it attempts to download the policy from the management module.

Figure 6.58 A Stealth Rule on a Nokia Cluster Rule Base

Figure 6.59 Installing the Security Policy for the Cluster

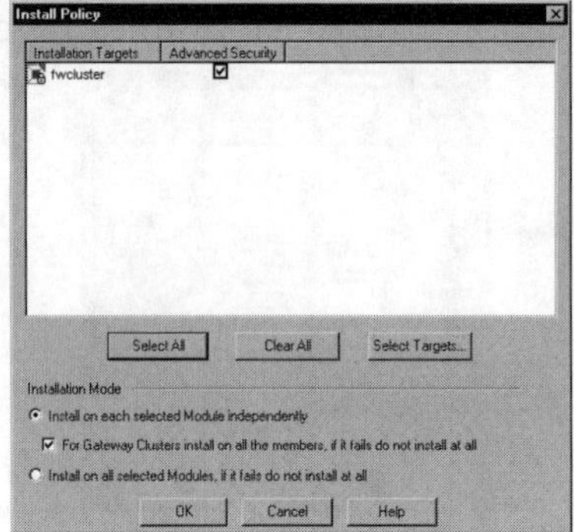

Once you have installed a policy, you have to complete the last step in configuring a Nokia load-sharing cluster: configuring the clustering on the Nokia appliances themselves.

Nokia Cluster Configuration on Voyager

When we configured the Gateway Cluster object in the SmartDashboard GUI, we did not configure the gateway cluster to have ClusterXL installed. This feature is not available on the Nokia platform; Nokia provides its own solution for load sharing. However, you have to configure it within the Voyager interface.

Note that you have to configure the cluster on each Nokia in the cluster, so you will have to repeat the procedure of configuring the cluster on each Nokia. This might sound obvious, but it is often something that is forgotten!

Voyager Configuration

Make sure that you have network connectivity from your browser to your Nokia FireWall-1 modules in your cluster, and make sure that the security policy you have installed on the Nokia appliances does not prevent you from accessing Voyager from your browser. Navigate to Voyager on the first member in your cluster. In our example, we do this by going to https://195.166.16.131 (see Figure 6.60).

Figure 6.60 Voyager's Main Screen

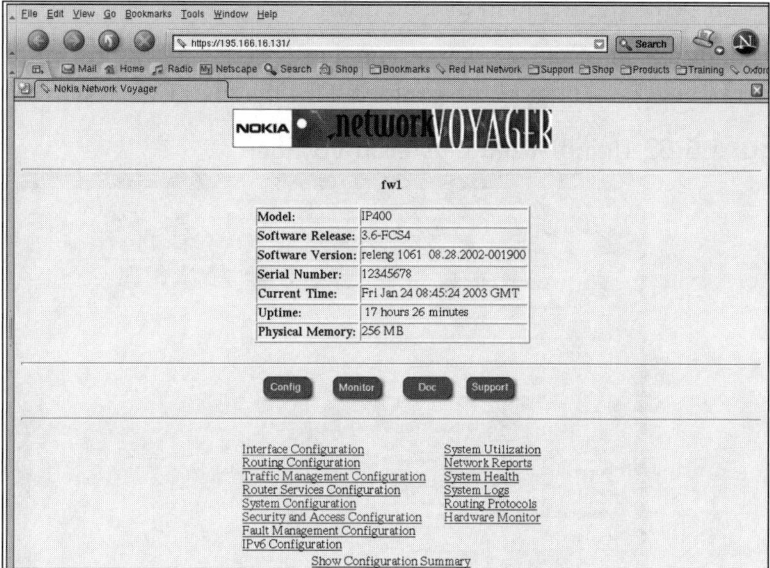

Here are the steps you need to follow after you have authenticated and are presented with the main screen:

1. From the main Voyager screen, click **Traffic Management Configuration**.
2. Click **Cluster**. The new screen will look something like Figure 6.61.

Figure 6.61 The Initial Cluster Configuration Screen

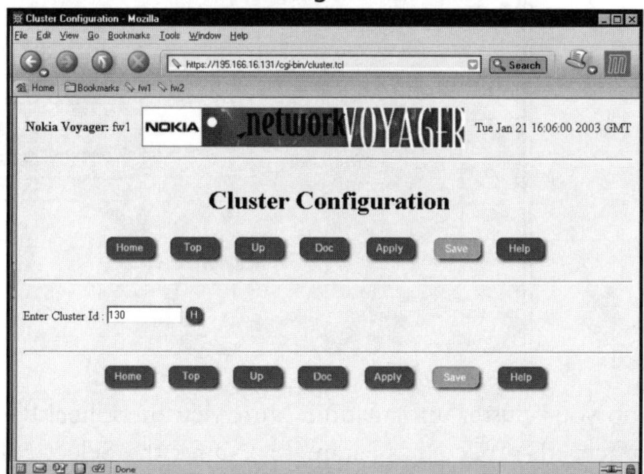

3. Enter a cluster ID. This can be any decimal number between 0 and 65,535. For simplicity, we chose 130 for our example. Once you've entered an ID, click **Apply** and then **Save**.
4. The cluster configuration screen will then expand to include more parameters that can be configured within the cluster.
5. The bottom half of the screen presented in Figure 6.62 is shown in Figure 6.63; it shows how to configure the clustering for member fw1 in our example.

Figure 6.62 Uninitialized Cluster in Voyager

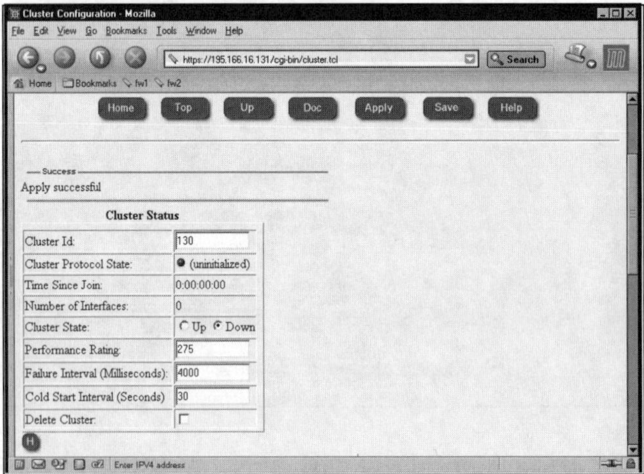

Figure 6.63 Cluster Configuration for the First Cluster Member

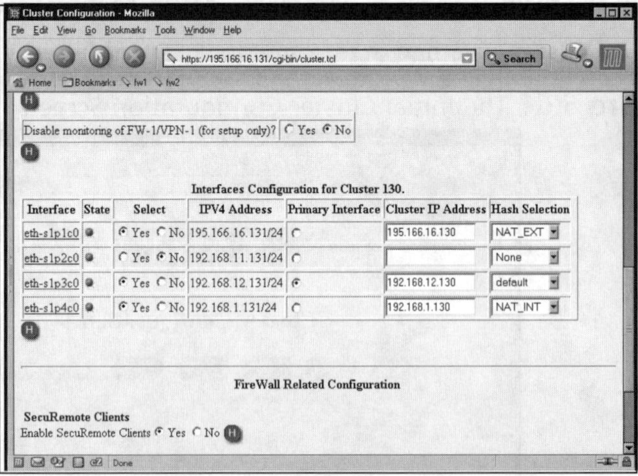

6. Set up your cluster information. Note that the CheckPoint state sync network interface, eth-s1p2c0, has parameter *No* for the Select column and the Hash

Selection column has *None*. The external interface eth-s1p1c0 has the hash algorithm *NAT_EXT* selected, and the internal interface eth-s1p4c0 has *NAT_INT* selected. The Cluster Control network has the Primary Interface radio button checked, and the hash selection is set to *default*.

7. Decide if you are going to use SecuRemote Clients and select **yes** or **no**. If you scroll further down the screen, you will see a section for defining VPN tunnel information. This is where you enter the remote encryption domain and remote gateway IP address so that this information is taken into account when the load-sharing algorithm is calculated. This ensures that the same member of the cluster participates in the VPN connection (as asymmetric routing would cause the VPN to fail).
8. Make sure that you click **Apply** and **Save** to save the changes you have made.
9. You can now make the cluster active, even with just one member. Click the **Cluster State Up** radio button, and then click **Apply** and **Save**, as shown in Figure 6.64. Once it is up and running, your cluster should route traffic through member fw1, if adjacent hosts are using the VIP address of the local subnet that they are connected to as their default gateway.

Figure 6.64 Bringing Up the First Cluster Member

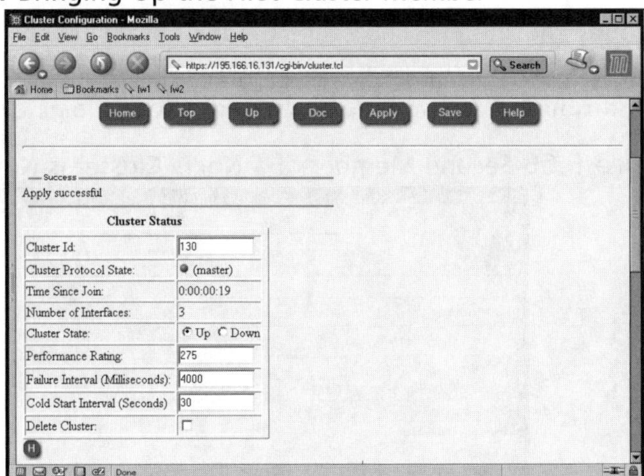

10. This completes member fw1 in the cluster configuration. You now need to point your browser to the second member and configure it to complement your configuration of member fw1. Note that the settings have to be correct and you have to use the equivalent interfaces on fw2 as fw1 and that the hashing algorithm you select must be identical to member fw1. When you change the **Cluster State** to **Up**, Voyager will inform you that the fw2 member is joining the cluster. This could take a little while (see Figure 6.65) and you will be informed as to whether the procedure succeeds or fails.

Figure 6.65 Member fw2 Joining the Cluster

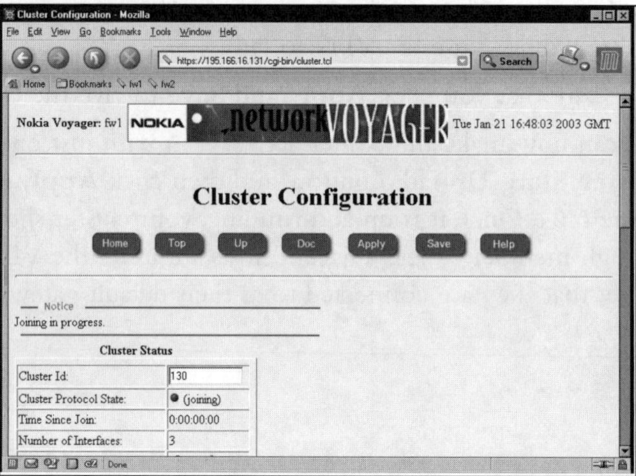

11. If joining the cluster is successful, the member will announce that it is now a member of the cluster (see Figure 6.66). Both members of the cluster are now up and running, and you are ready to test your Nokia cluster.

Figure 6.66 Second Member of a Nokia Cluster Is Now Online

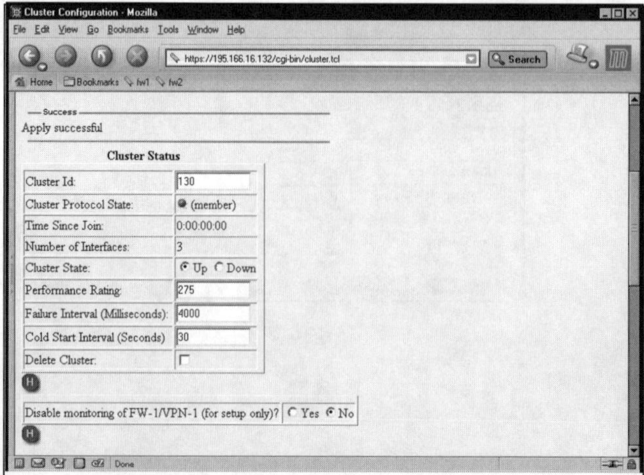

Testing the Nokia Cluster

Once your Nokia cluster is set up, you need to test it to make sure that it is functioning correctly. Again, you need to keep in mind the way that this particular clustering technology works and how it differs from the other clustering solutions we have covered so far.

Test 1: Pinging the Virtual IP Address of Each Interface

With Nokia clustering in load sharing, you should be able to ping the local VIP address of the cluster with a host that is on the same subnet as the cluster interfaces. You will receive a response if everything is working properly.

In the test we ran on our example network, a ping was initiated from the FireWall-1 management station (195.166.16.134) to the VIP of the cluster (195.166.16.130). A packet trace was run at the same time on the management station to analyze the packet for the ping session. If you look at the ARP cache of the local host initiating the ping, you should now have the multicast MAC address of the VIP. In our case, this is 01:50:5a:a6:10:82 (which you can check against Figure 6.51). This in itself does not tell you much—just that the VIP address is up and running and that a member in the cluster responded. But can we tell which member?

The answer is yes, we can, but only if we examine the packet trace we took when the ping session took place. If we look at the reply packet, in the data link layer, we can see the real MAC address of the member that responded, as shown in the packet analysis in Figure 6.67.

Figure 6.67 Analyzing the ICMP Echo Reply for the Source MAC Address

```
⊞ Frame 9 (98 bytes on wire, 98 bytes captured)
⊟ Ethernet II, Src: 00:c0:95:e2:b1:40, Dst: 08:00:20:a1:23:52
      Destination: 08:00:20:a1:23:52 (08:00:20:a1:23:52)
      Source: 00:c0:95:e2:b1:40 (00:c0:95:e2:b1:40)
      Type: IP (0x0800)
⊟ Internet Protocol, Src Addr: 195.166.16.130 (195.166.16.130), Dst Addr: 195.166.16.134 (195.166.16.134)
      Version: 4
      Header length: 20 bytes
    ⊞ Differentiated Services Field: 0x00 (DSCP 0x00: Default; ECN: 0x00)
      Total Length: 84
      Identification: 0x2fad
    ⊞ Flags: 0x04
      Fragment offset: 0
      Time to live: 255
      Protocol: ICMP (0x01)
      Header checksum: 0xa3a6 (correct)
      Source: 195.166.16.130 (195.166.16.130)
      Destination: 195.166.16.134 (195.166.16.134)
⊟ Internet Control Message Protocol
      Type: 0 (Echo (ping) reply)
      Code: 0
      Checksum: 0x551f (correct)
      Identifier: 0x1555
      Sequence number: 00:00
      Data (56 bytes)
```

In our example, we can see that the source MAC is 00:0c:95:e2:b1:40, which corresponds with member fw2 in the cluster (see Figure 6.51). Note that even though the real MAC address of the fw2 member was used, the source IP address for the ICMP echo reply was the virtual IP of 195.166.16.130.

Test 2: Determining the Status of Each Member in the Cluster

In a Nokia cluster, there are two tools you can use to monitor the status of the cluster and its members. One is the SmartView Status GUI, and the other is using Voyager monitoring.

The SmartView Status GUI shows you the health of each member and if it is in state table sync with other members of the cluster. What it won't show you is the correct status of each interface of each member. For this information, you have to use the Nokia Voyager screens on each member in the cluster.

Notice that in Figure 6.68, all the interfaces seem to be up; however, they would report this status even if one of the interfaces was unplugged. The giveaway that SmartView Status cannot monitor the interfaces is that the "Working mode" field says *Sync only*. This means that the only function ClusterXL is performing on a Nokia cluster is state table synchronization.

Figure 6.68 SmartView Status Does Not Show an Accurate Interface Status

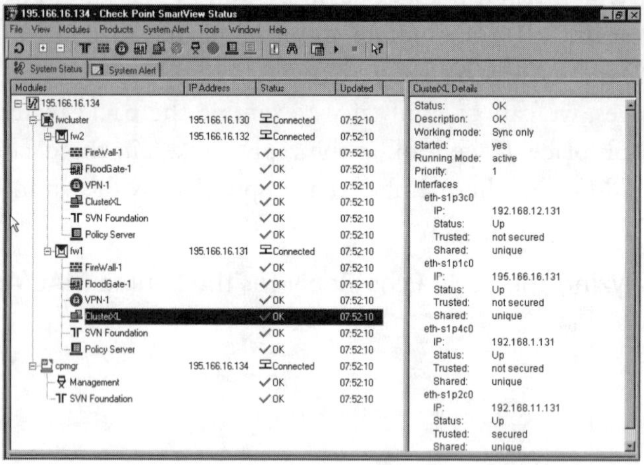

Checking the monitoring of the cluster through Voyager is straightforward. Connect your browser to one of the members, select the **Monitor** button, then click **Cluster Monitor**. This will show you the main statistics of each member in the cluster (see Figure 6.69) from the point of view of the member you are connected to. If everything is working correctly, it should not matter which member you connect to with Voyager, because they should all report the same status.

If a member in the cluster fails, you will see it removed from the cluster members table. If you only have one member left after a member fails (if you have a two-member cluster), the remaining member will also become master. Take note of the

Time Since Join parameter in the cluster members table. This parameter tells you how long a particular member has been online.

Figure 6.69 Both Members Are Online as Part of the Cluster

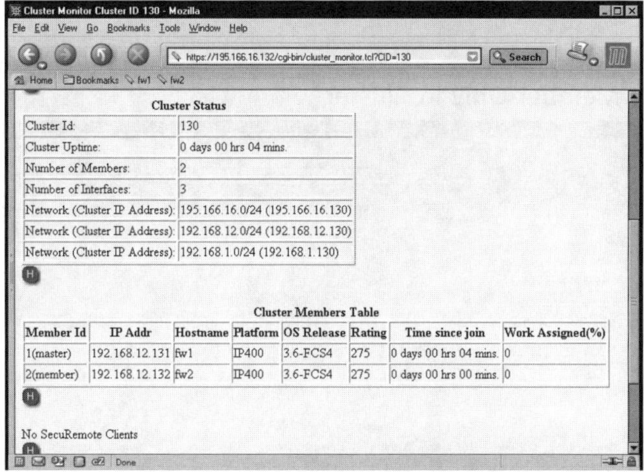

Cluster Status

Cluster Id:	130
Cluster Uptime:	0 days 00 hrs 04 mins.
Number of Members:	2
Number of Interfaces:	3
Network (Cluster IP Address):	195.166.16.0/24 (195.166.16.130)
Network (Cluster IP Address):	192.168.12.0/24 (192.168.12.130)
Network (Cluster IP Address):	192.168.1.0/24 (192.168.1.130)

Cluster Members Table

Member Id	IP Addr	Hostname	Platform	OS Release	Rating	Time since join	Work Assigned(%)
1(master)	192.168.12.131	fw1	IP400	3.6-FCS4	275	0 days 00 hrs 04 mins.	0
2(member)	192.168.12.132	fw2	IP400	3.6-FCS4	275	0 days 00 hrs 00 mins.	0

No SecuRemote Clients

One other place not to be forgotten when you're checking the health of your Nokia cluster is the system logs. These can be located in the /var/log/messages file. You should see entries from the *clusterd* process, which shows the status of the cluster.

In Figure 6.70, you can see a sample message of what will be seen in the /var/adm/message file when the internal Ethernet interface cable is removed from one of the members of the cluster, then restored. Note that when this happens, you will also see the cluster members table show one fewer member in the cluster (see Figure 6.71).

Figure 6.70 Sample of Nokia /var/log/messages After Internal Interface Was Removed, Then Restored

```
Jan 27 07:29:35 fw1 [LOG_NOTICE] clusterd[251]: Member(192.168.12.132)
    member id (2) left cluster(130):
Jan 27 07:30:15 fw1 [LOG_NOTICE] clusterd[251]: New member(192.168.12.132)
    joined cluster(130) with member id(2).
```

Test 3: FTPing Through a Load-Sharing Nokia Cluster During Interface Failure

Like ClusterXL load sharing and HA New mode, the best test you can perform is a real-world test. In load sharing, a simple test consists of starting a connection through the cluster and monitoring the cluster to determine which member the connection has gone through. If the test connection is the only connection, you might be able to see this from the "Work assigned" value in the cluster monitoring facility in Voyager, or you could use the FireWall-1 NG FP3 SmartView Tracker (with a hotfix applied to show origin IP addresses of the member in the cluster), or you could use SmartView Monitor.

Figure 6.71 One Member Only in Cluster

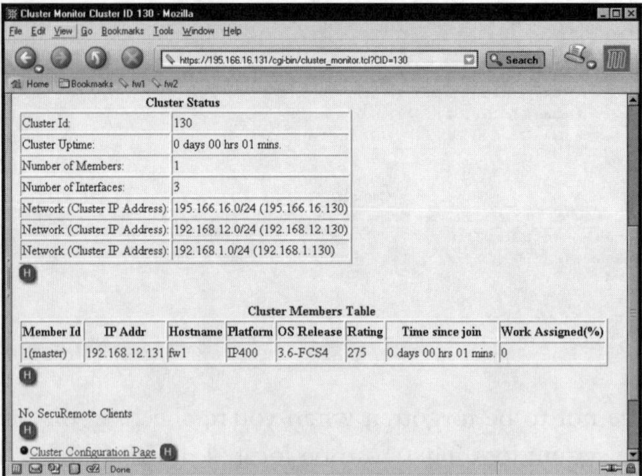

In this example, we have started an FTP session through the cluster, and we are using SmartView Monitor to monitor the traffic through the cluster. When we initiate the FTP session through the cluster and start downloading data, we can see that all the load is on member fw2 in the cluster (see Figure 6.72).

Figure 6.72 Display of Traffic Through SmartView Monitor

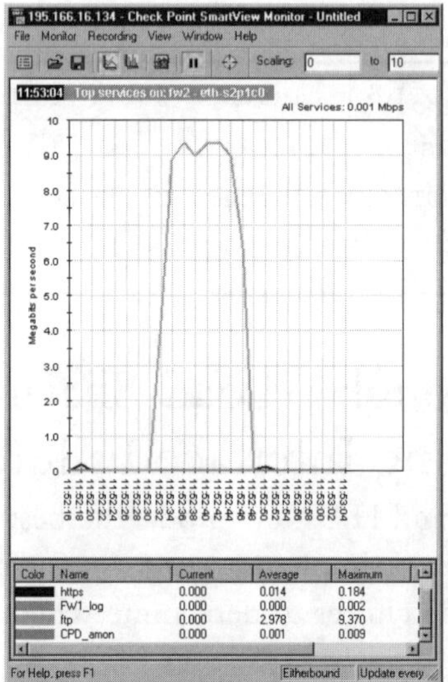

As we can see in Figure 6.72, the FTP session was started at 11:52:30, and failure occurred at 11:52:48 (actually, we pulled the internal interface connector out of member fw2). Figure 6.73 shows that member fw1 took over the session.

Figure 6.73 Display of Traffic Through Member fw1 When fw2 Fails

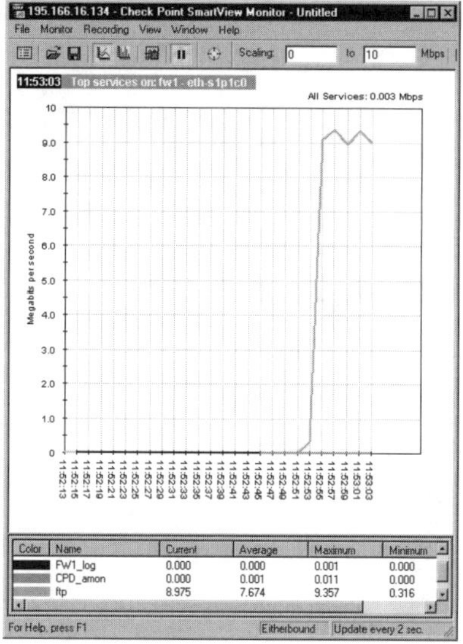

Note that the timeline shows that member fw1 did not take over the load for 3 seconds.

Command-Line Stats

We saw earlier that ClusterXL uses the *cphaprob* command to determine status of the cluster. We can use a similar Nokia command-line tool to check the status of a Nokia cluster.

On the Nokia platform, we use the Command Line Interface Shell (known as *clish*). This is an interactive command line, although a single command can be executed using the *–c* "command" option. Once in the shell, you can use the command *show clusters* to determine the status of the members in the cluster (see Figure 6.74).

Figure 6.74 Example of Use of the *clish* Command to Check the Cluster Status

```
fw2[admin]# clish
Nokia> show clusters
CID 130
    Cluster State up
    Member ID 1
```

Continued

Figure 6.74 Example of Use of the *clish* Command to Check the Cluster Status

```
    Protocol State master
    System Uptime At Join 1:02:58:57
    Performance Rating 275
    Failure Interval 4000
    Cold Start Delay 30
    Number of Interfaces 3
    Primary Interface eth-s2p3c0
    Interface eth-s2p1c0
        IP Address 195.166.16.132/24
        Cluster IP Address 195.166.16.130
        Hash NAT-external
    Interface eth-s2p3c0
        IP Address 192.168.12.132/24
        Cluster IP Address 192.168.12.130
        Hash default
    Interface eth-s2p4c0
        IP Address 192.168.1.132/24
        Cluster IP Address 192.168.1.130
        Hash NAT-internal

Member(s) information
    Number of Member(s) 2
    Member 1 (master)
        IP Address 192.168.12.132
        HostName(Platform) fw2(IP400)
        OS Release 3.6-FCS4
        Rating 275
        Time Since Join 0:19:20:57
        Cluster Uptime At Join 0:00:00:00
        Work Assigned 50%
    Member 2 (member)
        IP Address 192.168.12.131
        HostName(Platform) fw1(IP400)
        OS Release 3.6-FCS4
        Rating 275
        Time Since Join 0:19:14:34
```

Continued

Figure 6.74 Example of Use of the *clish* Command to Check the Cluster Status

```
        Cluster Uptime At Join 0:00:06:22
        Work Assigned 50%


Nokia> show cluster securemote
yes
Nokia> show cluster vpn-tunnels
VPN tunnel(s) configured
Network/Mask           Destination
192.168.254.0/24       194.155.13.33
Nokia> exit

Goodbye..
```

Many commands are variations of the *show cluster* command. See the *Nokia Command Line Reference Guide* for further information. You can use the *cphaprob* command on the Nokia platform if you like, but the information that it will tell you is limited. For example, it can't tell you which interfaces are up or down. It can tell you if the state table synchronization is working or not.

How Nokia Clustering Works

Nokia clustering has many similarities to the Check Point ClusterXL load-sharing solution, but because the clustering is not part of the Check Point product, you do get some differences that are significant. We can draw some parallels between ClusterXL load sharing and Nokia clustering as follows:

- Both ClusterXL load sharing and Nokia clustering use a VIP address and a multicast MAC address, so devices on the local subnet do not see any difference when initiating connections through the cluster. On a Nokia cluster, there is always a host that is assigned master in the cluster, and this member will respond to ARP requests.
- Both ClusterXL and Nokia clustering have a method for each member to tell the other members its status in the cluster. However, the ways that they do this are different. ClusterXL does this using the CPHA protocol, which is sent from each interface of the cluster member to all other cluster members. Nokia uses a dedicated network to communicate using its own protocols: IP protocol 0x90 (144 decimal), which is a multicast MAC destination and IP address, and

two TCP services (ports 11003 and 11004). Note that the protocol 0x90 traffic bypasses the firewall, so no policy rules are required.

- Both systems have a load-sharing hashing method that can be altered by the user. On Nokia, this method is set up in Voyager, based on whether your interface is external or internal (or a VPN gateway); on Check Point ClusterXL, this is based on three choices: IP addresses, ports, and SPI (VPN negotiation); IP addresses and ports; or just IP addresses.
- Like ClusterXL, connections through the Nokia cluster are directed through one member in the cluster on a per-connection basis. Asymmetric routing is avoided by the load-sharing algorithm, and although this would still work if it does occur, you could get some sessions dropped when they initiate, due to the reply being received from the remote host before the state tables have an opportunity to synchronize between the cluster members.
- Just like ClusterXL, the Nokia members still have valid IP addresses that you can connect to.

Let's walk through an example of how a connection would work through a Nokia cluster. In our example, host 192.168.1.200 will initiate a Telnet session through the Nokia cluster to our ISP router on IP address 195.166.16.129, and as before, in our ClusterXL HA New mode, we will hide the connection behind the cluster external IP address of 195.166.16.130, using a hide rule in our firewall NAT Rule Base.

When the Telnet session is initiated, the host 192.168.1.200 sends out an ARP request for 192.168.1.130, which is the default gateway on the network 192.168.1.0. The response in the ARP will be a multicast MAC address—a MAC address that applies to all members of our cluster for the internal interface. The Nokia member that is the master will always send the ARP response. (More on the master later.) In our example, the MAC address returned is 01:50:5a:a8:01:82. Our host on 192.168.1.200 then sends a SYN TCP packet, high source port, destination is to 195.166.16.129, destination MAC is 01:50:5a:a8:01:82 (the default gateway MAC address).

All members in the cluster will receive this packet, but only one of them will do anything with the packet—depending on which member in the cluster is meant to pick up the packet, which is based on the load-sharing algorithm. The member who will deal with the connection will pass the packet up through the IP stack to the Check Point FireWall-1 NG FP3 kernel for the incoming interface. The TCP SYN packet will pass through the Rule Base of the firewall and, providing everything is fine, it will then send the packet out of its external interface, with the source IP address of 195.166.16.130 (the external cluster IP address), with the source MAC address of the member that is taking the connection (in our example, the source MAC address is 00:c0:95:e2:b1:40, which corresponds with member fw2 external interface eth-s2p1c0), and the destination IP address will be 195.166.16.129 (see Figure 6.75).

Figure 6.75 Description of a Connection Through a Nokia Load-Sharing Cluster

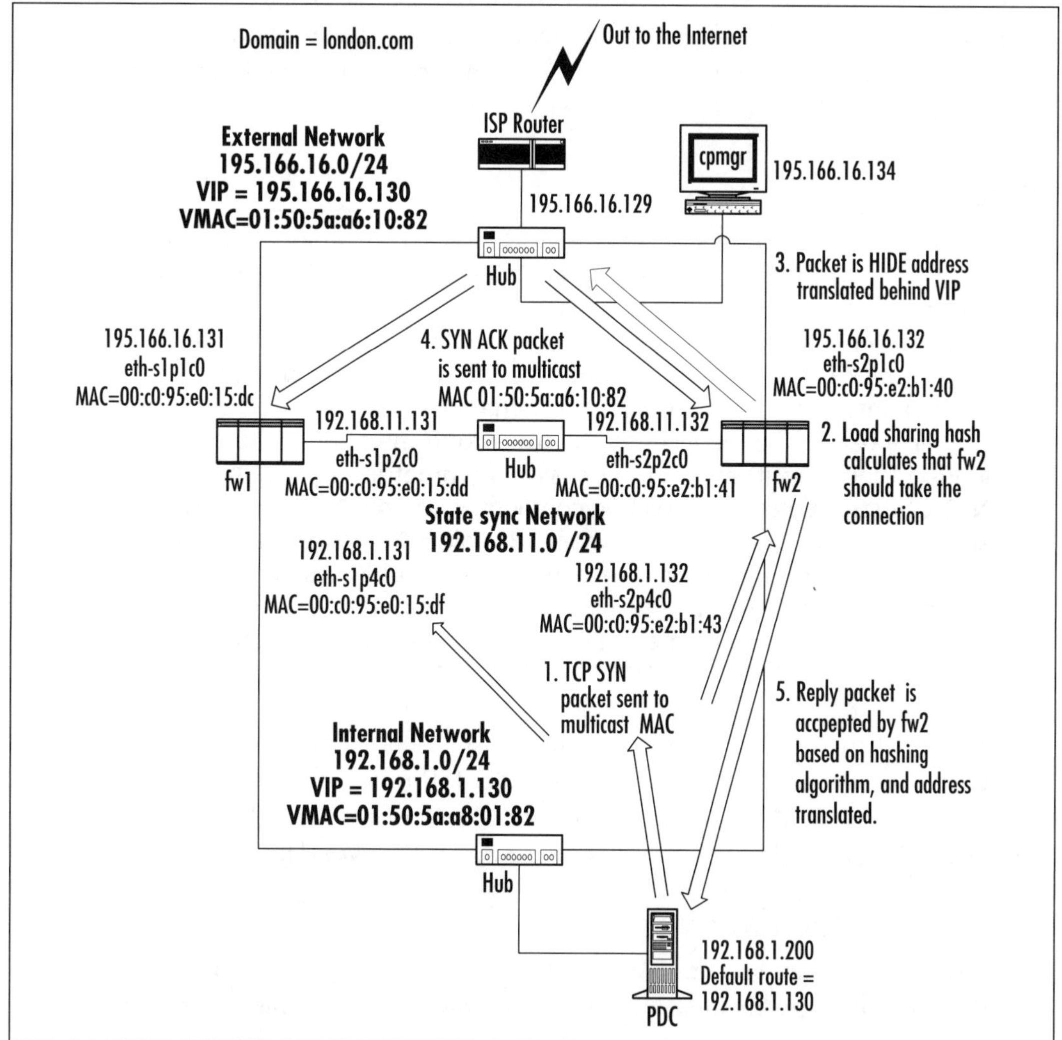

If the Telnet daemon is listening when the packet reaches the ISP router on 195.166.16.129, it will produce a response. Again, the ISP router will issue an ARP request for IP address 195.166.16.130, which is the VIP of the cluster. The master member will respond to the ARP request, sending the multicast MAC address as the MAC address associated with IP 195.166.16.130 (but it will keep the source MAC address of the ARP reply as its own physical external interface; this is one way to see which of your Nokia members is the master without using Voyager). Host 195.166.16.130 will then send a SYN,ACK TCP packet, the source IP will be 195.166.16.129, source port will be 23, and the destination MAC will be the multicast MAC address of the VIP 195,166.16.130, which is 01:50:5a:a6:10:82 in our example.

Again, the reply packet gets onto all members in the cluster, and the correct member that took the original SYN packet for the connection is selected by the hashing algorithm that was selected for that interface.

NOTE

It is important to understand the importance and meaning of the various hashing algorithms. The reply packets get sent back through the same member based on which hashing algorithms you select. For example, if you use Hide NAT when initiating a connection that leaves through the external interface, you have to pick hashing methods that take the NAT into account: NAT_EXT for the external interface, NAT_INT for the internal interface. Not doing this could cause the reply packets to be accepted by the wrong member in the cluster by the load-sharing algorithm, ending up with asymmetric routing. In some complex NAT configurations, there will be conflicts as to which hashing algorithms should be used—for example, where "double NAT" takes place. If these configurations cannot be avoided, other measures should be taken to avoid asynchronous routing, such as static routing via members. This could well lead to imbalances in load sharing and lack of resilience for some connections.

The packet then leaves the internal interface of member fw2 in our example; the source IP is the 195.166.16.129 IP address of the ISP router, the source MAC address is the internal interface MAC address 00:c0:95:e2:b1:43 of fw2, and the destination IP is now 192.168.1.200 (it has been address translated by FireWall-1).

Nokia Cluster Failover

In the event of a failure condition, network traffic taken by that member needs to be routed by an alternative member in the cluster. This is done on the cluster control network. Again, the key is the cluster control protocol that uses this network.

The Nokia cluster control protocol is utilized by the member that is the master. The master member sends out the status of the cluster to all other members in the cluster, using the cluster control protocol. The master member is usually the first member that is made active when you create a Nokia cluster. If the master fails, another member will take over and become master. There is only one master member in any cluster, but the member that is master can change depending on failures in the cluster.

When the master member in the cluster communicates with the other members in the cluster, it uses the Nokia cluster control protocol, which is IP protocol 0x90 (144 decimal). The cluster control network is used exclusively (unlike the CPHA protocol used in ClusterXL). When the master communicates with the other members in the cluster, it is from the real source MAC address of the master on the control network, the source is the real IP address of the master, the destination MAC address is a multicast MAC address, and the IP address is a multicast IP address. For example, if member fw1 were the master, it would send out a packet, source MAC 00:c0:95:e0:15:de, source IP 192.168.12.131, destination MAC 01:00:5e:00:01:90, destination IP address 224.0.1.144. All members that receive the packet will often respond, with their real source MAC and IP address, to the real destination MAC and IP address of the master.

In our example, if member fw1 were the master and member fw1 failed, fw2 would be the master. You would notice that fw2 would start to issue IP protocol 0x90 packets from its real IP, and the destination IP would be the multicast IP for the other members in the cluster. This is another method you can use to determine which member in the Nokia cluster thinks it is the master. Note that when a new master is chosen, it will stay the master until it fails and cannot be the master any longer. You will also see TCP ports 11003 and 11004 Nokia cluster control connections on the cluster control network.

Failover from the point of view of the networking devices on the same local subnet as the VIPs is transparent because the MAC address used by the cluster does not change. There will be a short delay during failover as the load-sharing algorithm determines which member in the cluster will take over the connections of the failed member. This process can take up to 4 seconds.

Nokia Failover Conditions

Failure of a Nokia cluster member is determined when one of the following occurs:

- IP forwarding fails or is stopped (e.g., by *cpstop*).
- The FireWall-1 process *fwd* dies.
- An interface goes down.

All these scenarios are monitored by the *clusterd* process on each Nokia member. When a failover occurs, the *clusterd* process logs the event in the Nokia system logs (/var/log/messages file).

Special Considerations for Nokia Clusters

We have talked a little about how the Nokia clustering solution works, so based on how the technology in Nokia clustering works, we need to take into account its effects when setting up our cluster and the Rule Base we are likely to use.

Network Address Translation

As with all clusters, the way you decide to implement your NAT rules needs to be taken into account. In ClusterXL in HA New mode, we noticed that you cannot use manual proxy ARP entries into the OS. In ClusterXL in Load-Sharing mode, we stated that all methods of NAT and proxy ARP should work fine.

In a Nokia cluster, you cannot use Check Point's own Automatic ARP setting in the **Policy | Global Properties | NAT – Network Address Translation | Automatic Rules for Automatic ARP Configuration** menu.

The reason for this is that each member will proxy ARP for the real MAC address of the member in the cluster as opposed to proxy ARPing the multicast MAC address of the cluster. For this reason, you cannot use Automatic ARP Configuration.

You can enter proxy ARP entries into Voyager for NATed IP addresses, using the multicast MAC address of the cluster interface. You can also use static routes on the ISP router to route traffic to the VIP address of the cluster for the NATed IP address.

If you plan to use proxy ARPs for multicast MAC addresses on the Nokia platform, you need to enable **Accept Multicast reply to ARP** on the **ARP** page of the Voyager interface. You need to do this for all members that make up your cluster.

NOTE

Accept Multicast reply to ARP must be enabled for the cluster to work properly.

Defining the Cluster Object Topology

When defining the gateway cluster object for the Nokia cluster, it is possible to define the cluster topology, listing the VIPs. However, this apparently harmless change results in a significant change in FireWall-1 behavior. Connections that originate from individual cluster members are subject to implicit Hide NAT behind the outgoing cluster VIP. This will affect traffic such as DNS lookups and outgoing FTP connections originating from cluster members. This is the same behavior we saw under ClusterXL. As with ClusterXL, once FP3 Hot Fix 1 is applied, packets routed back to the wrong member will be routed onward via the sync link. Check Point ClusterXL makes allowances for this when handling this traffic, dealing with it gracefully. A Nokia clustering solution will not deal with it as well, and the traffic involved will not be reliable. This behavior will also cause a problem with traffic between external interfaces of members. For these reasons, defining the cluster topology is not recommended when you're using a Nokia solution. Possibly this configuration will be made workable in future releases of NG.

Nokia IPSO VRRP Clusters

If a simple HA cluster solution is required for the Nokia platform, a VRRP configuration should be considered. In this section, we provide an overview of the VRRP protocol, how to configure it on IPSO, and how to configure FireWall-1 NG FP3 for a VRRP cluster. We'll then talk about how you can test the cluster and go over any special considerations that you need to keep in mind when using a cluster.

Nokia Configuration

To configure a Nokia VRRP cluster, you need to take the following steps:

- Configure the interfaces of a Nokia.
- Configure FireWall-1.
- Configure VRRP in Voyager.

We assume that you have installed IPSO 3.6 on your Nokia and that you have the Check Point FireWall-1 NG FP3 package installed and configured. As with setting up all clusters, it is recommended that you complete and test the physical connectivity first so that any problems that you encounter later aren't due to a misconfigured switch or interface, because these could be difficult to spot later.

In Figure 6.76, you can see an example Nokia VRRP configuration. It is a VRRP "Monitored Curcuits" configuration. This is the most common configuration and it is this flavor of VRRP that we will consider throughout this section. Plenty of the information shown won't make much sense yet, so just look at the topology and IP addresses for now.

Unlike Nokia clustering, a VRRP configuration does not require a separate cluster control network. As you can see from Figure 6.76, each network that has a VIP also has a virtual MAC address—a Unicast VRRP MAC that is used for the VIP. From a network perspective of neighboring equipment on the same network as the cluster interfaces, it looks the similar to Check Point ClusterXL in Load-Sharing mode, but with Unicast MAC addresses involved rather than multicast.

You should be able to perform basic IPSO configuration, install Check Point NG FP3, and configure the Gateway Cluster object in the same way as you would for IPSO clustering, with one exception: When configuring the gateway cluster object Availability Mode, select **High Availability**.

Configuring the Nokia VRRP Rule Base

You have some choices as to the Rule Base you want to install. You can either see if the configuration of your cluster object is going to work and install an open policy, or you can create a strict policy now. Remember, there is still one more step to do, which is to configure VRRP using Voyager, so you might want to install an open policy now and then tighten it later once you are happy that your clustering is working correctly.

Figure 6.76 Our Example Configuration: A Nokia VRRP Cluster

The VRRP protocol is multicast based. VRRP multicasts are sent by whichever member currently considers itself VRRP master. In IPSO 3.6, this traffic bypasses the firewall kernel, so no rules accepting the traffic are required in the security policy. If your switches are performing "IGMP snooping" to detect multicast group members, you need to allow the IGMP protocol from the cluster to multicast addresses, as shown in Figure 6.77.

Figure 6.77 Rule Allowing IGMP Multicasts from the Cluster

3	fwcluster	mcast	Any	igmp	accept

NOTE

If you are running IPSO 3.5 or earlier, your security policy must also allow the VRRP protocol from the cluster member addresses (use the cluster object) to multicast addresses.

As with other cluster solutions, it is a good idea to make sure that the time between the cluster members does not drift by implementing NTP time synchronization—so make sure that the Rule Base accepts NTP between cluster members.

You need to configure a group of host node objects that represent all the VRRP VIPs and use this in your "stealth" rule and elsewhere. For details, see the "IPSO Clustering" section.

Once you have configured your policy, install it to the cluster and test. You now have to complete the last step in configuring a Nokia VRRP cluster: Configure IPSO to use VRRP.

Nokia VRRP Configuration on Voyager

When we configured the Gateway Cluster object in the SmartDashboard GUI, we did not configure the gateway cluster to have ClusterXL installed. This feature is not available on the Nokia platform, but Nokia provides its own solution for HA: VRRP. However, you have to configure it within the Voyager interface.

NOTE

Remember that you have to configure VRRP on each Nokia in the cluster, so you will have to repeat the procedure on each Nokia.

In the section that follows, we deal with one particular VRRP configuration: VRRP monitored circuits with a single virtual router, and single virtual IP address, for each connected subnet, with two systems participating in the cluster. This is probably the most common and well-tested configuration, but VRRP provides many other possibilities. VRRP is a standard protocol for router redundancy and is well documented elsewhere, and brave readers might want to refer to RFC-2338. For more details regarding IPSO VRRP configuration, refer to *Nokia Network Security Solutions Handbook* (Syngress Publishing, ISBN 1-931836-70-1).

Voyager Configuration

Make sure you have network connectivity from your browser to your Nokia FireWall-1 modules in your cluster, and make sure that the security policy you have installed on the firewall does not prevent you from accessing Voyager from your browser. Navigate to Voyager on the system that you want to become the master member of the cluster. In our example, we would do this by going to https://195.166.16.131 (see Figure 6.78).

Figure 6.78 Voyager's Main Screen

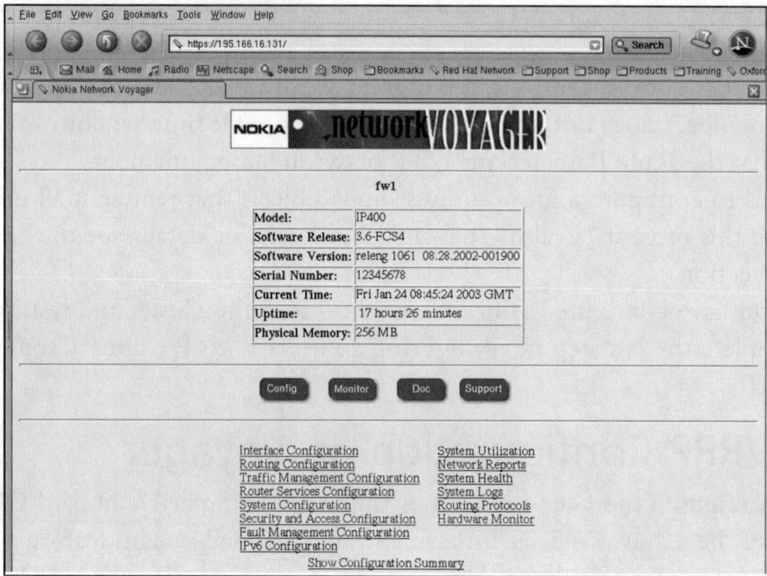

Here are the steps that you need to follow after you have authenticated and are presented with the main screen:

1. From the main Voyager screen, click **Router Services Configuration**.
2. Click **VRRP**. The initial configuration page appears.
3. Enter a cold start value. This introduces a delay after the VRRP system initializes, before it will consider itself a potential master router. A value of 30 seconds provides ample time for FireWall-1 to initialize (see Figure 6.79). Click **Apply**.
4. Select the VRRP mode for each interface on which redundancy is required. Typically, VRRP is enabled on all interfaces except the dedicated Check Point "sync" network. In this example, we use VRRP monitored circuits mode. The cluster configuration screen then expands to include more parameters that can be configured within the cluster. Click **Apply**.
5. Enter a virtual router ID (VRID) for each VRRP-enabled interface. Select a different VRID for each interface. In this case, we have simply based them on interface port numbers, but you could use, for example, network numbers (see Figure 6.80). Click **Apply**.

Figure 6.79 Initial VRRP Configuration Page in Voyager

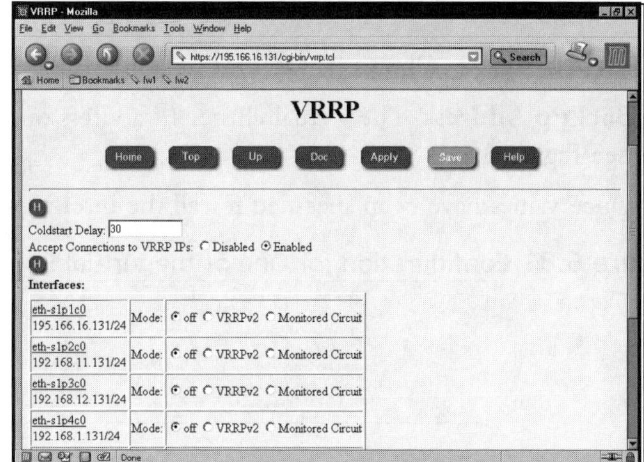

Figure 6.80 Cluster Configuration Defining VRIDs

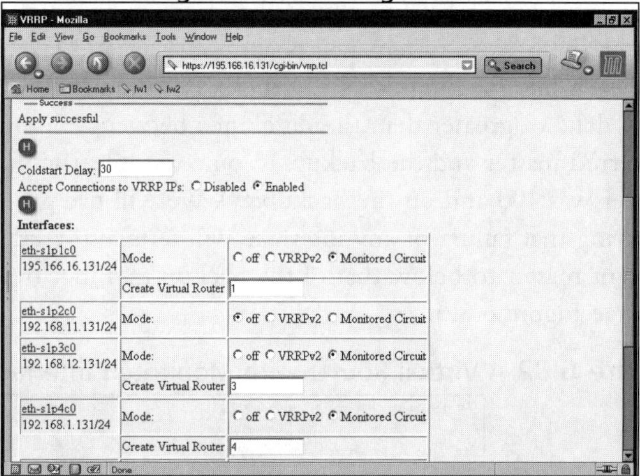

6. The next page allows you to configure VRRP for each interface. Supply values for each interface as follows:

   - **Priority** This should indicate your preference as to which member runs as master. In this example we give a priority of 100 to our preferred member for each interface. When configuring the other member, we give a value of 90.
   - **Hello interval** The interval in seconds between each announcement from the current master. We are using a value of 1 second to give the quickest failover. If bursts of serious network congestion results in loss of

some of these hello packets a greater value might be specified, resulting in slow failover but less chance of "false" failover.

- **VMAC Mode** Choose VRRP for default VRRP behavior.
- **Backup Address** The virtual cluster IP address on this interface's subnet (see Figure 6.81).

Once values have been specified for all the interfaces, click **Apply**.

Figure 6.81 Configuration for One of the Virtual Routers

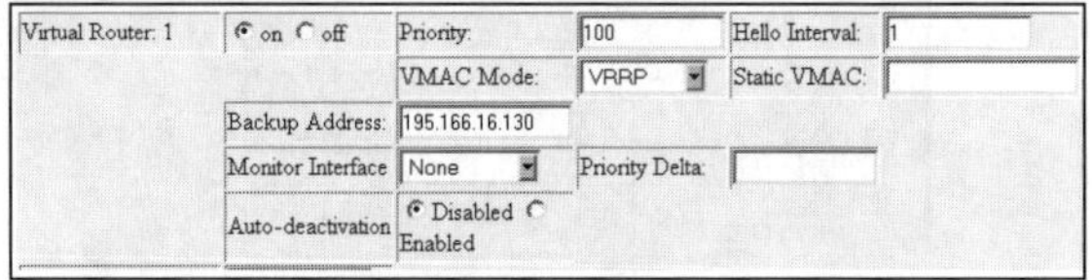

7. For each interface, we can now identify which other interfaces are monitored. This identification is key to the operation of Monitored Circuits mode. We want to ensure that if any one of the cluster interfaces fails on the current master, the backup system will become master and take over routing. To do this, each interface monitors all other VRRP enabled interfaces, with a priority delta of greater than the difference between the priority specified on the preferred master and the backup. In our example, the priority on our preferred master was 100 and on the backup, 90. We will use priority deltas of 15, ensuring that failure of any interface will reduce the effective priority of the current master to below that of the backup member (refer back to Figure 6.76 and see Figure 6.82).

Figure 6.82 A Virtual Router with Monitored Interfaces Enabled

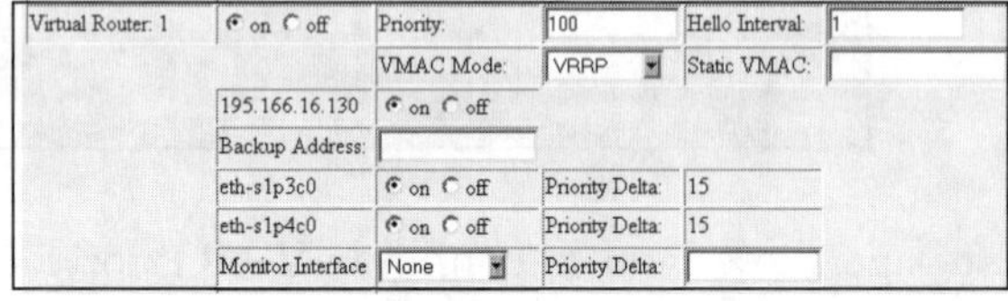

8. We will also configure authentication for each virtual router by enabling **Simple Authentication**, supplying a password, and clicking **Apply** (see Figure 6.83). This simple authentication is far from secure; the password given appears in Voyager after it is set and is transmitted in VRRP traffic as plaintext! It does, however, protect against simple attacks, or more likely, problems caused by other VRRP devices that have coincidentally been configured with the same VRID. Be aware that if the password (or lack of one) does not match that used by other members, this member will assume itself as master (there being no other devices

with "correct" passwords enabled)—so always set the password correctly immediately on configuration of a new member's VRRP interfaces.

Figure 6.83 Configuring VRRP Interface Authentication

9. Finally, don't forget to click **Save**.
10. To verify that the members have correctly identified themselves as master and backup, click the link at the bottom of the page to VRRP Monitor (see Figure 6.84). The preferred member should indicate that all its virtual routers are in Master mode. The backup member should indicate that its virtual routers are in Backup mode.

Figure 6.84 VRRP Monitor on Preferred Member Showing All Three Virtual Routers in Master Mode

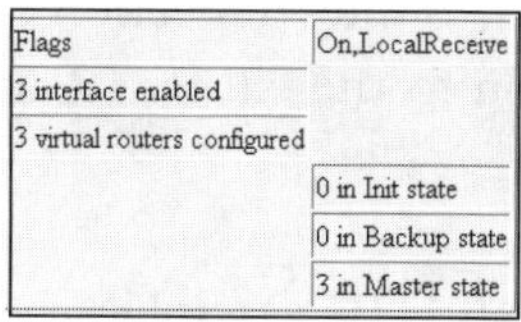

Flags
On,LocalReceive
3 interface enabled
3 virtual routers configured
0 in Init state
0 in Backup state
3 in Master state

Testing the Nokia VRRP Cluster

Once your Nokia VRRP cluster is configured, you need to test it to make sure that it is functioning correctly. Again, keep in mind the way that this particular clustering technology works and how it differs from the other clustering solutions we have covered so far.

Test 1: Pinging the Virtual IP Address for Interface

You should be able to ping the local VIP addresses (VRRP backed-up addresses) from a host that is on the same subnet as the cluster interfaces.

You will receive a response if everything is working properly. If you do not receive a response, verify that your Rule Base allows echo-request to the cluster IPs and that "Accept Connections to VRRP IPs" is enabled in the Voyager VRRP page.

In the test we ran on our example network, a ping was initiated from the FireWall-1 management station (195.166.16.134) to the VIP of the cluster (195.166.16.130). A packet trace was run at the same time on the management station to analyze the packet for the ping session. If you look at the ARP cache of the local host initiating the ping, you should now have the VRRP MAC address of the VIP. In our case, this is 0:0:5e:0:1:1 (which you can check against Figure 6.76). This in itself does not tell you much—just that the VIP address is up and running, and that a member in the cluster responded. But can we tell which member?

Unlike other solutions, because the source MAC address of the echo reply is the VRRP MAC address, there is no indication of which member actually replied.

However, if we ping a host behind the cluster—as long as doing so is allowed by the firewall policy—the source MAC address of the reply packet will be the real MAC address of the member that passed the packet. Running *tracert* from a Windows host to a host behind the cluster will also identify the master member.

Test 2: Finding Which Member Responds to Administrative Connections to the VIPs

A rather unconventional test for the cluster is to attempt an administrative connection—i.e. Telnet, FTP, Voyager (HTTP or HTTPS) to a cluster VIP. The responding member will indicate its hostname in its response, allowing you to deduce which member is the current master. If the connection fails, make sure that your Rule Base allows that type of connection to the cluster IP and that that type of access is supported by your IPSO configuration.

Test 3: Determining the Status of Each Member in the Cluster

In a VRRP configuration, there are two tools for monitoring the status of the cluster and its members. One is the SmartView Status GUI, and the other is Voyager monitoring.

The SmartView Status GUI shows you the health of each member and if it is in state table sync with other members of the cluster. What it won't show you is the correct status of each interface of each member. For this information, you have to use the Nokia Voyager screens on each member in the cluster.

Checking the monitoring of the cluster through Voyager is straightforward. Connect your browser to one of the members, and select **Monitor VRRP**. The summary information will indicate whether the member considers itself a master or backup (see Figures 6.85 and 6.86). More detailed information is available in the interface and stats pages (linked from this page).

Test 4: FTPing Through a VRRP Cluster During Interface Failure

We can follow the same steps as suggested for IPSO clustering configurations to perform a test. If SmartView Monitor is available, this provides a good method of observing the failover (or not).

Figure 6.85 The VRRP Monitor Interface Page

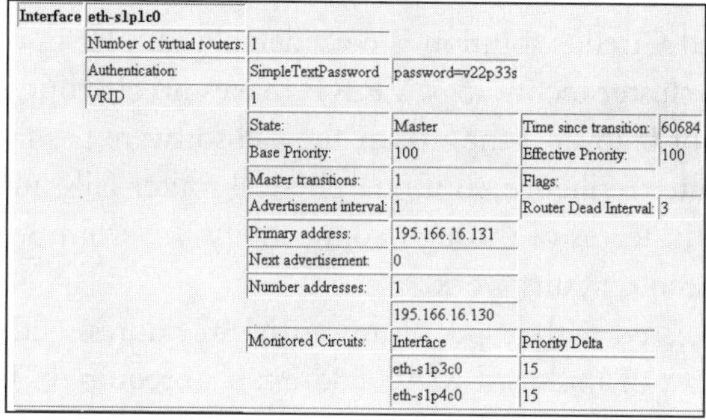

Interface eth-s1p1c0
Number of virtual routers: 1
Authentication: SimpleTextPassword password=v22p33s
VRID 1
State: Master
Time since transition: 60684
Base Priority: 100
Effective Priority: 100
Master transitions: 1
Flags:
Advertisement interval: 1
Router Dead Interval: 3
Primary address: 195.166.16.131
Next advertisement: 0
Number addresses: 1
195.166.16.130
Monitored Circuits: Interface
Priority Delta
eth-s1p3c0 15
eth-s1p4c0 15

Figure 6.86 The VRRP Monitor Stats Page

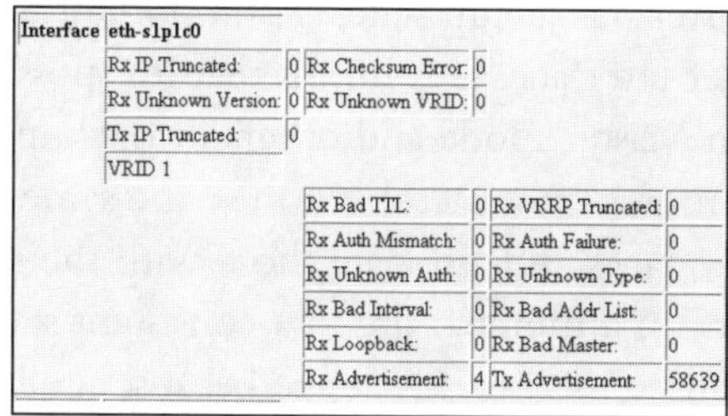

Interface eth-s1p1c0
Rx IP Truncated: 0
Rx Checksum Error: 0
Rx Unknown Version: 0
Rx Unknown VRID: 0
Tx IP Truncated: 0
VRID 1
Rx Bad TTL: 0
Rx VRRP Truncated: 0
Rx Auth Mismatch: 0
Rx Auth Failure: 0
Rx Unknown Auth: 0
Rx Unknown Type: 0
Rx Bad Interval: 0
Rx Bad Addr List: 0
Rx Loopback: 0
Rx Bad Master: 0
Rx Advertisement: 4
Tx Advertisement: 58639

Command-Line Stats

We can use the IPSO *clish* command to monitor VRRP from a console session. This command provides very similar information to that provided by Voyager but provides a useful alternative.

Once in the *clish* shell, you can use these commands:

- **show vrrp** Shows a summary of VRRP status.
- **show vrrp interface <*interface name*>** Provides for more details for a particular interface.
- **show vrrp interfaces** All interfaces.
- **show vrrp stats** Detailed VRRP statistics.

You can use the *cphaprob* command on the Nokia platform if you want, but the information that it will tell you is limited. For example, it can't tell you which interfaces are up or down, but it can tell you whether the state table synchronization is working or not.

How VRRP Works

The VRRP Monitored Circuits solution is considerably simpler in operation than the Check Point or Nokia cluster technology. VRRP makes no attempt to monitor the firewall software so does not failover if the master firewall software has failed. VRRP is designed to provide router resilience, so if one physical router fails, another takes over, hopefully transparently in terms of through connectivity. We will now take a detailed look at how VRRP Monitored Circuits work.

Each VRID is associated with a special unicast MAC address (although it can be configured to use any unicast or multicast MAC address, if so required). This MAC address comes from a range allocated for VRRP. Although it is a Unicast address, it floats between members so that devices on the local subnet see a single (virtual) router. When considering whether a member is in master or backup state, it is important to realize that the state is defined per virtual router per interface. This means that it is possible that a member has some of its virtual routers in Master mode and others in Backup mode. In our example, we configured each virtual router on a member to use the same priority and monitor all its other VRRP enabled interfaces and associate those with the same delta; this should ensure that all virtual routers on a member are in a consistent state. In more advanced configurations, this flexibility can be used to advantage because it allows a member to be a preferred master for some routes but backup for others by using multiple virtual routers.

Communication between members is simple; in fact, there is no two-way communication as such. There are reasonably straightforward rules governing when members switch a VR between Master and Backup state. However, VRRP was designed to handle single failures. More complicated configurations are possible, but usually when one interface fails on a router you want to fail over all the interfaces to the secondary, and if it looses an interface fail all over to the third and so on. Having a router with some VRIDs in backup and some master is prone to error and it is generally considered a misconfiguration.

- The member that believes itself to be the master for a given virtual router (VR) will send VRRP announcements for that VR at intervals as configured— in our example, every second—advertising its effective priority (that is, its base priority less the deltas of any failed interfaces). This concept is illustrated in Figure 6.87.
- If a member with a VR in master state sees an announcement with a lower effective priority than its own, it switches itself to backup state and stops sending announcements.
- If a member with a VR in backup state sees an announcement that has a higher effective priority, it will switch to master state itself and begin announcements.
- If a member with a VR in backup state does not see any announcements for three times the configured announcement interval, it will switch to master state.

Let's walk through an example of how a connection would work through a VRRP cluster. In our example, host 192.168.1.200 initiates a Telnet session through the cluster to our ISP router on IP address 195.166.16.129, and we address hide the connection behind the cluster external IP address of 195.166.16.130, using a hide rule in our firewall NAT Rule Base.

Figure 6.87 VRRP Announcements

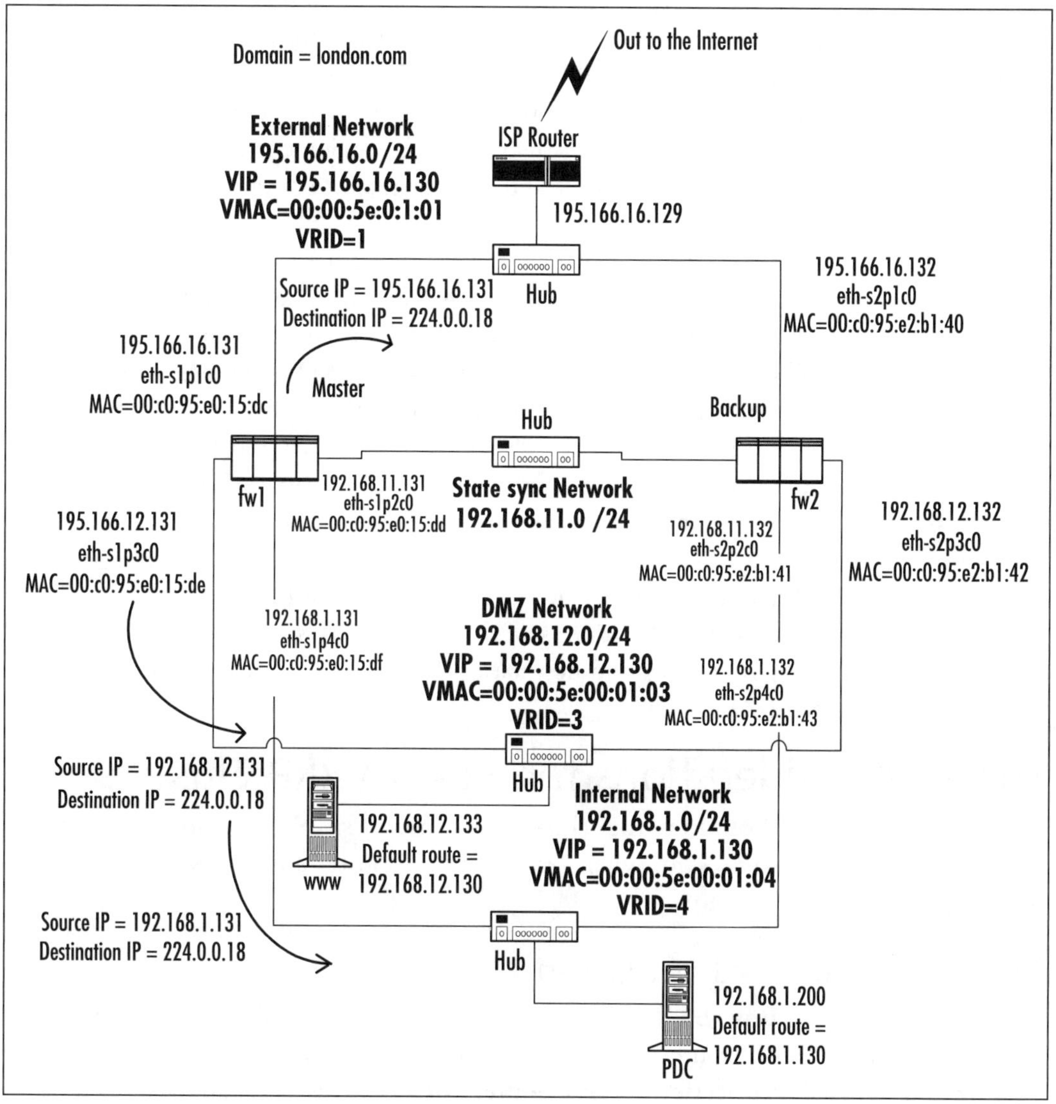

When the Telnet session is initiated, the host 192.168.1.200 sends out an ARP request for 192.168.1.130, which is the default gateway on the network 192.168.1.0. The address in the ARP response will be the VRRP MAC address for the VR on that network. The member that has the VR in master status will always send the ARP response. In our example, the MAC address returned is 0:0:5e:0:1:4. Our host on 192.168.1.200 then sends a SYN TCP packet, high source port, destination is to 195.166.16.129, destination MAC is 0:0:5e:0:1:4 (the default gateway MAC address).

Only one member of the cluster will do anything with the packet—the one with the VR in master state. This will pass the packet up through the IP stack to Check Point FireWall-1 for the incoming interface. The TCP SYN packet will pass through the Rule Base of the firewall and, providing that everything is fine, it will then send the packet out of its external interface, with the source IP address of 195.166.16.130 (the external cluster IP address), with the source MAC address of the member that has routed the packet (in our example, the source MAC address is 0:c0:95:e0:15:dc , which corresponds with member fw1 external interface eth-s1p1c0), and the destination IP address will be 195.166.16.129.

If the Telnet daemon is listening when the packet reaches the ISP router on 195.166.16.129, it will produce a response. The ISP router will issue an ARP request for IP address 195.166.16.130, which is the VIP of the cluster. The member with the external VR in master state will respond to the ARP request, sending the VRRP MAC address as the MAC address associated with IP 195.166.16.130. Host 195.166.16.129 will then send a SYN,ACK TCP packet, source IP will be 195.166.16.129, source port will be 23, destination MAC will be the VRRP MAC address of the VR master for 195.166.16.130. The reply packet arrives at all members in the cluster and is processed by the member with the VR in master state.

The packet then leaves the internal interface of member fw1 in our example, source IP is the 195.166.16.129 (IP address of the ISP router), source MAC address is the internal interface MAC of fw1 and destination IP is now 192.168.1.200 (it has been address translated by FireWall-1).

Special Considerations for Nokia VRRP Clusters

We have talked a little about how the VRRP solution works. Now we look at issues that should be taken into account when setting up our cluster and the Rule Base we are likely to use.

Network Address Translation

As with all clusters, the way you decide to implement your NAT rules needs to be taken into account. With VRRP, you cannot use Check Point's own Automatic ARP setting in the **Policy | Global Properties | NAT – Network Address Translation | Automatic Rules** for **Automatic ARP Configuration**.

The reason for this is that each member will proxy ARP for the real MAC address of the member in the cluster as opposed to proxy ARPing the VRRP MAC address of the relevant cluster VR. For this reason, you cannot use Automatic ARP Configuration.

You can enter proxy ARP entries into Voyager for NATed IP addresses using the VRRP MAC address of the cluster VR. Alternatively, you could add static host routes on the ISP router to route traffic for the NATed IP address to the external VRIP address. Note: It is *not* recommended to add the NATed IP address as a VRIP address, because doing so could cause problems with FireWall-1 antispoofing configurations.

Connections Originating from a Single Member in the Cluster

When defining the CP cluster object for the IPSO cluster, the cluster topology could be defined using the VIPs. This results in the same behavior as ClusterXL on connections from members out of the external if they implicitly hide NAT behind cluster VIPs. As with ClusterXL, once FP3 Hotfix 1 (or a more recent hotfix that includes Hotfix 1 features) is applied, packets routed back to the wrong member should be routed onward via the sync link, so this configuration will work—to a degree. However, in practice, there seem to be problems with this configuration in non-ClusterXL solutions that result in packet loss, and as such we recommend that the cluster topology *not* be defined when you're using a VRRP solution.

Third-Party Clustering Solutions

A range of solutions are available that provide HA and load-sharing functionality for FireWall-1. Some integrate with FireWall-1 on the cluster members themselves, others are located adjacent to the cluster and allocate traffic between members from there. The most widely used third-party solutions are probably Stonesoft StoneBeat and Rainfinity Rainwall; both have HA and load-balancing variants. For information on other OPSEC partner HA solutions, and indeed more about OPSEC, refer to the OPSEC Web site. It is wise to check the OPSEC site to match product version with supported FireWall-1 version for any third-party solution:

- **Stonesoft** www.stonesoft.com
- **Rainfinity** www.rainfinity.com
- **Other OPSEC partners** www.opsec.com

Clustering and HA Performance Tuning

If you have got this far after configuring and testing your cluster, you'll want to know what you can do in terms of improving your cluster's performance. A great deal of performance tuning on firewalls depends on how well you know the type of traffic that goes through the firewall and then tuning the firewall to handle the most common type of traffic more efficiently. In a clustering environment, you need to expand on the concept of tuning considerations, all the way down to hardware, depending on the clustering solution you have implemented. In this section, we discuss the main considerations for optimizing your cluster solution.

Data Throughput or Large Number of Connections

Firewall load-sharing clustering solutions are very good at increasing the overall data throughput of your firewall; the higher the throughput you require, the more members you add in your cluster. However, you will soon reach a stage where adding more members to your cluster just doesn't make any performance difference, because the bottleneck moves somewhere else on the data path—either the line speed of connecting equipment or cables or routers. Furthermore, consider the fact that a two-member load sharing of fast machines with fast network cards for cluster members will probably scale better than slower machines with slower network cards but more cluster members. This is where the price that you pay for hardware is probably significantly lower than paying for an extra enterprise license FireWall-1 module. On the other hand, if you are looking for higher resilience, more members in the cluster might be the way to go. When considering how many members to include in a load sharing cluster, always make sure that the cluster can cope with typical levels of traffic if one of its members is offline. If you don't, a single member failure could lead to the rest of the members being overwhelmed.

In large numbers of connections, clustering is less help than you might think. The reason for this is that if you have 50,000 connections going through one member and 50,000 connections going through the other member, and you only have two members in the cluster, and one member fails, you will have 100,000 connections going through one member. However, both members will still have a connections table showing 100,000 connections (assuming that the connections are synchronized between members), even when both members were online. The point here is that the connections tables are going to be large the more connections that you push through the cluster, because every member in the cluster should have its connections table synchronized with every other member in the cluster in case of a member failure. The rate of change of new connections makes the situation worse because it has a strong impact on the amount of data that is synchronized between cluster members. High rates of change of connections need to be identified wherever possible because these are prime services that you would target for not synchronizing across the cluster members.

Based on these two definitions of load on a firewall cluster, let's look at each type of load and what can be done to improve performance.

Improving Data Throughput

Improving data throughput is probably the easiest one of the two performance areas that can be addressed. It can be addressed in the following ways:

- Use good fast networking cards—100Mbps Ethernet full duplex or gigabit Ethernet cards—in the cluster members. Make sure that surrounding hubs and routers from the origin of the data through to the destination of the data have fast physical networking hardware. These are the key areas that will give you high throughput.
- Use fast single-processor members in the cluster, with lots of memory.
- Use a load-sharing cluster as opposed to an HA cluster. Traffic can be shared across the members in the cluster, which will give higher data rates of throughput.
- Keep your Rule Base short and compact. Larger numbers of rules will slow throughput. This applies to NAT rules and the security Rule Base.

You need good networking cards, and your hubs and routers—all the way from data source through the cluster to the data destination—need to be as good as you can get. This will define your maximum throughput, and it is this line speed that you will aim for.

Using fast single-processor members and plenty of memory is good practice. It enables the member in the cluster to deal with highly processor-intensive services, such as VPN connections, as quickly as possible. Different members in the load-sharing cluster will take different VPN connections between the cluster and the remote sites, so this means that one member will not be dealing with all the VPN traffic. If you just have one VPN set up between the cluster and the remote site, only one member in the cluster will take the load. If you have several VPNs set up, multiple members in the cluster will be dealing with the VPN connections. This will be based on the load-sharing algorithm used.

In addition, if you are using the security servers for passing traffic, such as FTP, HTTP, or Telnet, this is load shared across the cluster as well and will also give you efficiencies because it can also be CPU intensive. If you are using security servers, make sure that the DNS resolver on each member of the cluster is pointing at a high-speed DNS server or servers (which preferably have a very rich cache) so that DNS lookups do not hold up the performance.

Lots of memory will prevent your host from writing too much to the swap memory area, although some operating systems use their swap space regardless of how much physical memory you install.

If you are going for high throughput, you have to use a load-sharing clustering solution. This gives you scalability and allows big benefits for VPNs and security server connections. It gives big benefits for normal connections as well.

You can do many things with Rule Base tuning that will make a big difference to increasing the throughput of a member. Tuning the Rule Base will also give you some major connections-based performance as well. The types of things you need to do to a Rule Base to make it more efficient are as follows:

- Reduce the number of rules to a minimum.
- Try not to have rules that are sourced with group objects, destination group objects, because this will multiply out into individual rules when the policy is compiled. Instead, use network objects subnetted appropriately.
- Do not use group objects nested inside one another. Again, this causes the compiled Rule Base to have a large number of rules in it.
- Reduce the number of NAT rules to a minimum.
- Reduce the number of objects you reference in the Rule Base.
- Don't use resource rules or user authentication unless you need to. The throughput of the security servers is not as fast as a straight stateful connection through the FireWall-1 kernel.
- Place the most commonly accessed rules as close to the top of the Rule Base as you can get away with.
- Avoid using domain objects.
- Keep logging to a minimum on rules.

Tuning VPNs for throughput is a special case. You can always increase the overall performance of a VPN by making the member do less work to encrypt and decrypt packets, but this is usually at the price of security. For example, using weaker encryption strengths will reduce the security of encrypted packets, but it will mean that the firewall members have to do less work. Using perfect forwarding secrecy also causes a significant performance overhead, but changing this setting will reduce security.

If no compromise of security versus throughput is possible, you have two other options open to you. One is to use the Check Point Performance Pack, which will give you VPN acceleration. The other possibility is to use a hardware accelerator in each member of the cluster, which will aid DES and 3DES calculations for VPNs.

To summarize, anything that you can do on a single firewall member to improve performance is also true of a FireWall-1 member in a clustered environment.

Improving for Large Number of Connections

In many ways, improving for a large number of connections requires more thought than tweaking your cluster for maximum data throughput because it is less dependent on hardware. The first thing you need to be aware of that will reduce the performance of a cluster as far as a large number of connections is concerned is the rate of change of new connections. If this is very high, these particular types of connections are good candidates for not being synchronized between cluster members. On clusters, you need to reduce the number of connections in the connections state table, and you also need to reduce the number of connections that are synchronized statefully.

For example, DNS lookups through a member will be done often. These are small packets, which are often responded to very quickly, and most DNS resolvers are quite patient about waiting for a response. Many DNS lookups are done, especially by any HTTP clients, FTP clients, and the FireWall-1 management server itself if logging has been told to resolve hostnames.

DNS is a classic service for which you would turn off state table sync. It is a very transient UDP-based service, so synchronizing the state makes little sense. By default, the service is synchronized across the cluster members.

To do this, start the SmartDashboard GUI, log in, click **Manage | Services**, and select the service **domain-udp,** as shown in Figure 6.88. Click the **Edit** button, then click the **Advanced** button. Uncheck the **Synchronize on cluster** check box, and then click **OK** and install the policy.

Figure 6.88 Turning Off State Synchronization for a Specific Service

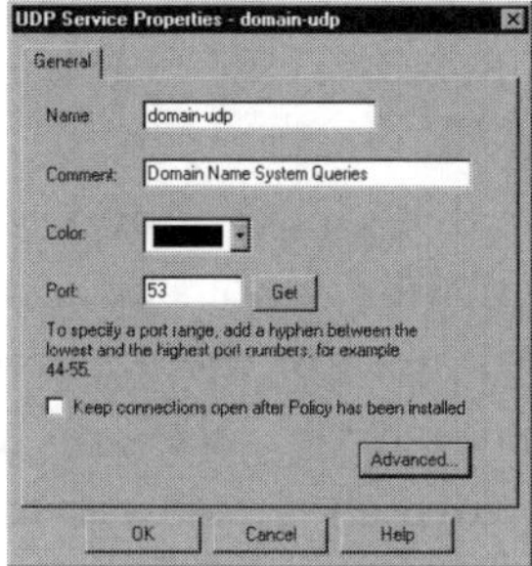

There are a large number of services to which you might want to do this. The more you reduce the state synchronization required, the better your members in your cluster will perform for connections.

The other weapon you have for reducing the number of connections in the state table is reducing the virtual session timeout for each service. This especially applies to UDP services, but it can also apply to many TCP-based services, such as HTTP.

Most HTTP sessions are short and transient, so unless you are hosting a Web site where it is vital that each HTTP session opened is longer than 3600 seconds (or 1 hour), it is a good idea to reduce this in the service itself. This means that if the session did not finish normally, the timeout will clear more quickly than the default of 1 hour. You can do this by clicking **Virtual Session Timeout** in the **Advanced** area of each service definition, as shown in Figure 6.89.

Once you have done as much as you can do to reduce the number of connections that each member will have and you have reduced the number of connections that will be synchronized across the cluster, you need to tune each member in the cluster to accept more than 25,000 connections and tune the kernel memory and NAT table sizes as well to cater for the increase in connections.

Figure 6.89 Advanced Settings of the DNS UDP Service

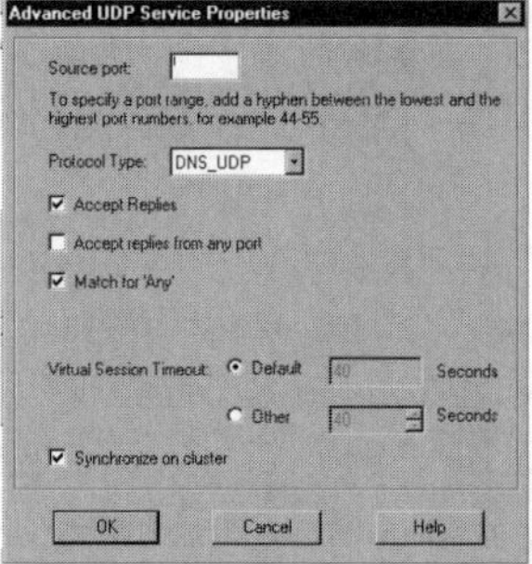

This process used to be a manual process of hacking text files previous to FireWall-1 NG FP3, but now it can all be done from the SmartDashboard GUI. Navigate to the **Manage** menu, choose **Network Objects**, then locate the **Cluster Gateway Object** of your cluster, and click **Edit**. On the left side of the popup window, select **Capacity Optimization**.

From Figure 6.90, you can see that you can modify all the parameters mentioned earlier. The automatic setting for memory pool size and connection hash table size is usually fine, but you might want to monitor these parameters (which we discuss next). If you need to manually tweak the hash table size and the memory pool size, you can also do this from this screen. Note that after policy install, the size of the connections table changes will take effect.

Figure 6.90 Configuring Capacity Optimization of Your Cluster

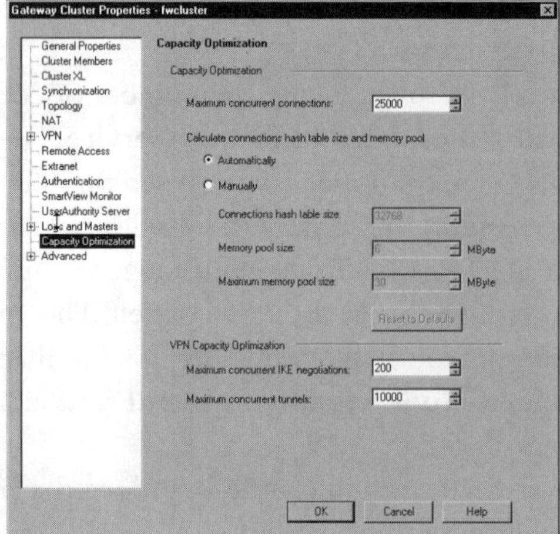

You'll want to monitor the connections table sizes, the memory pool size, and the table hash sizes. How can you do this? The best way is to get a console connection to one of your modules and run the diagnostic commands to reveal this information.

Monitoring the Connections Table

The first thing you will want to do is examine the connections table of a module to determine the current maximum limit for number of connections. This can be done with the *fw tab –t connections* command from one of the firewall modules in the cluster.

At the top of this command's output are the parameters of this table, which you need to take note of—including the maximum number of connections parameter.

```
-------- connections --------
dynamic, id 8158, attributes: keep, sync, expires 60, refresh, limit
    25000, hashsize 32768, kbuf 16 17 18 19 20 21 22 23 24 25 26 27 28
        29 30, free function 707138a0 0
```

Altering the number of connections up to 50,000 and then running the command will show the new table size for connections and a new hash value:

```
-------- connections --------
dynamic, id 8158, attributes: keep, sync, expires 60, refresh, limit
    50000, hashsize 262144, kbuf 16 17 18 19 20 21 22 23 24 25 26 27
        28 29 30, free function 707138a0 0
```

Note that when you change the connections size, you will also see that the SmartView Tracker logs show that connections table has changed, the connections table hash has changed, and the memory pool size has been changed.

If you want to monitor the number of connections going through a member at any one time, use the command *fw tab –t connections –s*. This will give you statistics of the current number of connections in the table (#VALS column) and the peak number of connections (#PEAK column):

```
fw1 # fw tab -t connections -s
HOST                 NAME                         ID #VALS #PEAK #SLINKS
localhost            connections                8158     5    20       8
```

You could get to the stage where you would like to identify a specific connection on a module and check that you can see that connection synchronized to another module in the cluster. To look at the connections table to make sure that it makes sense, use the command *fw tab –t connections –f*:

```
10:49:12          192.168.11.131 >      ----------------------------------
(+); Direction: 0; Source: 192.168.1.100; SPort: 4990; Dest: 192.168.1.
```

```
130; DPort: telnet; Protocol: tcp; CPTFMT_sep: ;; Type: 114689; Flags:
8405120; Rule: 2; Timeout: 3600; Handler: 0; Uuid: 3e37b13c0c3a610837b6;
Ifncin: 4; Ifncout: 4; Ifnsin: -1; Ifnsout: -1; Bits: 0000000002000000;
NAT_VM_Dest: 192.168.1.131; NAT_VM_Flags: 100; NAT_Client_Dest: 192.168.1
.130; NAT_Client_Flags: 100; NAT_Server_Flags: 0; NAT_Xlate_Flags: 32836;
 SeqVerifier_Kbuf_ID: 1076676608; Expires: 3495/3600; product: VPN-1 &
FireWall-1;

10:49:12        192.168.11.131 >      ----------------------------------
(+); Direction: 1; Source: 192.168.1.131; SPort: telnet; Dest: 192.168.1.
100; DPort: 4990; Protocol: tcp; CPTFMT_sep_1: ->; Direction_1: 0;
Source_1: 192.168.1.100; SPort_1: 4990; Dest_1: 192.168.1.130; DPort_1:
telnet; Protocol_1: tcp; FW_symval: 5; product: VPN-1 & FireWall-1;
```

Normally , the *fw tab –t connections –f* command would show all connections, but you can filter it down by piping into the *grep* command (such as *fw tab –t connections –f | grep telnet*, which was done in the preceding example).

The connection we are interested in is the connection which has an *Expires:* parameter. This shows the TCP timeout of the connection and so is a good method to prove that your changes to a services virtual session timeout is working (see Figure 6.86). The other connection we can see is present for the reply from the cluster IP address (as the session initiated was a Telnet from host 192.168.1.100 to the VIP address of 192.168.1.130).

The Telnet service is state synchronized, so we should see exactly the same connection in the connections table of fw2 in the cluster. State table synchronizes an update at least every 100ms to all members in the cluster.

Monitoring Pool Memory

Pool memory is fairly easy to monitor in FireWall-1 NG FP3. You need to make sure that kernel memory for the firewall kernel is not exhausted, or else you could end up with *halloc* memory allocation error messages in the system logs of your operating system. This can lead to the host becoming unresponsive and intermittently locking up—including locking up console access to the member.

You can monitor the kernel memory situation using the command *fw ctl pstat* on the firewall module:

```
fw2 #fw ctl pstat

Hash kernel memory (hmem) statistics:
   Total memory allocated: 20971520 bytes in 5118 4KB blocks using 2 pools
```

```
  Initial memory allocated: 6291456 bytes (Hash memory extended by
      14680064 bytes)
  Memory allocation  limit: 83886080 bytes using 10 pools
  Total memory bytes  used:   348308   unused: 20623212 (98.34%)   peak:
      369584
  Total memory blocks used:      114   unused:     5004 (97%)   peak:
      126
  Allocations: 71973 alloc, 0 failed alloc, 66671 free

System kernel memory (smem) statistics:
  System  physical   memory: 255074304 bytes
  Available physical memory: 59908096 bytes
  Total memory  bytes  used: 31724112   peak: 31869120
    Blocking  memory  bytes   used:  1531912   peak:  1636904
    Non-Blocking memory bytes used: 30192200   peak: 30232216
  Allocations: 3645229 alloc, 0 failed alloc, 3644952 free, 0 failed free

Kernel memory (kmem) statistics:
  Total memory  bytes  used: 11088212   peak: 11826720
      Allocations: 81792 alloc, 0 failed alloc, 76215 free, 0 failed free

Kernel stacks:
        262144 bytes total, 16384 bytes stack size, 16 stacks,
        2 peak used, 4124 max stack bytes used, 1028 min stack bytes used,
        0 failed stack calls

INSPECT:
         13746 packets, 2698521 operations, 43174 lookups,
         0 record, 702731 extract

Cookies:
         2309961 total, 0 alloc, 0 free,
         21 dup, 863658 get, 1243 put,
         1458553 len, 0 cached len, 0 chain alloc,
         0 chain free

Connections:
```

```
        4019 total, 436 TCP, 3381 UDP, 201 ICMP,
        1 other, 5 anticipated, 7 recovered, 10 concurrent,
        26 peak concurrent, 861843 lookups

Fragments:
        0 fragments, 0 packets, 0 expired, 0 short,
        0 large, 0 duplicates, 0 failures


NAT:
        215/0 forw, 1021/0 bckw, 1214 tcpudp,
        22 icmp, 1268-1410 alloc
sync new ver working
sync out: on  sync in: on
sync packets sent:
total: 9302 retransmitted: 0 retrans reqs: 0 acks: 49
sync packets received:
total 4911 of which 0 queued and 0 dropped by net
also received 0 retrans reqs and 38 acks to 17 cb requests
callback average delay 1 max delay 6
```

The area for kernel memory you should keep an eye on is the total memory bytes used, unused, and the peak usage. The peak usage will tell you whether in the past there has not been enough kernel memory. You will get some statistical count in the *failed alloc* field of hash kernel memory and system kernel memory if there is a memory allocation problem for connection load.

The output of this command also gives you connections statistics, fragmented packets stats, and NAT stats. It provides the state synchronization statistics as well.

Final Tweaks to Get the Last Drop of Performance

We have by no means covered everything you can do to the members in your cluster to maximize their performance. One particular area of note is optimizing the operating system that the members use. This varies considerably from one operating system to another in terms of the types and extent to which you can do this, but it is thoroughly worth doing.

Summary

Most of the hard work and decision making you'll encounter will be at the design stage. Are you using existing modules to upgrade to NG FP3, what platforms are the modules on, and what hubs and switches do you have available are all questions you will have to consider. Many of these issues are based on the type of clustering solution you choose. In a nutshell, the pertinent points of each clustering solution are as follows:

- **ClusterXL in HA New mode** High availability with monitoring of system, cluster, and network state, integrated with FireWall-1. Unicast MAC addresses are used for the VIP address on each subnet. Can be fully managed from SmartView status GUI. SmartCenter Server (management station) can be located on the secured network or elsewhere. Interfaces of the members in the cluster also have real IP addresses as well as the VIP address.
- **ClusterXL in HA Legacy mode** High availability with monitoring of system, cluster, and network state, integrated with FireWall-1. Included for compatibility with older FireWall-1 versions, limited by technology that leaves standby nodes unreachable except from management network. Can be fully managed from SmartView Status GUI, depending on failover conditions and location of GUI client on network. Unicast MAC for the VIP address, which is shared across the cluster, as is the MAC address for a particular subnet. SmartCenter Server *must* be located on the secured network and should have a second interface onto an Internet-routable IP address if managing other FireWall-1 enforcement points outside of the local network. Interfaces of the members in the legacy cluster do not have unique IP addresses or MAC addresses, apart from the secured network.
- **ClusterXL in Load-Sharing mode** Load sharing with monitoring of system, cluster, and network state, integrated with FireWall-1. Can be fully managed from SmartView Status GUI. Multicast MAC address responses for an ARP of the VIP (which is not a multicast IP address). This means each member in the cluster has the same MAC and VIP across the cluster for a particular subnet. The SmartCenter Server can be located on the secured network or elsewhere. Interfaces of the members in the cluster also have real IP addresses as well as the VIP address.
- **Nokia Load Sharing cluster** Load sharing with monitoring of system, cluster, and network state, limited integration with FireWall-1. Can be partially managed by SmartView Status GUI but also must use Voyager to find the status of the cluster. Multicast MAC address responses for an ARP of the VIP (which is not a multicast IP address). This means each member in the cluster

has the same MAC and VIP across the cluster for a particular subnet. The SmartCenter Server can be located on the secured network or elsewhere. Interfaces of the members in the cluster also have real IP addresses as well as the VIP address. The solution requires no license since it is part of the IPSO operating system.

- **Nokia VRRP cluster** Simple configuration but limited management. No monitoring of system or cluster state other than network interfaces. Unicast shared MAC for the VIP address, which is shared across the cluster. The SmartCenter Server can be located on the secured network or elsewhere. Interfaces of the members in the cluster also have real IP addresses as well as the VIP address. The solution requires no license since it is part of the IPSO operating system.

After you initially configure the cluster, make sure that you have the clustering solution working as you would expect before configuring a complex firewall Rule Base. The key here is to keep testing the functions of the cluster failover after each significant change to ensure that you have not done something to compromise the functionality of your cluster.

Once your cluster is configured and working and you have your security policy in place, take careful note of the configuration of your cluster and its members—and the settings of all the networking equipment on the same subnet as the VIP addresses of the cluster. This includes settings on routers, switches, and hosts. Taking note of these settings will be very useful if you ever need to troubleshoot the cluster. Sometimes configuration of adjacent devices has a habit of changing without advance warning to the firewall administrator.

The final step is to tune your cluster. Go through the procedure of examining your connections table to determine which services are most common in your connections table, and determine if you need to synchronize that service across the cluster. Is the service very transient? If so, it's a good candidate for switching off state table synchronization. Can you reduce the TCP or UDP timeout for a particular service? Additionally, make sure you increase the number of connections that your cluster will be able to handle and the kernel and hash allocation.

Solutions Fast Track

Designing Your Cluster

☑ Consider carefully the two things that a cluster will give you: resilience and increased capacity. If you are going for resilience, this can determine the type of equipment you put in surrounding your cluster, because the emphasis will be on maintaining the services through the cluster rather than the throughput, so you could decide that you will buy equipment that will enable you to find the cluster more easily (for example, using hubs rather than switches).

☑ Choose the operating system of the cluster modules carefully. They need to be the same platform and ideally the same specification. The Nokia platform has its own load-sharing solution, so you cannot use ClusterXL on it. Solaris and Windows and Linux do not have VRRP support with Check Point cluster on them.

☑ Make sure that you consider carefully where you put your management station in relation to your cluster. Are you going to manage just one cluster, or do you think you will have to manage additional clusters (or firewalls) from the same management station?

☑ Decide the type of address translation solution you will want to implement—and stick to it. Some of the clustering solutions will not allow you to implement certain types of address translation solutions.

Installing FireWall-1 NG FP3

☑ Do not forget the installation prerequisites. Especially make sure that the times between the cluster members and the firewall management station are the same.

☑ Make sure that you have a license available to you before installing. There is nothing worse than having your cluster working perfectly and all your users ecstatically happy, only to find out that after 15 days, nothing works because the evaluation license has expired!

☑ Once you have everything installed as you would like on your cluster, *back it up!* If you can, get a full disk image of each of the hosts in your cluster configuration, including the management module. Once the cluster is operational, make sure that you keep backing up any changes you make. Generally speaking, the management station needs care in backing up, because the modules can be reinstalled and the policy pushed to them relatively quickly once the management station is up and running.

Check Point ClusterXL

☑ Check that your network topology is configured properly before installing firewall modules. Make sure that routers on the same subnet have routes that point to the VIP addresses of your cluster (just so that you don't forget to change them when you have configured your cluster).

- ☑ Make sure that your management station has routes to reach the member interfaces directly (if using Legacy mode, the secured interfaces).
- ☑ Configure your gateway cluster object carefully and pay special attention to the cluster gateway topology.
- ☑ Once your cluster gateway is configured, test it.
- ☑ Configure your Rule Base and NAT, taking care to enter rules that will maintain cluster failover functionality.

Nokia IPSO Clustering

- ☑ Check that your network topology is configured properly before installing firewall modules. Use Voyager to configure your interfaces, making sure that there are two dedicated cluster networks: one for Check Point sync and one for IPSO Clustering traffic. Make sure that routers on the same subnet have routes that point to the VIP addresses of your cluster.
- ☑ Make sure that your management station has routes to reach the member interfaces directly.
- ☑ Use the SmartDashboard GUI to configure your gateway cluster object, avoiding the topology. Create and install a simple policy.
- ☑ Use Voyager to create a Nokia cluster on each member. Make sure that all members join the cluster.
- ☑ Install a Rule Base onto the cluster. Configure NAT. Test failover of members while traffic is traversing the cluster.

Nokia IPSO VRRP Clusters

- ☑ Check that your network topology is configured properly before installing FireWall-1. Use Voyager to configure your interfaces.
- ☑ Configure your gateway cluster object but not the topology. Push a simple policy to the cluster.
- ☑ Use Voyager to configure VRRP on each member. Check correct operation using the VRRP Monitor.
- ☑ Test a policy install again. Configure NAT if required. Test cluster failover.

Clustering and HA Performance Tuning

- ☑ Determine the services that are used through your cluster. Use firewall logs or the *fw tab –t connections –f* command.
- ☑ Make a decision on which services need to have full failover capacity to other members in the cluster. Turn off the cluster synchronization for these services.
- ☑ Reduce TCP and UDP service times to a practical minimum. Don't let the state table timeout be longer than it has to be. Conversely, don't make it too short, or else connections will be dropped prematurely.
- ☑ Modify the connections table, kernel memory pool, and hash table pools to cater for more than the default 25,000 connections.

Frequently Asked Questions

The following Frequently Asked Questions, answered by the authors of this book, are designed to both measure your understanding of the concepts presented in this chapter and to assist you with real-life implementation of these concepts. To have your questions about this chapter answered by the author, browse to **www.syngress.com/solutions** and click on the **"Ask the Author"** form.

Q: Why should we seek to avoid asymmetric routing on a cluster?

A: Generally, this is a bad idea. This is because the reply packet could get back to the wrong member in the cluster and be dropped by the firewall Rule Base because state table synchronization has not completed for the connection yet. The error message "Out of state TCP " will appear in the FireWall-1 logs.

Q: Why is consistent hostname resolution so important when using clusters?

A: It is always good practice to ensure that hostnames resolve consistently, i.e. hostname resolves to primary module IP, and these are the object name and general IP address. This is very important in clusters because each member will resolve its own hostname and then search the objects file with the resulting IP address. It must locate a cluster member object in order to know how to configure its ClusterXL module.

Q: Can I manage multiple clusters from the same management station? Can they be at the same site?

A: A single management station can manage as many clusters as you like. However, problems do occur if those clusters are attached to the same switching infrastructure. The reason for this is that Check Point cluster control and state sync traffic uses a fixed MAC address scheme that will result in duplicate MAC addresses on switch ports. Future releases of NG may resolve this issue; in the meantime, solutions should rely on changes to network infrastructure.

Q: I have configured earlier versions of ClusterXL and Check Point HA by editing files on the members. Is this still possible or required?

A: There is no need to edit member files. In fact, some will be overridden by the settings taken from the gateway cluster object.

Q: Which is the lower-cost option: Check Point ClusterXL or Nokia IPSO solutions?

A: The exact costs will vary with your requirements. ClusterXL is a licensed feature from Check Point. IPSO includes VRRP and clustering at no extra cost. However, the cost of the Nokia appliance should be considered relative to other Check Point platforms.

Q: Should I use Load-Sharing or HA mode ClusterXL?

A: Obviously, this depends on your requirements. If the traffic passing through the cluster can be comfortably processed by a single member, then load sharing introduces complexity (and unavoidably, problems) with little gain. It is worth noting that it is very easy to switch between HA New mode and load-sharing configurations, so starting with HA, then trialing load sharing, is a viable approach.

Q: Can I use the same interface for the Nokia cluster control and the Check Point state sync network ?

A: Yes, you could physically do this, but Nokia recommends that you don't.

Q: Can I configure the Nokia cluster or VRRP from the command line instead of using Voyager?

A: Yes. Refer to the Nokia IPSO 3.6 CLI reference guide for instructions on how to do this.

Q: Will a *traceroute* through a Nokia cluster tell me which member in the cluster the *traceroute* session is going through?

A: A Nokia IPSO Cluster will just report the VIP address of the cluster in the ICMP error packets back to your host. A VRRP cluster, however, will report the cluster members real IP address.

Q: When using Nokia VRRP or IPSO Clustering, why shouldn't I define the "Topology" in the FireWall-1 Gateway Cluster object ?

A: The result of doing so is that connections originating from cluster members are hidden behind these cluster interfaces. When connecting from the standby member, this will result in asynchronous routing. The ClusterXL solution handles this specific traffic gracefully, but VRRP and IPSO clustering do not.

Q: Why would I use VRRP when I could use Nokia clustering?

A: The VRRP solution is a standards-based solution, with well-documented and fairly simple behavior. If a well-established HA-only solution is required, VRRP should be considered. Nokia clustering brings load sharing and better integration with FireWall-1.

Q: Is it possible to have multiple VRs on one interface in order to provide basic load sharing with VRRP?

A: Yes, you can add multiple VRs and have each member master for some VRs and standby for others. Configuring routing accordingly can provide some load-sharing functionality. However, Nokia clustering should probably be considered if load sharing is a requirement.

Q: I have seen lots of documentation referring to various policy rules that are needed to accept the VRRP protocol. Which should I implement?

A: Happily, IPSO 3.6 ensures that VRRP traffic bypasses the firewall policy, so no special VRRP rules are required.

Q: [illegible] VERITAS [illegible] Clustering [illegible]
[illegible] Cluster [illegible]

A: [illegible]
[illegible]
[illegible]
[illegible] VERITAS [illegible]

Q: [illegible]

A: [illegible]
[illegible]
[illegible]
[illegible]

Q: [illegible]
[illegible]

A: [illegible]
[illegible]
[illegible]
[illegible]

Q: [illegible]
[illegible]

A: [illegible]
[illegible] required.

Chapter 7

SecurePlatform

Solutions in this chapter:

- The Basics
- Adding Hardware to SecurePlatform
- FireWall-1 Performance Counters

☑ Summary

☑ Solutions Fast Track

☑ Frequently Asked Questions

Introduction

Check Point has produced an operating system for use on *x*86 hardware to run its products. This purpose-built operating system is specifically hardened for network security purposes and tuned to operate Check Point Next Generation products on *x*86-based systems. SecurePlatform also provides exceptional throughput at a value price. This secure operating system includes the Performance Pack for Enterprise installations and boasts 3Gbps and higher throughput on a standard server-based platform.

SecurePlatform enables companies to utilize a high-performance platform without the worry of an additional license fee or support contract for the operating system. In addition, Check Point provides support for SecurePlatform, enabling the administrator to make a single support call for all nonhardware related issues.

This chapter provides SecurePlatform troubleshooting and functionality tips. We cover all the basic operations you will need to manage and maintain your SecurePlatform-based firewall, as well as troubleshoot the platform.

The Basics

In the first section of this chapter, we discuss the installation process using SecurePlatform FP3 Edition 2. We cover both installation options: the Web User Interface and the command line. Using the command line, you are required to use Check Point's restricted shell, CPShell. Lastly we discuss how you can grow your system by adding new packages to your SecurePlatform device as well as upgrading them. These are the basic requirements necessary for installing and maintaining a Check Point SecurePlatform system.

Installation

The installation of SecurePlatform is very straightforward. The product was designed to be quick and easy to configure. The installer loads some necessary drivers and asks for some localization information regarding type of keyboard.

Next, you are asked to configure an IP address for you to talk to this machine on. When you're configuring the interface during the installation process, this will be for the first NIC the system recognizes. In most cases, you will want to have the primary interface (and the IP address the hostname is tied to) be the external address—especially for VPNs. However, at this point, the address you specify here is just for you to get the system on the network after you have rebooted. Note: This system must be accessed from the same subnet because no default route or static routes are in effect at this point. This also stops people who are not on the local network from attacking the system before it is configured.

After you have set the IP address and netmask, the product verifies that you want to install SecurePlatform. At this point, nothing on the system has been irrevocably changed. However, when you click OK, the software will format the drive and install the operating system and the Check Point products.

Tools & Traps...

Hardware Considerations

Before you even buy the hardware for your SecurePlatform system, if you are not implementing it on a SecurePlatform appliance with performance numbers, you should really look at the hardware design to understand the type of throughput to expect from the system. In most cases, the limitation of the device that eludes administrators is the bus on the system. A single 32-bit/33MHz PCI bus will provide much less throughput capacity than a PCI-X (64-bit/133MHz) bus or a quad PCI-X bus. In addition, here are a few more recommendations:

- Always choose NICs that are directly supported in the SecurePlatform release.
- Hard drives do not need to be fast and large unless the system is a management station and you are storing a large number of logs.
- RAID should be done in hardware rather than software.
- The need for fast or multiple processors is mainly necessary when you're doing large amounts of encryption.
- The need for a large amount of RAM is mainly necessary when you're handling many connections.

An excellent resource for comparing appliances and platforms is the *Platform Selection Guide* available directly from Check Point's Web site.

Configuration

After you have rebooted the system, you will have to log in to finish the configuration. The default is *admin* for both the username and password. It does state this immediately before you reboot, but many people press Enter too quickly to read the screen and first-timers then start looking through documentation for what to do next. There are two methods to finish the configuration; one is via the command line (using a serial connections, *ssh* connection, or keyboard and monitor) and the other is via a Web browser. The simplest way to configure the system is via the Web User Interface (WebUI) because of its setup wizard. This is the method we discuss first and is also the supported configuration method.

Web User Interface Configuration

The WebUI for SecurePlatform first appeared in SecurePlatform NG Feature Pack 3, Edition 2. The motif is consistent with the user interface for Check Point SmallOffice and SofaWare's S-box. The WebUI requires Internet Explorer 5.0 or later. To connect, open your Web browser and connect to https://*<IP address you used during installation>*. This will bring you to the license agreement shown in Figure 7.1. Click **I Accept** to continue.

Figure 7.1 The SecurePlatform License Agreement

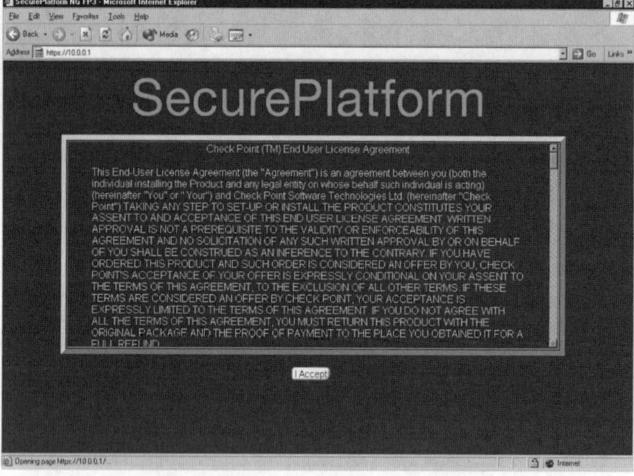

You must now log in. The first time you log in, use the default username (*admin*) and password (*admin*), as shown in Figure 7.2.

Figure 7.2 The SecurePlatform Login Screen

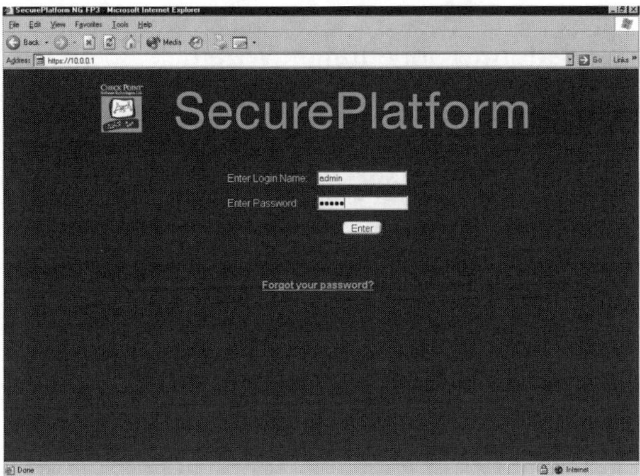

The installation requires you to change the password to a strong one, as shown in Figure 7.3. Type a new password into the appropriate box, verify it in the next box, and click **Apply** to save your new password. You can click the **Token** button to save a small file you can use to authenticate to the box if you forget the password. You should put the file on a diskette and store it in a safe place. This token can be used to reset the password and log into the WebUI. Click **Login** to continue.

Figure 7.3 Changing the Default SecurePlatform Password

You will now be presented with a wizard for configuring your SecurePlatform installation, as shown in Figure 7.4. Click **Next** to continue. If you click **Cancel**, no changes will be made, but you must still configure the system (either via the WebUI wizard or the command line). The WebUI wizard is the supported configuration method.

Figure 7.4 The SecurePlatform Configuration Wizard

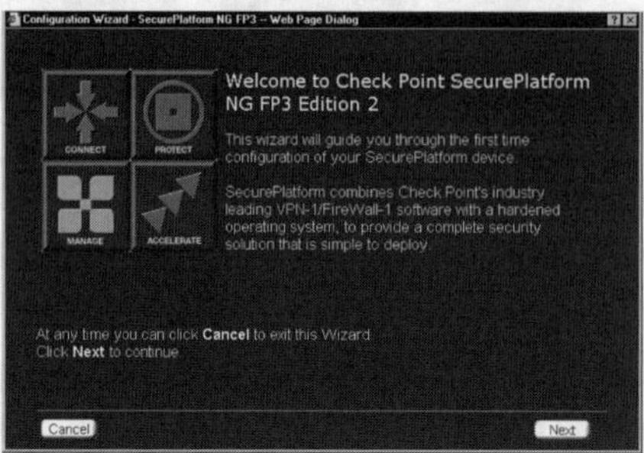

Here you can modify your interfaces as well as set the hostname, default route, and DNS servers for the system. You should set all these settings. Clicking **Edit** next to an interface will allow you to enter an IP address and netmask for the interface, as shown in Figure 7.5. If you happen to modify the interface you are connected through, the system will log you out and you will be required to log in again and restart the wizard. All other interfaces can be modified on the fly. If you want to add virtual local area networks (VLANs), you can do that after the wizard is finished. If you require that an interface be DHCP assigned, you should exit the wizard and use the command-line interface. You should also make sure you set the hostname and domain correctly. This is especially important if you are going to install a management station, because of the InternalCA and CRL lookups. Make sure to click **Apply** to any interface changes before clicking **Next** to continue.

Figure 7.5 SecurePlatform Network Configuration

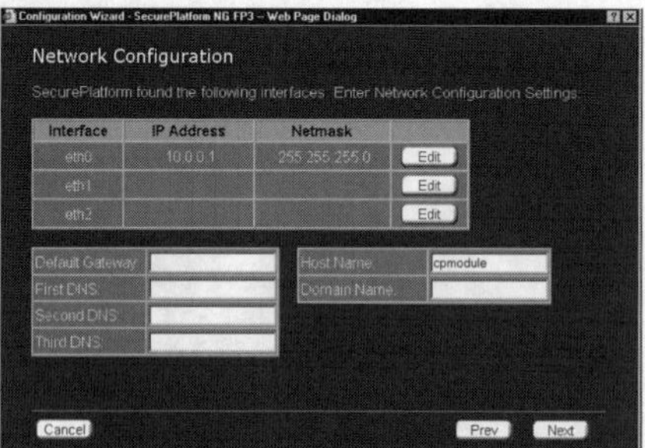

Next, as shown in Figure 7.6, you will be given the option to choose which Check Point products you ant to install. The default is to install a firewall module with the Performance Pack. You need a license for Performance Pack unless you are using an unlimited IP address gateway license that comes with it.

The option to select products to install is not available via the command-line interface. If you use the command-line interface and require more than the Check Point SVN Foundation (CPShared) and FireWall-1/VPN-1 package, which are installed by default, you need to add them manually, as described later in this chapter. In addition, after the wizard has completed, you need to add packages manually from the command line. There is no option to perform this task via the WebUI. Furthermore, to install a secondary management station, you have to cancel this configuration and do *cpconfig* from the command line.

Figure 7.6 SecurePlatform Product Configuration

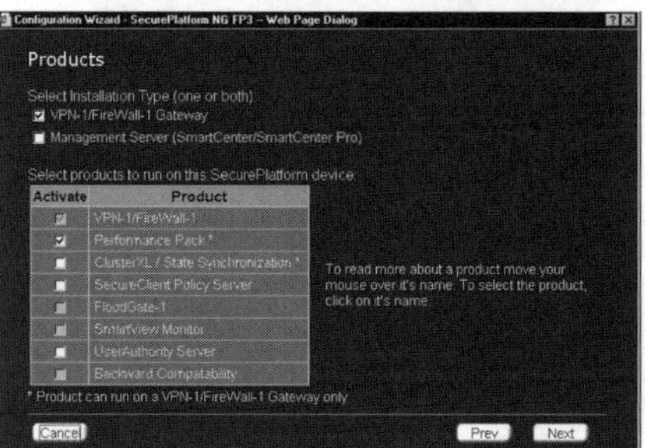

If you choose not to install a management station, you will be asked to set the activation key for Secure Internal Communication (SIC), as shown in Figure 7.7. This is a one-time password used only for authenticating a module to the management station. Once they have authenticated each other, a new digital certificate will be generated for the module; this certificate is used to secure all communications between the module and the management station.

Figure 7.7 Initializing SIC

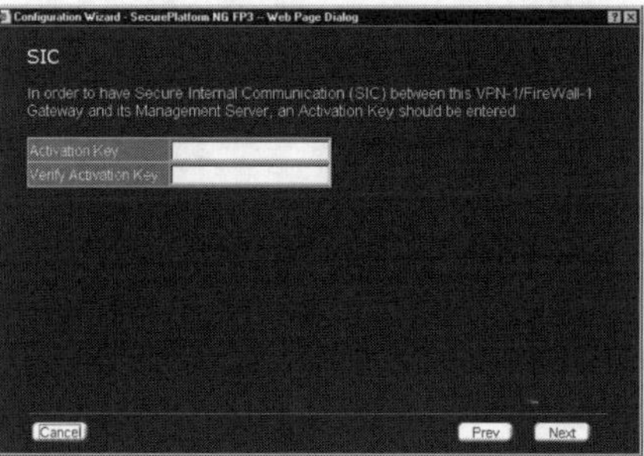

If you chose to install a management station on this system, instead of the screen shown in Figure 7.7 you will be prompted to define a username and password to log in using the Check Point SMART Clients, as shown in Figure 7.8. You will also have to define where you can log into the management station from using the Check Point SMART Clients. Even though this only allows you to define one administrator and GUI client, you can add more GUI clients later through the WebUI or the command line and more administrators via the SmartDashboard GUI.

Figure 7.8 SecurePlatform Administrator Configuration

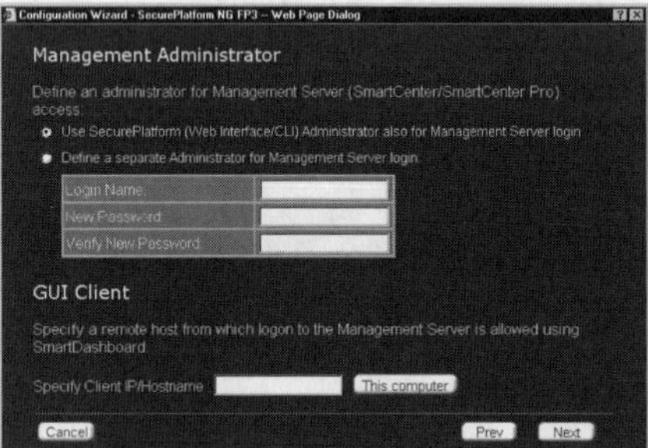

Of course, you have to license the Check Point products. Beginning with NG Feature Pack 3, you have the option of using a 15-day trial license. Note in Figure 7.9 that if you already have your license, you can enter the information here. You can also use the SmartUpdate GUI or the *cpconfig* command-line executable to add the license later.

Figure 7.9 The SecurePlatform License Setup Screen

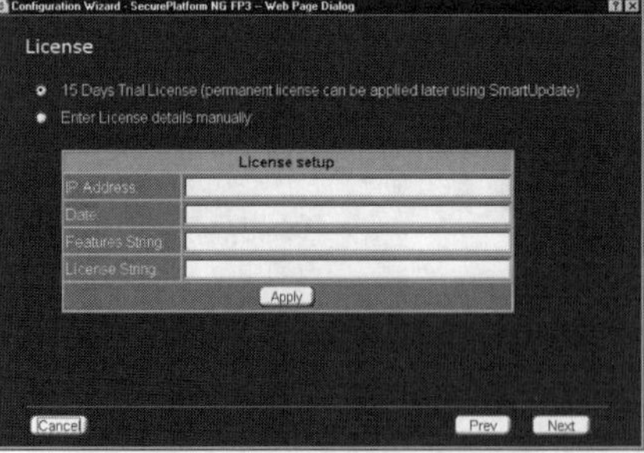

Because the validity of digital certificates is heavily based on date and time, you should pay special attention to the date and time on the system, as Figure 7.10 shows. This is extremely important if this is a management station, since the internal CA's certificate will have a creation date tied to it. In addition, your logs could have incorrect dates and other side effects.

Figure 7.10 Date and Time Setup

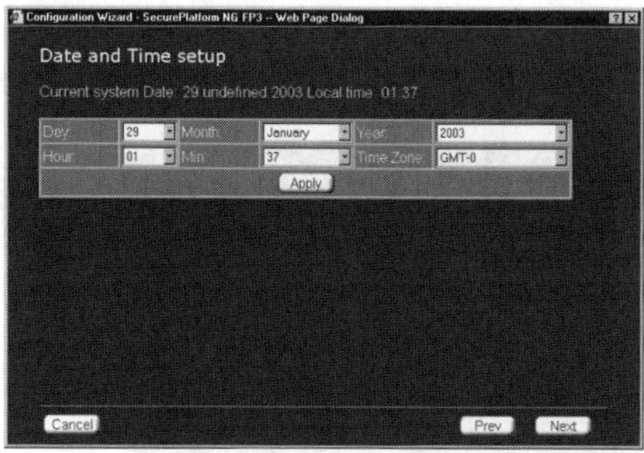

At this point the wizard has finished prompting you for information. When you click **Finish**, as shown in Figure 7.11, the system applies all the settings, sets up the firewall, and initializes the internal CA. It will also bring up the initial firewall policy. In most cases, this would lock you out of accessing the WebUI as well as *ssh* and *ping*. However, Check Point took this into account and allows you connect to the system via *https*, *ssh*, and the Check Point SMART Clients from the GUI client you specified earlier in the installation.

The initial policy the firewall loads is from the $FWDIR/conf/initial_management.pf file if it is a management module (or management and firewall module); if it is only a firewall module, it will load the $FWDIR/conf/initial_module.pf file. Within this file are references to two other files, webgui_clients_list.def and gui_clients_list.def. In these files are the IP addresses that are compiled into the initial policy that is loaded. This restricts all access to the system except from the management station (to establish SIC and push a policy to the firewall) and the GUI client. This system protects the firewall until the security policy is defined and applied.

Figure 7.11 The Configuration Summary Screen

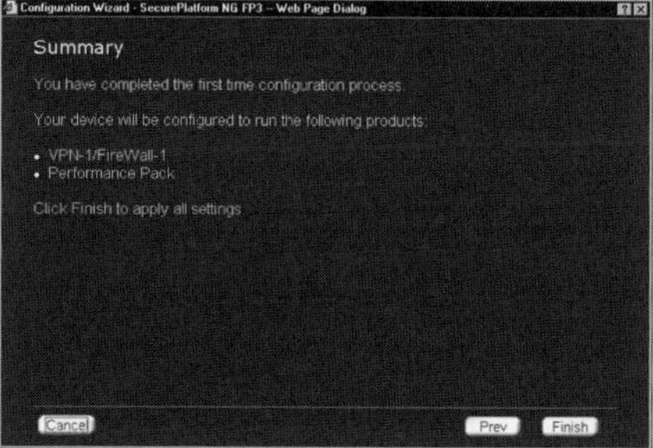

Now your configuration has finished. Figure 7.12 shows you the fingerprint of the internal CA's public certificate. This should be matched to the certificate presented when you connect to your management server. This is how you authenticate the validity of the management server and trust it. If you are presented with another fingerprint, you could be experiencing a man-in-the-middle attack.

Figure 7.12 Finishing Installation

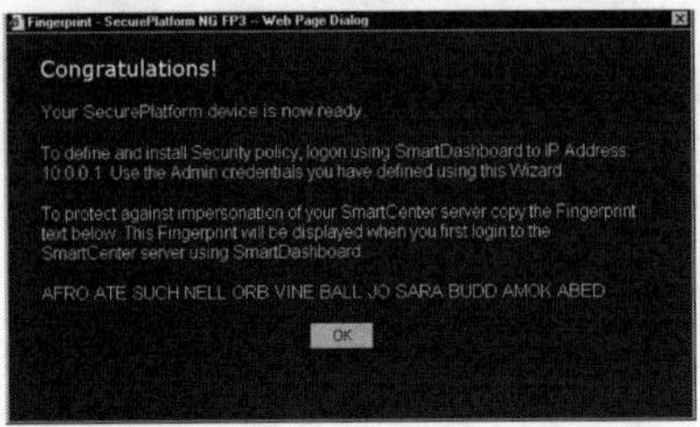

Command-Line Configuration

Although the supported initial configuration method is the WebUI wizard, you can access the command line the same way you installed the system, via a serial connection or via the console with a keyboard and mouse. If you choose to use a serial connection, you should set your terminal program to 9600 baud, 8 data bits, no parity, and 1 stop bit. This setting can be changed in /etc/grub.conf later.

In addition, you can access the SecurePlatform system via *ssh* if you so choose. Once logged in, you must change your password to a strong password. Doing so will drop you into the Check Point restricted shell (CPShell). This is much like a router in that you only have a few commands to choose from. You can enter **?** to get a listing of available commands. From there the easiest way to configure the system is to use the *sysconfig* utility.

The *sysconfig* utility is a text-based, menu-driven system used to configure the necessary pieces of the operating system, as shown here:

```
Choose a configuration item:

----------------------------------------------------------------

1) Network Interfaces          5) Domain name servers

2) Routing                      6) Time and Date

3) Host name                    7) Products Configuration

4) Domain name                  8) Exit

----------------------------------------------------------------

(Note: configuration changes are automatically saved.)

Your choice: 1
```

Configuring Interfaces

The first thing to do is configure all the interfaces to the correct addresses. For simplicity, it is easiest to get all the operating system-level parameters configured and checked before working with the firewall software, like so:

```
Choose a network interfaces configuration item:
------------------------------------------------------------------
1) Configure interface
2) Show configuration
3) Done
------------------------------------------------------------------
(Note: configuration changes are automatically saved.)
Your choice: 1
```

Next you will be presented with a list of interfaces that are known on the system. If you do not see the correct number of interfaces, you should make sure all your interfaces are supported and defined in /etc/modules.conf. Note that a card with multiple interfaces will only show up once for the first interface in /etc/modules.conf. (We explain how to get access to the file system in the CPShell section.) Here is a sample list of interfaces:

```
Choose an interface to configure:
------------------------------------------------------------------
1) eth0
2) eth1
3) eth2
4) Done
------------------------------------------------------------------
(Note: configuration changes are automatically saved.)
Your choice: 1
```

You are now presented with options to not only set the IP address but also to add or delete VLANs as well as set up the system for having a dynamic (DHCP assigned) IP address. Options 1 and 4 make changes to the /etc/sysconfig/network-scripts/ ifcfg-<*interface name*> file. All options here also make changes to the /etc/sysconfig/ cpnetstart file. Because these options are also updated here, we strongly suggest that you make interface and routing changes using one of the Check Point-provided methods (sysconfig or the WebUI) and not directly:

```
Choose eth0 item to configure:
------------------------------------------------------------------
```

```
1) Set interface network addresses  4) Mark it as having dynamic IP
2) Add VLAN interface                5) Done
3) Delete VLAN interface
-----------------------------------------------------------------
(Note: configuration changes are automatically saved.)
Your choice:
```

If you are configuring an interface to have a dynamic IP address, selecting option 4 seems to do nothing, but look carefully—it will change the word *dynamic* to *static* when it is configured to be DHCP assigned. In addition, when you're in the "Choose a network configuration item" menu, selecting **Show Interfaces** will show the interface as "not configured," even though it is configured to receive a DHCP assigned IP address. This concept is shown here:

```
eth0  ip: 192.168.0.3, broadcast: 192.168.0.255, netmask: 255.255.255.0
eth1  is not configured
eth2  is not configured
```

Configuring Routing

Once we have configured all our interfaces, we need to configure the routing. This is option 2 from the first menu:

```
Choose a routing configuration item:
-----------------------------------------------------------------
1) Add new network route       4) Delete route
2) Add new host route           5) Show routing configuration
3) Add default gateway          6) Done
-----------------------------------------------------------------
(Note: configuration changes are automatically saved.)
Your choice:
```

At a minimum, you should add a default route for the device. To add a network or host route, you need to know the IP address (or network and netmask in the case of a network route) as well as the gateway IP address and the interface from which you will be routing the traffic. Selecting option 5 shows the result of a *netstat –rn* from the command line. Configurations here also make changes to the /etc/sysconfig/cpnetstart file. Select option **6** to continue to the main menu.

Set the Hostname

Next we will configure the hostname by selecting **3**, Host name. The next thing we will do is choose a hostname and tie the hostname to the appropriate address.

```
Choose an action:
-----------------------------------------------------------------
1) Set host name
2) Show host name
3) Done
-----------------------------------------------------------------
(Note: configuration changes are automatically saved.)
Your choice: 1
```

If this is a firewall object, you should probably tie this hostname to the external address. If this is set as an internal (non-external) address of the firewall or an address other than the one in the General Properties page of the object in the SmartDashboard GUI, it can cause serious issues with establishing a VPN connection.

```
Enter host name: London
Enter IP of the interface to be associated with
this host name (leave empty for automatic assignment): 1.2.3.4
The host name is set.
```

This will return you to the above menu. Select **3** to go to the main menu and continue to the next section.

Set the Domain Name

Next we will set the default domain name the system will use. In this case, we will use example.com. First choose to set the domain name and then enter your chosen domain:

```
Choose an action:
-----------------------------------------------------------------
1) Set domain name
2) Show domain name
3) Done
-----------------------------------------------------------------
(Note: configuration changes are automatically saved.)
Your choice: 1
```

```
Enter domain name: example.com
The domain name is set.
```

Set the DNS Servers

Many functions of the firewall could require a DNS lookup of an IP address or name. Defining a domain name server (or better yet, multiple DNS servers) address is something that should be done on each and every firewall. You can choose the Add option multiple times to add multiple servers. Again, afterward select **4** to return to the main menu:

```
Choose a DNS configuration item:
-----------------------------------------------------------------
1) Add new domain name server          3) Show configured domain name
                                            servers
2) Remove domain name server           4) Done
-----------------------------------------------------------------
(Note: configuration changes are automatically saved.)
Your choice: 1

Enter IP address of the domain name server to add: 192.168.0.1
```

Set the Time and Date

As described earlier in the WebUI section, setting the correct date and time is essential because of the extensive use of digital certificates used to secure communications between Check Point devices. First you need to set the time zone, as shown here:

```
Choose a time and date configuration item:
-----------------------------------------------------------------
1) Set time zone                  4) Show date and time settings
2) Set date                       5) Done
3) Set local time
-----------------------------------------------------------------
(Note: configuration changes are automatically saved.)
Your choice: 1

Identify a location so that time zone rules can be set correctly.
Select a continent or ocean.
 1) Africa
```

```
 2) Americas
 3) Antarctica
 4) Arctic Ocean
 5) Asia
 6) Atlantic Ocean
 7) Australia
 8) Europe
 9) Indian Ocean
10) Pacific Ocean
11) none - I want to specify the time zone using the Posix TZ format.
12) cancel - I want to quit without changing the time zone.
#? 2
Select a country.
 1) Anguilla              18) Ecuador               35) Paraguay
 2) Antigua & Barbuda     19) El Salvador           36) Peru
 3) Argentina             20) French Guiana         37) Puerto Rico
 4) Aruba                 21) Greenland             38) St Kitts & Nevis
 5) Bahamas               22) Grenada               39) St Lucia
 6) Barbados              23) Guadeloupe            40) St Pierre & Miquelon
 7) Belize                24) Guatemala             41) St Vincent
 8) Bolivia               25) Guyana                42) Suriname
 9) Brazil                26) Haiti                 43) Trinidad & Tobago
10) Canada                27) Honduras              44) Turks & Caicos Is
11) Cayman Islands        28) Jamaica               45) United States
12) Chile                 29) Martinique            46) Uruguay
13) Colombia              30) Mexico                47) Venezuela
14) Costa Rica            31) Montserrat            48) Virgin Islands (UK)
15) Cuba                  32) Netherlands Antilles  49) Virgin Islands (US)
16) Dominica              33) Nicaragua             50) cancel
17) Dominican Republic    34) Panama
#? 45
Select one of the following time zone regions.
 1) Eastern Time
 2) Eastern Time - Michigan - most locations
 3) Eastern Time - Kentucky - Louisville area
 4) Eastern Time - Kentucky - Wayne County
 5) Eastern Standard Time - Indiana - most locations
```

```
 6) Eastern Standard Time - Indiana - Crawford County
 7) Eastern Standard Time - Indiana - Starke County
 8) Eastern Standard Time - Indiana - Switzerland County
 9) Central Time
10) Central Time - Michigan - Wisconsin border
11) Mountain Time
12) Mountain Time - south Idaho & east Oregon
13) Mountain Time - Navajo
14) Mountain Standard Time - Arizona
15) Pacific Time
16) Alaska Time
17) Alaska Time - Alaska panhandle
18) Alaska Time - Alaska panhandle neck
19) Alaska Time - west Alaska
20) Aleutian Islands
21) Hawaii
22) cancel
#? 1

The following information has been given:

        United States
        Eastern Time

Therefore TZ='America/New_York' will be used.
Local time is now:      Sun Feb  2 21:07:39 EST 2003.
Universal Time is now:  Mon Feb  3 02:07:39 UTC 2003.
Is the above information OK?
1) Yes
2) No
3) Cancel
#? 1
Updating time zone succeded.

Time zone is set.
```

Next you need to select **2** to set the date. Make sure to use numeric representations and the correct format when setting the date:

```
Enter date in format MM-DD-YYYY: 01-01-2003
Date is set.
```

And finally, select **3** to set the time in (24-hour format), and then select **4** to return to the main menu.

```
Enter time in format HH:MM: 13:00
Time is set.
```

Completing the Installation

The final thing that is required is to run 7, Products Configuration, which is essentially *cpconfig*. This will run you through a list of questions related to the products you have you selected to install and the part they play in your security infrastructure.

CPShell

When you log into SecurePlatform through the command-line interface via *ssh* or a serial connection, you will be presented with an application-specific configuration interface. This interface is much narrower in scope than a standard UNIX shell. The list of available commands is shown here:

```
[cpmodule]# ?
Commands are:
?              - Print list of available commands
SDSUtil        - Software Distribution Server utility
arp            - Display/manipulate/store the arp table
audit          - Display/edit commands entered in shell
backup         - Backup configuration
cpconfig       - Check Point software configuration utility
cphaprob       - Defines critical process of High Availability
cphastart      - Enables the High Availability feature on the machine
cphastop       - Disables the High Availability feature on the machine
cpinfo         - Show Check Point diagnostics information
cplic          - Add/Remove Check Point licenses
cpshared_ver   - Show SVN Foundation version
cpstart        - Start Check Point products installed
cpstat         - Show Check Point statistics info
cpstop         - Stop Check Point products installed
```

```
date            - Set/show date
diag            - Send system diagnostics information
dns             - Add/remove/show domain name resolving servers
domainname      - Set/show domain name
exit            - Switch to standard mode/Logout
expert          - Switch to expert mode
fw              - VPN-1/FireWall-1 commands
fwm             - Compile the merged Scroll Policy for the host
help            - Print list of available commands
hostname        - Set/show host name
hosts           - Add/remove/show local hosts/IP mappings
idle            - Set/show auto logout time in minutes
ifconfig        - Configure/store network interfaces
log             - Log rotation control
netstat         - Show network statistics
passwd          - Change password
ping            - Ping a host
reboot          - Reboot gateway
restore         - Restore configuration
route           - Configure/store routing tables
scroll          - Allow scrolling the output of various commands
shutdown        - Shut down gateway
sysconfig       - Configure your SecurePlatform Gateway
time            - Set/show time
timezone        - Set/show the time zone
top             - Show the most active system processes
traceroute      - Trace the route to a host
username        - Change the user name
vconfig         - Configure Virtual LANs
ver             - Print the version
vpn             - Control VPN
```

For very advanced debugging and configuration, the *expert* command can require a separate password (much like Enable mode on a router) to access its privileged level. Once authenticated, you will be dropped into a *bash* shell with full access to the underlying operating system and its files. You can always tell that you are in Expert mode by the prompt containing *Expert@* preceding the hostname of the device. The first time you enter Expert mode, you will be prompted to set a password for it. This password can be the same as your normal login password or a separate one as required by your written security policy:

```
[cpmodule]# expert
Enter current password:

This is the first time you enter the expert mode.
Expert password must be changed.

Enter new expert password:
Enter new expert password (again):

You are in expert mode now.

[Expert@cpmodule]# pwd
/home/admin
```

Backup and Restore

Another common pair of utilities is backup and restore, for obvious reasons. Backup allows you to create a backup of the system configuration files, Check Point configuration files, or both and save them locally or send them to a TFTP server. In this version of SecurePlatform, to back up the Check Point configuration files, you need to issue a *cpstop* before running the backup program. After a backup file is created, it will display an MD5 checksum on the file you should save to ensure that it has not been tampered with. When you restore, it will ask you to verify the checksum before restoring this backup. All backups are stored in the /opt/CPbackups directory.

Restore allows you to rebuild a system quickly once it is on the network. Using the *-list* option gives you a list of available backups to restore. Like the backup utility, *cpstop* must be issued for the command to be run. Before you restore the files, however, you must install the packages you had previously installed and configured. Because this process replaces a great number of files and requires a reboot afterward, it is unlikely that this restriction will be lifted.

```
[cpmodule]# backup
Usage: backup system name [<tftp> <ip>]
       backup cp     name [<tftp> <ip>]
       backup all    name [<tftp> <ip>]
```

```
[cpmodule]# restore
Usage: restore [-v] <name> [tftp <ip-address>]
       restore -list

[cpmodule]#
```

Tools & Traps...

Beware the Backups

An important thing to remember is that the backups will only back up the configuration of the operating system that Check Point does through its own tools. This includes anything configured through CPShell as well as the WebUI. Changes to base.def or the OS files that stock Check Point utilities do not touch will not be backed up using the backup utility. To understand what is backed up and what isn't, perform a backup and then open the backup file—or you can just execute *tar ztvf /opt/CPbackups/<filename>.tgz* to view a list of the files backed up. This does, however, restore all the certificates, rule bases, and so on. Basically, it restores all the Check Point-related pieces needed to bring the system back to where it was, with a little preparation. Although it's not a supported option, if you want to modify the files that the utility will back up or the default backup partition, you can edit the /bin/backup_start file since it is only a Bourne shell script. Note, however, that these changes will likely be overwritten during upgrades.

Applying OS and Application Updates

Periodically, new packages might need to be added or updated. Adding packages can be done from three places:

- From the WebUI wizard as you are setting up the system
- From the SmartUpdate GUI
- From the command line in Expert mode

When the system is installed, other Check Point packages are copied into the /sysimg/CPrpm/ directory on the file system. Adding a package is as simple as logging into the command line, entering Expert mode, and executing an *rpm -i <package file>*. Once the package is installed, you have to enable it in the object's definition in the SmartDashboard GUI.

If you add the FloodGate, Policy Server, Real-Time Monitor, or User Authority Gateway package, you should also install the related CPShell package. Doing so will add the relevant commands to the CPShell when you are in it. Adding this package will not replace the CPShell executable with a new one; it will just modify the config file /etc/cpshell/cpshell.cfg. This means that the CPShell packages are not mutually exclusive, so you can install the CPShell package for both FloodGate and the Policy Server without any decreased functionality.

```
[Expert@cpmodule]# cd /sysimg/CPrpm/
[Expert@cpmodule]# ls
CPdtps-50-03.i386.rpm  CPrtm-50-03.i386.rpm  CPshell-uag.i386.rpm
CPfg1-50-03.i386.rpm   CPshell-fg.i386.rpm   CPuag-50-03.i386.rpm
CPfwbc-41-00.i386.rpm  CPshell-ps.i386.rpm
CPppak-50-03.i386.rpm  CPshell-rtm.i386.rpm
[Expert@cpmodule]# rpm -i CPfg1-50-03.i386.rpm
[Expert@cpmodule]# rpm -i CPshell-fg.i386.rpm
[Expert@cpmodule]#
```

If you are upgrading packages (including the operating system itself), you follow basically the same procedure. You can use SmartUpdate or do it manually from the command line. SmartUpdate is definitely the easiest way to upgrade, but if you have a management station running SecurePlatform or do not have a SmartUpdate license (which is included with a SmartCenter Pro license), you will be required to upgrade from the command line.

You should always read the release notes before upgrading, but at the moment the first thing you should do when updating the operating system is update the *CPpatch* command. You can do this by entering the following command on the command line:

```
[Expert@cpmodule]# patch add /mnt/cdrom/SecurePlatform/patch/CPpatch_
    command.tgz
```

After you have upgraded the *patch* command, you can upgrade SecurePlatform by simply issuing a *patch add cd*. This command searches the CD for the upgrade to SecurePlatform itself. It begins something like the following example:

```
[Expert@cpmodule]# patch add cd
Choose a patch to install:
```

```
1) SecurePlatform FP3 Edition 2 (CPspupgrade_FP3_e2.tgz)
2) Exit

Your choice:
 1

The MD5 checksum of the patch is: c0082b61d4ef79763c8f6ef9a8390285
Is that right (Y/N)?
y
Start Upgrading ..
```

To upgrade the Check Point products you have installed to a new version, you first have to move the new files to the SecurePlatform system. This can be done via CD or an FTP initiated from the SecurePlatform system. Once the package is on the system, you can install it by issuing an *rpm -i --replacefiles <RPM package file>*.

Adding Hardware to SecurePlatform

The wonderful part about a system running SecurePlatform rather than a black-box solution is that you can service and upgrade it. As your network grows, bandwidth increases, and as your VPNs become more popular and mission critical, you could be put in the position of needing to upgrade the hardware on the box. This is a very quick, simple, and inexpensive way to add more capacity to your gateway. The most typical changes you make to the physical configuration of your gateway include adding memory, adding a second processor, adding network interface cards, and adding more hard drive space.

Adding Memory

Many times the first thing you need as your network grows is more RAM because what is most likely growing is your number of connections. Each connection takes up a small amount of RAM in the state table during the duration of the connection. The amount of memory a connection takes depends on a number of factors. A normal firewalled connection takes less memory than one that involves NAT, which takes less than one that involves encryption. The connections that take up an especially large amount of RAM are ones that utilize a security server.

Adding memory is quite easy. All you have to do is shut down the machine, add the RAM, and boot it up. Utilizing the memory available is a little different. If you are adding more memory because you believe you are reaching the limitation of your connections table, you should first check the size of your connections table. Go to the firewall and execute a *fw tab -t connections -s* to find out how many connections you have. You should also execute the *top* command to see how much RAM you have available. This information is shown in bold in the following:

```
[cpmodule]# fw tab -t connections -s
HOST                 NAME                      ID #VALS #PEAK #SLINKS
localhost            connections             8158    38   273     143
[cpmodule]# top
 12:00pm  up 16 days,  8:30,  1 user,  load average: 0.11, 0.03, 0.01
40 processes: 39 sleeping, 1 running, 0 zombie, 0 stopped
CPU states:  0.0% user,  0.0% system,  0.0% nice,  2.6% idle
Mem:   128552K av,  121068K used,    7484K free,    0K shrd,    9752K buff
Swap:  257000K av,       0K used,  257000K free               52408K cached
```

If you have plenty of RAM free and your connections table is near 25,000 (the default limit), you don't need to buy more RAM—you only need to raise the number of concurrent connections allowed through the firewall in the Advanced properties of this object in the SmartDashboard. To make it take effect, raise it to 50,000 or whatever you feel is appropriate, push the policy to the module, and reboot the system. You can verify that it has taken effect by looking at the result of an *fw tab -t connections* command, as shown here after the word *limit:*

```
[cpmodule]# fw tab -t connections
localhost:
-------- connections --------
dynamic, id 8158, attributes: keep, sync, expires 60, refresh, limit
    25000, hashsize 32768, kbuf 16 17 18 19 20 21 22 23 24 25 26 27 28
         29 30, free function c83734b8 0
```

Adding NICs

Another common need in growing companies is the addition of new network interfaces on the firewall. Sometimes this addition is to accommodate more DMZs, sometimes it is to separate servers from workstations or servers from other servers, and sometimes it's used to handle more capacity or add redundancy. Any way you slice it, though, at some point it is very likely you will need to add more interfaces to your firewall.

To add a NIC, simply install the NIC, and during the boot process the system will automatically probe for new hardware. If it finds a new NIC it recognizes, it will automatically create an entry in /etc/modules.conf for the new driver (if necessary) and a new file, /etc/sysconfig/network-scripts/ifcfg-<*interface*>, to hold the configuration. At this point you can use the WebUI or *sysconfig* to configure it with the correct addresses. If either of these two things does not happen, you might be required to configure the NIC manually according to the needs of the specific driver. In addition, Check Point does not support third-party NIC drivers that have not been QA tested and included in the distribution.

A growing way to solve port density issues is to leverage VLAN tagging (802.1q), which allows you to leverage a single, fast network connection and make virtual network interfaces that allow networks to stay separate and have traffic routed through the firewall but without the hassle of adding many physical network cards. In addition, adding network cards requires you to shut down the firewall to install a card, whereas adding and removing VLANs can be done on the fly. SecurePlatform supports 802.1q and allows an administrator to manage them via *sysconfig* or the WebUI. If configuring this interface to support 802.1q and it's been previously defined with an IP address, it will recommend you set the interface's physical interface to 0.0.0.0, which will overwrite the interface's previous definition. When you look at the physical interface, it will show up as "not configured":

```
Enter new VLAN id for eth0 [1-4094]: 1
New VLAN interface eth0.1 created successfully.
Enter IP address of the interface eth0.1: 192.168.0.1
Enter network mask of the interface eth0.1: 255.255.255.0
Enter broadcast address of the interface eth0.1 (leave empty for default):

The interface is configured.
Current interface configuration is:

eth0.1  ip: 192.168.0.1, broadcast: 192.168.0.255, netmask: 255.255.255.0
It is recommended to set the physical interface IP to 0.0.0.0.
Do you want to set eth0 IP address to 0.0.0.0 (Y/N)?
```

Adding a Second Processor

If you install the system with multiple processors, it will automatically install the Symmetric Multiprocessor (SMP) version of the kernel and boot it by default. You will be given two options in the Grub bootloader: SecurePlatform NG FP3 Edition 2 and SecurePlatform NG FP3 Edition 2 Single CPU. The first one is the SMP kernel and the second is the standard single processor kernel. You will also see Maintenance Mode as well as Debugging Mode options. The Maintenance Mode option is installed automatically with the kernel. This is the same kernel, but when it boots, it boots into single-user mode. (You can compare the differences in the /etc/grub.conf file.) The Debugging Mode option actually boots a different kernel, the debugging kernel with all the debugging options enabled. This will severely degrade performance on the system if used in production, so it should not be used unless absolutely necessary.

The most typical symptom of high load on a firewall is use of the security servers. Use of the security servers dramatically reduces the throughput of the services running through the firewall and significantly increases the CPU load. In this case, your choices are to either add another processor or add another firewall and cluster them.

Another reason that a system is running out of processing capacity involves the overhead of doing a great deal of encryption. To offload this from the processor, you can always install a VPN accelerator card or an IPSec NIC card. Another way to ease the burden of doing a large amount of encryption is to change the encryption algorithm you are using. AES was written to be done in software, so it performs much better than 3DES, since DES (and by the same token, 3DES) was written to be done in hardware. In many tests, the same Check Point firewall can do upward of three times more traffic when the encryption algorithm is set to AES instead of 3DES, even when the AES algorithm is set to do 256-bit encryption versus 3DES's effective 112-bit encryption. DES and 3DES encryption accelerators have been on the market for a while, and AES accelerators are just recently coming to the market. Whichever you choose, make sure that it is OPSEC compliant (www.opsec.com) to ease your integration.

Before you start adding more processing power to your firewall, make sure that another processor will actually help your situation. In some cases, the firewall's limitation could be the speed of the bus on the system or the capacity of your network interfaces. You can easily view the average CPU usage using the SmartView Status GUI. This is done by selecting the system and viewing the information/statistics of the SVN Foundation. It may show N/A at first, but if you leave the GUI open it will gather the statistics and average them over the time you have it open. If your average usage is 80 percent or more, you probably need to add another CPU (if possible) or another system for clustering.

Configuring SecurePlatform for a Second Processor

Currently, there is no documented method for migrating from a uniprocessor to a multiprocessor system. The simplest way is probably to back up the configuration to another system, reinstall the OS, and restore the Check Point configuration files. If you would rather upgrade the current system to support multiple processors, you can *rpm* install the multiple-processor kernel. This is an unsupported method, but it did work in SecurePlatform FP3 Edition 2. Consult Check Point directly for the supported method on your running version.

Installing the *rpm* for the multiple-processor kernel will yield a new option (the default) on the Grub bootloader. If you plan to install the debugging option as well, you should install it first, because the last kernel you add is the one that will be booted by default. If you happen to install the debugging version second, you can change this behavior by editing the /etc/grub.conf file manually. The following text shows how to install the SMP kernel if you add the second processor after SecurePlatform has been installed and configured. Note the additions to the grub.conf file in bold:

```
Last login: Sat Feb  1 14:49:08 2003

? for list of commands
sysconfig for system and products configuration

[cpmodule]# expert
Enter expert password:

You are in expert mode now.

[Expert@cpmodule]# uname -a
Linux cpmodule 2.4.9-36cp #1 Tue Jan 7 11:02:42 IST 2003 i686 unknown
[Expert@cpmodule]# mount /dev/cdrom /mnt/cdrom
mount: block device /dev/cdrom is write-protected, mounting read-only
[Expert@cpmodule]# cd /mnt/cdrom/SecurePlatform/RPMS/
[Expert@cpmodule]# ls kernel*
kernel-2.4.9-36cp.athlon.rpm          kernel-kdb-2.4.9-36cp_kdb.i686.rpm
kernel-2.4.9-36cp.i386.rpm            kernel-kdb-smp-2.4.9-
36cp_kdb.
   athlon.rpm
kernel-2.4.9-36cp.i586.rpm            kernel-kdb-smp-2.4.9-36cp_kdb.i586.rpm
kernel-2.4.9-36cp.i686.rpm            kernel-kdb-smp-2.4.9-36cp_kdb.i686.rpm
kernel-kdb-2.4.9-36cp_kdb.athlon.rpm kernel-smp-2.4.9-36cp.athlon.rpm
kernel-kdb-2.4.9-36cp_kdb.i386.rpm   kernel-smp-2.4.9-36cp.i586.rpm
kernel-kdb-2.4.9-36cp_kdb.i586.rpm   kernel-smp-2.4.9-36cp.i686.rpm
[Expert@cpmodule]# rpm -i kernel-kdb-smp-2.4.9-36cp_kdb.i686.rpm
[Expert@cpmodule]# rpm -i kernel-smp-2.4.9-36cp.i686.rpm
[Expert@cpmodule]# cat /etc/grub.conf
# grub.conf generated by anaconda
#
```

```
# Note that you do not have to rerun grub after making changes to this file
# NOTICE:  You have a /boot partition.  This means that
#          all kernel and initrd paths are relative to /boot/, eg.
#          root (hd0,0)
#          kernel /vmlinuz-version ro root=/dev/hda2
#          initrd /initrd-version.img
#boot=/dev/hda
default=0
timeout=10
splashimage=(hd0,0)/grub/splash.xpm.gz
background 777777
serial --unit=0 --speed=9600 --word=8 --parity=no --stop=1
terminal --silent --timeout=5 console serial
password --md5 $1$GGZTBGBB$NijpJ4R4eD9Uf/EBJYMa4/
title Check Point SecurePlatform NG FP3
        root (hd0,0)
        kernel /vmlinuz-2.4.9-36cpsmp ro root=/dev/hda2 console=ttyS0 3
        initrd /initrd-2.4.9-36cpsmp.img
title Check Point SecurePlatform NG FP3 [Maintenance Mode]
        lock
        root (hd0,0)
        kernel /vmlinuz-2.4.9-36cpsmp ro root=/dev/hda2 debug console=
            CURRENT single
        initrd /initrd-2.4.9-36cpsmp.img
title Check Point SecurePlatform NG FP3 [Debugging Mode]
        root (hd0,0)
        kernel /vmlinuz-2.4.9-36cp_kdbsmp ro root=/dev/hda2 console=ttyS0 3
        initrd /initrd-2.4.9-36cp_kdbsmp.img
title SecurePlatform NG FP3 Edition 2
        root (hd0,0)
        kernel /vmlinuz-2.4.9-36cp ro root=/dev/hda2 console=ttyS0 3
        initrd /initrd-2.4.9-36cp.img
title SecurePlatform NG FP3 Edition 2 [Maintenance Mode]
        root (hd0,0)
        lock
```

```
        kernel /vmlinuz-2.4.9-36cp ro root=/dev/hda2 debug 7 console=
            CURRENT single
        initrd /initrd-2.4.9-36cp.img
title SecurePlatform NG FP3 Edition 2 [Debugging Mode]
        root (hd0,0)
        kernel /vmlinuz-2.4.9-36cp_kdb ro root=/dev/hda2 console=CURRENT 3
        initrd /initrd-2.4.9-36cp_kdb.img
```

At this point, you need to reboot the machine. When it comes back up, the first two (three, if you installed the debugging kernel) options are the new SMP kernel. Even though it does not say *dual CPU* or *single CPU*, log in and go into Expert mode. Verify that the new processor is being utilized by SecurePlatform. First you should verify that the new kernel is being used. You can do this can by issuing a *uname -a* from the command line and seeing that the new version is reflected, as shown in bold in the following code. Next you should also run *top* to make sure the operating system recognizes the new processor and is using it.

```
[Expert@cpmodule]# uname -a
Linux cpmodule 2.4.9-36cpsmp #1 SMP Tue Jan 7 10:36:23 IST 2003 i686
    unknown
[Expert@cpmodule]# top
  3:07pm  up 2 min,  1 user,  load average: 0.56, 0.23, 0.08
31 processes: 29 sleeping, 2 running, 0 zombie, 0 stopped
CPU0 states:  8.4% user, 11.4% system,  0.0% nice, 79.0% idle
CPU1 states:  8.1% user, 11.2% system,  0.0% nice, 80.0% idle
```

Adding Hard Drives

Adding a hard drive is the most manual process we describe in this chapter. Even if you have two drives when you install SecurePlatform, unlike with processors, it will not utilize them both. The system will only format and use the first disk. From this point you will have to work from the command line in Expert mode. In this example, we assume that we're adding a drive and that all our firewall logs will be stored there. After the drive has been installed, we'll first check what drive we're using to boot from. In this case, it's /dev/hda:

```
[Expert@cpmodule]# df -k
Filesystem           1k-blocks      Used Available Use% Mounted on
/dev/hda2               388693    149961    218651  41% /
/dev/hda1                46636     11545     32683  27% /boot
```

```
/dev/hda5              505605     66994    412507  14% /opt
none                    62964         0     62964   0% /dev/shm
/dev/hda3              798508     21496    736448   3% /sysimg
/dev/hda7            36471848     40232  34578924   1% /var
```

Now we ask the system which drives it sees and run *fdisk* on the new drive (hdb):

```
[Expert@cpmodule]# dmesg |grep sectors
block: queued sectors max/low 82565kB/27521kB, 256 slots per queue
hda: 78198750 sectors (40038 MB) w/2000KiB Cache, CHS=4867/255/63, (U)DMA
hdb: 12594960 sectors (6449 MB) w/512KiB Cache, CHS=784/255/63, (U)DMA

[Expert@cpmodule]# fdisk /dev/hdb

Command (m for help): m
Command action
   a   toggle a bootable flag
   b   edit bsd disklabel
   c   toggle the dos compatibility flag
   d   delete a partition
   l   list known partition types
   m   print this menu
   n   add a new partition
   o   create a new empty DOS partition table
   p   print the partition table
   q   quit without saving changes
   s   create a new empty Sun disklabel
   t   change a partition's system id
   u   change display/entry units
   v   verify the partition table
   w   write table to disk and exit
   x   extra functionality (experts only)

Command (m for help):
```

Next let's look at the partition table and delete the existing file system partitions:

```
Command (m for help): p
```

```
Disk /dev/hdb: 255 heads, 63 sectors, 784 cylinders
Units = cylinders of 16065 * 512 bytes

   Device Boot    Start       End    Blocks   Id  System
/dev/hdb1             1       784   6297448+   0   Empty

Command (m for help): d
Partition number (1-4): 1

Command (m for help): p

Disk /dev/hdb: 255 heads, 63 sectors, 784 cylinders
Units = cylinders of 16065 * 512 bytes

   Device Boot    Start       End    Blocks   Id  System

Command (m for help):
```

Repeat the deletions until you have an empty partition table. Once you have a clean partition table, create a partition the size you want. In our example, we use the defaults to make one partition for the entire drive:

```
Command (m for help): n
Command action
   e   extended
   p   primary partition (1-4)
p
Partition number (1-4): 1
First cylinder (1-784, default 1): 1
Using default value 1
Last cylinder or +size or +sizeM or +sizeK (1-784, default 784): 784
Using default value 784
```

Verify that the partition has been created and write the partition table to the disk. If you do not write the information to the disk, no changes will be made to the disk:

```
Command (m for help): p

Disk /dev/hdb: 255 heads, 63 sectors, 784 cylinders
```

```
Units = cylinders of 16065 * 512 bytes

   Device Boot    Start       End    Blocks   Id  System
/dev/hdb1             1       784   6297448+  83  Linux

Command (m for help): w
The partition table has been altered!

Calling ioctl() to re-read partition table.

WARNING: If you have created or modified any DOS 6.x
partitions, please see the fdisk manual page for additional
information.
Syncing disks.
[Expert@cpmodule]#
```

Now that we have created the partition, we need to create the file system (in other words, we need to format it). We use *mkfs* to do this and specify the partition on which to create the file system. This will automatically create an ext3 (Linux) file system:

```
[Expert@cpmodule]# mkfs /dev/hdb1
mke2fs 1.23, 15-Aug-2001 for EXT2 FS 0.5b, 95/08/09
Filesystem label=
OS type: Linux
Block size=4096 (log=2)
Fragment size=4096 (log=2)
788704 inodes, 1574362 blocks
78718 blocks (5.00%) reserved for the super user
First data block=0
49 block groups
32768 blocks per group, 32768 fragments per group
16096 inodes per group
Superblock backups stored on blocks:
        32768, 98304, 163840, 229376, 294912, 819200, 884736

Writing inode tables: done
Writing superblocks and filesystem accounting information: done
```

```
This filesystem will be automatically checked every 33 mounts or
180 days, whichever comes first.  Use tune2fs -c or -i to override.
[Expert@cpmodule]#
```

In the next step, we're going to create a place to put the drive (/fw1-logs) and mount it. Once it's mounted, we will stop the firewall, then move the all the log files to their new location. Finally, we will remove the current log directory and make a symbolic link to the new location so that the firewall knows where the files should go:

```
[Expert@cpmodule]# mkdir /fw1-logs
[Expert@cpmodule]# mount /dev/hdb1 /fw1-logs
[Expert@cpmodule]# df -k
Filesystem           1k-blocks      Used Available Use% Mounted on
/dev/hda2               388693    150987    217625  41% /
/dev/hda1                46636     11546     32682  27% /boot
/dev/hda5               505605     68215    411286  15% /opt
none                     62964         0     62964   0% /dev/shm
/dev/hda3               798508     21496    736448   3% /sysimg
/dev/hda7             36471848     41712  34577444   1% /var
/dev/hdb1              6198404        20   5883512   1% /fw1-logs
[Expert@cpmodule]#
[Expert@cpmodule]# cpstop
SecureXL device disabled
FW: stopping VPN-1 module -- OK
FireWall-1: disabling IP forwarding

SVN Foundation: cpd stopped
SVN Foundation: cpWatchDog stopped
SVN Foundation stopped
[Expert@cpmodule]# mv log/* /fw1-logs/.
[Expert@cpmodule]# rm -rf log
[Expert@cpmodule]# ln -s /fw1-logs log
[Expert@cpmodule]# cpstart

cpstart: Start product - SVN Foundation


SVN Foundation: Starting cpWatchDog
SVN Foundation: Starting cpd
```

```
SVN Foundation started

cpstart: Start product - FireWall-1

FireWall-1: Starting external VPN module -- OK
FireWall-1: Starting fwd
FireWall-1: Starting fwm (SmartCenter Server)


Installing Security Policy Standard on all.all@cpmodule
Fetching Security Policy from localhost succeeded
FireWall-1 started
[Expert@cpmodule]#
[Expert@cpmodule]# cd /fw1-logs/
[Expert@cpmodule]# ls
cpca.elg               fw.log               fw.vlog               fwui.log
cpmad.err              fw.logLuuidDB        fw.vlogaccount_ptr   lost+found
fw.adtlog              fw.logaccount_ptr   fw.vloginitial_ptr   sam.dat
fw.adtlogaccount_ptr   fw.loginitial_ptr   fw.vlogptr
fw.adtloginitial_ptr   fw.logptr            fwd.elg
fw.adtlogptr           fw.logtrack          fwm.elg
```

At this point, we need to add a line to /etc/fstab (probably at the bottom) to make sure that our new file system is loaded at boot time. The structure of the file can be defined in the following way: The first field is the physical device we're working with. The second field is the place we are going to mount the file system. The third field is the type of file system the partition is formatted as. The fourth field is a list of options that *mount* will use when actually mounting the file system. The fifth field is used by the dump utility, if you are using it for backups. (The backup utility described in this chapter does not use dump. Dump is used to backup an entire partition, not just specific files.) If this field is set to 0, dump will disregard it. The final field is used by *fsck* (the utility used to check and repair the file system). You should set this to 2 unless it's the root partition, which should be set to 1, or a file system you do not want to *fsck,* which requires a 0. In the /etc/fstab file, we will use *vi* to add the following line:

```
/dev/hdb1                /fw1-logs                ext3     defaults          0 2
```

The purpose of adding this line is that when we reboot the system, it will automatically check and mount the drive. You can also change a few of these steps and mount the drive exactly where the log directory was.

FireWall-1 Performance Counters

A great deal of documentation is available on how to effectively use the utilities built into Linux to check its performance (and we have mentioned some of them in this chapter), but there is very little information about how to measure the performance of the firewall. This section discusses some very important utilities for measuring firewall performance. This is very important for capacity planning and identifying where you are reaching limits within the device when you run into issues.

Firewall Commands

Many, many commands are available within a normal firewall installation. These commands can be used to see what's going on internally for capacity planning as well as for debugging and troubleshooting. The following sections describe how to use some of the most useful commands and give a few examples.

cpstat

The *cpstat* command gives a wealth of statistical information about the system or another system, if the command is run from the management station using the AMON OPSEC API. The *-f* option allows you to specify the "flavor" of the flag you specify. The easiest way to think about this is that the flag is the general area and the flavor is the more specific area. For example, if you execute *cpstat -f all os*, it will show you all the operating system information, but if you execute *cpstat -f cpu os,* it will only show you the CPU-related information:

```
[Expert@cpmodule]# cpstat

Usage: cpstat [-h host][-p port][-f flavour][-o polling [-c count]
     [-e period]] [-d] application_flag

-h A resolvable hostname, a dot-notation address, or a DAIP object name.
   Default is localhost.

-p Port number of the AMON server.
   Default is the standard AMON port (18192).
```

```
-f The flavour of the output (as appears in the configuration file).
   Default is to use the first flavour found in the configuration file.

-o Polling interval (seconds) specifies the pace of the results.
   Default is 0, meaning the results are shown only once.

-c Specifying how many times the results are shown.
   Default is 0, meaning the results are repeatedly shown.

-e Period interval (seconds) specifies the interval over which
   "statistical" oids are computed. Ignored for regular oids.

-d Debug mode

Available application_flags:

-------------------------------------------------------------
|Flag        |Flavours                                      |
-------------------------------------------------------------
|os          |default, routing, memory, old_memory, cpu,    |
|            |disk, perf, all, average_cpu, average_memory, |
|            |statistics                                    |
-------------------------------------------------------------
|persistency |product, TableConfig, SourceConfig            |
-------------------------------------------------------------
|fw          |default, policy, perf, hmem, kmem, inspect,   |
|            |cookies, chains, fragments, totals, ufp, http,|
|            |ftp, telnet, rlogin, smtp, sync, all          |
-------------------------------------------------------------
|vpn         |default, product, IKE, ipsec, traffic,        |
|            |compression, accelerator, nic, statistics,    |
|            |watermarks, all                               |
-------------------------------------------------------------
|polsrv      |default, all                                  |
-------------------------------------------------------------
|mg          |default                                       |
-------------------------------------------------------------
```

```
[Expert@cpmodule]# cpstat -f cpu os

CPU User Time (%):    8
CPU System Time (%): 20
CPU Idle Time (%):   73
CPU Usage (%):        28
CPU Queue Length:     -
CPU Interrupts/Sec:  50
CPUs Number:          2

[Expert@cpmodule]#
```

fw ctl pstat

The fw ctl pstat command allows you to quickly see a concise view of how the memory is being used and what pieces of the Check Point subsystem are doing a great deal of work. This information can easily show you the peak amount of memory used, the number of INSPECT operations, peak concurrent and total connections, fragmented packets reassembled and ones that weren't, and more:

```
[Expert@cpmodule]# fw ctl pstat

Hash kernel memory (hmem) statistics:
  Total memory allocated: 6291456 bytes in 1535 4KB blocks using 1 pool
  Total memory bytes  used:   111416   unused:  6180040 (98.23%)   peak:
         253680
  Total memory blocks used:     59   unused:     1476 (96%)    peak:  93
  Allocations: 2807675 alloc, 0 failed alloc, 2805577 free

System kernel memory (smem) statistics:
  Total memory  bytes  used:  8616108   peak:  9191484
    Blocking  memory  bytes   used:   196576   peak:   213172
    Non-Blocking memory bytes used:  8419532   peak:  8978312
  Allocations: 522409 alloc, 0 failed alloc, 522230 free, 0 failed free

Kernel memory (kmem) statistics:
  Total memory  bytes  used:  2429332   peak:  3027596
```

```
        Allocations: 2982493 alloc, 0 failed alloc, 2980218 free, 0
            failed free

Kernel stacks:
        0 bytes total, 0 bytes stack size, 0 stacks,
        0 peak used, 0 max stack bytes used, 0 min stack bytes used,
        0 failed stack calls

INSPECT:
        23154360 packets, 620258087 operations, 7042944 lookups,
        0 record, 197214487 extract

Cookies:
        55641139 total, 0 alloc, 0 free,
        22315091 dup, 315688042 get, 24785793 put,
        11513069 len, 10602 cached len, 0 chain alloc,
        0 chain free

Connections:
        148473 total, 107539 TCP, 27134 UDP, 13800 ICMP,
        0 other, 63 anticipated, 62 recovered, 8 concurrent,
        273 peak concurrent, 55977060 lookups

Fragments:
        21218 fragments, 10602 packets, 14 expired, 0 short,
        0 large, 0 duplicates, 0 failures

NAT:
        4884574/0 forw, 6963979/0 bckw, 11799051 tcpudp,
        49502 icmp, 146537-146557 alloc

[Expert@cpmodule]#
```

vpn tu

The VPN Tunnel utility (also known as *vpn tunnelutility* or *vpn tu*) allows you to view all the IKE (Phase 1) and IPSec (Phase 2) security associations (SAs) that the firewall knows about. This utility allows you to quickly see what VPN connections are nailed up and to which peers. It allows you to take down or reset a VPN connection very quickly if necessary by using the Delete options. You can also choose option **8** to take down *all* the VPN tunnels and make all the peers re-establish their VPNs. This is a very effective way to cut off remote access VPN users if necessary. Once you know the users' IP addresses, you can revoke/reset their credentials and then use this utility to tear down the VPN tunnel.

```
[Expert@cpmodule]# vpn tu


**********      Select Option      **********


(1)               List all IKE SAs
(2)               List all IPsec SAs
(3)               List all IKE SAs for a given peer
(4)               List all IPsec SAs for a given peer
(5)               Delete all IPsec SAs for a given peer
(6)               Delete all IPsec+IKE SAs for a given peer
(7)               Delete all IPsec SAs for ALL peers
(8)               Delete all IPsec+IKE SAs for ALL peers

(A)               Abort

*******************************************
```

fwaccel

If you happen to be leveraging the software or SecureXL hardware acceleration features built into Check Point, you can use the *fwaccel* command to turn the acceleration on and off as well as get and set configuration information. The main SecureXL feature on SecurePlatform is the Performance Pack, the license for which comes with an unlimited IP address gateway license. This license leverages Check Point's patented SecureXL API to optimize how security functions are handled at both the processor and NIC level. Command usage is shown here:

```
[Expert@cpmodule]# fwaccel
Usage: fwaccel on | off | ver | stat | cfg <...> | conns | dbg <...> | help

Options:
   on                       - turn acceleration on
```

```
    off                      - turn acceleration off
    ver                      - show SecureXL version
    stat                     - show acceleration status
    cfg <options>           - configure acceleration parameters
    conns <options>         - print the accelerator's connections table
    dbg <options>           - set debug flags
    help                     - this help message

[Expert@cpmodule]#
```

Summary

SecurePlatform is a very simple, efficient, fast, and inexpensive platform on which to run Check Point's products. This product allows an administrator to quickly set up a very high-capacity system that is fully supported—from the OS to the application—by one vendor, Check Point. SecurePlatform removes the focus and the difficult decisions (as well as a great deal of the cost) from the hardware and puts the focus on the important piece, the software.

Configuration of the system can be done in two ways: via the WebUI or via the command line. The WebUI allows you to configure many things, but the most complete way to configure the system is via the command line. A difference between SecurePlatform and a normal Linux distribution is that when you log in to the command-line interface, you will receive an application-specific configuration and management interface. The CPShell environment allows an administrator to access the commands essential to firewall administration, but it further limits access to the underlying operating system with another separate password. The advanced debugging and troubleshooting mode is referred to as Expert mode.

This chapter also reviewed the reasons for adding hardware to a SecurePlatform system as well as the commands you need to execute to take advantage of the new hardware. Related to the requirements of new hardware, we discussed being able to effectively check the performance and capacity of the system and forecast the need to raise the capacity of the system.

Solutions Fast Track

The Basics

☑ Check the bus speed of the machine to accurately determine possible throughput.

☑ Make sure that you choose NICs that are directly supported in the SecurePlatform release. Adding drivers is not supported.

☑ Configuration of SecurePlatform can be done via the WebUI or from the command line.

☑ You can use a 15-day evaluation license or enter your permanent license during the installation.

☑ CPShell is the restricted shell you use when you log in via the command line. To get to a full UNIX shell, use the *expert* command.

- ☑ Backups can be done locally or sent to a TFTP server.
- ☑ Adding and upgrading packages can be done via the WebUI, SmartUpdate, or manually from the command line.

Adding Hardware to SecurePlatform

- ☑ Check to make sure that you actually do need more memory before you add to it. You might only need to raise the size of the connections table.
- ☑ If changing an interface to utilize VLANs, remember that the main address on that NIC will be overwritten with the IP address of 0.0.0.0.
- ☑ To take advantage of a second processor after the OS has been installed, you need to install the RPM for the SMP kernel.
- ☑ To offload work from the processor, encryption traffic can be processed by an IPSec encryption card.

FireWall-1 Performance Counters

- ☑ The *cpstat* command gives a wealth of statistical information about the system or another system if run from the management station using the AMON OPSEC API.
- ☑ The *fw ctl pstat* command allows you to quickly see a concise view of how the memory is being used and what pieces of the Check Point subsystem are doing a great deal of work.
- ☑ The *vpn tu* command allows you to view all the IKE (Phase 1) and IPSec (Phase 2) SAs that the firewall knows about.
- ☑ You can use the *fwaccel* command to turn the acceleration on and off as well as get and set configuration information if you are leveraging the software or SecureXL hardware acceleration features built into Check Point.

Frequently Asked Questions

The following Frequently Asked Questions, answered by the authors of this book, are designed to both measure your understanding of the concepts presented in this chapter and to assist you with real-life implementation of these concepts. To have your questions about this chapter answered by the author, browse to **www.syngress.com/solutions** and click on the **"Ask the Author"** form.

Q: How much does SecurePlatform cost? Who do I pay for support?

A: SecurePlatform is free and there is no cost for support. Check Point provides support for the OS all the way up to the application, but the company does not support interoperability with other Linux packages or packages that do not come on the SecurePlatform installation CD. The support for the operating system comes with a valid support contract for the firewall application at no additional cost.

Q: SecurePlatform doesn't have support for <*insert package name here*>. Can I just add the RPM?

A: Yes. However, Check Point does not support anything that does not come on SecurePlatform. If you install other packages, you might be invalidating the support for the system if it happens to conflict with other packages.

Q: The system I have came with a bunch of hard drives, and I want to do RAID on them, but SecurePlatform does not have the necessary packages. What should I do?

A: If you require RAID support for your disks, you should do it in hardware, not software using SCSI disks as IDE RAID controllers are not yet supported. It is more reliable, and SecurePlatform only sees it and treats it as one disk. You could add the RPM, but you would possibly be invalidating your support.

Q: I installed SecurePlatform, but it doesn't see one or more of my NICs. Can I just add the driver?

A: Yes, you can add the driver, but since it is not officially part of SecurePlatform, it's not necessarily supported by Check Point. In addition, upgrades to the operating system might cause the NIC driver to stop working or create other issues. The best recommendation is to only use supported NICs from common manufacturers. Consult Check Point's Web site, your reseller, or your local Check Point office for information on the currently supported NICs.

Q: What NICs are supported on SecurePlatform?

A: You can always get an up-to-date list directly from Check Point's Web site at http://support.checkpoint.com, searching specifically for Solution ID 55.0.4089734.2604361. These are the NICs Check Point has actually tested on the various OSs. In reality, anything supported in the equivalent release of RedHat should work. The easiest way to get a system with fully supported components is to buy a Secured By Check Point appliance that runs SecurePlatform. Numerous vendors provide these solutions. An updated list of prices and hardware can always be found at Check Point's main Web site, in the *Platform Selection Guide*. These also help you accurately estimate performance.

Chapter 8

SmartCenter Management Server, High Availability and Failover, and SMART Clients

Solutions in this chapter:

- SmartCenter Server: The Roles of a Management Server
- Management Server Backup Options
- Installing a Secondary Management Server
- SMART Clients

☑ Summary

☑ Solutions Fast Track

☑ Frequently Asked Questions

Introduction

The most important system in any Check Point FireWall-1 configuration is the management server, renamed SmartCenter Server in FP3. Some of you might have used FireWall-1 in "standalone" configurations only, but the majority of deployments are distributed. Regardless of deployment, every FireWall-1 design has a management server.

The management server handles major functions of the firewall enforcement point and provides all connectivity for the SMART Clients. The management server provides the connectivity and data for all SMART Client connections and stores enforcement point logs, enforcement point configuration, and all other aspects of the firewall architecture. Therefore, maintaining your management server is an important task. If you lose your management server, your life can become difficult in a very short time.

Of course, your management server should be backed up to a trusted medium, such as a local tape drive or local DVD burner. However, you can back up your management server on a regular basis and still face the possibility of losing this system, regardless of how careful you are. For this reason, Check Point provides the ability to have multiple, highly available management servers in your environment. In this chapter, we discuss how to set up those servers and how they function. FP3 adds new and modified functionality for SMART Clients. The functionality and name changes are discussed in the second half of this chapter.

SmartCenter Server: The Roles of a Management Server

Have you ever lost your Check Point management server? If you have, you know the pain involved in reviving this patient. Hopefully, though, you will never need to experience this challenging moment. Regardless of your organization's classification of mission criticality, you probably have some level of redundancy and high availability (HA) in your infrastructure. The goal is to remove or mitigate the potential for a single point of failure. Toward this end, the management server is the single most important element in your Check Point installation. Every single customization made through the SmartDashboard is maintained on this server. The importance of having redundant and automatically replicated management server(s) should not be overlooked.

In either a standalone or distributed configuration, the management server is still a distinct component from both the enforcement point (the firewall) and the SMART Client. The management server is the server that your SMART Client software connects with in order to manage one or many enforcement points, depending on configuration and licensing. In the configuration in which enforcement point, management server, and SMART Client software are all installed on a single computer, these components all function distinctly within the same server. This centralized management and client/server architecture is one of the Check Point solution's strengths. There is a many-to-one relationship between SMART Clients and the SmartCenter Server and a one-to-many relationship between SmartCenter Server to enforcement points (see Figure 8.1).

Figure 8.1 Check Point Architecture

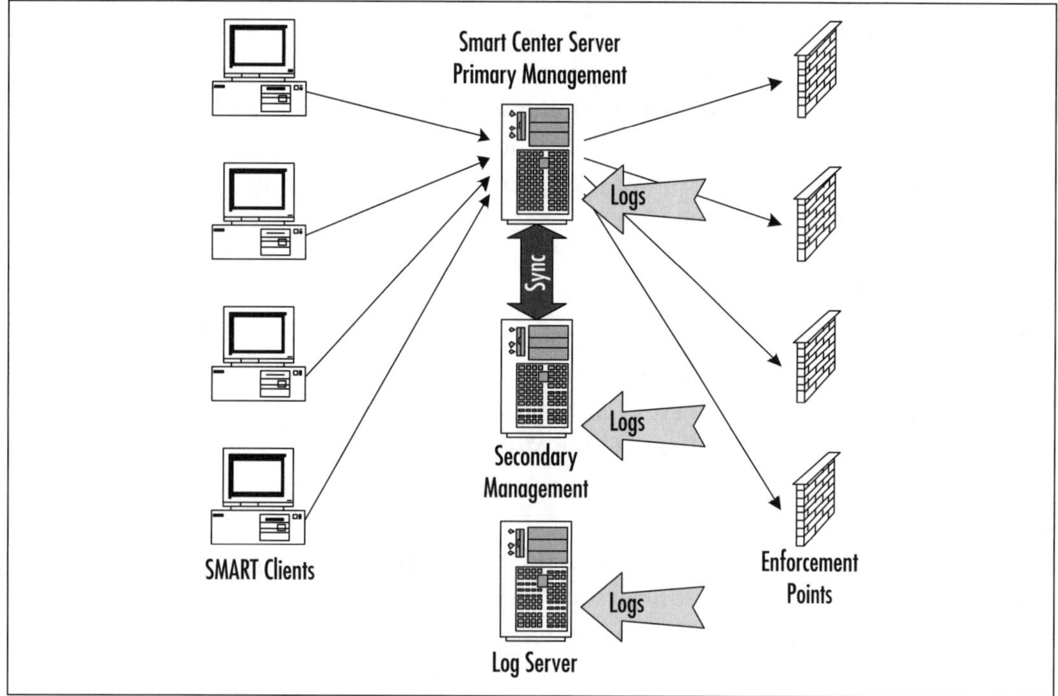

NG has increased the functionality of the management server; now it is much more than just a repository for your objects, rules, and logs. It is your internal certificate authority (CA) enabling Secure Internal Communications (SIC) for the NG components and the use of certificates for authentication. Centralized licenses are maintained and managed on this server using SmartUpdate. SmartUpdate also has the ability to upgrade the software on managed systems. This functionality also resides on the management server.

With the increased importance of the management server, you have an option to remove the logging overhead. A log server component is licensed separately. This ability to have logs maintained on a different server is an operational decision you need to make depending on your environment. In a management HA configuration, a decision must be made whether to send logs to every management server. The primary management server will automatically be listed as a log server on the firewall object. You can then add the secondary management server as a log server as well. The issues start to compound here. Do you want to have duplicate logging taking place on both the primary and secondary management servers? You should realize that the logging server is an alternative to having the logging directed back to management stations.

Internal Certificate Authority

The internal certificate authority function of the management server is used for a few functions. The first of the functions is ensuring communications between SMART Clients, SecureServer, and enforcement points, called SIC. Another use for the CA function is to provide certificates for firewall administrator accounts to be used for authentication. The last application of these certificates is to authenticate either site-to-site or client-to-site VPN connections.

VPN Certificates

When you create a Check Point gateway and enable either VPN-1 Pro or Net, the management server will automatically generate a certificate for this object when you click **OK** to finish. This is the certificate this object will use to authenticate to establish an IKE VPN tunnel with another gateway. When both gateways are managed by this management server, there are no issues in trusting the CA that issued the certificates, since the same CA issued both.

If you are using internal users configured locally on your management server, you have the option to generate certificates for user authentication. To use SecuRemote or SecureClient to authenticate to a gateway for a client VPN, the gateway must have a certificate from the same CA that issued the user certificate. A problem could occur if for some reason you need to reset the CA on your management server.

Management Server Backup Options

Pre-NG Check Point installations had no automated internal method to provide the backup or replicate the management server. We were forced to use some other method to provide backup. The initial configuration of backup management servers is still manual in the earlier NG Feature Packs. Administrators need to perform a *cpstop* and manually copy files from the primary management server to all secondary management servers. Now the process is a button click away during the initial configuration. This is a great option if you have chosen to purchase a Management HA license. If you have not, you can take some manual steps to create your own backups.

Check Point resolution skl4680, *Which Files to Back Up in Order to Restore the NG Management Server*, lists the steps and files necessary for restoring a management server. It is important to note that these steps are only for restoring on the same operating system. The issue with this solution is that it might be an incomplete list for your configuration. Another option is available in Check Point Knowledge Base Solution sk16625, *The Ultimate Upgrade Guide: How to Upgrade a Management Server from 4.1 to NG*. A hyperlink in this resolution, *How to Upgrade the Management Server,* links to http://support.checkpoint.com/kb/docs/public/firewall1/ng/pdf/upgrade_mgmt_srvr.pdf and is the ultimate upgrade guide for taking a 4.1 through NG FP2 management server to FP3. (This is the same solution mentioned in Chapter 1.)

In this document, you'll find steps explaining the files necessary for first replicating a management server to be used for the upgrade. These same steps are helpful in listing the critical files necessary to back up manually. Specific files and directories are listed under both the $CPDIR that contains the CPSHARED configuration and the $FWDIR that contains firewall configurations. It is important to note that you must perform a *cpstop* prior to copying these files. The best action for you to take is to copy both the $CPDIR and $FWDIR directories completely, including their subdirectories, to make a backup. When you need to perform a restore, you should copy these directories completely and not just specific files you want, or you risk a corruption due to a lack of synchronized states.

The importance of the management server is obvious from the previous discussion. For many environments, a license for Management HA should be considered.

Next we cover the setup and configuration of the secondary management server. This will take away the opportunity for mistakes that can occur as a result of a manual process.

Protecting the Configuration

If you are familiar with the simplicity of backing up your 4.1 management server, it is important to note that NG is significantly more complex. You cannot just copy the objects.C, rulebases.fws, *.W files from the $FWDIR/conf directory. You can use the steps listed in Chapter 1 regarding replication of management servers to back up specific files. The easiest method of protecting the configuration files is to completely back up the $FWDIR and $CPDIR directories.

Enforcement Point Functions

The databases are compiled before they are downloaded to the enforcement points. No functional files on the enforcement points can be used to recreate the objects or rule base files. Copies of these files are available on the management server in subdirectories of the $FWDIR/conf directory. In a distributed installation, there will be a directory with the name of the firewall object, or in a single gateway environment, the directory will have the name of the management server. In the respective directory, there is a copy of the objects_5_0.C and rulebases_5_0.fws files. Check Point Knowledge Base

Solution sk11754 documents how these files can be used to repair a situation in which there are no objects available or no rules populating the Security Policy screen in SmartDashboard.

Logging

When an enforcement point loses the logging connection to the designated logging server(s), it will log locally. You can retrieve these files using SmartView Tracker; refer to the SmartView Tracker portion of the "SMART Client" section of this chapter for details.

Installing a Secondary Management Server

The Management HA license provides a way for administrators to create their own insurance against loss of their management servers. The name of the license feature could lead to some confusion, however. The configuration using secondary management servers is not high availability from the automatic failover perspective. Configuration files and installation state information can be defined to automatically synchronize across multiple management servers from the current active management server. The state change from an active to a standby is a manual process and must be initiated by the administrator.

There are a couple of important restrictions to keep in mind. The primary management and all the secondary management servers must be running the same operating system. You must be using a distributed configuration. There is no limit to the number of secondary servers, aside from purchasing the correct number of licenses.

The secondary management server should be licensed with a local license. All other licenses should be central licenses from the primary management server. Certificates and all other configurations are based on the primary management server's license and IP. To install a secondary management server, follow the same steps as you used to install the primary server until you come to the screen shown in Figure 8.2. During the installation process, select **Enterprise Secondary Management** and initialize the SIC password.

Figure 8.2 Choosing Secondary Management

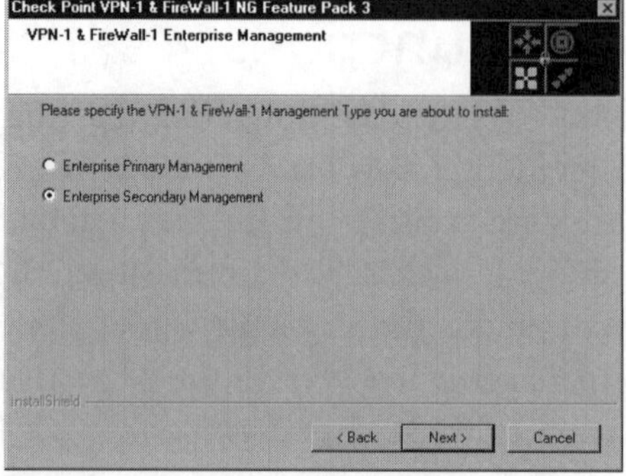

On the Primary Management screen, define a new Check Point host and the communication, and initialize SIC with the password you selected during installation. At this point, you need to save the object in SmartDashboard. Then from the menu select **Policy | Management High Availability** to open the high availability window. This window will display the status of synchronization between primary and secondary management servers (see Figure 8.3). The secondary management station has a status of *Never Synched*. Highlight the peer and click the **Synchronize** button to manually replicate the configuration. The status will change to *Synchronized*.

Figure 8.3 The Management High Availability Server Screen

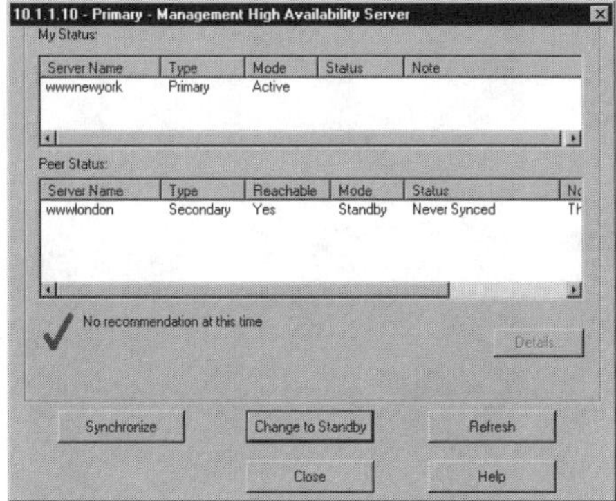

Now that the initial synchronization is complete, we need to define the synchronization settings to be used from this point forward. There are automatic settings for synchronizing the management servers in the Global Properties. Select **Policy | Global Properties** to open the Global Properties window. In the tree on the left side of the window, select the **Management High Availability** option (see Figure 8.4). There are three options that are exclusive of each other; any or all may be selected:

- When policy is saved
- When policy is installed
- On scheduled event

Enabling the **When policy is saved** option means that databases will synchronize every time an administrator elects to save in SmartDashboard. The **On scheduled event** option allows for defining a time object to determine when to synchronize. This is a good place to define a set time before the daily system backups are performed. Both of these options only replicate the configuration databases. The other choice, **When policy is installed**, will replicate both the databases and the state information for the policy installed on an enforcement point. This will allow a *properly configured* firewall to fetch the appropriate policy from the secondary management servers if it is unable to communicate with the primary. *Properly configured* means that you have defined the secondary management servers as masters under the Logs and Masters | Masters screen (see Figure 8.5). The primary management server (wwwnewyork) will already appear in the Masters window. Click the **Add** button and then add your secondary server (wwwlondon). When trying to fetch the policy from the master(s), the firewall will first try to fetch from the first listed master, in this case the primary. If it unable to fetch from the first master, it will attempt the next master, in this case the secondary. All three of these choices back up your databases so that your configuration settings are protected.

Figure 8.4 Global Properties Management High Availability

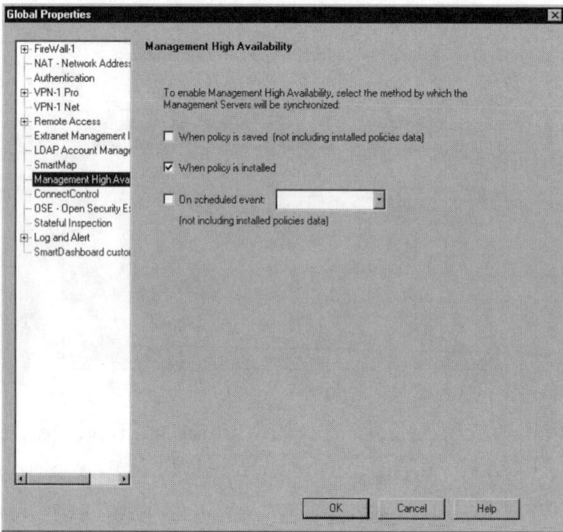

Figure 8.5 Gateway Masters Configuration

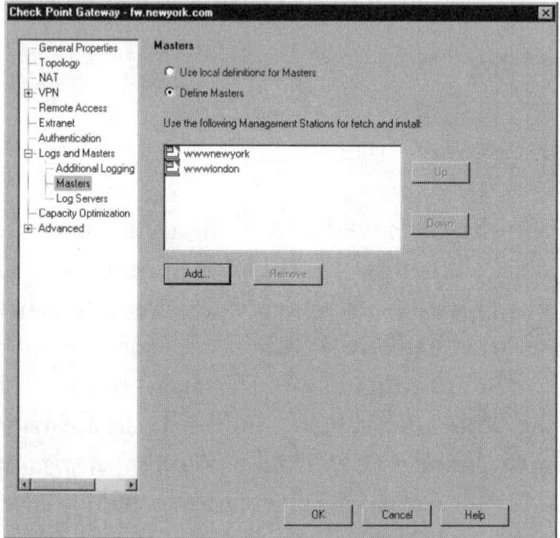

The last consideration in a Management HA environment is how to handle logging. The primary management server is automatically defined as a log server. In the case of secondary management, you will need to decide if you want logs directed there as well. The main consideration is whether you want the firewalls to duplicate logging across multiple servers. There is the option of logging to a secondary management server when the primary becomes unreachable. This is where the option of a logging server becomes an interesting one. A log server can be used to offload the logging function from a primary or secondary management server. These options provide the flexibility you desire in your Check Point infrastructure. In Figure 8.6, you will see the option for always sending logs to a particular server or, in the case in which a server is unavailable, you can have logs directed to a different server.

Figure 8.6 Gateway Log Servers Configuration

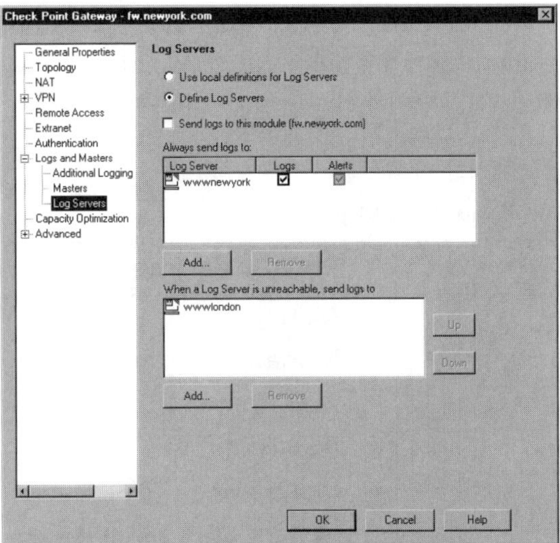

Don't forget that if these firewalls and management servers are separated over a wide area network (WAN), logging decisions may also depend on available bandwidth or other infrastructure considerations. The important points are that you have flexibility in where you choose to maintain log files and it is possible to configure duplicate logging.

The connectivity of a management server or whether or not you are using an HA Management configuration might not be the only logging decisions you need to make. Earlier we mentioned the license option available for a logging server. There are some other considerations you should keep in mind. The first is to have an understanding of the volume of logging going to a particular logging server, whether a management server or just a logging server. In a high-traffic, high-volume log environment, you might choose to use multiple logging servers.

The second consideration is the bandwidth available. When you have a small bandwidth connection to a remote office or a remote site, you might not want to utilize that circuit for logging. In some scenarios, it might make more sense to use a local logging server. You, the firewall administrator, need to understand the options available and make the best decision based on your infrastructure and budgetary constraints while being able to provide a business case to justify the choices.

SMART Clients

Here we list the components that are part of the SMART Client installation. Use of some of these components requires a specific license on the different modules. An important modification with FP3 is the addition of an automatic 15-day evaluation license. Instead of needing to go to the user center to obtain an evaluation license; one installs automatically. If a module has a component enabled without the specific license the feature will be activated using this automatic evaluation license.

The naming conventions have all changed in NG-FP3. Table 8.1 lists the name changes.

Table 8.1 Feature Pack 3 Name Changes

New FP3 Name	Previous Name
SmartCenter	Management
SmartCenter Server	Management Server
SMART Clients	Management Clients
SmartDashboard	Policy Editor
SmartView Tracker	Log Viewer
SmartView Status	System Status Viewer
SmartMap	Visual Policy Editor
SmartUpdate	SecureUpdate
SmartView Monitor	Traffic Monitor
SmartView Reporter	Reporting Tool
SmartLSM (Large Scale Manager)	Atlas
Provider-1/SiteManager-1	Provider-1

SMART Client Functions

The SMART Client software enables the configuration of the management server. The management server is always an implied management client (the GUI Clients parameter has been renamed in FP3); all other clients must be defined. This configuration requirement has not changed. The secondary management servers must also be defined as management clients if you want to use SMART Client software to connect to the primary management server. They will be implied only if connecting to themselves as the management station.

Some new methods are available in FP3 for designating management clients. In addition to name and IP address; you can define a range of addresses, wildcard matching, or any (see Figure 8.6). Using any means, there is no restriction on the management client IP address. The IP range or wildcards make the process of adding multiple management clients quick. When you use the range or wildcard designations, you must create an explicit rule allowing these addresses as a source to the SmartCenter Server as destination with the predefined Check Point Management Interface (CPMI) service, TCP port 18190. If a firewall sits between the SMART Client and the SmartCenter Server, the Rule Base must be reinstalled after defining additional management clients (see Figure 8.7).

Figure 8.7 Defining Management Clients

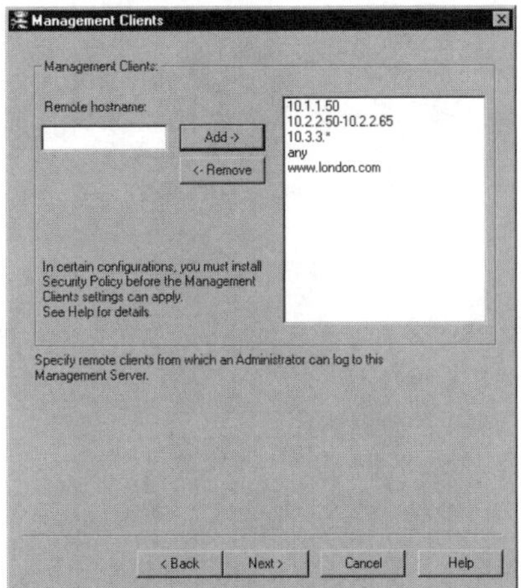

SMART Client Login

SMART Client tools are used to connect with your management server. The default authentication window that opens contains Identification Method and Connect to Server sections with options for read only and Demo mode. If you're new to Check Point NG, Demo mode is a great way to get a feel for the different management interfaces. Provided that your authentication is valid and your IP address is a valid management client, you will be connected with the appropriate rights. It is recommended that you use an IP address or name in the SmartCenter server section of this screen, even if you use a SMART Client local to the management server. There are knowledge base articles on the Check Point Web site describing some strange behavior linked to using *localhost*. Please see the Tools & Traps sidebar, "Firewall Administrator Accounts."

Some new options are available in FP3. By selecting **More Options** in the authentication screen, you will expand the screen as shown in Figure 8.8. The new areas are Certificate Management, Connection Optimizations, and Advanced Options. Certificate Management allows the administrator to change the password on his or her certificate. Using compression will use an internal method to optimize communications. Information entered into the Session Description field will populate a field called Session ID, available in the Audit mode of SmartView Tracker. This field can be used to explain why a particular administrator is making this particular connection. The last line of this expanded window is a check box, **Do not save recent connections information**. By checking this box, you set all SMART Client tools on this individual client to not display the last administrator and management server to which an administrator successfully connected.

Figure 8.8 SmartDashboard Login with More Options Enabled

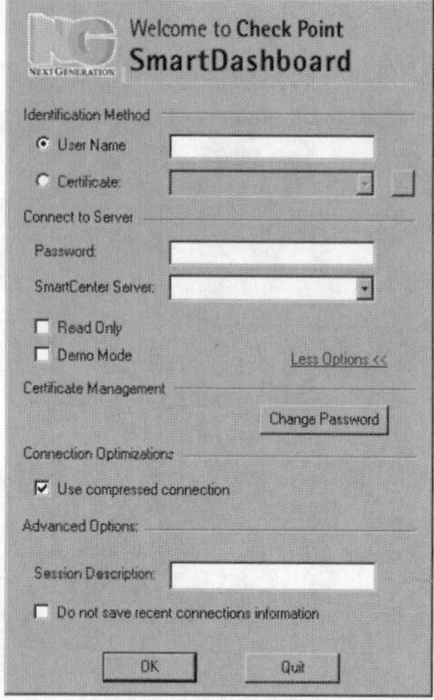

Tools & Traps…

Firewall Administrator Accounts

Creating firewall administrator accounts has been limited to the *cpconfig* configuration tool authenticating with a static password in the pre-NG and recent feature packs. NG versions provide the ability to create administrator accounts from SmartDashboard. There is increased granularity for defining specific rights to the various components. A new feature in FP3 is an option to control accounts that can manage the administrators. The administrative users can be authenticated using SecurID, VPN-1 and Firewall-1 Password, OS Password, and Radius. If you want to use a two-factor method to authenticate; you can

Continued

generate a certificate or FP3 for Check Point to allow the use of a CAPI certificate (Microsoft) for authentication.

From the Objects tree pane, you can right-click the **Administrators** branch to open a window to create a single administrator account. From the menus, select **Manage | Users and Administrators** to open the Users and Administrators window. Click **New... | Administrator...** to open the Administrator Properties window. The general screen contains the Login Name and Permissions Profile parameters. You will first need to create a permissions profile before defining additional options.

In the Permissions Profile Properties window, you have the increased granularity for defining administrative rights. In a large environment, you might not want all administrators to have read/write all permissions with the ability to manage administrators (see Figure 8.9). One common situation to define an account with read-only rights is for use during an audit. The ability to define accounts with more limited rights can be helpful in the distribution or delegation of duties to make your life easier.

Figure 8.9 Administrator Permissions

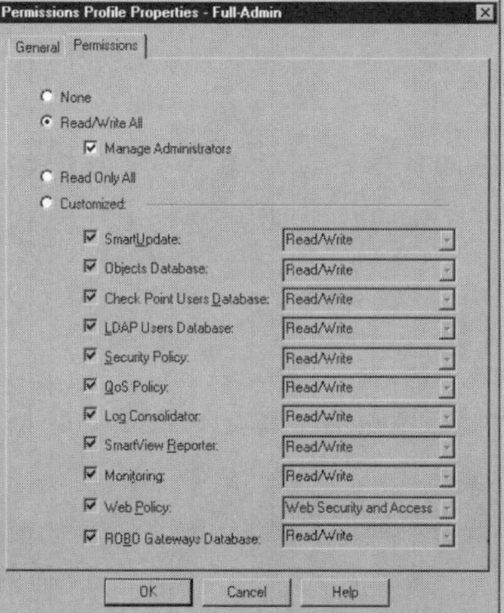

There is one last issue regarding administrator accounts for auditing purposes. In many environments, people like to create a common shared account for firewall administration. There are far too many installations out there with a shared administrator account of *fwadmin* that has a password of *abc123*. Although this combination is functional for a training environment, it is a very bad idea for production. Create specific administrator accounts for the individuals who will be administering the firewall. Doing so will enable you to see who is connected in SmartView Status and will provide audit logging to track specific changes made by an administrator in SmartView Tracker.

SmartDashboard

This is the renamed Policy Editor, where nearly all configurations take place; SmartDashboard is the console driving your enterprise security. Four panes make up the SmartDashboard window; they are the Objects tree, the Objects list, the Rule Base, and SmartMap. Ongoing modifications and additions have been made in this tool through all the NG Feature Packs. The ability to add header lines to the security policy is a new feature available with FP3. These are used in large policies to separate rules for readability.

The Objects tree shows the different types of objects relative to the selected tab from the top of this pane. The objects list displays the individual objects for the highlighted branch of the Objects tree pane. In the Rule Base section of the screen, an administrator can define one of the six different types of policies: the Security Policy (Rule Base), Address Translation, VPN Manager, Desktop Security, Quality of Service, and Web Access. All six might not be visible, depending on your licensing and configuration. The SmartMap pane represents a graphical version of your objects. You can create a map of your topology that allows you to search for objects and rules in relation to connectivity across the enterprise.

Damage & Defense…

Implied Rules

Check Point has taken care to add popup windows for new installations that warn about implied rules. By default, four implied rules are enabled with a matching order designation:

- Accept VPN-1 and Firewall-1 control connections—First
- Accept outgoing packets originating from Gateway—Before Last
- Accept CPRID connections (SmartUpdate)—First
- Accept dynamic address Module's DHCP traffic—First

The matching order designations are First, Before Last, and Last. *First* places the implied rules before the first numbered rule. *Before Last* places the implied rules before the last numbered rule. *Last* places the implied rules after the last numbered rule. The last numbered rule in any rule base should be the cleanup rule. In this case, a packet being compared to the rules will never reach implied rules with a Last designation.

The rules created by these settings do not appear in the Security Policy tab of SmartDashboard. In order to view these, you must select **View |**

Continued

Implied Rules. These rules are designed to enable many types of communication between Check Point modules and other common servers in your environment. They are designed to make a firewall administrator's life easier by allowing communication through the firewall before the explicit rules. The benefit is mitigated by performance and security issues.

Packets are compared to the rules in a top-to-bottom fashion. The default settings have over 30 rules before a packet ever reaches the first explicit rule. In a high-traffic environment, you will experience performance degradation for rules you might not need. The security considerations are another important consideration. These default implied rules accept the services that allow fingerprinting of Check Point devices.

All the implied rules should be disabled. Create explicit rules for only the services you require in your specific environment. This will improve performance by reducing the number of rules a packet must be compared to before being accepted, dropped, or rejected. Security is improved by reducing the opened ports for which your firewall may respond. *Warning:* Always verify that explicit rules are properly configured to allow SMART Clients to communicate with the management server *before* installing the policy!

A significant change is introduced in FP3 for how an enforcement point handles existing connections when installing a new policy (see Figure 8.10). This is defined in the Gateway object; select **Advanced | Connection Persistency** to display the choices. **Keep all connections** will maintain all established connections until they finish. **Keep data connections** will maintain data streams from established control connections until they finish but will force the control connections to be matched against the current policy. **Rematch connections** forces all connections to be compared against the current policy before the enforcement point will accept them. These settings are superceded when a service is configured to keep connections open after a policy is installed (see Figure 8.11).

SmartDefense

SmartDefense is a new configuration option available from the menu bar or the SmartDashboard screen. This feature can be licensed separately to allow you to update various signatures from Check Point on a subscription basis. This is the integration of the Check Point Malicious Activity Detection (CPMAD) from earlier versions. An administrator can configure automatic and discretionary parameters. The default settings here may impact traffic in your environment. You should use the SmartView Tracker to analyze packets that may be dropped with these settings and modify as necessary. To open the Smart Defense Settings screen shown in Figure 8.12, simply click the **SmartDefense** button or select **Policy | SmartDefense...** from the pull-down menus.

Figure 8.10 Connection Persistency

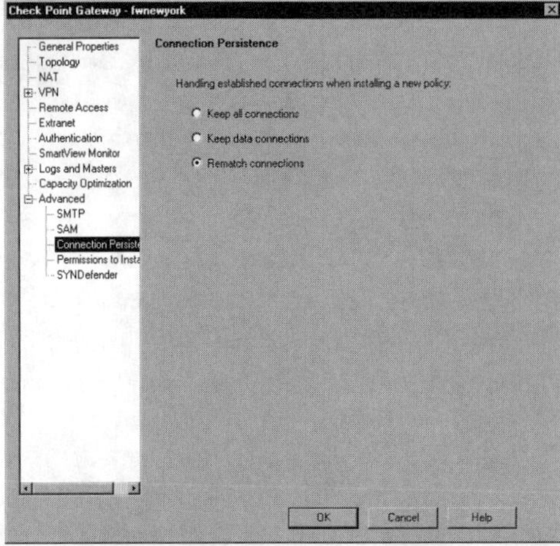

Figure 8.11 Service Persistency Setting

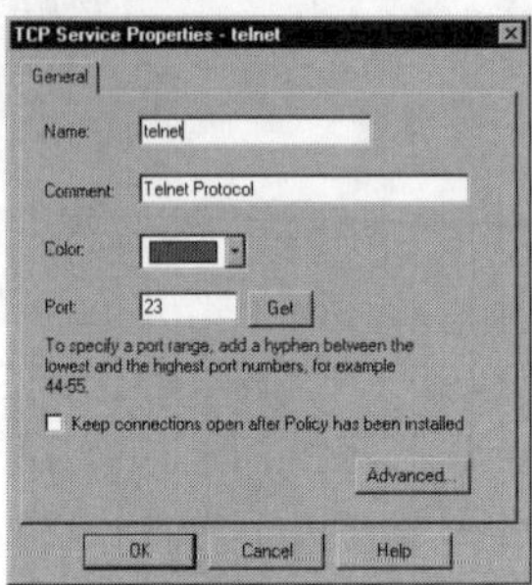

Figure 8.12 The SmartDefense Screen

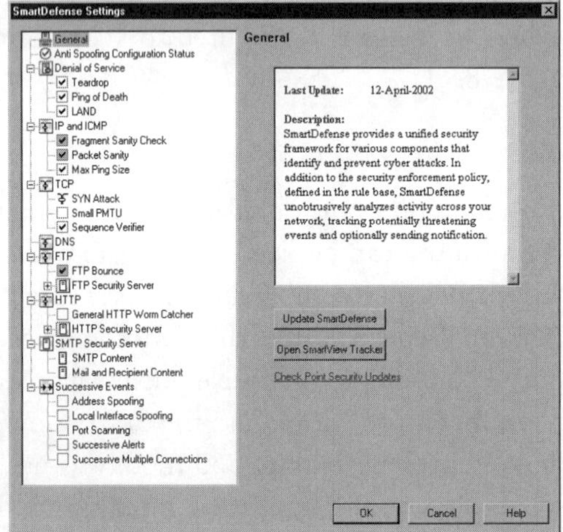

A few of the default settings can trip you up during an upgrade. The first of these is the TCP Sequence Verifier. This setting not only forces a connection to match a valid connection in the state table, but it makes sure the sequence numbers are valid. The DNS UDP protocol enforcement may cause domain name queries to be dropped. The settings for the HTTP and SMTP security servers can be set to match all connections or only those that match a rule using a resource. In upgrading from a 4.1 environment to FP3, these settings may adversely impact legitimate traffic on your network. Verify in SmartView Tracker to see if SmartDefense is dropping traffic.

From the SmartDefense settings screen, you can click the hyperlink **Check Point Security Updates** to open the link www.checkpoint.com/techsupport/documentation/smartdefense/index.html. This page provides specific advisories and attack information. Clicking **Attack information hyperlinks** and then the solution number will open a page providing Common Vulnerability and Exposures (CVE) numbers as well as candidates for inclusion in the CVE list. If you have the appropriate license, you can click the **Update SmartDefense** button to update signatures. After clicking the Update SmartDefense button, you will see a screen telling you what signatures have been upgraded, as shown in Figure 8.13.

Figure 8.13 SmartDefense Update

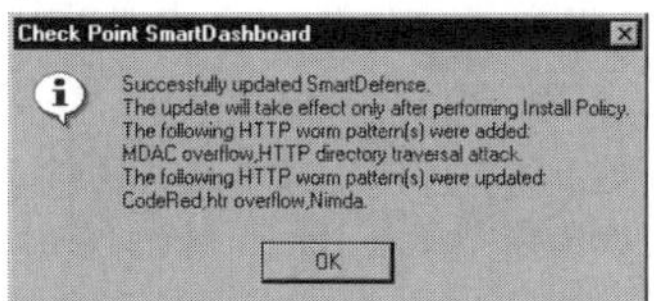

SmartView Status

SmartView Status is the renamed System Status Viewer, where information regarding the status of Check Point and OPSEC is displayed. Three panes make up the SmartStatus window; they are the Modules, Details, and Critical Notifications. The Modules pane contains a tree with all the objects currently managed by the management server. Expanding the tree on a particular object displays the specific modules. The Details pane lists specific details for the installed modules under each object. Error messages and warnings appear in the Critical Notifications pane.

The status in the window is updated automatically and can be updated manually. The timing for automatic updates is configured in the SmartDashboard window. Open the Global Properties by selecting **Policy | Global Properties**. Highlight the **Log and Alert** branch of the tree on the left side of the window to display the log and alert settings. In the **Time Settings** portion of the screen, the **Status fetching interval** setting defines the number of seconds the management server waits between queries for managed object status updates.

FP3 has a new feature for disconnecting clients from the management server. In the Modules pane, expand the management server object and select the **Management** module by highlighting it. Select **Tools | Disconnect Client** to open a window showing the current administrator connections. You can then select any connection to enable the **Disconnect** button; subsequently pressing this button will drop an administrative SMART Client connection.

SmartView Tracker

SmartView Tracker is the renamed Log Viewer, where you can review log entries. Three panes make up the SmartTracker window; they are the Query tree, Query Records, and Records. The Query tree allows selection of predefined queries for specific records matching a filter for product or type, in the case of the account query. Part of the query involves defining the fields that are visible when a particular query is selected. Showing a particular column in a view along with the width and filters is configured in the Query Records pane. The predefined queries are read only, but modifications can be saved and are available in the Custom branch of the query tree.

Three log file modes can be viewed by selecting the respective tab; they are the Log, Active, and Audit modes. The Log mode displays the security event-related records. The Active mode displays the active connections through the managed firewalls. The Audit mode displays both successful and unsuccessful logins, policy installation and uninstallation, and modifications. The Audit mode log is a tremendous help in diagnosing problems and the changes that may have caused them. The best practice is to have individual accounts for all administrators.

Another new feature is the ability to simultaneously open multiple log files or multiple instances of the same log file. This can assist you in defining filters, previously referred to as selection criteria, to search for particular entries or correlate events. A limit of five windows can be opened at one time in the application. You even have the ability to retrieve local log files that a firewall created while unable to communicate with the designated log server(s). Initiate this process from the menu bar by selecting **Tools | Remote Files management...** to open a Check Point Modules List window. Select a particular module, and you have the option to get a list of the log files on this module or to perform a log switch. Select the appropriate button for your desired action.

SmartView Monitor

SmartView Monitor is the renamed Traffic Monitor, in which performance statistics can be measured in real time or used to generate historical reports. This component may be licensed separately or bundled with SmartCenter Pro. Real-time monitoring is available for Check Point system counters, traffic, and virtual links (see Figure 8.14). Traffic can be monitored by service, network object IP, QoS, and top firewall rules.

Figure 8.14 SmartMonitor Session Properties

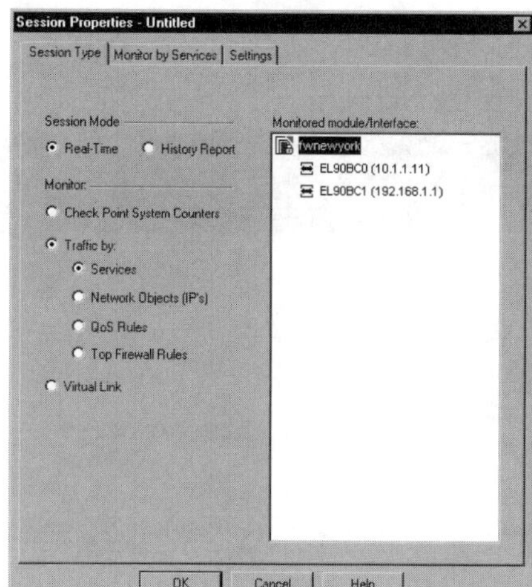

User Monitor

User Monitor is a new tool that allows firewall administrators to monitor users who are connected to a policy server. There are three panes in the User Manager window: Query Selector, Policy Servers View, and Query Editor. The Query Selector allows selection of a specific query. In the Query Editor, the parameters of the query are defined. Queries may include filters defined for the username, policy server, IP address, Secure Configuration Verification (SCV), and logon time with a record-number limit. The Policy Servers View pane displays whether or not a policy server has synchronized data with the SmartCenter Server.

This tool is not fully functional in FP3; it requires FP3-HF1 to be applied, plus a few modifications. These steps are documented in Check Point Knowledge Base Solution sk16494, *What to Do When It's Not Possible to Perform Any User Monitor Queries*. You need to edit the objects_5_0.C and tables.C files in the $FWDIR/conf directory. A default *query1* is predefined and will list all users currently connected to a particular policy server. In Figure 8.15, you can see that user *jnoble* is logged into the policy server.

SmartUpdate

SmartUpdate is the renamed SecureUpdate tool that is used for managing licensing and updating Check Point module software and, in some cases, their operating systems. Currently, only IPSO and SecurePlatform operating systems are supported for upgrade using this tool. SmartUpdate is automatically installed with a management server. Only the license component may be used without an additional license purchase. This licensing component enables the centralized license options for NG. Centralized licensing enables licensing for various Check Point modules using the IP address of your management server.

Figure 8.15 The User Monitor Screen

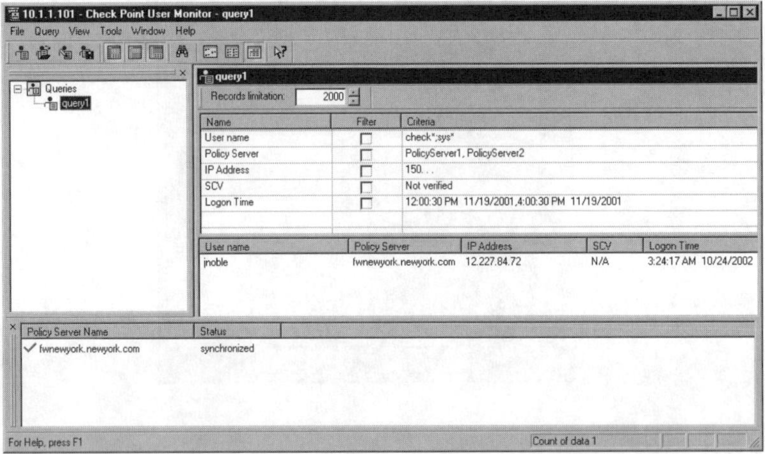

There are two main sections of the SmartUpdate tool: Products and Licenses. In the Products screen, you can view all the modules and their installed components that are managed by the management server. The Licenses screen allows you to view and attach licenses to the managed modules. Optionally, an administrator can turn on and off additional windows—the Product Repository, License Repository, and Operation Status windows. The Product Repository is where administrators can add products for remote installation. Products may be added to the repository from the Download Center, a CD, or a particular file. Licenses may be added to the repository form the User Center, manually, or from a file. To add a centralized license to the license repository, select **Licenses | New License**, and select where you want to get the license. You may add a license from the User Center, manually, or by importing a file. After successfully adding the license to the repository, you can attach it to an enforcement module. The trick is that you must already have created the object, initialized SIC, and then completed a save from SmartDashboard. Some SmartUpdate functions will not work properly with SmartDashboard opened, because it locks the databases; therefore, you should always close SmartDashboard before attempting to use SmartUpdate.

The real muscle of SmartUpdate is in the software upgrade capabilities. Administrators can upgrade NG modules from the SecureServer independently or in a group. The Secure Virtual Network (SVN) Foundation component must be installed and SIC initialized with the management server. The ability to upgrade version 4.1 modules is also supported. The module must be at least a Service Pack 2 and have the Check Point Remote Installation utility (CPutil) installed. Additionally, a *putkey* must be established with the device. This feature uses the Check Point Remote Installation Daemon service, TCP port 18208; any firewalls between the management server and the module must allow this service. This is enabled by default as an implied rule. (See the Damage & Defense sidebar, "Implied Rules," for more details.)

The software upgrade capability also requires that an object already be created and saved. The screens that follow are the exact steps used to upgrade an enforcement point to FP3-HF1. Prior to doing this upgrade, the SmartCenter server and the management client software had to be upgraded to FP3-HF1. Three packages needed to be downloaded: the HF1 for CPSHARED, FW1, and GUI. Running setup after extracting the ZIP files is all that was required to upgrade CPSHARED and FW1. The GUI upgrade required uninstalling the FP3 SMART Client software, then reinstallation using the HF1 software. Just running the HF1 software gave an error stating that FP3 SMART Client software was already installed.

Once the management server and client software were at FP3-HF1, this is how the enforcement point was upgraded. Select **Products | New Product | Add from Download Center** to add a product to the repository directly from the Check Point Download Center (Requires a Login), as indicated in Figure 8.16.

Figure 8.16 SmartUpdate: Add Product

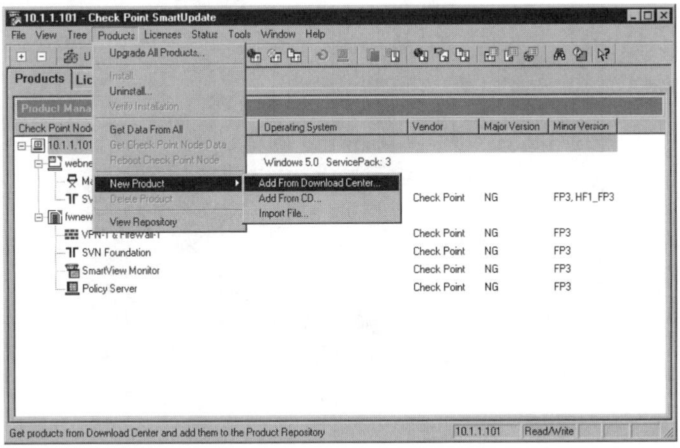

After electing to add a product from the download center, click the **Download** button. We need to get both the SVN Foundation FP3-HF1 and VPN-1/FireWall-1 FP3-HF1 for Windows, as illustrated in Figures 8.17 and 8.18. You need to make sure you download the package that's appropriate for the operating system you want to upgrade.

Figure 8.17 SVN Foundation

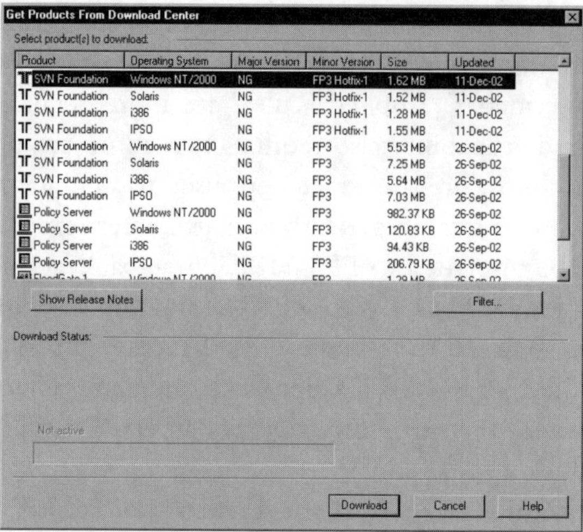

Figure 8.18 VPN-1/FireWall-1

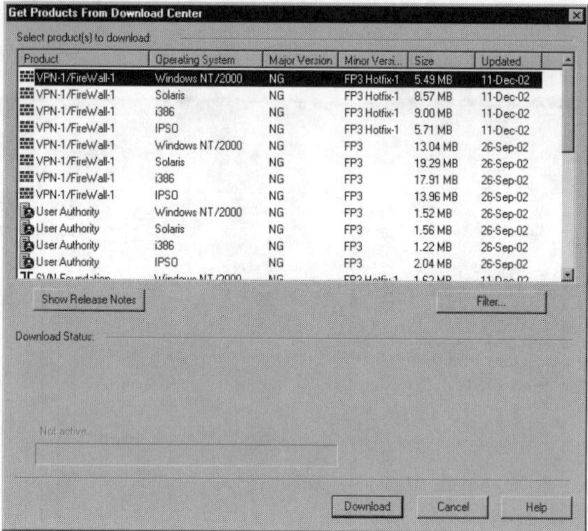

You can verify that both products have been added to the software repository by looking at the screen in Figure 8.19. This screen shows the products in the repository and the status of the operation of adding them.

The steps to upgrade for FP3-HF1 state to add the products individually instead of all at once. By right-clicking the object you want to upgrade, you can select **Install Product** (see Figure 8.20). This will cause a warning that can be ignored to pop up (see Figure 8.21).

Figure 8.19 Product Repository

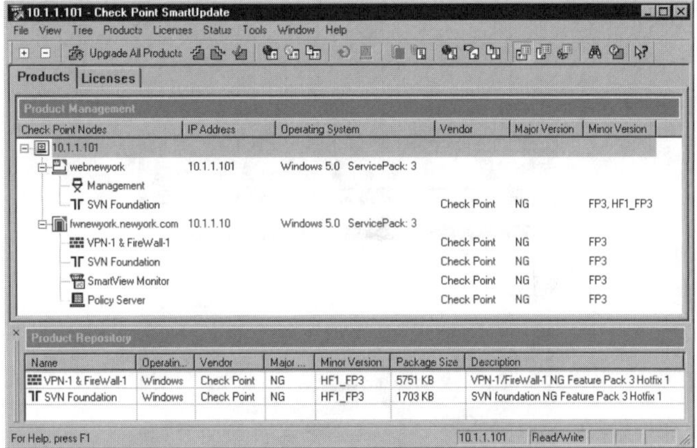

Figure 8.20 Install Product

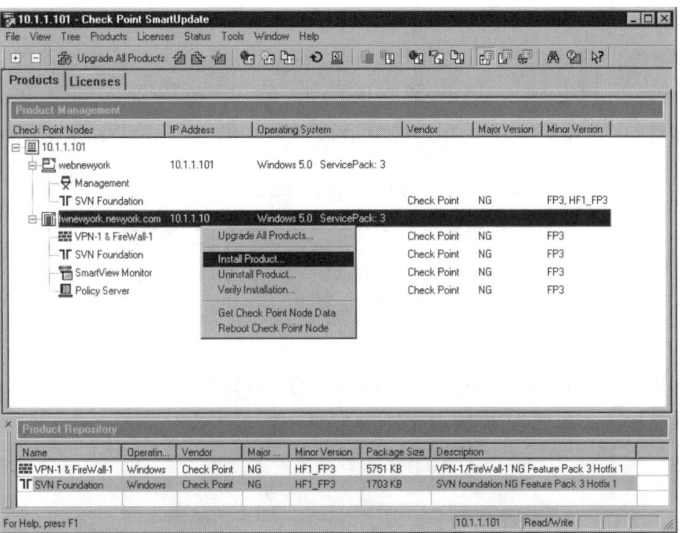

Figure 8.21 SmartUpdate Warning

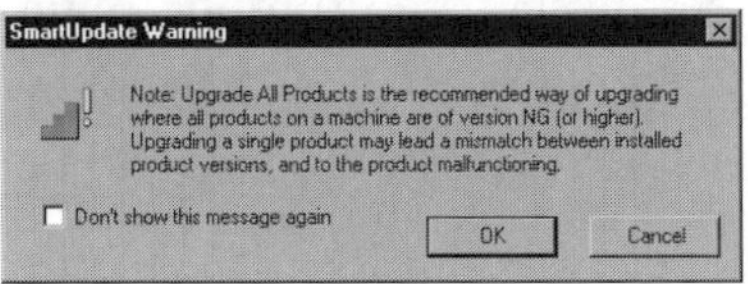

You then need to select the product to install, and click the **Install** button. For our installation, SVN Foundation was selected first, followed by VPN-1/FireWall-1. There is a check box for rebooting after install; this box is ignored after upgrading the SVN

Foundation. The application has the intelligence to know that the VPN-1/FireWall-1 software must be upgraded also before rebooting. Figure 8.22 shows the Install Product selection screen.

Figure 8.22 Product Selection

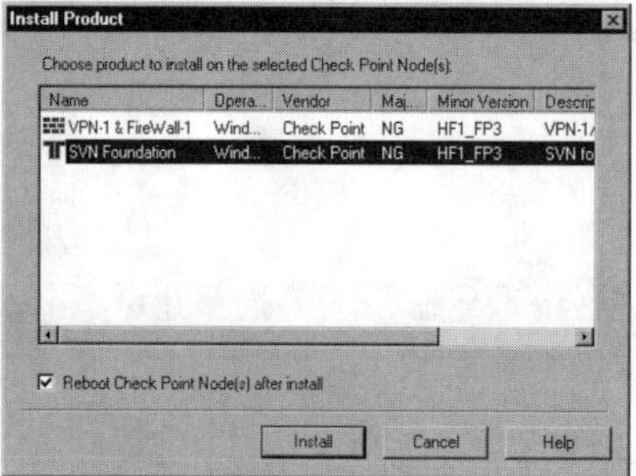

Once you select either of these packages and click the **Install** button, a warning screen will appear. This warning, shown in Figure 8.23 for SVN Foundation or in Figure 8.24 for VPN-1 and FireWall-1, informs you that the object being upgraded will perform a *cpstop*. This is a reminder that the object will stop all Check Point applications in this step of the process and that packets will not be forwarded.

Figure 8.23 The SVN Installation Warning Screen

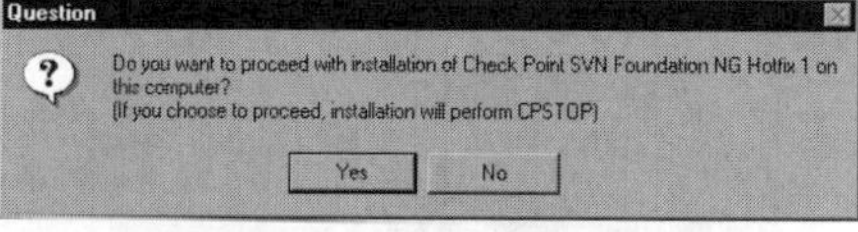

Figure 8.24 The VPN-1 and FireWall Warning Screen

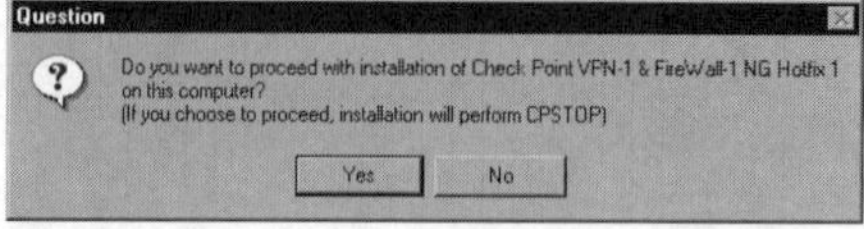

During the upgrade process, the value in the status column in the Operation Status screen will change. You will see the status go through these steps of the process:

1. Operation Started
2. Testing Module
3. Testing Completed
4. Transferring Package to Module
5. Installing Package on Module

6. Product Was Successfully Applied
7. Rebooting Module (if necessary)
8. Rebooting Completed Successfully (if necessary)

The screen in Figure 8.25 shows the completed process. There is a slight bug in what is displayed in the minor version immediately after the upgrade. It initially read *HF1-FP3*, then it changed to *FP3, HF1_FP3* after updating the installed product list. Notice the whole process summarized in the Operation Status window.

Figure 8.25 SmartUpdate Products

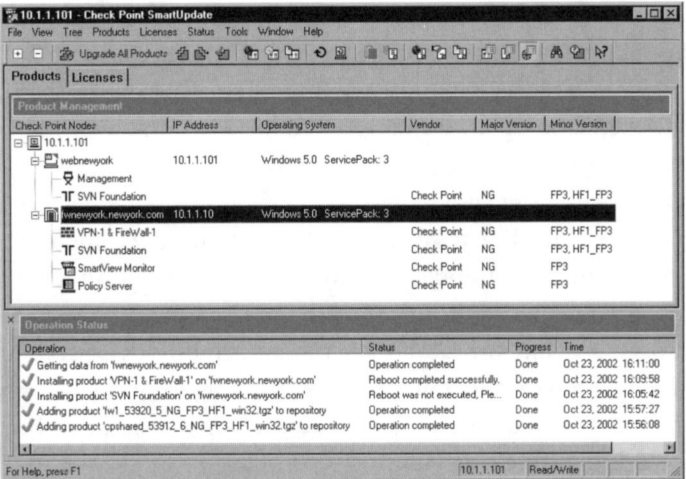

Summary

The SmartCenter management server is the cornerstone of a Check Point NG installation. In either a standalone or a distributed environment, this component maintains every configuration option. The objects and services that are used to define your Rule Base, address translation, desktop security policy, and VPN configurations are just one of this server's responsibilities. The internal certificate authority controlling certificates used in the SSL-based SIC with SMART Clients and enforcement points is a function of the management server. Housing the central repository for applications and licenses is another of the management server's functions. The management server is the single most important component of your Check Point installation.

The flexibility and complexity of the management server add to the importance of backing up this device. We have a manual method of backing up the critical configuration files. However, the manual process to restore includes downtime that might be unacceptable. The ability to license and configure multiple secondary management servers is critical for your environment. There are many different infrastructure designs in use across complex information technology architectures. The NG product line is designed to offer the solutions necessary to accommodate the many installation possibilities.

The SMART Clients used to connect to the management server and modify the configuration have many functions. We have different methods of authenticating the administrative users who have the appropriate rights for using these tools. The source IP addresses are restricted to predefined management clients to add another layer of security. These tools used to define our enterprise security are built around a secure architecture. The proper implementation is a requirement to maintain this security.

The SMART Clients have added functionality in FP3 to assist in the day-to-day operation and management of your Check Point environment. Remember that SmartDefense directly impacts how your enforcement points pass packets. Understanding the new features of FP3 along with their intended security controls is imperative to configuring and managing the Check Point architecture.

Solutions Fast Track

SmartCenter Server: The Roles of a Management Server

☑ The SecureServer is the most important component of a Check Point VPN-1/Firewall-1 installation.

☑ Configuration files contain every single configuration modified in the environment.

- ☑ The internal certificate authority on the management server maintains certificate information used to authenticate administrators, initiate SIC between modules, and authenticate IPSec VPNs.
- ☑ Using SecureUpdate, you can manage the licensing and version upgrades for the various Check Point modules.

Management Server Backup Options

- ☑ The database files are no longer able to be backed up in the simplistic fashion used for version 4.1.
- ☑ Follow the *Ultimate Upgrade Guide* for the minimum necessary files needed to replicate an NG management server.
- ☑ The objects_5_0.C and rulebases.fws files are backed up in a subdirectory of $FWDIR/conf. These files are insufficient for performing a full restoration in NG.

Installing a Secondary Management Server

- ☑ Installation of a secondary management module is simplified in the current NG feature pack.
- ☑ The secondary management server is to be licensed using a local license (licensed to the IP address of the secondary server). All other license-specific functionality replicated from the primary management server will be derived from the primary management server's license.
- ☑ The failover is not an automatic process and must be done manually.
- ☑ Database and install information is automatically synchronized across all management servers.

SMART Clients

- ☑ The SmartDashboard controls more than just the objects and rules. There are settings in the global properties, objects, and services that affect establishing and the statefulness of connections.
- ☑ SmartDefense is a modification of CPMAD to incorporate basic intrusion detection functionality with the firewall operations.

☑ SmartView Status displays the state of different modules installed on a Check Point or OPSEC module. A new tool allows for disconnecting management client connections to the management server.

☑ SmartView Tracker provides different views of logged information useful in troubleshooting a Check Point configuration.

☑ SmartView Monitor enables an administrator to generate real-time or historical reports on communications that are useful for baselining or optimizing your firewall's performance.

☑ User Monitor is a new tool that allows queries to be run against a policy server to manage SecureClient devices connected to your infrastructure.

☑ SmartUpdate is a dual-functionality management tool that enables the use of centralized licensing and centralized version upgrade capabilities.

Frequently Asked Questions

The following Frequently Asked Questions, answered by the authors of this book, are designed to both measure your understanding of the concepts presented in this chapter and to assist you with real-life implementation of these concepts. To have your questions about this chapter answered by the author, browse to **www.syngress.com/solutions** and click on the **"Ask the Author"** form.

Q: How can I keep track of changes to a policy without saving it with a new name?

A: From the Global Properties window, select **SmartDashboard Customization**. Check the box in the **Database Revision Control to create new version upon Install Policy operation**. This action will ask for a name for this version of the Rule Base. Then, by selecting **File | Database Revision Control...** or by clicking the button for **Database revision control**, you can change between revisions of the policy without changing the name.

Q: What is the If Via column in the Rule Base used for?

A: When creating policies in simplified mode, you can match traffic based on VPN communities.

Q: How can I tell what NAT rule caused an address translation?

A: There is a new field that will list the NAT rule that was applied in the SmartView Tracker.

Q: Can multiple administrators make different secondary management servers active?

A: Yes, this is one major limitation of Management HA. The problem is that when you have an active management server synchronize with the other management servers, there is no merging of the configuration database. The management server that is synchronizing will overwrite the other servers. With multiple management stations active, administrators can overwrite other administrator changes. You will need to coordinate this logistically in your environment.

Q: When I first install FP3, my management station is configured as a gateway object, but it is only a host. Can I change it to a host?

A: Right-click the object and there will be an option at the bottom to convert to host.

Q: If I upgrade an object to FP3-HF1, will this change be reflected in the Version field of the object?

A: No, the Version field will still read *NG Feature Pack 3*. HF1 will only show up in the SecureUpdate screen.

Chapter 9

Integration and Configuration of CVP / UFP

Solutions in this chapter:

- Using CVP for Virus Scanning E-Mail
- URL Filtering for HTTP Content Screening
- Using Screening without CVP

☑ Summary

☑ Solutions Fast Track

☑ Frequently Asked Questions

Introduction

Despite an airtight rule base, stateful inspection, and a well thought-out SmartDefense implementation, your network still remains susceptible to viruses. Users may inadvertently contract a virus through e-mail or over the Web. Once infected, a user's work station, sitting behind your firewall, grants the virus access to the entire network segment, allowing it to spread unobstructed throughout your network. In addition, you may be inclined to block your users from accessing certain URLs, and CVP allows for this based on a variety of factors.

To combat the threat of virus infection, Check Point Firewall-1 provides content-level filtering via the Content Vectoring Protocol (CVP). CVP allows you to utilize any OPSEC-certified product to perform such tasks as virus scanning, e-mail content screening, and URL filtering via the Uniform Filtering Protocol (UFP). For a complete list of vendors that are part of the OPSEC alliance, see www.opsec.com. These vendors also develop tools that can be used through CVP to enhance the ability of your firewall to combat content-related threats.

In this chapter, we cover several methods of implementing content-level inspection, specifically scanning e-mail for viruses. We also touch on some other CVP/UFP-based OPSEC products and detail any traps and pitfalls you may encounter.

Using CVP for Virus Scanning E-Mail

Although any thorough security policy should include virus protection at the desktop level, it makes sense to consider scanning incoming e-mail for viruses to prevent malicious code from even reaching the PC. The combination of these two levels of virus scanning further reduces the chances of a virus infecting your network.

We first cover a generic CVP solution that will provide you with a good basis for developing a CVP configuration for any environment. Then we describe a practical, real-world environment and the steps required to fit CVP into this environment to alleviate the risk of virus infection via e-mail. The combination of a generic configuration and a specific, practical application will give you the perspective to adapt CVP to your network.

Configuring CVP

To configure CVP, you must first define a CVP server, which is an OPSEC service running on a server; that server may be dedicated to the OPSEC application or shared with other applications.

Next, you must add a resource for virus inspection. The type of resource to add depends on what type of service you are implementing. In this case, we are implementing virus scanning for e-mail, so the appropriate resource type is SMTP (Simple

Mail Transport Protocol), which is the protocol used to deliver mail. There are a number of additional options available in the resource CVP and Action tabs to fine tune how the firewall will handle e-mail filtering and checking, which we cover in the "CVP Configuration" section.

The third and final step required to configure CVP for virus scanning e-mail is to add a rule to your security rule base that has a service type that includes the resource you defined above. When traffic passing through the firewall matches the source, destination, and service specified in the rule, it will redirect this traffic to the resource you defined and use the information gathered by this resource to determine whether to permit or deny the traffic.

Figure 9.1 outlines the steps required to configure CVP.

Figure 9.1 CVP Configuration

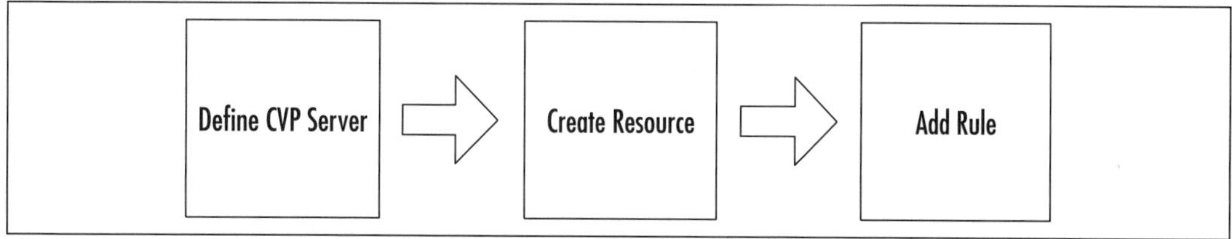

A Generic CVP Solution

Although in this case we describe how to configure CVP for e-mail virus scanning, note that CVP is useful for a number of other applications. For example, some OPSEC applications can filter URLs based on content, inspect the content of Java and Active X applets, and even perform filtering based on SQL database contents.

Although functionality of the OPSEC applications varies, the process of configuring your firewall to utilize any application is quite similar.

Network Layout

As a general CVP configuration, we consider the case of a network with one firewall, one mail server, and a number of user workstations. The users send and receive mail through the mail server, and are protected from the Internet by the firewall by sitting on one of its internal interfaces, and by residing on nonroutable IP addresses. The mail server is also protected by the firewall, but on a different interface, and is also assigned an unroutable IP address. Since the firewall will be communicating with external mail servers, it is not necessary for the actual mail server to reside on a routable IP address; this adds an additional level of security to the network.

The rule base used in this configuration is shown in Figure 9.2. Rule 2 permits internal users to reach external Web servers on the Internet. Rule 3 permits internal users to send mail to the mail server. Rules 4 and 5 permit the mail server to reach and be reached by external mail servers, respectively. Finally, Rule 1 is a standard hide rule, and Rule 6 is a standard cleanup rule, to drop all other traffic.

Figure 9.2 Sample Rule Base

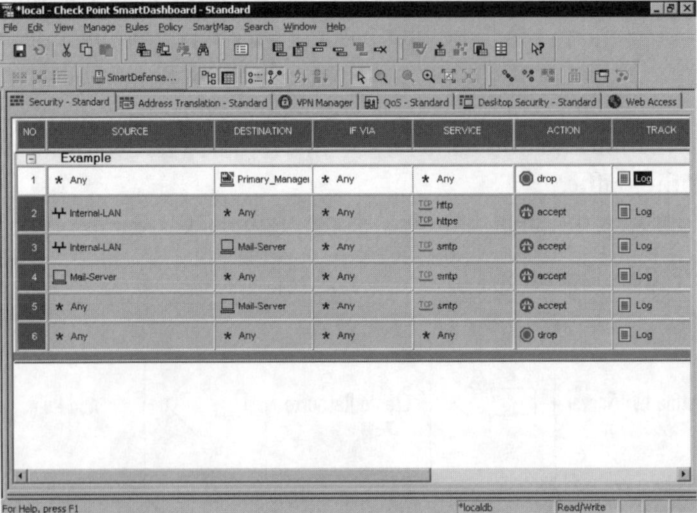

CVP Configuration

Now that you have a good idea of the network configuration, you can begin configuring CVP to protect the internal users from viruses in their e-mail. The first step is to add a CVP server. Before you can add a CVP server to your Check Point configuration, the CVP server itself must already be configured and operational. Setting up a CVP server involves installing an OPSEC-compatible application and configuring it to perform the content check you desire. CVP server configuration is outside the scope of this chapter.

To add a CVP server, first you need to define a host that points to this server. Open the Check Point SmartDashboard and choose **Manage | Network Objects**. Click on **New**, then **Node**, then **Host** (see Figure 9.3).

Here, enter a descriptive **Name** for the CVP server—in this case use "SMTP-CVP". Specify the **IP Address** of the server, and optionally enter a **Comment** to help you identify this object in the future.

The next step is to define the OPSEC application on the CVP server. Choose **Manage | OPSEC Applications**. Click on **New** and then **OPSEC Application** (see Figure 9.4).

Figure 9.3 New Node Properties

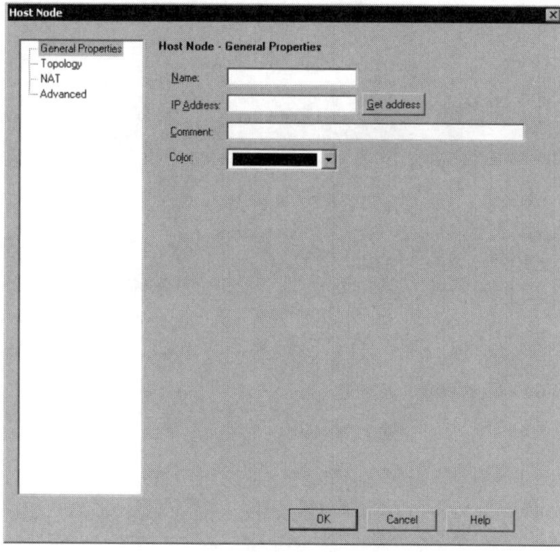

Figure 9.4 New OPSEC Application General Properties

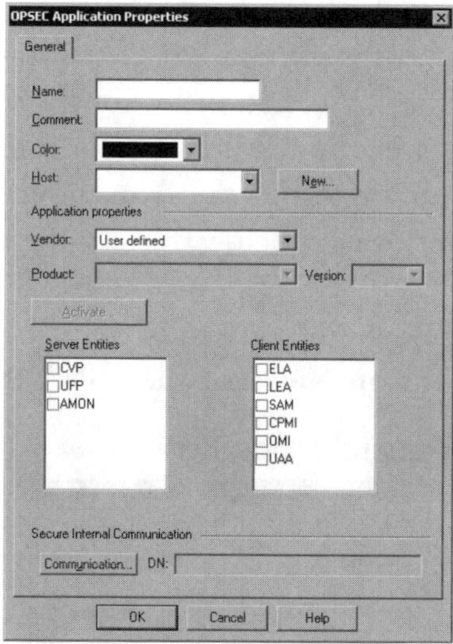

These are the general options for the OPSEC application. Enter a descriptive **Name**—in this case use "Email-virus-CVP". Optionally enter a **Comment**, and choose a **Color** to easily identify this object. For the **Host**, choose **SMTP-CVP**, which is the name of the host object you just defined. For **Vendor**, you may choose the name of the vendor of your particular CVP application, or you may choose **User Defined** if that vendor is not listed. Under **Server Entities**, choose **CVP** and leave all the other check boxes unchecked. Next, click on **CVP Options** (see Figure 9.5).

Figure 9.5 OPSEC Application CVP Options

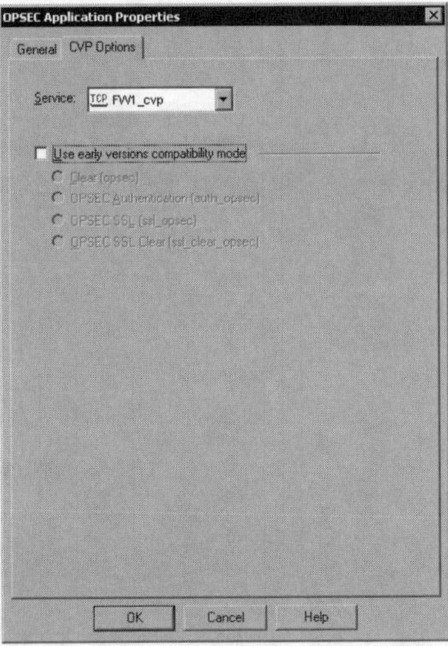

In most cases, you should leave the **Service** set to **FW1_cvp**, which is the TCP port that the CVP application will run on (in this case port 18181). The only case in which you would change this port is if the OPSEC application you are using does not use the standard CVP port, either by design or by your custom configuration.

Enable **Use early versions compatibility mode** if the OPSEC application is written for Firewall-1 4.1 or earlier. In this case, you should consult the OPSEC application's documentation to determine which early version compatibility mode option (Clear, OPSEC Authentication, OPSEC SSL, or OPSEC SSL Clear) to select.

Next, you need to configure an SMTP resource that has CVP enabled. Choose **Manage | Resources** and click on **New** and then **SMTP** (see Figure 9.6).

Figure 9.6 SMTP Resource General Properties

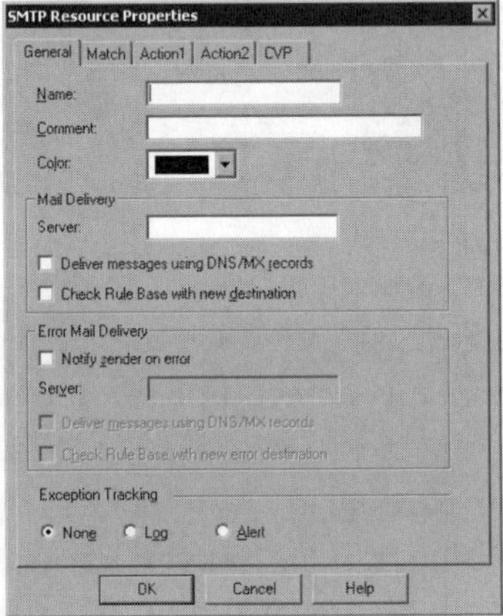

Enter a descriptive **Name**—in this case use "SMTP-Server". Optionally enter a descriptive **Comment**, and choose a **Color** to easily identify this object. Under **Mail Delivery**, set the **Server** to the IP address of your SMTP server. Check **Deliver messages using DNS/MX records** if you would like mail to be delivered based on the MX records for the destination domain. In this case, the mail will not be delivered to the server specified earlier; instead, the firewall will retrieve the MX record for the destination domain and deliver the mail to the first available server found.

Selecting **Check Rule Base with new error destination** instructs the firewall to check the address found from the MX record against the rule base to determine whether traffic should be allowed to this address, and if so, the rule will also determine whether a resource should be used.

The following section deals with what action should be taken if there is an error in mail delivery, such as when mail is sent to an invalid domain or when the destination mailbox does not exist. Selecting **Notify sender on error** instructs the firewall to send a bounce message to the sender with details about why the message was undeliverable. The server specified determines what mail server the bounce message should be sent to. Just as in the Mail Delivery section, here you also have the option to leave the server field empty and check **Deliver messages using DNS/MX records**, as well as setting the option for the firewall to check the rule base before forwarding mail to the server found via the MX record.

The final general option for an SMTP resource is for exception tracking. The choices here are None, Log, or Alert, which specify the method of tracking for actions that are matched from the Action tabs for this resource.

The Match and Action tabs allow for manipulation and control over e-mail outside of CVP functionality. Since the focus of this chapter is CVP configuration, we do not cover these tabs here.

Next, enable and configure CVP for this resource. Go to the **CVP** tab shown in Figure 9.7.

Enable **Use CVP** and then select the **CVP server** you defined earlier: **Email-Virus-CVP**. If you enable **CVP server is allowed to modify content**, the firewall is given the leeway to actually make changes to various properties of e-mail that passes through. You must decide whether or not to enable this option depending on how intrusive you want your SMTP filtering to be.

Check the next option, **Send SMTP Headers to CVP server**, if you would like the CVP server to check e-mail header content, in addition to the content of the body of the e-mail. Enable this option if your CVP application has the ability to screen messages based on variables in the message header.

The **Reply Order** settings specify when the CVP server returns the data it inspects to the security server (in this case, SMTP server). If you select **Return data**

after content is approved, the CVP server waits until it has received and approved all the data for a particular e-mail before returning it to the SMTP server. On the other hand, selecting **Return data before content is approved** instructs the CVP server to return each approved packet as it arrives. Which setting you choose here will largely depend on the nature of the CVP application you are using—consult its documentation for guidance.

Figure 9.7 SMTP Resource CVP Properties

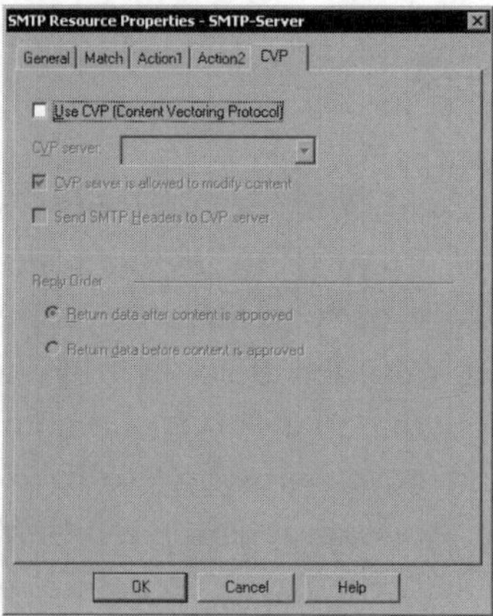

The final step to enabling virus scanning for e-mails is to add the appropriate rules to your rule base (see Figure 9.8).

Figure 9.8 Rule with SMTP Resource

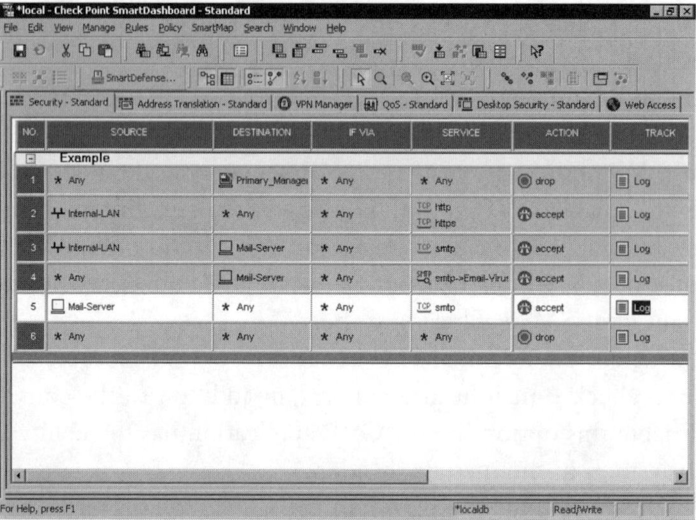

Rule 4 is for SMTP mail services. It permits all sources to send mail via SMTP, but you will notice that in the SERVICE section, the service is listed as "smtp->Email-Virus-CVP". This means that the firewall will redirect traffic that matches this rule to the resource you configured earlier, which will then verify the content of the message with the CVP server you defined.

To add a service with a resource, right-click on the **SERVICE** section and select **Add with Resource** (see Figure 9.9).

Figure 9.9 Adding Service with Resource

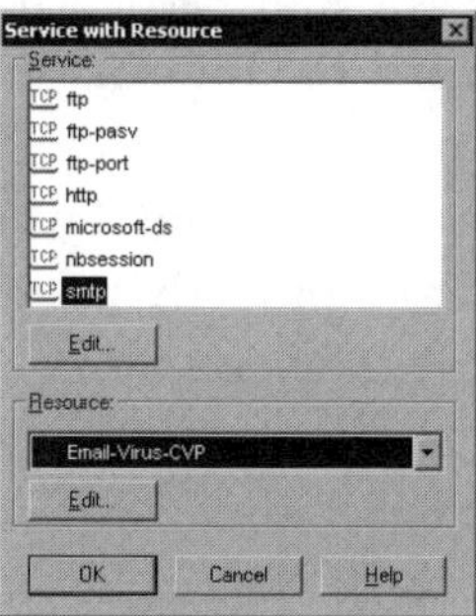

In this case, highlight **smtp—**in other cases you would highlight the service you are configuring—and you will then see the **Resource** section become available. In the drop-down box, select the CVP server you have configured—in this case, **Email-Virus-CVP**—and click **OK**.

Troubleshooting CVP

The most sensible way to troubleshoot CVP is to examine each component and use process of elimination to determine where the problem lies. Because there are a number of components involved—the CVP server, the resource, the SMTP server, and the firewall—troubleshooting can quickly become complex if you look at the process as a whole. Looking at each component separately makes for a much more manageable troubleshooting exercise.

In the case of scanning e-mail for viruses, the first thing you need to do when troubleshooting is accurately collect the symptoms of the problem. What exactly is happening to the e-mail, assuming it has not been delivered successfully? The first place to check is the mail server that hosts the users' mailboxes. Its log files should give you a good indication of whether the e-mail in question even made it as far as the server.

If the server log files show that the e-mail arrived at the server, the reason that e-mail was not delivered may have nothing to do with the firewall—the server may be the culprit. However, if the server log files show no sign of the e-mail, you need to step back and look at the firewall to see what went wrong.

The first thing to check on the firewall is the SmartView Tracker, to make sure the external mail server on the Internet actually attempted to connect and deliver the mail. If you see this connection as dropped, check your rule base to ensure that you have a rule defined to allow SMTP traffic (with a resource in this case) inbound from any source.

If the inbound SMTP connection was accepted, double-check the setup of your CVP server under **Manage | OPSEC Applications** to ensure that you have the correct object and that the object has the correct IP address. If this is correct, the firewall has passed the e-mail to the CVP server, so the next place to check is the CVP server log file. Consult the documentation of your particular CVP server to determine how to access its log files and how to interpret the information contained in them. What you are looking for is proof that the e-mail arrived at the CVP server and information about what happened to the e-mail at that point. For example, the CVP server may indicate that an error prevented it from properly processing the e-mail, in which case you need to troubleshoot that problem by consulting the CVP server documentation.

Once the CVP server is operating normally, it will have returned the e-mail to the firewall. At this point you should recheck the mail server logs to see if the e-mail has arrived there. If not, recheck the SmartView Tracker to determine if anything in your rule base is preventing the e-mail from being delivered.

Finally, if you continue to have difficulties and none of these techniques helps to find the problem, your last resort is to use the **fw monitor** command to monitor packets entering and leaving the firewall, to prove where the problem component is that is preventing the normal flow. Usage of **fw monitor** is outside the scope of this chapter, but your firewall documentation will have syntax and examples.

URL Filtering for HTTP Content Screening

Blocking access to particular Web sites via URL filtering is an effective way to enforce your network or corporate security policies around accessing inappropriate content. The challenge is to ensure that your filtering does not prevent users from accessing sites they legitimately need to view, while blocking access to as many inappropriate sites as possible.

To accomplish this goal, Check Point Firewall-1 integrates with OPSEC applications that conform to the URL filtering protocol, or UFP. There are various UFP servers, but in general a UFP server's role is to maintain a regularly updated list of URLs that users may and may not access. Then, when the firewall receives a request from a user to access a particular URL, it first checks with the UFP server to see whether that URL is permitted and allows or denies the request based on that information.

Setting Up URL Filtering with UFP

Configuring your firewall to have UFP functionality is similar to the earlier exercise where you set up e-mail content filtering. Just as with CVP configuration, this guide assumes you already have a functional CVP application running on a server. For more information on configuring a CVP application, see the documentation provided by each of the OPSEC vendors for their respective products.

The first step to configure URL filtering with UFP is to add a network object that references the IP address of your CVP server. To do this, open the SmartDashboard and choose **Manage | Network Objects**. Choose **New**, then **Node,** then **Host**, since you want to define a server with a single IP (see Figure 9.10).

Figure 9.10 New Host Properties

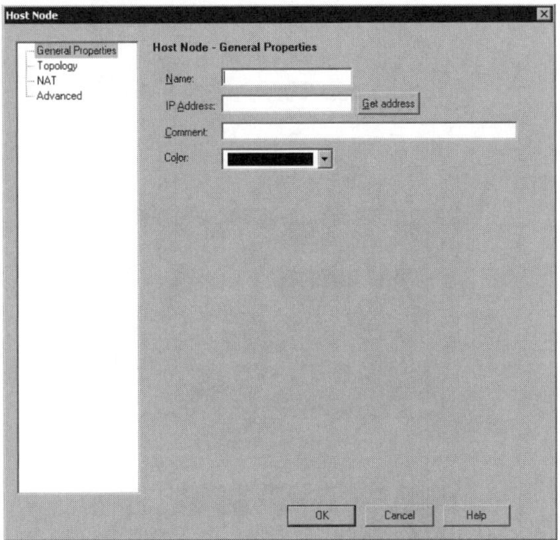

Enter a descriptive **Name** for the UFP server—in this case we will use "UFP-Server-1". Then enter the **IP Address** of the server, and an optional **Comment** and **Color**.

The next step is to define the UFP server as an OPSEC Application. To do this, open the SmartDashboard and choose **Manage | OPSEC Applications**. Here, click on **New** and then **OPSEC Application** (see Figure 9.11).

Select a descriptive **Name** for your UFP server—in this case use "URL-Screener". Enter an option **Comment** and **Color**, and under **Host** choose the network object you defined earlier: **UFP-Server-1**. If the vendor of your UFP server is listed in the **Vendor** drop-down box, select it, as well as the specific product name under **Product** and **Version**. Then, check the **UFP** check box under **Server Entities**, which will cause the UFP Options tab to appear. Click on this tab, which is shown in Figure 9.12.

Figure 9.11 OPSEC Application General Properties

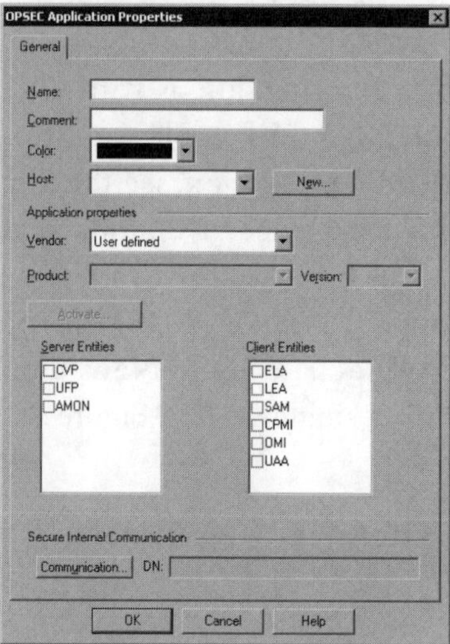

Figure 9.12 UFP Options

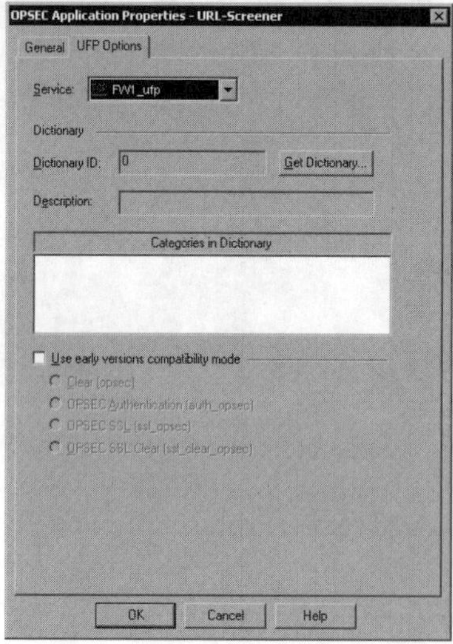

Here, you will generally want to leave **Service** as the default: **FW1_ufp**. This is defined as TCP port 18182, which is the default for most OPSEC applications. The only time you should change this is if the documentation of your OPSEC application specifies a different default port, or you have manually changed the port that your UFP application uses for communication with the firewall.

The next section, **Dictionary**, defines a list of content categories that are used for filtering. Clicking on **Get Dictionary** will result in the firewall requesting a dictionary from the UFP server you have defined. You will then see the **Dictionary ID**, **Description**, and category list populated by the UFP server.

Choose **Use early versions compatibility mode** if your UFP server is designed for Firewall-1 4.1 or earlier. In this case, you must also choose the encryption and/or authentication method compatible with the server.

Next, you need to define a URI resource. To do this, choose **Manage | Resources**, and choose **New** and then **URI** (see Figure 9.13).

Figure 9.13 URI Resource Properties

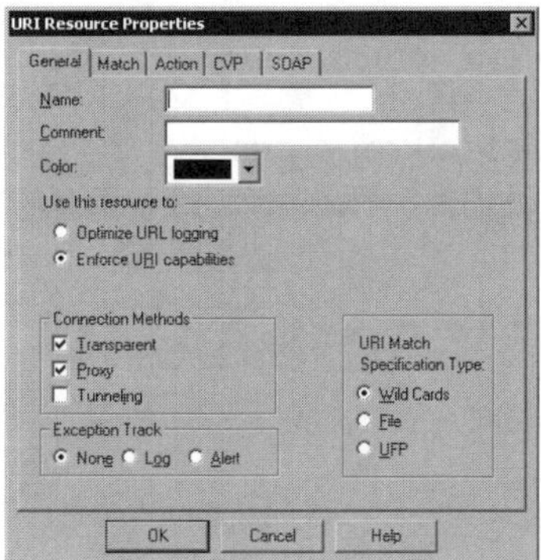

Here, choose a descriptive **Name** for the resource—in this case use "HTTP-with-CVP". Optionally enter a **Comment** and **Color**. Choose **Enforce URI capabilities** in the next section, which instructs the firewall to use this resource to permit or deny HTP traffic based on the information returned from this resource.

The **Connection Methods** options relate to the different ways users can open connections to Web sites. In general, you should select **Transparent**, which matches requests that do not come through a proxy, and **Proxy**, which matches requests that do come through a proxy. Selecting **Tunneling** removes your ability to define content security for this object, so do not select it in this case.

Tools & Traps…

Tunneling Connection Method

Choosing the tunneling connection method restricts the firewall to checking only the hostname and port number of the HTTP request. As a result, your ability to screen requests for content is limited. Use this option only when a Check Point security server is used as a Web proxy for your users, since in this case the security server can provide additional control through authentication.

For **Exception Track**, choose the destination of informational messages generated as a result of this object. In general, at least select **Log** initially to gather information in case of difficulties that require troubleshooting.

Set the **URI Match Specification Type** to **UFP** in this case, since you are defining this resource in order to use a UFP server for URL screening. In other cases, you could select **File** to list URLs you would like to block in a file that the firewall will reference, or **Wild Cards** to manually enter a list of URLs, in wild card format, to have the firewall block. Note that the option you select here affects the makeup of the subsequent tabs for this resource.

Next, click on the **Match** tab, which is shown in Figure 9.14.

Figure 9.14 URI Resource Match Properties

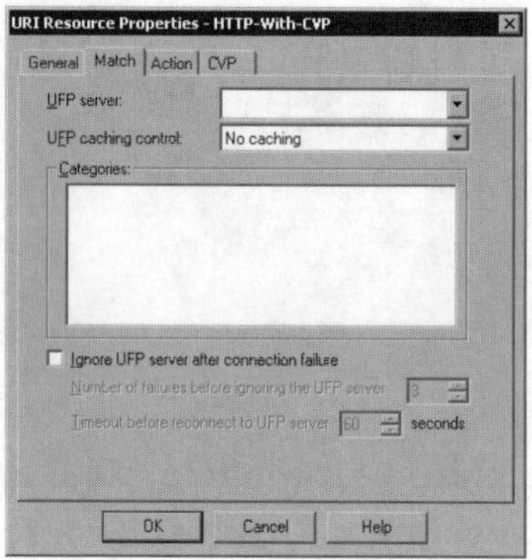

For **UFP Server**, select the UFP server you defined earlier: **URL-Screener**. Next, you will need to choose a caching method under **UFP caching control**. Caching allows you to increase the performance of the UFP filtering mechanism, but at the risk of using outdated data to decide whether or not to block a URL. Choices here are **No caching**, which disables caching completely, resulting in the best data accuracy but poorest performance; **UFP Server**, which allows the UFP server to perform caching; and **VPN-1 & Firewall-1**, which enables caching via the firewall. The last option allows you to specify **one request** or **two requests**, which indicates the number of identical requests the firewall must receive for a particular URL before updating its cache.

The list of **Categories** will be filled in once you retrieve the dictionary from the UFP server as outlined earlier in this section. Then, you can choose which categories you would like to trigger a match. This allows you to customize your content screening to a high degree because you can base your category selection on corporate etiquette policies.

Choose **Ignore UFP server after connection failure** to instruct the firewall to prevent against a failed UFP server from disabling all Web access from your network. In the case of a UFP server failure, the firewall will begin to ignore the UFP server after the specified number of connection attempts, and for the specified timeout, thereby allowing Web access during that time.

Next, choose the **Action** tab, which is shown in Figure 9.15.

Figure 9.15 URI Resource Action Properties

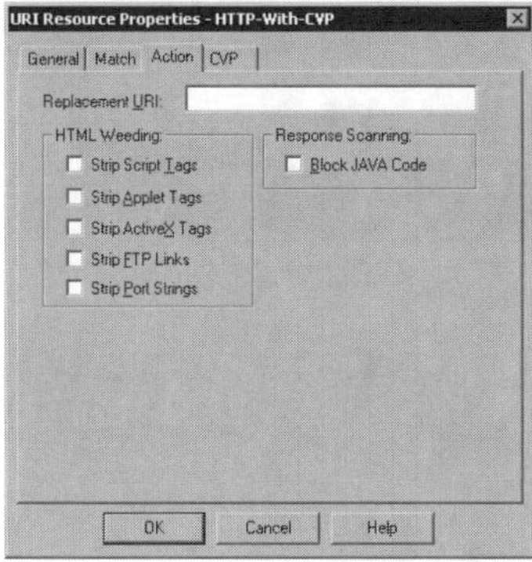

Here, enter a **Replacement URI** of a Web page you would like users to see if they attempted to access a URI that matches and is rejected as appropriate by the firewall. For example, you could create a Web page on a local Web server explaining your corporate security policy, that the URI the user was attempting to access was rejected, and what action the user could take if they felt this restriction was in error.

You may also choose from a variety of **HTML Weeding** and **Response Scanning** options, which further allow you to screen URL content through the removal of tags, links, strings, and code.

Damage & Defense…

HTML Weeding

Removing potentially harmful items in an incoming Web page is an important factor to consider when designing your security model. For example, malicious Web designers may include links to scripts or ActiveX programs that could potentially do damage to a user's workstation. By configuring your firewall to strip these tags, you eliminate this threat. However, be careful to consider potentially legitimate content that may end up removed.

The final step to enabling UFP to screen URL content is to add a rule to your general rule base that specifies the resource you created earlier. To do this, open the SmartDashboard (see Figure 9.16).

Figure 9.16 Rule Base with Resource Rule

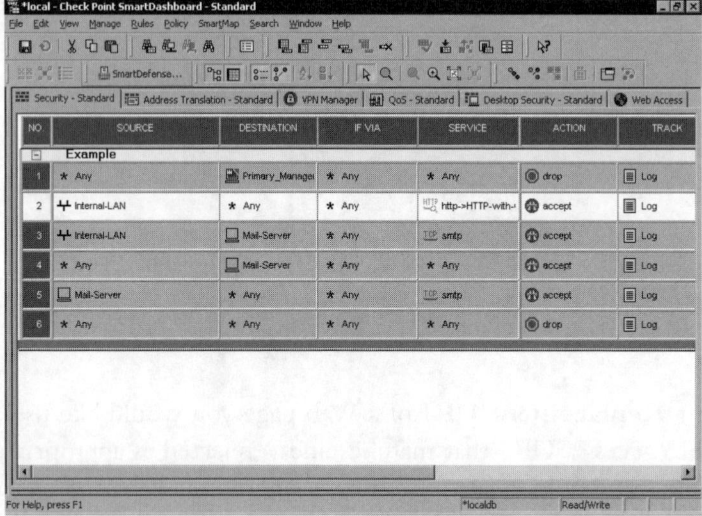

Rule 2 specifies that traffic from any of your internal networks destined for any external source, with service HTTP, will be directed to the "HTTP-with-CVP" resource, which will then examine the request and deal with it as specified. To add the service with a resource, right-click on the **SERVICE** box and choose **Add with Resource** (see Figure 9.17).

Figure 9.17 Adding HTTP with Resource

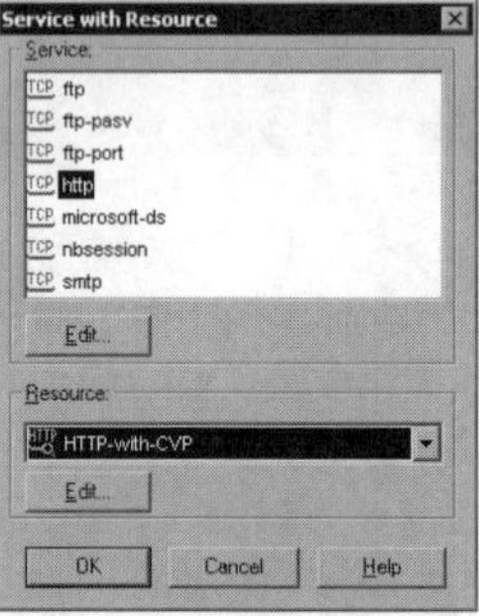

Here, for **Service** choose **http**, and then under **Resource** select the UFP-based resource you defined earlier: **HTTP-with-CVP**.

Using Screening without CVP

Screening URLs for content can also be accomplished without CVP. There are two other options Firewall-1 provides in this case: wild card and file-based matching.

To configuring your firewall for non-CVP-based URL screening, follow the same procedure used for CVP-based screening (see the earlier section "CVP Configuration"). The only difference comes when setting up the resource. In this case, we go through the available options in the case of wild card and file matching.

To create a resource with wild card matching, from the SmartDashboard choose **Manage | Resources**, choose **New**, and then **URI**. The options for the General tab should be filled in as you did back in Figure 9.13, but choose **Wild Cards** under **URI Match Specification Type**. Choose the **Match** tab, which is shown in Figure 9.18.

Figure 9.18 URI Resource Match Properties

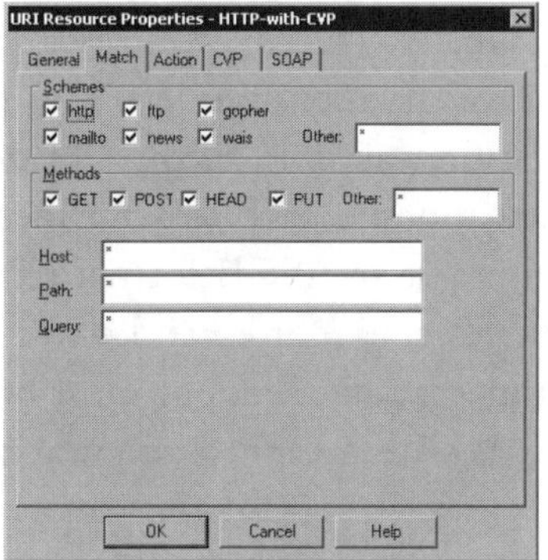

The Match tab specifies the properties of the user's URL request that must be present in order for the firewall to conclude a match and take the action specified in the Action tab. Choose from a variety of **Schemes**, which dictate the general type of request (http, ftp, gopher, and so on), or even specify a custom scheme under **Other**. Next, select the **Methods** that must be matched, from **GET**, **POST**, **HEAD**, or **PUT**, and again you have the option of specifying a custom method under **Other**. Finally, you can specify **Host**, **Path**, and **Query** text to match from the user's requests. All of these fields accept wild card characters, which means you can enter a host such as "www.sports*" to match all hosts that begin with "www.sports".

The Action tab behaves just as in the UFP section.

To create a resource with file matching, from the SmartDashboard choose **Manage | Resources**, choose **New**, and then **URI**. Again, the options for the General tab behave as shown earlier, but choose **File** under **URI Match Specification Type**. Choose the **Match** tab, which is shown in Figure 9.19.

Figure 9.19 URI Resource Match Properties

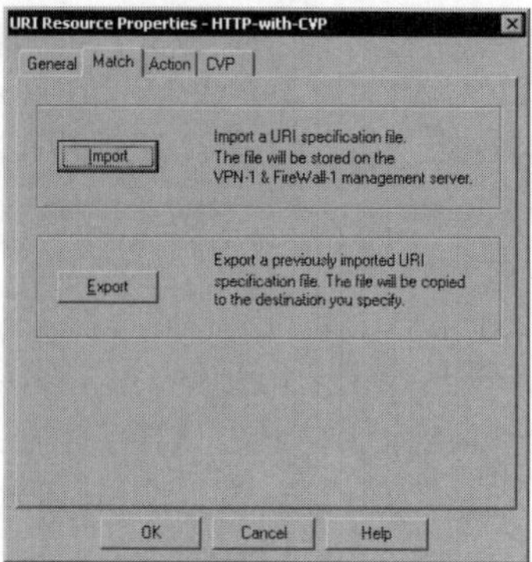

Notice that the Match tab contains only two options: **Import** and **Export**. The **Import** option allows you to specify a file on your local computer that contains data about what constitutes a match of the user's request. This file is subsequently stored on the management module of the firewall. The **Export** option allows you to save a copy of that data on the management module back to your local workstation.

The file that you import must be in ASCII format (plain text), and contain three fields per line, each line representing a record. Field one specifies an IP address, field two the URI path, and field three is not used, but must not be blank, so enter any "1". Again, the **Action** tab behaves as with a UFP configuration.

Summary

A security policy that works on a variety of levels is most likely to be effective. One such level is content screening, and this level of security provides for a great deal of control over network access.

Check Point's Content Vectoring Protocol is a powerful tool that, among other things, allows you to scan e-mail for viruses to prevent malicious code from ever arriving in a user's mailbox. The URI Filtering Protocol allows you to control what Web sites users may visit, thereby enforcing corporate policies on appropriate Web access.

Due to the flexible nature of CVP, OPSEC vendors are free to develop applications to solve any number of problems related to content. There are currently more than 300 OPSEC partners, and although the purpose of many of the OPSEC applications are the same, the variety of choice allows you to pick the application with the feature set that best suits your needs.

Combine content filtering with a solid overall security policy, and the risk of security issues is greatly reduced.

Solutions Fast Track

Using CVP for Virus Scanning E-Mail

- ☑ Add a network object that references the IP address of the CVP server.
- ☑ Add and configure the CVP server OSPEC application, setting the desired options.
- ☑ Configure a resource that makes use of the CVP server, to be referenced in the rule.
- ☑ Add a rule to the rule base that will match SMTP to the mail server and set it to use the CVP resource.

URL Filtering for HTTP Content Screening

- ☑ Add a network object that references the IP address of the UFP server.
- ☑ Add and configure the UFP server OPSEC application, setting the desired options.
- ☑ Configure a resource that makes use of the CVP server, to be referenced in the rule.

☑ Add a rule to the rule base that will match HTTP traffic and set it to use the UFP resource.

Using Screening without CVP

☑ Add a network object that references the IP address of the CVP server.

☑ Add and configure the CVP server OPSEC application, and choose the wild card method to manually enter URLs to match or choose the file method to import a file with a list of URLs to match.

☑ Use the file method when the list of URLs is too long to enter manually, so that the list can be maintained in an external file.

Frequently Asked Questions

The following Frequently Asked Questions, answered by the authors of this book, are designed to both measure your understanding of the concepts presented in this chapter and to assist you with real-life implementation of these concepts. To have your questions about this chapter answered by the author, browse to **www.syngress.com/solutions** and click on the **"Ask the Author"** form.

Q: Can I use CVP to screen both incoming and outgoing e-mail?

A: Yes. The firewall knows when to use CVP to screen e-mail based on the rule base. So to add CVP-based screening for outgoing e-mail, add a rule with a resource that will be matched for outgoing SMTP requests.

Q: Once I set up UFP to prevent users from accessing certain URLs, can I make a user exempt?

A: Yes, as long as you know the user's IP address—you should ensure that it is static. In this case, add a rule in the rule base above the UFP rule that does not contain a resource. The user's HTTP requests will match this rule and bypass the UFP check.

Q: Can I use the same server for both CVP and UFP?

A: Yes. In this case, when defining the OPSEC application object, check both UFP and CVP and configure both tabs. Then, reference the same OPSEC application object when defining resources.

Q: When should I use CVP as opposed to wild card or file-based matching?

A: This depends mostly on your security policy for filtering. CVP allows for more dynamic and versatile filtering; the other two methods are more static, and they change only when you choose to manually update your configuration. If your policy is only to block an unchanging number of URLs, a CVP server is probably not necessary.

Q: What caching control method should I use for UFP?

A: The level of caching to use is a balance between speed and accuracy. If you disable caching, you are guaranteed accurate results, but performance may become unacceptably slow. You may also opt to have the server perform the caching, if your UFP server supports that option. Overall, you may have to adjust your caching level based on observing performance and accuracy over time.

Chapter 10

SecureClient Packaging Tool

Solutions in this chapter:

- Creating a Profile
- Managing SecureClient Profiles
- Creating SecureClient Installation Packages
- Deploying SecuRemote Packages

☑ Summary

☑ Solutions Fast Track

☑ Frequently Asked Questions

Introduction

Once you've decided to enable remote users to access your internal network through a VPN connection, you still face the tricky issue of configuring the remote users' machines. Fortunately, Check Point provides the SecureClient Packaging Tool, which can largely automate this process.

The SecureClient Packaging Tool, which consists mostly of two wizards for creating profiles and packages, allows administrators to create customized SecuRemote and SecureClient installation applications. These installation packages can provide seven specific benefits:

- The administrator can create, test, and debug an installation package and then provide a consistent, working, repeatable process for what can be a tricky installation.
- Users need only run the installation package and reboot.
- The installation can be automatically configured with specific default settings.
- The package can be configured for "silent installation," in which the user does not have to make configuration decisions.
- The administrator can customize the flow of the end user's installation process.
- The administrator can manually configure additional options for the client installation.
- It's easier to distribute a single executable to users than an entire directory of configuration files.

Notes from the Underground...

If There's Any Doubt

If you're not sure whether you should roll out your VPN solution to remote users using the SecureClient Packaging tool, it's often best to err on the side of implementing with an installation package rather than without. Check Point FireWall-1 is fairly complex; this is a good opportunity to shield your end users from some of that complexity.

Installing the SecureClient Packaging Tool

It's easy to install the SecureClient Packaging tool. You will usually find that it's already been installed for you by default. If it has not been installed, you can easily add it to your existing suite of installed SMART Clients.

Installing by Default

If you have installed the Check Point SMART Clients, the default installation option includes the SecureClient Packaging tool. Since the application is small, it's recommended that you accept the installation utility's default choices and allow the packaging tool to be installed along with the rest of the SMART Clients.

Installing Explicitly

It's also easy to explicitly install the tool:

1. Run the **Check Point Management Clients** installation.
2. In the Installed Products window, select **SecureClient Packaging Tool** and continue with the installation utility.

Starting the SecureClient Packaging Tool

There are two ways to start the SecureClient Packaging Tool:

- Launch it from the operating system, *or*
- Have FireWall-1 launch it for you.

The first method is fairly simple; just run **Start | Programs | Check Point SMART Clients | SecureClient Packaging Tool NG FP3**.

Experienced FireWall-1 administrators also know that a fast and easy way to launch one of the SMART Clients if they're already logged into another of the SMART Clients is to use the **Window** menu or the keyboard shortcuts and launch the client directly without having to reauthenticate. In all the SMART Clients except SmartView Dashboard, the menu choice is **Window | SecureClient Packaging Tool**. and the keyboard shortcut is **Ctrl + Shift + K**.

There's one hitch that needs to be considered, however. You cannot be logged in to the SmartView Dashboard and the SecureClient Packaging Tool simultaneously if you're requesting read/write permissions in both. For example, if you're editing your security policy with SmartView Dashboard and try to launch the SecureClient Packaging tool, you'll see the dialog box in Figure 10.1.

Figure 10.1 Read-Only Requirement Dialog Box

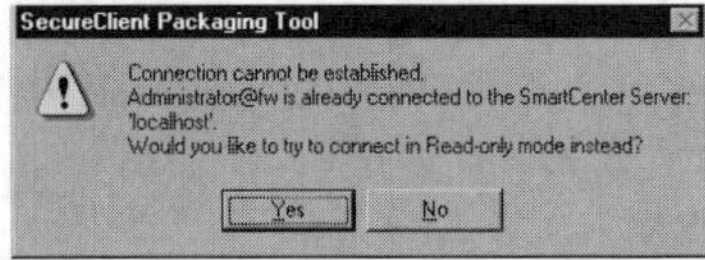

It's probably best to log out of SmartView Dashboard before building any SecureClient installation packages anyway, because you don't want the opportunity to change your firewall configuration in the middle of building an installation package that relies on that very configuration. It is probably for this reason that the menu choice and keyboard shortcut for the SecureClient Packaging tool are both absent in the SmartView Dashboard client.

When you see the screen shown in Figure 10.2, you've successfully installed and launched the SecureClient Packaging tool. You're now ready to begin creating a profile.

Figure 10.2 Successfully Launching the SecureClient Packaging Tool

Creating a Profile

The first step in creating a SecureClient Installation package is to create a new user profile. This is done through the SecureClient Packaging Tool wizard. To launch the wizard, choose one of these three methods:

- Select **Profile | New** from the menu.
- Press **Ctrl-N**.
- Click the **New** icon on the toolbar.

Let's now walk through the windows you will see.

The Welcome Window

The first window (see Figure 10.3) is the Welcome window. Seeing this window is your confirmation that you've successfully launched the wizard. Click **Next** to continue.

Figure 10.3 The Welcome Window

The General Window

The second window (see Figure 10.4) is the General window.

Figure 10.4 The General Window

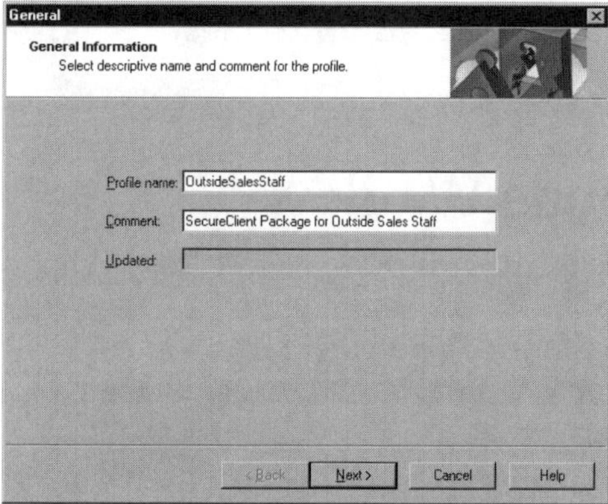

In the General window, the administrator defines two properties for the new user profile and can verify the last time this profile was changed. There are three fields on this screen to pay attention to:

- **Profile name** Enter a descriptive profile name. (Remember that you might be selecting this profile later from a list of profiles.) The name cannot contain any spaces and may not be longer than 256 characters. In this example, we've entered **OutsideSalesStaff** because it's a good, clear name of a group of employees who need remote access.

- **Comment** Enter a descriptive comment. Here the text can be in natural language. This will provide further clues to someone reviewing a list of profiles later.
- **Updated** The date and time of the last update to this profile will appear in this field. The field is currently grayed out because this is a new profile.

Once you've entered the profile name and comment, click **Next** to continue.

Tools & Traps...

Naming and Describing Your Policies

Be sure to use a fully descriptive name and comment for your profiles. The point is to ensure that the next human who comes along (it might very well be you!) can instantly understand the purpose of a given profile. You also might start appreciating the benefits of having multiple profiles and need to keep clear on their different uses as the count starts increasing.

The Connect Mode Window

The third window (see Figure 10.5) is the Connect Mode window.

Figure 10.5 The Connect Mode Window

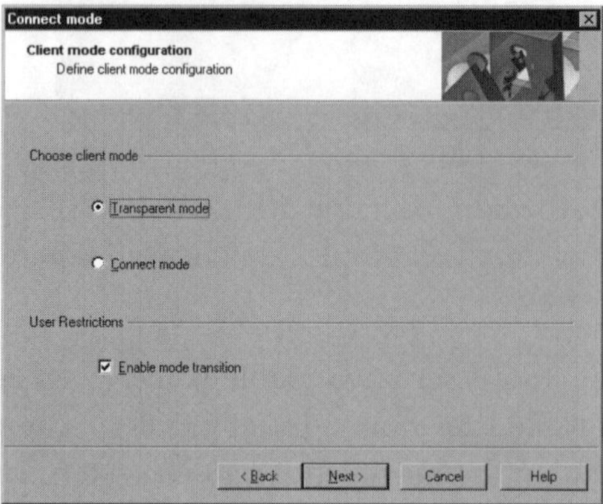

There are two ways to initialize an encrypted connection between SecuRemote/SecureClient and a VPN-1 gateway: Transparent mode and Connect mode. The Connect Mode window allows the administrator to select the mode that will be used and whether the user can switch from one mode to the other (mode transition). Once you have made your selection on the Connect Mode window, click **Next** to continue. Before you do so, let's take a look at these three options.

Transparent Mode

In Transparent mode, the user simply attempts to connect to resources behind the VPN-1 gateway as though the encrypted connection already existed. Only when the first packet tries to reach a host within the encryption domain will the encrypted connection become initialized. This is known as *Transparent mode* because the initialization is transparent to the user.

NOTE

Transparent mode was the only mode available in versions prior to NG Feature Pack 1.

Connect Mode

In Connect mode, connection and disconnection events are specifically defined. The user is required to connect to the site before attempting to access hosts within the encryption domain. Prior to this explicit connection event, packets that might otherwise travel over the VPN are simply dropped.

Table 10.1 shows the differences between the two modes.

Table 10.1 Transparent Mode vs. Connect Mode

Client Mode	Transparent mode	Connect mode
User Input	None required (hence, it's "transparent")	Explicit connect and disconnect events are required
SecuRemote/ SecureClient Versions	All versions	Only NG Feature Pack 1 and later
What Happens If User Tries to Connect to Host in Encryption Domain	First packet initiates the encrypted connection	Packets dropped until explicit event is completed
When Typically Preferred	For remote users who generally don't come in to the office and want a simpler experience	For users who need to connect on occasions both from over the Internet and while connected to the local LAN

Mode Transition

The user might want to change from one mode to the other. By setting this check box, the administrator can explicitly allow or disallow this transition.

The SecureClient Window

The fourth window (see Figure 10.6) is the SecureClient window. There are several options to choose from on this window:

- **Allow clear connections for Encrypt action when inside the encryption domain** Checking this box allows a special exception to a rule the administrator may establish in the Desktop Security Rule Base. If a rule specifies that the action is Encrypt, the connection is normally allowed only if it is encrypted. However, if both the source and destination are within the encryption domain, it might be unnecessary to encrypt the connection. Checking this option allows these special unencrypted connections to be accepted with this rule.
- **Accept DHCP response without explicit inbound rule** If the administrator has not explicitly created a rule in the Desktop Security Rule Base allowing DHCP packets to flow, remote users may be denied access even to the fundamental step of getting an IP address. Checking this option allows DHCP packets to flow, even if they aren't explicitly permitted by the Rule Base.
- **Restrict SecureClient user intervention** The SecureClient Policy menu normally contains a *Disable Policy* command, allowing the user to entirely opt out of the desktop security policy. Checking this option disables this menu choice.
- **Log on to Policy Server at SecureClient startup** If this option is enabled, SecureClient will automatically attempt to log on to the default policy server.
- **Choose default Policy Server** Choose the policy server that SecureClient will attempt to log on to at startup.
- **Enable Policy Server Load sharing at SecureClient startup** Enabling this option instructs SecureClient to log on to any available policy server.

Figure 10.6 The SecureClient Window

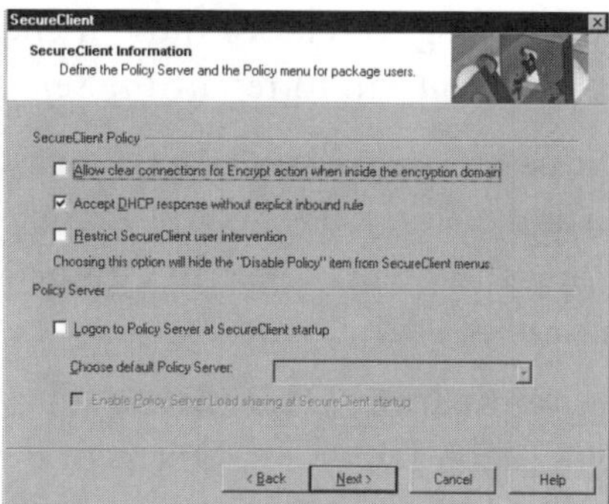

Notes from the Underground…

Encrypting Connections Within the Encryption Domain

Decide if you really need to encrypt connections for which both the source and destination are within the encryption domain. If the main purpose of a VPN is to provide a private, encrypted, authenticated tunnel through the public Internet, it might not be worth the encryption overhead to do the same through your internal network. Some organizations may require this additional security within the encryption domain; most will not.

Once you have made your selections, click **Next** to continue.

The Additional Options Window

The fifth window (see Figure 10.7) is the SecureClient window. The options in this window include the following:

- **IKE over TCP (with supporting gateways)** Phase 1 of IKE negotiations is normally conducted over UDP. Enable this option if you want to use TCP instead.
- **Force UDP encapsulation for IPSec connections** IPSec connections are normally conducted over TCP. However, this can cause some incompatibilities with some NAT implementations. Enable this option to encapsulate IPSec connections within UDP packets to possibly resolve these issues.
- **Do not allow the user to stop SecuRemote** By default there is a Stop VPN-1 SecuRemote or Stop VPN-1 SecureClient menu option in the

System tray menu and in the File menu of the SecuRemote/SecureClient application. Enable this setting to remove those menu options. A SecureRemote Watchdog will run to restart the service if it is stopped.

- **Block all connections when passwords are erased** The SecureClient Passwords menu contains an Erase Passwords option. If you enable this option for the profile, choosing this menu command immediately blocks all encrypted communications.
- **Use third-party authentication DLL (SAA)** Third-party OPSEC partners can provide an authentication DLL compliant with the Secure Authentication API (SAA). The functionality of these products can include challenge/response tokens, biometrics, PKI, smartcards, authentication servers, and directory servers. If you are using one of these products, identify the appropriate DLL here.

Click **Next** to continue once you have made your selections.

Figure 10.7 The Additional Options Window

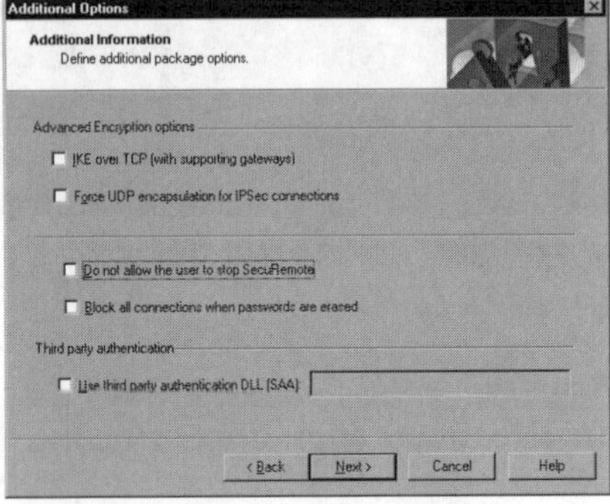

Tools & Traps...

Advanced Encryption Options and Connect Mode

Previously, in the Connect Mode window, you chose between Transparent mode and Connect mode. If you chose Connect mode, these two Advanced Encryption options will not be effective in the SecureClient profile.

The Topology Window

The sixth window (see Figure 10.8) is the Topology window.

Figure 10.8 The Topology Window

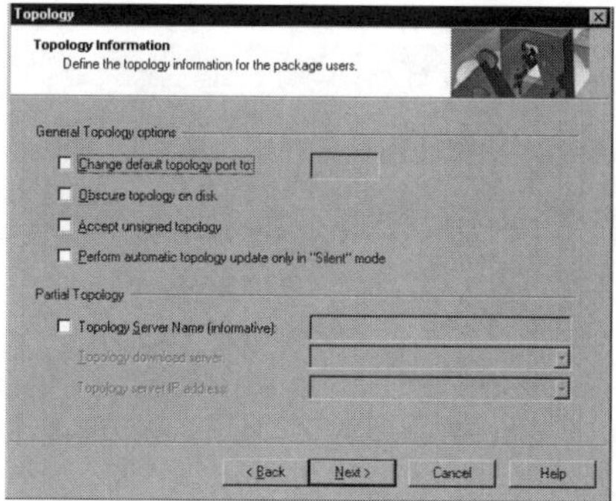

From the Topology window, we can set the following:

- **Change default topology port to** By default, the SecuRemote client connects to port 264 on the firewall and obtains the topology information. In the rare event that port 264 is in use by another application, you may select another port number here. Remember that a change here needs to be matched with a corresponding change in the firewall policy itself.
- **Obscure topology on disk** By default, the topology information is stored in plain text in the userc.C file. This could present a security risk. By selecting this option, the topology information is stored in an obscured (encrypted) format.
- **Accept unsigned topology** To ensure that the topology information has not been compromised, it should be authenticated in some way. The preferred method is through user authentication, in which the user and the VPN-1/FireWall-1 identities are mutually authenticated. A less preferred method is for the management server to sign the topology information with its FWZ key, allowing the client to authenticate the information. If you want the client to also accept unsigned topology information, select this option.
- **Perform automatic topology update only in "Silent" mode** If this option is selected, the client will silently download a new topology after every key exchange, without informing the user.
- **Topology Server Name (informative)** Enter a descriptive name for the partial topology site here.
- **Topology Download Server** Select a single object to be the server used for the initial topology download.
- **Topology server IP address** Enter the IP address of the interface on the topology download server to be used for the topology download.

Damage & Defense...

Publishing Your Installation Packages

After you've created your installation package, you need a way to easily distribute the package to your users. A common method is to publish it on a Web site accessible to remote users. If the package contains topology information, this might be a way for sensitive network configuration information to fall into the wrong hands. A clever way to solve this problem is to use Partial Topology. This method delays the distribution of the topology information until after the user authenticates to the firewall. The user will be prompted with "Click here to update site," and if the management server is configured to require authentication for topology exchange, your rollout can still limit topology information to authenticated users. If Partial Topology is not used, the customized package will contain no site information.

Once you have made your selections, click **Next** to continue.

The Certificates Window

The seventh window (see Figure 10.9) is the Certificates window. From this window we set the following:

- **Certificate Authority IP address** Enter the IP address and port number for the Entrust Certificate Authority. This information will be written to entrust.ini.
- **LDAP server IP Address** Enter the IP address and port number for the LDAP server. This information will be written to entrust.ini.
- **Use Entrust Intelligence** Choose this option and the client will attempt to use the Entrust Entelligence toolkit, if it is installed.

Click **Next** to continue once you have made your selections.

Figure 10.9 The Certificates Window

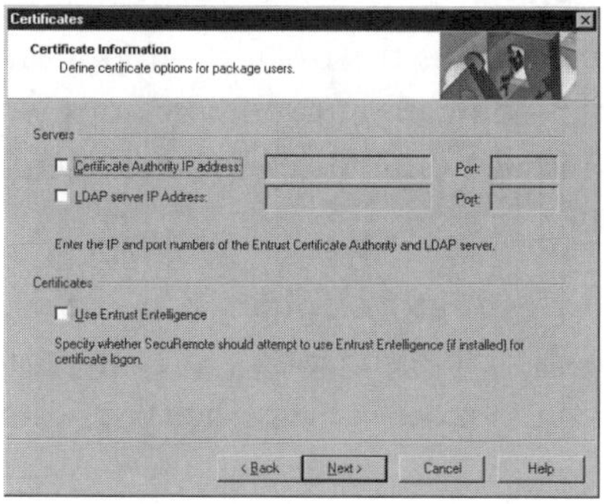

The Silent Installation Window

The eighth window (see Figure 10.10) is the Silent Installation window.

Figure 10.10 The Silent Installation Window

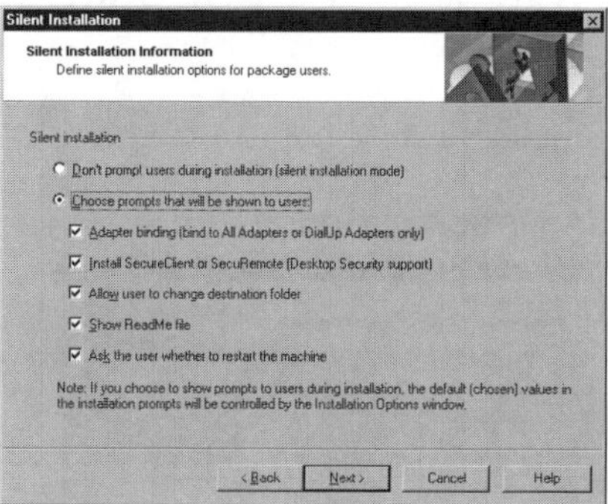

As we like to say in the IT business, what if your end users are just "normal" people? What if they use IT simply as a means to an end? After spending years "in the trenches," it might be hard for an IT specialist to believe that not everyone shares his or her desire to tweak and fiddle with every possible configuration option. Here in the Silent Installation window ,you'll find an opportunity to shield your users from unnecessary complexity and possibly shield yourself from unnecessary support issues, which is, of course, an important goal of the SecureClient Packaging tool anyway.

The only decision that you cannot shield your users from during the installation process is whether to accept the end-user license agreement. Other than that, here you have the opportunity to make the process completely silent.

Once you have made your selections, click **Next** to continue.

The Installation Options Window

The ninth window (see Figure 10.11) is the Installation Options window. This configuration window is something of a companion to the previous window in that you're able to set the defaults for the key installation choices you considered allowing the user to make. Your options here include:

- **Default installation destination folder** Choose whether you want the client to install in the default destination folder (typically C:\Program Files\Check Point\SecuRemote) or whether you want to specify a different default folder.
- **Adapters installation** Choose whether you want to install SecuRemote/SecureClient on all adapters (including Ethernet) or on just the dialup adapters.
- **Install SecureClient by default** If this option is selected, the installation program will install SecureClient by default. Otherwise, SecuRemote will be installed by default.

Make your selections and click **Next** to continue.

Figure 10.11 The Installation Options Window

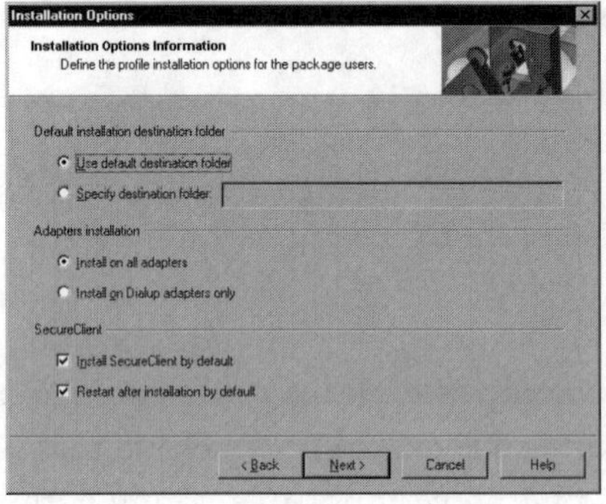

The Operating System Logon Window

The tenth window (see Figure 10.12) is the Operating System Logon window.

Figure 10.12 The Operating System Logon Window

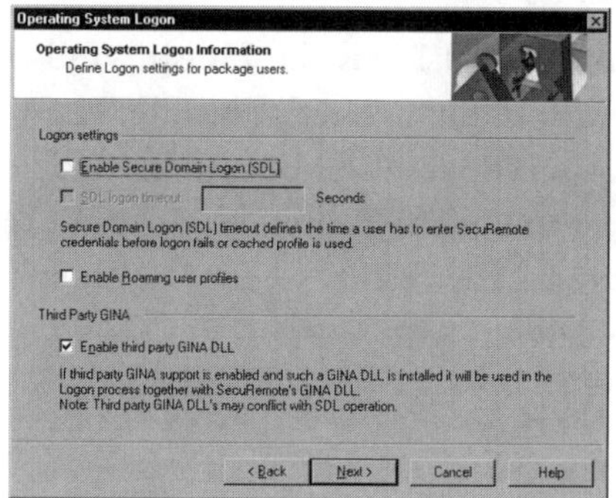

Secure Domain Logon (SDL) allows clients to securely log on to a Windows NT domain controller within the encryption domain, with both LAN and dial-up connections. With SDL, SecuRemote initializes before the domain controller authenticates the domain user. This allows the user's credentials (username and password) as well as the user profile to travel over an encrypted tunnel between the client and the domain controller. Options available on this screen include:

- **Enable Secure Domain Logon (SDL)** Checking this option ensures that SecuRemote/SecureClient is activated before Windows authentication credentials are sent to the domain controller.
- **SDL Logon Timeout** Configure the time (in seconds) during which the user must enter domain controller credentials. The logon will fail if there are no cached logon credentials and the proffered credentials are not entered during this period.
- **Enable Roaming user profiles** Choosing this option will quietly allow the opening of encrypted connections with the domain controller, despite that fact that the connection has been closed by SecuRemote/SecureClient logoff or shutdown. These open connections may be required to enable the proper synchronization of user profiles with the domain controller.
- **Enable third-party GINA DLL** Winlogon is a component of Windows (versions NT and later) that provides interactive logon support. The Winlogon executable works with the Graphical Identification and Authentication (GINA) DLL to implement the authentication policy. By default, Windows loads and executes the standard Microsoft GINA DLL (MSGina.dll). Check this box if your clients might need to authenticate with a third-party GINA DLL replacement.

Make your selections and click **Next** to continue.

The Finish Window

The eleventh window (see Figure 10.13) is the Finish window. Congratulations! You've successfully completed the wizard and created a profile. The profile is stored in a database on the management server and will be available to edit or copy or be the basis for generating a different package in the future. If you were to choose **YES, Create profile and generate package**, the SecureClient Packaging Tool Package Generator wizard would launch immediately.

Figure 10.13 The Finish Window

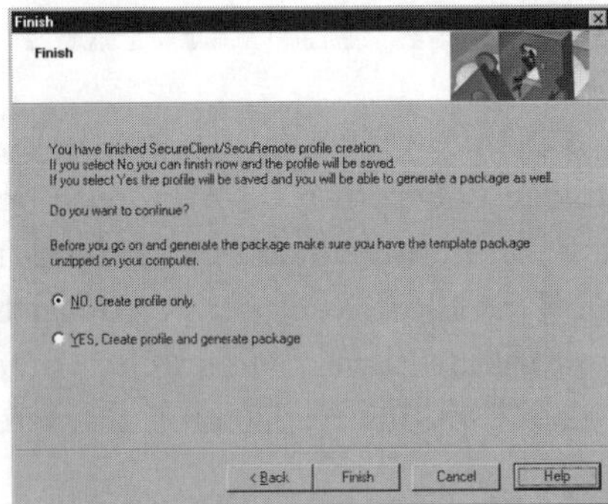

NOTE

The SecureClient Packaging tool uses the configuration options chosen in this wizard to configure the userc.C and Product.ini files (usually located in the SecuRemote\database directory on the client machine). These files can also be edited with a text editor, allowing all the options to be configured.

Click **Finish** to continue and close the wizard.

Managing SecureClient Profiles

Once you're satisfied with the profile that you've created, you'll probably want to create other, related profiles that have minor changes, either for testing purposes or to provide different functionality for different groups of remote users. You might also want to delete or edit an existing profile. These tasks are easy to accomplish in the SecureClient Packaging tool.

Creating a New Profile From an Existing Profile

A perfectly reasonable way to create additional profiles is to copy an existing profile under a different name and then modify its configuration. To do this, follow these steps:

1. Highlight the profile's name in the **Main** window (see Figure 10.14).

Figure 10.14 Selecting an Existing Profile

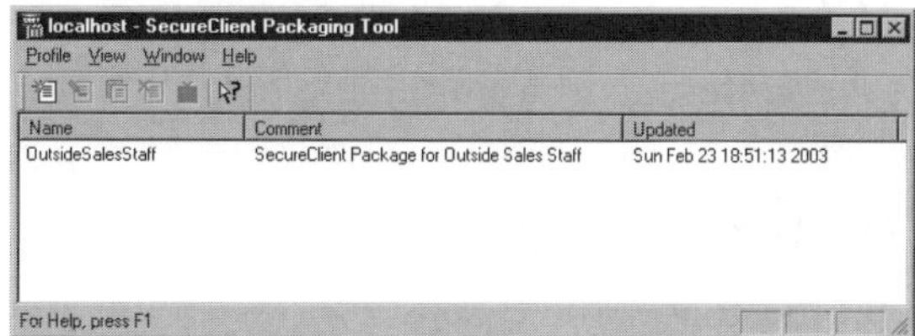

2. Open the **Copy [profile name] to** dialog box (see Figure 10.15) by doing one of the following:
   - Select **Profile | Copy** from the menu.
   - Right-click and then select **Copy** from the menu.
   - Press **Ctrl + C**.
   - Select the **Copy** icon from the toolbar.
3. Enter the new profile name and comment. In this example (see Figure 10.15), we're creating a profile for software developers who work from other locations.

Figure 10.15 The "Copy [profile name] to" Dialog Box

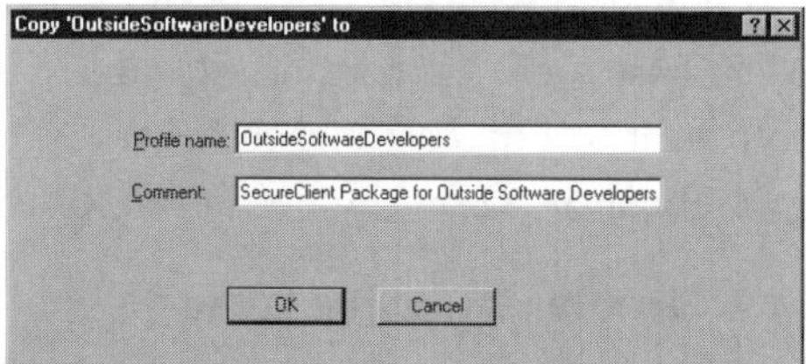

4. Click **OK** to copy the profile and close the dialog box.
5. You can now double-click the new profile name and edit its options.

Deleting a Profile

Deleting a profile is easy. Complete the following steps:

1. Highlight the profile's name in **Main** window (refer back to Figure 10.14).
2. Delete the profile by doing one of the following:

- Select **Profile | Delete** from the menu.
- Right-click and then select **Delete** from the menu.
- Press **Del**.
- Select the **Delete** icon from the toolbar.

Editing a Profile

To edit an existing profile, follow these steps:

1. Highlight the profile's name in **Main** window (refer back to Figure 10.14).
2. Edit the profile by doing one of the following:
   - Select **Profile | Edit** from the menu.
   - Right-click and then select **Copy** from the menu.
   - Press **Ctrl + E**.
   - Select the **Edit** icon from the toolbar.

Creating SecureClient Installation Packages

To create SecureClient Installation packages, launch the SecureClient Packaging tool (if it's not already open) and view the existing profiles (refer back to Figure 10.14). Highlight the profile you want to build a package for and then start the SecureClient Packaging Tool Package Generator wizard by doing one of the following:

- Select **Profile | Generate** from the menu.
- Right-click and then select **Generate** from the menu.
- Press **Ctrl + G**.
- Select the **Generate** icon from the toolbar.

Let's walk through the process window by window.

The Welcome Window

The first window you will see is the Welcome window (see Figure 10.16). Seeing this window is your confirmation that you've successfully launched the wizard. Be sure to heed the warning in the third paragraph in this window. For this wizard to execute, it needs to have access to the special SecuRemote/SecureClient directory so that it can copy all the files it needs. Be sure to have it copied over in advance. Click **Next** to continue.

Figure 10.16 The Welcome Window

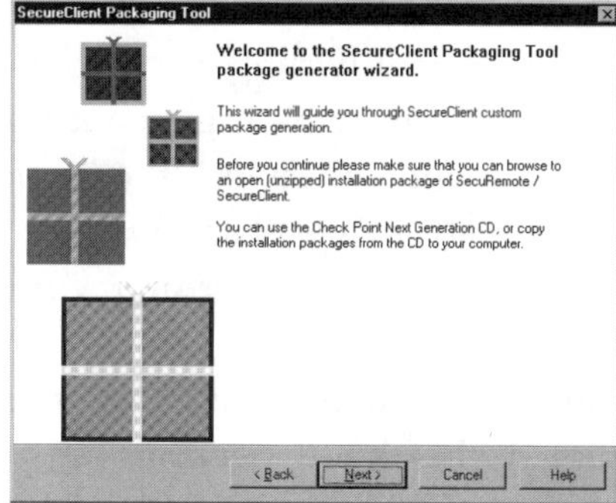

The Package Generation Window

The second window (see Figure 10.17) is the Package Generation window. You shouldn't have a reason to change the offered defaults unless you have an unusual configuration. Keeping it standardized is a way to reduce complexity and errors. Click **Next** to continue.

Figure 10.17 The Package Generation Window

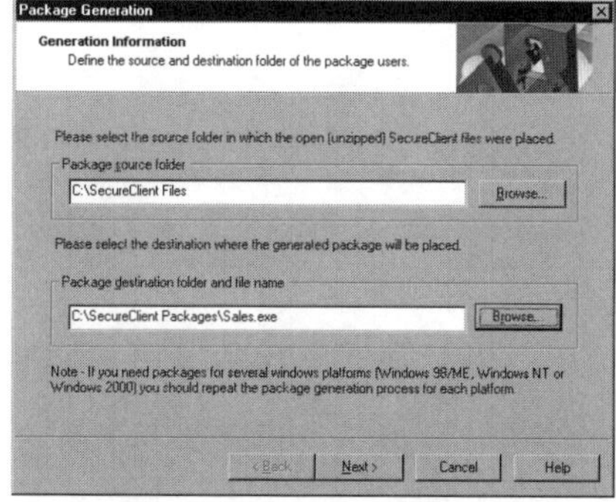

As you can see from Figure 10.18, we've successfully created the installation package. Distribute it to your remote users and you're ready to go!

Figure 10.18 Success!

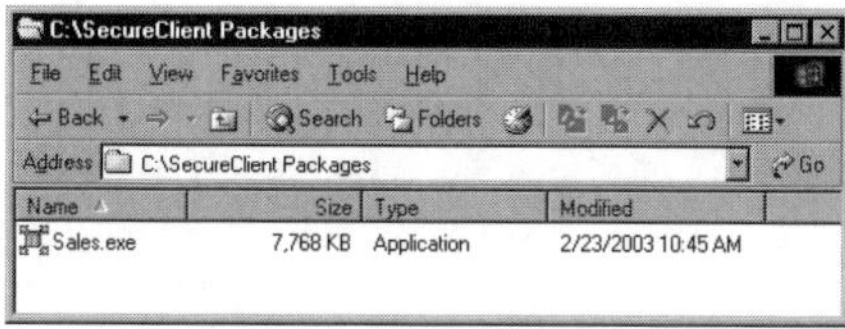

Deploying SecuRemote Packages

The SecureClient Packaging tool is a fairly simple, self-contained utility program. It creates profiles and then creates installation packages containing the profiles. There's really nothing complicated at all about "deploying" them; you just post them on your Web site or send them out on CD-ROMs. In fact, that's the whole point of this utility; once the installation packages are created, the user simply runs them and reboots and they're done.

More sophisticated administrators might want to add some complexity to the deployment process. Even though there's little security risk in a user receiving a spoofed installation package (after all, the software is publicly available and the user still needs to authenticate to the server), you might want to digitally sign the packages (in a ZIP file, say) before distributing them.

A typical installation package is 7MB or 8MB, so it's probably too large to be conveniently e-mailed. Posting on a Web site for downloading could be ideal.

Summary

The SecureClient Packaging tool can significantly reduce complexity in a VPN rollout by enabling you to generate customized installation packages comprising a single executable file to be distributed to users. Within this package, you can set default options, configure for silent installation if desired. and set additional options manually. The user only has to launch the executable, approve the end-user license agreement, and the rest of the installation is automated, presenting to the user only the choices determined by the administrator.

The SecureClient Packaging Tool provides a wizard to assist you, the administrator, in creating user profiles and an easy interface for managing these profiles. The SecureClient Packaging Tool Profile Generator wizard combines the completed profile with the necessary SecuRemote/SecureClient installation files to create a single executable file for distribution to users.

All that's left for the administrator is to distribute the packages to end users. The packages are designed for easy self-installation by users without advanced skills. For more sophisticated enterprises, the administrator might want to implement version control or digital signing of the packages.

Solutions Fast Track

Creating a Profile

- ☑ Close the SmartView Dashboard before trying to launch the SecureClient Packaging tool, because they cannot simultaneously be open with read/write privileges.
- ☑ Use the SecureClient Packaging Tool wizard to create profile for your users.
- ☑ Follow the screen in the wizard to configure all the settings for the automated installation.
- ☑ By configuring the profile to obscure (encrypt) topology information in the userc.C file and to include only partial topology information, you can make the installation package safer for public distribution.

Managing SecureClient Profiles

- ☑ Copy an existing profile and save it under a new name to create new, similar profiles.

- ☑ Edit existing profiles when you need to make changes.
- ☑ Experiment with different versions of your profiles until you get them working properly, and then delete the unneeded copies.

Creating SecureClient Installation Packages

- ☑ Run the SecureClient Packaging Tool Profile Generator wizard to combine a completed profile with the necessary installation files to create an installation package. Be sure to specify the target location for your completed installation packages.
- ☑ Complete the two-screen wizard and you're done!

Deploying SecuRemote Packages

- ☑ Copy the necessary files to the management server before trying to generate a package from a profile.
- ☑ Use the SecureClient Packaging Tool Package Generator wizard to generate ready-to-go installation packages.
- ☑ Be sure to do thorough testing with a small sample before launching a large-scale rollout.
- ☑ Distribute the installation package to your remote users.

Frequently Asked Questions

The following Frequently Asked Questions, answered by the authors of this book, are designed to both measure your understanding of the concepts presented in this chapter and to assist you with real-life implementation of these concepts. To have your questions about this chapter answered by the author, browse to **www.syngress.com/solutions** and click on the **"Ask the Author"** form.

Q: For one-time installations and testing, isn't it faster and easier to copy the SecuRemote/SecureClient directory over to the remote machine and run the installation program from there?

A: Even for single installations, using the packaging tool may prove beneficial, because creating a profile and then generating a package goes very quickly, and it gives the added benefit of a repeatable installation process.

Q: Where can I find the special directory of files that the package generator needs to build the package?

A: Download the SecuRemote/SecureClient self-extracting installation package from the Check Point Web site. Run the package and the directory will be created for you. The default destination location is C:\SecureClient Files.

Q: I want to be able to post our installation packages on our public Web site so that our users can download them and run them from anywhere, without having to authenticate first. Is this safe?

A: The SecureClient Packaging tool and the SecuRemote/SecureClient software are distributed with every copy of VPN-1/FireWall-1 NG, so you won't be able to prevent anyone from getting access to them. But since remote users need to authenticate as part of initializing a VPN, there's no risk that unauthorized persons could connect to your encryption domain. As for information that might be contained in your particular userc.C file, this is more of a concern because topology information might be included in this file. Be sure to check **Obscure topology on disk** in the Topology window in order to encrypt topology information in the userc.C file. Also, enable **Partial Topology** in the same window in order to reduce the amount of topology information included in the userc.C file.

Q: If the SecureClient Packaging tool is one of the SMART clients, why can't I launch it directly from the SmartView Dashboard?

A: You can't have the SmartView Dashboard and SecureClient Packaging tool both open at the same time in read/write mode. This prevents your creating a package based on a configuration that's being edited. Therefore, the option to launch the SecureClient Packaging tool directly from the SmartView Dashboard isn't available, and if you try to launch it from the operating system, you'll get a warning dialog box reminding you that you can't have them open simultaneously for read/write access.

Q: Is the SecureClient Packaging tool just for preparing installation packages for SecureClient, or can I also prepare a package for SecuRemote?

A: The SecureClient Packaging tool can prepare installation packages for either product.

Chapter 11

SmartDefense

Solutions in this chapter:

- Understanding and Configuring SmartDefense

☑ Summary

☑ Solutions Fast Track

☑ Frequently Asked Questions

Introduction

SmartDefense is a new product that was first available for FireWall-1 NG FP2 and was designed to be part of Check Point's new line of Active Defense security solutions. The new active solutions are designed to take immediate action to prevent an attack, instead of only notifying the administrators that an attack has taken place. This can be viewed as an extension to the packet inspection that already takes place on your firewall. FireWall-1 previously had the capability to understand a small number of application layer protocols, such as FTP, to allow the firewall make the correct decision on the validity of a connection. FireWall-1 now understands additional protocols and has some idea of what should be considered a valid data stream based on user-defined parameters.

SmartDefense takes a different approach than a standard Intrusion Detection System (IDS) because it does not attempt to counter each new attack that is discovered, but instead it protects your network against entire classes of attacks. SmartDefense performs strict sanity checks on packet headers and protocol data to prevent any malformed information into your network. For example, instead of watching for an extensive list of attacks that can be used against DNS servers, SmartDefense will check DNS packets for compliance with the RFC standard for DNS packets. This behavior can protect against a large number of current and future exploits without the need for continual signature updates. This, of course, will not protect against every available attack because many attacks are difficult to distinguish from valid traffic flows. Some of these checks may also be too strict and will subsequently drop valid traffic that is required for your applications to function properly, which is why you have the ability to change the sensitivity levels or even turn off the protection entirely.

Not everything that you will see in SmartDefense is a new feature, because Check Point has combined some longstanding features with new attack defenses and placed it all into a single user interface. This user interface is available for use without any extra licensing, but if want to be able to update the attack definitions you will need to purchase the subscription service, which gives you the ability to receive all of the latest updates directly from Check Point with the click of a button.

This chapter covers the SmartDefense features available in FireWall-1 NG FP3. SmartDefense is constantly being updated via the subscription service, and the user interface will likely be modified in future updates, so it is likely that you will see features that were not available during the writing of this book. Fortunately, many of the major attack classes already exist in SmartDefense and the information in this chapter should still be valid in future versions.

The help files that are currently included with the FP3 SmartClients are lacking in both information and accuracy. You may see discrepancies between what is printed in this chapter and what is contained in the help files. Most of the features in SmartDefense were tested in a lab environment so that the most accurate information about the behavior of SmartDefense could be presented to the readers.

Understanding and Configuring SmartDefense

The SmartDefense configuration window is the new home for some firewall features that have been available for years. Since not all of these options can be turned off, SmartDefense cannot be disabled as a whole, but you have the ability to pick and choose which features you would like to activate. Before enabling any features in a production environment for the first time, it would be prudent to do extensive testing to verify that valid traffic is not affected by false positives. In addition, some of the options can be configured for sensitivity, and the thresholds should also be thoroughly tested before being applied to production firewalls. As part of the testing process, you should read through the release notes for SmartDefense, because a few of the features still have problems that can have adverse affects on your network. Knowing the kinds of applications that are used on your network and how they communicate can also help you identify any possible problems before modifying the SmartDefense policy.

The options for SmartDefense can be accessed from the SmartDashboard, either via the SmartDefense toolbar button or through the menus by selecting **Policy | SmartDefense**. The SmartDefense configuration window is made up of three different components. On the left half of the screen, you will see the configuration tree, which contains all of the available attack signatures categorized by attack type. You can enable and disable attacks in the configuration tree by clicking on the check box next to each option. In the top right portion of SmartDefense is an informational window. This window will display a brief description of the selected attack and usually some basic information about how the attack is countered. Below the information window is where the configurable options are placed, if any are available for a particular attack.

The following sections describe the attacks that SmartDefense is able to recognize and the configurable options available to the firewall administrator.

General

The General section of the SmartDefense configuration tree, shown in Figure 11.1, contains some general information and some links to quickly perform other tasks related to SmartDefense. The information window contains a section called "News flashes," which contains some announcements about SmartDefense features. Below the information window is a button labeled **Update SmartDefense**. This button causes the management server to connect to Check Point's site and download any attack signature updates that are available.

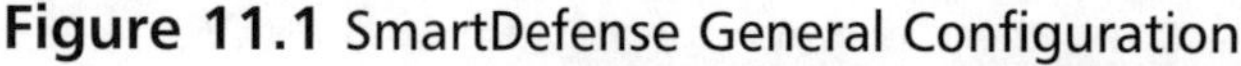

Figure 11.1 SmartDefense General Configuration

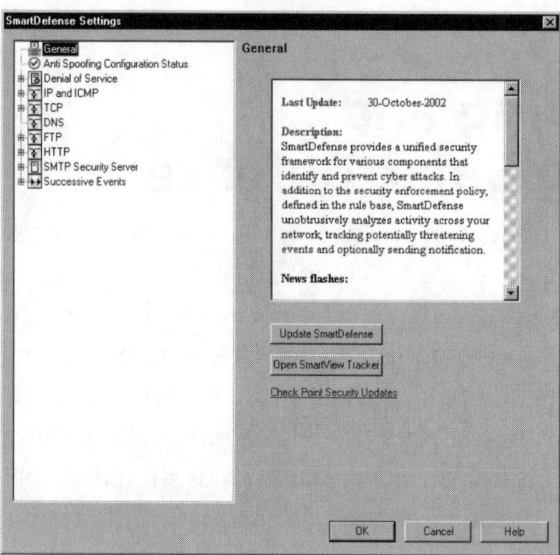

The second button, labeled **Open SmartView Tracker**, is a way to quickly jump to SmartView Tracker if you want to see any log entries that SmartDefense may have added to the logs. The final link, **Check Point Security Updates**, opens your Web browser and takes you to the Check Point Security Updates page, which contains advisories about new vulnerabilities and instructions on how to configure your enforcement points to protect against the attacks.

Updating SmartDefense to use the latest attack signatures is an extremely simple process, assuming you have purchased the subscription service. If you do not have access to the subscription service, you will not have access to the update button. To update your current signatures, just click the **Update SmartDefense** button. If updates are available, a pop-up window appears describing what has been updated, as shown in Figure 11.2. Just like it says in the pop-up window, these updates will not take effect until you install the policy. This also assumes that you use the **OK** button to exit the SmartDefense configuration. If you press **Cancel** to close the window, the updates will not be saved. If you are already using the latest attack signatures, you will get a pop-up message saying so, as shown in Figure 11.3.

Only two outbound services are used for updating SmartDefense: DNS (UDP only) and HTTPS. When you click on the **Update SmartDefense** button, the GUI Client (*not* the management server or enforcement point) will perform a DNS query for support.checkpoint.com and then initiate an HTTPS session to support.checkpoint.com to download any updates. If the GUI Client is unable to resolve support.checkpoint.com or is unable to initiate the HTTPS session, the update will fail.

Figure 11.2 Successful Update of SmartDefense

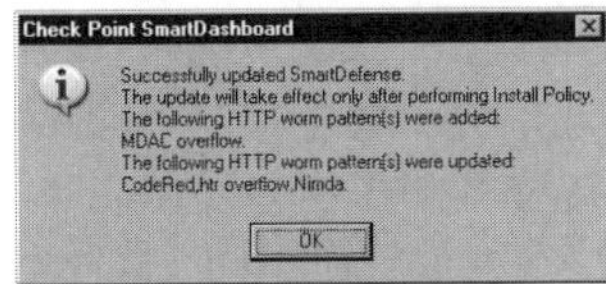

Figure 11.3 SmartDefense Already Up to Date

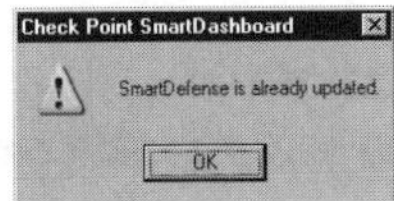

Anti-Spoofing Configuration Status

When an attacker is said to be spoofing packets, he is usually bypassing the standard TCP/IP stack of the OS and building packets with a source address that is not the real address assigned to the originating workstation. When the source address of a packet is changed, or spoofed, to another address, the response packets will not be returned to the attacking machine because the packets will be routed to the real owner of the spoofed source address. Often, the return packets aren't needed when performing an attack, such as a SYN attack, which is discussed later in the chapter in the "SYN Attack" section. When performing a SYN attack, the source address is spoofed to hide the real source of the attack and to make the attack much more difficult to block because the target server will see connections from thousands of different IP addresses. Other times, the source address will be spoofed to try and fool a gateway device into thinking that the packet is originating from a machine in the internal network.

FireWall-1 has long had an anti-spoofing feature that prevents packets with spoofed internal addresses from passing through the firewall from the external interface. More specifically, if a packet is not sourced from the network that is defined behind an interface, it will not be allowed through the firewall.

The anti-spoofing portion of SmartDefense doesn't block an attack itself, but it is meant to be an easy way to verify that you have anti-spoofing configured on all the gateways in your network. Any enforcement points that are not correctly configured for anti-spoofing will be displayed in a list on this page. From the page, you can select the gateway that you would like to configure and go straight to the topology page for the selected gateway. SmartDefense will not consider a gateway to be correctly configured for anti-spoofing, unless the IP addresses behind all interfaces are defined and the **Perform Anti-Spoofing based on Interface Topology** box is checked.

You can quickly see if you have any gateways that are not performing anti-spoofing by looking at the icon next to **Anti Spoofing Configuration Status** in the SmartDefense settings tree. The icon for the menu item will either be a red triangle with an exclamation point inside (see Figure 11.4) or a green check mark with a circle around it (see Figure 11.5). If you see the red warning symbol, you have gateways that are not configured to perform anti-spoofing, and they will be listed in the bottom-right corner of the SmartDefense window. If you select the gateway and click the **Edit** button, you will be taken directly to the topology page for that gateway. Once you have configured all gateways for anti-spoofing, the gateway list will be removed and you will see a message that "Anti-spoofing configuration is set on all gateways."

Figure 11.4 Anti Spoofing Not Configured on All Gateways

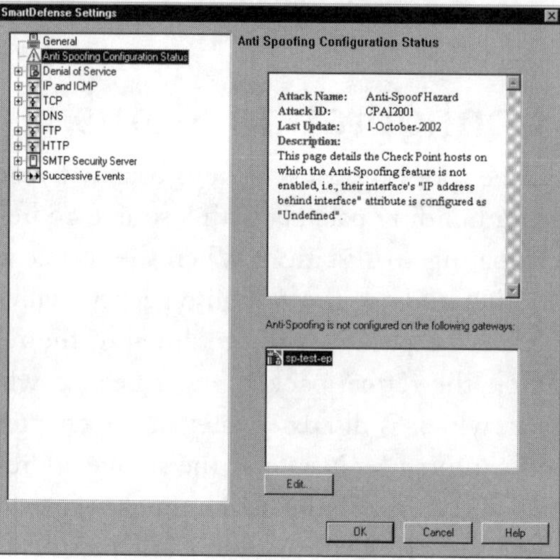

Figure 11.5 Anti Spoofing Configured Correctly

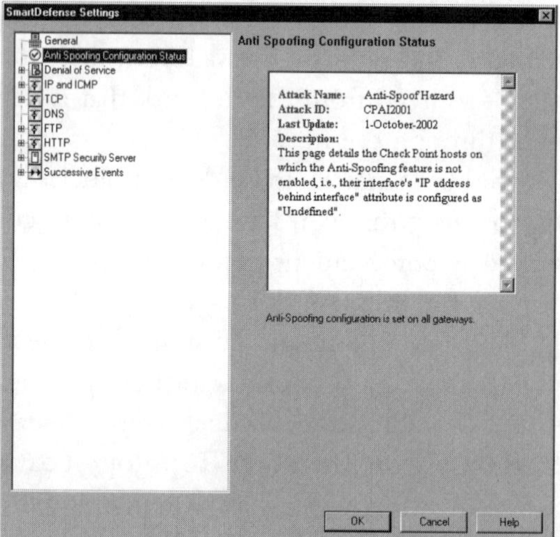

If you are not using this feature on your firewall, an attacker may be able to get a packet through your firewall by setting the source address of a packet to an IP that belongs to your internal network. When you are not using anti-spoofing, the firewall will not keep track of which interface a source address should be originating from and will allow any packets through that match an "accept" rule in the policy. Someone with experience writing code in C or some other programming language can write his own programs to forge these kinds of packets. Instead, someone could use one of the many tools available on the Internet, such as RafaleX, which can be found at http://www.packx.net. Packets builders such as these can be used by a firewall administrator to test the security policy and verify that such attacks will be dropped by the firewall before an attacker attempts to access your systems.

Denial of Service

This section of SmartDefense deals with some common Denial of Service (DoS) attacks that are used to crash the target machine. These particular attacks are able to crash systems by sending illegal packets (packets that do not conform to the RFC standard for the specific protocol) that the receiving system is unable to process correctly.

There is very little to configure in this section (see Figure 11.6); your only decision is which attacks you want SmartDefense to watch for. You can disable checking for any individual attack by removing the check mark next to the attack name. For the attacks that you do want to defend against, you have the option of selecting what action should be taken when an offending packet is detected.

Figure 11.6 Denial of Service Category Settings

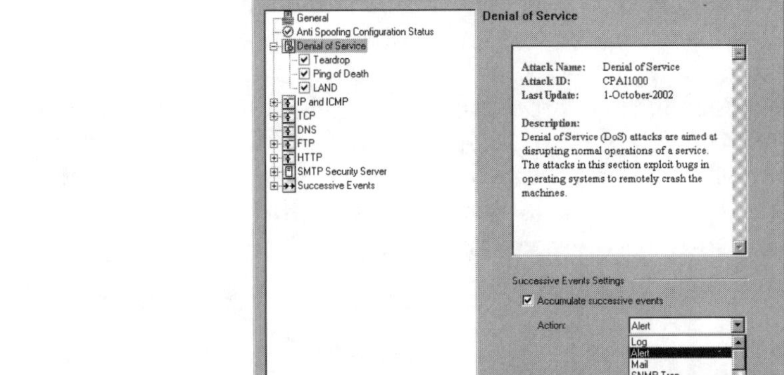

If, in your environment, you are constantly under a range of attacks and you do not want to be alerted every time the attack happens, you can use the **Accumulate successive events** feature available on the main **Denial of Service** category menu, which is also shown in Figure 11.6. If you select the **Accumulate successive events** option, you will need to select the alert you would like to receive when a certain threshold of events has been reached. There is also an **Advanced** button where you select how many events will trigger the selected action. The settings here are exactly the same as the ones available for the other attacks under the Successive Events category in the configuration tree, and these advanced settings are covered in the "Successive Events" section.

Tools & Traps...

Review of Alerts

All of the actions available for use in SmartDefense (some are shown in Figure 11.6) are user configurable. If you want to change the parameters for a specific alert, you do so in the global properties of your security policy under **Logs and Alerts | Alert Commands**.

You need to configure most of the alerts before you can do anything useful with them. FireWall-1 contains an *internal_sendmail* command that you can use to generate SMTP mail messages and send them through a designated SMTP server, and an *internal_snmp_trap* command that generates and sends an SNMP trap message to the configured destination (by default, local host). These scripts are only accessible from within FireWall-1, and cannot be accessed from the command line of the management server or enforcement point.

You can configure the *internal_sendmail* command with additional parameters to allow the mail to be properly formatted for transit through your network. Many mail servers are configured to reject messages with a blank sender field, or they will only permit mail from specific e-mail addresses. These options are configured by adding additional tags to the *internal_sendmail* command. The format of this command is as follows:

```
Internal_sendmail -t mail_server [-f sender_address] [-s "subject"]
    recipient_address
```

Here is a description of each option in this command string:

- **mail_server** The IP address or hostname of your SMTP gateway that will be forwarding the generated e-mail message to the proper destination. This option is required, because *internal_*

Continued

sendmail does not perform the DNS lookups to deliver the SMTP message itself.

- **sender_address** The e-mail address that will be listed as the sender of the e-mail message. This option is not required, but you can use it if your SMTP gateway requires a valid e-mail address before relaying SMTP messages, or if you want firewall messages sent from a certain e-mail address.
- **subject** The subject message that you want in the generated e-mail message. The subject cannot contain any spaces, unless you enclose the entire subject in quotation marks, such as "Firewall Alert Message".
- **recipient_address** The e-mail address that the e-mail message will be sent to. You must define at least one recipient (otherwise, what is the point of sending an e-mail?), and you can separate multiple e-mail address with spaces.

The body of the e-mail message is determined by FireWall-1 depending on what alert triggered the action. This cannot be changed, as the only configurable options available are used to facilitate proper delivery of the e-mail alert messages.

Teardrop

In the case that an IP datagram is larger than the maximum allowed packet size in a network, the packet can be fragmented into smaller pieces so it can pass through that network. Within the IP protocol header is a flag that specifies that more fragments are coming, and a field that contains an offset value. The offset value informs the receiving device at what position in the data stream to place the data in packet. The Teardrop attack exploits this feature of the IP protocol by sending packet fragments that overlap with each other. This is done by setting the offset value to something closer to the beginning of the packet than where the previous packet ended, meaning the server thinks there are two different sets of data that belong in the same exact place in the data stream. This condition should not occur under normal circumstances, and many operating systems were unable to handle the overlapping fragments, which caused the machine to crash.

Enabling this option does not provide any extra protection against this attack because FireWall-1 already does strict sanity checking of fragmented packets (which is covered in the next section). Illegal packets will automatically be dropped, and a fragmentation error log entry will be created. Even though you are already protected from this attack, it was added to SmartDefense so that you can specify a different action for the Teardrop attack than for other fragmentation errors. For example, you may want to receive e-mail alerts when someone has launched this attack against you, but do not want to receive an e-mail for every fragmentation error that is encountered.

Ping of Death

The Ping of Death is another Denial of Service attack that functions by breaking the rules defined for an IP packet. This particular attack consists of a machine sending an ICMP echo request that is larger than the maximum IP datagram size. This can be accomplished by sending IP fragments to the destination machine that, when combined, add up to more that 65,535 bytes. As the fragments are being reassembled into memory, packet buffer will overflow, which can cause unpredictable results ranging from no effect to a system crash.

As with the Teardrop DoS attack, this attack will be prevented regardless of how you configure this option, but you have the ability to specify a different action for this specific attack than when other packet sanity checks fail.

LAND

The LAND Denial of Service attack confuses the target machine by sending a spoofed TCP packet with the SYN flag set, and the source and destination address and port numbers are exactly the same. The target machine will interpret this packet as a TCP session that is being initiated from itself. At the time that this vulnerability was discovered, most operating systems did not know how to handle this condition and would crash or reboot.

Although this attack will normally be countered by the anti-spoofing configuration on your gateways, you can still defend against this DoS attack even if you have decided not to perform anti-spoofing at your enforcement points.

IP and ICMP

This section of SmartDefense deals with IP- and ICMP-based attacks and requires even less configuration than the Denial of Service category. This is because most of these options cannot be disabled. You will notice that the check boxes next to the **Fragment Sanity Check** and the **Packet Sanity** check are grayed out and locked in the "checked" position. There is one available option under **Packet Sanity** called **Enable relaxed UDP length verification**, which is shown in Figure 11.7. This option will prevent the enforcement point from imposing such strict checks on the length field in the UDP packet header. This option may be needed because not all applications calculate the UDP length field in the same manner, and the firewall will drop some of these packets because it thinks the length is incorrect. Removing the check mark from this option will offer a little more protection, but if you use applications that don't calculate the length field correctly (from FireWall-1's perspective), you will need to leave this option enabled.

Figure 11.7 IP and ICMP Options

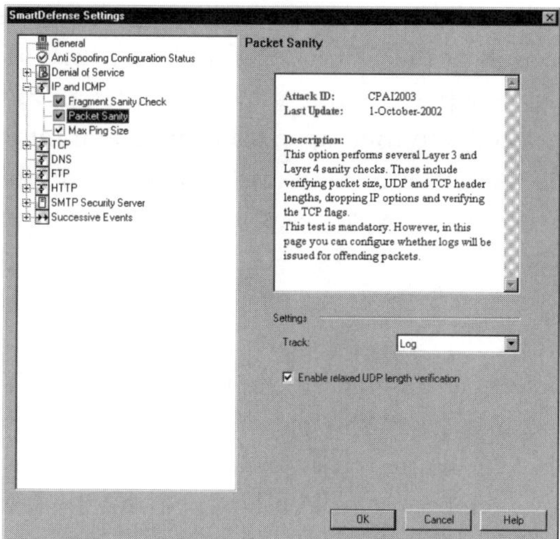

The other configurable option in the IP and ICMP Configuration Tree is **Max Ping Size**. To configure this option, select **Max Ping Size** in the configuration tree, and modify the **Ping Size** field to specify the maximum number of bytes that will be allowed in a ping.

Fragment Sanity Check

This feature of SmartDefense cannot be disabled, but is listed here to let you decide how you want the firewall to respond to problems detected by the strict fragment sanity check that is performed. Some firewalls and IDS systems will not detect an attack if it is fragmented into smaller pieces. This happens because each packet is inspected individually as it passes through the device, and a fragment of the attacker's data won't be recognized as an attack. To avoid this problem, FireWall-1 collects all fragments and checks the reassembled packet before passing the information to the destination.

Packet Sanity

Again, this is an option that cannot be disabled, and it's only in SmartDefense so that you can choose what action should be taken when a packet fails this check. This is a sanity check on all information in the packet at layer 3 and layer 4. This sanity check looks for a wide range of problems in the packet structure, such as the following:

- Invalid packet length
- Invalid header length
- Improper TCP flags
- Use of IP options

If any information in the packet is inconsistent with the state of the communication or the data within the packet, the firewall will drop the packet. This check also prevents the Options section of the IP header from being used. IP options can be configured to do such things as supply routing information telling intermediate routing devices how the packet should be routed, or to record route information as the packet traverses the network. These options can be useful tools for troubleshooting, but they also give an attacker the ability to bypass security measures, so they are not allowed through the enforcement points.

Max Ping Size

This feature of SmartDefense is designed to drop echo requests if they are larger than the specified amount in this section. You can set the maximum byte size that you want to allow from an ICMP echo request. If an echo request is larger than the byte count configured in this section, the packet will be dropped and the specified action will be taken. When choosing what action you want performed, keep in mind that the action will be taken for each ICMP packet that is dropped. This check is performed before the packet is checked against the rule base, so you will receive alerts for pings that are too big, even if no ICMP is allowed through the gateway.

This feature was not designed to combat the Ping of Death attack, which creates an illegal size packet, but instead limits the amount of data that can be sent in a correctly sized echo request. Large echo requests are not usually needed for troubleshooting and can easily cause congestion on links that are already near capacity. For this reason, you may want to keep your allowed echo request size low.

WARNING

The default setting for Max Ping Size is 64 bytes. If your security policy allows pings into your network, keep in mind that this option, at its default setting, will prevent certain devices from being able to ping. For example, Cisco routers use a default ping size of 100 bytes, so while a Microsoft Windows workstation will be able to ping through your enforcement point, the Cisco router would not.

Keep in mind when you are choosing your max ping size and action method that every ping larger than your threshold will be considered an attack. For example, if you configure SmartDefense to send you an e-mail if someone exceeds the max ping size, you will receive an e-mail for each individual oversized ping that is received; if you receive 1,000 oversized pings, you will receive 1,000 e-mails.

TCP

This section of SmartDefense contains categories of attacks that attempt to exploit the TCP protocol, such as out of sequence packets, invalid session requests and excessively small fragment sizes. No options are available for the TCP category itself; all configuration is on the individual object within the TCP tree.

SYN Attack

A SYN attack is a Denial of Service attack that abuses the flags that are used to initiate a TCP session. This attack can cause the destination server to stop accepting new connections from valid hosts because it is busy waiting for responses from the attacker's false sessions.

> **Notes from the Underground…**
>
> **TCP 3-Way Handshake**
>
> When a client wants to transfer data with another server, it will request a new session by sending an empty (no data) TCP packet with the "synchronize" (SYN) flag set. The SYN flag tells the destination host that the client is requesting a TCP session be opened. If the server decides to accept this new connection, an empty TCP packet will be sent in response with both the SYN and acknowledge (ACK) flags set. The SYN/ACK tells the client that the server has acknowledged its request for a new session and is accepting the request by trying to establish the connection in the opposite direction. As the final step of the three-way handshake, the client will send a response packet with only the ACK flag set. This completes the TCP handshake, as both sides have sent a SYN request and an ACK response that is required for two-way communication.
>
> A session can be rejected by sending the reset (RST) flag to the other host. This is different from the graceful closing of a session that uses the finish (FIN) flag in a similar way as the initial handshake. The RST flag is used when either host detects an error and decides to reset the communication channel, or if it does not want to accept the communication at all. If a client initiates a TCP connection by sending a SYN packet to a port that is not currently being used, the server will respond with a RST/ACK, telling the client that it has acknowledged the request but is refusing to allow the communication. Along those same lines, if a client receives a SYN/ACK packet for a session that it has not sent the initial SYN for, the client will respond to the server with a RST flag, telling the server it does not wish to complete the handshake.

When a server receives a SYN request, it puts the partially established connection information into a separate table from where established connections are tracked, which Check Point refers to as the backlog queue. If the server does not receive a response to the SYN/ACK packet that is sent to the client, the uncompleted connection will stay in the backlog queue until the server times out the connection and removes it from the table. If the backlog queue is full of incomplete connections, the server will stop accepting new requests until space is made available in the queue. This process is illustrated in Figure 11.8. The attacker will take advantage of this limit by sending a constant stream of SYN requests, but will not respond to the SYN/ACK packets that are sent back to the source. This will keep the backlog queue full of invalid connections, and valid users will not be able to connect to the server.

Figure 11.8 TCP Three-Way Handshake

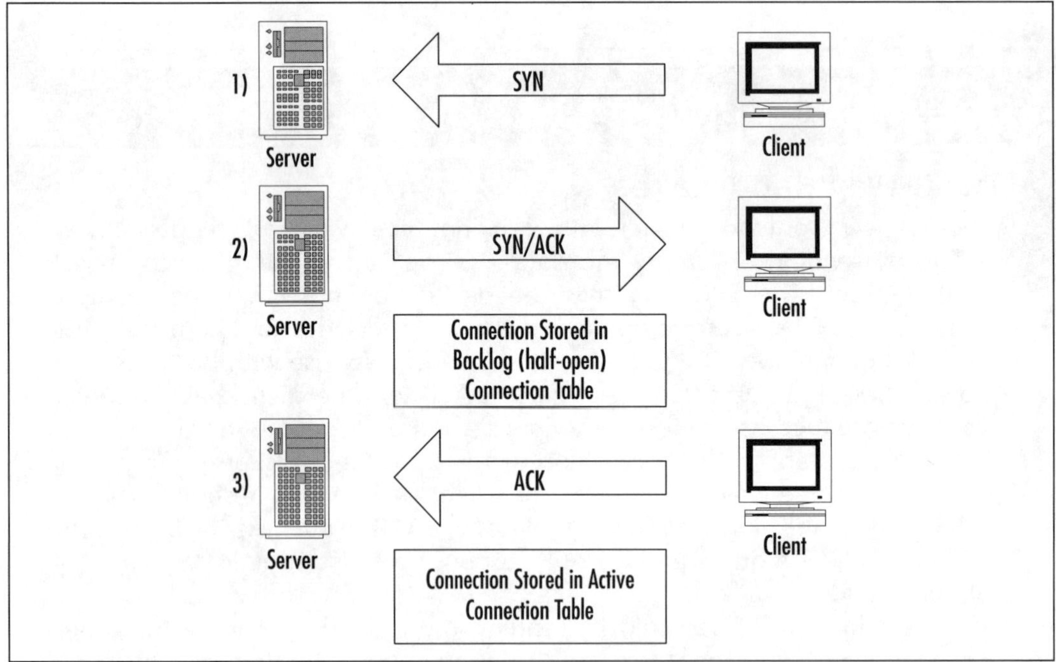

To prevent the target from blocking all incoming packets from the IP address of the attacker, the source address of the packets will usually be spoofed, which makes it difficult to identify the attacker and filter out the invalid packets. During the attack, the attacker needs to make sure that the spoofed source addresses are not used by valid machines. If a real host receives a SYN/ACK for a connection it didn't initiate, that host will send a RST back to the server. Once the server receives the RST packet, it will remove the connection from the backlog queue, which frees space for another new connection. If the majority of the attacker's packets are spoofed with IP addresses of active hosts, the backlog queue will never fill up, because the connections will be reset in milliseconds.

A feature designed to combat SYN attacks, called SYNDefender, was added to previous versions of FireWall-1. Three different defense methods were available in SYNDefender, and each had its strengths and weaknesses:

- **SYN Gateway** When the server sends the SYN/ACK back to the client, the firewall will immediately send the ACK packet to the server. This will move the connection out of the backlog queue and into the active connection table. This is done because servers can handle a much large number of established connections than partially established connections. If the ACK is not received from the client within the timeout period, the firewall will send a RST to the server, closing that particular session. Figure 11.9 illustrates the steps taken when using SYN Gateway.

Figure 11.9 SYN Gateway

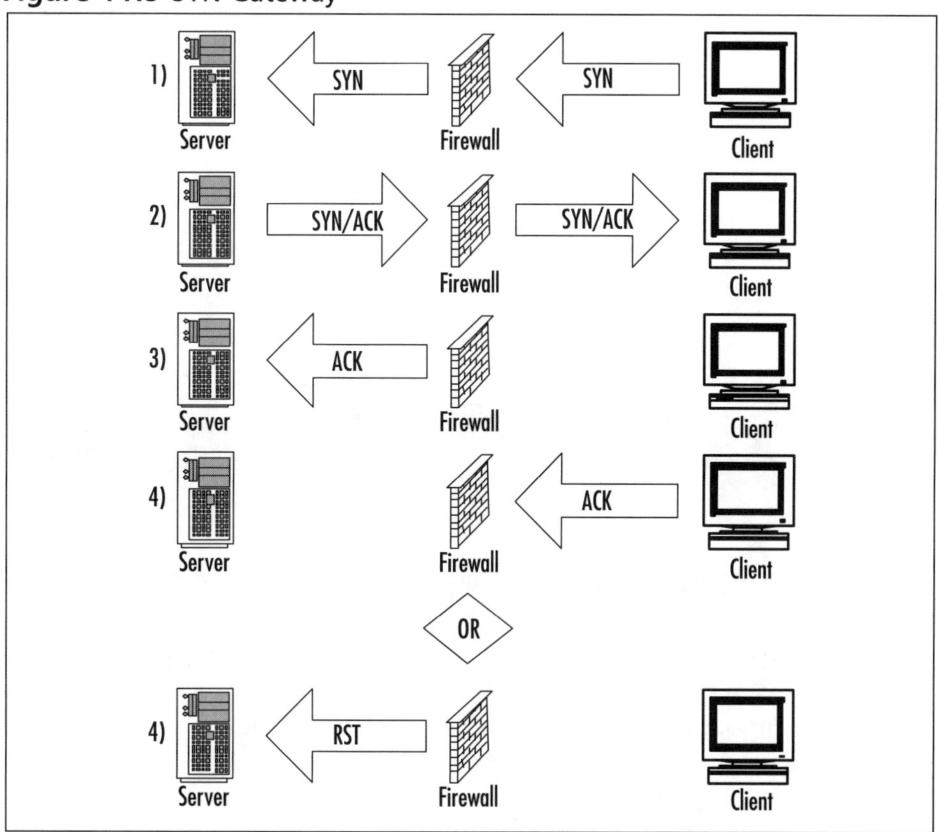

- **Passive SYN Gateway** This is the least intrusive method, because it allows the connection request to proceed as normal, in the backlog queue. If the ACK isn't received within the timeout period, the firewall will generate a RST packet to remove the session from the server's backlog queue. The timeout period on the firewall is much less than the default timeout from the server. This will not entirely prevent an attack, but it makes sure that entries in the backlog queue do not linger. The challenge is finding an appropriate timeout value that makes an attack very difficult, but will not reset sessions coming over slower links. Figure 11.10 illustrates Passive SYN Gateway.

Figure 11.10 Passive SYN Gateway

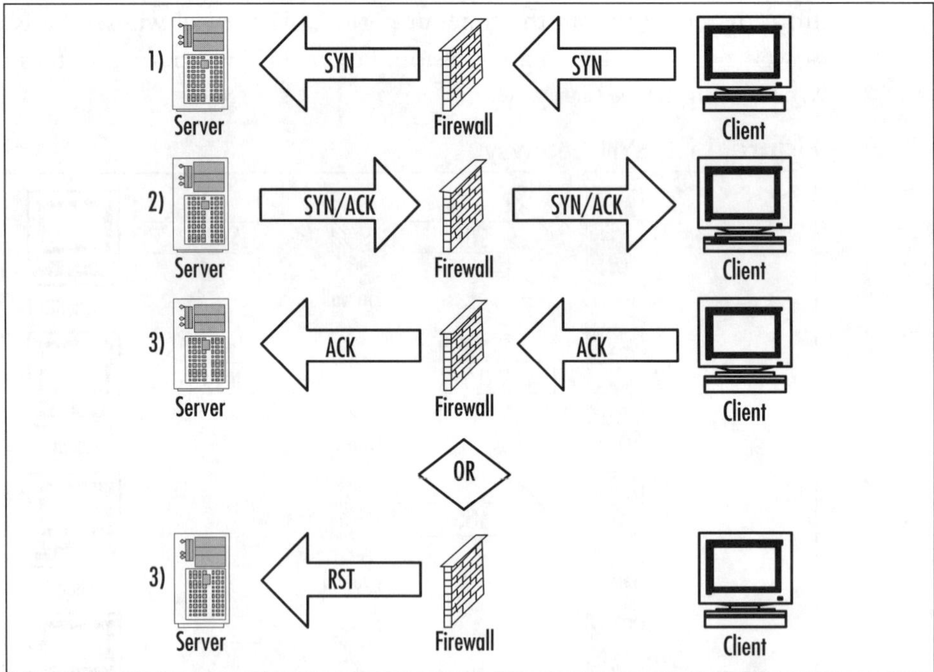

- **SYN Relay** When this method is used, the Firewall will respond to all SYN packets on behalf of the server by sending the SYN/ACK to the client. Once the ACK is received from the client, the firewall will pass the connection to the server. With this method, the server will never receive invalid connection attempts, because the firewall will not pass on the original SYN packet until it has received the corresponding ACK from the client. This method offers the best protection for the target server, but also has the most overhead because the firewall is required to respond to all connection requests passing through. This option was not available in FireWall-1 4.*x*, but was added to NG as a kernel-level process to keep delay to a minimum, although it will still add some amount of overhead.

With the introduction of SmartDefense to FireWall-1 NG FP2, the SYNDefender functionality was moved into the SmartDefense configuration. A new method to combat SYN attacks, called SYN Attack protection, was also added to SmartDefense, although Check Point left an option to use the older SYNDefender if you are so inclined.

The new SYN Attack protection automatically switches between two different modes of operation: passive mode and active mode. Under normal condition, SYN Attack protection runs in passive mode and only switches to active mode when it detects a SYN attack in progress. Once the attack has passed, the enforcement point will switch back to passive protection. Configurable options allow you to set SmartDefense's sensitivity to SYN attacks.

When SmartDefense SYN Attack protection is operating in passive mode, it is using the Passive SYN Gateway feature described earlier in this section. This keeps the overhead to a minimum while still ensuring that uncompleted handshakes do not stay in the backlog queue too long. If the threshold of attack attempts is exceeded, the Enforcement Point (EP) will switch to active protection until the number of offending SYN packets drops below the threshold level. When using active protection mode, the EP is operating as a SYN Relay. The combination of these two methods ensures that your gateways operate as quickly as possible, but will also completely protect your servers from SYN attacks when one is detected.

By default, SYN protection is disabled, because the SYNDefender configuration has been overridden on all modules, but the new SYN Attack protection hasn't yet been enabled. The default settings for the SYN Attack configuration are shown in Figure 11.11. To enable SYN flooding protection on your gateways, you need to use either active SYN Attack protection or use the SYNDefender configuration if you have modules that need to use the older protection.

As was mentioned in the anti-spoofing section, there are many tools that can be used by an attacker to try to disable your servers. RafaleX, allowing you to set any variable in the layer 3 and 4 packet headers, can be used to generate a SYN flood condition. Another tool, nmap (www.insecure.org), is a port scanning tool that identifies open ports by sending a SYN packet and seeing how the server responds. This tool can be configured to use spoofed "decoy" addresses and could possibly trigger a SYN flood condition if the probing was configured too aggressively. Both of these tools can be used by an attacker to exploit your firewall, but they are much more useful to the firewall administrator for testing the security policy and verifying that you are protecting against these types of attacks. Port scanners like nmap can also tell you which ports are being filtered and which are not. This can tip you off to a problem in your rule base before an attacker finds and exploits the problem.

Figure 11.11 SYN Attack Protection Methods

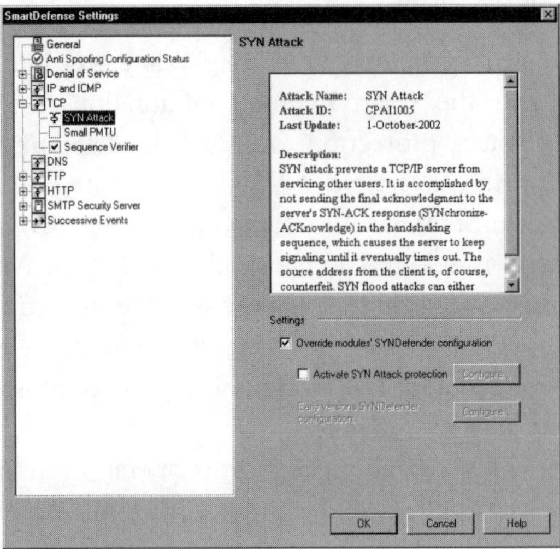

After selecting the **Activate SYN Attack protection** box, you will be able to select the **Configure** button to change the SYN Attack settings. The available options for SYN Attack protection are shown in Figure 11.12.

Figure 11.12 SYN Attack Settings

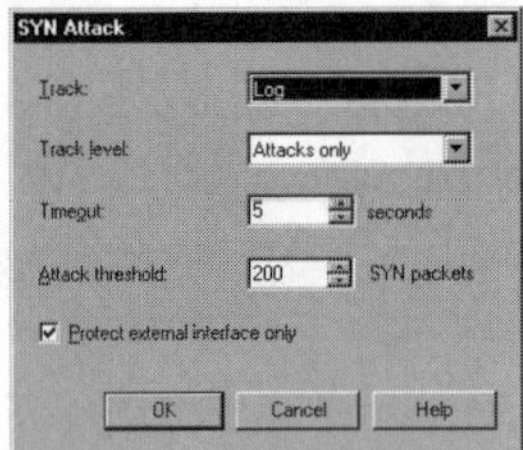

Tools & Traps...

Using SYN Protection

It would be very beneficial to have a solid understanding of the traffic that is flowing through your firewall before you enable this feature. Every network is different with respect to the types of traffic flows that are considered "normal" for that environment. These SYN protection options have configurable parameters because a threshold of partially open sessions that could be considered an attack for a small network may be a normal number for a much larger network.

Continued

If your thresholds are set too high, your firewall may be ineffective at preventing a DoS attack against one of your servers, and setting the thresholds too low will mean that your firewall is often operating in active protection mode. Because the firewall is responding to all connection requests on behalf of the server, the performance of your network can slow to a crawl if the number of connection requests overwhelms the enforcement point. I would not recommend blindly enabling this feature without performing some form of traffic analysis on your network. This can become even more important if you plan on enabling SYN Protection for all interfaces of the firewall. Some firewalls have a large number of interfaces (10+), and configuring the firewall to watch all interfaces can significantly increase the load on the firewall.

The following options are available for configuration:

- **Track** Choose the action that you would like to be taken when a SYN Attack is detected. This feature ties in with the Track Level selection.
- **Track level** The track level determines how much detail you want to receive about possible attacks. Table 11.1 details each of the track level options.
- **Timeout** The timeout value tells the gateway how many seconds it should wait before considering a SYN packet to be part of an attack. After this timeout period passes, the gateway will send an alert based on the Track action and Track Level options.
- **Attack threshold** This is the level of unanswered SYN packets that should be considered an attack. When this threshold is crossed, the gateway will switch to active protection and relay all TCP sessions after the handshake has been completed with the firewall. Once the number of attacks has dropped back below the threshold number, the gateway will move back to passive mode.
- **Protect external interface only** If this option is checked, the gateway will only look for SYN attacks coming from the external interface, as defined in the gateway's topology. If you feel that you could experience SYN attacks from other interfaces, uncheck this option, and the gateway will watch for SYN attacks on all interfaces.

Table 11.1 Track Level Options for SYN Attack Protection

Track Level	Track Level Description
Individual SYNs	When this track level is selected, the Track action will be taken for each individual SYN packet that does not receive the corresponding ACK from the client. You will receive notifications for events such as **SYN->SYN/ACK->RST** and **SYN->SYN/ACK->Timeout**. In addition, you will receive notification when SYN Attack protection switches between active and passive defense modes.
Attacks Only	This track level takes the specified action only when the defense mode changes between passive and active modes. You will not receive any notification when individual SYNs time out or receive a RST in response.
None	In this mode, SYN Attack protection will continue to operate as normal, but you will not receive any notifications of suspicious SYN packets or when the gateway changes defense modes.

If you have a need to stick with the older SYNDefender configuration, you will need to uncheck the **Override modules' SYNDefender configuration** option. This will enable the **Configure** button for the SYN Defender features, as shown in Figure 11.13. Your options here include the following:

- **Method** Lets you choose between no protection, SYN Gateway mode, or Passive SYN Gateway mode as described earlier in this section.
- **Timeout** This is the amount of time that the firewall will wait for the client ACK packet before considering the session to be part of an attack. This is the timer used by SYN Gateway and Passive SYN Gateway when deciding when to reset a session.
- **Maximum sessions** This is the maximum number of sessions that the firewall will keep track of. The higher the number, the more memory will be used for the connection tables, but if the number of sessions exceeds this setting, the gateway will track new sessions.
- **Display warning messages** When this option is checked, SYNDefender will send status messages to the log file.

Figure 11.13 Earlier Versions SYNDefender Configuration

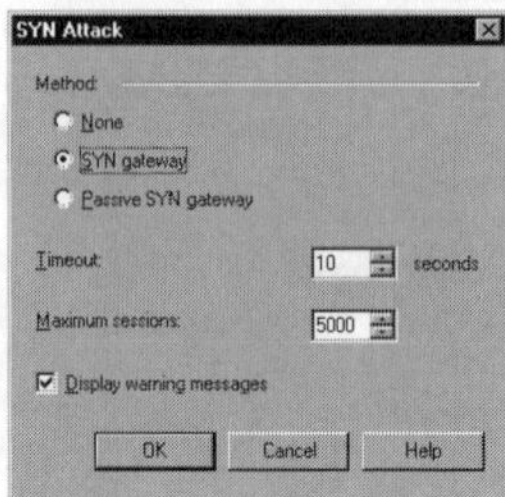

Small PMTU

PMTU stands for Path Maximum Transmission Unit. Each hop between the client and server may have a different maximum packet size. PMTU is a method for a server to discover what the smallest MTU is when communicating with a client. Once the client discovers the smallest MTU of any hop along the path between client and server, all packets can be made small enough so that they do not need to be fragmented in transit. Enabling this option prevents ICMP messages requesting an excessively small MTU (determined by you) from reaching the server. This attack works by fooling the server into the thinking that the MTU is small enough that any normal packet is broken into a large number of fragments. When sending small-sized fragments, you use more bandwidth, because the header size is the same for every packet, no matter how much data follows. So, if the server is incorrectly sending lots of small packets, the header information will use a larger percentage of bandwidth. If the minimum PMTU is set too small, an attack will not be prevented, and if the minimum MTU is set too large, the firewall may drop the wrong traffic.

Sequence Verifier

Every packet in a TCP session contains a sequence number in the TCP header information. The sequence number is important because it is the mechanism used to allow reliable communications between hosts. The sequence number identifies each chunk of data so the receiving host can reassemble the stream in the correct order and can acknowledge each individual packet as it is received. If a sequence number is not acknowledged within the set period of time, the sender knows to retransmit the unacknowledged packet. In the case that a retransmission and the acknowledgement pass each other on the network, the receiving host will know to discard the duplicate packet because it has already seen the sequence number.

In FireWall-1 NG FP3, the Sequence Verifier was moved from the Global Policy settings to the SmartDefense configuration. This feature watches all traffic flows going through the gateway and keeps track of the sequence numbers in the packets. If it sees a packet is received with an incorrect sequence number, the EP will consider the packet out of state and drop the packet.

You have the option of turning off this feature, since it is not currently supported in certain configurations, such as firewall clusters using asymmetric routing. When this feature is disabled, the firewall changes some of its behavior with respect to certain TCP packets. For example, the RST flag is not trusted, and instead of removing a session from the state table when a RST is encountered, it sets a 50-second timeout on the connection before it considers it closed. This can cause problems if the client, within the 50-second window, tries to reconnect with the same source port because the firewall will consider the SYN flag an out-of-state packet and drop it.

When the sequence verifier is enabled, you are given three different tracking options when deciding what sorts of problems you want to receive alerts/logs on. These options are shown in Figure 11.14 and include the following:

- **Every** This option will take the selected tracking option for every out-of-state packet that is dropped by the gateway.
- **Anomalous** This tracking option is less sensitive than the previous one, because it will only track out-of-sequence packets that suggest some sort of communication problem may exist.
- **Suspicious** When this option is selected, the gateway will only track out-of-state packets that the gateway thinks may be part of an attack.

Figure 11.14 Sequence Verifier Configuration Settings

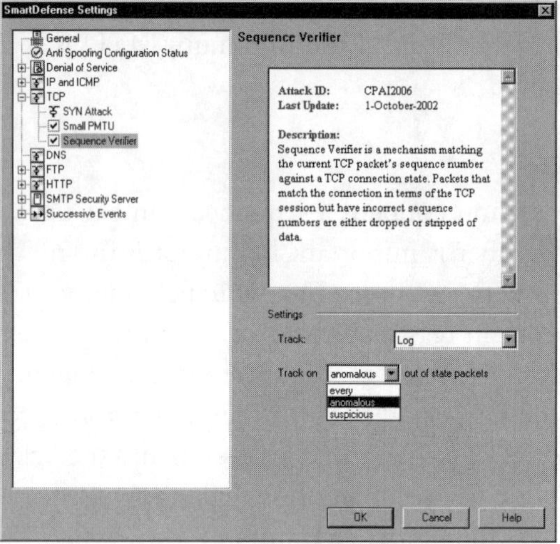

DNS

When this feature is enabled, the enforcement point will perform sanity checks on all DNS packets to verify that they have been formatted to comply with the standard DNS format as described in RFC 1035. More specifically, the enforcement point will inspect all UDP packets flowing over port 53 to verify that they are DNS packets and formatted properly. As of FP3, SmartDefense will only inspect UDP DNS packets, so any TCP DNS traffic, such as zone transfers, will not be checked for DNS packet integrity.

If you are running a Windows 2000 Active Directory domain, you will want to perform extensive testing before using this feature in your network. According to the FP3 release notes, DNS protocol enforcement will drop DNS communications made to AD domain controllers. If you have any hosts that communicate with a domain controller through the firewall, you will likely not be able to use DNS protocol enforcement.

No other configurable options related to DNS protocol enforcement exist for UDP packets. The only decision you have to make is if you want to enable the feature. If you would like to use the strict DNS checks, make sure to check the **UDP protocol enforcement** box, shown in Figure 11.15, and select the type of tracking for malformed DNS packets.

Figure 11.15 DNS Protocol Enforcement

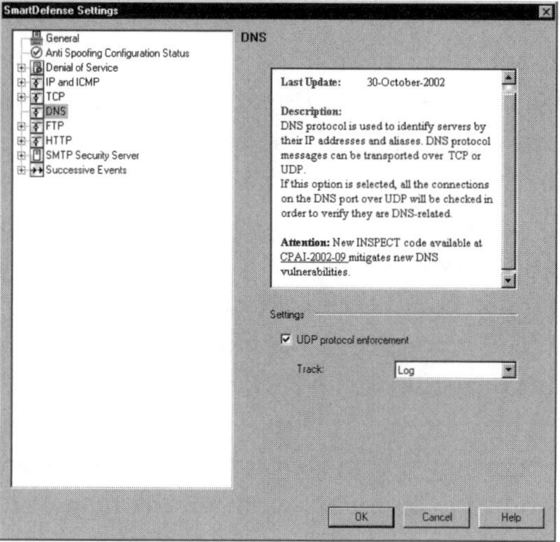

WARNING

According to the release notes, this feature currently does not recognize Active Directory DNS traffic as being valid. If you have hosts that need to send AD traffic through the firewall (that is, hosts and domain controllers are on separate networks), you will not be able to use this feature.

FTP

This section of SmartDefense protects against attacks using the File Transfer Protocol (FTP). No options apply to the entire FTP category, and all other settings are under their individual categories.

NOTE

Security Server alerts (FTP, HTTP, and SMTP) are reported in the logs as coming from FW-1/VPN-1, instead of SmartDefense, because you are making changes to the Security Server that are invoked when filtering a protocol with resources and not directly to SmartDefense.

FTP Bounce Attack

An easy way to hide the source of an attack is to exploit a design flaw in the FTP protocol that allows the client to specify the IP address and port number the FTP server should attach to for a data connection. All the attacker needs is anonymous write access to a directory on a vulnerable FTP server, where he can upload a file containing the data stream that is going to be sent to the target machine. The attacker can then exploit the flaw by asking the FTP server to send the file to an arbitrary IP address and port number. For example, the file could contain a malformed HTTP request and the attacker could have the FTP server open a connection to port 80 on the target machine and send the malformed request. As far as the Web server can tell, the connection came from the IP address of the FTP server, not the IP address of the attacker. The attacker is effectively "bouncing" the attack off the FTP server, and the victim will not be able to discover the source of the attack without the help of the administrator of the vulnerable FTP site.

Check Point has added a check to all FTP traffic to prevent this attack. When the *PORT* command is seen passing through the firewall, it will verify that the address specified in the *PORT* command is the same address as the machine requesting the file transfer. This will force all FTP data transfers to go only to the originating IP address and prevent an attacker from initiating a connection to a different machine.

FTP Security Servers

The options listed here are extra configurable options that apply to the FTP Security Server built into Firewall-1. By default, these options will not affect any traffic unless you have already configured your FTP rules to use an FTP resource, as shown in Figure 11.16. If you want the FTP Security Server to be invoked for every FTP connection that flows through your firewall, you have the option of changing the behavior in this section. If you have large amounts of traffic flowing through your enforcement points, this option may cause performance problems on your gateways.

Figure 11.16 FTP Security Server Settings

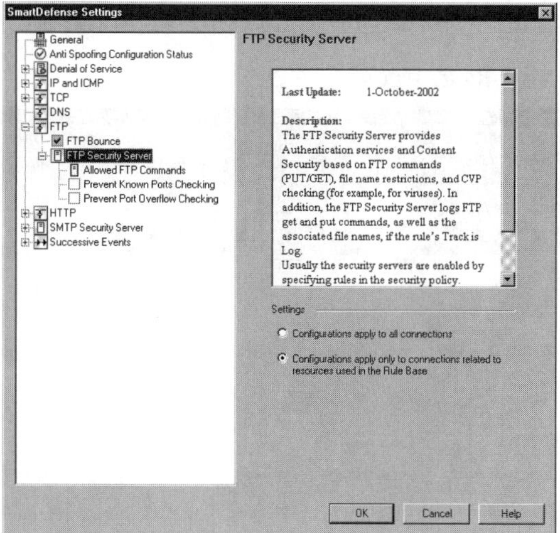

NOTE

Selecting **Configurations apply to all connections** will make the firewall call the security server for every FTP connection on port 21, no matter which direction the traffic flows. This setting works exactly the same for HTTP and SMTP security servers. If you have a high throughput through your gateway, the additional overhead could cause some performance problems. Also, when this option is selected, it will not apply to FTP traffic on nonstandard ports, even if the service is configured with a protocol type of FTP (under advanced configuration for a service).

To better illustrate how rules with FTP, HTTP, or SMTP resources are used, Figure 11.17 shows two rules that use HTTP resources. Please note the SERVICE column for rules 30 and 42 to see an HTTP rule which uses an HTTP resource (Security Server) to apply additional restrictions to particular traffic flows. To view or define new resources, you can go to **Manage | Resources** in the main menu.

For those FTP connections that do go through the Check Point Security Server (whether you have configured it for all FTP, or only FTP resources), you have the ability to choose individual commands that you want to allow. By selecting the **Allowed FTP Commands** menu, you will see two lists in the configuration area of the SmartDefense window. This list on the left displays all the commands that are allowed; the list on the right is all the commands that will be blocked. By default all commands are enabled, but you can easily disallow the use of a command by highlighting it in the allowed list and clicking **Add**. If you decide later that you want to move a command back into the accepted list, just highlight the command and click **Remove**.

Figure 11.17 Rules with Resources

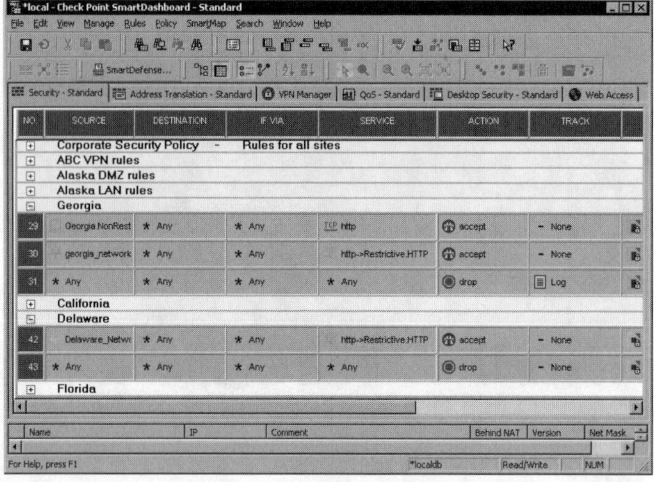

NOTE

The **Allowed FTP Commands** configuration is shown in Figure 11.18. Please keep in mind that this figure represents random commands moved into the blocked category and does not reflect an appropriate way to protect your FTP server.

Figure 11.18 Allowed FTP Commands

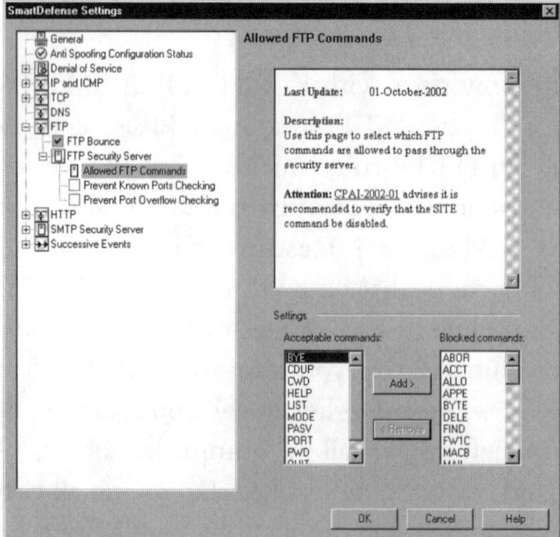

Two other additional measure are automatically enabled when using the FTP Security Server. These two options are called **Prevent Known Ports Checking** and **Prevent Port Overflow Checking**. The known ports check is in place to prevent an FTP *PORT* connection from requesting a connection to a known port (for example, port 80 for HTTP). If you would like to disable this feature and allow data transfers to be sent to a well-known port, place a check mark in the box.

The other feature, called port overflow checking, keeps track of the *PORT* commands that have been issued and will drop multiple *PORT* requests to the same destination port. Again, this feature can be *disabled* by placing a check mark in the box labeled **Prevent Port Overflow Checking**.

HTTP

This section contains the attacks that exploit vulnerabilities in the HTTP protocol. Most of these features are designed to filter malformed requests that usually are not seen in a valid HTTP stream by checking for excessive field lengths and abnormal characters. In addition, Check Point has added a new feature that scans for HTTP worms and prevents them from reaching your servers.

Worm Catcher

One of the newer and more devastating variety of attacks to come about recently is HTTP worms, such as Code Red and Nimda. A HTTP worm is a virus that self-propagates, among other ways, though HTTP protocol to infect other Web servers. These worms exploit vulnerabilities in Web servers that allow the worm to load itself into the running memory of the target machine. Once in memory, it will start scanning other IP addresses in an attempt to spread onto more machines. Usually just the traffic load of thousands of machines scanning for vulnerable hosts is enough to slow down Internet traffic across the globe, not even considering other damages the payload can cause. Because these worms communicate over standard HTTP traffic streams (TCP port 80) you cannot protect yourself against these attacks with rules in your rule base, because there is no way to differentiate valid Web traffic and the worm at layer 4 or below.

To combat these worms, Check Point has designed a scanning process that reads the HTTP protocol data and searches for specific patterns before deciding to allow the packet. The worm catcher comes with some predefined worm definitions and is updated with new patterns when performing a SmartDefense update. In addition, you can also manually add new patterns using standard regular expressions. This book gives only brief coverage on writing regular expressions, because an entire book could be (and is) dedicated to the topic.

Tools and Traps...

Regular Expressions

Regular Expressions are an extremely flexible method of performing pattern matching and are implemented in many tools and programming languages. This section is meant to be a (very) brief overview of regular expressions. If you would like to learn more, you can find a multitude of introduction pages with a simple Web search.

In Regular Expressions, most characters will match themselves, meaning the expression "abc" will only match the exact phrase "abc". Some characters, however, have special purposes when matching characters. For example, the * character is a wildcard used to match any number of the preceding character. If you want to match the actual character instead of its special meaning, you must precede the character with a backslash (\ ), so your expression would contain * if you wanted to match the asterisk character, and \\ if you wanted to match a backslash. Here is a list of some special characters:

. (period)

*

?

^

$

+

(

)

\

|

The use of regular expressions makes the worm catcher an extremely powerful tool. The ability to manually add new worm definitions means that you can filter HTTP packets based on any data pattern that you can describe with a regular expression. You will also be able to protect yourself against future HTTP worms without having purchased the SmartDefense subscription service, if you don't mind taking the time to research the infectious data stream and writing a regular expression to describe it.

The worm catcher is an independent process from the HTTP Security Server, so you can use the feature without invoking the HTTP Security Server on connections.

The worm catcher is a kernel-level process and should not cause any significant performance impacts when enabled. Even so, thorough testing is recommended before enabling the feature in a production environment.

First, let's take a look at the attack signature for the Code Red worm. Code Red spread by overflowing an unchecked buffer that could be accessed by calling an Internet Data Administration (.ida) file. Data can be passed to an .ida file by following the file with a question mark (?) and then the data you wish to pass to the server. For example, the HTTP header "GET /default.ida?abcdefg" will send "abcdefg" to the default.ida script.

The pattern that is used to prevent the Code Red worm in the worm catcher is "\.ida\?", which is shown in Figure 11.19. Because both "." and "?" are special characters that have other meanings in a regular expression, they must be preceded with the \ character to let the worm catcher know that you want to match the actual characters. This regular expression looks for the string ".ida?" and will drop any requests with this pattern. Notice that this will prevent any files with the .ida extension from being called, so if you use these files, you will want to disable this worm check and make sure that your Web server is patched against this vulnerability. You could also try to rewrite the regular expression to look for a more specific match that will not trigger every time someone accesses your Web site.

Figure 11.19 General HTTP Worm Catcher

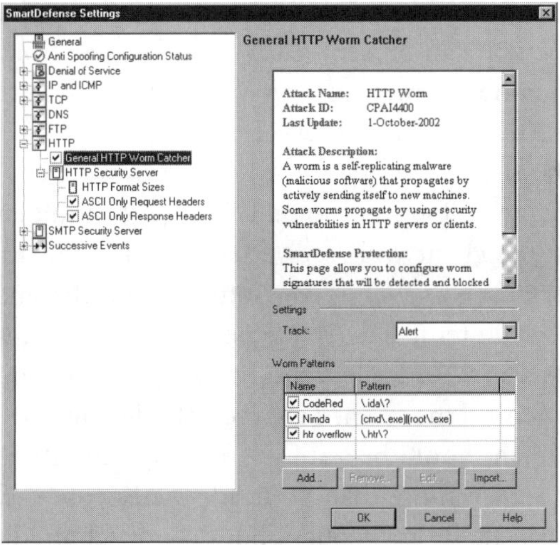

The signature for the Nimda worm tries to access either cmd.exe or root.exe through an HTTP request. In order to prevent a request with either "cmd.exe" or "root.exe" in the data stream, the logical OR operation (|) needs to be used. The regular expression for the Nimda worm is "(cmd\.exe)|(root\.exe)", as shown in

Figure 11.19. The parentheses are control characters that group everything listed between them. The two sets are separated by the logical OR operation, and as mentioned in the last worm signature, the period character must be preceded by a backslash if you want to match a period (instead of any character). So, the regular expression is written to drop any HTTP request that contains "cmd.exe" or "root.exe" in the request.

WARNING

As of FP3, when you enable the **General HTTP Worm Catcher**, all active connections through the firewall will be broken when you push policy.

HTTP Security Servers

The options in this section are a part of the HTTP security server and will only apply when the HTTP Security Server is invoked for a connection. As with the FTP Security Server, you can choose to apply these settings to all HTTP traffic (port 80 only), or only to connections that use HTTP resources. The additional settings in this configuration tree allow you to set limits on some of the HTTP protocol information that passes between client and server.

One section, shown in Figure 11.20, is dedicated to setting limits on the HTTP header sizes and URL lengths. These features are used as general protection against buffer overflows because you can prevent URLs and headers from being long enough to overflow unchecked buffers. When you type a URL into your Web browser, it will initiate a TCP session to the destination server and send the HTTP GET request along with some HTTP headers that describe what sorts of data types and encoding types that browser will accept, as well as send some other general information such as browser type. In return, the client will receive response headers that give additional information to the client, such as Web server software and the encoding and content type of the data that is being returned. As a general sanity check you can prevent excessively long URL requests and header lengths. In addition you can limit the number of headers that are sent by either the client or server. By default, the maximum number of headers is set to 500, which should be a sufficiently high number to identify an attack since most pages won't return more than 10 headers. Also, the default settings prevent more than 2 kB of data in the URL request, but do not set any limits on how long each individual header can be. These settings are all configurable to allow you to define your own parameters for normal HTTP traffic.

Two other options that are available and enabled by default are called **ASCII Only Request Headers** and **ASCII Only Response Headers**. These two options will restrict the header data to contain only printable ASCII characters. Some buffer overflow attacks use the header fields to store the payload information that is supposed to be written to memory, and limiting the header fields to containing only ASCII characters will prevent binary code from being stored in the header fields. Although both of these options apply to the HTTP headers, they were separated into two separate options so you could enforce this check on the client's request headers only, the server's response headers only, or both request and response headers.

Figure 11.20 HTTP Format Sizes

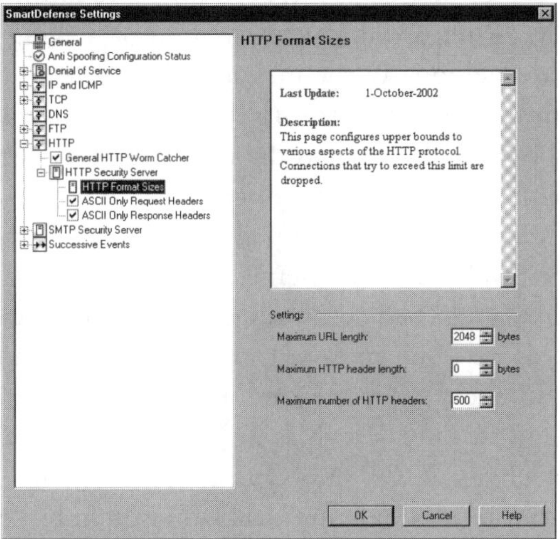

SMTP Security Server

As with the other security servers, you have the option to use the security server for all SMTP traffic, or for only the SMTP resources defined in the rule base.

WARNING

More than likely you do not want to enable the SMTP security server for all connections, because your enforcement point will act as an open relay to anyone on the Internet. This can cause your IP to get added to an open relay blacklist, which can prevent you from sending e-mail to domains that block SMTP traffic from sites on the blacklist. If you want to use the SMTP security server features, you should create a SMTP resource with *@mydomain.com in the Recipient field of the Match tab. You can then add this resource to the rules where you would like to use the SMTP security server.

There are two categories under the SMTP security server. **SMTP Content** deals with the content in the actual SMTP commands that are passed between a client and server. The **Mail and Recipient Content** category scans the SMTP data that is passed as the body of an e-mail message. These two categories are covered in more detail in the following sections.

SMTP Content

The SMTP content category provides security options that attempt to identify attack attempts by watching the commands that are passed between client and server.

When the security server intercepts SMTP traffic passing through the firewall, it is basically acting as an SMTP relay. You have the option of making FireWall-1 add a "Received by" header to the body of the message when it relays mail by selecting the **Add "received" header when forwarding mail** option. If you uncheck this option, no additional lines will be added, although the next SMTP server's received header will state that the e-mail was received from the enforcement point, instead of the previous SMTP server, so the SMTP security server will not be entirely transparent.

You can also set the SMTP Security Server to watch for "bad" SMTP commands. There are two different types of bad commands, from SmartDefense's point of view, and you can define thresholds for both kinds of bad commands. One type of bad command are the ones that have no effect when they are used. Only a certain number of commands are needed to send an e-mail, such as *MAIL FROM:*, *RCPT TO:*, and *DATA*, and other commands, such as *NOOP* (No Operation), do nothing but keep the TCP session from timing out. You can configure a maximum number of "no effect" commands that are allowed before the session is terminated.

The other type of "bad" commands are those that are not known to the security server. The security server is aware of all RFC standard commands, so it is unlikely that another SMTP server will be sending illegal commands. The logic behind this feature is that if more than a small number of "no effect" or unknown commands are sent to the server, the e-mail is not likely being delivered by an SMTP daemon, but an attacker snooping around your server. These features should keep an attacker from snooping around too much, and they can create a log entry when the session is terminated.

All of the options discussed in this section are shown in Figure 11.21. Also, notice that there isn't an **Action** field defined in this section, so your only choice is to log the dropped connections. You cannot send any other form of alert when this type of attack is detected.

Mail and Recipient Content

This SMTP category focuses on scanning the data that is passed in an e-mail, specifically the Multipurpose Internet Mail Extensions (MIME) information that is used to identify the accompanying data in the e-mail message. When an e-mail message is created, MIME information is placed in the e-mail header to describe to the recipient how to interpret the data that follows. One of the MIME headers used is content-type, which specifies what sort of data follows, such as text/plain or text/html. When there are multiple types of data being sent in a single message, such as an HTML e-mail with a Word document attached, then the content-type is set to "multipart." Multipart indicates to the receiver to expect multiple MIME sections, or parts, each with their own set of headers describing each chunk of data. Another header called "content-transfer-encoding" is used to describe what encoding method has been used on the attached data, such as 7bit, 8bit, and so on. 7bit and 8bit data must follow certain guidelines about how many octets per line, and what values are acceptable (CR and LF are not allowed). Binary can be specified as the encoding type when the data hasn't actually been encoded.

Figure 11.21 SMTP Content

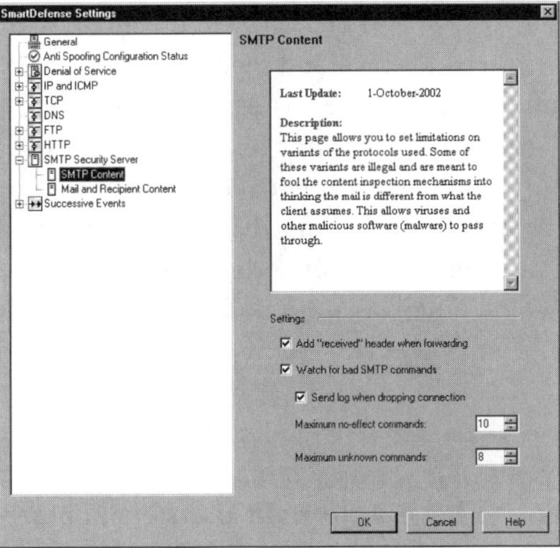

When an SMTP message is passed through the SMTP security server, it will scan the data for possible problems with the MIME headers in the message. One of the problems that can be detected is when multiple content-type headers are listed in the message. When there are multiple content-types listed, the receiving workstation has contradictory information it must deal with, and different programs will handle this exception in different ways. Another check that the SMTP security server performs is for multiple encoding headers, which can cause similar problems as with multiple content-type headers. This check will not block multipart messages, because they will have multiple content-types by definition. The difference is that there are boundary lines that separate each MIME part in the message. Each content-type header applies to a different MIME part, so there is no contradictory information. The problem occurs when there are multiple content-type or content-transfer-encoding headers that try to describe the same section of data.

NOTE

These settings will not apply if you have chosen to apply the security server to all SMTP connections passing through your firewall. For these settings to work, you *must* define and apply an SMTP resource to the traffic that you want scanned.

The Security Server also gives you the option of denying "non-plain" and unknown encoding types. A plain encoding method does not modify the data, but just describes how it is represented. Standard ASCII characters are represented by a 7-bit value, and extended ASCII characters are represented with 8-bit characters, so when 7bit or 8bit encoding is used, these characters are represented as themselves. Even encoding schemes such as Base64 can be considered plain, because this method takes a group of three 8-bit characters (24 bits) and separates it into four 6-bit pieces. Each 6-bit section is represented by a character, as described in RFC 1521. Even though this won't be humanly readable, the data has not been modified as it would be if another process like compression was applied to the data before it was encoded. You can prevent more exotic encoding types by making sure that the **Allow "non-plain" encoding types** option is *un*selected. Some of the encoding types that will pass through as "plain" encoding types are 7bit, 8bit, binary, Base64, and quoted-printable. As new encoding schemes are made available, the Security Server may not understand what the new encoding scheme is, and if you have your enforcement points configured to strip out unknown encoding types, these newer encoding formats will be dropped. You have the option of allowing or disallowing unknown encoding types.

The **Force recipient to have a domain name** option prevents mail from being delivered through the security server if the destination e-mail address doesn't contain a domain name for the user. For example, a SMTP server that is responsible for the mail of a single domain name may be configured to accept a *RCPT TO*: line that contains only the username, instead of username@domain.com.

The **Perform aggressive MIME strip** option defines how the security server will go about searching for and removing MIME headers. When this option is disabled, the security server will only look in the header area of each MIME part for information that needs to be stripped. If aggressive mode is enabled, the security server will search the entire body of the message for MIME information that should be removed.

Figure 11.22 shows the available options in the Mail and Recipient Content configuration window. As with the previous SMTP section, you can only log when the Security Server detects a suspicious transmission because the **Action** option is not available.

Figure 11.22 SMTP Mail and Recipient Content

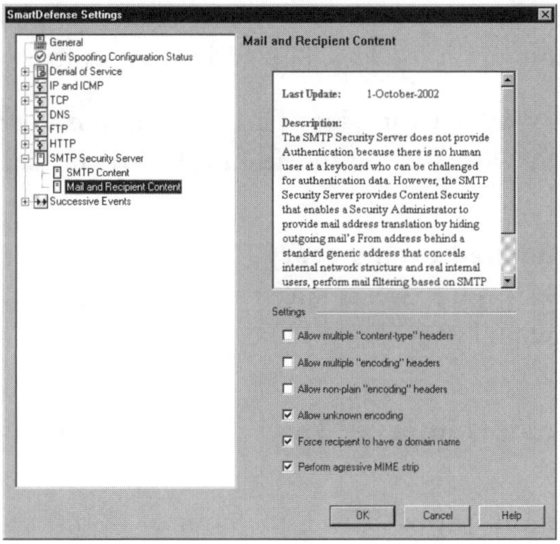

Successive Events

The Check Point Malicious Activity Detection (CPMAD) daemon was integrated with SmartDefense as the Successive Events tree. All of the options in this branch of the tree work by scanning the FW-1 logs for signs of suspicious activity, and they all have an **Advanced** configuration button, which lets you tweak the sensitivity of the alerts. This Advanced Configuration window is shown in Figure 11.23, and we cover these settings here because the window looks exactly the same for each subsection that will be described below.

Figure 11.23 Successive Events Advanced Configuration

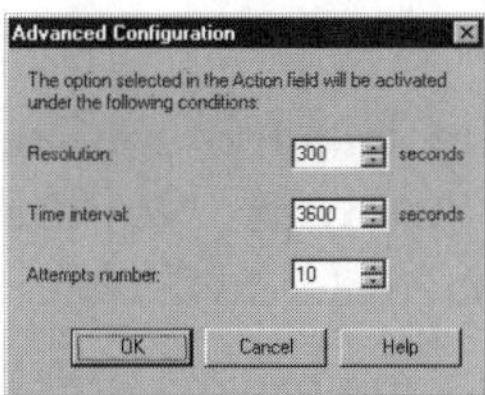

Note

The Successive Events section scans the log entries for evidence of the attacks listed in the configuration tree. Packets that are dropped by the implicit deny at the end of the rule base will be logged. This means that if you have not configured an explicit drop rule that logs all packets that are denied, then most of these features will not report when an attack has occurred.

The main Successive Events category contains some options that apply to all sub-options in this category. These options define how much memory will be used for tracking events that show up in the logs. The options are as follows:

- **Max Memory allocation size** This is the amount of memory that will be allocated to the Successive Events feature, for use in tracking log entries that are related to an attack.
- **Reset accumulated events every** This is the number of seconds that each entry in the Successive Events table can live. This prevents the table from continuously growing by removing old entries that should no longer be taken into account.
- **Logging attempts interval** This is the interval of time that log entries are counted.
- **Max logging attempts** This is the number of times an entry has to occur before the action is taken.

Each option within the Successive Events category contains an **Advanced** button that lets you configure the sensitivity levels of each feature. This menu allows you to set a threshold by defining how many events in a certain time period will be considered an attack. Once the threshold is crossed, the selected action will be taken.

These options are also available under the advanced settings of the Denial of Service category, and are as follows:

- **Resolution** This is the length of the interval that SmartDefense uses when tracking pertinent log entries. Check Point recommends the resolution to be one-tenth of the **Time Interval** option, and should never be set less than one-fifth.
- **Time Interval** This is the length of time that log entries will be considered valid for an attack. If the **Attempts Number** of attacks is detected during this time period, the selected alert will be used.
- **Attempts Number** The number of attacks that needs to be exceeded within the above time limit to signal an attack.

The following five subsections describe each option available under the Successive Events configuration tree, which is shown in Figure 11.24.

Address Spoofing

As was mentioned at the beginning of the chapter, the Anti-Spoofing configuration section does not block any attacks by itself, nor does it even look for evidence of a spoofing attack. It only tells you which gateways are not configured for anti-spoofing protection. Once you have your gateways configured for anti-spoofing, this feature can be used to send alerts when spoofing attempts are detected. If this feature is enabled, it will scan the logs for drops due to the anti-spoofing protection. If the thresholds that are defined in the advanced configuration are exceeded, the selected alert will be sent.

Figure 11.24 Successive Events

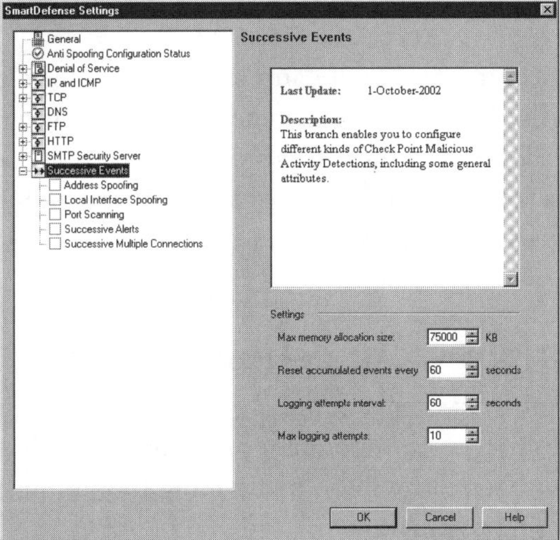

Local Interface Spoofing

This section will look for packets that are sourced from local interfaces of your gateways. If packets are dropped because they contained spoofed addresses of the firewall interface, this feature will send an alert when the defined thresholds are crossed.

Port Scanning

An attacker will perform port scans on a server when he is trying to find out which ports are accepting connections. The easiest way to find out which ports are accepting connections is to initiate a connection to that port and see if he receives a response. If the server responds with a SYN/ACK, the attacker knows that the port is open and accepting connections. If a RST/ACK is returned, the attacker knows that the particular port is closed and the server is not accepting connections from that server. Finally, if no response is received from the SYN request, the attacker can assume that port is being filtered by a firewall because a firewall will just drop the packet instead of returning a response as the server will do. This is performed for every port that is being checked, and usually thousands of ports will be checked to determine which networked applications are running on a server.

Since a log entry will be generated for each SYN packet that is sent to a blocked port (assuming you have a cleanup rule that logs), SmartDefense can alert when port scans are being attempted because a large number of packets will be sent in a short period of time. A patient hacker will perform his port scan over a period of days, which will be not be detectable unless you have extremely sensitive thresholds defined, although this will also drastically increase your number of false positives.

Successive Alerts

Certain SmartDefense features can create an excessive amount of alerts when an attack is taking place, such as the HTTP worm catcher. Check Point designed **Successive Alerts** to give a single alert when these types of attacks take place. For example, you can set the original attack to send a pop-up alert when the offending packets are detected, but have **Successive Alerts** send an e-mail alert when a certain threshold of attacks are detected.

Successive Multiple Connections

This will scan the logs of an excessive number of connections to the same destination IP and port number within the configurable time limit. The advanced settings let you decide how sensitive this log scan will be by defining the number of attempts that can happen within a certain time limit.

Summary

With the addition of SmartDefense to Check Point's FireWall-1 NG, you now have additional protection within your enforcement points that was not previously available. SmartDefense allows you to look for abnormalities in packets and can take immediate action to prevent the malformed packets from entering into your network. To prevent these types of attacks, the Firewall has been given additional understanding about the structure of some commonly used protocols, such as HTTP, SMTP, and FTP. Most of the exploitations of these protocols are caused by sending a stream of data that the server never expects to see, such as an HTTP header that is larger than the memory space allocated to hold that piece of information.

Other features watch for suspicious behavior in the protocol data streams, such as in the SMTP protocol where someone may be snooping around and trying different commands to probe the server for information. In these situations, SmartDefense can end a session when it detects that an unusual number of commands are issued that are not directly needed to send an e-mail message. You are also given the ability to limit which commands are available when communicating with an FTP server; you have the option of removing commands that do not have a valid use in your environment.

In each case, you are tightening down what sort of behavior is acceptable on your network, and you can prevent a range of attacks, both new and old, by performing extra sanity checks on the protocol data. In some cases, these features can cause problems in certain network configurations, so Check Point has made most of the SmartDefense features optional, allowing you to pick which types of protection would be most beneficial in your environment.

Solutions Fast Track

Understanding and Configuring SmartDefense

☑ SmartDefense is designed to prevent classes of attacks, instead of individual ones.

☑ Since many attacks are performed by sending malformed packets, SmartDefense contains many options for performing strict checks on commonly used protocols.

☑ Not only does SmartDefense perform sanity checks on Layer 3 and Layer 4 protocol information, it can also scan commonly used Layer 7 protocols such as DNS, HTTP, FTP, and SMTP.

☑ You can choose how FireWall-1 should notify you when an attack is detected. You can use any of the built-in features of FireWall-1 or call your own scripts.

- ☑ The Denial of Service options let you specify only what sort of alerting you would like to see, since these attacks are already prevented by the standard protocol sanity checks.
- ☑ The HTTP worm catcher can be used to block any HTTP URL that you want to write a definition for. All you need to do is write a regular expression defining the URL you wish to prevent.
- ☑ Although you may want to use some of the features available as part of the security servers, you may not want to enable the use of security servers if you are in anything other than a small office environment, due to the amount of overhead that security servers can add. The only way to know if the security servers will work in your environment is with thorough testing.
- ☑ If you enable the SMTP security server for all connections through your firewall, your firewall will act as an open relay and can be abused by spammers and other people that want to mask the source of their e-mails.

Frequently Asked Questions

The following Frequently Asked Questions, answered by the authors of this book, are designed to both measure your understanding of the concepts presented in this chapter and to assist you with real-life implementation of these concepts. To have your questions about this chapter answered by the author, browse to **www.syngress.com/solutions** and click on the **"Ask the Author"** form.

Q: A new attack has recently been released. How can I configure my firewall to prevent this attack from affecting me?

A: In the General section of the SmartDefense window is a link to **Check Point Security Updates**. This will open your Web browser and take you to a page that describes how to defend against some of the latest attacks.

Q: I want to update my SmartDefense configuration, but the **Update** button is grayed out and I cannot click on it. Why?

A: You cannot update SmartDefense unless you purchase the subscription service. Contact Check Point to get pricing for this service.

Q: Can SmartDefense detect when any of my machines have been infected with a worm?

A: You can use SmartDefense to indirectly detect when one of your systems has been compromised. Some worms create a lot of network traffic while trying to scan for other vulnerable hosts. If you are using **Successive Multiple Connections** in SmartDefense, you will see when a certain connection threshold is reached. This can be used to identify machines that may possibly be infected by a worm.

Q: How can I make SmartView Tracker display only messages that are generated by SmartDefense?

A: In the Query Tree of SmartView Tracker is a predefined log query that will only display messages generated by SmartDefense. This has the same affect as adding a filter to the product field that displays only the SmartDefense product messages.

Chapter 12

SmartUpdate

Solutions in this chapter:

- Licensing Your Products
- Updating Your Products

☑ Summary

☑ Solutions Fast Track

☑ Frequently Asked Questions

Introduction

You have deployed 4 enforcement points, 2 management servers, 100 client VPN connections; Check Point produces a new feature pack. You have a business requirement to upgrade all of your software as quickly as possible. Most security engineers will groan and shake their heads—another massive undertaking to perform a simple upgrade. Check Point has created the SmartUpdate Client for this reason. SmartUpdate is the tool that you will use to perform product updates and to push licenses to products.

Since the advent of NG, licensing has significantly changed. Licenses in 4.*x* were always "local" with the license files always installed directly on the Check Point product platform. With the new method of licensing, you can install all of your licenses on the management server and "push" the licenses to all Check Point products. This method of licensing provides a new level of flexibility. If you have a remote enforcement point in Chicago, and the office moves to New York, you can remove the license from the Chicago firewall and redeploy the license to New York, all from your central management server. Central management of your licenses will ensure that you have control over the deployment of your firewall products.

As mentioned above, SmartUpdate also allows you to update the code on your firewall products. SmartUpdate will show your currently licensed products and allow you to push updates to them. You can add the updates to your management server by copying them from a CD, or by simply connecting and downloading them from the Check Point site.

Licensing Your Products

Managing licenses for your Check Point products is an important component of overall firewall management. Although licensing is a straightforward concept—each firewall component must be licensed for the features it will use—the actual process of licensing your products can quickly become confusing when dealing with a large, diverse, and physically dispersed environment.

Before we discuss the procedures for managing licenses with SmartUpdate, an overview of the underlying components of a Check Point license will be useful. A license consists of the following:

- **Certificate key** A unique string issued by Check Point, used to identify the license
- **Product** A string that identifies to what features the license applies
- **Version** The Check Point version to which the license applies
- **Customer name** The name of the customer to whom the license is issued

- **Expiration date** The date the license will expire, if any
- **Host ID** The IP address of the management module (for central licensing), or the IP address of the Check Point node (local licensing)
- **SKU** A unique string issued by Check Point, also used to identify the license
- **Signature** A unique string generated by Check Point to verify its authenticity

Figure 12.1 shows the main components of the SmartUpdate tool, which you'll find in the **Check Point SMART Clients** program group. Open it, then choose the **Licenses** tab. Then choose **Licenses | View Repository**. This displays the list of licenses currently installed in SmartUpdate.

Figure 12.1 SmartUpdate Licenses

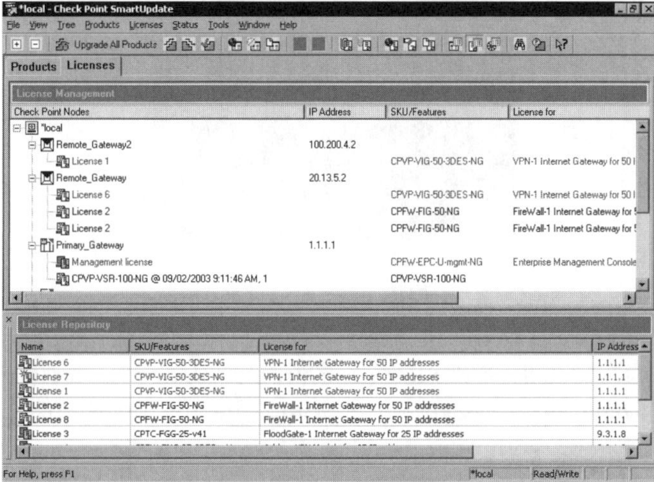

The first section, **License Management**, is a good general overview of the Check Point nodes configured in your firewall. For each node, any licenses that are attached to that node are displayed. The second section, **License Repository**, is essentially the same information, organized differently. Here you'll find a list of licenses, with information about the features, IP addresses, expiration dates, types, and attached nodes of each.

Management Server

Licensing your management server requires a management license, identified by "mgmt" in the product string. This type of license may have the capability to manage a specified number of enforcement modules or an unlimited number of modules.

An important caveat to using the SmartUpdate tool for license management is that you must install a license on the management server before using this tool. This means that you cannot use SmartUpdate to initially install the management server license.

Installing Licenses via the Management Server

To initially install a license on the management server, you may use the **cpconfig** or **cplic put** commands from the command-line interface of the server running the management module. Once the management server has a license on it, you can use SmartUpdate to install a new license, just as you would any other node.

To install a license, the first step is to get to a command-line interface on the management server. Then, type **cpconfig** (see Figure 12.2).

Figure 12.2 cpconfig

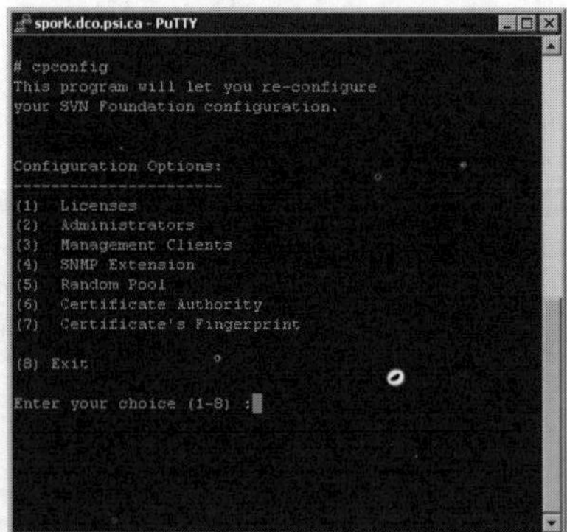

Enter **1** for licenses, and a list of licenses currently installed on this management module, if any, will be displayed. Enter **A** to add a license, and then enter **M** if you want to manually enter the details of the license as prompted, or **F** to fetch the license from a file. In the case of fetching the license data from a file, this file should be downloaded from your User Center account and saved to a text file on the management server.

Instead of using **cpconfig**, you may use **cplic put** to add a license to the management server:

```
cplic put -l <license file>
```

Here *<license file>* is a text file saved on the server that contains the license data from your User Center account. Or, you may specify the license details manually:

```
cplic put host expiration-date signature SKU/features.
```

Removing Licenses via the Management Server

You can also remove licenses from a management server by using the **cpconfig** command. To do this, log on to the command-line interface of the management server, and enter **cpconfig**. Enter **1** for licenses, and a current list of installed licenses will be displayed. Enter **D** to delete a license, and you will then be prompted for the license signature of the license you want to remove. Copy and paste the license signature of this license from the list displayed.

Resetting SIC

When the firewall's Secure Internal Communications (SIC) is reset, either via the **cpconfig** interface or the GUI, note that the licenses must be reinstalled on the management console. Until this is done, you will not be able to use the management console to install the security policy on any enforcement modules.

Enforcement Points

Licensing your enforcement points can be performed entirely from the SmartUpdate tool. No matter what type of license you want to install, the process is identical. Note that enforcement points may be integrated into the same physical firewall as the management server, but this does not change the license installation procedure.

Installing Licenses via SmartUpdate

Licenses may be downloaded from the Internet, added manually, or imported from a file. We cover each of these options.

To install a new license into SmartUpdate, choose **Licenses | New License**. Then choose **Add From User Center**, which will open a new window that prompts you to log in to your User Center account. After you log in, you will see a list of available products.

Tools & Traps...

Missing License

If the license you are looking for is not listed in your User Center account, there are several possible explanations. If you recently purchased the license, check with your Check Point reseller to find out whether your order has been fully processed—it takes time for newly ordered licenses to appear. Or, the license may be associated with another User Center account, perhaps to someone else within your organization. If all else fails, you may also contact Check Point licensing support.

Select the action **Download License File**, check the licenses you want to add to SmartUpdate, and click **GO**. After the license files download, SmartUpdate will ask if you would like to add them to its inventory. You should then see the added licenses in the license repository list. Note that when you add a license, the IP address assigned to that license must be assigned to a Check Point module that SmartUpdate knows about, or you will not be permitted to install that license.

Once you have downloaded the license, the next step is to attach it to the node. In the License Management section, right-click on the node you want to attach the license to, and choose **Attach Licenses** (see Figure 12.3).

Figure 12.3 Attach Licenses

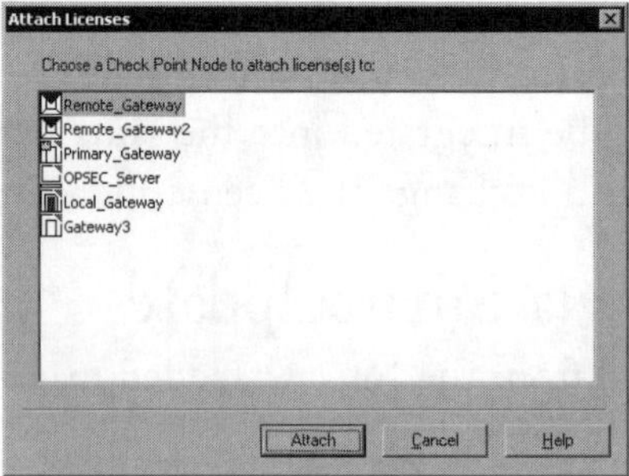

Here, you will see a list of all licenses that are not currently attached to any node. Select the license you want to attach to this node and click **Attach**. Back in the License Management window, you should now see this license listed under its node.

Removing Licenses via SmartUpdate

Removing a license from a node is as simple as detaching the license from that node. To do this in SmartUpdate, right-click on the license you want to detach and choose **Detach License**. If you do not want to keep this license to use on another node, you may uninstall it from SmartUpdate by right-clicking on the license in the License Repository and choosing **Delete License**.

Other License Types

Aside from the standard license types we have discussed, a number of other Check Point products require licensing. You can also use Smart Update to install these licenses.

SecuRemote

Before using SecuRemote to allow remote users to connect to your network, you need to ensure that sufficient SecuRemote licenses are installed on your Check Point nodes. The good news is that SecuRemote licenses are free from Check Point.

To obtain these free SecuRemote licenses, log in to your User Center account and click on the **Add VPN-1 SecuRemote Product to your account** link. You will be asked how many remote users the license is for, and you will then be prompted for details about the license. Be sure to select central licensing and enter the IP address of your management module. You will then see this new license listed in your product list.

You can download the SecuRemote license and install it into SmartUpdate just as you would any other license. Once it is installed, simply attach the license to the management server, and you are licensed for SecuRemote use.

SecureClient

Use of SecureClient requires the purchase of sufficient SecureClient licenses from Check Point. Once a SecureClient license is listed in your User Center account, select it to enter its licensing details—be sure to select central licensing and enter the IP address of your management module. You can then download and attach the SecureClient license just as with SecuRemote licenses.

FloodGate

FloodGate licenses must be purchased from Check Point, and they are installed on the enforcement module. Use the procedure described in "Installing Licenses via SmartUpdate" to install these licenses with SmartUpdate.

Connect Control

Connect Control licenses must be purchased from Check Point, and are installed on the node running this software. Use the procedure described in "Installing Licenses via SmartUpdate" to install these licenses with SmartUpdate.

Updating Your Products

Using SmartUpdate to keep your Check Point products up-to-date is an extremely efficient process compared to the daunting task of manually updating multiple nodes. Note that in order to use Smart Update for this purpose, you must have a license that allows you to do so—the CPMP-SUP-1-NG (for one node) or CPMP-SUP-U-NG (for unlimited nodes). These licenses can be installed via SmartUpdate to the management module.

The first step to using SmartUpdate to update your products is to open the SmartUpdate program and go to the **Products** tab. Then choose **Products | View Repository** (see Figure 12.4).

In the Product Management area, you will see a list of all the Check Point nodes available and the products installed on each, including their IP addresses, operating systems, vendors, and versions. This gives you a good overview of your product base and allows you to quickly determine what upgrades are required.

Figure 12.4 SmartUpdate Products

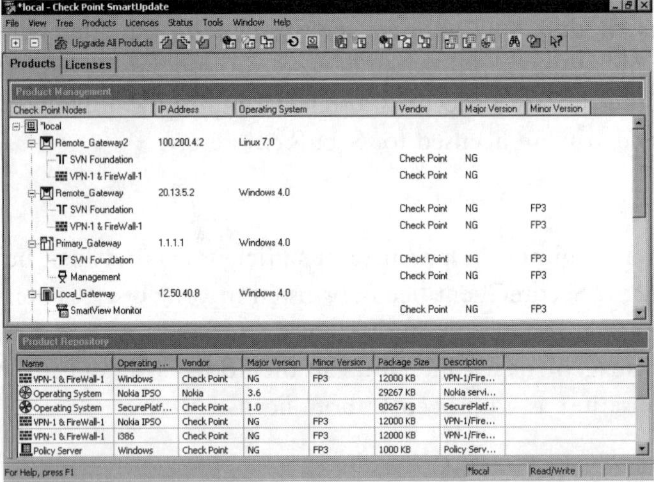

The Product Repository section lists each product available to SmartUpdate for installation. The name, operating system, vendor, version, size, and description are displayed to give you full information on each.

Adding a New Product

To add a new product to the Product Repository, choose **Products | New Product**. You have the option of adding the product from the Check Point Download Center (valid login ID and password are required), from a Check Point CD, or from a file. Once the product is added and listed in the repository, it is available for installation.

Installing a Product

To install a product listed in the repository on a node, right-click on that product and choose **Install**. You will be presented with a list of nodes for which this product is applicable—SmartUpdate will automatically detect which nodes match this product's operating system. Choose the node or nodes on which you want to install the product, and SmartUpdate does the rest. Note that you also have the option to reboot the node following the installation, which is advised.

Summary

In a network that consists of only one or two Check Point components, keeping software versions up-to-date and organizing licensing is not a difficult task, and can be done manually. But in the case of a larger environment with many varied components, these tasks can be daunting.

Because updating software may be a time-sensitive task, especially in the case of a security-related update, SmartUpdate is an important tool to enable you to perform updates quickly and accurately.

SmartUpdate also allows you to quickly and easily keep track of licensing. Given the wide variety of license types available, manually managing licenses for a high number of devices quickly becomes tedious. Smart Update avoids this unnecessary effort, saving you time and energy.

Solutions Fast Track

Licensing Your Products

- ☑ Manually install a management license on the management server.
- ☑ Download licenses from User Center, enter them manually, or import them from a file.
- ☑ Attach and detach licenses to nodes as required.

Updating Your Products

- ☑ Add products into SmartUpdate via the Internet, from CD, or from a file.
- ☑ Install products on Check Point nodes either individually or on all nodes at once.
- ☑ Have SmartUpdate reboot the nodes following installation.

Frequently Asked Questions

The following Frequently Asked Questions, answered by the authors of this book, are designed to both measure your understanding of the concepts presented in this chapter and to assist you with real-life implementation of these concepts. To have your questions about this chapter answered by the author, browse to **www.syngress.com/solutions** and click on the **"Ask the Author"** form.

Q: Why are some licenses in SmartUpdate red?

A: These licenses are expired. If you want to continue using them, you need to order a renewal.

Q: When I try to add a license to SmartUpdate, why do I get an error that it cannot be added because of its IP address?

A: There is no node known to SmartUpdate that matches the IP address of the license. Either relicense with a different address or make sure the node is defined in your firewall so it will show up in SmartUpdate.

Q: Is it best to install updates on all nodes at once or each individually?

A: If possible, keep versions of software the same on all nodes, to prevent possible compatibility problems. If you need to move one node to a different version by itself, be sure to read the release notes carefully for potential issues.

Q: Do I have to pay for SecuRemote licenses? What about SecureClient?

A: SecuRemote licenses are free, and you can add them to your User Center account directly from the Web interface. SecureClient licenses must be purchased from your Check Point reseller.

Q: If I upgrade a product manually, can I use SmartUpdate to upgrade the product in the future?

A: Yes. SmartUpdate can be used to upgrade any product, whether or not that product was upgraded manually in the past.

Q: Once a product is upgraded, does it need to have its license reinstalled?

A: This depends on the versions before and after the upgrade. For example, if you are upgrading a component from Check Point 4.1 to NG, you would also have to upgrade the license in the User Center, and then install that new license. However, upgrades within a version, such as NG FP2 to NG FP3, do not require the license to be reinstalled.

Chapter 13

Performance Pack

Solutions in this chapter:

- How Performance Pack Works
- Installing Performance Pack
- Command Line Options for Performance Pack
- Troubleshooting Performance Pack

☑ Summary

☑ Solutions Fast Track

☑ Frequently Asked Questions

Introduction

When it comes to your VPN-1/FireWall-1 platform's performance, more is definitely better. However, until very recently, high performance came at a high price. In order to lower the high cost of high performance, Check Point has developed a software add-on to VPN-1/FireWall-1 NG FP3 that will enable over 3Gbps of throughput on standard server hardware. This Performance Pack runs on Check Point SecurePlatform and Solaris. Support for the Nokia IP series is planned for the upcoming IPSO 3.7/NG FP4 release, in addition to the existing Nokia Flows. For sites that do not desire to use the Nokia IP series, SecurePlatform, or Solaris, there are other options such as Nortel's Alteon Switched Firewall or RapidStream's VPN/Firewall Appliances.

Performance Pack can provide midsize organizations with high-throughput solutions for sites that use FireWall-1 on high-speed links, particularly when high VPN throughput is desired.

Check Point gives the technology behind Performance Pack the name *SecureXL*. The terms *Performance Pack* and *SecureXL* can be used interchangeably, as we do in this chapter.

How Performance Pack works

Performance Pack works by taking advantage of specific design features in the host OS and CPU. In other words, Performance Pack replaces some parts of FireWall-1 with code that is highly specific to the OS and CPU that Performance Pack will run on and highly optimized for that OS and CPU.

Examples of such enabling technology include separating performance-critical code from the main firewall executable; moving that code into "kernel space," where it can run with higher priority and higher privileges as well as potentially "closer" to such key elements of the OS as the TCP/IP stack and the routines that handle NIC input/output; taking advantage of CPU features such as HyperThreading; binding NIC interrupts to a specific processor in a SMP (multiprocessor) environment; and creating Connection Templates to increase the session rate. Many accelerated connections, once established, essentially bypass the firewall, instead being handled by the low-level SecureXL driver.

Performance Pack accelerates general network throughput as well as certain CPU-intensive key security functions of VPN-1/FireWall-1, such as:

- Encryption (VPN throughput)
- NAT
- Connection/session rate

- Accounting
- Access control
- General security checks

Check Point adds to the areas of VPN-1/FireWall-1 that Performance Pack accelerates with each Feature Pack. Expect FP4 to expand on the preceding list of functions.

Notes from the Underground...

Invalid Sequences

When Performance Pack is activated, TCP Sequence Validation, a new feature of FireWall-1 NG, is turned off. Checking of the statefulness of TCP traffic remains enabled, unless you disable it manually, of course. However, TCP sequence numbers are no longer verified for correctness. This will not be a problem as long as you follow the philosophy of "multilayered security" and keep your host systems up to date, so that attacks on their TCP/IP stacks using invalid sequence numbers are not viable.

Working on Interfaces While Using Performance Pack

Because of the way that Performance Pack ties into the low-level functions of the host OS it runs on, you are required to turn acceleration off with an *fwaccel off* command before you start work on an interface, such as bringing that interface up or down or assigning a new IP address to it. The Release Notes contain a detailed list of activities that require you to turn acceleration off first.

As of Performance Pack NG FP3, you have to turn acceleration off before:

- Modifying, adding, or deleting interfaces
- Executing *ifconfig up/down/plumb* or *unplumb*

On SecurePlatform, use *sim uninstallin* before performing *fw ctl uninstall*. After *fw ctl install*, use *sim installin*.

Installing Performance Pack

Before you install Performance Pack, be sure to download the latest Release Notes from www.checkpoint.com/techsupport/installation/ng/release_notes.html. These notes contain important information about current limitations of Performance Pack and precautions to take when working with network interfaces while Performance Pack is installed and running.

Performance Pack can only be installed on an enforcement module, not on a management station without an enforcement module. As of Performance Pack NG FP3, Performance Pack does *not* support the following products:

- ClusterXL in load-sharing mode
- Floodgate-1
- SmartView Monitor

Hardware Requirements

The minimum requirements for Performance Pack are those of FireWall-1 NG. Since Performance Pack is about *performance*, though, let's have a look at the recommended system configurations and their relative performance.

One thing Performance Pack simply loves is raw CPU power. You can scale throughput almost linearly by adding a second CPU. The second thing Performance Pack loves is memory. A good I/O bus is also essential. Without I/O, your CPU won't be able to flex its muscle. The system should come with at least a dual 64-bit/66MHz PCI bus—better yet, multiple PCI-X buses, to facilitate high throughput.

Check Point recommends a Dual SPARC 64-bit machine with 512MB of memory or more, GigaSwift network interfaces, and 400MB of disk space as a platform for Performance Pack on Solaris. Platforms specifically recommended are a SunBlade 1000 or SunFire V480. Supported interface cards are the GEM Ethernet NIC, 10/100 QuadEthernet NIC, GigaSwift NIC, and Sun HME 10/100 Ethernet NIC.

A read into Check Point's platform selection guide gets more specific: The High Performance Solaris platform is identified as a SunFire V480, Dual UltraSPARC-III Cu, 4GB of memory, 2x Sun GigaSwift, and a Dual PCI bus. Such a configuration achieves 900Mbps+ throughput, according to Check Point.

If you want to use Performance Pack on SecurePlatform, Check Point recommend a Dual Intel Xeon machine with 512MB of memory or more, Intel Pro 1000XF or 1000XT network interfaces, and 400MB of disk space as well as at least two 64-bit/66MHz PCI buses on ServerWorks or Intel E7500 chipsets.

The platform selection guide is, again, edifying as to the expected performance of different SecurePlatform-based machines. The "basic" SecurePlatform is identified as a Celeron or Duron processor, 256MB RAM, one 32-bit/33MHz PCI bus with standard 10/100 network interfaces. The throughput of this configuration is given as 200Mbps. Next up is the "midrange" SecurePlatform, which sports a Pentium or Athlon CPU, 512MB of RAM, two Intel Pro/1000 network interfaces, and 64-bit/66MHz PCI buses. Throughput is stated as 1Gbps+. Lastly is the "high performance" SecurePlatform, with dual Xeon or Athlon MP processors, 1GB of RAM, four Intel Pro/1000 network interfaces, and four separate PCI-X buses. The stated throughput here is 3Gbps+.

The importance of the I/O bus for raw TCP/UDP throughput cannot be overstated, as this example shows: a dual Xeon 1.7 GHz machine, 1GB RAM, two independent 64-bit/66MHz PCI buses: 1.7Gbps. A dual Xeon 2.2 GHz machine, 1GB RAM, four independent PCI-X buses: 3.1Gbps. Comparing the raw CPU speeds, one would expect a performance increase to about 2Gbps, not 3Gbps. It is the I/O bus that is slowing the first configuration down.

That said, these throughput figures are large TCP streams without encryption. Read on for some qualifying statements about performance.

Performance Considerations

Keep in mind that 900Mbps+ (Solaris) or 3Gbps+ (SecurePlatform) is maximum FireWall-1 throughput using 1500-byte packets. Throughput is lower in a real-world situation. Look at some numbers: You can expect around 4 percent of your packet volume, which equals approximately 20 percent of your byte volume, to come from these 1500-byte packets. About a third of the packets are dataless ACKs (40 bytes), with maybe another fourth coming from 552-byte packets. The median packet size is about 256 bytes; a good 85 percent of all "streams" are under 1KB in length. Now throw encryption (VPN-1) into the picture, and your performance drops dramatically from the quoted 900Mbps+ or 3Gbps+.

We'd love to give you real figures. Unfortunately, we can't—not for a high-performance Sun Solaris platform. We can make some educated guesses, however. We'd expect a raw FW-1 throughput, with real-world traffic, on the order of 600Mbps to 700Mbps. VPN-1 throughput is hard to estimate. Judging from what other platforms achieve, 30Mbps to 50Mbps seem reasonable.

For SecurePlatform, Check Point states it offers 710Mbps encrypted throughput using AES-128 on a high-performance platform. Clearly, then, when encryption comes into play, the field is leveled between a platform with four PCI-X buses and a platform with two PCI 64-bit/66MHz buses. Playing our guessing game again, we would expect between 2.3Gbps and 2.5Gbps throughput with real-world traffic and between 200Mbps and 250Mbps VPN-1 throughput.

We hasten to say that these are guesstimates, based on other platforms for which we have performance data. Nothing will replace a real RFC2544 performance graph. Insist on this information when you shop for a FireWall-1/VPN-1 platform.

An area of performance that we have never seen graphed is throughput while using security servers. Security servers are *the* most performance-eating application you can run on your firewall. For this reason, they are not usually deployed on a firewall that has been specified for maximum throughput. If, however, you do use security servers, and you are hurting for performance, give Performance Pack serious consideration. It does accelerate security servers. This will be even truer, we expect, in the upcoming FP4 and later releases, since Check Point has moved certain security server functions into kernel streams, and Performance Pack does accelerate kernel streams in FP4.

Installing Performance Pack on Solaris 8

You can install Performance Pack NG FP3 on Solaris 8 with minimal downtime for your firewall. You do not have to halt the VPN-1/FireWall-1 processes to perform the installation, although established streams might break when enabling Performance Pack and will have to be reestablished. This could change with future releases. Be sure to read the Release Notes to find out whether installation requirements have changed. You might have to reboot.

There are two methods of installation. You can use the FireWall-1 Comprehensive Install package, or you can add the Performance Pack package using *pkgadd*.

Prerequisites

You need *root* privileges for the installation of Performance Pack. If you are not already logged in as *root*, become *root* by typing **su –**.

Performance Pack requires the same Solaris patch level as VPN-1/FireWall-1 NG. As of FP3, all needed patches are included in Sun's 8_Recommended patch cluster. In the unlikely case that you have not updated your 8_Recommended patch cluster when you installed or upgraded to FireWall-1 NG FP3, you should do so now.

If you use the Solaris FireWall-1 wrapper install, you also need about 130MB of free space on one of your partitions to hold the installation files—around 60MB for the compressed wrapper file and another 70MB for the uncompressed files and space during installation. Allow for more space during installation if you install Performance Pack at the same time you install VPN-1/FireWall-1.

Installation Using the Solaris Comprehensive Install Package

You can install Performance Pack with the help of the *UnixInstallScript* that Check Point provides with its Solaris VPN-1/FireWall-1 Comprehensive Install or *wrapper* package. The *UnixInstallScript* contained in that package lets you add Performance Pack to a system that already has VPN-1/FireWall-1 NG installed. You may also use it to install Performance Pack at the same time that you install VPN-1/FireWall-1 NG.

Since Check Point recommends using the wrapper install over installing individual packages, this is the preferred method of installing Performance Pack. If disk space is at an absolute premium, you might instead want to try the individual package install, covered in the "Installation as a Separate Package" section. Or invest in a bigger hard drive.

Unpack the *solaris_wrapper.tgz* file into a directory with sufficient free space. Then start the install by typing **./UnixInstallScript**. Continue through the first few pages and the License Agreement until you come to the Product Selection Screen, shown in Figure 13.1.

Figure 13.1 Product Selection Screen with Performance Pack Selected

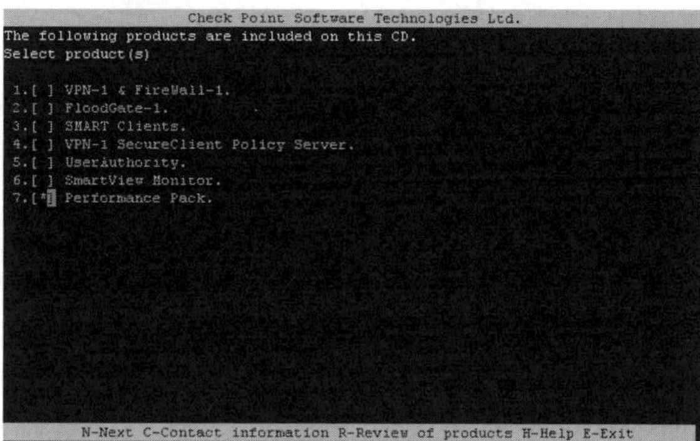

Choose **Performance Pack**, then **Next**. Verify that you have correctly chosen Performance Pack, then choose **Next** again. The script will now install Performance Pack and finish with a screen that informs you of what you need to do to activate the newly installed software.

Let's activate Performance Pack now. Log out and then back in again as user *root*. Next, type **cpconfig**, You will see an option to enable or disable Check Point SecureXL. This choice determines the default state of Performance Pack after boot: acceleration on (enabled) or off (disabled). You can always manually enable or disable SecureXL through the command line while FireWall-1 is running.

Next, type **cpstart**. This command starts SecureXL, if you selected it as enabled in cpconfig, and fetches policy so that acceleration is enabled. In the output of *cpstart*, you expect to see a line telling you that the SecureXL device has been enabled:

```
# cpstart


cpstart: Start product - SVN Foundation
```

```
SVN Foundation: cpWatchDog already running
SVN Foundation: cpd already running
SVN Foundation started

cpstart: Start product - FireWall-1

FireWall-1: starting external VPN module -- OK
FireWall-1: Starting fwd
FireWall-1: Starting fwm (SmartCenter Server)

SecureXL device is enabled

Installing Security Policy Standard on all.all@syngress-fw
Fetching Security Policy from localhost succeeded
FireWall-1 started
```

If you desire, you can now clean up the installation files by removing the solaris2 directory, the wrappers directory, and the UnixInstallScript and ReadmeUnix.txt files.

Installation as a Separate Package

This method of installation needs considerably less temporary disk space than the wrapper install. About 10MB of free space will be plenty, plus another 2.5MB on */opt*.

To install Performance Pack, first unpack the package's .TGZ file. The NG FP3 Performance Pack installation package unpacks into a directory called *CPppak-53*.

The Check Point instructions tell you to use *pkgadd –d CPppak-53* to install the package. If you attempt this, you will get an error message telling you that no package was found. Instead, while in the parent directory of *CPppak-53*, type **pkgadd –d .** and then choose to install **CPppak-53**. Answer **y** to the next two questions. CPppak-53 will install and warn you to reboot. If you are presented with a prompt to install CPppak-53 once again, break out of it by typing **q**.

Contrary to what the *postinstall* script tells you, you do not need to reboot to activate Performance Pack NG FP3. Follow the same steps as after a wrapper install of Performance Pack NG FP3. Execute **cpconfig** and enable SecureXL. Exit the *cpconfig* utility and type **cpstart** to fetch policy and enable acceleration.

If you are installing a later release of Performance Pack NG, read the Release Notes to see whether installation requirements have changed.

Uninstalling Performance Pack

You can uninstall Performance Pack NG FP3 without any downtime to your firewall—not even a glitch in traffic. Do, however, see the Tools & Traps sidebar for a vital warning about a possible system crash during uninstall with FP3.

To uninstall, first execute **fwaccel off**, then remove the package with the command **pkgrm CPppak-53**. For future Feature Packs, the name of the package will change accordingly. The FP4 package will likely be named *CPppak-54*. When in doubt, use **pkginfo** to see the names of all installed packages.

When you uninstall this way, the SecureXL module might remain in memory until the next reboot, although acceleration is no longer possible. If you desire a clean uninstall, you will have to reboot.

Should you be tempted to manually remove the *fwaccel* binary that the uninstallation script seemingly left behind, we advise against it. *Fwaccel* is actually part of the FireWall-1 package proper, not of Performance Pack.

Tools & Traps...

Crash and Burn

The uninstallation script for Performance Pack NG FP3 does not perform an *fwaccel off* command as its first step. As a result, your firewall will crash, and crash hard, if you attempt to remove the CPppak-53 package without turning acceleration off first. This is true even if you *cpstop* the firewall first. It will crash on the subsequent *cpstart* if acceleration was not turned off. In our testing, the server rebooted into single-user mode and needed minor console intervention (an *fsck –y* followed by a *reboot*) to come back up again. Now imagine that we had done this work remotely, without an out-of-band console connection.

Always turn acceleration off first before uninstalling. It is likely that future Feature Packs will sport a more forgiving uninstallation routine. Still, better to be safe than sorry.

Installing Performance Pack on SecurePlatform

SecurePlatform installs Performance Pack by default. Unless you expressly deselected it, SecurePlatform has been installed for you. You may install Performance Pack as an individual package if you opted out of its installation during initial installation of SecurePlatform.

Prerequisites

You have to be in *expert* mode to install the Performance Pack package. *Expert mode* is what Check Point calls the root shell in SecurePlatform. Because you are going to install an rpm package, you need a root shell.

Installing the rpm Package

Unpack the contents of the Performance Pack package into a temporary directory. Execute the command **rpm –i CPppak-50-03.i386.rpm** to install Performance Pack NG FP3. After installation, use **cpconfig** to enable SecureXL if you want acceleration to be enabled by default; then execute **cpstart** to start acceleration.

Command-Line Options for Performance Pack

Because Performance Pack, or more precisely the SecureXL driver, gets "in the way" of interface-level changes to the host machine, we need a way to stop and start Performance Pack at will. The ability to stop Performance Pack is also useful in troubleshooting; it enables you to narrow a problem to "no, it is not caused by Performance Pack" or "yes, it is caused by Performance Pack." Lastly, you might want to see what goes on "under the hood" or change some of the settings of Performance Pack. This is where the command line comes in.

Stopping and Starting SecureXL

You can determine whether acceleration should be on by default with the help of the *cpconfig* utility. It offers an option to enable or disable Check Point SecureXL:

- **fwaccel on** Turn acceleration on while FireWall-1 is running.
- **fwaccel off** Turn acceleration off while FireWall-1 is running.

Checking the Status of SecureXL

You can get the current status of SecureXL by typing **fwaccel stat**. This command shows you whether acceleration is enabled and whether Connection Templates are currently being used:

```
# fwaccel stat
Status : on
Templates : enabled
Accelerator Features Mask : 0x0006f167
```

To see the number of connections SecureXL currently accelerates, type the command **fwaccel conns –s.** You will see two connections per TCP stream there, one for each direction. To see more detail about the connections, such as source and destination addresses and ports and the physical interfaces the accelerated traffic passes through, use **fwaccel cons** or **fwaccel cons –m <*max_entries*>**. The latter form limits the maximum number of connections shown to <*max_entries*>.

You can also filter the connections shown using **fwaccel conns –f <*flags*>**. You can use one or more of these flags:

```
F/f  - forwarded to firewall/cut-through
U/u  - unidirectional/bidirectional connections
N/n  - entries with/without NAT
A/a  - accounted/not accounted
C/c  - encrypted/not encrypted
```

On SecurePlatform only, there are two more ways to gain some status information about SecureXL. To view the affinity settings of all interfaces—that is, a list of interfaces and the processors that handle each interface on a multiprocessor system—use **sim –l**. To view a list of currently generated Connection Templates, use **sim tab templates**.

To get a configuration overview or view general statistics, use the command **cat /prot/ppk/conf | ifs | statistics**. The Performance Pack configuration is displayed if you view *conf*, the interfaces Performance Pack is bound to if you view *ifs*, and some general Performance Pack statistics are available through *statistics*.

Configuring SecureXL

A few aspects of SecureXL's configuration can be controlled through the command line:

- **fwaccel –l <*number*>** Limit the amount of Connection Templates that SecureXL can generate.
- **fwaccel –l 0** Reset to defaults.

On SecurePlatform only, you can set the *affinity* of the network interface cards. Affinity determines which processors in a multiprocessor system handle that particular NIC:

- **sim –a** Affinity is set automatically, according to the load on each interface. Retuning of the affinity happens every 60 seconds. This is the default mode.
- **sim –s** Affinity is set manually. For each interface, you will be asked to either enter a space-separated list of processor numbers that will handle this interface or the keyword *all*, which will allow all processors to handle that interface.

Troubleshooting Performance Pack

Few areas of Performance Pack will need troubleshooting. Check Point has made Performance Pack a very simple product. It seamlessly improves the performance of Firewall-1/VPN-1, with very little configuration necessary.

If you do suspect Performance Pack is causing trouble, turn it off using **fwaccel off**, then see whether your issue remains.

That being said, there is one area of Performance Pack that deserves a closer look: Connection Templates. Connection Templates improve the setup and teardown rate of connections that differ only by source port. A typical example is a Web server: One client will initiate many connections to the server in the course of one session. These connections differ by source port only.

Connection Templates will be generated only for simple TCP or UDP connections. Connection Templates are subject to a few restrictions:

- If SYN Defender is enabled, Connection Templates will only be created for UDP connections.
- Connection Templates will never be created for:
  - NAT connections
  - VPN connections
  - Complex connections such as H.323, FTP or SQL
  - Connections involving a security server

Connection Templates will be disabled completely if the Rule Base contains a rule containing one of the following:

- Service(s) with a source port range
- A time object
- Dynamic objects and/or Domain objects
- Services of type "other" with a match expression
- Services of type RPC/DCERPC/DCOM

If your Rule Base contains a rule with one or more of the preceding factors, you will receive console and log messages telling you that Connection Templates have been disabled and identifying the restricted rules. To enable Connection Templates, you will have to either rewrite or delete those rules. To merely disable them is not sufficient.

Summary

Performance Pack, also called SecureXL, is a software solution to accelerate CPU-intensive FireWall-1/VPN-1 operations, including but not limited to setup and tear-down of connections, encryption, authentication, accounting, and NAT. It is supported on Solaris and SecurePlatform, with support on Nokia IPSO planned in the near future. Performance Pack is an alternative to performance solutions found on other FireWall-1/VPN-1 platforms.

Care must be taken when working with the physical interfaces of the host platform; turn acceleration off before enabling, disabling, or changing an interface.

The ideal hardware platform for Performance Pack has multiple high-powered CPUs, multiple independent very fast I/O buses, and at least 1GB of memory. Lower-specification hardware will still benefit from Performance Pack but will not reach the 3Gbps+ throughput on high-end hardware that Check Point states.

Real-world throughput will be lower than the numbers quoted by Check Point, but by no means will they be low. Impressive throughput of well over 2Gbps TCP throughput and over 600Mbps encrypted VPN can be achieved.

Performance Pack can be installed with the Comprehensive Install package on Solaris and comes preinstalled by default on SecurePlatform. If so desired, it is possible to install Performance Pack as a separate package after initial system install.

Performance Pack is very easy to use, but its configuration options are limited. You can turn acceleration on and off, and you have some tools to optimize performance, particularly on multiprocessor systems. Session setup and teardown optimization through Connection Templates might require changes to your Rule Base to work.

Solutions Fast Track

How Performance Pack Works

☑ Performance Pack accelerates CPU-intensive functions of FireWall-1/VPN-1. It does so by moving routines into "kernel space," taking full advantage of the host OS and CPU it runs on, and using Connection Templates and other low-level techniques.

☑ Performance Pack will very likely gain new functionality, such as the ability to accelerate security server connections, in future Feature Packs.

Installing Performance Pack

- ☑ On Solaris, use the Comprehensive Install wrapper and choose *Performance Pack* as one of the products to install.
- ☑ On SecurePlatform, Performance Pack is installed by default when you install FireWall-1/VPN-1.
- ☑ Be careful when you uninstall Performance Pack on Solaris; turn acceleration off first.

Command-Line Options for Performance Pack

- ☑ Acceleration can be turned on with *fwaccel on* and off with *fwaccel off*
- ☑ To get the status of Performance Pack, use fwaccel stat
- ☑ To see a list of accelerated connections, use *fwaccel conns*
- ☑ On SecurePlatform, the *sim* command can be used to control the processor affinity of individual NICs.

Troubleshooting Performance Pack

- ☑ Connection Templates will be disabled if the Rule Base contains certain rules. These rules will have to be deleted, not just disabled, for Connection Templates to start functioning.
- ☑ Disable Performance Pack using *fwaccel off* if you suspect it of causing problems.

Frequently Asked Questions

The following Frequently Asked Questions, answered by the authors of this book, are designed to both measure your understanding of the concepts presented in this chapter and to assist you with real-life implementation of these concepts. To have your questions about this chapter answered by the author, browse to **www.syngress.com/solutions** and click on the **"Ask the Author"** form.

Q: Does Performance Pack on Solaris support VLANs?

A: As of NG FP3, no.

Q: I see deviations from the TCP quotas I have established. Why?

A: Small deviations from the TCP quotas may indeed occur when Performance Pack is enabled. This is a side effect of the way Performance Pack works.

Q: Accounting information seems to be somewhat lower than actual traffic. Why?

A: If you have a high-availability configuration, some accounting information for accelerated connections might get lost during HA failover. The accounting information reported may thus be somewhat lower than actual traffic. If this is very noticeable, your HA solution is likely failing over more often than it should—a situation that you should look into.

Q: How can I downgrade Performance Pack from FP3 to FP2?

A: Uninstall the package, then reinstall once your firewall is on FP2.

Q: Is Performance Pack supported on Solaris 9?

A: Not as of NG FP3. It will install, but upon activating, it will crash your firewall to the point where you need to remove Performance Pack in single-user mode to become operational again.

Q: Is Performance Pack the only implementation of SecureXL?

A: No. SecureXL technology is also used to enable more tightly integrated FireWall-1 platforms (platforms without a "general-purpose" host OS and possibly with dedicated coprocessors that SecureXL offloads work to), such as the Nortel Alteon Switched Firewall or RapidStream VPN/Firewall Appliances.

Q: The VPN-1 throughput figures given in this chapter seem somewhat arbitrary. How do I get accurate figures?

A: Ask your vendor. RFC-2544 Performance Figures, also known as the "Bradner Run," are an industry standard to measure throughput, although other test methods also deliver reliable results. These results are arrived at using traffic generator/ analyzer hardware that can be priced in the $150,000 range. Keep in mind that the median packet size is likely to be around 256 bytes for typical "Internet traffic." On a vendor platform that does offer RFC-2544 data but does not implement Performance Pack, VPN-1 throughput figures tripled on 1450-byte packets, as compared to throughput on 256-byte packets. The real throughput you get will depend heavily on your application.

Chapter 14

UserAuthority

Solutions in this chapter:

- Defining UserAuthority
- Installing UserAuthority
- Implementing UserAuthority Chaining
- Utilizing UserAuthority Logging
- Understanding Credentials Management and Domain Equality
- Deploying UserAuthority

☑ Summary

☑ Solutions Fast Track

☑ Frequently Asked Questions

Introduction

Single sign-on (SSO), centralized security, LDAP and Active Directory integration… these are all things that many organizations are trying to achieve. FireWall-1 NG can now start closing some of those gaps, particularly where Web applications are involved. UserAuthority can, for example, authenticate external visitors to your Web site against a centralized Windows Active Directory, without modifying the Web site. Check Point supplies WebAccess, a plug-in for IIS, that—when combined with the UserAuthority Server—gives you the capability to have Check Point control the authentication and traffic flow to your Web server.

UserAuthority can also provide an SSO mechanism for internal users, encompassing internal Web applications and authenticated Internet access. This chapter discusses the features of UserAuthority and the methods for deploying it.

Defining UserAuthority

At the heart of UserAuthority is the UserAuthority server. This application performs two functions:

- Storage and management of the UA credentials database
- Provision of a secure interface, allowing remote applications access to the UA credentials database and context details relevant to a connection or user ID

The user credentials database is called the *UA Credentials Manager (UACM)*. It could be thought of as holding user "wallets," each of which stores application authentication credentials for a particular user. So, for example, user Bob could have different usernames and passwords for accessing a Web-based e-mail gateway and an intranet server. This information can be stored in Bob's "wallet" in the UA credentials database. When Bob accesses a UA-enabled Web application for the first time, he will be able to store the credentials he supplies in his wallet. We refer to a user's credential store as a *wallet* because this seems a fitting description, but this is not a term you will find in Check Point manuals.

The UACM secures this information by providing a lock on each user's wallet that can be undone if the user provides valid UA authentication credentials—for example, by supplying a FireWall-1 username and password. If the FireWall-1 authentication method is strong, we are providing strong authentication that protects access to credentials, themselves probably based on weaker authentication methods. Taking the example of our user Bob, he connects to the office from home, authenticating via a secure method and over an encrypted SecureClient session. Bob has already been authenticated by the corporate firewall, so when Bob attempts to access his *BobB* mailbox (over HTTP) or the intranet server, UA can supply Bob's relevant credentials to these servers.

Bob has authenticated access to the internal servers after authenticating just once, when he started his SecureClient session. This concept is illustrated in Figure 14.1.

Figure 14.1 Bob and Jane at Work with UserAuthority

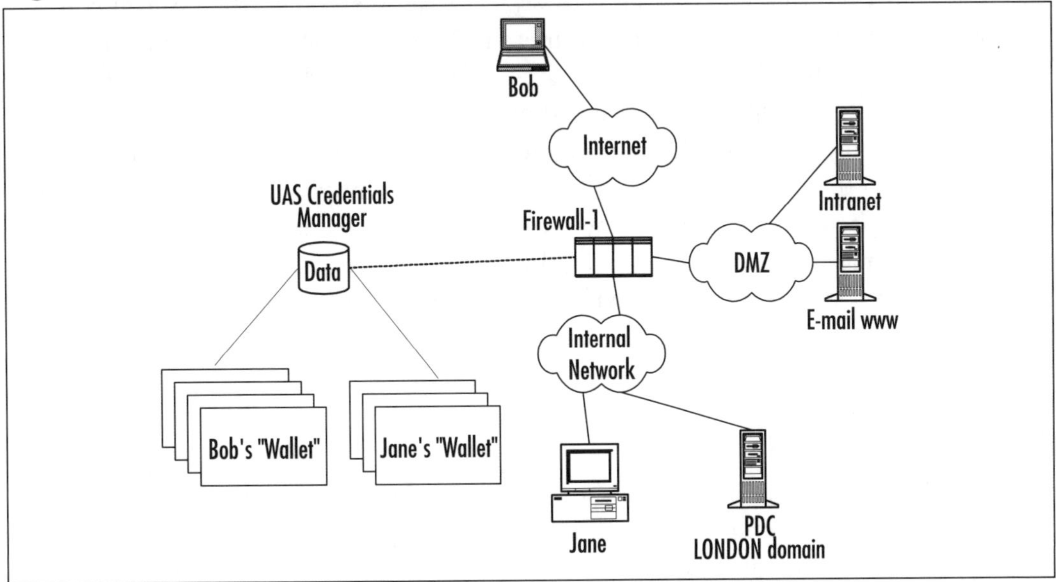

In order to provide this UA functionality, the Web servers involved should run the UA Web Access Module (WAM). This module is available for Microsoft IIS and—at time of writing—in beta for Linux Apache. The module integrates with the Web server's authentication mechanisms in order to seamlessly authenticate connections to the server. The UA Web Access software also gives users the ability to manage their UA wallets—for example, they can view the credentials that are stored; usually a Web server is configured specifically for users to perform credentials management. The latest incarnations of WAM also allow for very granular and powerful access control to Web sites. Authorization rules can be defined down to just about any property of the HTTP request—the Web site, path, query, type of HTTP request, or other headers. Permissions can be based on more than just username: integration with FireWall-1 means that the context of the connection can be considered, whether it is made over a VPN, the source IP address, the strength of authentication, and time of day. Other context details supplied by the UAS can be considered, commonly user group membership. WAM can also be used to add authentication to a server that itself allows anonymous access.

The example of Bob is based on a UA server installed on the firewall gateway, and it is authentication against FireWall-1 that gives Bob access to his wallet. A UA server can also be installed on a Microsoft Windows domain controller (Windows NT or 2000). A domain controller UAS does not provide the functionality of a firewall gateway UAS, but it *is* able to supply authentication details for a given client IP address. The domain controller UAS can verify the identification of a domain user, thanks to a lightweight agent, UA SecureAgent, which is automatically installed to users' PCs when they log in to a domain. The firewall gateway UAS can then query the domain controller UAS to obtain user details for an internal client—a process known as *chaining*. This means that although internal users have not authenticated against the firewall, the users may access their UACM wallet based on their Windows domain authentication.

Looking at another example from Figure 14.1, a user "Jane" working at her desk and logged into the corporate domain might need to connect to a restricted area of the intranet. This special area requires authentication, and Jane has a username *hr* on that server. When Jane connects to the server, she is transparently authenticated because her *hr* credentials are stored in her UACM wallet. The WAM on the Web server was given the *hr* credentials from Jane's wallet by the firewall gateway UAS because Jane had been authenticated by the UAS server on the domain controller.

WAM in Detail

Now let's look in a bit more detail at how WAM works. We know it is a plug-in for Web servers, and it communicates with a UserAuthority server to allow SSO. It can also be configured to authenticate access to the Web server at a very granular level. What is actually happening when a user makes a connection to a Web server?

Consider an incoming Web request for which the native Web server requires authentication. WAM can intercept the request, then contact the local gateway UA server and request credentials and any context details that match the incoming connection. The incoming connection could have passed through the firewall from a SecureClient user, in which case the UA server will be able to access the wallet of the SecureClient user and supply the credentials—if any—relating to that Web server. If there is a UAS on a Windows domain controller and the connection to our WAM-enabled server is from an internal user, it could be that the gateway UAS will be able to retrieve the client Windows username via chaining, and then supply that user's credentials to WAM. If WAM does receive valid credentials from the gateway UAS, it will pass those to the local Web server and the connection can continue without prompting the user for authentication.

If WAM does not receive valid credentials from the UAS, it can give the user the chance to authenticate directly to WAM. The user will be prompted for authentication, but the credentials supplied by the user are processed by WAM instead of the Web server's own authentication handlers (in fact, the Web server itself might not require authentication for the request involved). WAM will pass the credentials the user supplied to the gateway UAS, which checks them against the FireWall-1 user database and responds to WAM with the results. WAM will allow access to the Web server only if the UAS confirmed the credentials. We can use this feature to add authentication to an existing unauthenticated Web server, and the authentication mechanism will be via a FireWall-1 user database, giving access to the wide range of authentication methods supported by FireWall-1, including strong authentication servers, certificates ,LDAP, and Windows Active Directory integration.

Combining multiple UserAuthority servers with WebAccess modules gives the potential for very powerful configurations. In this chapter we take a look at three simple configurations that provide the building blocks for more elaborate SSO solutions.

Tools & Traps…

Guide to UserAuthority Acronyms

There are plenty of acronyms to be found when you're working with UserAuthority. Here is a quick reference guide:

- **UA** UserAuthority
- **UAS** UA server
- **UACM** UA Credentials Manager
- **WAM** UA WebAccess Module
- **UAA** UA application—an application that has been UA enabled so that it can participate in the SSO process; WAM is Check Point's own UAA for Web servers

You could also come across some acronyms that have been superseded:

- **UAG** UserAuthority Gateway—now known as UAS; still found in underlying configuration files and commands
- **UAM** User to Address Mapping—an early ancestor of UA that integrated with the Meta IP product to provide some SSO capability

Supported Platforms

Here is a quick rundown of the components and the platforms they can be installed on:

- **UserAuthority Server on FireWall-1 NG FP3** IPSO 3.5/3.51, IPSO 3.6, Linux, Solaris 2.8, Windows 2000, NT

- **UserAuthority Server on domain controller** Windows NT4, Windows 2000
- **WebAccess plug-in module** Windows 2000 with IIS v5, Windows NT with IIS v4, Linux Apache (beta)
- **UserAuthority SecureAgent** Windows 98, ME, NT, 2000, and XP

Installing UserAuthority

In this section, we discuss how to install the various parts of UserAuthority, from the UserAuthority server to the UserAuthority SecureAgent. We also discuss basic configuration that will allow you to test your UserAuthority installation.

Installing the UserAuthority Server

The main component to UserAuthority is the UserAuthority server. Here we cover how to install the UserAuthority server on a FireWall-1 enforcement module and on a Windows domain controller.

UserAuthority Server on a FireWall-1 Enforcement Module

Installation of the UserAuthority server on a FireWall-1 enforcement module can be performed as part of the standard "CD wrapper" process for installing a normal firewall enforcement module: When you are presented with the screen that asks you which Check Point products you want to install, make sure you select **UserAuthority Server**, as shown in Figure 14.2.

Figure 14.2 Installing UAS on a Firewall Enforcement Module During CD Wrapper Install

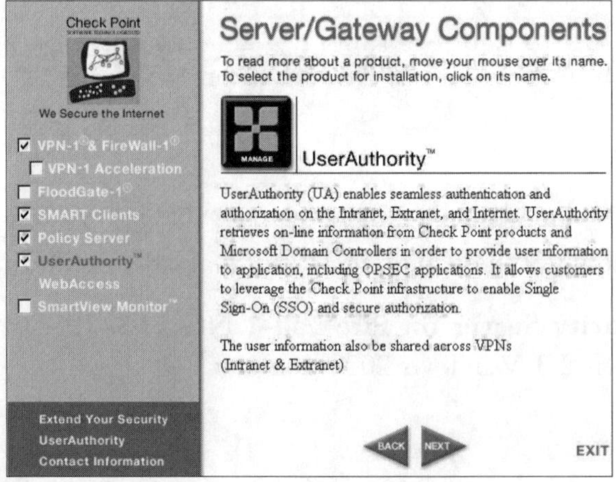

Alternatively, if you have an existing enforcement module that does not have UserAuthority installed, it is possible to download the individual UserAuthority FP3 package and install that. The installer will probably request a reboot in order to complete installation of the package.

In SmartDashboard, edit the object representing the enforcement module and enable the UserAuthority Server package, then push a security policy to the enforcement policy in order to check that it still installs correctly.

Once UserAuthority Server has been installed, it can be tested using one of the simple deployment examples we describe later in the chapter.

UserAuthority Server on a Windows Domain Controller

Installation of a UserAuthority Server on a domain controller can be achieved using the standard NG FP3 CD wrapper. In this section, we cover the essentials of installing and configuring UserAuthority Server on a domain controller using the wrapper. Note that in order to fully test this domain controller installation, we need to install and configure UAS on a FireWall-1 enforcement module as well.

During the install process, the main area to pay attention to is the Server/Gateway Components screen, as shown in Figure 14.3. Here you need to make sure you select **UserAuthority**. The SVN package will be installed as well because it is required.

Figure 14.3 Installation of Server/Gateway Components

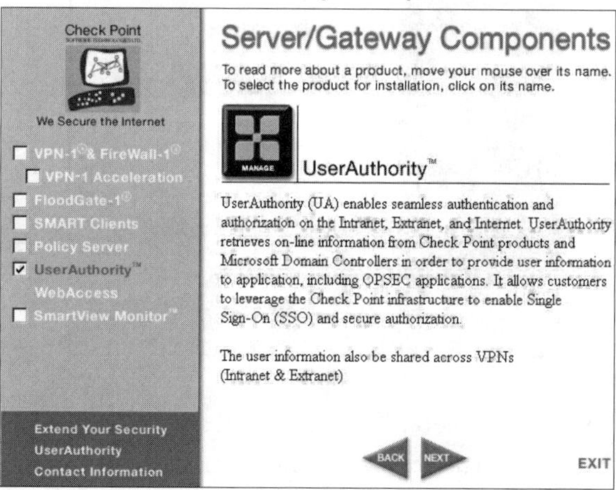

You will then see a verification screen popup, as shown in Figure 14.4. Click **Next** when you are ready to proceed.

The installation process will proceed to install the SVN software and then the UAS product.

Following the installation, you will be prompted to perform some initial configuration—licensing and SIC trust. You will see the same screens when you install a WAM module; they are described later and illustrated in Figures 14.20–14.22. You do not need to install a license on the domain controller UAS; the configuration utility will warn you that you have not added a license, so don't worry about that. Don't forget to make a note of the password you specify when you initialize SIC trust.

Figure 14.4 Verification of Components to Install

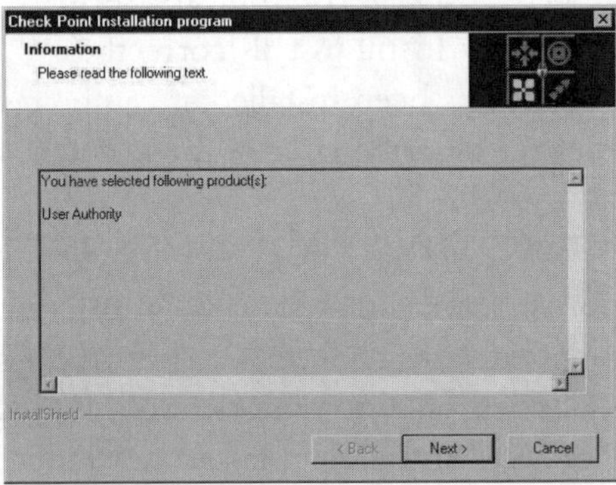

Once you have completed the initial configuration, you will be asked if you would like to reboot your machine, as shown in Figure 14.5.

Figure 14.5 Installation Complete—Reboot?

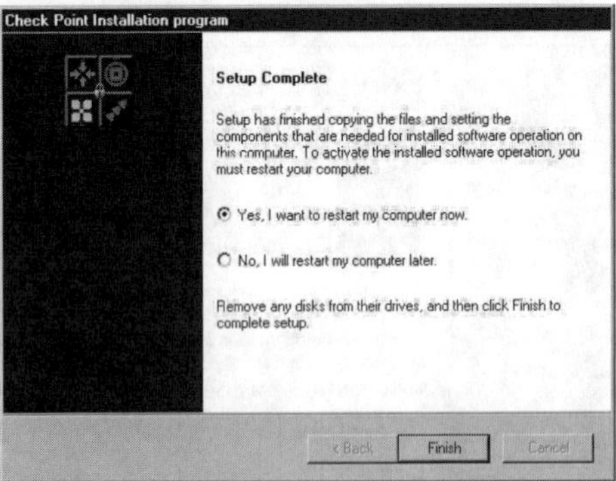

The installation is now complete. The next section describes how to use SmartDashboard to configure trust between the management station and the UserAuthority Server-enabled domain controller.

Setting Up Trust to the UserAuthority Server

To set up trust to UserAuthority server, follow these steps:

1. First you need an object for your domain controller. If you already have a node object for it, you can right-click on that node in the **Object** tree, and

choose **Convert to Check Point Host**. Otherwise, go to the **Manage Menu | Network Objects** menu in the SmartDashboard GUI. Click **New** and select **Check Point | Host**. You will then see a popup window appear. Fill in the details of your domain controller (see Figure 14.6). Check the **UserAuthority Server** product.

Figure 14.6 Defining the Domain Controller UserAuthority Server Object

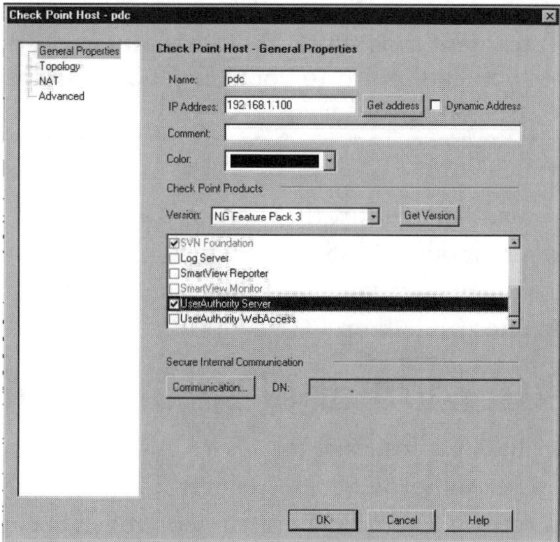

2. Click the **Communication** button. You will see the window shown in Figure 14.7. Fill in the activation key as supplied during the installation of the UAS on the domain controller. Confirm the activation key using the same password. Click the **Initialize** button. Once the trust has been established, click **Test SIC status** to make sure that it says *Communicating*.

Figure 14.7 Initiating Trust Between the Management Module and the Domain Controller

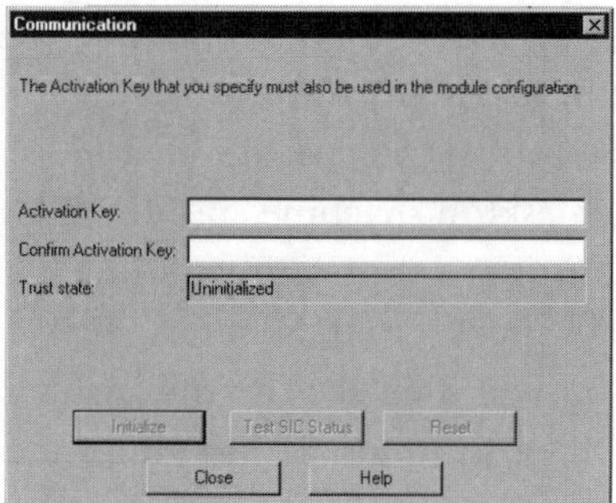

WARNING

If there is a firewall between the management station and the UserAuthority server, you will need to set it to allow communications from the management server to the UserAuthority Server through the firewall enforcement module policy. If that firewall is managed from your management station, there is an easy way to ensure that the correct ports are opened: *Before* clicking your new UAS object's **Communication** button, click **OK** and then push the policy to the firewall enforcement module(s). The necessary implied rules will then be in place so that you can return to your object and successfully initialize the SIC trust to the UserAuthority server.

Once the trust has been set up, the domain controller UAS is ready to be integrated with the enforcement module UAS. However, to take advantage of UserAuthority Server on a domain controller, you need to ensure that the UserAuthority SecureAgent is installed on the internal desktop PCs.

Installing UserAuthority SecureAgent

This section describes how to install the UserAuthority SecureAgent on a Windows desktop PC. The UserAuthority SecureAgent is used in conjunction with UserAuthority Server on a Windows domain controller. SecureAgent will run on Windows 98, ME, NT 4, 2000, and XP.

Manual Installation on Desktop

This is the simplest way to install SecureAgent—but not by much! If you only have a handful of desktop Windows machines that require SSO, you can copy the appropriate files to the users' desktop machine.

The files will have been installed on the domain controller when you installed the UserAuthority Server. The files for installing the UserAuthority SecureAgent can be located in the C:\WINNT\sysvol\sysvol\<*domain name*>\scripts directory. In our example, the files were installed to the C:\WINNT\sysvol\sysvol\london.com\ scripts directory, as shown in Figure 14.8.

All you need do here is copy all the files that are shown in Figure 14.8 (apart from the login.bat file) to the desktop machine, and then run the command **InstUatc.exe /shortcut /icon /debug** from the command line. This will install the necessary files to the C:\Program Files\Check Point\SecureAgent\ directory on the local machine. Within this directory, you will then see the files uatc.exe, uatc.log, and uatcs_acl.txt (and maybe a backup of this file). To uninstall, just run the uatcs_uninstall.bat from the files you copied from the domain controller.

Figure 14.8 Location of the UserAuthority SecureAgent Files on the Primary Domain Controller

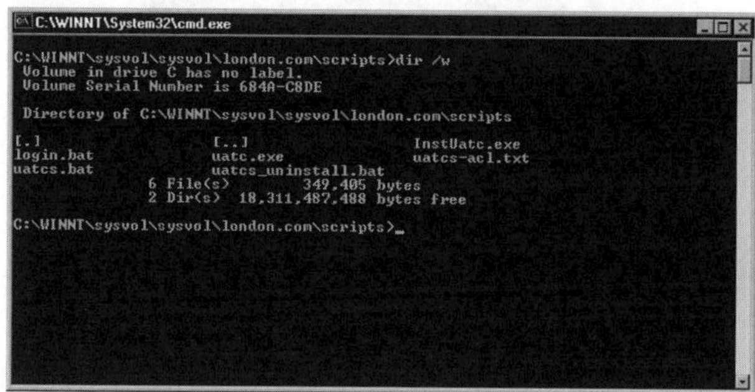

NOTE

SecureAgent will not appear in the Add/Remove Programs section of the Windows Control Panel.

Automatic Installation on Login to the Domain

Automatic installation on domain login is the preferred way of getting the UserAuthority SecureAgent installed to all of your desktops that log in to your domain. All you need to do is add the **InstUatc.exe /shortcut /icon /debug** entry to the login script for your domain users and it will install to their desktops and run every time they log in to your domain. You could do this for just one user on the primary domain controller if you want to test first. In the example in Figure 14.9, we created a user called Jane on the primary domain controller, and in the Profiles tab of her user definition, we have the scripts set to login.bat, a batch file we created that runs the command *InstUatc.exe /shortcut /icon /debug.*

When Jane next logs in to the London domain, the login script will run and the UserAuthority SecureAgent will install and start. The system tray of her desktop will show the icon for the UserAuthority SecureAgent, as shown in Figure 14.10.

In order to configure and test your domain controller UAS and SecureAgent installation, you need to configure the enforcement module UAS to use them. (Take a look at the relevant deployment example later in this chapter.)

Figure 14.9 User Login Script Definition to Auto-Install to the Desktop for User *Jane*

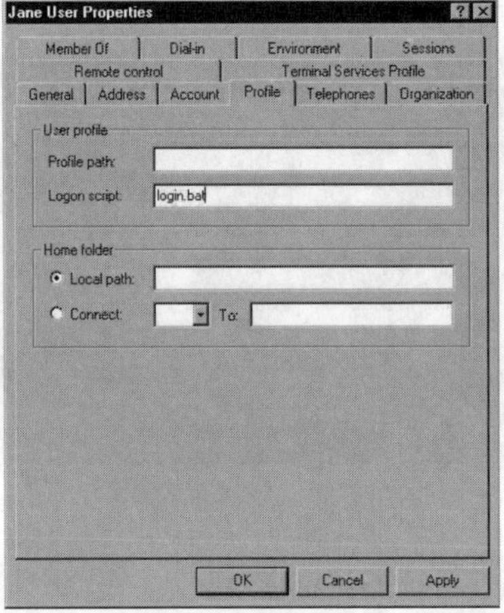

Figure 14.10 SecureAgent Icon in the System Tray

Installing the UserAuthority WebAccess Plug-In

In this section, we install the WebAccess plug-in module (sometimes referred to as the *WAM*). This component of UserAuthority is installed on the Web server itself. In this example, it will be installed on Microsoft IIS version 5 on a Windows 2000 SP3 host.

It is recommended, but not essential, to have your firewall management module and your UserAuthority server already set up and configured at this point.

Prerequisites for the WebAccess Plug-In

Here are the things you need in order to install the UserAuthority WebAccess plug-in:

- A Windows 2000 or Windows NT server with Microsoft IIS version 4 or 5
- A single network card (more can be used if required)
- The NG FP3 SVN package, located on the NG FP3 CD or downloadable
- WebAccess plug-in, usually a separate package and not included on the NG FP3 CD (you will have to download it from the Check Point Web site)

Installing the WebAccess Plug-In

Here are the steps you need to take to install the WebAccess plug-in. Before starting, make sure that the Microsoft IIS service is stopped.

1. Insert the **Check Point NG FP3** CD into the CD drive of your Windows 2000 or NT host that has IIS installed. You could find that the CD auto-runs the Check Point install wrapper. If it does, cancel this process; it is not possible to install WebAccess from the CD. However, we do need to install the SVN package from the CD, and we need to do this manually.
2. Click the Windows **Start** menu, then select **Run.** Type in the path where the SVN package is located on the CD (or the location to which you have downloaded it). For a CD, this location should be ***<Drive letter>*:\windows\CPshared-50\Setup.exe**. Click **OK** to start the installation (see Figure 14.11).

Figure 14.11 Installing the SVN

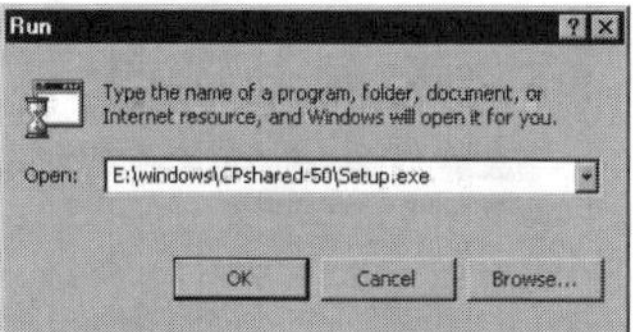

3. You should then see the Check Point Installation wizard for the Check Point SVN (see Figure 14.12). Click **Next** to proceed.

Figure 14.12 The Check Point SVN Installation Wizard

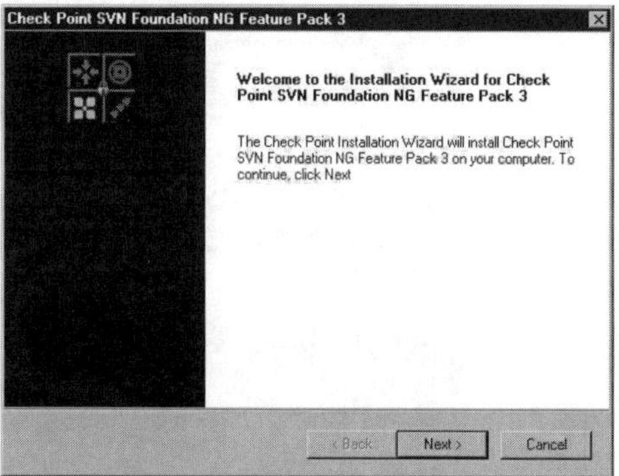

4. You will then see the License Agreement screen (see Figure 14.13). Scroll down to read the license agreement. If you agree with the license terms and conditions, click **Yes**.
5. You will then be prompted to give the location on your hard drive to which you require the SVN software to install (see Figure 14.14). Select the area and then click **Next**.
6. The installation of the SVN software will now proceed (see Figure 14.15). Wait while it completes.

Figure 14.13 The Check Point License Agreement

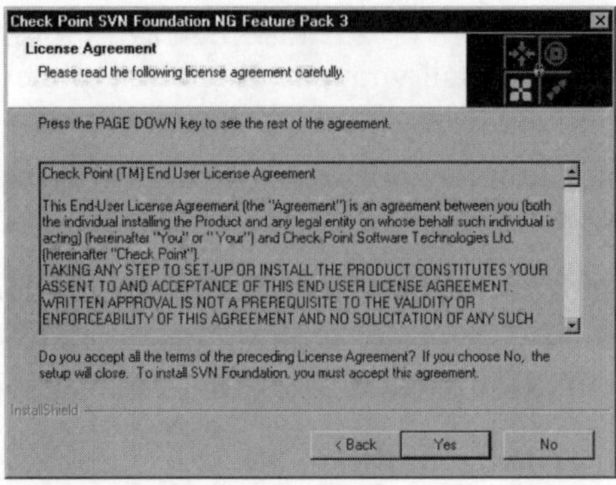

Figure 14.14 The Installation Location of SVN

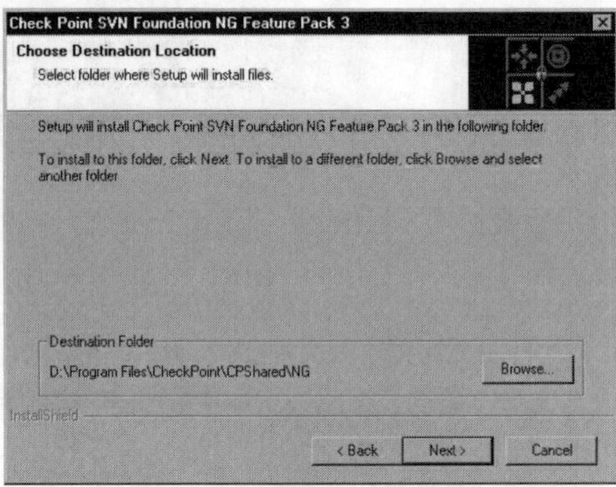

Figure 14.15 SVN Proceeds to Install

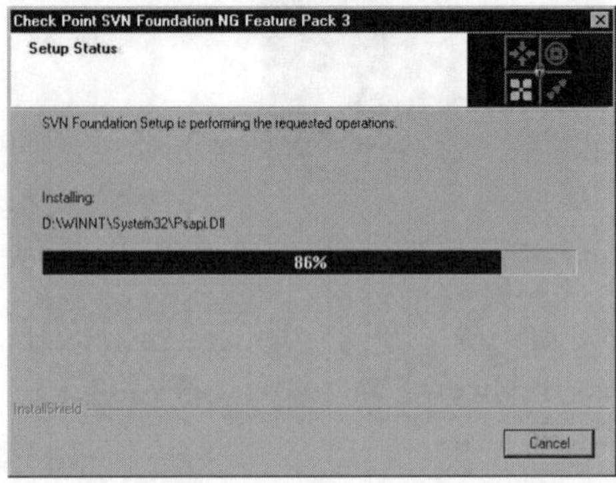

7. Finally, the last screen of the wizard will appear (see Figure 14.16). At this point, you should be asked to reboot. Reboot the host before installing the WebAccess plug-in.

Figure 14.16 The Finish Screen of SVN installation

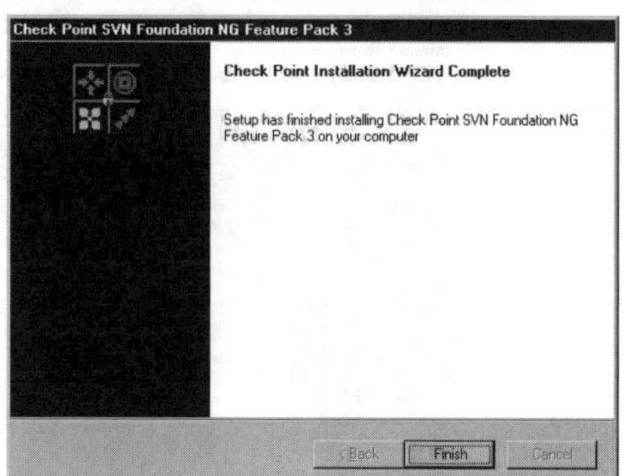

8. Once the host has rebooted, you are ready to install the WebAccess plug-in module. Download the **WebAccess plug-in module** from the Check Point site. Unzip it to a directory on the local hard drive of the host on which you have just installed the SVN package. Run the **Setup.exe** file. You will see a screen like the one in Figure 14.17.

Figure 14.17 The Installation Wizard for the WebAccess Module

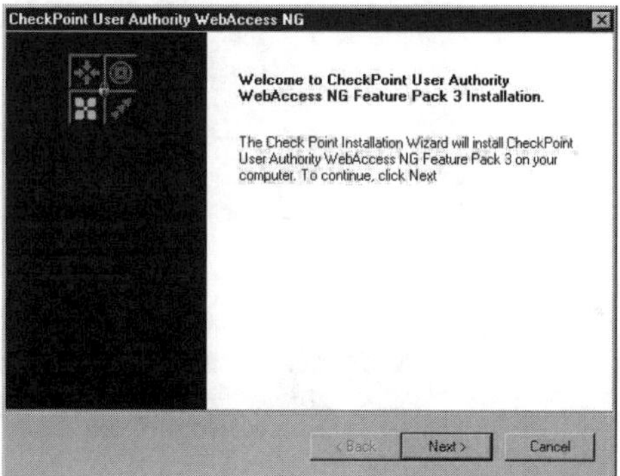

9. Click **Next**. You will see the Check Point License Agreement screen (see Figure 14.18). Scroll down to read it and if you agree to the terms, click **Yes**.
10. You will then be presented with the screen shown in Figure 14.19. Decide where you would like the WebAccess software to install on your hard drive, then proceed by clicking **Next**.
11. You will then see the Check Point Licenses screen, as shown in Figure 14.20. UserAuthority is licensed at a management station and UAS level, not WAM, so click **Next**. You will be warned that you have not added a license (see Figure 14.21)—that's fine, so click **Yes**.

Figure 14.18 The Check Point License Agreement

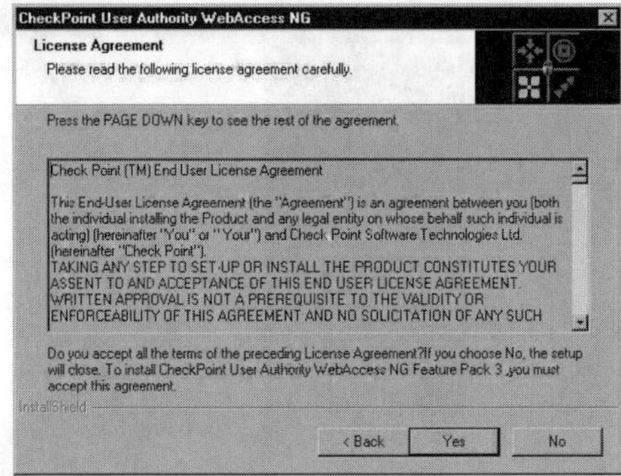

Figure 14.19 The Installation Location for the WebAccess Module

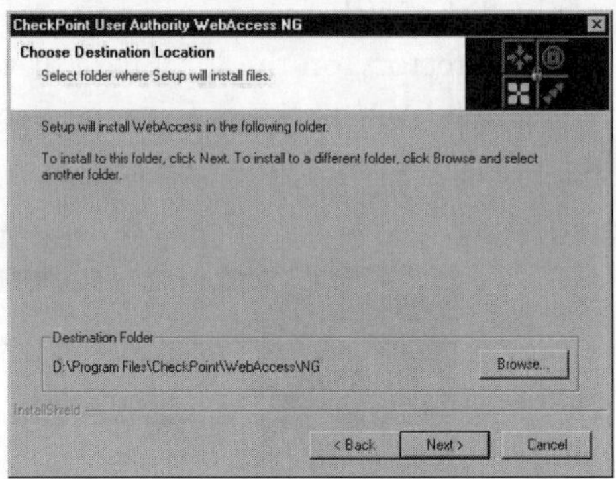

Figure 14.20 The Check Point Licenses Screen

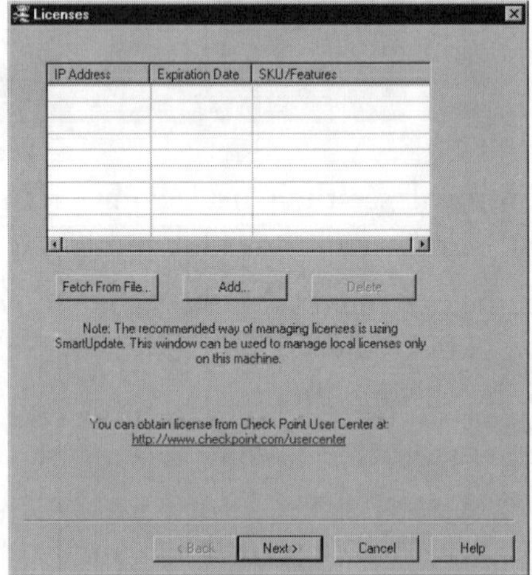

Figure 14.21 Warning of No License

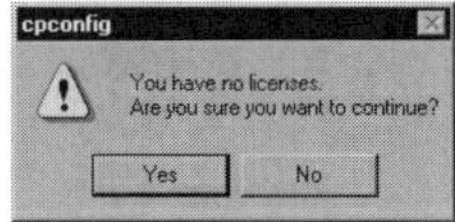

12. You should now see the Secure Internal Communications screen. As with all Check Point NG components, you will have to establish trust with the management station ICA so that the WebAccess module can communicate with the UserAuthority server and the management station in a secure manner. Enter a password in the **Activation Key** field, and then type the same password into the **Confirm Activation Key** field. Click **Finish** when you are ready to proceed.
13. Wait while the installation completes. You will be asked if you want to reboot. Select **Yes, I want to restart my computer now** and then click **Finish**. The host should reboot.

The WebAccess module is now ready to be configured by the management server.

Establishing Trust Between the WebAccess Module and the Firewall Management Station

The WAM module has been installed, but it has not been initialized by the management module, so the first thing we need to do is set up trust between the FireWall-1 management module and the WAM:

1. First we need an object for our WAM-enabled Web server. If you already have a node object representing the Web server, you can right-click that node in the **Object** tree, and choose **Convert to Check Point Host**. Otherwise, go to **Manage | Network Objects** in the SmartDashboard GUI. Click **New** and select **Check Point | Host**. You will then see a popup window. Fill in the details of your WebAccess module (see Figure 14.22). In our example, the WebAccess module is on 192.168.12.133. Check the **UserAuthority WebAccess** product. At this point, do *not* click Communication—we will come back to initializing SIC later.
2. Once we check the UserAuthority WebAccess option, another option appears on the left side menu: **UserAuthority WebAccess**. Click this option. You will now see a screen similar to that in Figure 14.23.

Figure 14.22 Defining the WebAccess Module in the SmartDashboard GUI

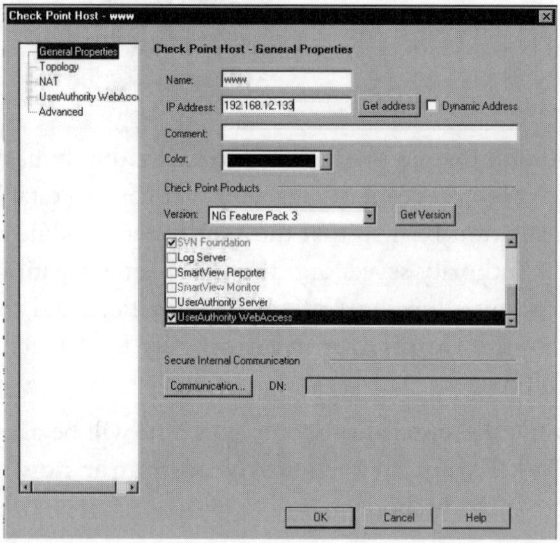

Figure 14.23 Defining the WebAccess Server: Clicking UserAuthority WebAccess

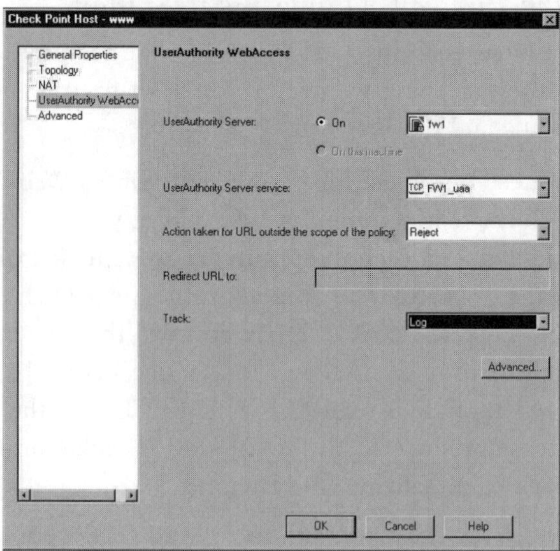

Make sure you select a UserAuthority server. In our example, the UAS is installed on the firewall enforcement module (called *fw1*). You might also want to change the **Track** selection to **Log**, as shown in the example in Figure 14.23. You'll see more settings if you

click the **Advanced** button, but you don't need to do that right now. Click **OK** to save our new object.

Install the applicable security policies to the enforcement module referenced earlier, and also install any enforcement modules between the management station and the WAM host.

Return to the WAM object and click the **Communications** button. Supply the password that you used when you installed the WAM plug-in on the Web server, and initialize SIC.

Click **Close** and then click **OK**. Now install the policy again to the enforcement module referenced as the UAS for this WAM host. This will ensure that the certificate for the new WAM module is distributed to the UAS.

Your WAM module is now installed and trusted by the Check Point management station. The deployment examples later in the chapter give instructions for configuring and testing your installation.

Implementing UserAuthority Chaining

UserAuthority chaining is the term used to describe one UserAuthority server querying one or more other UserAuthority servers in order to find out if a user has already authenticated. The reason that a UserAuthority server would perform this action is for the purpose of SSO: If a user has authenticated already on one UAS server, other UAS servers can be configured to trust the remote UAS server.

UserAuthority chaining is possibly best explained with a couple of examples. Perhaps the simplest example is the case of a UserAuthority server installed on a Windows domain controller. Desktop machines log into the domain, and then the same desktop machines need access to the Internet via SSO client authentication rules on the FireWall-1 enforcement module. If the FireWall-1 enforcement module also has UserAuthority Server installed, it can be configured to use chaining to query the UserAuthority server on the PDC. This configuration is described in detail later in the "Authenticated Internet Access" example deployment.

Another example in which you might use chaining is when one UserAuthority server on one FireWall-1 enforcement module would query another UserAuthority server on another firewall module. In addition, the UserAuthority server can be configured to query the remote FireWall-1 enforcement module UAS down a VPN that has been set up between the two modules. This gives the ability to allow users behind a remote firewall to access the WAM-enabled intranet Web site or customer Web server.

In the example in Figure 14.24, *PC1* has client authenticated against the *fw1* enforcement module for user *Bob* and is connecting down the *fw1* to *fw2* VPN to access the Web server *www*. The Web server is WebAccess enabled and is configured for SSO using the UserAuthority Server on *fw2*. When *Bob* at *PC1* attempts to access the Web server, the WebAccess module will ask *fw2* for authentication data related to this HTTP connection. Module *fw2* checks locally and has no relevant authentication data but is configured to chain down the VPN and ask the UAS at *fw1*. It asks *fw1* if the user has authenticated based on IP address and ports of the HTTP connection. Because *fw1* originally performed client authentication for that connection, it will respond with user *Bob's* details—his username and group. This information will be passed to the WebAccess module by *fw2* and the WAM will determine, based on its policy, if user *Bob* is allowed access or not. If authentication is successful, he will be allowed access to the Web site.

Figure 14.24 Example of UAS Chaining Across a VPN

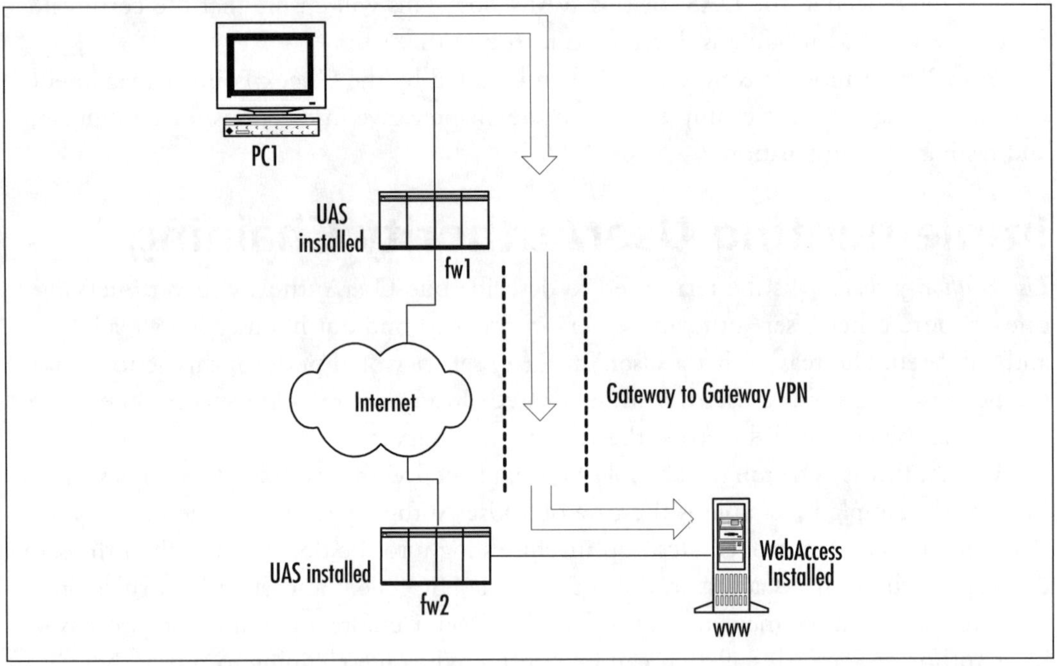

Chaining is configured in the firewall enforcement module object itself, within the SmartDashboard GUI. If we take a quick look at the object again, you will be able to see some of the options. Our *fw1* object is shown in Figure 14.25, configured to chain to its local Windows PDC UAS.

Note that to define chaining you need to create a UserAuthority Server group and make the target UAS servers part of the group.

The settings under Export Policy are also useful because they determine what aspects of the credentials will be made available to other UserAuthority servers that are not managed by your management server.

Figure 14.25 UserAuthority Server on a Firewall Gateway

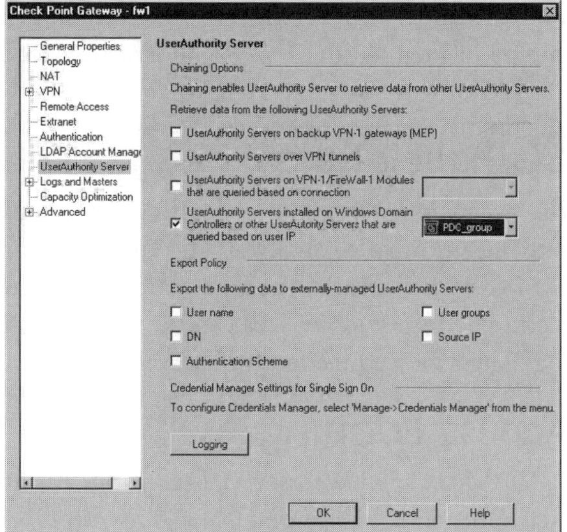

Utilizing UserAuthority Logging

The SSO mechanism makes it easy for users to access resources without requiring repeated authentication using different credentials. A further benefit is the ability to track user activity for security and usage accounting purposes. All UA-enabled applications—including FireWall-1 enforcement modules running UAS—can obtain authentication details either from an initial FireWall-1 authentication action or from a Windows domain user's UA SecureAgent.

Possible applications of this logging ability include:

- **Internet usage accounting** Install UAS on Internet gateway FireWall-1 modules and domain controllers, then use security policy client authentication (SSO) rules for Internet access with log tracking.
- **External Web application usage accounting** Install UAS on FireWall-1 modules protecting the extranet Web server. Install WAM on the extranet server itself. Configure WAM to log access by external user groups to the Web application.
- **Internal secure Web application tracking** Install UAS and WAM on a FireWall-1 SecureServer enforcement module protecting the secure Web application. The Web Access policy restricts and logs access to sensitive areas (by URL) of the application.

The logging generated by the different components is controlled in different locations in the SmartDashboard and viewed in SmartView tracker. In the following sections, we look at each type of logging, the type of information recorded, and where it is configured.

FireWall-1 SSO Policy Rules

Logging of connections accepted by FireWall-1 due to SSO is configured via the Track action of the client authentication rules involved. The authentication events are configured in the Properties of the Client Authentication action. Different tracking for each user group and connection address and services can be configured by creating several SSO rules. The logging is best viewed using the FireWall-1 predefined query.

WAM Web Access Logging

Logging of access to a WAM-enabled Web server is controlled in the Web Access policy. Selection of events logged is highly granular—down to URL, action, user group and event, security control, authorization control, and SSO. Access that is rejected by the policy is logged according to the Rejection Policy settings for the WebAccess Web site objects. Access that is rejected because no policy applies is configured in the Check Point object for the WAM server. The logging is best viewed using the UA WebAccess predefined query. An example of WAM logging is shown in Figure 14.26.

Figure 14.26 An Example of WAM Logging

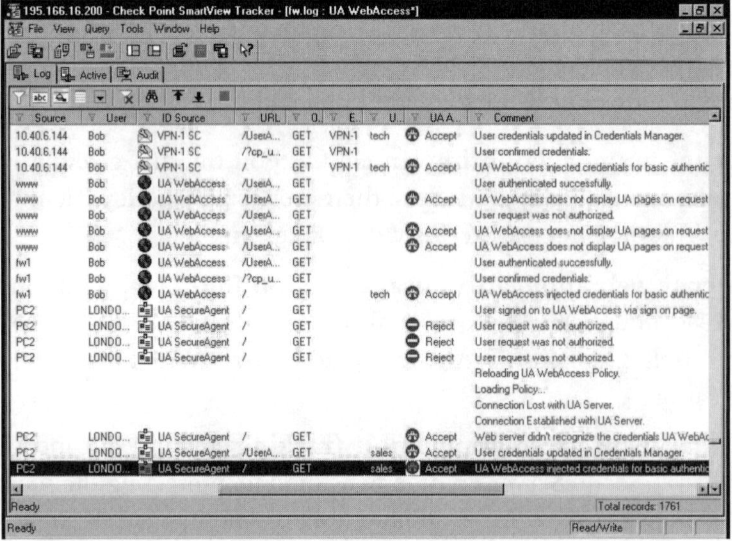

UAS Event Logging

Logging of events by the UA Server and Credentials Manager is configured in the Check Point object for the UAS server (in the object, choose **UserAuthority Server | Logging**). Logging of these events should be enabled only for troubleshooting purposes, because they can generate high volumes of logging. Everyday logging of access and rejected access to services should be performed by either the FireWall-1 module or the involved WAM. The logging is best viewed using the UA Server predefined query. An example of UAS logging is shown in Figure 14.27.

Figure 14.27 An Example of UAS Logging

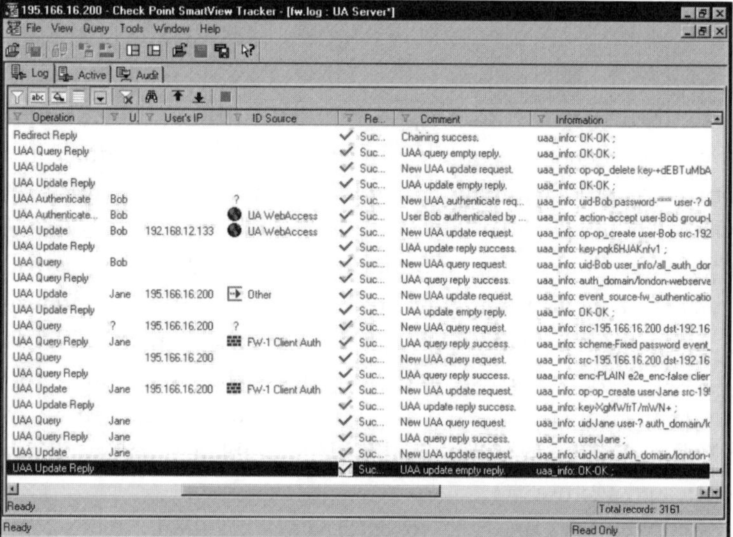

Understanding Credentials Management and Domain Equality

We have discussed how the Credentials Manager on the UAS stores user credentials in the user's "wallet." The UACM will store credentials when a UAA such as WebAccess "learns" them, after they are supplied by the user. If a UAA requests the credentials in order to perform SSO, credentials from a wallet may be supplied by the UAS.

There are two ways that these credentials may be managed:

- **UACM credentials management utility, *uacmutil*** This command-line utility can be run on the enforcement module UAS. It provides a means for an administrator to manage the credentials database.

- **WAM credentials management Web page** Users accessing a WAM-enabled server can access a Web page allowing them to edit their credentials and manage their personal wallets. An example of this is shown in our final deployment later in the chapter.

Domain Equality

The first thing to remember before using domain equality is to know when it should and definitely should not be used! Domain equality should be used only when a UAS is chaining to other UAS hosts that are fully trusted. We effectively lower the authentication strength for our users to that used by users of the same name on any chained UAS server.

By default, the credentials manager on a UAS stores the domain that a person logs into. It uses this information to uniquely identify users irrespective of which chained UAS we received their details from. Take, for example, a UAS module on a firewall that chains to a domain controller for the *LONDON* domain. If user *bob* were to log onto the domain controller and then later access a WAM that stored his Web server credentials, these credentials would be stored under the ID of *LONDON\bob*—if you like, the name on that wallet. If *bob* later authenticated against a FireWall-1 gateway, his credentials would be stored with ID *FIREWALL\bob*—the domain name *FIREWALL* is reserved for the local FireWall-1 user authentication database. So, the same person may end up with more than one wallet—one holding credentials learned when authenticated via FireWall-1 and one for each of the UAS-enabled Windows domains that the user has authenticated against.

Domain equality enables the UAS to determine that the domains *FIREWALL* and *LONDON* are the same, and therefore user *bob* in FireWall-1 and *bob* on the domain controller for the *LONDON* domain are referring to the same person. Bob will then always see the same wallet, wherever he authenticates.

WARNING

If you plan to implement domain equality and to create users manually on your firewall gateway, make sure that you pay attention to the fact that FireWall-1 usernames are *case sensitive*. For example, user *Bob* is a different user than *bob*. This means that you need to make sure that the usernames you define on the firewall match the case of usernames that are on your domain controller.

If you did not have domain equality implemented, you could create a user *LONDON\bob* on the firewall, and this would refer to the user *bob* on the domain controller UAS. This user could then be used in user groups and policy rules.

Configuring Domain Equality

Domain equality is configured on the UASs on which you want to have domain equivalence. Domain equality is configured in the netso.ini file, which can be located in the /opt/CPuag-50-03/conf directory on UNIX and in the C:\Program Files\Check Point\UAG\NG\conf folder on Windows. Alternatively, you can use the $UAGDIR environment variable to navigate to the correct area. (For example, by using the command *cd $UAGDIR/conf*, you can get to the directory of the netso.ini file.)

Edit the netso.ini file and find the section [CREDENTIAL_MANAGER_DOMAINS]. Uncomment this section by removing the semicolon from the front of the line. To enable domain equality, the following line needs to be added just below the section title:

```
equal = FIREWALL, <DOMAIN NAME1>, <DOMAIN NAME2>
```

For example, to make the users on host *fw1* equal to the users on the domain controller for the *LONDON* domain, the entry would be:

```
equal = FIREWALL, LONDON
```

Save the file netso.ini, and then issue a *cpstop* and *cpstart* from the command line to restart the UAS. The netso.ini file needs to be changed on all the UASs to which the domain equality is relevant.

Once domain equality is configured and the UASs are stopped and started, user *bob* on the host *fw1* will now be the same user as user *bob* on the domain controller for *LONDON*.

If SSO is configured in the firewall Rule Base, this will take into account the domain equality.

Deploying UserAuthority

There are countless arrangements of UASs and WAM modules that can be configured to provide SSO functionality. Here we describe three simple configurations that illustrate how the different components can work together:

- **Authenticated Internet access** FireWall-1 UAS, domain controller UAS and SecureAgents
- **Authenticated Web server** FireWall-1 UAS with WAM
- **SSO Internet access and Web server** FireWall-1, domain controller UAS and WAM

Authenticated Internet Access

This configuration uses authentication provided by SecureAgent. In order to do this, we also need to use the UAS on the domain controller as well as the UAS on the domain controller. Then we must have UAS installed on a firewall module that can query the UAS on the domain controller!

As a starting point, the firewall management station and firewall enforcement module with UAS must be installed. UAS should already be installed on the domain controller, and the trust between the UAS on the domain controller and the firewall management station should be established and working. The login script on the domain controller for the users logging into the domain needs to have been modified so that the SecureAgent has been installed to the users Windows desktop PCs. The configuration is illustrated in Figure 14.28.

The aim of this configuration is to achieve sign-on to the domain controller via the user logging into the domain; then the user should be able to go out through the firewall to a Web site that is protected by a single sign-on Client Authenticated rule. When they go through the firewall SSO rule, the firewall UAS server will query the UAS on the primary domain controller to check that the user has authenticated to the domain. If so, they will be allowed through the firewall.

Figure 14.28 The Servers Involved in the Single Sign-On Process

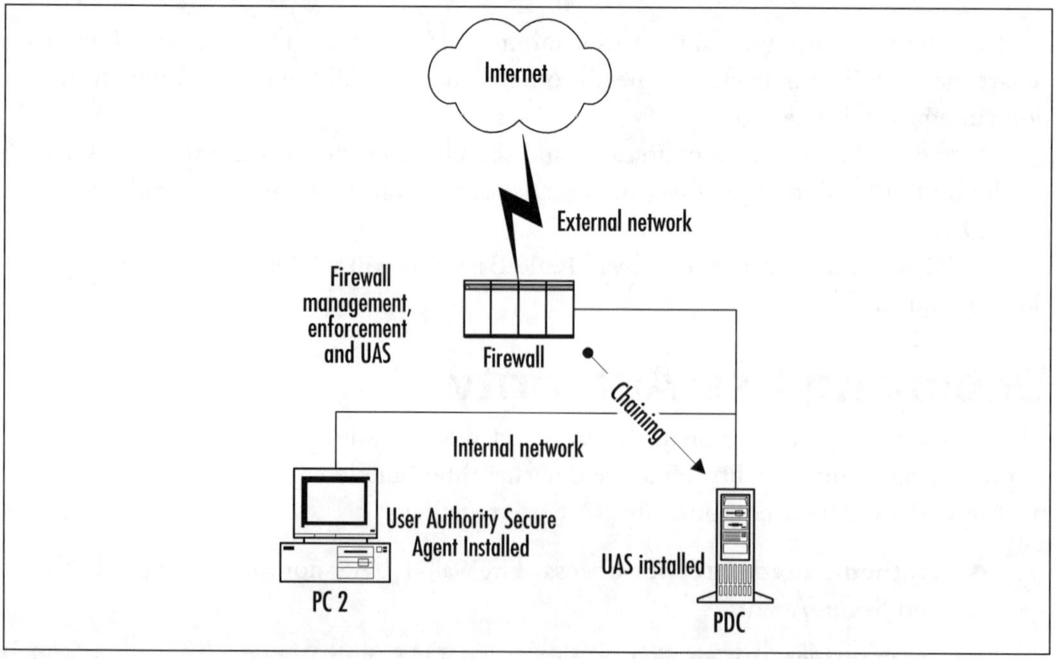

Configuring Objects in the SmartDashboard GUI

As with all configuration, there are many starting points. In this case, we start with configuring the objects in the SmartDashboard GUI. We start by setting up the UserAuthority Chaining and Domain Equivalence.

Go to the **Manage | Network Objects** and click **New**. Select **Group | UserAuthority Server Group**. You should see a popup window like the one shown in Figure 14.29. Give the group a name and add the UAS that is installed on your primary domain controller. (You should already have setup the trust for this object.)

Figure 14.29 Adding the PDC UAS Object to the UAS Group

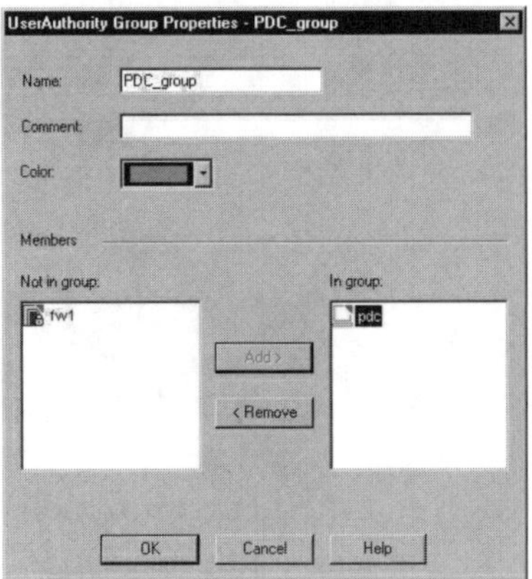

Click **OK** and then click the firewall enforcement module that has the UAS installed. In our example, this is *fw1*. Click **Edit**. Select **UserAuthority Server** from the left side. You should see the screen shown in Figure 14.30. Under **Chaining Options**, select the check box **UserAuthority Servers installed on Windows Domain Controllers or on UserAuthority Servers that are queried on user IP**. In the field next to this setting, select the UserAuthority Server group that you just created. In our example, this is **PDC_Group**.

Click **OK**. Now install the policy to the firewall module.

Configuring Domain Equivalence Between the Firewall UAS and the Domain Controller UAS

Now let's configure domain equivalence between the firewall UserAuthority server on the enforcement module and the UAS installed on the primary domain controller (PDC). If we don't do this, the firewall will need to have users defined on it that are of the format *<domain>**<userid>*. For example, if user *bob* were created on the domain controller for domain *london*, we would have to create the user *london\bob* as a user in a group for our SSO client authentication rule. If we just had user *bob* on our firewall, it would fail without setting up domain equivalence.

Figure 14.30 Setting Up the UserAuthority Server Chain

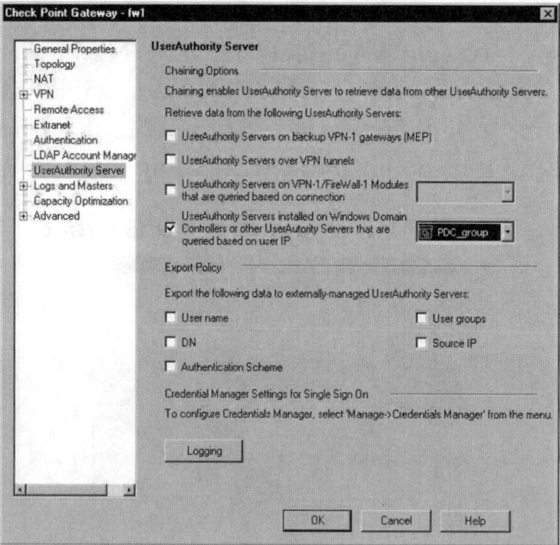

To set up domain equivalence, edit the netso.ini file on both the UAS on the firewall module and the UAS on the domain controller. On a UNIX system, this can be found in the /opt/CPuag-50-03/conf directory and on the Windows domain controller; it can be located in the C:\Program Files\Check Point\UAG\NG\conf directory.

Scroll down the file until you get to the section marked [CREDENTIAL_MANAGER_DOMAINS]. Make sure that this heading is uncommented by removing the semicolon (;) from the start of the line. Now enter a new line that reads **equal = FIREWALL, *<domain>*,** where domain is your PDC's domain name:

```
[CREDENTIAL_MANAGER_DOMAINS]

equal = FIREWALL, LONDON
```

Make sure you make the same change on the UAS on the firewall and the domain controller. Stop and start the servers using the *cpstop* and *cpstart* commands from the command line on each of the UASs.

This completes the process of setting up domain equivalence between the firewall UAS and the PDC UAS.

Creating Users on the Firewall

You might be wondering why we need to create users on the firewall when we are basing our authentication on Windows domain authentication and the Windows user database. The answer is that typically we base our security policy on groups of users—not just anyone who managed to authenticate on our Windows domain. In order to create these groups, we have to refer to users who are members of these groups. One way of doing this is to create FireWall-1 users with the same names as our Windows domain users and place these users in FireWall-1 user groups. There is no need to configure the user details; they are just there to provide references for our Windows usernames. A better solution is to use LDAP integration. If the domain controller is providing Windows 2000 Active Directory services, in our FireWall-1 security polices we can refer directly to groups in the Active Directory user database. With LDAP, we really do have SSO; FireWall-1 policies link directly into our existing AD user database, and the authentication that was performed when the user logged into the Windows domain is all that is needed for their authenticated access to all UA-enabled resources. Note that LDAP integration is a licensed FireWall-1 feature.

In this example, to demonstrate UA working in a simple manner, we create the user and the user group on the local firewall.

Go to the **Manage | Users and Administrators**. Click **New | User by Template | Default**. Enter a username here that matches exactly—case included—the user on our Windows domain. (See the section on Domain Equivalence for more on this topic.) In our original example (refer back to Figure 14.1), Bob's FireWall-1 user is defined as *Bob*. We must rename this user *bob* because this is Bob's username in our Windows user database. In the **Authentication** tab, we have selected **VPN1 and FireWall-1 Password**. Note that with domain equivalence configured, the password in the Authentication tab does not *have* to be the same as on the PDC, although if Bob authenticates against FireWall-1 sometimes—maybe in SecureClient—it's probably easier if it is. Click **OK** when complete. Create as many more users as you require.

Now create a group by clicking the **New | Group** button, as shown in Figure 14.31. In our example, the group *Sales* was created and users *bob* and *jane* were added.

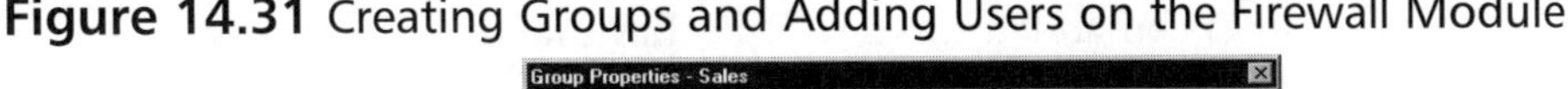

Figure 14.31 Creating Groups and Adding Users on the Firewall Module

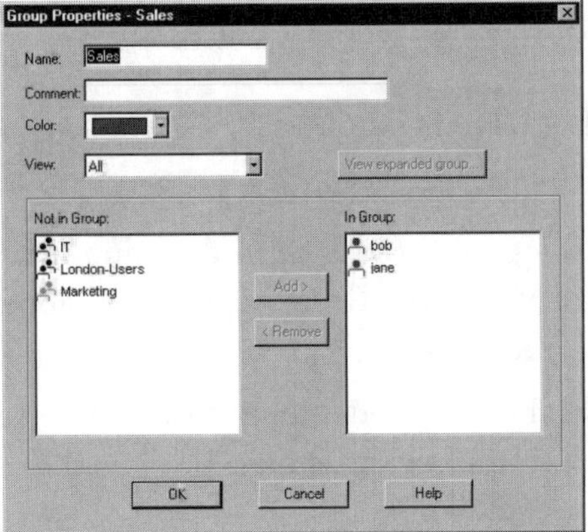

Once complete, click **OK**. Now click **Install** to update the user database on the management server.

Creating the Rule Base

Creating the Rule Base is the final stage. Here we create some client authentication (SSO) rules for Web access to the Internet. The aim here is that if users have not logged into the domain, their Internet access will fail. If they have logged in to the domain, we will log their usernames when they access the Internet.

The rule we have set up is shown in Figure 14.32. The clever bit here is the client authentication rule. If you right-click the **Client-Auth** action and select **Edit Properties**, the SSO method is selected, as shown in Figure 14.33.

Figure 14.32 Client Auth Rule for Web Access Using SSO

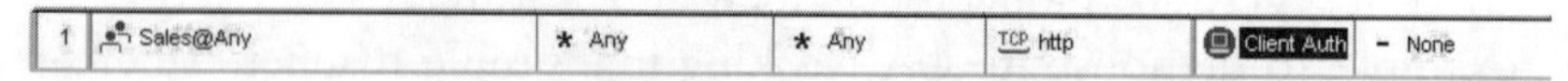

1
Sales@Any
* Any
* Any
TCP http
Client Auth
- None

Figure 14.33 Properties of the Client Auth Action

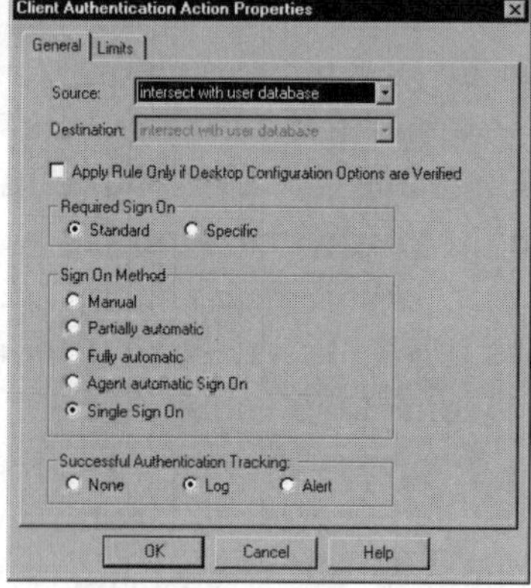

When the SSO rule has been added to your Rule Base, install the policy to the firewall module on your Internet gateway. In our example, this will be *fw1*.

Testing the Configuration

To test the configuration, all we need to do is:

1. User *bob* needs to log in to the *London* domain. After he has authenticated, he should see the UserAuthority SecureAgent icon appear in his desktop system tray, as shown in Figure 14.10.
2. Bob then starts his browser and attempts to browse to a site on the Internet. This should work seamlessly; he should not be asked to authenticate, nor

should he be refused access. The client authentication rule we set up should grant him access via UA SSO.

3. In the SmartView Tracker, we can see a log entry for Client Authentication. In the Info field, we see *reason: SSO Authentication*.

You could also test the configuration using a user who is not in the group and test to make sure that they can't access the Internet for Web browsing.

Authenticated Web Server

In this configuration example, we assume that you have installed the UserAuthority server on a Check Point FireWall-1 enforcement module and that you have installed the WebAccess module on a host with Microsoft IIS version 5 on a DMZ of your FireWall-1 enforcement module. We will then allow users who are internal and external to the firewall to access the Web server, and the WebAccess software on the IIS server will challenge the users for authentication. Our example network is shown in Figure 14.34.

Figure 14.34 An Example Network for UserAuthority with WAM

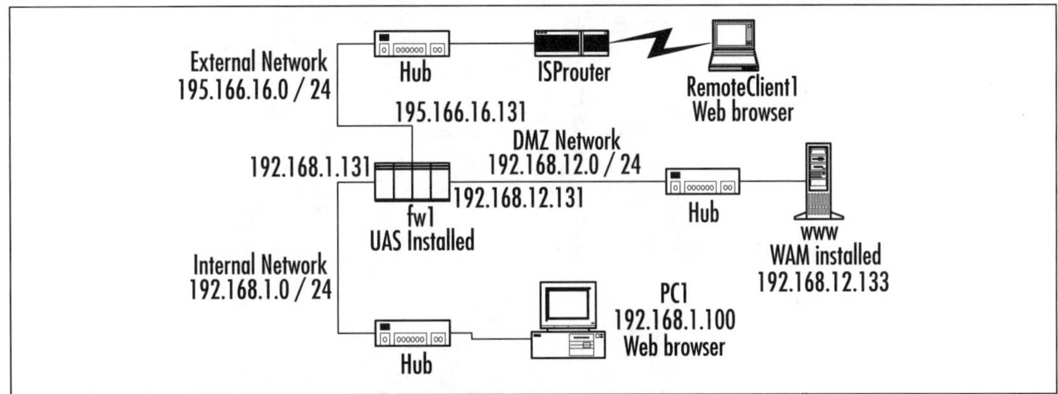

In Figure 14.34, UserAuthority Server is installed on the firewall gateway (fw1), and we are accessing the Web site on host www using internal and external Web browsers. The WebAccess module is installed on the www server and is managed by the firewall management station (which is not marked on this diagram).

Creating a Simple WebAccess Policy

At the moment, if you attempt to connect to your Web server, you will be denied access. This is because we have not yet installed a policy to the WebAccess module. For example, if host 192.168.1.100 were to browse to 192.168.12.133 using her browser, the connection would get through the firewall fine, but the WebAccess plug-in module would deny them access, and they would see a response similar to that shown in Figure 14.35.

Figure 14.35 Access to the Web Server Is Denied When There Is No Policy Installed to the WAM

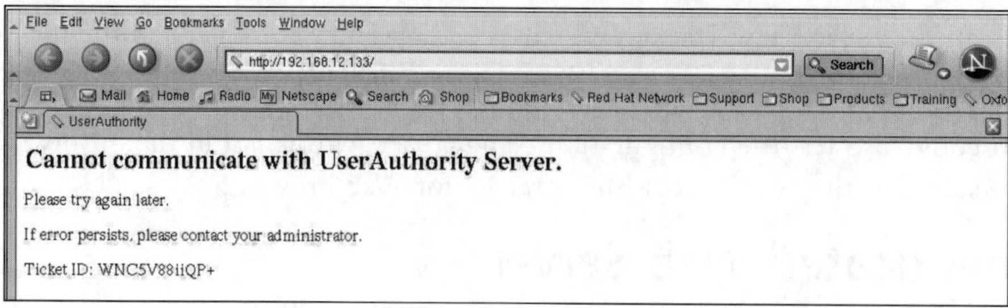

At this stage, if you haven't already, you will need to switch on the WebAccess tab in your SmartDashboard GUI. This can be done by clicking **Policy | Global Properties | Smart Dashboard Customization**. You should see a screen similar to the one shown in Figure 14.36.

Figure 14.36 Enabling the WebAccess Tab on the SmartDashboard GUI

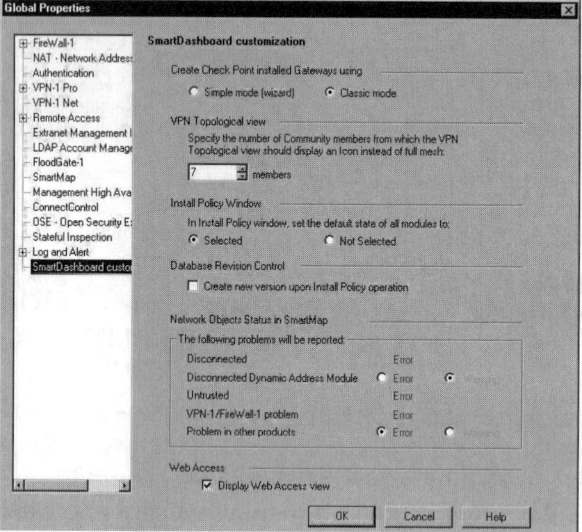

At the bottom of Figure 14.36, you can see that **Display Web Access view** needs to be checked. When you do this, an extra tab will be displayed in your SmartDashboard GUI. Click **OK**.

We now need to create some users who can use the Web site. We create the users on the firewall, but they could easily be defined on an external server, such as an LDAP or RADIUS server. Let's create groups and users as shown in Figure 14.37.

Figure 14.37 Groups of Users to Define for WebAccess

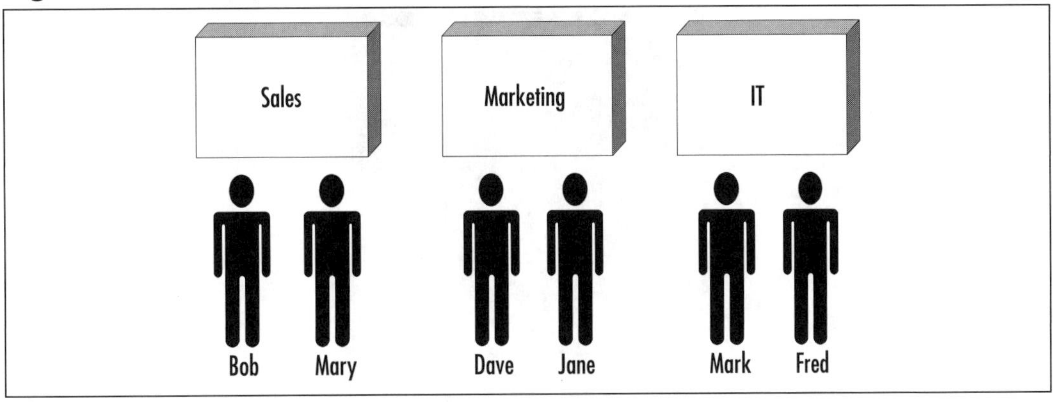

First, let's create the groups. Click **Manage | Users and Administrators**. Click **New | Group**. Fill in the group definition. We have defined the Sales group, as shown in Figure 14.38. Follow the same steps to create the Marketing and IT groups.

Figure 14.38 Creating Groups on FireWall-1 NG FP3

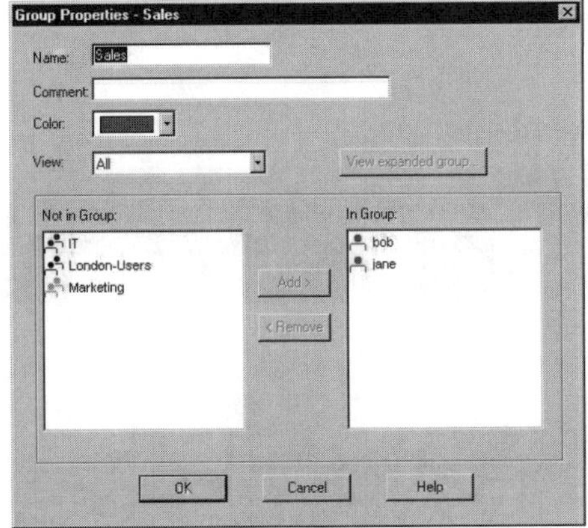

Once the groups are created, we can start creating the users and adding them to the groups. In our example, we started with Bob. Click **New | User by Template | Default**. You will then see a popup window as shown in Figure 14.39. Enter the username, then click **Personal**; set an **Expiry date**, then click **Groups**, select the **Sales** group we created earlier, then click the **Authentication** tab and select the method of authentication. In our example, we selected **VPN and FireWall-1 password**. Location, time, certificates, and encryption can all be set up if required, but they are not needed for this example.

Now create all the other users and put them into the correct groups.

Figure 14.39 Creating Users and Assigning Them to Defined Groups

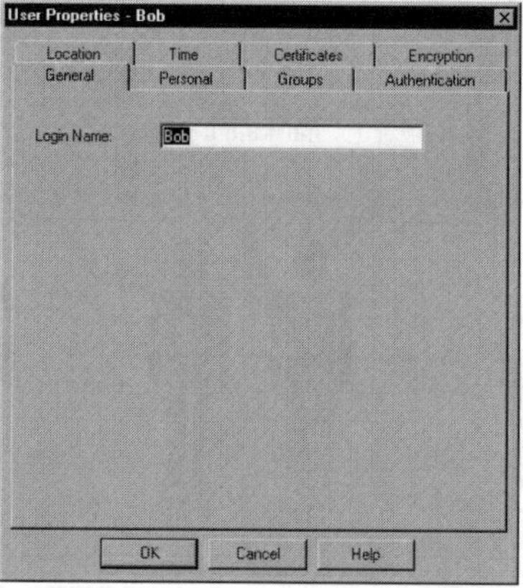

When you're finished defining the users, click **Install**. Then click **OK**, and let the user database install to the management server. This is also a good point to install the security policy to the firewall enforcement modules.

You are now ready to start defining your WebAccess policy. Click the **WebAccess** tab of your SmartDashboard. You will be greeted with a screen that looks something like Figure 14.40.

Figure 14.40 WebAccess Blank Policy

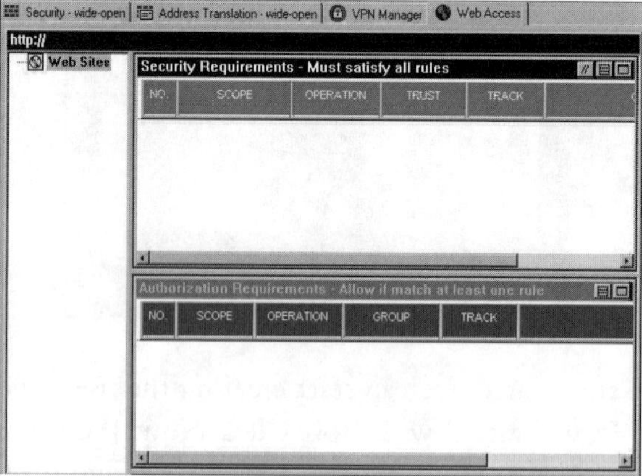

The first thing we need to do is create a Web site. This is done by right-clicking on the **Web Sites** icon in the top-left side of the screen. Select **New | Web Site**.

You will then be presented with a popup window like the one shown in Figure 14.41. Enter the name of the Web site. In our example, we have given the name **www.london.com**. Click the **Add** button. You will see a second popup window that shows all the existing WebAccess servers. Select a WebAccess server from the list. In our example, this is **www** (see Figure 14.42).

Figure 14.41 Web Site Properties

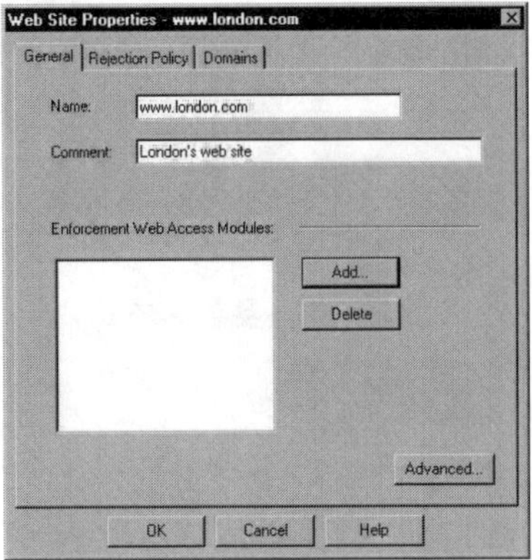

Figure 14.42 WebAccess Server Selection

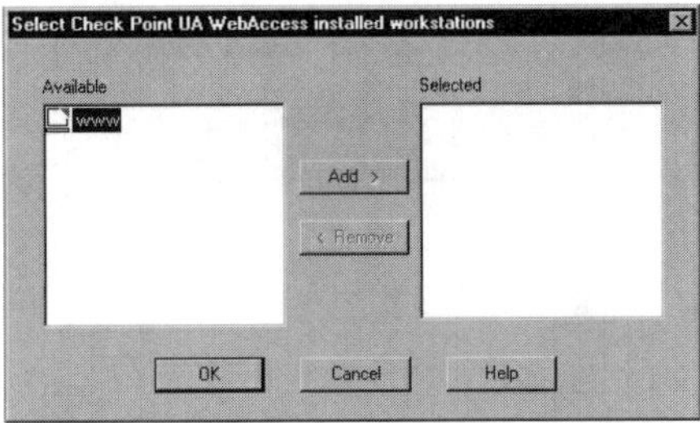

Click **OK** when you have made your selection.

Now click the **Rejection Policy** tab. You might want to alter the setting here, because it will control what happens if the WAM module decides to prohibit access to a page on the server. In Figure 14.43, you can see that we selected the tracking **Log** option. Click the **Domains** tab. This option defines which domains used in the URL of a user's request are covered by the site definition. For the purposes of getting something running quickly, we have set this to **Any**, which is the default, as shown in Figure 14.44. We could have used www.london.com.

Click **OK** when you have completed your changes. You will notice that you now have a Web site defined in the top-left side of the screen, just under the Web Sites icon, as shown in Figure 14.45.

You now need to create a policy for this Web site. Select the new Web site (www.london.com, in our case) and click the **Security Requirements** window. We now need to create a rule in this policy. It is possible to add rules using the same methods we used for standard Security Policy rules: the toolbar icons or the Rules menu.

Figure 14.43 Rejection Policy

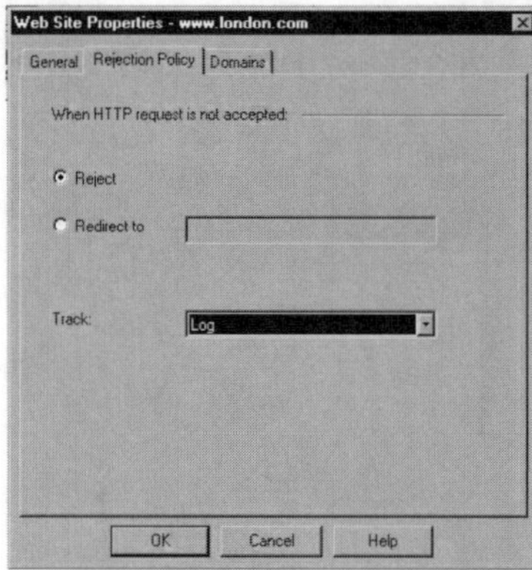

Figure 14.44 Domains

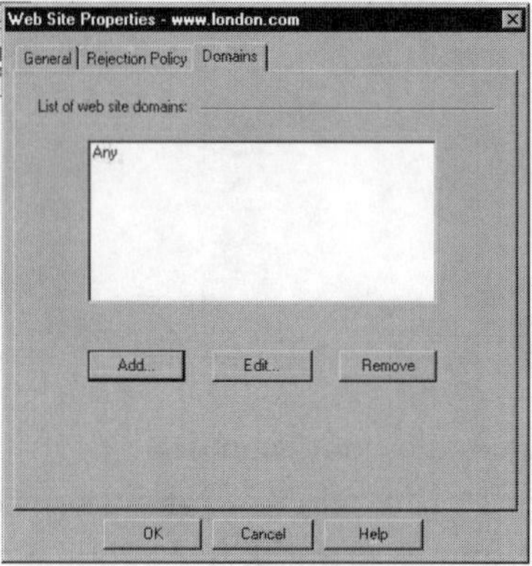

Figure 14.45 Moving on to Policy Creation After Web Site Creation

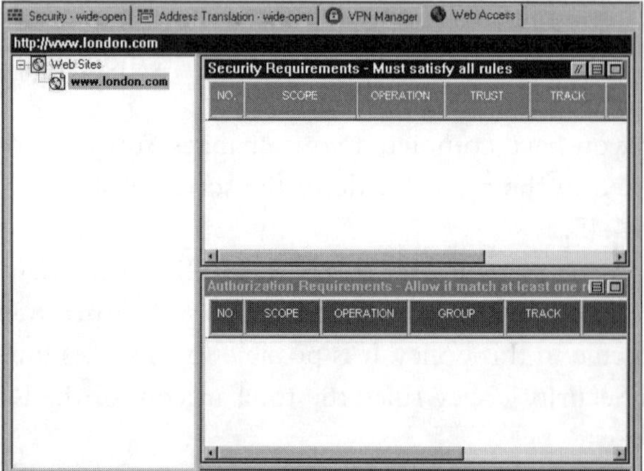

We now have a blank rule in the Security Requirements window, which should look like Figure 14.46. You need to modify this rule by right-clicking each individual rule element and selecting the value that you require.

Figure 14.46 Default Settings When You Create a New Rule

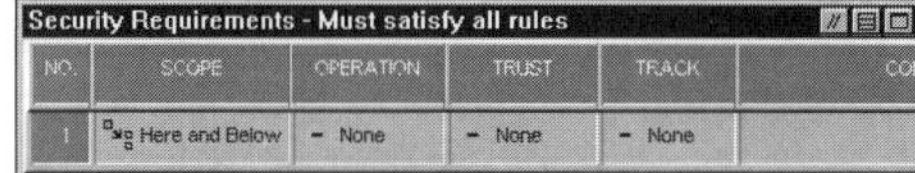

In our example, shown in Figure 14.47, we selected the operation Any, the trust Any, and the track Log. The scope is Here and Below, which means the rule will apply to every subdirectory of this Web site.

Figure 14.47 The Configured Rule

NO	SCOPE	OPERATION	TRUST	TRACK
1	Here and Below	* Any	* Any	Log

Now click the **Authorization Requirements** window and create a new rule. Modify the rule by right-clicking each element in the options and selecting the options that you require. For our example, we chose the operation **Any** (which could perhaps be restricted to Read for everyone, to block, for example, HTTP *GET* and *PUTs*). For the Group element, we selected the user groups that we created earlier. For Track, we selected **Log**. Once complete, we have something like the screen shown in Figure 14.48.

Figure 14.48 Authorization Requirements

Authorization Requirements - Allow if match at least one rule

NO.	SCOPE	OPERATION	GROUP	TRACK
1	Here	* Any	IT Marketing Sales	Log

We have now defined our simple WebAccess policy and need to install this policy to the WebAccess server. To do this, right-click the icon for your Web server and select **Install,** as shown in Figure 14.49. In our case, we clicked **www.london.com | Install** to install our policy to our WebAccess server, as shown in Figure 14.49.

When you have selected **Install**, you will see a popup window. This window verifies your policy before installing it on the WebAccess module, as shown in Figure 14.50.

If everything has gone well, the policy is now being enforced by the WebAccess module. We have made limited use of the WAM functionality that's available; it is possible to define far more complex policies using multiple rules, each applying different restrictions to areas of the Web site. Before moving on to testing our new policy, let's look at how more complex rules could be created.

Figure 14.49 Installing the WebAccess Policy

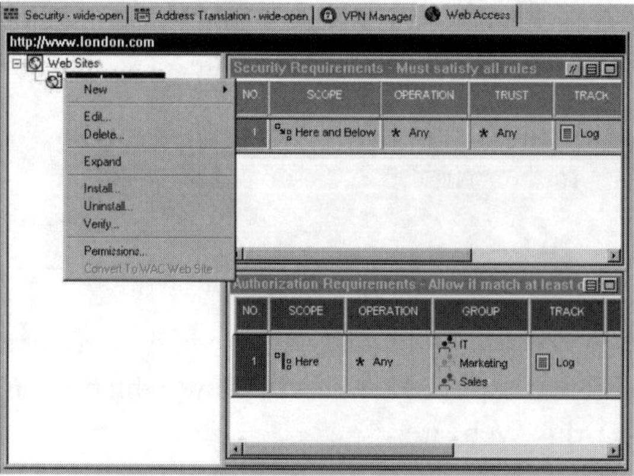

Figure 14.50 Policy Installation Screen for a WebAccess Module

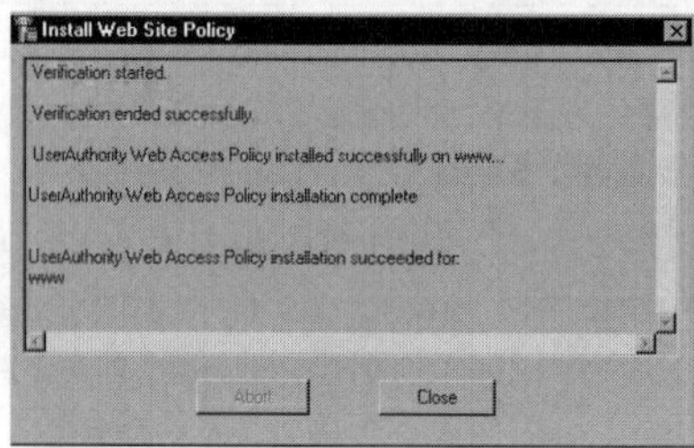

The WebAccess policy consists of three Rule Bases for each defined site and sub-URL:

- **Security Requirements** This Rule Base defines the level of trust required in order to access the URL. An HTTP request must match every rule in order to be permitted by WebAccess.
- **Authorization Requirements** This Rule Base defines the type of HTTP access allowed to the URL per user group. When a connection is made, the user is identified either by the WAM directly or via the UAS, and the user's group is matched against these rules. The user must be a member of one of the groups specified in order to gain any access, unless a rule specifying the Any group is present.
- **Application Settings—Effects**. This Rule Base is optional and specifies an action (effect) that will take place if the rule is matched.

The rules are defined using the following elements:

- **URL** We can define different rules for each area of the Web site by defining new URL objects in the Web Sites tree. Right-click the Web site or an existing URL and choose **New..URL** to do this. A new policy can then be defined for that URL.

- **Scope** Each rule is defined with a scope. This controls whether a rule applies to just this URL (Here), or all "lower" URLs (Here and Below). If a "lower" URL has inherited rules, these are indicated with the scope From Above.
- **Operation** Rules can apply to specific types of HTTP operation only—for example, a simple page *GET* request or form data *PUT* methods. New Operation objects can be defined that specify particular HTTP headers.
- **Trust** A security requirements rule can specify the level of trust required to access a URL—both trust in the user and the user's HTTP connection. This element can be used to provide a high level of integration with the firewall module UAS because we can base rules on state information held by FireWall-1 for the incoming HTTP connection. Four types of trust can be required by a rule, as defined by the Trust object selected:
  - **Trust—Encryption** FireWall-1 VPN encryption or SSL can be required from the client to the FireWall-1 and optionally right through to the Web server.
  - **Trust—Authentication** Strong authentication (token or certificate) can be required, as can membership of particular FireWall-1 user groups. User group access permissions can also be defined in the Group element of the authorization rules.
  - **Trust—Networking** Access to a URL can be limited to particular source client and destination Web server IP addresses based on FireWall-1 Network objects.
  - **Trust—Time** FireWall-1 Time objects can be used to restrict URL access by time.
- **Group** Used in authorization rules to specify the user groups to which a rule applies.
- **Effects** The action that is triggered by an Application Settings rule. These are predefined as follows:
  - **Effect: Single Sign On** It is this action that enables the WAM SSO functionality. If this action is enabled, WAM will query the firewall UAS in order to collect connection data, which is then used when considering the WebAccess policy. WAM will also update the UAS with Web server credentials supplied by the user, storing them in the user's wallet.

- **Effect: Redirection** The user attempting to access a URL matching the rule is sent an HTTP redirect as specified.
- **Effect: Insert Header** An HTTP header is added to the request passed to the Web server. This action can be used to pass FireWall-1 connection information to the Web server application (e.g., the FireWall-1 username).
- **Effect: Delete Header** If the specified headers are found in the HTTP request, they are removed before the request is passed to the Web server.

- **Track** Matching on a rule can generate a log entry that tracks access to a URL. The logging is seen via the SmartView Tracker UA WebAccess query.

An HTTP request is matched against a Web site/URL policy and will be blocked by WAM if:

- Any security requirements rule is not matched
- No authorization requirements rule is matched

The action on block is defined in the Web site rejection policy. Be aware that if no Web site or URL matches the policy, the action can be Accept or Reject, as defined in the UA WebAccess-enabled Check Point object.

Before attempting to define a complex policy, it is best to test the WebAccess module using a simple policy such as we have defined. Install the WebAccess policy, then start a Web browser and enter the address of the Web server. In our example (shown in Figure 14.51), we go to www.london.com and are asked to authenticate by the WebAccess module.

Figure 14.51 Testing the WebAccess Policy

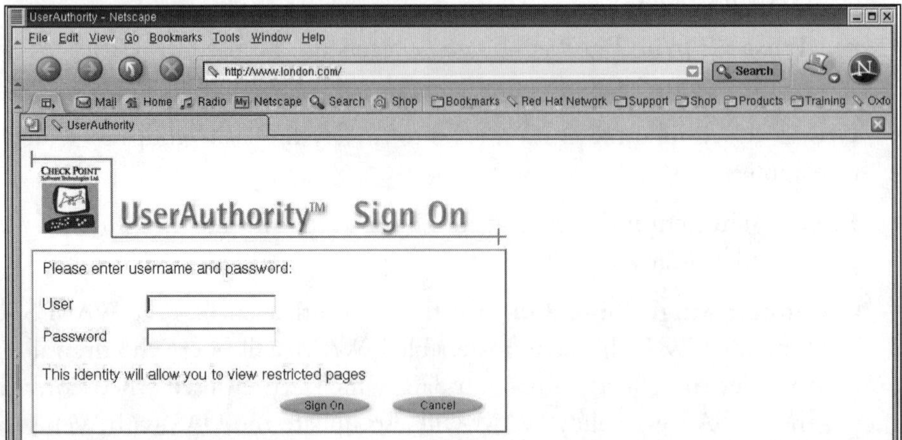

Here, we can enter the Web site if we enter a username and password for any of the users we created earlier who are members of the Sales, Marketing, or IT groups. If you fail to authenticate correctly, you will be presented with the same screen again, as shown in Figure 14.51; however, the firewall logs will show a failed authentication and the source IP address of the Web client that attempted the authentication (if logging has been switched on in the appropriate place).

If you authenticate correctly, your browser will show you the main page of your Web site. Our site's impressive home page is shown in Figure 14.52.

Figure 14.52 Successful Authentication: Access Granted to Main Web Page

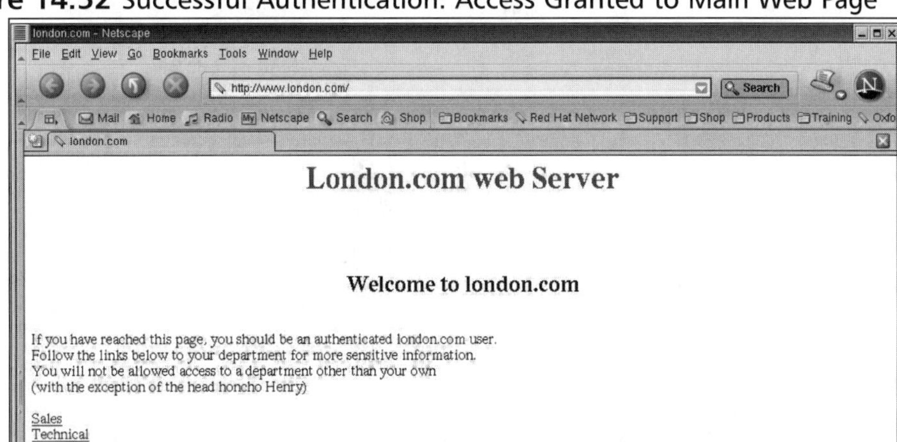

SSO Internet Access and Web Server

We now look at an example that combines our two previous configurations. We provide single sign-on so that just by logging into the domain, the user can access the Internet as his or her client authenticated SSO rules allow, and the user can access the intranet server, without having to authenticate to either the firewall module or the WebAccess server after logging into his or her domain.

Users accessing the network from the Internet using SecuRemote will also be able to benefit from this configuration because they will be authenticated by FireWall-1 and so gain SSO access to the intranet server.

Configuration

This example deployment requires domain controller UAS, SecureAgents, and WAM installed and configured as described in our first two examples: with **Authenticated Internet access** and **Authenticated Web server**. This setup is illustrated by Figure 14.53. This setup should put you in a position where PC2 can log in to the domain *LONDON* and then get access to the Internet via the firewall without having to authenticate.

Figure 14.53 An Example of Single Sign-On

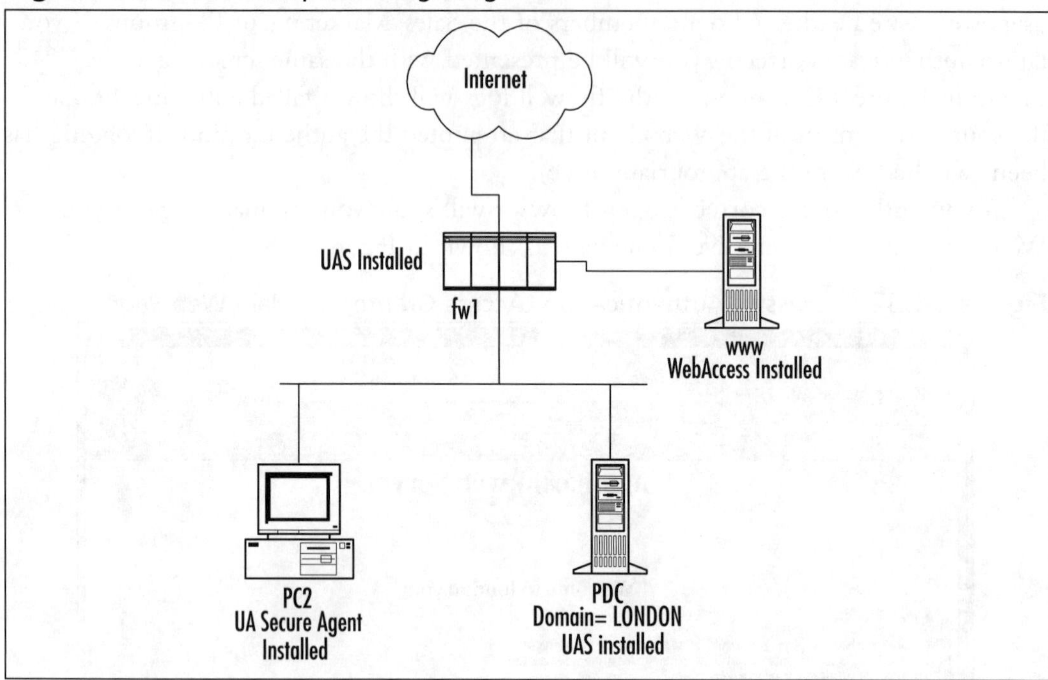

We first consider the FireWall-1 Rule Base. The SSO client authentication rule(s) will be the rules by which connections to the Internet are accepted. Check to make sure by looking at your SmartView Tracker logs.

You should also be able to Web-browse to the www server through a FireWall-1 Accept rule. Make sure that this does not occur through one of your SSO client authentication rules.

We assume that WAM is installed and configured as described in the previous example. Currently, when you attempt to connect to the intranet (www.london.com) Web server, WAM should ask you to authenticate. If you do so correctly, you should be granted access to the Web server.

Let's now examine how to allow users to access the intranet Web server via SSO. Each user's Web server credentials will be stored by the Credentials Manager on the firewall, in their wallets. To achieve this goal, we need to complete the following steps:

1. In SmartDashboard, choose **Manage | UserAuthority | UserAuthority Domains** and click **New**. You will be presented with a popup window, as shown in Figure 14.54. Fill in the name as you require (it can be anything). In our example, we called it **www-access**. This domain represents applications that use the same authentication credentials—perhaps a bank of intranet servers.

Figure 14.54 Creating a UserAuthority Domain for SSO

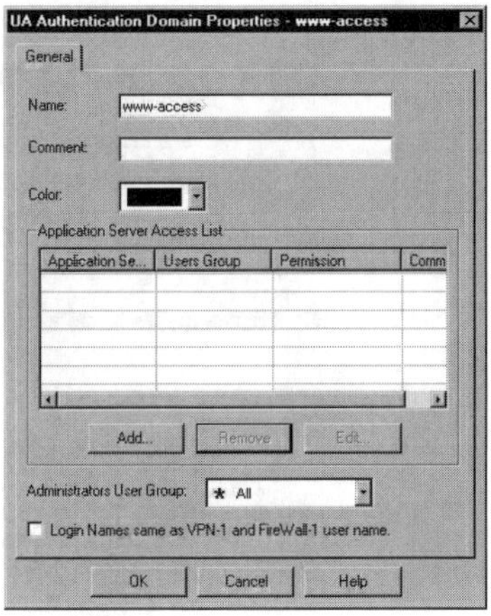

2. Click the **Add** button. You will see a popup window, as shown in Figure 14.55. Select the object that represents your WebAccess server. In our case, this is server **www**.

Figure 14.55 Defining Application Server Access List

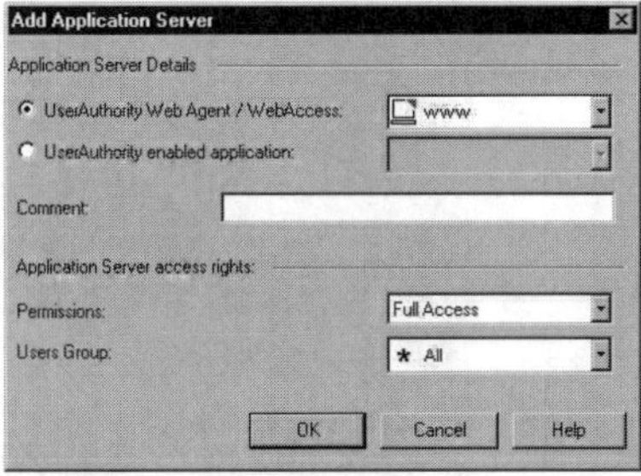

3. Click **OK** when you're finished. You should now have a screen that looks like Figure 14.56. Click **OK**, then click **Close**.
4. Click the **WebAccess** tab of the SmartDashboard GUI main screen. You should already have a Security Requirements rule and an Authorization Requirements rule. If you move the Authorization Requirements Rule Base divider up a little bit, you should then see the Application Settings—Effects Rule Base, which is blank at the moment. Click the **Application Settings** Rule Base, then go to **Rules | Add rule | Top**. You should see a default rule appear in the Application Settings—Effects Rule Base, as shown in Figure 14.57.
5. Right-click the entry **None** for the operation column. Select **Add**, select **Any**, and then click **OK**.

Figure 14.56 A Completed Authentication Domain with a Application Server Added

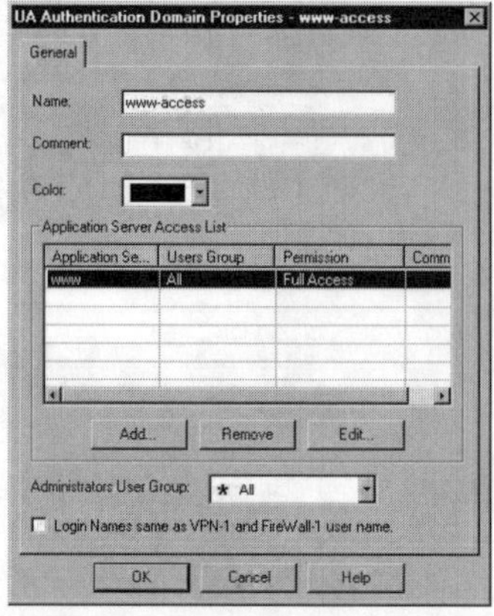

Figure 14.57 Application Settings—Effects Rule Base

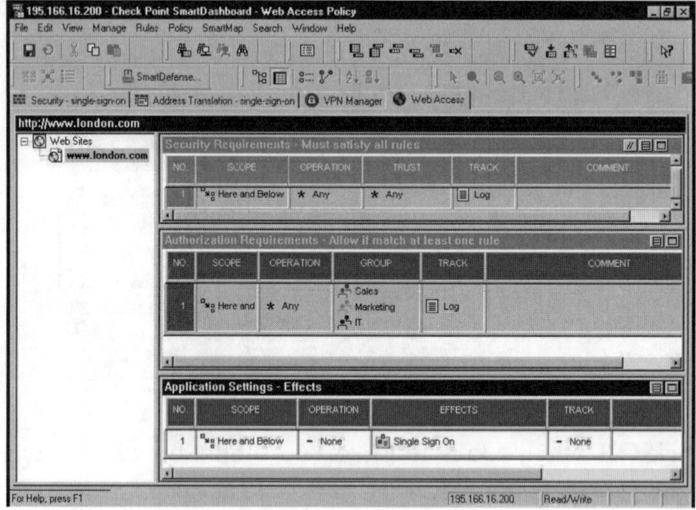

6. Right-click the **Single Sign On** entry in Effects. Select **Edit Properties**. You should see a popup window as shown in Figure 14.58. Keep the Single Sign On Type set to **Basic**, and for the Authentication domain, select the domain object that you created earlier. In our example, this was called **www-access**. You can leave the application name blank. You might want to click the **Track** tab and select **Log** while you are testing. Click **OK** when you are finished.
7. In the **Track** column, you might want to select **Log** while you are testing. Once that process is complete, you should install the policy by right-clicking

the **www.london.com** Web site on the left side and click **Install**, as shown in Figure 14.59.

Figure 14.58 Editing the Properties of Single Sign-On Effects

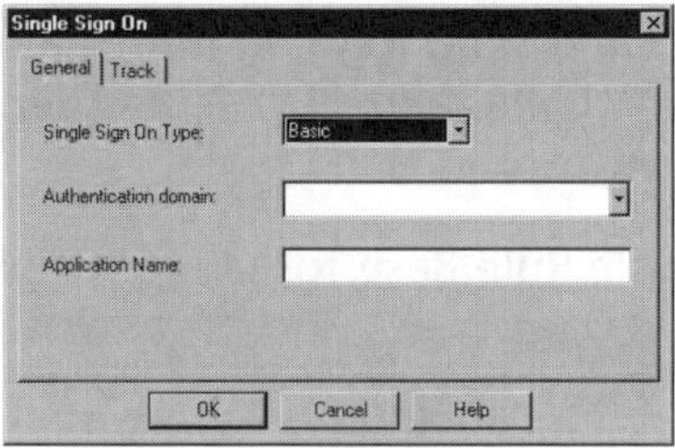

Figure 14.59 Installing the Policy to the *web-access* Server

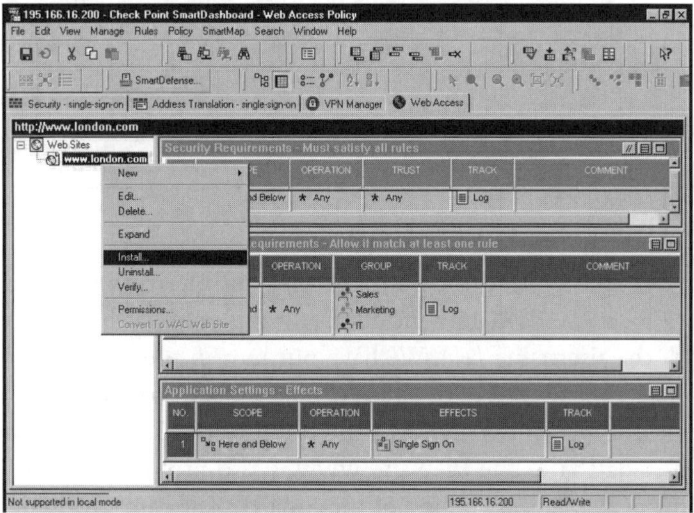

8. Once the policy is installed, you are ready to test the configuration to see if it works.

NOTE

We have not discussed the FireWall-1 Security Rule Base in much detail here. In the examples in this chapter, a very simple Rule Base was used with *no address translation rules*. If you use address translation, be aware that this can interfere with your SSO system if any of the hosts or workstations participating in SSO have NAT rules that apply to them such that it changes the client source address. This is because the IP address seen by the WAM-enabled Web server may be different from that seen by UAS servers. The same problems may occur when a client Web browser is accessing the Web server via a proxy.

The simplest Rule Base that can be made to work with the configuration so far would be as shown in Figure 14.60. This is not a real-world example, but it shows you the rules that have any effect. It does not show the intercommunication rules that are required so that the firewall UAS objects can speak to each other correctly and send logging information. You should also allow the services FW1_uaa, FW1_ela, and CP_SecureAgent_udp between all the UAS and UA SecureAgent devices.

Figure 14.60 Sample Rule Base for Our SSO Example

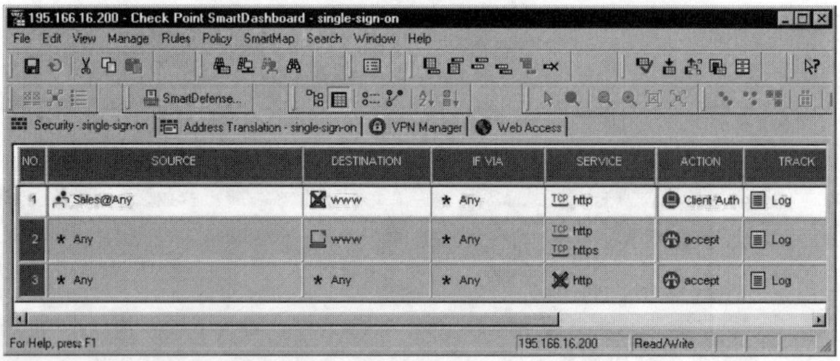

Testing the Configuration

Testing the configuration is hopefully the pleasant bit. In this test example, we have created a user *bob* on the domain controller, and this user has been created on FireWall-1 as well (with the username *bob*). We have put him in the group *sales* on the firewall.

The Web server on www has a userid of *sales* and password of *sales* to access the front page of the Web site. This was configured in the IIS security properties and Windows user database. The Web site www is also protected by the WebAccess policy, as shown in the Web access policy of the SmartDashboard GUI.

Here is what user *bob* will observe when he logs into the domain *LONDON*:

1. User *bob* needs to first authenticate to the PDC—in other words, log in to the Windows domain. A typical dialog box is shown in Figure 14.61. Note that the username specified here is not case-sensitive for the purpose of logging in to the domain. When the domain controller UAS is queried to obtain the name of the user, it will supply the name in the case defined on the domain controller, not necessarily the case used in this login dialog box.
2. After user *bob* has authenticated to the domain, he will notice his domain login script running. The UserAuthority SecureAgent will start and the SecureAgent icon will be present in his system tray.
3. Bob then starts his browser and connects to an Internet Web site on the other side of his firewall. He is not asked to authenticate, but looking at the

FireWall-1 logs in SmartView Tracker, he can observe that he went out through a client-authenticated HTTP rule—rule 1 in our example.

Figure 14.61 User *bob* Authenticating to the Primary Domain Controller

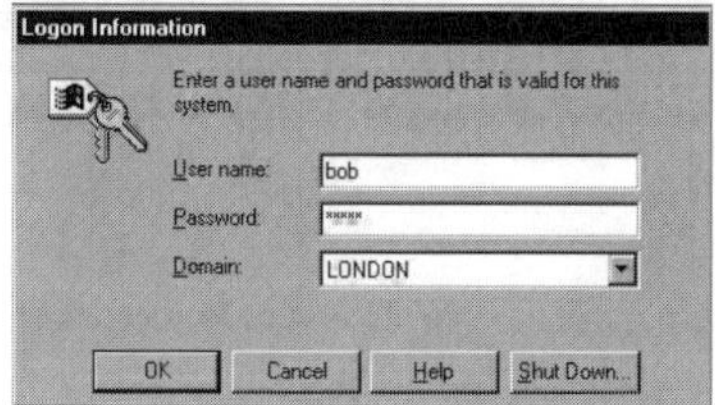

Figure 14.62 The Second Time User *bob* Visits the www Server

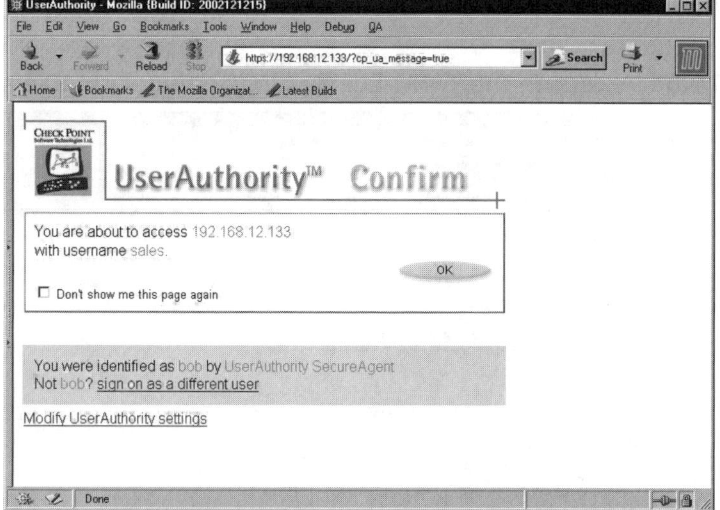

4. Bob then uses his Web browser to go to the intranet server www on the DMZ. He is presented with the screen shown in Figure 14.62. This is because he has been to this site before and he has already saved his credentials for this Web site.
5. Clicking **OK**, Bob then gets to the home page of the Web server, shown in all its glory in Figure 14.63.

There are a number of additional things that user bob can now do. He can access the site again after restarting his browser, and he can modify his credentials as well.

If he now goes to the www server after having just logged into the PDC, he will see the screen shown in Figure 14.64.

Figure 14.63 Bob Is Allowed Access to the Web Server www

Figure 14.64 Accessing the WAM-Enabled Web Server Using SecureAgent SSO

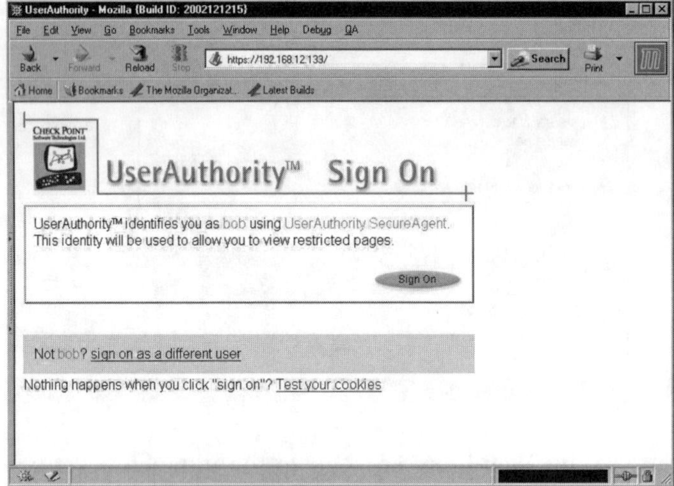

Notice that the UserAuthority server knows who Bob is and that he is using the UserAuthority SecureAgent. If Bob was connecting from home using SecureClient, this page would reflect that fact.

Note

For the WebAccess server to work with the browser, you must allow cookies on your browser. A "Test your cookies" link is available on the WebAccess sign-in page when you confirm your credentials. If you are in any doubt about your cookies support, click the link to check.

If Bob clicks **Sign on**, he is then greeted with the Web page shown earlier in Figure 14.62. If user *bob* wants to modify his credentials, he can click the **Modify UserAuthority Settings** link. Doing so will show him a screen like the one shown in Figure 14.65.

Figure 14.65 Credentials Management Screen

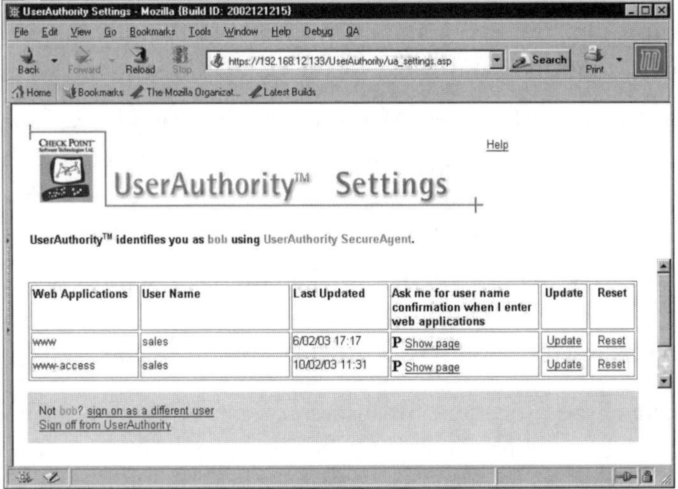

Here Bob can update his credentials for a particular Web server, or he can remove a particular Web server from his credentials. This page can be thought of as a view of Bob's wallet. If he wants to remove a particular server from his wallet, he clicks the **Reset** link. If he wants to update his credentials for a particular Web server, he clicks the **Update** link. Clicking the **Update** link will produce a popup window like the one shown in Figure 14.66.

Figure 14.66 Updating the Credentials for a Particular Web Server

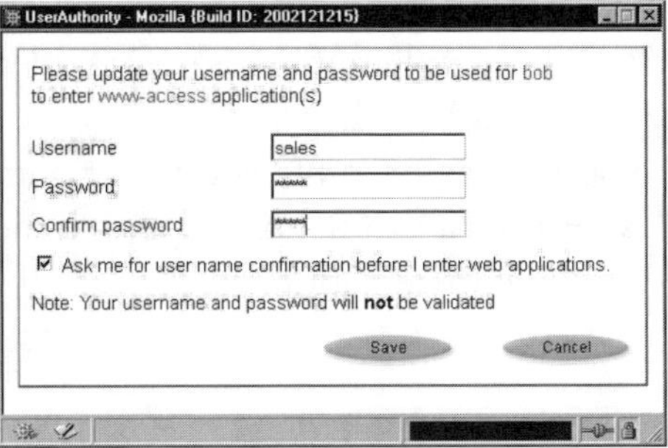

Figure 14.66 is the screen where Bob would enter the user ID and password for the Web server (e.g. IIS) authentication. This information is then associated with the user *Bob* as part of Bob's credential wallet. The changes are saved when he clicks the **Save** button.

Summary

In this chapter, we have talked about UserAuthority, outlined its functionality and shown how it can help you along the path toward single sign-on for your desktop users and your remote access users. We have described all the components that make up UserAuthority:

- **UserAuthority Server** Can be installed on a firewall enforcement module or domain controller; also holds the credentials manager.
- **UserAuthority WebAccess Module** Installed on a IIS version 4 or version 5 Web server (Apache in beta). Adds authentication protection to a Web site that does not have any authentication on it, or if there is already IIS authentication on the server, adds the username and passwords to the users' credential wallets.
- **UserAuthority SecureAgent** Installed on the desktop. Used exclusively when logging in to a domain controller that has UAS installed on it, so that other UAS servers installed on firewall modules can query the domain controller.

We also described the procedure for installing each of the components. We looked at how chaining can be used to extend SSO to incorporate multiple firewalled sites and Windows domain controller authentication.

The rich logging options throughout UA were described, including how to view the logs and some possible applications.

We explained the importance of domain equality in providing full SSO integration and the security risks involved. We looked at how to implement this on the UAS and the resulting behavior of the credentials manager.

We also described how users can use the Web-based credentials management tool in order to update their stored credentials for particular Web sites.

We ran through a couple of example configurations that will enable you to test the UAS and WAM installations. The first scenario illustrated SSO Windows domain-authenticated Internet access. The second configuration provided FireWall-1 integrated authentication for a Web server using WAM.

To wrap things up, we described an example configuration that pulls together all the major components of UserAuthority to provide SSO intranet and Internet access integrated with Windows domain authentication.

Solutions Fast Track

Defining UserAuthority

☑ UserAuthority enables authentication and SSO solutions that integrate Web applications with FireWall-1 and Windows domain authentication.

☑ UserAuthority can enable SSO-authenticated Internet access integrated with Windows domain authentication.

☑ UserAuthority includes several components, including UA Server, the UA WebAccess module, and UA SecureAgent.

Installing UserAuthority

☑ Installing UserAuthority Server on a Windows domain controller is a more or less identical procedure to installing UserAuthority Server on a firewall module.

☑ Installing the WebAccess module requires that you download it from the Check Point site. It does not come on the NG FP3 media by default.

☑ Use the PDC login script to install the UserAuthority SecureAgent to users' desktops.

☑ Once the components of UAS are installed, set up the trusts between the UAS servers and the Check Point management module. Make sure the time and date are correct on all the components.

☑ Work out your strategy for where you are going to create your users: on the Windows domain controller only (and use LDAP on the firewall to query the Windows 2000 Active Directory or use RADIUS to query Microsoft IAS), or using a separate RADIUS server, or creating the users on the firewall as well as on the Windows domain. Make sure the usernames on the Windows domain and on the firewall are consistent in terms of case.

☑ Set up chaining as you require it—for example, to integrate the domain controller UAS with the firewall.

☑ Set up domain equivalence to complement any chaining that you use.

☑ Be very careful of NAT rules when using chaining, especially the address translation of desktops. Make sure that the desktops are not address-translated between a domain controller and a WAM-enabled Web server.

Implementing UserAuthority Chaining

- ☑ Determine the other UserAuthority servers that you have and determine if they are managed by the same management module.
- ☑ Create UserAuthority Server groups for domain controllers and firewall modules. Use these groups in the Firewall objects when referring to UASs that you need to chain to.
- ☑ Be aware of the security implications of setting up domain equivalence. Make sure you are aware how this will change the security of the Rule Base based on who can access what and on the WebAccess servers you have.

Utilizing UserAuthority Logging

- ☑ Logging can be generated by the UAS and WAM.
- ☑ Applications include internal and external Web access reporting and Internet access user logging.
- ☑ SmartView Tracker queries provide different log views.

Understanding Credentials Management and Domain Equality

- ☑ Users can manage their credential "wallets" via WAM-enabled Web servers.
- ☑ Administrators on the UAS can use the *uacmutil* utility.

Deploying UserAuthority

- ☑ Set up UserAuthority with a PDC on a domain controller, and set up chaining and domain equivalence on both the PDC and the firewall enforcement module. Then create client-authenticated SSO rules in the Rule Base.
- ☑ Set up WebAccess separately and make sure you can authenticate to the WebAccess server using a FireWall-1 defined user and group.
- ☑ Create a UserAuthority domain object, and then use this object when you create a rule in the Web Access | Application Settings—Effects Rule Base for single sign-on.

Frequently Asked Questions

The following Frequently Asked Questions, answered by the authors of this book, are designed to both measure your understanding of the concepts presented in this chapter and to assist you with real-life implementation of these concepts. To have your questions about this chapter answered by the author, browse to **www.syngress.com/solutions** and click on the **"Ask the Author"** form.

Q: Where can I install UserAuthority Server?

A: UserAuthority Server can be installed on Check Point FireWall-1 enforcement modules and/or it can be installed on Windows domain controllers (Windows 2000 or NT 4).

Q: Where can I install the WebAccess module?

A: The WebAccess module can be installed on multiple Microsoft IIS version 4 or version 5 Web servers. There is a beta version of the WebAccess module for the Apache Web server on Linux.

Q: Where can I install the UserAuthority SecureAgent?

A: The UserAuthority SecureAgent can be installed on the desktop PC of your users who authenticate to your windows domain (where the domain controller has the UserAuthority Server installed).

Q: Why can't I see the WebAccess tab in the SmartDashboard GUI?

A: This is not enabled by default. You need to click **Policy | Global Properties | Smart Dashboard Customization**. At the bottom of the window is a check box for **Display Web Access view**, which needs to be checked.

Q: How do I install a policy to the WebAccess module? It does not show up when I attempt to install the FireWall-1 Security policy or if I try to install the User Database.

A: You can only install the WebAccess policy from the **WebAccess** tab screen in the SmartDashboard GUI. Right-click the **WebSites** icon and then select **Install**. You can install to a specific WebAccess module only if you right-click the specific object and click **Install**.

Q: When I configure SSO to a WebAccess module and log in using the SecureAgent on a desktop host and authenticate against the PDC, then use a browser to access the WebAccess server, the WebAccess server fails to identify my user ID. Why? My WebAccess server does not identify my user ID, although I'm sure I have UserAuthority working correctly on my domain controller and firewall. What could be the problem?

A: A common cause of this problem is that the connection to the WebAccess server is being address-translated—either by the firewall module or by another host between yourself and the WebAccess server. Using a proxy to access the Web server will have a similar effect. You need to avoid NAT and proxying on the connections to the WebAccess server. If you must use a proxy, WAM can interpret an HTTP header that identifies the original source IP address of the client, if your proxy supports that.

Q: Can I use SecureClient as a remote user and achieve SSO?

A: Yes. When you authenticate using SecureClient, you will register with the UAS on the firewall enforcement module that your secure client module authenticated against, and then the WebAccess server can query the module to see if you have authenticated (or if not, the firewall module you authenticated against can use chaining to query other firewall modules).

Q: We have personal firewalls on our internal PCs. Will this cause a problem for UA SecureAgent?

A: Yes. SecureAgent must be able to receive queries from the domain controller UAS, UDP port 19194. Your personal firewall must be configurable to allow this traffic. Note that Check Point SecureClient version 4.1 cannot be configured to this level of granularity, so it is not suitable for use with SecureAgent if the SecureClient policy is blocking incoming connections to the client. SecureClient NG allows finely granular polices so is fully compatible.

Q: We are running a gateway cluster. Can we run UAS on the cluster members?

A: Yes, UAS can be run on a cluster. However, the cluster mechanism will not synchronize the UACM databases between the members. Check Point supplies a utility called *db_sync* that will update cluster members. The synchronization must be scheduled manually by the administrator.

Chapter 15

Firewall Troubleshooting

Solutions in this chapter:

- SmartView Tracker
- SmartView Monitor
- Using fw monitor
- Other Tools

☑ Summary

☑ Solutions Fast Track

☑ Frequently Asked Questions

Introduction

Traffic is not flowing, the phone is ringing, and you are scrambling to figure out why. As the administrator of your firewall, you have a large selection of tools at your disposal. There are also a number of tools that you should have close in the event of trouble.

SmartView Monitor, SmartView Tracker, a local network sniffer—you should know how to use all of the tools possible to ensure you can troubleshoot the problems that you will no doubt face. We review the Check Point tools and some third-party tools that we recommend that you have in your arsenal.

Check Point has provided the SmartView Tracker so that you can view the traffic as it flows through the firewall. This should be the first line of troubleshooting your firewall. SmartView Monitor allows you to view interfaces and links in real time. Immediate traffic flow analysis is available to determine how the system is functioning. Along with these tools, Check Point provides command-line utilities that expose the FireWall-1 Kernel statistics, VPN and encryption, and other performance metrics.

Check Point also has other tools that will allow the more technical personnel to perform *fw monitor* functions. *Fw monitor* is a command-line facility that allows you to analyze the traffic flowing through your firewall on a systematic basis. We review the best methods of using this utility, and how it can provide insight as to where your firewall may not be functioning as you expect.

SmartView Tracker

Typically the first thing you'll want to do when analyzing firewall behavior is to log in to the SmartView Tracker and watch the traffic as it flows through your firewall. This tool is installed along with the other Check Point SMART Clients on an NG FP3 Windows workstation or server by default. If you are running a pre-FP3 management module, this same tool will be named Log Viewer.

The FP3 SmartView Tracker provides a new view into the FireWall-1 logs, with three modes accessible via tabs (Log, Active, and Audit). As shown in Figure 15.1, you also have several options in a drop-down menu format within each view for customizing and searching the log records that are displayed. The nicest feature about the FP3 interface is the modular views, where you can have multiple instances of the logs open within the Tracker frame by selecting **File | Open In New Window** and selecting the filename you wish to open.

Filtering Traffic

You can make certain selections within the SmartView Tracker to limit the log records viewable, which can help you to isolate certain traffic and more effectively troubleshoot your firewall. There are a number of predefined selection criteria that you can choose from in the menu display on the left. The default is to show All Records, but you can also choose to view only FireWall-1, VPN-1, or FloodGate-1 traffic for instance by simply right-clicking on the name and choosing **Open**. You can determine exactly what is being filtered by looking for a green icon next to the column where the filter is applied. For example, the FireWall-1 predefined filter sets the Product column to SmartDefense and VPN-1 & FireWall-1 only; the VPN-1 filter sets the Encryption Scheme column to IKE and FWZ; and the FloodGate-1 filter sets the Product column to FloodGate-1 only.

Figure 15.1 SmartView Tracker Log View

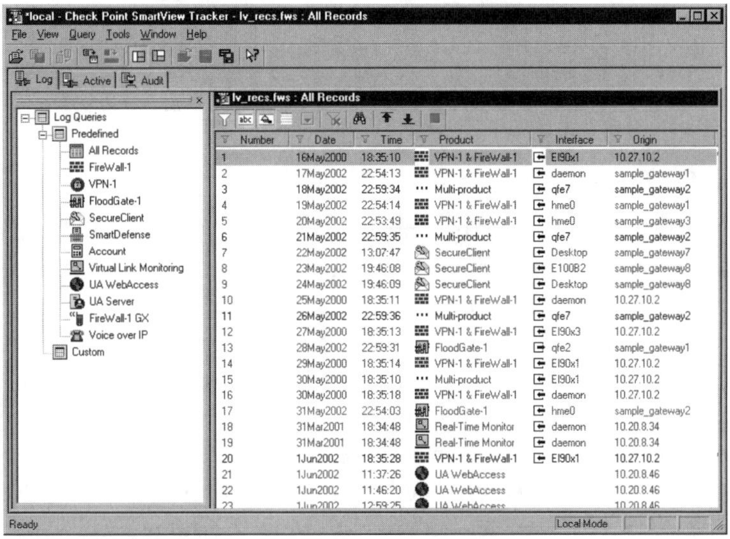

If you would prefer to create your own filters, each of the columns in the frame that displays the logs has a filter option, which you can activate by simply right-clicking on the column and selecting **Edit Filter**. See Figure 15.2 for an example of the service filter window in which we have selected SMTP as the protocol we hope to scan for in the logs. To do this, follow these steps:

1. Log in to SmartView Tracker.
2. Ensure that **All Records** are displayed.
3. Right-click on the column labeled **Service** and choose **Edit Filter**.
4. Type in **smtp** in the selection window on the right-hand side, or scroll down to the service you wish to choose in the list.
5. Click **Add**. You can add as many services as you want to see in the logs to this window.
6. Click **OK**.

To remove a filter, simply right-click on the column and choose **Clear Filter**. You can configure multiple filters and search for all SMTP from a specific source address that was dropped also. You can then save the filters you have created as a "Custom" filter and then load them again anytime. Use the Query menu to save customer filters and to perform other filter operations.

Figure 15.2 SmartView Tracker Service Filter

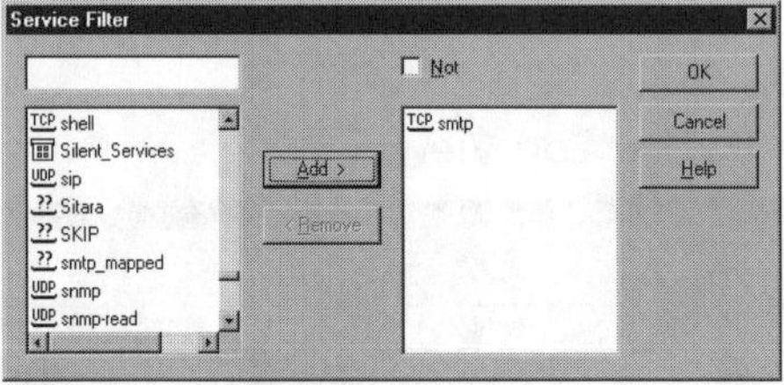

Active and Audit Logs

The other tabs available to you in the SmartView Tracker are the Active and Audit logs. The Active view shows you any active connections in your firewall(s) in real-time. The Audit view shows you what the firewall administrators are doing, such as who logs into the various Smart Clients and when, as well as any changes they may make while logged in with write permission. If something suddenly stops working one day, and you have others administering the policy, it might be a good idea to see if any changes were made that correspond to the outage in service. The Audit view will give you such detail as the color of an object that was changed, or new objects that were created, a policy was installed, and so on. You can set up filters in both the Active and Audit logs the same way you did it in the Log view.

Tools & Traps...

GUI Administrators

It is best to use individual admin usernames instead of a generic username like fwadmin. The problem with using a generic login ID is that you cannot properly audit the activities of the firewall administrators. It may be important for you to know who installed the last security policy when you are troubleshooting a problem. This becomes more and more important when there are several people administering a firewall system.

It is also important to limit the activities of your administrators to only those functions that they will need. You may not want to give an entry-level

Continued

sys admin write access to the security policy if he will only need to managed network objects and users. FireWall-1 is very flexible in the permissions you can customize for each administrator, so take advantage of it.

SmartView Monitor

SmartView Monitor is included free with all SmartCenter Pro licenses. With this product you can receive up-to-the-minute information about your firewalls and networks due to status alerts, security threat alerts, and defense capabilities monitored and reported in SmartView. In addition, SmartView Monitor can assist in long-term decision making and policy planning due to data mining, trending, and detailed analytical tools included in SmartView.

In order to view real-time monitor data from your FP3 SmartCenter, you will need to install the SmartView Monitor on your firewall modules, and check the box labeled **SmartView Monitor** in the Check Point products list for the relevant Check Point objects defined through SmartDashboard, and then install the security policy. You will also require an additional license for monitoring and reporting per module if you are not running a SmartCenter Pro. SmartView Monitor (a.k.a. Real-Time Monitoring) is very useful for environments where troubleshooting through the firewall is common, and SmartView Monitor can be used in lieu of other monitoring software, thereby saving money.

Log in to the SmartView Monitor from the SMART Clients menu, and you will be presented with a screen similar to the one shown in Figure 15.3. In this screen, you will need to select the type of session you wish to start. You can select only one firewall or interface to monitor at a time. You are also able to record a session and play it back later.

Figure 15.3 Session Type

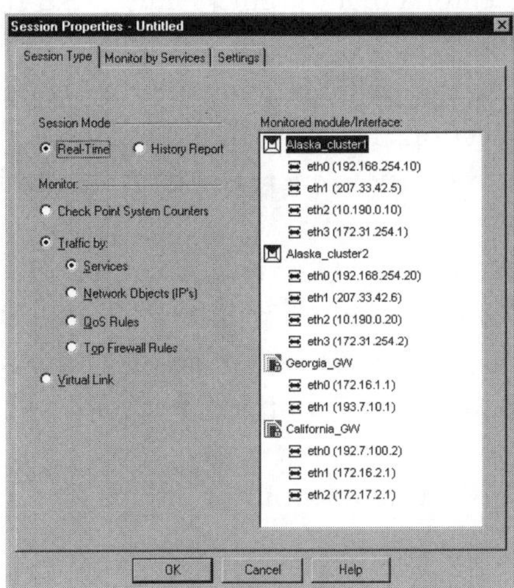

The other tabs listed will depend on your selections on the Session Type tab. If you choose **Real-Time** for the **Session Mode**, you will be able to monitor **Check Point System Counters**, **Traffic**, or a **Virtual Link**. From the Settings tab, you can control the monitor rate, which is set to 2 seconds by default, and you can choose between a line or bar graph. You may also have the options to choose the type of measurement by **Data Transfer Rate**, **Packets per Second**, **Line Utilization (%)**, **Percent**, or **Milliseconds**, and to set the scale for the graphs that you are viewing. These choices are shown in Figure 15.4.

Figure 15.4 Session Properties Settings

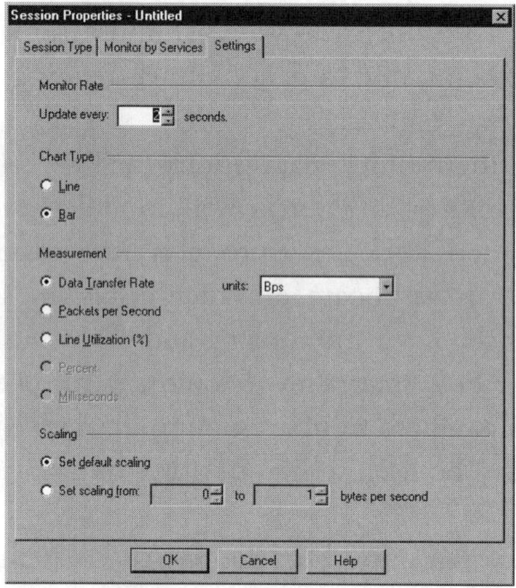

Monitoring Check Point System Counters

Check Point System Counters allow you to monitor and report on system resources and other statistics for your enforcement points. Figure 15.5 shows a monitoring session on a cluster that measures the size of the connection table in FireWall-1. This data can be very valuable for analyzing the traffic at your site. You could possibly identify a problem if you see the connections reaching the maximum of 25,000 at any time, which will give you the opportunity to increase that value to better fit the needs of your connection.

There are a number of counters categories for you to choose from in the Counters tab in your SmartView Monitor properties window. Choose **Basic: FireWall-1** from the pull-down menu to monitor the number of active connections as shown in Figure 15.5. You could also choose to monitor dropped, rejected, and/or accepted packets, memory and cpu, encryption parameters, security servers, and FloodGate-1 traffic. You don't have to choose just one setting to monitor either; you can select as many counters as you wish and each one will be displayed on the same graph with a different line color. Don't get too carried away though, or you won't be able to read the output.

Figure 15.5 Monitoring FireWall-1 Active Connections

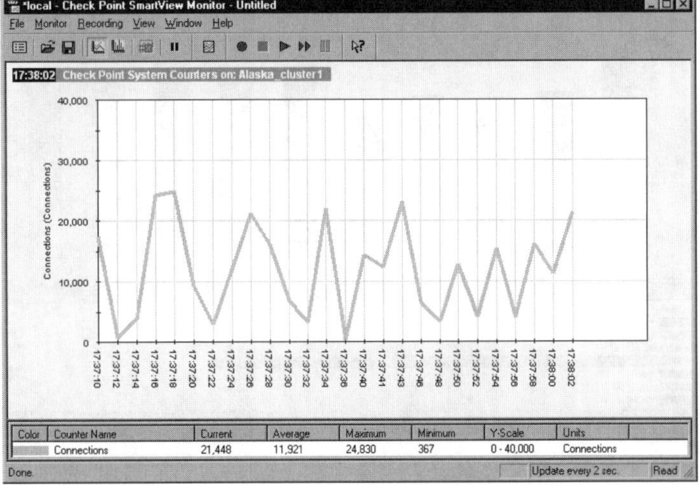

Monitoring Traffic

Using the SmartView Monitor to monitor traffic is another way to view the statistics on your firewall. When choosing **Session Type**, select **Traffic by:** and then select from **services**, **Network Objects (IPs)**, **QoS Rules**, or **Top Firewall Rules**. If you take the default, **services**, the **Monitor by Services** tab will be available in the SmartView Monitor properties window, and you can select the method that you would like to view services. You could again take the default of **Top 10 Services**, as shown in Figure 15.6, or you can narrow it down to a particular service that you may wish to monitor.

Monitoring by network objects is similar to monitoring by service, the default is to display the **Top 10 Network Objects**, or you can select specific objects that you wish to display instead. You can also choose if you want the object monitored in the source, destination, or both. **Top Firewall Rules** allows you to choose how many (10 is the default) firewall rules you wish to monitor. This feature may help you to better order your rules, since you should attempt to write your policy such that the most frequently used rules are placed closest to the top of the policy for better performance. If you are running FloodGate-1, you can also monitor QoS Rules through the SmartView Monitor. The **Monitor by QoS Rules** tab in the Session Properties window allows you to choose the rules that you wish to display, and then you can watch how they are utilized.

Figure 15.6 Monitoring Top 10 Services

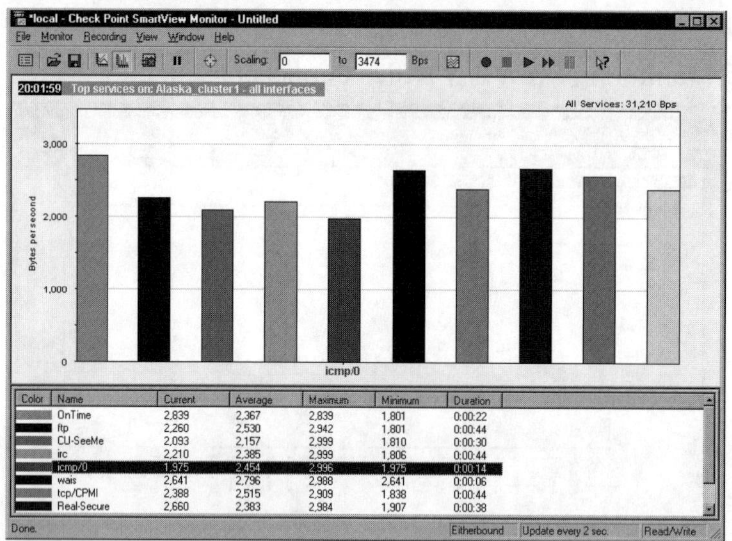

Monitoring a Virtual Link

To monitor a Virtual Link, you must first define one or more Virtual Links through the SmartDashboard from the Virtual Links tab in the Objects Tree. You will need to give the link a name and specify two firewall modules as end points. End point A must be an internal FireWall-1 module, and end point B may be either internal or external. If you wish to monitor the link between these modules, you must check the box to **Activate Virtual Link**. You can also define SLA parameters from the Virtual Link Properties window in the SmartDashboard to ensure that the SLA is being met.

NOTE

Check Point uses the Check Point End-to-End Control Protocol (E2ECP) service to monitor the link between gateways in a Virtual Link configuration. You may need a rule to allow the communication for this protocol on both end points. E2ECP uses UDP port 18241.

Once you have selected the Virtual Link you wish to monitor in the Session Properties window in SmartView Monitor, select the **Virtual Link Monitoring** tab to choose the type of graph you wish to have displayed. You can choose to view **Bandwidth** or **Bandwidth Loss** from point A to B, B to A, or both directions (as shown in Figure 15.7), or you can choose **Round Trip Time** to monitor the total time it takes for a packet to travel round trip between the gateways.

Next you will need to select data type: either **Application Data** or **Wire Data**. Application Data is monitored as the application would see it in an unencrypted and uncompressed form. Wire Data on the other hand analyzes all data on the wire in its encrypted and compressed form. This method should be selected to compare SLA Guarantees, for example.

Figure 15.7 Monitoring a Virtual Link

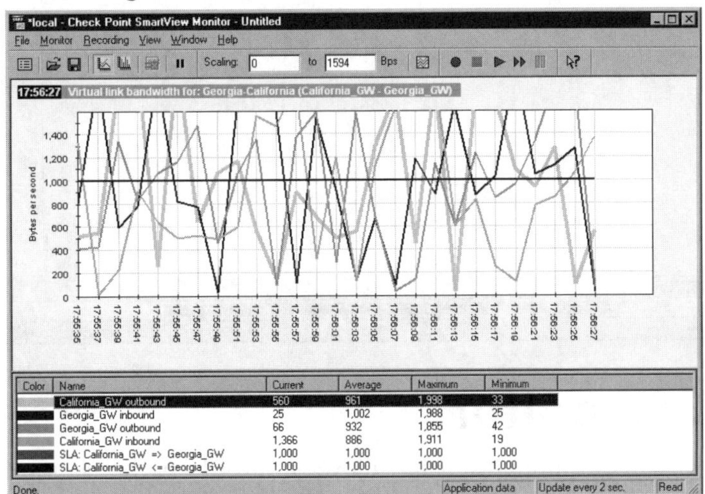

Running History Reports

You can use the SmartView Monitor to generate history reports by selecting **History Report** as the **Session Type**. As opposed to Real-Time Monitoring, the History report will show you static data over the last hour, day, week, and month or since the time of installation. You can run reports on Check Point counters (see Figure 15.8 for a monthly report on FireWall-1 connections) or traffic, however, your choices are somewhat limited from the options you had in the Real-Time mode. For traffic, your only options for reports are:

- Service (bytes per second)
- Top Destinations (bytes per second)
- Top Sources (bytes per second)
- Top FireWall-1 Rules (bytes per second)
- Top Services (bytes per second)

Figure 15.8 Reporting on FireWall-1 Active Connections

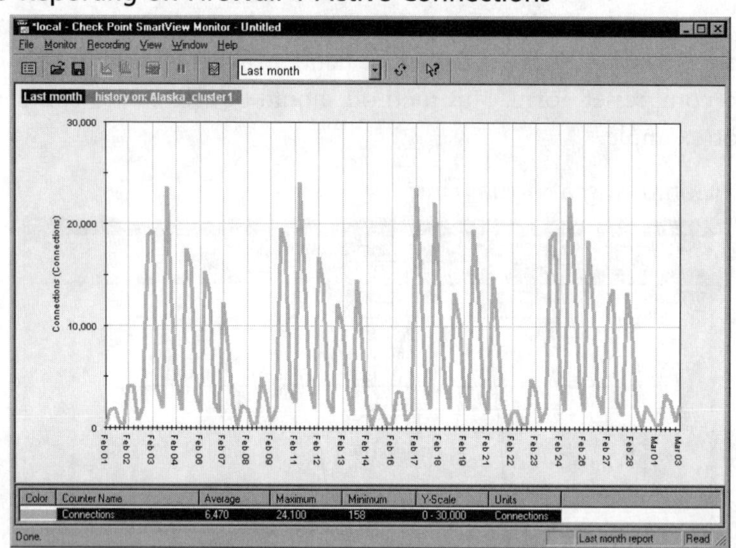

Using fw monitor

Fw monitor is a command-line utility that allows you to do packet captures on your firewall. This tool is available on all platforms on VPN-1/FireWall-1, which means even those running Windows can utilize it. *Fw monitor* comes in very handy when troubleshooting particularly tricky firewall problems, like when you can't figure out why an FTP session is failing or whether NAT is functioning properly. By the end of this section, you should understand how *fw monitor* works, how to create your own INSPECT filters for use with the command, and how to review the output. The syntax for *fw monitor* follows, see Table 15.1 for a description of each switch:

```
fw monitor [-d] [-D] <{-e expr}+|-f <filter-file|->> [-l len] [-m mask]
[-x offset[,len]] [-o <file>]
```

Table 15.1 Switches Used with *fw monitor*

Switch	Description
-d	A lower level of debugging of the INSPECT filter as it's loading.
-D	A higher level of debugging output of the INSPECT filter as it's loading.
-e	Specify an INSPECT filter on the command line.
-f	Load the INSPECT filter from a file.
-l	Length of the packet to be displayed.

Continued

Table 15.1 Switches Used with *fw monitor*

Switch	Description
-m	Mask the inspection points to be captured. You can use any of the inspection points i, I, o, or O as described in Table 15.2. The default, if this switch is not used, is to capture from all.
-o	Output file where the captured packet data will be logged. You will need to use a network protocol analyzer to view the output of the file.
-x	Hex dump of IP and protocol information can be displayed with console output only using this switch.

How It Works

The *fw monitor* command works by first loading an INSPECT filter, which analyzes and matches packets as they pass through each interface of your firewall both in the inbound and outbound direction. This filter is similar to the one compiled from your Security Policy. If you run the command without any arguments, all packets will be captured and printed to standard output (text printed on the screen), and each packet will be displayed four times, two for each interface and direction. See Figure 15.9 and Table 15.2 for an explanation of inspection points.

Figure 15.9 Interface Direction Inspection Points

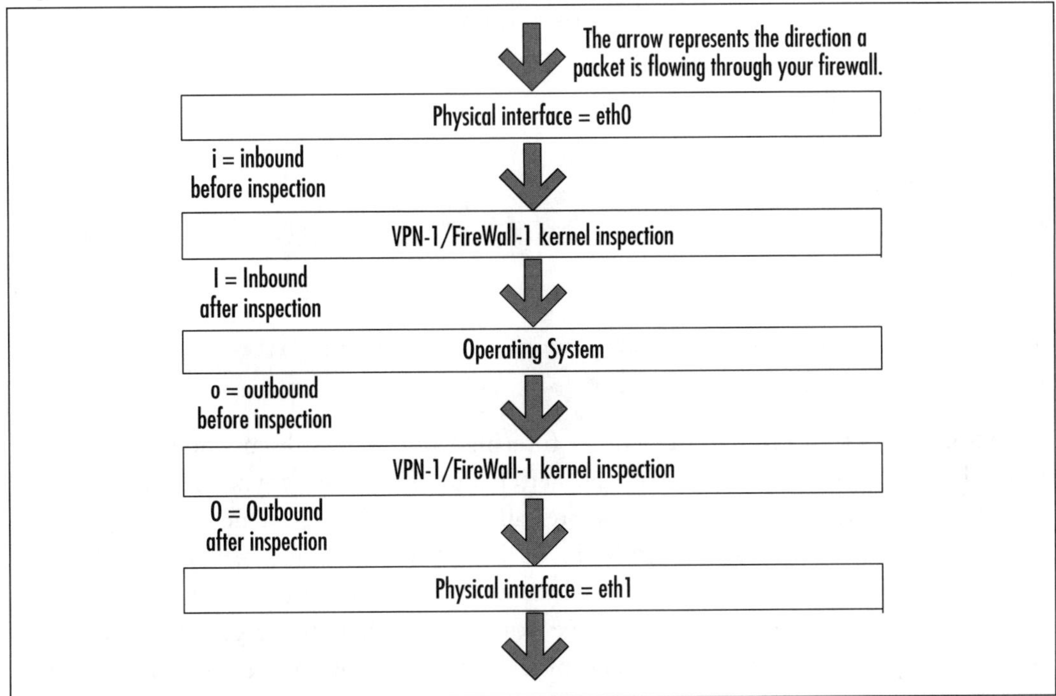

Table 15.2 Interface Direction Inspection in *fw monitor*

Inspection Point	Description
i	Before VPN-1/FireWall-1 kernel inspection in the inbound direction
I	After VPN-1/FireWall-1 kernel inspection in the inbound direction
o	Before VPN-1/FireWall-1 kernel inspection in the outbound direction
O	After VPN-1/FireWall-1 kernel inspection in the outbound direction

Writing INSPECT Filters for *fw monitor*

If you don't want to just dump every packet to the terminal, which is the default if you give *fw monitor* no arguments, you may wish to set up some specific filters for capturing certain traffic. A simple *fw monitor* filter like this, *fw monitor –e "accept;" –o monitor.out* will capture every packet, but will save the output to a file. Then you will need some kind of network protocol analyzer that can interpret and read packet capture data, such as *snoop* or Ethereal. See the following section, "Reviewing the Output," for more information.

The *accept* action that you specify means only that you want the filter to accept and match on packets as you specify them, it doesn't mean that you want to see only packets that the firewall has accepted. It's also important to remember to use the semicolon at the end of the filter, otherwise it won't load. If you successfully compile an *fw monitor* filter, you will see the following output (as the last line explains, simply press **Ctrl-C** when you want to stop capturing packets):

```
tampagw[admin]# fw monitor -e "accept;"
monitor: getting filter (from command line)
monitor: compiling
monitorfilter:
Compiled OK.
monitor: loading
Feb 28 09:24:46 tampagw [LOG_CRIT] kernel: FW-1: monitor filter loaded
monitor: monitoring (control-C to stop)
```

Before we get into some of the other filtering options, let's discuss how an IP packet header is put together, so you can better understand the syntax used in the examples that follow. Figure 15.10 illustrates an IP packet header, which contains 20 total bytes, and each byte is equal to 8 bits of data. When counting the bytes in the header, we are going to begin with zero; byte zero in the diagram contains the IP version and header length of the packet. If we skip down to byte 9, we get the IP protocol (for example, TCP, UDP, and so on), and byte 12 is where the source IP address begins.

When specifying INSPECT filters with *fw monitor*, you will be specifying the start byte to determine what you want to capture. The syntax for specifying a specific value is *[<offset>:<length>,<order>]*. The *offset* specifies the start byte, *length* specifies the total bytes to read (four bytes is the default), and *order* specifies either *b* for big endian or *l* for little endian or host order (*l* is the default). For example, if you want to search for all TCP traffic, you could use the command *fw monitor -e "accept [9:1,b]=6;"*. This expression says that if you start at the ninth byte and read the first byte, then this value should be equal to 6, which is the protocol number for TCP. For a list of protocols and their associated numbers, go to www.iana.org/assignments/protocol-numbers for the most up-to-date information. The most commonly used protocols are ICMP, TCP, and UDP, which are represented by numbers 1, 6, and 17 respectively.

Figure 15.10 IP Packet Header

0		1	2		3
IP Version (4 bits)	Header Length	Type of Service (TOS)	Total Packet Length (in Bytes)		
4		5 16-bit Identification	6 Flags	7 13-bit Fragment Offset	
8 Time to Live (TTL)		9 Protocol (Transport Layer Protocol)	10	11 Header Checksum	
12		13	14 32-bit Source IP Address		15
16		17	18 32-bit Destination IP Address		19

If you are interested in capturing data to or from a specific IP address, you might use the following syntax: *fw monitor -e "accept [12,b]=10.10.10.1* or *[16,b]=10.10.10.1;" –o monitor.out*. In this example, *[12,b]* represents the source IP address, which starts in the twelfth byte of an IP packet header (starting from 0, as shown in Figure 15.10). In this case, you do not need to specify the number of bytes to read, as in *[12:4,b]* since *fw monitor* will read four bytes by default from the start byte specified. We recommend a filter like this if you are analyzing traffic from a specific source or destination address, say for example FTP is failing to a specific destination. You should choose the FTP server IP address as both the source and destination in this filter, since you want to see the traffic flowing in both directions, and your source IP address may be translated at the firewall, so you may not capture all packets if you choose the FTP client address. Here is a step-by-step example where we are trying to FTP to or from 192.168.0.8:

1. Run *fw monitor -e "accept [12,b]=192.168.0.8 or [16,b]=192.168.0.8;"*.
2. Start the FTP connection from your client and reproduce the problem.
3. When done capturing data, press **Ctrl-C** on the firewall to end the *fw monitor* capture.
4. Review the output.

The last example of an *fw monitor* command filter is one in which you are looking for a specific source or destination port number. Let's say that you want to capture all HTTP (TCP port 80) traffic—you might write a filter like this:

```
fw monitor -e "accept [20:2,b]=80 or [22:2,b]=80;" -o monitor.out
```

For more help with the INSPECT language, review the NG CP Reference Guide available online at www.checkpoint.com/support/technical/documents/docs-5.0/cp_ref_ng_sp0.pdf.

Reviewing the Output

If you use the *–o* option with *fw monitor* to save the output to a file, you will need some kind of network protocol analyzer that can interpret and read packet capture data. You can use tools such as *snoop* or Ethereal. If you don't use the *–o* option, the data will be displayed to standard output, and you can redirect the output from the command to a text file. It's easiest to use Ethereal to view the data since you can easily do searches and configure filters for the output, so we use that in the following examples. Ethereal is a freeware program that you can download at www.ethereal.com.

NOTE

To use *snoop* (available on most Solaris systems), use the *–i* switch to import the file, as in the following examples:

- Ex. snoop –i monitor.out
- Ex. snoop –i monitor.cap -V -x14 tcp port ftp or tcp port ftp-data

See Figure 15.11 for an example output of *fw monitor* in Ethereal. In the top frame, you can view the time elapsed in milliseconds, the source, destination and protocol, and then in the Info field you can see the source and destination port numbers, TCP flags, sequence number, ACK number, window, and length. If you highlight one of the packets, you can get more detailed data in the second frame. Finally, in the third frame, you can determine at which inspection point the packet was captured, for the example in Figure 15.11, you can see *i.eth-s4p1c0*, which tells you that the packet was caught before VPN-1/FireWall-1 kernel inspection in the inbound direction on *eth-s4p1c0*.

Figure 15.11 Ethereal Output

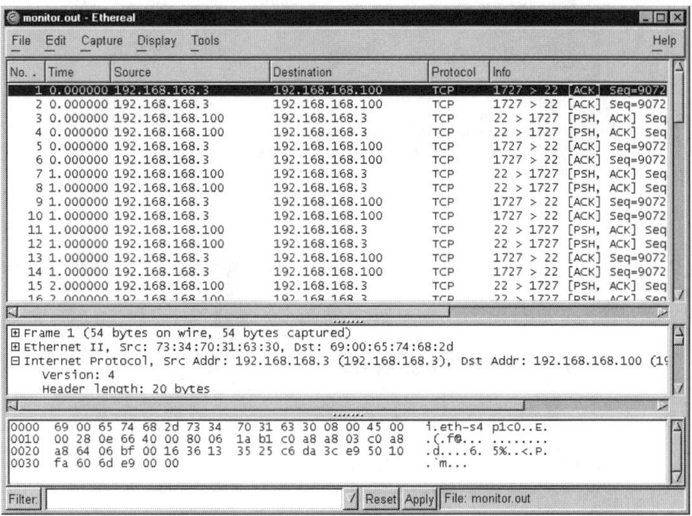

You can also use Ethereal to set up filters. You can type in a filter in the window at the bottom, such as **ip.addr == 192.168.168.3** or **tcp.port == 80**, then click **Apply**, or you can use the **Filter** button on the bottom of the page to select the filter you are interested in applying. Figure 15.12 illustrates how this is done.

1. Click on **Filter**.
2. Click on **Add Expression…**.
3. Select a **Field name**, such as **Source or Destination Address**.
4. Choose a relation:
   - **Is present**
   - **==** Equal to
   - **!=** Not equal to
   - **>** Greater than
   - < - Less Than
   - **>=** Greater than or equal to
   - **<=** Less than or equal to
5. Finally, enter the IP address you wish to search for in the box provided. When you are done, click **Accept**.
6. Click **OK** to apply the filter.
7. Click on **Reset** when you want to remove the filter.

Figure 15.12 Ethereal Filter

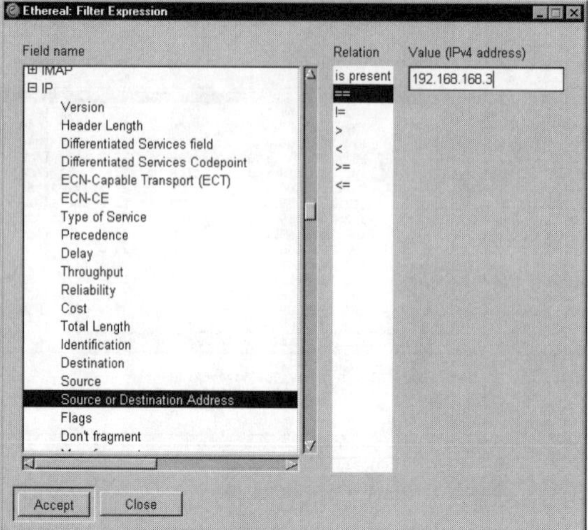

Other Tools

Several other tools are available when troubleshooting your firewall. Some of them are available on your VPN-1/FireWall-1 system, and others are available with your operating system.

Check Point Tools

You may find that the tools mentioned previously may not be too helpful if you are troubleshooting a performance issue or a specific system error message, especially if you don't have a license for the SmartView Monitor; the following sections provide more options for your problem-solving arsenal.

Tools & Traps...

CSP Tools

If you happen to be a Check Point Certified Support Partner, you have access to several tools that allow you to do additional troubleshooting in NG. Sorry, only CSPs are given access to these.

- **DNS-Info Wizard** Generates the dnsinfo.C file for use with SecuRemote/SecureClient and split DNS configurations

Continued

- **FW-Monitor GUI** Uses the FireWall-1 4.0/4.1 GUI interface to generate INSPECT scripts for use with *fw monitor* using the *–f* switch.
- **IKE view** If you enable IKE debugging on your firewall or in SR/SC, you can use this tool to view the IKE.elg output file.
- **INFO tab** Displays kernel table information as generated with *fw tab* or *cpinfo*. Some kernel tables are displayed in a more readable format for easy review.
- **Info view** A robust tool that takes an input of *fwinfo*, *cpinfo*, *srinfo*, and/or *mipinfo* files and displays them in a graphical format; it allows you to test for certain conditions using the input file, display the security policy, run Infotab on the kernel tables, parse the objects file, launch IKEView, read the user database, and verify all file builds on a firewall.
- **Lic view** Provides a graphical representation of license string features in a tree format to analyze licenses.
- **Monitor for SecuRemote** Utility that is installed on a SecuRemote client that is run to monitor a SecuRemote installation.
- **Tunnel Utility** Installed on your firewall module, Tunnel Utility manages IPSec and IKE Security Associations (SAs) allowing you to list or delete SAs.

Log Files

Don't forget how useful log files can be. Check Point has several useful text files (not viewable via SmartView Tracker) in the $FWDIR/log directory, which can provide you with additional information:

- **cpca.elg** Check Point Certificate Authority logs
- **dtlsd.elg** Policy Server Logging daemon logs
- **dtpsd.elg** Policy Server logs
- **fwd.elg** FireWall-1 daemon logs
- **fwm.elg** FireWall-1 Management logs
- **mdq.elg** SMTP Security Server dequeue logs
- **vpnd.elg** VPN daemon logs

fw stat

Displays VPN-1/FireWall-1 status, including the name of the last policy installed.

```
fw.toronto[admin]# fw stat
HOST       POLICY      DATE
localhost 121202      3Mar2003 16:06:24 :   [>eth-s1p4c0] [>eth4c0]
    [>eth2c0] [>eth3c0] [<eth3c0] [>eth1c0]
```

fw ctl pstat

Displays VPN-1/FireWall-1 kernel parameters and statistics, including kernel memory, connections, and NAT information. You can use this command to gain valuable insight into how your system is performing. Here are some of the more interesting fields:

- **Total memory allocated** Displays the total amount of kernel memory assigned to FireWall-1.
- **Total memory bytes used** Displays the amount of memory used, unused, and peak. You can use this to determine if the total memory allocated is sufficient for your system. If you see that you are using all of the kernel memory allocated, you can increase this value. For information on how to do this, see page 365 in the *Check Point Next Generation Security Administration* book (Syngress Media, Inc. ISBN: 1928994741).
- **Allocations** What you care about here are the failed allocations. If your system is running well, you should always have **0 failed alloc** displayed here.

You can also use *fw ctl pstat* to view information about your system if it is in a HA configuration. If you scroll all the way to the end of the output displayed, you will see information about sync. If sync is not configured properly, you may see that no sync packets were received or that sync is not on.

```
fw.toronto[admin]# fw ctl pstat


Hash kernel memory (hmem) statistics:
  Total memory allocated: 6291456 bytes in 1535 4KB blocks using 1 pool
  Total memory bytes  used:    369748    unused:  5921708 (94.12%)    peak:
        871940
  Total memory blocks used:       122    unused:      1413 (92%)    peak:
        243
  Allocations: 12101262 alloc, 0 failed alloc, 12095655 free
```

```
System kernel memory (smem) statistics:
  Total memory  bytes  used: 13879436   peak: 14500728
    Blocking  memory  bytes   used:  1505496   peak:  1563272
    Non-Blocking memory bytes used: 12373940   peak: 12937456
  Allocations: 40812699 alloc, 0 failed alloc, 40812353 free, 0 failed free

Kernel memory (kmem) statistics:
  Total memory  bytes  used:  7948424   peak:  8538800
        Allocations: 12559037 alloc, 0 failed alloc, 12553085 free, 0
            failed free

Kernel stacks:
        0 bytes total, 0 bytes stack size, 0 stacks,
        0 peak used, 0 max stack bytes used, 0 min stack bytes used,
        0 failed stack calls

INSPECT:
        371804 packets, 265643860 operations, 4963757 lookups,
        0 record, 63361113 extract

Cookies:
        25767245 total, 0 alloc, 0 free,
        204 dup, 80057678 get, 624 put,
        24502341 len, 0 cached len, 0 chain alloc,
        0 chain free

Connections:
        307750 total, 223 TCP, 14081 UDP, 293446 ICMP,
        0 other, 51 anticipated, 39 recovered, 89 concurrent,
        1539 peak concurrent, 3297600 lookups

Fragments:
        0 fragments, 0 packets, 0 expired, 0 short,
        0 large, 0 duplicates, 0 failures

NAT:
        192/0 forw, 192/0 bckw, 384 tcpudp,
```

```
        0 icmp, 40-25202 alloc
sync new ver working
sync out: on  sync in: on
sync packets sent:
total: 423172 retransmitted: 0 retrans reqs: 0 acks: 39
sync packets received:
total 4605511 of which 0 queued and 0 dropped by net
also received 0 retrans reqs and 19 acks to 0 cb requests
```

fw tab

This command will display kernel table information. If you run it with no arguments, it will dump all the tables and their first 16 elements to standard output. If you want to view only one table, you must specify the table name on the command line with the *–t* switch. The *–s* switch (for short display) can be very useful also, since you can read the #VALS column to see the total number of entries in the table, and #PEAK shows you the maximum value the table has reached. The *–x* switch will completely clear out a table, which may be useful if you need to refresh the firewall's host count, but be careful with this option since you don't want to accidentally clear out your active connections in the middle of the day. See Table 15.3 for a list of some of the *fw tab* options.

```
Usage: fw tab [-t <table>] [-s | -c] [-f] [-o <filename>] [-r] [-u | -m
    <maxvals>] [[-x | -a] -e entry] [-y] [hostname]
```

This is an example of an *fw tab* output, which is a short display of the connections table:

```
fw.toronto[admin]# fw tab -t connections -s
HOST    NAME                                 ID #VALS #PEAK #SLINKS
localhost    connections                   8158    102   1539    284
```

Table 15.3 *fw tab* Options

Option	Description
-all	Displays info for all targets.
-conf <filename>	Displays info for the targets defined in *<filename>*.
-a	Displays all tables.
-s	Short display.
-h	Displays the usage.
-f	Displays in decimal format (hex is the default).

Continued

Table 15.3 *fw tab* Options

Option	Description
-u	Do not limit the number of table entries displayed.
-m <number>	For each table, display the first *<number>* of elements. Sixteen entries will be displayed by default.
-t <table>	Specifies the table that you wish to display.
-x	Deletes/clears all table entries.
Targets	Specifies that target(s) that you wish to have displayed.

Here is a list of common tables that you may find useful to review on an NG firewall:

- **connections** Contains all active connections. By default, FireWall-1 limits the size of this table to 25,000. If you are reaching this value at peak times, you may want to consider increasing the size of your connection table through the SmartDashboard. Edit the firewall module object, select **Capacity Optimization**, and increase the value for **Maximum concurrent connections**.
- **pending** Contains connections that are pending, such as FTP PASV connections.
- **host_table** Exists on systems with limited host licenses. Contains each host that the firewall has counted towards the license.
- **IKE_SA_table** Contains all active IKE Security Associations.
- **fwx_alloc** Contains all ports allocated for translation.
- **fwx_auth** Contains original destination and port prior to translation.
- **fwx_cntl_dyn_tab** Contains currently allocated IP Pool NAT addresses for SecuRemote users.

fw lichosts

On systems with a limited license, this command will display all hosts that the firewall has counted towards the license. If you have exceeded your license limit, use this command to help you identify the hosts that the firewall has counted. The philosophy Check Point uses for licensing is that anything that is not external to the firewall is being protected by the firewall, and hence you must have a license to cover all those devices. FireWall-1 does not count hosts by the number of objects created, but rather by the IP addresses that it sees on its internal interfaces.

cpinfo

If you need to escalate a problem to Check Point, they will want to get a *cpinfo* off of the management module and enforcement point for review. The *cpinfo* file replaces the *fwinfo* file that used to be distributed with all Check Point systems. You can download *cpinfo* from Check Point at www.checkpoint.com/techsupport/downloadsng/utilities.html; it is not installed with your VPN-1/FireWall-1 software. Most of the time, you will be running the command *cpinfo –o <filename>* to produce a file to send to Check Point. See Table 15.4 for other options.

Table 15.4 *cpinfo* **Options**

Option	Description
-o *<filename>*	Directs output to filename
-r	Obtains the entire Windows System Registry info
-v	Displays version info
-t	Gathers SecuRemote/SecureClient kernel tables only
-n	Turns DNS resolving off
-c *<cmaname>/<ctx>*	Fetches either a Provider-1 CMA info or a VSX CTX info
-l	Include Log files
-h	Help; prints usage

Operating System and Third-Party Tools

Some other useful tools for troubleshooting your firewall or network are available on your operating system, such as *ping* and *traceroute*. If you have a Windows firewall, and you want to have several Unix tools available at your disposal, you might want to consider running a Unix shell environment on your firewall so you can use these tools, such as Cygwin (www.cygwin.com). You can even run an SSH daemon through Cygwin and gain remote access to your Windows system through a secure shell. Also, don't forget the value of system files; on Windows systems, check the System and Application Event logs; on Unix systems, check the messages and syslog files for additional information.

Platform-Friendly Commands

The following commands are available on Unix and Windows systems:

- ***ping*** Connectivity testing and round-trip time.
- ***traceroute*** (*tracert* on Windows) allows you to see each hop that a packet goes through to reach the destination.

- ***netstat*** Used with the *–an* switch, you can view listening TCP/UDP ports and established connections; with the *–rn* switch, you can see the routing table; and *–in* displays interface information (input packets, output packets, collisions, and errors).
- ***nslookup*** Allows you to do DNS lookups.
- ***telnet*** You can use *telnet* to connect to TCP ports other than the default 23. For example, you can *telnet* to a Web site on port 80 or *telnet* to a mail server on port 25 to see if you get a connection.

Unix Commands

These are some Unix commands that are available on most systems (Solaris, Linux, and Nokia):

- ***df –k*** Displays disk partitions and usage.
- ***vmstat n*** Displays information about your system, including memory and CPU utilization every *n* seconds.
- ***top*** Displays system processes that are utilizing the most system resources at the top, and refreshes periodically.
- ***ps*** Displays system processes; use *–aux* switch with BSD-like systems and *–ef* on Solaris or System V–like systems.
- ***dig*** Another DNS lookup utility, which looks like it may replace *nslookup* in the near future.
- ***tcpdump*** A packet capture and analyzer utility available on Linux and Nokia systems. Use the *–i* switch to specify the interface you want to listen on.
- ***Snoop*** A packet capture and analyzer utility available on Solaris systems. Use the *–d* switch to specify the interface you want to listen on.

Third-Party Tools

Sometimes the tools available on your system just aren't enough and you really want something more. Consider using some of these third-party tools for additional troubleshooting on your firewall:

- **Netcat** A robust network debugging and exploration tool that reads and writes data across network connections. The possibilities are almost limitless with netcat. There is a Unix as well as a Windows version for download at www.atstake.com/research/tools/network_utilities.

- **Ethereal** A network protocol sniffer and analyzer tool available for Unix and Windows systems at www.ethereal.com.
- **Firewalk** Determines what packets a device will pass, thereby determining its access control lists (ACLs) by using a *traceroute*-like approach. Firewalk can be downloaded at www.packetfactory.net/firewalk.
- **Sniffer Pro 4.7** Another network protocol sniffer and analyzer tool. For more information about this tool, check out *Sniffer Pro Network Optimization and Troubleshooting Handbook* (Syngress Media, Inc. ISBN: 1-931836-57-4).
- **Cygwin** Allows you to run a Unix-like environment on your Windows PCs (www.cygwin.com).
- **NMAP** A network exploration tool that can also be used for security audits, NMAP can determine several characteristics about available hosts including open ports, operating system and version, and much more. Available for download at www.insecure.org/nmap.
- **Retina** A network vulnerability assessment scanner, Retina was rated number-one by *Network World* magazine. Available for download at www.eeye.com/html/Products/Retina.
- **ISS Scanner** Another network vulnerability assessment scanner, available at www.iss.net.

Summary

When working with VPN-1/FireWall-1 you are going to find yourself in situations where you will need to do some troubleshooting from time to time. Hopefully the tools found in this chapter will help you to do your job and resolve problems accurately and in a timely manner. Most likely, the first tool you will use for evaluating the firewall and the traffic flowing through it is the SmartView Tracker. This is the same tool that firewall administrators familiar with previous versions of Check Point would call the Log Viewer, and although it performs largely the same function, it does have some added features in NG, such as predefined filters to search for certain types of logs. Also you can open multiple log windows at one time within the Tracker tool so you can perform multiple searches. You can also see what your other administrators are up to by clicking on the Audit tab.

Another invaluable tool available in NG is the SmartView Monitor. This tool is available on any SmartCenter Pro consoles or can be purchased separately with other Reporting tools. To run the Monitor, you must install it on a firewall module first, and select that firewall as having the SmartView Monitor installed through the SmartDashboard. Once this is done, you will be able to monitor the firewall in real-time or via history reports. In real-time, you can choose from three options: Check Point System Counters (memory, CPU, kernel values, and so on), Traffic (Top Ten Services, Top Firewall Rules, and so on), and Virtual Links.

Every Check Point firewall module out there has the packet capturing *fw monitor* tool installed and available for your use. You can define some simple filter options to capture only certain traffic, or you can capture all packets going through the firewall and use a tool such as Ethereal to review and filter the output. This utility is very useful for particularly tricky problems, where you must see what is happening on the wire to understand the problem.

There are a large number of tools available for troubleshooting your firewall, from watching Check Point and system logs to downloading and installing additional third-party software. Some Check Point command-line tools include various *$FWDIR/bin/fw* commands and *cpinfo*. Your operating system also has many tools for checking system resources and testing network conditions. You may also want to add some third-party tools onto your system for additional troubleshooting gratification, such as netcat or Firewalk.

Regardless of which tools you choose to use on your Check Point firewalls, there is definitely something for everyone when it comes to the tools available. These tools don't take away from the operator finesse and people skills required to successfully troubleshoot a problem, but they will certainly assist you and make you sound like you know what you're talking about. We wish the best of luck to you in your troubleshooting endeavors.

Solutions Fast Track

SmartView Tracker

- ☑ Multiple log views can be open at the same time with the SmartView Tracker.
- ☑ Predefined filters are used to limit the entries displayed in the Log view to display more relevant data.
- ☑ Filters can be defined manually within each of the SmartView Tracker views to search for specific criteria.
- ☑ Manual filters can be saved as customer filters, which can be used over and over again by simply selecting opening the filter.

SmartView Monitor

- ☑ In Real-Time mode, you can monitor Check Point Systems Counters, Traffic statistics, and Virtual Links.
- ☑ Check Point System Counters allow you to analyze data such as memory, CPU, FireWall-1 connections, encryption parameters, and much more.
- ☑ Traffic statistics include Services, Network Objects, QoS Rules, and Top Firewall Rules.
- ☑ You can monitor only one firewall, interface, or Virtual Link at a time.
- ☑ History reports allow you to view past data for Check Point Systems Counters or Traffic statistics.

Using *fw monitor*

- ☑ *Fw monitor* is a packet-capture utility available on all VPN-1/FireWall-1 enforcement points.
- ☑ You can write INSPECT filters for *fw monitor* to capture specific traffic.
- ☑ If you save *fw monitor* output to a file, you will need to use a packet analyzer such as *snoop* or Ethereal to review the output.
- ☑ Filters can be configured in Ethereal to search for a specific traffic.

Other Tools

- ☑ Check Point provides some command-line tools that help you to troubleshoot your firewall, such as *fw ctl pstat*, *fw tab*, and *fw lichosts*.
- ☑ You will need to download *cpinfo* and run it on any Check Point management module and enforcement point before escalating a ticket to Check Point.
- ☑ Several operating system commands can help you troubleshoot system or network issues (*ping*, *traceroute*, *netstat*, and so on).
- ☑ Many third-party tools can assist you in problem solving as well. Netcat, Ethereal, Firewalk, Sniffer Pro, and Cygwin are a few.

Frequently Asked Questions

The following Frequently Asked Questions, answered by the authors of this book, are designed to both measure your understanding of the concepts presented in this chapter and to assist you with real-life implementation of these concepts. To have your questions about this chapter answered by the author, browse to **www.syngress.com/solutions** and click on the **"Ask the Author"** form.

Q: How can I confirm that my NAT is performing properly?

A: You can start by watching the SmartView Tracker. You could select the FireWall-1 predefined query, or if you are in the All Records view, you will need to enable the NAT fields in the query. Choose **View | Query Properties**. Then you can select NAT rule number, NAT additional rule number, XlateSrc, and XlateDst. Then you can compare the source/XlateSrc and then destination/XlateDst to determine if NAT is working properly.

If that doesn't give you what you are looking for, or if the logs in the SmartView Tracker are not what you expect, then you can run an *fw monitor* command on the firewall to confirm how NAT is working. If you are trying to do a static NAT from IP_A to IP_B, you might set up a filter like this to see if the translation happens in the source:

```
fw monitor -e "accept [12,b]=IP_A or [12,b]=IP_B;"
```

If that produces too much data, and you want to further filter based on port number, try the following:

```
fw monitor -e "accept [12,b]=IP_A or [12,b]=IP_B and [20:2,b]=80 or
    [22:2,b]=80;"
Example output:
```

```
eth-s4p1c0:i[40]: 192.168.1.3 -> 207.171.185.16 (TCP) len=40 id=39382
    TCP: 3273 -> 80 F...A. seq=12f51366 ack=0000fb02
eth-s4p1c0:I[40]: 192.168.1.3 -> 207.171.185.16 (TCP) len=40 id=39382
    TCP: 3273 -> 80 F...A. seq=12f51366 ack=0000fb02
eth-s3p1c0:o[40]: 192.168.1.3 -> 207.171.185.16 (TCP) len=40 id=39382
    TCP: 3273 -> 80 F...A. seq=12f51366 ack=0000fb02
eth-s3p1c0:O[40]: 172.16.1.3 -> 207.171.185.16 (TCP) len=40 id=39382
    TCP: 12551 -> 80 F...A. seq=12f51366 ack=0000fb02
eth-s3p1c0:i[40]: 207.171.185.16 -> 172.16.1.3 (TCP) len=40 id=0
    TCP: 80 -> 12551 ....A. seq=0000fb02 ack=12f51367
eth-s3p1c0:I[40]: 207.171.185.16 -> 192.168.1.3 (TCP) len=40 id=0
    TCP: 80 -> 3273 ....A. seq=0000fb02 ack=12f51367
eth-s4p1c0:o[40]: 207.171.185.16 -> 192.168.1.3 (TCP) len=40 id=0
    TCP: 80 -> 3273 ....A. seq=0000fb02 ack=12f51367
eth-s4p1c0:O[40]: 207.171.185.16 -> 192.168.1.3 (TCP) len=40 id=0
    TCP: 80 -> 3273 ....A. seq=0000fb02 ack=12f51367
```

The first four entries here show the packet on its way from the client to the server, and the first three inspection points (*i*, *I*, and *o*) show that the source IP address remains the same. Then in the fourth entry, as the packet is leaving the firewall, the source address is translated to 172.16.1.3. You may notice that the source port is also translated, this is how FireWall-1 performs hide NAT.

In the last four entries, you see the return packet from the server to the client. The first inspection of the return packet is destined for the translated address 172.16.1.3 (notice the same source port also). Then the packet is translated back to its original IP and source port for the remainder of the inspection process.

Q: What is the right tool for viewing which rule passes which connections: *fw monitor*, SMARTView Monitor, or SMARTView Tracker?

A: SmartView Tracker is the only tool that will show you the rule number associated with the log entry.

Q: How would I use the tools described in this chapter to troubleshoot a problem where I'm not receiving inbound email?

A: The first thing to check if someone calls with an inbound email problem would be the SmartView Tracker. If a security server is being used, you may see important information in the Info field, such as the virus scanner may not be responding, or the mail server (final MTA) may not be accepting email. If you can't determine the problem via the logs alone, try to *ping*, *traceroute*, and then do a *telnet* to their external mail server address on port 25 and try to deliver a mail message manually. You might also do the same thing from the firewall to the internal mail server address. If you don't know the external address of their mail server but do know their domain name, use the *nslookup –q=mx domain.com* command to find their mail exchanger record. The MX entry with the lowest priority number will be the first attempted. If the solution is still elusive, check that NAT is defined properly and that there are no system resource problems on the firewall preventing processing of inbound mail. Check log files and run an *fw monitor* and/or *tcpdump* to find out if there is a virus/worm causing problems or to determine how far the mail is getting before it is stopped. At this point, it would be a good idea to get a *cpinfo*, and then as a last resort, try a *cpstop/cpstart* and/or reboot the firewall to try to get things moving again.

Q: What are the SMTP commands to deliver a mail message manually?

A: Here is a sample connection to a mail server. The commands used to send a message manually are in bold:

```
220 CheckPoint FireWall-1 secure SMTP server
hello
250 Hello
mail from:<someone@somedomain.com>
250 <someone@somedomain.com... Sender ok
rcpt to:<you@yourdomain.com>
250 <you@yourdomain... Recipient ok
data
354 Enter mail, end with "." on a line by itself
Subject: Internet email test message
Dear me,
This is just a test. Testing 123.
.
250 Ok
quit
221 Closing connection
```

Q: How can I test a connection to a Web server with *telnet*?

A: Most Web servers will listen for connections on port 80, however, there are some exceptions. If you know that this is a standard port 80 HTTP connection, just run *telnet www.cisco.com 80*, for example, and if you want to verify that you have a connection established, type **GET /** and press **Enter** once or twice. You should see HTML scroll across the screen, and then your connection will be closed.

Q: I'm trying to set up synchronization on a Nokia pair, but under ClusterXL in the SmartView Status window it says "Problem!". How can I resolve this?

A: Here are some things for you to check:

- Run *cpconfig* on each module and verify that synchronization is enabled; if it is not, enable it and reboot.
- Run *fw tab –t connections –s* on both hosts at the same time. If sync is working, you should see a number (under #VALS) that is very similar, within about 200 connections.
- Ensure that the firewalls are using NTP to synchronize their time. The closer they are to having the same time, the better state sync will work; it is recommended that they are not more than a few seconds off from one another.
- Ensure that you have the cluster object defined properly:
    1. Check that you have the correct Availability mode selected (High Availability or Load Sharing).
    2. Check that you have Synchronization enabled and a secure network defined.
- Run *fw ctl pstat* and review the sync information displayed on the modules.
- Run *tcpdump* on the sync interface to see if sync is working and packets are being sent and received.

If sync is working properly, you should see output similar to the following by monitoring the sync interface via *tcpdump*. Notice the second column in the output contains both *I* and *O* packets, indicating that there is sync traffic both inbound and outbound on this interface.

```
00:42:23.630410 O 0.0.0.0.8116 > 192.168.254.0.8116:  udp 28
00:42:23.720021 O 0.0.0.0.8116 > 192.168.254.0.8116:  udp 24
00:42:23.720109 I 0.0.0.0.8116 > 192.168.254.0.8116:  udp 36
00:42:23.831756 I 0.0.0.0.8116 > 192.168.254.0.8116:  udp 28
00:42:23.832244 I 0.0.0.0.8116 > 192.168.254.0.8116:  udp 1292
00:42:23.850223 O 0.0.0.0.8116 > 192.168.254.0.8116:  udp 28
```

Q: How do I use the *fw tab* command to see how many hosts my firewall has counted?

A: Use the command *fw tab –t host_table –s*. The output will look something like the following output. The number under #VALS is the current number of hosts counted.

```
HOST            NAME                     ID #VALS #PEAK #SLINKS
localhost       host_table             8185    22    22       0
```

Index

B

C

E

G

K

L

M

N

O

P

R

T

U

V

W